# The Political Thought of the Civil War

Nov. 2019.

For Danielle Allen,

In gratitude.

Tom Merrill

For Danielle,
Nice to meet you!
Alan Levine

American Political Thought

WILSON CAREY MCWILLIAMS AND LANCE BANNING
*Founding Editors*

# The Political Thought of the Civil War

Edited by
Alan Levine, Thomas W. Merrill, and
James R. Stoner, Jr.

University Press of Kansas

© 2018 by the University Press of Kansas

All rights reserved Published by the University Press of Kansas (Lawrence, Kansas 66045), which was organized by the Kansas Board of Regents and is operated and funded by Emporia State University, Fort Hays State University, Kansas State University, Pittsburg State University, the University of Kansas, and Wichita State University

Library of Congress Cataloging-in-Publication Data

Names: Levine, Alan, 1961– editor. | Merrill, Thomas W. (Thomas Westneat), 1974– editor. | Stoner, James Reist, editor.

Title: The political thought of the Civil War / edited by Alan Levine, Thomas W. Merrill, and James R. Stoner, Jr.

Description: Lawrence, Kansas : University Press of Kansas, [2018] Series: American political thought | Includes bibliographical references and index.

Identifiers: LCCN 2018016379
ISBN 9780700626694 (cloth : alk. paper) |
ISBN 9780700629114 (pbk. : alk. paper) |
ISBN 9780700626700 (ebook)

Subjects: LCSH: United States—Politics and government—1857–1861. | United States—Politics and government—1861–1865. | United States—Politics and government—1865–1869. | United States—History—Civil War, 1861–1865—Causes. | Reconstruction (U.S. history, 1865–1877)

Classification: LCC E459 .P635 2018 | DDC 973.7/11—dc23.
LC record available at https://lccn.loc.gov/2018016379p.

British Library Cataloguing-in-Publication Data is available.

Printed in the United States of America
10 9 8 7 6 5 4 3 2 1

# Contents

Part III: Pyrrhic Victories?

# Preface

This volume was conceived during the sesquicentennial years of the Civil War. It was the editors' firm belief that the ideas, events, and trauma of the Civil War continued to haunt American life—and do so even today. We did not then foresee the specific debates over statues or the resurgent attempt to mainstream white supremacy by the so-called alt right, but we are not surprised by these developments either. These current battles are—as many future such events will be—signs that the ideas and events of antebellum America, the Civil War, and the war's aftermath have not been fully digested and settled but remain with the regime. Through serious and systematic study, this volume hopes to shed light on the issues and ideas underlying today's (and tomorrow's) headlines. Every chapter in this volume not only addresses its topic as understood in nineteenth-century America but also reflects on what is living and what is dead in those largely forgotten issues and debates for today. Each chapter further attempts to show the ways in which the Civil War either resulted in the completion of the great American political experiment begun in 1776 and 1787 or served as a new beginning for it. We hope these reflections and this framework enable thoughtful citizens and statesmen to better understand and deal with today's issues and events.

Many of this volume's chapters originated as lectures delivered at the Political Theory Institute (PTI) in the School of Public Affairs at American University between 2011 and 2015. We are grateful to PTI's faculty, students, friends, and supporters for making these events, and thus ultimately this book, possible. Other chapters were presented at the 2013 annual meeting of the American Political Science Association and the 2014 annual meeting of the Southern Political Science Association.

*The Political Thought of the Civil War*

# Introduction: The Civil War as a Regime Question

Thomas W. Merrill, Alan Levine, and
James R. Stoner, Jr.

In the wake of the sesquicentennial of the Civil War, faced with a multitude
of books on the topic, a reader might well ask: Why another book about the
war? Why a book about the political thought of the Civil War in particular?
Do we not already know enough about Abraham Lincoln, John C. Calhoun,
slavery in the territories, secession, emancipation, and the details of battles and
commanders?

To this question it is perhaps appropriate to respond with another: Why
does the Civil War still speak to us, so much so that we could easily be overwhelmed by the books and articles about it? The answer, we suspect, is that
the war, together with the long conflict of which it was the culmination, was
a genuinely constitutional moment, a moment that forced participants and
onlookers alike to face up to the fundamental question of the soundness or
unsoundness of the American regime itself. By constitutional, we do not mean
a merely technical or legalistic question of the meaning of this or that clause
of the Constitution or of managing disputes within the terms of a system that
is fundamentally sound and uncontroversial. Although well and good under
normal circumstances, such an approach takes the basic premises of the constitutional order for granted and thereby tacitly encourages us to ignore the
full range of alternatives to our own way of doing things. In moments of crisis,
however, mere management of the existing system no longer suffices. In those
times, painful and divisive issues, tactfully buried for the sake of social comity
in normal times, come to the fore. No longer is it possible to rely on the inertia
of institutions or on the transmitted wisdom of the founders for guidance. No
longer is it possible to avoid the question of the viability or defensibility of the
regime. Citizens must think anew, and think again, about elemental questions
of justice and injustice, about the tension between morality and prudence, and
about the most basic meaning of American political identity. Both the parts of
the war that touch on nobility, such as the emancipation of enslaved people,

and those that terrify us, such as the war's grinding, fratricidal violence, bear witness to the war's character as a constitutional moment in which the meaning and soundness of the regime was put in doubt.

Perhaps the war still speaks to us, even at this great distance from its events, because we suspect or worry that we too are living through a constitutional moment. Twenty-first-century America feels cleaved by mistrust; is keenly aware of divisions along lines of political identity, class, and race; and is skeptical of the political and cultural institutions that are supposed to bring us together. Congress seems barely able to find agreement on even the most minimal functions of government, and the Supreme Court is often viewed as a vehicle of partisanship and so lacking the authority to bridge our differences. The idea of "fake news," so much discussed as we write, illustrates our condition: whether any particular piece of news is fake or not, the idea only reveals the extent to which Americans feel themselves to be living in different realities from significant numbers of their neighbors. Not being able to agree on the basic facts of our situation, we feel that we cannot speak to each other as fellow citizens who perhaps disagree but also seek some common good. In these circumstances, it would be surprising if we did not worry about the soundness of our regime. After all, a regime is not simply a list of abstract ideas. More fundamentally, it is a way of life characterized by a particular spirit or ethos and made possible by a sense of trust and mutual accommodation among its members. When that trust seems to evaporate, we naturally begin to wonder about the foundations of our political community.

It is not surprising, then, that Americans living in our time might be attracted to the Civil War. Perhaps we see some kinship between our situation of polarization and mistrust and the situation before and during the war. But perhaps we are also attracted by the differences: although we might feel paralyzed by our inability to resolve the conflict between today's competing ideologies, most Americans find it easy to recognize "good guys" and "bad guys" in the Civil War. Slavery in America was indeed a great evil and ending it a great good, even if slavery's demise was accompanied by significant costs and the "badges and incidents" of segregation and second-class status for blacks lingered for more than a century.[1] Yet it must also be admitted that the very reasons for our attraction to the war might well present certain obstacles to seeing both it and ourselves whole. It is tempting to see the war by way of contrast with our own situation as a morality play and to think that, although slavery was America's original sin, the war took care of all that. But it would be wrong to conceive of ourselves as the contented inheritors of the wrenching choices of previous generations and think that all we need do is sit back and cheer on yesterday's heroes and deplore yesterday's villains. There is a twofold danger here. On the one hand, because we take pleasure in morality plays, we easily avert our attention from the moral ambiguities, even failings, of our appointed heroes and from the virtues of our appointed villains. On the other hand, by assuring ourselves that all the hard work was done long ago, the morality-play version might make us complacent about our own current moral responsibilities. This morality-play view of the war, common enough in works about the war, assumes history can be safely sealed away in the past and does not continue to shape the present. In this view, facing up to the war requires no painful self-examination on our part, asks for no sacrifice from us. Being entertained and diverted by the war from our own morally ambiguous situation, we run the risk of preening ourselves on our moral superiority to the past and so avoiding the task of self-knowledge.

The present volume is animated by the conviction that a critical engagement with the main thinkers, events, and ideas of the war is illuminating, both for its own sake and for the help it gives us in thinking through our own situation. The authors of the chapters included here share the belief that the source of the war's enduring importance is its ability to provoke reflection on questions we might otherwise be tempted to avoid. The war tested all those who lived through it by forcing them to confront the question of the fundamental soundness of the regime. As a practical matter this presented itself as a question of allegiance: In the American regime, who is the final judge of disputes between citizens—the federal government, the states, or citizens taking matters into their own hands? But inextricably entangled with the practical question are theoretical questions: Are the avowed principles of the regime sufficient to the case at hand? Are they true? Doing justice to the war requires taking these questions seriously, and that requires trying to take a comprehensive view of the war and of the American political tradition, one that does not take for granted the war's justice, nobility, or even success. It also requires considering the legacy of the war in reflecting on the constitutional health and justice of our regime today.

## A DELIBERATIVE APPROACH

The chapters in the present volume share what we are calling a *deliberative approach* to politics. We mean this to be a clear-eyed engagement with the words and deeds of the most thoughtful political actors associated with the war, as they understood themselves and in the light of fundamental questions about the regime. Our approach starts from the points of view of the actors themselves—the statesmen, citizens, others without an official place in the regime, even the enslaved or formerly enslaved whom the regime oppressed—facing a practical problem or controversy. It is they, confronted with difficult choices with no easy answer, who first had to articulate what needed to be done and how and why. Starting with the actors, we then try to think through the theoretical dimensions of the controversy and the decisions made in response to it. We examine the role of those political actors who deliberated about politics and who offered reasoned, articulate accounts of the alternatives that confronted them and the choices they made. What the chapters included here share is less a set of conclusions or views about the main substantive issues in question than a common approach to thinking about and studying politics, an approach that might be initially described simply as taking the political thought of the Civil War seriously.

This deliberative approach can serve as an indispensable antidote to the tendency toward complacency about the war—and ourselves. We believe that, after we set aside the morality-play version of the war, the close study of the war and the issues it raises compel reflection on fundamental questions about the character of the American regime and American political identity, to say nothing of perennial controversies of political life relevant beyond the United States. To that end, we offer here studies of some of the most thoughtful, farsighted, and representative political actors and observers of the war itself, the long conflict that preceded it, and its consequences and ramifications in its aftermath.

The starting point of the chapters that follow are those political actors, North and South, black and white, who, faced with political choices, deliberated about what to do and offered reasoned accounts of the alternatives confronting them and the choices they made. We proceed in this way because we are ultimately interested in trying to understand for ourselves the truth or falsity of the political ideas animating our actors. However, because practical deliberations are often deeply entangled in theoretical commitments, the best point of entry for coming to terms with those commitments (at least to begin with) is taking seriously the explanations and arguments made by the political actors as they tried to justify their actions. This approach leads us to focus on those actors and observers who offered the most thoughtful and farsighted articulations of their own situations. These are sometimes, but by no means always, the holders of high office. It is often the case that the holders of high office have incentives not to see, or at least not to say, the whole truth about their situations, and so the political analyst will often find it indispensable to seek out the minority or dissident view in a given society. By the same token, however, sometimes those who achieve high office, such as Lincoln, happen to have clarity and farsightedness, and sometimes being in high office spurs them to see some things that the rest of us miss. Our aspiration, then, is to take seriously the opinions and the reasons of those who deliberated most intelligently about the political problems facing them whatever their position in society may be.

The rationale for this approach to the Civil War is explained most easily by contrasting it with two approaches with which it might be confused, the historical approach and a philosophical one. The task of a historian is to understand the past as it was and not as we might like it to be, whereas the task of a philosopher is to seek universal truths, especially about morality and politics. Although we respect each of these approaches, we come to the war from a different angle. In our view, the historical and philosophical (or theoretical) dimensions of human life are not as easily separable as it might seem, especially when we study human beings deliberating about a course of action. For when they deliberate, human beings always rely on some view of what might loosely be called the theoretical dimensions of political life: justice, the character of a good society, or human nature. If the task of the historian is to understand historical actors as they understood themselves, then history cannot avoid paying attention to these dimensions of those actors' beliefs. The converse is true as well. Philosophers often act as though political ideas can be discussed in abstraction from circumstance. But practice often has something other, and richer, to say than might be expected from mere ratiocination. It reveals complications that force familiar ideas to be formulated more precisely; by presenting political actors hard choices between competing goods, it compels them to clarify their priorities; and it throws up new circumstances revealing unforeseen implications or tensions within familiar beliefs. Sometimes the full meaning of political ideas is revealed most clearly in the scrum of practical life, not at the seminar table, so attention to the fate of ideas in practice is an important part, perhaps even an indispensable part, of our efforts to figure out whether those ideas are true. The approach to the political thought of the Civil War taken in this volume, then, is to ponder the practical dilemmas our thinkers faced and to assess the theoretical principles they asserted in the course of responding to those dilemmas. Although the historical situation of the war and the philosophical questions raised by the war are and remain distinct, we believe a student of the war cannot think fruitfully about the one without the other. However, this "methodological" point is perhaps understood most easily in terms of some examples of how a practical question implicates regime questions that in turn cannot be addressed without some attention to the properly theoretical dimension of politics.

## REGIME QUESTIONS

To illustrate our deliberative approach, consider three regime questions, each of which underlies one of the three parts of this volume. First, what was the place of slavery in America prior to the Civil War? Although the 1860s was the decade of actual fighting, earlier decades were times of deliberation about and preparation for the conflict. The main issue leading up to the war was slavery in the territories, which acquired its urgency from the nation's vast expansion of territory via the Louisiana Purchase and the US victory in the Mexican War and the westward pressure of Americans eager to settle in it. Would Congress and the Supreme Court allow, mandate, or prohibit slavery in the territories of Kansas, Nebraska, and elsewhere? The question that lurked behind this controversy was whether America was at bottom a proslavery country or not. That question had been present in American politics from the start. The Convention of 1787 had been able to write and get the Constitution ratified only on the basis of a fundamental compromise on slavery in which the Constitution let the institution be protected where it existed but offered it no explicit endorsement. That compromise had long since been accepted by almost all major forces in American politics. Slavery in the territories, however, presented the old issue in a new light. No longer was it possible for the country to look at slavery and believe it was only a regrettable inheritance about which nothing could be done. Slavery in the territories was an open question, not an unfortunate necessity; the country had to choose one way or the other, and that meant facing slavery on its merits. As is often noted, the success of American imperialism in manifest destiny had destabilized the regime by forcing its underlying ambiguity into the open. Did the regime accept slavery only as something imposed that must be tolerated, or did it actually endorse slavery? By the 1850s, it was not so easy to say where the regime actually stood on this basic question.

The ambiguity over slavery pointed to a second, more theoretical regime question concerning the tension between substantive morality and procedural constitutionalism. Even if the American regime tolerated slavery only as an unavoidable evil (a claim disputed by the 1850s by many slave owners), it represented a compromise with a moral evil. It is legitimate to compromise on matters of mere policy dispute, but is it really possible to compromise with moral evil and not become evil? In the decades before the war, many Southerners had grappled with this question, as had the abolitionists, some of whom believed the Constitution was a "covenant with hell" in William Lloyd Garrison's provocative phrase. Rather than look to the Constitution as the ultimate authority for the American regime, the abolitionists thus looked to the dictates of morality and what William Seward called the "higher law." We today find it easy to sympathize with this point of view. However, there are weighty counterarguments to the abolitionist position. In a memorable speech on the perpetuation of our political institutions, Lincoln argued that the rule of law depends, in the last analysis, not on force but on the attachment of the people. Actions that break constitutional forms, even (or especially) if they are carried out in the name of a just cause, undermine that attachment. Such actions encourage mob rule—mob rule in the name of one cause encourages mob rule in other causes—but the mob might well be wrong in a specific case; and so those who engage in extrajudicial actions one day might well be the victims of extrajudicial actions the next. Constitutional government depends on the willingness of the citizens to obey even decisions with which they disagree, and extraconstitutional actions undermine that willingness. This is not to deny that the Constitution was entangled in injustice (notably, but not only, slavery) but only to point out the difficulty of the issue. Nor is the problem automatically resolved by appeal to the higher law. For one thing, the slave owners claimed to have their own divine sanction.[2] The problem was not to resolve the theoretical question but to persuade the many who were unconvinced by theoretical arguments. The dilemma of the antebellum antislavery movement, then, was this: Given the realities of American life, was it possible to act against slavery without undermining constitutional government? Or, to reverse the question, can constitutional government overcome deeply entrenched injustice, or is it doomed to perpetuate such injustice?

A third regime question, one that arose out of the war but that came to the fore only afterward, asks whether the principles of the American regime are adequate to the challenge of building a multiracial, multicultural society. To be sure, this was hardly a pressing issue in the minds of most Americans in the 1850s or before, and it should be remembered that even those most loudly opposed to slavery in the 1850s were by no means open and were in most cases opposed to political and social equality for black Americans. (This is one reason the morality-play version of the war is basically deceptive.) Limiting or ending slavery was by no means the same thing as supporting racial equality. Yet in a sense this issue, so important after the war, had shaped the racial landscape of antebellum America from the beginning. In his well-known analysis of the problem of slavery in the founding generation, Thomas Jefferson famously explained the contradiction between slavery and the principles of the Declaration of Independence and thus the need to end slavery. But he also articulated a profound pessimism about the feasibility of ending slavery in the short term. Blacks and whites would never be able to live together in America, Jefferson believed, precisely because of the legacy of slavery. Blacks would resent the injustices done them, whites would claim innocence and blame their ancestors, and the difference in color would always be there to keep the old animosities alive. For this reason, Jefferson's support for emancipation was always conditional on colonization, which never seemed feasible. It is thus wrong to say that Jefferson failed to recognize the conflict between slavery and his political principles, but it is not wrong to say that the practical problem of slavery was rooted in Jefferson's and other founders' inability or unwillingness to imagine a multiracial society. No doubt Jefferson's position on this point was something of a self-fulfilling prophecy and self-serving to boot. Nonetheless, it is an open question with us as it was with Jefferson: Do the principles of the regime provide the help we need in building a multiracial society in light of America's very complicated racial history? Or do we need some sense of positive engagement beyond just the agreement to protect each other's natural rights and tolerate their varied exercise, as recommended by Jefferson's natural rights doctrine?

All three of these regime questions—the status of slavery, the tension between morality and constitutionalism, and the viability of the principles of the Declaration to meet the challenge of a multiracial society—point to a more elemental and more problematic question about the meaning of the war for the American political tradition. Did the war simply correct American institutions in order to bring them into accord with the true meaning of the original principles of the regime? Or did the war introduce new, perhaps better, principles? At bottom, is the war best understood as a completion of the regime begun in 1787, albeit with some significant details changed, or was it a genuine refounding, perhaps even a regime change? This question can be pursued on several different levels, and the three questions just reviewed are best understood as aspects of this more fundamental issue. The chapters in the present volume do not share a single answer to these questions, nor do their authors claim to have answered them definitively. We do claim, however, that these are the questions with which any serious student of the war and its place in the American political tradition will have to wrestle. And we believe that readers, no matter how they are inclined to answer these regime questions, will be instructed and stimulated by the chapters that follow. We conceive of these chapters not as the last word on their various topics but as invitations to a conversation that in the nature of things can only be completed by the reader.

## DEBATING THE WAR

No inquiry starts simply de novo, especially not on this topic. Many scholars have written on these topics before, and we are the grateful inheritors of their work, not least of their enduring controversies and conflicting opinions. In order to pay due homage to our fellow scholars, but also to indicate where we believe we have something new to add to the conversation, it will be useful to mention some of the works that have shaped our thought on these issues, whether in agreement or disagreement. Because of our deliberative approach, our work must be (and, we hope, is) informed by the best histories of the war itself, including the long period of struggle over slavery and sectionalism in antebellum America and the difficult and in some respects still unresolved aftermath. Our task in this volume is not to offer another narrative of the historical events in all their particularity but to use those particulars as a means of raising and thinking though the theoretical questions just beneath the surface of most histories. Our task would be impossible without the work of the historians. To this end we gladly acknowledge the histories of the war itself, especially by James McPherson and Allen Guelzo, as indispensable reference points for the present volume.[3] For the period before the war, we relied on the work of Daniel Walker Howe and Sean Wilentz as general histories, William Freehling's work on the South and secessionism from 1776 to 1861, and Don Fehrenbacher's work on the 1850s.[4] For the period after the war, we have relied on Eric Foner's classic work on Reconstruction.[5] We also learned from Drew Gilpin Faust's work on the suffering caused by the war.[6]

When we turn to the great number of worthy studies of particular topics related to the Civil War, the deliberative point of view suggests that the best way to think about them is less by academic field than by specific decision points that have sparked scholarly debate and discussion. Although each chapter in this volume is in dialogue with the scholarship on its particular issues, there are five bodies of literature on the war and its meaning for the American political tradition that we would like to acknowledge here because each of these five literatures is focused on a key decision point or controversy and thus partakes of something akin to our deliberative approach. First, there is an excellent literature on the tension between abolitionism and constitutionalism in the 1850s. Was it better for a person who believed slavery was immoral and contradictory to the natural rights principles of the Declaration to work within the constitutional order, knowing that the consensus of the time was that the Constitution ruled out any direct action against slavery where it existed and even obligated officeholders and citizens to act in support of slavery in some important respects? Or was it better for that person to refuse to compromise with evil and instead stand as a critic of the constitutional order from the outside? This was the issue between Lincoln and abolitionists such as Garrison, and articulate proponents of each side can be found among scholars down to our own day. Defenders of Lincoln, such as Harry Jaffa, George Anastaplo, Guelzo, and others argue that the real obstacle for the antislavery movement was not the Constitution but the power of the slave states and that the only way to oppose that power effectively was to build a coalition to act politically under the Constitution.[7] To refuse to participate in politics or to seek the dissolution of the Constitution, these scholars argue, would have left the slave owners free to act as they pleased, with no assurance of future progress. In light of events, of course, this position seems to have been vindicated and is still probably the consensus view among scholars. Nevertheless, other scholars such as Foner, George Kateb, John Stauffer, Manisha Sinha, and Daniel Malachuk have a weighty response.[8] They point out that it is easy to conflate the result of the Civil War, emancipation, with Lincoln's intentions or with what would have been the best guess available at the time as to the consequences of his actions. Lincoln always claimed that the national government had no power to do anything about slavery where it existed and in early 1861 even supported a constitutional amendment to give slavery explicit protection as an attempt to avoid secession.[9] Had the Southern states not seceded—an event out of Lincoln's control—slavery would almost certainly have lasted considerably longer than it did. The defenders of the abolitionists thus argue that the case for Lincoln rests on something like victor's history; had any one of a hundred events turned out differently, we would have less reason to praise Lincoln. And because we should judge historical actors not only by the results of their actions (given those are often accidental) but also based on their intentions and reasonable expectations, these scholars suggest, the abolitionists should be judged far more positively than they usually are.

Second, there is a robust, deliberative literature on the decision to make and accept war in 1861. Decisions of war and peace are paradigmatic moments of choice in which political beliefs are revealed, tested, and sometimes even revised or abandoned. Lincoln's decision to accept war in 1861 (and the Confederacy's decision to make it) has been one of the great cruxes of the literature of the war. Most scholarly and popular opinion endorses Lincoln's decision. However, not all scholars do, and those who contest it argue that we should not allow the human suffering caused by the war to be eclipsed by a morality-play version of the war. For that cost was truly staggering by anyone's standard, with an estimated death toll of 620,000 persons, suffering that would be hard to parallel in American history.[10] Would Lincoln have accepted this carnage, critics ask, had he known in advance how heavy it would be? Would the Southern leaders have accepted it? Many Americans today would say that the cost of the war was justified by the emancipation of the slaves, but Lincoln's original justification for the war was preserving the Union, not freeing the enslaved.[11] Southerners and those sympathetic to the Southerners reject Lincoln's proclaimed justification, arguing that secession and the idea of dissolving the Union was much less shocking in 1861 than it is today and even had some precedent in the right of revolution in 1776. Some scholars sympathetic to the abolitionist cause also reject Lincoln's justification for the war. For example, Jeffrey Hummel, who has made one of the most articulate critiques of Lincoln's choice of war from an antislavery point of view, writes that justifying the war on the grounds of preserving the Union absent any intention of ending slavery was "bankrupt and reprehensible," and Mark Graber has argued that John Bell, not Lincoln, was the right choice for prudent antislavery citizens in the election of 1860.[12] Against this, defenders of Lincoln such as Stephen Oates and James Read argue that 1861 was not 1776 because the morality of the two causes (independence versus slavery) was not equivalent; that if a polity allows disgruntled minorities to leave, it will quickly find itself being pushed around by all disgruntled minorities; and that the Southern leaders bore as much of the responsibility for the length of the war as Lincoln did.[13]

A third robust, deliberative debate concerns the defensibility of the compromises with slavery in the Constitution. Lurking behind the previous two debates lie the status and defensibility of the Constitution as it was in 1861, and settling those debates requires consideration of the compromises with slavery in the Constitution itself. Lincoln famously argued that the founding generation accepted slavery only as an unfortunate necessity that could not be eradicated at that time but was "in the course of ultimate extinction." Lincoln's view implied that what in 1861 had come to be called the slave power was not in the original spirit of the founding but had grown up afterward. Garrisonian abolitionists disagreed. For them, the Constitution was so thoroughly entangled with slavery as to be beyond saving. Both sides of this debate have articulate and able scholarly proponents today. Kateb argues that slavery was not just a blemish on, but an integral part of, the Constitution, so that the Constitution was "unworthy of obedience," and Graber has defended the *Dred Scott* decision not as morally acceptable but as in accord with the original understanding of the Constitution.[14] Similarly, scholars of the American founding such as Paul Finkelman, George Van Cleve, David Waldstreicher, and Alan Taylor argue that the Constitution of 1787 did not merely compromise with slavery but actively supported the institution and made it difficult if not impossible to do anything about it.[15] On the other side, scholars such as Fehrenbacher, Freehling, Thomas West, and Paul Rahe point to numerous statements by members of the founding generation about the inconsistency of slavery with their political principles.[16] They point out that South Carolina and Georgia made it perfectly clear at the Constitutional Convention that the price of any Constitution was the toleration of slavery, and that the Constitution purposefully avoids endorsing the moral legitimacy of slavery and even seems to understand the toleration of slavery as temporary (as in the clause allowing Congress to abolish the slave trade in 1808). Whether these defenses of the framers of the Constitution are entirely successful is a question that readers will have to resolve for themselves, but the fact remains that the ambiguity of the Constitution provided ample support for proslavery and antislavery causes throughout the antebellum period.[17]

A fourth worthy literature debates the meaning of the American political tradition for African Americans. As we have said, starting from the deliberative point of view means being open to the possibility that in the light of unforeseen cases, our principles might turn out to have unanticipated consequences. And we should remember that those who first articulate a principle do not necessarily get to say just how far that principle extends; principles have a way of leading to places we did not expect to go. In no other case is this fact clearer than in the case of enslaved people and their descendants in America. Largely excluded from any direct role in antebellum American politics, the victims of a system of human bondage based on race turned out to be among the greatest thinkers and rethinkers of the meaning of the American political tradition. If white society, South and North, had little place for free blacks, might not the avowed principles of the political order still offer a ground for the enslaved and formerly enslaved to assert their right to freedom and to respect? Or were the principles so tainted by their proximity to an oppressive society that self-respecting blacks would have to seek other principles and other ways of life? As Frederick Douglass asked long before the war itself, "What country have I?" Douglass himself famously changed his mind on that issue, thereby setting the terms for a debate that still resonates for thoughtful Americans in our own day. In his younger days Douglass held that a free black could not and should not want to be a citizen of the United States because the Constitution failed to embody the principles of the Declaration. But in the 1850s Douglass publicly changed his mind, holding that the Constitution itself was good and defensible but that the institutions of the regime had been captured by the slave power.[18] Thanks to the work of scholars such as David Blight, Peter Myers, and Nicholas Buccola, we now have a much better sense of what was at stake in these questions for Douglass.[19] And despite Douglass's case for the Constitution, it should come as no surprise that African Americans have been divided about this question ever since. After the war, the debate between W. E. B. DuBois and Booker T. Washington echoed the difference between the young and the mature Douglass; arguably the same basic disagreement is visible in the differences between African American thinkers such as Ta-Nehisi Coates and Shelby Steele today.[20] Not surprisingly, the debate between DuBois and Washington divides scholars as well, with David Levering Lewis and Lawrie Balfour taking the side of DuBois and Robert Norrell and Herbert Storing taking the side of Washington.[21]

A fifth body of literature vividly debates whether the Civil War was a reaffirmation of the American regime or a refounding. Here some differences correlate with scholarly discipline: leading legal scholars such as Bruce Ackerman and Akhil Reed Amar argue that the postwar Reconstruction produced a fundamental alteration in the nature of the Union and the legal-political understanding of rights,[22] whereas constitutional historians such as Michael Les Benedict, Herman Belz, and Morton Keller argue that basic constitutional structures, particularly decentralized federalism, endured in the new era of emancipation and nationally guaranteed constitutional rights.[23] Among social scientists, the basic disagreement often turns on the interpretation of the intent and the legacy of Lincoln. Before the war, Lincoln claimed to be a constitutional conservative, wishing only to restore the original constitutional understanding of the place of slavery in the constitutional order. Yet in the aftermath of the war, with the abolition of slavery settled on the battlefield, the question of how much the rest of the constitutional order ought to change proved controversial even among those who considered themselves friendly to Lincoln. To understand this, it is important to distinguish between the way this question arises on the constitutional level and on the moral level. On the constitutional level, partisans of the "Lost Cause," as Southerners wistfully or bitterly referred to their secessionist dream, argued that the Fourteenth Amendment had effected a reversal of the antebellum understanding of the relation between the states and the federal government, which in their view was one much for the worse. Strangely, as scholars such as Ronald Pestritto and Jason Jividen have argued, prominent Progressives otherwise unsympathetic to the Lost Cause agreed with this basic point.[24] They thought that the original Constitution had been as the Confederates described it and that Lincoln's actions in the war had been a radical break with the tradition. However, whereas the Southerners had seen this as a calamity, the Progressives saw Lincoln's innovation as praiseworthy, even a spur for further innovation for the sake of progress.[25] In this way, even though Lincoln claimed to be upholding constitutionalism in the original sense of the term, his actions became an inspiration for what would be called the *Living Constitution* view of the American regime. On the moral level, a similarly strange reversal occurred with regard to the Declaration of Independence. Progressives such as Herbert Croly and Woodrow Wilson held Lincoln in high regard, but less for his advocacy of natural rights than for his actions as a strong executive.[26] Indeed, for Wilson and many other Progressives, the Declaration's self-evident truth of human equality had to be revised in light of history and the findings of the new science of race.[27] One version of that science, first proposed by Samuel Morton and George Gliddon and others, encouraged antebellum Southern statesmen to defend slavery. Another version of that science, based on Darwin's science of evolution, claimed there were fundamental differences between the races with regard to intelligence and self-control. Curiously enough, principles used to justify the side that lost in the Civil War thus continued to thrive after the war and even to make their way into the mainstream of American political thought. This is not the place to discuss the complexity and contradictions of American political thought in the twentieth century; suffice it to say that the different, even contradictory, lessons drawn by different observers from Lincoln's example provide a crucial entry point into the politics of our own era.

## THE PRESENT VOLUME

The chapters in the present volume are organized by stages of the deliberative point of view, which forms the common "methodological" approach of our contributors: the problem or controversy that calls for choice (Part One); the decision point or moment of choice itself (Part Two); and the consequences (and limits) of choice (Part Three).

The chapters that make up Part One of our volume all deal with some aspect of the practical dilemma to which the war was the response. They show antebellum America's most prominent judicial, scientific, philosophical, and political strategies for dealing with the founding's unresolved problems.

Thomas W. Merrill starts the volume by offering a novel angle on the debate about the status of slavery in the founding, arguing that the Missouri Crisis of 1819–1820 is a more important moment for understanding the role of slavery as a political issue in antebellum America than the ratification of the Constitution in 1787–1788. By 1819 Jefferson and the other members of the Republican dynasty had dropped their opposition to the expansion of slavery in the territories and had articulated a political outlook that would be profoundly influential on the antebellum South. Jefferson's main legacy, Merrill argues, was the contradiction between his fundamental political commitments: the doctrine of natural rights, which became the intellectual basis for the antislavery movement, on the one hand, and his support for agrarian political economy, states' rights, and the expansion of slavery throughout the territories, which became pillars of the distinctively Southern political program, on the other. By 1819, the Jeffersonian contradictions could no longer be covered by polite silence. The crisis revealed that the framers' inability to forge any real consensus on the issue of slavery had left the country with fundamental and enduring political disagreement.

The other chapters in Part One show several antebellum thinkers striving in opposing ways to resolve the fundamental tension in the regime they inherited from the founding generation. Keith Whittington examines the institution most obviously charged with holding the regime together, the Supreme Court. Building on Rogers Smith's claim that America has not just one political tradition (Lockean liberalism) but multiple traditions, Whittington carefully disentangles several court cases to uncover the different and often competing ideological traditions that shaped the Court's jurisprudence: the rule of law, union, liberty, and race. It is far too simple to say that the American regime is committed to liberty above all else, Whittington suggests; the challenge of jurisprudence in antebellum America was wrestling with the tension among the regime's basic commitments.

Daniel Malachuk and Alan Levine examine thinkers who try to resolve the tension of the antebellum regime on the philosophical or ideological level. Speaking directly to the theoretical issues only implicit in most of our other chapters, Malachuk defends the abolitionists against critics who charge them with moral fanaticism based on dubious metaphysical and theological claims. Of these modern critics, some are defenders of Lincoln against what they regard as the abolitionists' extremism, and others simply reject as fantastical their metaphysical commitments, accepting instead something like John Rawls's notion of an "overlapping consensus" as the ground for political obligation. Malachuk responds by pointing out the lack of consensus in antebellum America, the extent to which the abolitionists prodded moderate antislavery politicians such as Lincoln to do the right thing, and the fact that Lincoln was far closer to the abolitionists' philosophical and theological assumptions than to Rawlsian skepticism. If we were to bracket all foundational assumptions from political life, Malachuk suggests, we would deprive the deliberative point of view of one of its sources of vitality.

Levine's chapter shows us that Southerners too were troubled by the tension between the natural rights doctrine of the founding and the reality of slavery, although they tried to resolve that tension in a direction opposite to that of the abolitionists. As a significant portion of Southerners, seeing and wanting no way out of slavery, explicitly jettisoned Jefferson's natural rights doctrine, many sought and found a philosophical or ideological foundation for slavery in new scientific doctrines of race. As Levine points out, American scientists were only too willing to offer such foundations in the form of accounts of African racial inferiority, foundations that Southern statesmen trumpeted as the basis for their new regime, as Confederate vice president Alexander Stephens did in his well-known Corner-Stone Speech of 1861. Levine reads this episode as a kind of parable of how well-intended scientists can be tempted by the desire for praise or political power to use their science to rationalize morally problematic institutions. The solution, he argues, is not to ignore science but to temper it by keeping it in conversation with other sources of practical wisdom, so as to encourage scientists to speak with a greater sense of humility and self-criticism when they engage in politics.

The final chapter in Part One is James Read's analysis of the Southerner Calhoun's political program, which defined the antebellum South by linking a defense of slavery as a positive good with a robust account of states' rights, including both nullification and secession. Read admits that Calhoun was trying to preserve American constitutionalism as he understood it and that he offered a penetrating analysis of the problems of majority government worthy of study still. However, it would be a grave mistake, Read argues, to think that one could separate Calhoun's constitutional thought from his defense of slavery. Whereas Jefferson exemplified Southern ambivalence about slavery, Calhoun believed that the South's sense of self-respect must be bolstered by an uncompromising assertion of slavery's rightness. As Read shows, although there were more moderate strands of Southern political thought, Southern statesmen effectively followed the political strategy sketched by Calhoun right down to the eve of secession.

With secession we come to the second stage in our deliberative point of view, the moment of choice. Part Two of the volume deals with the decisions

Americans made as the regime they inherited from the founders broke down, most obviously in the crisis that began the war itself. Part Two begins with a chapter that, although it concerns events of the 1850s, offers a subtle commentary on how Lincoln transcended the contradictions inherent in the Jeffersonian regime on race and slavery and thus offered something new in the American political tradition. Diana Schaub gives a close reading of Lincoln's rhetoric not on slavery but on race in his 1854 Kansas-Nebraska Speech and his 1857 *Dred Scott* Speech. Schaub's Lincoln recognizes that antislavery feeling in his time was deeply entangled with antiblack sentiment, and she argues that Lincoln subtly used, without endorsing, white prejudice and self-interest to encourage his audience to act against slavery. What some commentators have seen as evidence of Lincoln's own racism, Schaub sees as a masterful attempt to coax human beings into rising above themselves.

The chapters of Steven Smith, Caleb Verbois, and W. B. Allen all deal with aspects of the political choice par excellence, the choice to make or accept war. Smith's chapter examines Lincoln's justification to accept war in 1861 by means of close readings of Lincoln's First Inaugural Address and his July 4 Message to Congress in Special Session. Although not dismissing the importance of the slavery question, Smith suggests that the significance of the decision to accept war ultimately turned on the correct understanding of what it means to be a constitutional people. Although there is a natural right of revolution, Smith's Lincoln argues, there cannot be a constitutional right of secession, and a con stitutional people that allows the losers in a free and fair election to walk away from the polity sets itself up for unending bullying. In refusing to allow the Southern states to secede unilaterally, Smith argues, the people of the United States (as instructed by Lincoln) stood up not primarily for an abstract concept of justice but for their own self-respect.

War brings its own dilemmas, unanticipated by the text of the Constitution or an abstract theory of morality, and the next chapter in the volume addresses one of these: Can constitutionalism survive war? Or must the necessities of national self-preservation override the standards of peacetime? Verbois's chapter takes up these questions by reconsidering three of Lincoln's most controversial wartime actions: his mustering of the militia in 1861 before Congress could act, his suspension of habeas corpus, and his Emancipation Proclamation. Verbois argues that although Lincoln did step outside the bounds of normal executive action, he was always sensitive to the need to respect and bolster public attachment to the Constitution. Lincoln's greatest achievement, Verbois suggests, might have been holding and winning the election of 1864 while making the case for the constitutionality of his actions as executive.

Allen's chapter brings us back to the issue underlying the war, slavery, with a close examination of the Emancipation Proclamation. By 1862, it was clear both that the war would not end quickly and that the practice of slavery represented a major weakness for the Confederacy. For the first time, the end of slavery seemed to be in the direct interest of white Americans, at least Northern whites. Yet, Allen suggests, in contemplating the end of slavery, Lincoln faced a new version of the tension between constitutionalism and morality because if he acted unilaterally to emancipate all the slaves, he would likely lose the support of the border states and face the likelihood of a challenge from the Supreme Court. As Allen shows, the Emancipation Proclamation navigated this dilemma by appealing to military necessity and restricting the proclamation's reach. The proclamation thus strengthened the Union war effort, both materially and in terms of Northern morale, and prepared the way for the American people to end slavery constitutionally with the Thirteenth Amendment.

Taken together, the chapters by Schaub, Smith, Verbois, and Allen show Lincoln as a master of using low, sometimes even ignoble motives for the sake of nobler ends. Whereas Jefferson had used the tension between morality and self-interest as an excuse for not acting, and the abolitionists had used morality to hector Americans without regard to self-interest, Lincoln aimed to use his audience's less-than-admirable motives for admirable ends.

Although moments of decision are contingent, it is all too easy for us to think the war had to turn out as it did, to think the victors had to win because they did win. James Stoner, Jr., offers a challenge to this familiar tendency in his chapter on the understudied Confederate Constitution. As he argues, the authors of the Confederate Constitution claimed merely to be restoring the true original understanding of the US Constitution, and as such their work stands as an important challenge or reference point for constitutional originalists today. For example, the Confederate Constitution explicitly endorses slavery, suggesting that its authors understood the US Constitution's silence on slavery as a rebuke, though in most other respects they duplicated that Constitution rather than, say, reviving the Articles of Confederation. Like the chapters by Read and Whittington, Stoner's chapter thus reminds us of the existence of multiple, conflicting traditions within American political thought and suggests that, in at least some respects, the Civil War was indeed a kind of refounding that rejected an earlier understanding of the US Constitution. Stoner argues that the Confederate Constitution, as the road not taken, helps us gain clarity by throwing into relief the choices made in establishing the postwar order, especially in the Reconstruction amendments.

Part Three of our volume examines the consequences, but also the limits, of choice. The chapters by Michael Zuckert and Philip Lyons each examine the political aftermath of the war. Zuckert's chapter examines the Thirteenth, Fourteenth, and Fifteenth Amendments and argues that, far from signifying a refounding of the American regime, these amendments complete the original US Constitution not only by ending slavery but also by bringing it closer to James Madison's original vision of the Constitution. At the Convention of 1787, Madison had argued for national power with regard to the states, including a congressional veto over state laws. Zuckert suggests that the Fourteenth Amendment aims at a similar goal, albeit through the courts rather than Congress.

As Lyons's chapter on Reconstruction shows, however, the overall success of the war was mixed by any standard. In the aftermath of the war, Americans faced for the first time the problem of how to build a genuinely multiracial society. Yet, Lyons suggests, many Southerners, embittered by the war and still believing that whites should not share power with blacks, rejected equality for the freedpeople. Was justice for blacks compatible with the self-government of whites? Lyons argues that this fundamental dilemma was exacerbated by the excessively punitive attitude of the radical Republicans in Congress toward the now-defeated Confederates. Having failed to heed the example of Lincoln, who had taken a more conciliatory approach while he lived, the radical Republicans ended up undermining the progress of African Americans for a century to come.

Our final two chapters take a broader view of the meaning of the war by taking seriously the points of view of both the freedpeople and the heirs of the former slave owners. Myers uses the thought of the greatest abolitionist of the nineteenth century, Douglass, himself formerly enslaved, to look back over the war and the long struggle over slavery that preceded it. Douglass, Myers suggests, believed that by means of the war the nation was finally making good on the promise of human equality in the Declaration of Independence. Yet formal freedom was only a beginning: Would whites and blacks be able to live together as genuine equals? And would the natural rights doctrine of the Declaration serve to support that project or undermine it? Myers finds in Douglass a Jeffersonian hopefulness about progress, but now sobered and chastened by a Thucydidean realism about the enduring tension between justice and self-interest.

Johnathan O'Neill concludes the volume by examining the aftereffects of the war on the political and constitutional thought of Southerners well into the twentieth century. O'Neill identifies a crucial irony for the story of this volume: although the South lost on the battlefield in 1865, it largely managed to win the battle for the interpretation of the war for at least a century. According to that interpretation, the war was no mere completion or perfection of the original regime but was a genuine and violent revolution in the American regime. Some, like Wilson and other Progressives, welcomed this result and found inspiration for going further. Others, building on the postwar apologias for the South by Jefferson Davis and his vice president, Stephens, lamented the loss of constitutional, limited government. O'Neill finds something admirable in the constitutionalist tradition of Southern political thought in the twentieth century, something, he thinks, that the mainstream of American constitutional thought has lost. Nonetheless, as he makes clear, the Southern tradition he discusses, however attractive in other ways, was marred by a fundamental unwillingness or inability to acknowledge the extent to which slavery and racism have been at the heart of Southern political life.

## OUR REGIME QUESTION

Taken as a whole, the chapters in this volume bespeak the moral complexity, even ambiguity, of the war, the problem to which it responded, and the results it produced. The story of the war is one of triumph and disappointment; of nobility mixed with ugliness; of the dignity, but also limits, of political choice and deliberation. By raising fundamental questions of the soundness or unsoundness of the American regime, the war and the events surrounding it tested those who lived through it and still test us today. We trust that the chapters in this volume make vivid the exemplary thinkers who rose to the occasion of thinking though these regime questions, and we hope we will inform our readers by bringing understudied moments of the American political tradition to light and spurring those readers to see figures they thought they knew more fully with new eyes. Yet we would be remiss if we did not mention a most practical dimension of the inquiries we have pursued here. Our historical question has been whether the Civil War was a reaffirmation (or completion) of the original American regime of the founders or something new, a refounding or even a regime change. The practical version of that question asks about the viability or defensibility of the regime: Should we here and now affirm and defend or alter and abolish the regime in which we live, or can we both affirm and alter?

The chapters that follow provide ample intellectual stimulation for readers wrestling with the question of the worthiness of our regime. We hope to have shown the dignity and importance not only of the regime question itself but also of issues and questions still with us today. Moreover, all of these questions have contemporary analogues for us. Is the regime in which we live a viable, defensible one? Are its intellectual foundations strong and its political institutions worthy of defense? Although we hope that the present volume, by showing exemplary Americans wrestling with their own versions of these questions, encourages thoughtfulness about these questions in and for our own times, in the final analysis the decision rests with the reader.

## NOTES

1. For the background of this phrase in Thirteenth Amendment jurisprudence, see Jennifer Mason McAward, "Defining the Badges and Incidents of Slavery," *University of Pennsylvania Journal of Constitutional Law* 14, no. 3 (2012): 561–630.

2. Elizabeth Fox-Genovese and Eugene D. Genovese, *The Mind of the Master Class: History and Faith in the Southern Slaveholder's Worldview* (New York: Cambridge University Press, 2005).

3. James McPherson, *Battle Cry of Freedom: The Civil War Era* (New York: Oxford University Press, 1988); Allen Guelzo, *Fateful Lightning: A New History of the Civil War and Reconstruction* (New York: Oxford University Press, 2012).

4. Daniel Walker Howe, *What God Hath Wrought: The Transformation of America, 1815–1848* (New York: Oxford University Press, 2007); Sean Wilentz, *The Rise of American Democracy: Jefferson to Lincoln* (New York: Norton, 2005); William Freehling, *The Road to Disunion*, vol. 1: *Secessionists at Bay, 1776–1854* (New York: Oxford University Press, 1990) and vol. 2: *Secessionists Triumphant, 1854–1861* (New York: Oxford University Press, 2007); Don Fehrenbacher, *The Dred Scott Case: Its Significance in American Law and Politics* (New York: Oxford University Press, 1978)

5. Eric Foner, *Reconstruction: America's Unfinished Revolution, 1863–1877* (New York: HarperCollins, 1988).

6. Drew Gilpin Faust, *This Republic of Suffering: Death and the American Civil War* (New York: Knopf, 2008).

7. Harry Jaffa, *Crisis of the House Divided: An Interpretation of the Issues in the Lincoln-Douglas Debates* (Chicago: University of Chicago Press, 1958); George Anastaplo, *Abraham Lincoln: A Constitutional Biography* (Lanham, MD: Rowman and Littlefield, 1999); Allen Guelzo, *Abraham Lincoln: A Very Short Introduction* (New York: Oxford University Press, 2009); Allen Guelzo, *Redeeming the Great Emancipator* (Cambridge, MA: Harvard University Press, 2016).

8. Eric Foner, *The Fiery Trial: Abraham Lincoln and American Slavery* (New York: Norton, 2010); John Stauffer, *The Black Hearts of Men: Radical Abolitionists and the Transformation of Race* (Cambridge, MA: Harvard University Press, 2004); Manisha Sinha, *The Slave's Cause: A History of Abolition* (New Haven, CT: Yale University Press, 2016); Daniel Malachuk, *Two Cities: The Political Thought of American Transcendentalism* (Lawrence: University Press of Kansas, 2016). See also Andrew Delbanco, with

commentaries by John Stauffer, Manisha Sinha, Darryl Pinckney, and Wilfred McClay, *The Abolitionist Imagination* (Cambridge, MA: Harvard University Press, 2012).

9. On this point, see Daniel Crofts, *Lincoln and the Politics of Slavery: The Other Thirteenth Amendment and the Struggle to Save the Union* (Chapel Hill: University of North Carolina Press, 2016).

10. Faust, *This Republic of Suffering*. Some scholars have recently suggested that the actual number of casualties might have been considerably higher. See J. David Hacker, "Recounting the Dead," *New York Times,* September 20, 2011, https://opinionator.blogs .nytimes.com/2011/09/20/recounting-the-dead/.

11. On the emergence of emancipation as the aim of the war, see James Oakes, *Freedom National: The Destruction of Slavery in the United States, 1861–1865* (New York: Norton, 2013).

12. Jeffrey Hummel, *Emancipating Slaves, Enslaving Free Men: A History of the American Civil War* (Chicago: Open Court, 1996), 352; Mark Graber, Dred Scott *and the Problem of Constitutional Evil* (New York: Cambridge University Press, 2006).

13. Stephen Oates, *With Malice toward None: A Life of Abraham Lincoln* (New York: HarperCollins, 1977); James Read, *Majority Rule versus Consensus: The Political Thought of John Calhoun* (Lawrence: University Press of Kansas, 2009).

14. George Kateb, *Lincoln's Political Thought* (Cambridge, MA: Harvard University Press, 2015); Graber, Dred Scott *and the Problem of Constitutional Evil.*

15. Paul Finkelman, *Slavery and the Founders: Race and Liberty in the Age of Jefferson,* 2nd ed. (New York: Routledge, 2001); David Waldstreicher, *Slavery's Constitution: From Revolution to Ratification* (New York: Hill and Wang, 2009); George Van Cleve, *A Slaveholders' Union: Slavery, Politics, and the Constitution in the Early American Republic* (Chicago: University of Chicago Press, 2010); Alan Taylor, *American Revolutions: A Continental History, 1750–1804* (New York: Norton, 2016).

16. Fehrenbacher, *The* Dred Scott *Case;* Freehling, *Road to Disunion;* Paul Rahe, *Republics Ancient and Modern,* vol. 3: *Inventions of Prudence* (Chapel Hill: University of North Carolina Press, 1994); Thomas G. West, *Vindicating the Founders: Race, Sex, Class, and Justice in the Origins of America* (Lanham, MD: Rowman and Littlefield, 1997). Some observers, such as Frederick Douglass, Gerrit Smith, and Lysander Spooner, argued before the war that the text of the Constitution actually makes no concessions to slavery. See Peter Myers, *Frederick Douglass: Race and the Rebirth of American Liberalism* (Lawrence: University Press of Kansas, 2008), chap. 3.

17. For an evenhanded discussion of this question, see Alan Gibson, *Understanding the Founding: The Crucial Questions,* 2nd ed. (Lawrence: University Press of Kansas, 2010).

18. For Frederick Douglass's question and his early, critical view of the Constitution, see The Right to Criticize American Institutions, a Speech to the American Antislavery Society, May 11, 1847, in *Frederick Douglass: Selected Speeches and Writings,* ed. Philip S. Foner and Yuval Taylor (Chicago: Lawrence Hill, 1999), 75–83. For Douglass's changed view of the Constitution, see Change of Opinion Announced, May 21, 1851, in *Frederick Douglass: Selected Speeches and Writings,* 173–174, and The Constitution of the United States: Is It Pro-slavery or Anti-Slavery? March 26, 1860, in *Frederick Douglass: Selected Speeches and Writings,* 379–390.

19. David Blight, *Frederick Douglass's Civil War: Keeping Faith in Jubilee* (Baton Rouge: Louisiana State University Press, 1991); Myers, *Frederick Douglass;* Nicholas Buccola, *The Political Thought of Frederick Douglass: In Pursuit of Liberty* (New York: New York University Press, 2012).

20. Ta-Nehisi Coates, *Between the World and Me* (New York: Spiegel and Grau, 2015); Shelby Steele, *The Content of Our Character: A New Vision of Race in America* (New York: HarperPerennial, 1990).

21. David Levering Lewis, *W. E. B. DuBois: A Biography, 1868–1963* (New York: Henry Holt, 2009); Lawrie Balfour, *Democracy's Reconstruction: Thinking Politically with W. E. B. DuBois* (New York: Oxford University Press, 2011); Robert Norrell, *Up from History: The Life of Booker T. Washington* (Cambridge, MA: Belknap Press of Harvard University Press, 2011); Herbert Storing, "The School of Slavery: A Reconsideration of Booker T. Washington," in *Toward a More Perfect Union,* ed. Joseph M. Bessette (Washington, DC: American Enterprise Institute Press, 1995).

22. Bruce Ackerman, *We the People,* vol. 2: *Transformations* (Cambridge, MA: Belknap Press of Harvard University Press, 1998); Akhil Reed Amar, *The Bill of Rights: Creation and Reconstruction* (New Haven, CT: Yale University Press, 1998).

23. Michael Les Benedict, *Preserving the Constitution: Essays on Politics and the Constitution in the Reconstruction Era* (New York: Fordham University Press, 2006); Alfred H. Kelly, Winfred A. Harbison, and Herman Belz, *The American Constitution: Its Origins and Development,* 7th ed., vol. 1 (New York: Norton, 1991), 317–318, 360–361; Morton Keller, *America's Three Regimes: A New Political History* (New York: Oxford University Press, 2007), 131–134. See also Richard Franklin Bensel, *Yankee Leviathan: The Origins of Central State Authority in America, 1859–1877* (New York: Cambridge University Press, 1990), and Hummel, *Emancipating Slaves, Enslaving Freemen,* who see the buildup of the federal government to win the war as the genesis of the modern American central state.

24. Ronald J. Pestritto and Jason R. Jividen, "Lincoln and the Progressives," in *Lincoln and Liberty: Wisdom for the Ages,* ed. Lucas Morel (Lexington: University Press of Kentucky, 2014).

25. Often inspired by Charles R. Kesler's definitive essay "Woodrow Wilson and the Statesmanship of Progress," recently reprinted in *Progressive Challenges to the American Constitution: A New Republic,* ed. Bradley C. S. Watson (New York: Cambridge University Press, 2017), 226–253, several scholars have revaluated the Progressive understanding of presidential leadership and Lincoln in particular. For an overview, see Jason R. Jividen, *Claiming Lincoln: Progressivism, Equality, and the Battle for Lincoln's Legacy in Presidential Rhetoric* (DeKalb: Northern Illinois University Press, 2011).

26. See James W. Ceaser, "Progressivism and the Doctrine of Natural Rights," in Watson, *Progressive Challenges,* 67–86; Ronald J. Pestritto, "Woodrow Wilson and the Meaning of the Lincoln Legacy," in *Constitutionalism in the Approach and Aftermath of the Civil War,* ed. Paul Moreno and Johnathan O'Neill (New York: Fordham University Press, 2013), 183–201; J. David Alvis and Jason R. Jividen, *Statesmanship and Progressive Reform: An Assessment of Herbert Croly's Abraham Lincoln* (New York: Palgrave Macmillan, 2013).

27. On science, race, and eugenics in the Progressive era, see Thomas Leonard,

*Illiberal Reformers: Race, Eugenics, and American Economics in the Progressive Era* (Princeton, NJ: Princeton University Press, 2016). On Woodrow Wilson's policies with regard to race, see Eric Yellin, *Racism in the Nation's Service: Government Workers and the Color Line in Woodrow Wilson's America* (Chapel Hill: University of North Carolina Press, 2013).

# Part One

*The Problem*

# CHAPTER 1

# The Later Jefferson and the Problem of Natural Rights

Thomas W. Merrill

In his speeches in the 1850s arguing for the restriction of slavery in the territories, Abraham Lincoln wrapped himself in Thomas Jefferson's mantle, citing Jefferson's authority as author of the Declaration of Independence and as originator of the policy of prohibiting slavery in the territories. Yet this last claim must have struck informed contemporaries as somewhat misleading because Jefferson had changed his mind about slavery in the territories and had famously opposed the very line between free and slave territories Lincoln was campaigning to restore. For today's readers, informed by Lincoln's interpretation of the founding, Jefferson's change of heart on slavery in the territories must appear anomalous and painful.[1] The author of the most comprehensive study of Jefferson and slavery describes the episode as the "strange death of Jeffersonian liberalism."[2]

How could the author of the Declaration of Independence square his attachment to natural rights with his recommendation to expand slavery throughout the territories? Jefferson, however, does not regard the expansion of slavery as contradicting natural rights but uses the logic of natural rights to justify it. According to Jefferson's most famous statement on the Missouri Crisis, his letter to John Holmes of April 22, 1820, slavery presents a profound dilemma for American slave owners because justice for the enslaved people and the self-preservation of the slave owners are at odds. But because self-preservation is the first natural right, slavery presents a conflict between two legitimate rights. Because slave owners have a legitimate interest in avoiding rebellions, he argues, they are justified in seeking to extend slavery across the territories, thus diluting concentrations of rebellious slaves.

Jefferson's reaction to the Missouri Crisis is well known,[3] and political theorists have offered innumerable treatments of Jefferson's natural rights doctrine. Yet rarely have scholars read Jefferson's reaction for what light it sheds on his understanding of natural rights. The status and meaning of Jefferson's natural rights doctrine has, of course, long produced both anxiety and defensiveness among scholars of American political thought. Some scholars, such as Herbert Storing and the early Harry Jaffa, have seen Jefferson's natural rights doctrine as essentially egoistic, eventually leading to a weakening of the communal responsibility necessary to a healthy polity. In this view, rights precede and eventually trump duties in Jefferson's natural rights doctrine, and the egoism of the natural rights doctrine contribute to the lack of forceful action on the part of Jefferson and the founding generation generally on slavery. Yet other scholars of American political thought, such as Michael Zuckert (and sometimes the same scholars at different points in their careers, such as Jaffa) argue that there is nothing inherently destabilizing for the polity in Jefferson's natural rights doctrine. These scholars thus aim to vindicate Jefferson's natural rights doctrine, arguing that Jefferson's record on slavery stems not from his political theory but from his racism and personal hypocrisy, factors extrinsic to his political theory.[4]

This chapter uses Jefferson's reaction to the Missouri Compromise and related texts to think through what it is about Jefferson's natural rights doctrine that invites such divergent reactions of condemnation and exculpation. It does not offer a purely theoretical discussion of the merits and flaws of the natural rights doctrine in the abstract. Nor is it intended to shed new light on the historical facts of the case, which are well known. Instead, the chapter aims to elucidate the problematic but interesting phenomenon of Jefferson's words and deeds on slavery and natural rights as a way of getting at the underlying theoretical questions. I proceed on the hypothesis that the use of a political theory in particular circumstances and in response to the necessities of the moment may reveal more about how a given political actor thinks about a political theory than a discussion of the theory in the abstract does. I find that Jefferson's invocations of natural rights with regard to the Missouri Crisis reveal a tangled set of intentions too complex to be adequately captured by either the egoistic or the moral interpretations of Jefferson's doctrine. Although the egoistic interpretation is correct to point out that the slave owner's right to self-preservation trumps his duty to respect the rights to life and liberty of enslaved persons, that interpretation fails to do justice to Jefferson's attempt to defend the moral innocence of American slave owners in the face of real or anticipated moral criticism, an attempt visible both in the letters about the Missouri Crisis and in Jefferson's draft of the Declaration of Independence. Paradoxically, it seems to have been Jefferson's need to vindicate the moral guiltlessness of American slave owners that led him to radicalize the egoistic dimension of the natural rights doctrine.[5] I begin with the puzzle of Jefferson's position on the Missouri Crisis, then widen the focus to show that Jefferson uses the natural rights doctrine in a similar way in his draft of the Declaration, and conclude with some reflections on the meaning of Jefferson's natural rights doctrine.

## JEFFERSON'S CHANGE OF HEART

In 1784 Jefferson, then a member of the Continental Congress, produced a report for the government of the western territories recently acquired by the new country. That report remarkably proposed that neither involuntary servitude nor slavery should exist under the temporary or the permanent governments that might be established in the new territories after 1800. Had Jefferson's recommendation been accepted and enforced, it would have prohibited slavery in all the western lands, not just those north of the Ohio. Jefferson's recommendation, however, fell short of passing the Continental Congress. One vote prevented the prohibition on slavery in the territories from passing. "The voice of a single individual," he wrote in 1786, "would have prevented this abominable crime from spreading itself over the country. Thus we see the fate of millions unborn hanging on the tongue of one man, and heaven was silent in that awful moment." Yet Jefferson looked forward to a time when this "crime" could be restrained: "It is to be hoped that [heaven] will not always be silent and that the friends of the rights of human nature will in the end prevail."[6]

Jefferson's failed attempt to bar slavery in the territories was, of course, the basis of what became the Northwest Ordinance of 1787, which, although not going as far as Jefferson's draft, did prohibit slavery north of the Ohio.[7] And Jefferson's youthful position was in fact quite aggressively antislavery. Jefferson was, after all, the author of the Declaration of Independence, whose natural rights principles were, as everyone recognized, incompatible with slavery and whose implications for slavery in America would have been even more obvious had Jefferson's original draft been published. Jefferson had also attempted to end slavery in Virginia, proposing a scheme of gradual emancipation in the Virginia legislature in 1776. Although that scheme had been rejected by his fellow legislators, Jefferson discussed it in his *Notes on the State of Virginia* in one of the most outspoken discussions of the injustice of slavery of the time and a frank and painful treatment of the core dilemma of American slave owners.[8]

By the last decade of his life, however, Jefferson had changed his mind. By the time of the Missouri Crisis in 1819–1820, Jefferson no longer believed slavery could be restricted to the existing states by the power of the federal government, or indeed that it should be. Quite the contrary: in a series of letters in this period, some of which were intended for public distribution, Jefferson argued strenuously that the expansion of slavery into the territories was the prudent course of action and that, in any event, Congress lacked the power to restrict it. In making such arguments, Jefferson did not speak for himself alone. The other prominent members of the Republican dynasty from Virginia, James Madison and James Monroe, concurred.[9] This policy position became a defining commitment of Southern statesmen throughout the antebellum period, from Jefferson to John C. Calhoun to Jefferson Davis. To be sure, Jefferson had not changed his mind on the basic injustice of slavery, and he would have been horrified by the rejection of natural rights by Calhoun and others. He claimed, as he had always done, that slavery was both contrary to the natural rights of the slaves and a calamity for the slave owners, albeit one of which there was no easy way out. In the last decade of his life, Jefferson argued that diffusionism, or the extension of slavery throughout the territories, was the best way of ameliorating the evils of slavery and perhaps even the best way of ultimately ending the institution.[10]

Given the important role the disagreement about slavery in the territories played in antebellum politics, Jefferson's change of heart is an important turning point in the political history of the early republic. Certainly Jefferson's final position in favor of the expansion of slavery was well known to antebellum America and often cited by Southern statesmen in support of their own political positions.[11] Yet the timing and the meaning of Jefferson's change of heart is elusive because we have little direct evidence of when, precisely, the change occurred.[12] But the more important question is the meaning of his shift. How is it, after all, that the man who saw the extension of slavery to the territories as the spread of an "abominable crime" across the continent decided that spread was in fact the best thing to do? How could the author of the Declaration of Independence argue that natural rights were compatible with the expansion of slavery?

*THE LETTER TO HOLMES*

Jefferson gave his best-known answer to that question in his letter to John Holmes of April 22, 1820. The letter is famous for its unforgettable description of the situation of American slave owners as holding "the wolf by the ear"[13] and is often read without reference to the political context or to Jefferson's intention in writing the letter, which he well knew would become public. The political context is the controversy over whether slavery would be allowed to spread into Missouri and the other territories, and Jefferson's intention was to make the case that restricting the spread of slavery would be both imprudent and unconstitutional. In order to understand the full significance of the "wolf by the ear" image, then, we need to understand what Jefferson was trying to accomplish with the letter.

Holmes was a member of the House of Representatives from the Maine district of Massachusetts when the Missouri Crisis broke out in 1819.[14] When James Tallmadge, representative from New York, proposed that Missouri, then a territory qualified to become a state, be admitted to the Union only if slavery were prohibited within its borders, slave state representatives fought back by asserting the right to carry their slaves wherever they wished in the territories. They also threatened to block Maine's request to become a state. The compromise that resolved the crisis allowed Missouri to come into the Union as a slave state in exchange for Maine coming in as a free state and established the 36° 30′ latitude line as the division between potential free and slave states from the territories. As the representative from Maine and the man who would become Maine's first senator in 1820, Holmes was at the center of the controversy. In the interest of having Maine become a state, Holmes sided with the slave states. Yet this position was unpopular with his largely antislavery constituency in Maine in his campaign for Senate in 1820. Caught between his constituency and his political bargain, Holmes needed help. As one scholar of the Missouri Crisis remarks: "It could be argued that nothing less than an endorsement from the author of the Declaration of Independence himself could have salvaged Holmes's political career in Maine. Fortunately for him, he had exactly that."[15]

Jefferson's letter, written in response to a request from Holmes, was payback for an ally who had supported the Southern position and was suffering as a result. And because Jefferson had every reason to think Holmes would publicize the letter, the letter in effect speaks to Holmes's constituents in particular and antislavery opinion in the North generally. The primary theme of the letter is the threat posed by the Missouri Compromise line to the Union, which Jefferson describes as the death knell of the Union. A geographical line corresponding to a moral and political principle, he writes, will be an unending source of rancor for the polity. The North and the South will come to blows, Jefferson predicts, tearing apart the America envisioned by the founding generation.

The letter to Holmes is often praised for its prescience. Yet Jefferson's blame for the looming struggle between North and South is not evenhanded.[16] In the controversy over slavery in the territories, Jefferson is firmly on the side of the South. That is why diffusionism is such a prominent theme in the letter and why Jefferson describes those pushing the nation toward a civil war as moved by "an abstract principle more likely to be effected by union than by scission."

The abstract principle is moral opposition to slavery; it is Jefferson's own "self-evident truth" that all men are created equal. By heedlessly pressing the South on something the South considers a vital interest, the antislavery Northerners are threatening the Union. It is they who perpetuate "an act of suicide on themselves, and of treason against the hopes of the world."

For us, who tend to see antebellum America through a Lincolnian lens, Jefferson's argument might seem surprising and counterintuitive. His argument is this. Slavery is indeed a moral wrong, but the spread of slavery across the territories is the best means of weakening it under the circumstances. More importantly, congressional noninterference with slavery in the territories will reassure Southern slave owners that Congress will not try to emancipate the enslaved directly. "An abstinence" from restricting slavery in the territories, Jefferson remarks, "would remove the jealousy excited by the undertaking of Congress to regulate the condition of the different descriptions of men composing a State." For this is "the exclusive right of every state, which nothing in the Constitution has taken from them and given to the General Government." Lurking behind the controversy about Missouri is the far more dangerous question of slavery in the states. Jefferson implies that if Congress does restrict slavery in the territories, the slave states would have a legitimate reason to fear a later attempt to emancipate the enslaved where they already are. In that case, the slave states would almost certainly dissolve the Union rather than accept emancipation of the enslaved. Jefferson thus darkly predicts, or threatens, Southern secession as the likely outcome of Northern aggression over slavery in the territories.

It is here that the image of the "wolf by the ear" plays an important, even indispensable, role in Jefferson's argument. We Southerners, Jefferson suggests, never wanted to enslave these people and would get rid of them if we could. But the slave owners are in a terrible bind: "We have the wolf by the ear and can neither hold him, nor safely let him go. Justice is in one scale, and self-preservation in the other."[17] Of course, because self-preservation is itself a natural right, what Jefferson means is that justice is on both sides. Natural rights confront natural rights. Jefferson never denies that the slaves would be justified in using violence to acquire their freedom. But the slave owners are under no obligation to free the enslaved if that would endanger their own self-preservation. Indeed, they are equally justified in doing whatever they must in order to secure their lives. Jefferson seems to treat the right to self-preservation as an absolute, as a trump that automatically outweighs other considerations. The conflict at the heart of American slavery is morally undecidable precisely because natural rights as Jefferson understands them are absolute.

The emotional anchor of the letter to Holmes is this existential conflict between master and slave. In effect Jefferson says to his Northern audience, you think you are choosing the moral course in attempting to restrict slavery. But you do not understand that slavery is a life-or-death issue for the South. If you do not allow slavery to expand, you lock us slave owners into an ever-closer entanglement with the wolf, a situation that only grows more dangerous as the slave population expands. If you go further and attempt to emancipate the existing slaves, you will confront us with the terrible choice between justice and self-preservation.[18] Your actions will force us to dissolve the Union long before the tragic choice of justice versus self-preservation becomes a reality. Under this scenario, the actor might be the Southern states, but the responsible party would be the Northern states, who recklessly force the Southern states' hand.[19]

## A QUESTION OF EXISTENCE

The letter to Holmes was not, of course, the only time Jefferson expressed his reaction to the Missouri Crisis. In a series of remarkable letters to John Adams, Albert Gallatin, Charles Pinckney, the Marquis de Lafayette, and others written around the same time, Jefferson makes the same argument in different ways.[20] These letters confirm the interpretation of the letter to Holmes proposed above and shed light on important aspects of Jefferson's position only alluded to in the public letter to the Maine senator. For a fuller understanding of that position, especially on the role played by the language and logic of natural rights, we turn briefly to these private letters on the Missouri Crisis.

The private letters are franker than the letter to Holmes about key aspects of Jefferson's view, including the existential threat to the South in any restriction of slavery in the territories, the possibility that the South will be compelled to secede from the Union, and the character of the Northern statesmen who advocate for restriction. Jefferson sketches his analysis of the Missouri Crisis in his letter to Gallatin of December 26, 1820:

[The Missouri question] served to throw dust in the eyes of the people and to fanaticize them, while to the knowing ones it gave a geographical and preponderant line of the Potomac, throwing fourteen states to the North and East, and ten to the South and West. With these, therefore, it is merely a question of power; but with the geographical minority it is a question of existence. For if Congress once goes out of the Constitution to arrogate a right of regulating the condition of the inhabitants of the states, its majority may, and probably will, next declare that the condition of all men within the United

States shall be that of freedom; in which case all the whites south of the Potomac and Ohio must evacuate their states, and most fortunate those who can do it first.[21]

For the Northerners, the Missouri question is not moral at all, but only a means of exercising power over the slave states. But for the slave states the issue is an existential one. As Jefferson wrote to John Adams on January 22, 1821, "The real question is, Are our slaves to be presented with freedom and a dagger? For if Congress has a power to regulate the conditions of the inhabitants of the states, within the states, it will be but another exercise of power to declare that all shall be free."[22] The Southern states would sooner secede, Jefferson thinks, than face such a possibility. Were the Northern states to move decisively toward emancipation, he writes, "there would be a secession of the members south of the line [marked out by the Potomac and Ohio] and probably of the three Northwestern States, who, however inclined to the other side, would scarcely separate from those who would hold the Mississippi from its mouth to its source."[23]

The private letters make it clear that in Jefferson's mind the antislavery leaders are cynics, whipping up the fanaticism of the Northern masses for advantage over their political opponents. Those leaders are, he remarks to Gallatin, old Federalists, trounced in politics, now trying to replace the old party divisions with "a new one of slave-holding and non-slave-holding States."[24] The cynical few are manipulating the morally naïve many purely for the sake of increasing their power and the sectional power of the North. The painful irony, of course, is that the principle to which these cynics appeal is the natural rights doctrine of the Declaration of Independence itself. Yet, in Jefferson's mind, the appearances are backward. It is the slave owners whose backs are against the wall, whose very existence is in question, and it is the allegedly antislavery leaders who are the Machiavellians, pursuing pure self-interest under the cover of moral principle. When he says they are committing "treason against the hopes of the world," he means it literally.

Read with the letter to Holmes, these letters bring out a striking dimension of the role of the conflict of natural rights in Jefferson's reaction to the Missouri Crisis. In all these letters Jefferson shows himself concerned to demonstrate that the moral blame for the current crisis belongs not to slave owners but to Northerners. Contra appearances, it is not the slave owners who are power-hungry amoralists, for they are compelled, by virtue of their terrible situation, to continue being slave owners and to seek to extend slavery. Rather, moralistic Northerners are the real cynics. Jefferson uses the natural rights doctrine, then, to deflect blame from the slave owners. They are tyrants only by necessity, but in truth they are innocent. Jefferson tells a morality tale with clear innocents and clear villains; it is only an accident of fate that the innocents are compelled to exercise tyrannical power, whereas the tyranny of the villains is cloaked under the name of morality. One need not deny that the slave owners were in a genuine bind or that moralistic denunciations of the slave owners was a cheap way for Northerners to claim the moral high ground. But these truths should not distract us from the fact that Jefferson uses the natural rights doctrine to shift blame in ways that are quite dubious. The effect of Jefferson's appeal to the natural rights doctrine is to suggest that slave owners are not guilty for the ugly things they are compelled to do. The natural rights of some provide a ready excuse for the continued deprivation of the rights of others.

Jefferson's appeal to the natural rights doctrine in this context raises some disquieting questions. Is Jefferson's use of natural rights here merely personal, a sign of the dark and rather paranoid side of his personality? Or is there something in the doctrine of natural rights, as Jefferson understands it, that lends itself to this kind of use?

## THE CONFLICT OF RIGHTS IN THE DECLARATION OF INDEPENDENCE

To address these questions, it is worth noting that the letter to Holmes was not the first time Jefferson had used the doctrine of natural rights in this way. To be sure, that letter was the first time Jefferson had made the case in public for the extension of slavery. But it was not the first time Jefferson had used the thought of an irreconcilable conflict of legitimate rights as a means of defending American slave owners from criticisms of injustice and hypocrisy. He had already done so, or at least tried to do so, in his draft of the Declaration of Independence, in a paragraph excised from the final version by the Continental Congress. That paragraph is well known, of course, for Jefferson's scathing denunciation of slavery as a violation of natural rights. Less often noticed is the fact that the paragraph portrays American slavery as a fundamental conflict of rights in just the way that the letter to Holmes does, and that the paragraph is also meant to deflect predictable criticism, also in a way very similar to the letter to Holmes. To see this, it helps to read the excised paragraph in the context of the argument of the Declaration as a whole.

As is well known, the structure of the Declaration is a syllogism of practical reason.[25] The assertion of natural rights at the beginning provides the major premise, the list of the crimes of the king of Great Britain form the minor premise, and the final declaration of independence is the conclusion.

The paragraph on slavery in Jefferson's draft has an important place in this structure. The crimes of George III are listed in ascending order from minor to major offenses. Thus the accusations rise from mere inactivity—refusing "his assent to laws the most wholesome and necessary"—to obstructionism—calling together "legislative bodies at places unusual, uncomfortable, and distant"—to the ominous—keeping standing armies in times of peace. As the list develops, the king comes to seem malign and conspiratorial. The final phase of the crescendo, both in the draft and in the final version, is the king's direct attacks on American life and property. The king and his agents have plundered the Americans' ships, ravaged their coasts, and burned their towns. Large armies of mercenaries bent on acts of "cruelty and perfidy" have been transported to America. American sailors have been impressed by the British navy and even compelled to become "executioners of their friends and brethren or to fall themselves by their own hands." Moreover, the king has excited "the merciless Indian savages," whose "known rule of warfare is an undistinguished destruction of all ages, sexes, and conditions," to attack Americans. There, with the royal attacks on the natural rights of life and liberty of the Americans, the published version of the list ends.

In Jefferson's draft, however, there is one more paragraph describing what he evidently sees as the king's crowning crime. The king has "waged cruel war on human nature itself, violating its most sacred rights of life and liberty in the persons of a distant people, who never offended him, captivating them and carrying them into slavery in another hemisphere or to incur miserable death on their transportation hither." Nor has the king simply enslaved the Africans and left them in America. He has also resisted any attempts by the Americans to stop the slave trade, even "prostituting his negative" to do so. And so that "this assemblage of horrors might want no fact of distinguished die," the king now makes matters worse. He or his agents are "exciting those very people to rise in arms among us, and to purchase that liberty of which he has deprived them, by murdering the people on whom he also obtruded them, thus paying off former crimes committed against the LIBERTIES of one people, with crimes which he urges them to commit against the LIVES of another."[26] The king excites the enslaved people to assert their natural rights to liberty at the expense of the natural rights to life of the slave owners. The king's culminating crime is to set the rights of liberty and life in irreconcilable and apparently mortal conflict. In this respect the king's incitement of revolts seems to be a more fiendish version of what the British navy does to impressed sailors by forcing them to choose between executing their friends and killing themselves. By inciting revolts, the king forces American slave owners to choose between allowing themselves to be killed and killing innocents attempting to assert their natural rights. In this respect the culminating crime of the king is different from those that precede it. Those earlier crimes are all things Americans have had done to them. In slavery, however, the king puts the Americans into a situation in which they are compelled to act like tyrants no matter their intentions. The crowning crime, it seems, is not to make Americans suffer but to compel them to make others suffer. He makes them act as he does. In this telling, Americans are innocent tyrants, slave owners through no intention of their own.

At the peak of the king's crimes in Jefferson's draft of the Declaration is the same thought so memorably expressed in the letter to Holmes. There is a fundamental conflict between the natural rights of enslaved people and the natural rights of the slave owner, a conflict irresolvable in terms of the doctrine of the Declaration. Indeed, the treatment of slavery in the excised paragraph forms a rather tragic counterpoint to the stirring words of the document's opening lines. Having confidently asserted the doctrine of natural rights at the beginning of the document, the paragraph on slavery reveals that doctrine's limits. To be sure, in order for Jefferson to present it as an irreconcilable, tragic conflict, he must cast all the responsibility for slavery's origins and continued existence on King George. Had the Americans chosen to enslave the people, the moral dilemma would not be as stark as Jefferson presents it because the Americans would be simply to blame.

In his autobiography, written in the 1820s, Jefferson described the decision to excise the paragraph about slavery as a victory of unrepentant slave owners from South Carolina and Georgia.[27] There is some truth to this description, but the reality was more complex. Many readers, from Jefferson's time to the present, have felt that the excised paragraph exaggerated both the guilt of the king and the innocence of the Americans for slavery.[28] Thus John Chester Miller remarks, "More aware than was Jefferson— who was obviously carried away by zeal for pillorying the king—of the dangers of propagandistic overkill, Congress wisely took the position that the monarch, already burdened by Jefferson with culpability for 'murder,' 'piratical warfare,' and inflicting 'miserable death,' could not be held accountable for all the evil extant in the British Empire."[29] One need not have been an advocate of slavery to have doubts about the wisdom of including Jefferson's paragraph.

Yet if the paragraph is overkill, the interesting question is why Jefferson felt the need for overkill in the first place. Part of the answer surely has to do with anticipated moral criticism of the American revolutionaries. It was, after all, only to be expected that when Americans justified their revolution from Great Britain, they would be charged with hypocrisy. As Samuel Johnson wrote in

1774, "How is it that we hear the loudest yelps for liberty from the drivers of Negroes?"[30] The excised paragraph is best read as a preemptive strike against such criticism. However implausible its argument as a historical matter, the intended rhetorical effect is clear: to deflect the predictable moral criticism of Americans for enslaving people back onto the king. The very implausibility of Jefferson's claims in the excised paragraph suggests that we have here a sensitivity to moral criticism and a strong, perhaps not fully self-conscious, desire to assert and secure his own moral blamelessness with regard to slavery. As Joseph Ellis remarks, the excised paragraph was "less a clarion call to end slavery than an invitation to wash one's hands of the matter."[31]

Although written with quite different practical goals in mind, the excised paragraph and the letters about the Missouri Crisis nonetheless have definite similarities. Both analyze American slavery in terms of competing sets of legitimate natural rights, and both leave the reader with the disquieting sense that there is no morally acceptable solution to that conflict. It is difficult to deny that there is a genuine moral problem here, and most of the founding generation likely shared Jefferson's view of the character of the problem. Yet there is something distinctive about the way Jefferson uses the conflict of rights that goes beyond the mere recognition of the problem. Whereas others might regard the problem as an unfortunate truth that must be worked around, there is in Jefferson a tone of despair and a sharp sense of the injustice of the slave owner's plight. As Peter Onuf remarks, "The passionate, blood-soaked language of rage and betrayal that Jefferson's colleagues excised from the Declaration—and that he restored in his *Autobiography* in 1821—was the same language that spilled out, seemingly beyond authorial control, in his despairing response to the Missouri crisis."[32] Whereas others might minimize the problem, Jefferson wallows in the existential conflict, making the conflict of rights his theme.[33]

The interesting question is why. In both the draft of the Declaration and the later letters Jefferson is concerned to deflect real or anticipated moral criticism. In effect, he uses the doctrine of natural rights in both cases to admit that American slave owners have committed, are committing, and will commit some awful wrongs. But it is not their fault because they are compelled to do so in order to protect their own natural rights. In truth, the fault is elsewhere: with the king of Great Britain, who foisted slavery on the colonies, in the one case, and with the Northern politicians, who cynically manipulate antislavery sentiment to gain power over the South, in the other. In both cases Jefferson uses the doctrine of natural rights to turn moral criticism of American slave owners back on their enemies. If Jefferson had used the notion of a conflict of rights in this way only once, we might dismiss it as a coincidence. But the fact that he did it more than once raises difficult questions. Is there something about the doctrine of natural rights itself that lends itself to this kind of use? And if so, what is it?

## JEFFERSON'S NATURAL RIGHTS DOCTRINE

The status and meaning of Jefferson's natural rights doctrine have long been sources of both anxiety and defensiveness in scholars of American political thought. It sometimes seems as though the question of the ultimate worth of the American project can be reduced in the eyes of these scholars to the theoretical question of the viability of the natural rights doctrine itself. Thus in a classic essay on slavery and the moral foundations of the American republic, Herbert Storing writes that the problem with Jefferson and the other founders is not that they betrayed their principles. The problem lies in their principles themselves. Writing about the letter to Holmes, Storing concedes that only an "invincible naïveté" would deny that Jefferson had identified a genuine moral dilemma for the founding generation. Nonetheless, Storing argues, there is a "tendency under the Declaration of Independence for justice to be reduced to self-preservation, for self-preservation to be defined as self-interest, and for self-interest to be defined as what is convenient and achievable."[34] In this view there is an anarchic individualism implicit in the natural rights doctrine that will sooner or later undermine the political order itself. Yet such worries have provoked their own defensiveness among those who wish to affirm the stability and justice of the American project. Michael Zuckert, for example, argues that there is no organic or necessary connection between Jefferson's record on slavery and his natural rights doctrine. Zuckert tries to show how Jefferson's version of natural rights necessarily points to and is completed by a system of duties and mutually recognized rights. Jefferson's record on slavery, he says, is the result of Jefferson's racism and personal hypocrisy, factors essentially external to, and separable from, the natural rights doctrine itself.[35] Jefferson was guilty, Zuckert argues, but the natural rights doctrine was innocent.

Does our reading of Jefferson's treatment of natural rights and slavery in these texts shed any light on this moral drama of condemnation versus exculpation? The answer is complicated because neither the "egoistic" interpretation nor the "moral" interpretation does justice to the tangled reality of Jefferson's thought. On the one hand, both the letters about the Missouri Crisis and the draft of the Declaration show that Jefferson believed there was a fundamental conflict of equally legitimate natural rights in slavery, one that was, for the foreseeable future, irreconcilable. And although he admitted (at least as a theoretical matter) that the doctrine of natural rights would justify enslaved people in attempting to rebel, he also believed that the same doctrine justified the slave owners in doing what they must to preserve themselves, regardless of the consequences for the enslaved. This means, contra the "moral" interpretation, that there is indeed a conflict between the rights of the individual and the common good, at least in this particular case. What else could it mean for Jefferson to assert that justice and self-preservation are at odds? On this point, the egoistic interpretation is more accurate about the actual consequences of Jefferson's thought. The practical upshot of Jefferson's use of the natural rights language is a kind of egoism and justification for actions that Jefferson himself, at other times in his career, thought were morally unacceptable, such as extending slavery across the territories.

A brief look at Zuckert's recent defense and rearticulation of Jefferson's natural rights doctrine helps us understand why. Unlike some defenders of Jefferson's political theory, Zuckert does not claim that the natural rights theory is really a natural law theory. He admits that the core of Jeffersonian morality is self-concern in the form of an assertion of natural rights, and he emphasizes that, whereas human beings originally or naturally assert rights, they do not naturally recognize others' legitimate claims. Nonetheless, Zuckert claims that there is a clear path from the original rights assertions, which he calls "proto-rights," to mutually recognized, fully moral rights, which he calls "rights-in-the-proper-sense." Because the "proto-rights" cannot be secure without a scheme of mutual recognition, Zuckert argues, they point beyond themselves toward "rights-in-the-proper-sense." Their natural deficiency points toward completion in "a system of mutual recognition" that is necessarily a "system of natural duties correlative to natural rights."[36]

Zuckert's argument is a plausible account of how Jefferson thought about rights and duties under nonextreme circumstances. But the key point here is that, in both Jefferson's draft of the Declaration and the letters about the Missouri Crisis, slavery makes the extreme case normal. It reverses the development that Zuckert traces from "proto-rights" to "rights-in-the-proper-sense" and stands as a permanent bar to Americans making the transition to "rights-in-the-proper-sense" completely. Put differently, slavery shows that "proto-rights" are the inalienable core of "rights-in-the-proper-sense." This need not mean that the egoism of Jefferson's natural rights doctrine is necessarily in conflict with the interests and rights of others. There is no reason to think that the natural rights doctrine as Jefferson understood it would counsel choosing the institution of slavery if it did not already exist. But matters are different if it does already exist and today's slave owners have merely inherited it. It is precisely because American slavery is, for Jefferson, an historical accident, not a choice, that slavery presents an especially problematic example of the conflict of natural rights.

The "egoistic" interpretation is therefore more right than wrong in arguing that there was a tendency in Jefferson's natural rights doctrine toward reducing justice to self-interest. Yet seeing Jefferson as simply egoistic does not do justice to the full phenomenon revealed in these texts either. Neither the draft of the Declaration nor the letters about Missouri reveal a cold calculator shrewdly gauging his self-interest. They reveal a man struck to the quick by criticism of American slave owners, a man passionately concerned to defend himself and his fellows against the charge of hypocrisy. Jefferson does emphasize the "egoistic" dimension of natural rights, but he does so in an effort to turn the moral tables on his opponents. The very weakness and implausibility of Jefferson's arguments, which his colleagues in the Continental Congress seem to have recognized, suggests that we have here a deeply rooted psychological conflict. There is defensiveness and even self-righteousness in Jefferson that cannot be reduced to mere egoism and is hard to explain on the basis of Jefferson's own natural rights doctrine. The "egoistic" reading of Jefferson thus needs to be supplemented by attention to this dimension of Jefferson's character and his arguments.

Was there something about Jefferson's version of the natural rights doctrine that lent itself to these results? On the one hand, one would not want to say that the natural rights doctrine by itself was the cause of Jefferson's tendency to reduce justice to self-interest. There were other statesmen who, although starting from the same basic premises as Jefferson, did not emphasize the necessities imposed on Americans by the conflict of rights. Even if one accepted the reality of a profound moral dilemma in American slavery, one can easily imagine a different practical course of action in the light of that reality. Nonetheless, trying to pin the blame for Jefferson's record on slavery on allegedly external factors (racism, hypocrisy) avoids facing up to the deeper entanglement between that record and the natural rights doctrine.

It is more accurate to say that the doctrine of natural rights was a necessary but not sufficient cause of those uses. Put differently, even if Jefferson misused and subtly perverted the natural rights doctrine, there must be something in the doctrine that lent itself to that misuse. It is not, perhaps, surprising that a doctrine that begins with the assertion of an indefeasible natural right to preserve oneself should lend itself to being used as an excuse for otherwise problematic actions. It might be precisely the absolute character of natural rights as

Jefferson understands them that lends itself, not so much to a straightforward selfishness, but to an unmoderated moralism. To be sure, the fate of Jeffersonian liberalism was mediated by powerful historical contingencies. Without the historical accident of slavery in the early republic or the distinctive personality of Jefferson himself, the natural rights doctrine might not have been radicalized in this particular way. Nonetheless, that radicalization reveals a genuine possibility implicit in the natural rights doctrine. There is, it seems, a kind of absolutism or moralism in the natural rights doctrine as Jefferson understands it that can serve as an excuse not to face up to all the consequences of one's actions.

## THE "STRANGE DEATH OF JEFFERSONIAN LIBERALISM"

Many have said that the problem of slavery revealed the inherent limitations of the natural rights doctrine. A doctrine of the natural right of each individual to preserve him- or herself, it might be said, cannot provide a persuasive argument for why that individual should risk his or her life or sacrifice significant interests for the sake of someone else's rights. Having motivated the Americans to throw off foreign tyranny, the doctrine of natural rights could not move them to put an end to their own tyrannizing. This analysis is a familiar one. As the letter to Holmes reveals, it seems to have been Jefferson's own. Slavery revealed the implicit egoism of the natural rights doctrine. Yet our reading of these texts suggests that it may not be the most important criticism to be made of Jefferson and his understanding of natural rights. After all, it is very much an open question whether any political theory could have resolved this dilemma in an easy or acceptable fashion. It behooves us to remember there was a real problem inherent in American slavery. Nonetheless, recognizing the gravity of the problem by no means clinches Jefferson's innocence. Even if a problem is intractable or merely very difficult, how a person handles it makes a difference. One could, for example, resolve not to make matters worse.

The truth is that Jefferson did make it worse. Even while he remarked on the injustice and imprudence of slavery, Jefferson also pursued a political agenda that strengthened slavery and contributed to the political disposition that would come to characterize the antebellum South after his death. Think here not simply about his position on extending slavery to the territories but of his defense of states' rights and local government, his opposition to "consolidated" government, and above all his support for agriculture as opposed to manufactures. From early on, Jefferson believed that agriculture was more conducive to free and self-governing citizens than manufacturing and cities were. But the predominantly agricultural part of the nation was also the part most deeply entangled in slavery, and the most important consequence of supporting agriculture was strengthening slavery.[37] By the time of the Missouri Crisis, after the invention of the cotton gin and after the Louisiana Purchase, it was clear or should have been clear that, far from withering away, slavery was getting stronger and expanding, in part because of the preference for agriculture of Jefferson's own party. In any event, it would not have taken great insight to see that Jefferson's policies and his own doctrine of natural rights were in deep tension; nor is it surprising that, in the decade after his death, Jefferson's political heirs would explicitly affirm agriculture, states' rights, and slavery and reject the doctrine of natural rights. As Robert Shalhope writes, "If . . . Jefferson's antislavery actions contributed to the creation of the moral posture that eventually propelled the North into war, it must also be recognized that the Virginian helped to create the ideological underpinning of the southern proslavery stance that made the war inevitable."[38] Some scholars even think that Jefferson's letter to Holmes set an important precedent for the tactic of later Southern statesmen in dealing with slavery in the territories: threaten to secede unless their demands were met. Jefferson is surely not responsible for the actions and beliefs of those who came later, but neither is he wholly innocent. It is that tension, even contradiction, between the main commitments of Jefferson's statesmanship, far more than any merely personal hypocrisy, that was Jefferson's main practical legacy to antebellum America. It is no wonder, then, that Miller calls the Missouri Crisis the "strange death of Jeffersonian liberalism."[39]

The case of the later Jefferson is thus more complex and disquieting than either the "egoistic" or the "hypocritical" interpretations allow. On the political level, Jefferson exhibits grand self-contradiction and blindness to the ways in which some of his political commitments undermine his other commitments. In light of the developments that occurred in the last decade of Jefferson's life and after, it is hard not to wonder, How could he have missed all this? This question is not easy to answer. Human motivation is always a tangled web. But perhaps part of the story is visible in the letter to Holmes itself. There is a bitter moralism in Jefferson's letter as he tries to turn the criticism of slavery back onto the Northerners themselves. You say we slave owners are immoral? He in effect says, in reality, you are forcing us to contemplate secession by making it likely we will face the existential choice between justice and self-preservation. Jefferson thus appeals to natural rights in order to defend himself and other slave owners, even while entrenching slavery in the American polity ever more firmly. He fails to see, it seems, that his appeal to natural rights makes it inevitable that his own political coalition will collapse. Is it not likely that Jefferson's strong desire to vindicate his own moral innocence blinded him to the predictable effects of his actions? Is it not Jefferson's moralism, and not any mere egoism, that accounts for both the emotional force of the letter to Holmes and his apparent inability to face up to the meaning of his actions?

Our reading of the letters about the Missouri Crisis and the draft of the Declaration has attempted to do justice to the curious intertwining of self-interest and angry, even self-righteous, defensiveness in Jefferson's thought. Paradoxically, Jefferson seems to have been led to emphasize the existence of an irreconcilable conflict of rights—and so the primacy of an "egoistic" concern for self-preservation—out of a deeper desire for moral vindication. If slavery could be defined as an unavoidable conflict of equally legitimate natural rights, then Jefferson could claim that he and other slave owners were not to blame. Despite the terrible actions they were compelled to do, they were, at the end of the day, innocent. To think that Jefferson's natural rights doctrine unleashed egoism is troubling. Yet more disturbing, perhaps, is the thought that it did so because that doctrine was a vehicle for an angry moralism.

*NOTES*

1. Those who defend the founders' record on slavery along Lincolnian lines sometimes overlook Jefferson's change of heart on this topic. See Thomas G. West, *Vindicating the Founders: Race, Sex, Class, and Gender in Origins of America* (Lanham, MD: Rowman and Littlefield, 1997), 23. I dedicate this essay to the memory of Walter Berns, who saw both the necessity of and the paradoxes within the natural rights doctrine.

2. John Chester Miller, *The Wolf by the Ears: Thomas Jefferson and Slavery* (Charlottesville: University of Virginia Press, 1991).

3. See ibid.; Paul Finkelman, *Slavery and the Founders: Race and Liberty in the Age of Jefferson*, 2nd ed. (New York: M.E. Sharpe, 2001).

4. For the first view, see Herbert Storing, "Slavery and the Moral Foundations of America," in *Toward a More Perfect Union*, ed. Joseph M. Bessette (Washington, DC: American Enterprise Institute Press, 1995), 142–144; and Harry Jaffa, *The Crisis of the House Divided: An Interpretation of the Issues in the Lincoln-Douglas Debates* (Chicago: University of Chicago Press, 1959). For the second view, see Michael Zuckert, *The Natural Rights Republic: Studies in the Foundation of the American Republic* (Notre Dame, IN: University of Notre Dame Press, 1996), and Zuckert, "Response," in *Thomas Jefferson and the Politics of Nature*, ed. Thomas S. Engeman (Notre Dame, IN: University of Notre Dame Press, 2000), 191–210, along with Jaffa's revised position in *A New Birth of Freedom: Abraham Lincoln and the Coming of the Civil War* (Lanham, MD: Rowman and Littlefield, 2000).

5. Charles Griswold makes a similar argument about Jefferson's moral theory, but he characterizes the tension in Jefferson's thought differently than I do. He sees Jefferson's moral theory as a synthesis of epicureanism and moral sense theory and argues that the pressure of slavery exposed the incoherence of that synthesis. See Griswold, "Rights and Wrongs: Jefferson, Slavery, and Philosophical Quandaries," in *A Culture of Rights: The Bill of Rights in Philosophy, Politics, and Law—1791 and 1991*, ed. Michael J. Lacey and Knud Haakonssen (Cambridge, UK: Cambridge University Press, 1991), 144–214.

6. See "Jefferson's Observations on Demeunier's Manuscript," June 22, 1786, in *Papers of Thomas Jefferson*, vol. 10, ed. Julian P. Boyd (Princeton, NJ: Princeton University Press, 1954), 58.

7. Donald L. Robinson points out that although the Northwest Ordinance prohibited slavery above the Ohio River, the Southwest Ordinance of 1790 failed to prohibit slavery south of the Ohio. Robinson, *Slavery in the Structure of American Politics, 1765–1820* (New York: Harcourt Brace Jovanovich, 1971), 385–386.

8. Thomas Jefferson, *Notes on the State of Virginia*, in Jefferson, *Life and Selected Writings*, ed. Adrienne Koch and William Peden (New York: Modern Library), 237–243, 257–258.

9. For Madison's opposition to the Missouri Compromise and support of diffusionism, see James Madison to Robert Walsh, November 27, 1819, in *Papers of James Madison: Retirement Series*, vol. 1: *1817–1820*, ed. David Mattern, J. C. A. Stagg, Mary Parke Johnson, and Anne Mandeville Colony (Charlottesville: University of Virginia Press, 2009), 553–558. For discussion, see Drew McCoy, *The Last of the Fathers: James Madison and the Republican Legacy* (Cambridge, UK: Cambridge University Press, 1989), 260–276; Walter Berns, "The Constitution and the Migration of Slaves," in Berns, *In Defense of Liberal Democracy* (Chicago: Gateway Editions, 1984), 199–230, esp. 214–230.

10. Miller, *Wolf by the Ears*, chaps. 24–26.

11. John Calhoun read the entire letter to Holmes on the floor of the Senate in 1848. Cited in *Union and Liberty: The Political Philosophy of John C. Calhoun*, ed. Ross Lence (Indianapolis, IN: Liberty Fund, 1992), 551–553.

12. On diffusionism, see Lacy Ford, "Reconfiguring the Old South: 'Solving' the Problem of Slavery," *Journal of American History* (June 2008): 95–122.

13. Jefferson's famous phrase is often misquoted as "wolf by the ears," although Jefferson actually wrote "wolf by the ear." See http://memory.loc.gov/master/mss/mtj/mtj1/051/1200/1238.jpg. Quotations in this section are from Thomas Jefferson to John Holmes, April 22, 1820, in Jefferson, *Life and Selected Writings*, 637–638.

14. See Robinson, *Slavery in the Structure of American Politics*, chap. 10; Robert Pierce Forbes, *The Missouri Compromise and Its Aftermath: Slavery and the Meaning of America* (Chapel Hill: University of North Carolina Press, 2007).

15. Forbes, *Missouri Compromise and Aftermath*, 103.

16. Peter Onuf and Brian Steele emphasize Jefferson's fears about the preservation of the nation rather than slavery. Onuf, *Jefferson's Empire: The Language of American Nationhood* (Charlottesville: University of Virginia Press, 2000), chap. 4; Steele, *Thomas Jefferson and American Nationhood* (Cambridge, UK: Cambridge University Press, 2012), 168, 179. Steele reads Jefferson as articulating a Lincoln-like recognition of

national guilt for slavery. Stewart Leibiger, however, persuasively argues that Jefferson conveys a barely veiled threat that the South will secede if slavery is not allowed to extend throughout the territories. Leibiger, "Thomas Jefferson and the Missouri Crisis: An Alternative Interpretation," *Journal of the Early Republic* 17, no. 1 (1997): 121–130.

17. Jefferson alludes to the slave rebellion in Haiti and Gabriel's Rebellion in Virginia.

18. Similar arguments were made in the congressional debates about Missouri: "Calling attention to blacks in the galleries, a Virginian shouted that Northerners were stirring up insurrection by their careless remarks about the immorality of slavery." Robinson, *Slavery in the Structure of American Politics*, 411–412.

19. Noting differences between Jefferson's letters to Northerners and Southerners, Leibiger suggests that Jefferson's despair at the Missouri Crisis was exaggerated for effect. Jefferson was, he argues, trying to coerce a compromise by frightening his audience, thus anticipating "Southern pro-slavery intransigence" throughout the antebellum period. Leibiger, "Thomas Jefferson and the Missouri Crisis," 130.

20. See *Works of Thomas Jefferson*, vol. 12, ed. Paul Leicester Ford (New York: Putnam, 1905), 164–166, 179–181, 185–189, 189–191; *The Adams-Jefferson Letters: The Complete Correspondence between Thomas Jefferson and John and Abigail Adams*, ed. Lester Cappon (Chapel Hill: University of North Carolina Press, 1959), 570.

21. *Works of Thomas Jefferson*, vol. 12, 187–188.

22. *Adams-Jefferson Letters*, 570.

23. *Works of Thomas Jefferson*, vol. 12, 188.

24. Ibid., 187.

25. Quotations from the Declaration of Independence and Jefferson's draft in this and the next paragraph are from Jefferson, *Life and Selected Writings*, 23–29.

26. Lord Dunmore proclaimed in November 1775 that all slaves joining the British forces would be set free. For Jefferson's reaction, see Miller, *Wolf by the Ears*, 10–11.

27. Jefferson, *Life and Selected Writings*, 23.

28. Pauline Maier, *American Scripture: Making the Declaration of Independence* (New York: Knopf, 1997), 146–147; Joseph Ellis, *American Sphinx: The Character of Thomas Jefferson* (New York: Vintage, 1996), 60; Onuf, *Jefferson's Empire*, 139.

29. Miller, *Wolf by the Ears*, 9.

30. Cited in ibid., 8.

31. Ellis, *American Sphinx*, 61.

32. Onuf, *Jefferson's Empire*, 141.

33. For example, James Madison's letter about the Missouri Crisis to Robert Walsh, has a quite different tone from Thomas Jefferson's letter to John Holmes. Madison focuses on (perhaps dubious) constitutional arguments against congressional authority to restrict slavery in the territories, rather than the existential threat of slave rebellion. Unlike Jefferson's letter to Holmes, Madison's letter does not come across as a threat of secession. See Madison to Walsh, November 27, 1819.

34. Storing, "Slavery and the Moral Foundations of America," 143.

35. Zuckert, "Response," 191–210.

36. Zuckert, *Natural Rights Republic*, 73-77; the passage quoted is on 74.

37. See Paul Rahe, *Republics Ancient and Modern*, vol. 3: *Inventions of Prudence:*

*Constituting the American Regime* (Chapel Hill: University of North Carolina Press, 1994), 203, 205.

38. Robert Shalhope, "Thomas Jefferson's Republicanism and Antebellum Southern Thought," *Journal of Southern History* 42, no. 4 (1976): 529–556. Walter Berns remarks: "One cannot help wondering what the course of American history might have been if Madison and Jefferson had resolutely and publicly maintained their early hopes that Congress could do something about the evils of slavery and that it would 'countenance the abolition' of the slave trade and adopt regulations forbidding the introduction of slaves 'into the new States to be formed out of the Western Territory.' Instead they chose to act in ways that inspired men such as John C. Calhoun." Berns, "Constitution and Migration of Slaves," 229.

39. Miller, *Wolf by the Ears*, 232. Of course, Jefferson's problematic conception of natural rights does not necessarily clinch the "guilt" of the natural rights doctrine either. The Continental Congress, after all, chose not to include the paragraph on slavery, and its members might have done so for good reasons, despite Jefferson's accusation that they caved in to the proslavery contingent.

CHAPTER 2

# Slavery and the US Supreme Court

KEITH E. WHITTINGTON

Judges are lawyers and policy makers, not philosophers. Their primary concern is with resolving legal disputes and arbitrating among competing claims of legal rights and duties. Nonetheless, their opinions can provide useful insights into American political thought. Unlike most policy makers, judges are routinely called upon to provide elaborate written justifications for the decisions they make. Although often technical in their concerns, such opinions can range more broadly. Legal scholars such as Henry Hart and Alexander Bickel have emphasized that the peculiar role of judges in the American political system is to be "a voice of reason" and to develop and articulate "impersonal and durable principles."[1] The nature of constitutions in the United States gives further importance to that judicial role. The fundamental law invokes basic values and deep principles of American society, and the judicial function of interpreting those constitutional provisions regularly calls on judges to clarify those values and suggest how they ought to be balanced and reconciled with each other.

Judicial opinions can be a particularly valuable lens through which to examine the problem of slavery in American political thought. Throughout the first several decades of the nation's existence, judges regularly resolved legal controversies involving enslaved people and the institution of slavery.[2] Because slavery was understood to be a local institution created and maintained by local laws, state judges were the ones most commonly asked to provide decisions interpreting the law of slavery. Federal judges were called upon to render far fewer decisions relating to slavery, but when doing so they carried the sensibilities of national political actors addressing what was often a regional body of law and legal problems. Judges were hardly the only set of political actors in the first half of the nineteenth century to grapple with the problem of how to reconcile human bondage with American ideals, but they were somewhat insulated from the political pressures surrounding the issue and faced with institutional responsibilities to integrate slavery into a larger web of principles and commitments.

The institution of slavery poses particular challenges for American political thought. Political scientist Louis Hartz famously identified what he thought was a liberal consensus in American political life. The apparent liberal hegemony in the United States was perhaps particularly striking in the middle of the twentieth century. As political debate in Europe involved not only liberals but robust radical movements from both the right and the left, with options ranging from fascism to communism seeming like viable possibilities, politics in the United States might have seemed surprisingly truncated by contrast. With anticommunist liberals such as Harry Truman and post–New Deal conservatives such as Dwight Eisenhower dominating politics and radical activists pushed far to the political margins, Hartz believed that the United States was unusually liberal at its core. Moreover, the liberal consensus was not merely a recent development. Rather, the nation had, according to Hartz, always been defined by a "liberal tradition." The American political spectrum had always been occupied in its entirety by Lockean principles. The "national folklore" of American exceptionalism was true. The "outstanding thing about the American community in Western history" is that it is "a liberal community," with America "skipping" such defining historical stages as feudalism and settling into an unconsidered, almost instinctual liberalism.[3]

Writing in the early days of the Cold War, Hartz was particularly moved by a question over which many commentators of the period puzzled: Why are there no radical movements in the United States? Or perhaps more specifically, why no socialism? For Hartz, the answer could be found in the origins of the United States. The country was born in bourgeois equality. Without feudalism, liberal ideals and politics would not develop in reaction to feudal ideas and institutions. The ideas of class, Hartz believed, that emerged hand-in-hand with a revolutionary liberalism that needed to actively reject an aristocracy carried the seeds of socialism. Without the class consciousness that supported liberal revolution, there could be no class consciousness to support a socialist revolution. Everyone would share the values of and identify with the middle class. The American political tradition would be one dominated by a commitment to such Lockean values as individualism, rights, formal equality, limited government, and private property. Political disputes would be fought out within the narrow confines of that tradition.

The Hartzian narrative is both powerful and problematic. Because it was laid down by Hartz and others at midcentury, scholars have challenged the framework of a liberal consensus from a variety of perspectives. The prominence of intellectual influences within the history of American political thought that do not fit neatly within the liberal paradigm have been repeatedly identified, suggesting that the liberal consensus has not always been as overwhelming as Hartz posited. Even so, the surprising resilience and pervasiveness of liberal ideals in American political discourse have been hard to ignore or minimize.[4]

Slavery is a particular puzzle for the dominance of the liberal tradition.[5] The practice of slavery had some rather obvious inconsistencies with liberal ideals. The political and legal acceptance of slavery within the United States stood in some embarrassment with Jefferson's resounding invocation of the liberal belief that "all men are created equal" and "endowed by their Creator with certain unalienable rights." Although it might have been possible to mount a defense of slavery within the confines of liberalism, it was no doubt easier to justify the practice in nonliberal terms.[6] The political and intellectual need to rationalize the presence of slavery within the borders of the United States invited the development of arguments, ideas, and even entire value systems inconsistent with liberalism and found nourishment in other ideological traditions.[7]

Believers in the liberal consensus have deployed a variety of tactics for dealing with the slavery problem. Two options are simply to ignore slavery or minimize its significance as a factor in American political ideology (if not necessarily in American social and economic life). Another option is to treat slavery as something of an embarrassing exception. The exception might simply indicate that the facts on the ground did not wholly match American ideals. Such a "gap . . . between American political ideals and American political institutions and practice" might pose more of a challenge to the political practices than to the ideals, feeding reform movements dedicated to bringing ideals and reality into closer alignment and closing the gap.[8] Rather than generating alternative ideologies that might challenge or subvert the liberal consensus, institutions such as slavery might have tended to reinforce and reaffirm the ideological dominance of liberalism by encouraging purifying movements. Hartz himself saw slavery as something of a "feudal remnant" within American society and thought its defenders were engaged in intellectual "fraud." Proslavery thought was wracked by internal contradictions precisely because it tried to simultaneously embrace slavery and liberalism and as a consequence could not offer a genuine alternative to the liberal paradigm. After the final collapse of slavery, the ideas associated with proslavery thought swiftly disappeared with little impact on mainstream currents of American political thought.[9]

There are many ways of approaching the question of how slavery was integrated into American political thought. Was it ignored by American political thinkers who proceeded to articulate political ideals as if no such practice existed? Was it apologized for as an exceptional or peculiar divergence from received ideals with no real significance for governing norms and fundamental commitments? Was it defended as either consistent with dominant values or integral to some alternative and superior normative system?

The US Supreme Court offers some valuable perspective on these issues. Justices were called upon to address slavery questions as part of their normal functions. They were obliged to explain their actions in reasoned opinions, and in doing so to provide elaborations of American values and rationalizations for the practice of slavery within that system of values. Even when supporting slavery as an institution, justices can be distinguished from many proslavery advocates in that they were not otherwise invested in the maintenance and defense of that institution. Proslavery arguments might have influenced justices and played a role in their actions, but generalist justices primarily occupied with other tasks were unlikely to be defined by proslavery ideology. Considering how justices attempted to make sense of slavery can help illuminate the impact of slavery on American political thought broadly.[10]

An examination of how the justices on the US Supreme Court dealt with slavery suggests that there have been multiple values at play within American politics. The "presence of the liberal idea" has not precluded the presence of competing values and concerns.[11] Other values that have also held sway within American politics are not all inconsistent with liberalism, but a single-minded emphasis on a liberal consensus obscures some of the complexity of the American experience. The record of the Court reinforces the criticisms mounted against the idea of a liberal consensus and emphasizes the rich tapestry of ideals within the American political tradition. Given a Hartzian liberal consensus, we might expect justices to shade their decisions against the interests of enslaved people, to bend the law so as to maximize liberal values within the constraints imposed by the existence of slavery as a political and legal reality. A review of judicial opinions relating to slavery indicates a more complex story. In particular, four alternative values make an appearance in those opinions, with justices sometimes appealing to the preeminence of liberty within the American constitutional scheme but sometimes appealing to other fundamental commitments, such as the rule of law, union, and race.

## SOME BACKGROUND ON SLAVERY AND THE SUPREME COURT

The institution of slavery was deeply rooted in American law, and as a consequence many courts encountered slavery as part of their routine business. Slavery was, however, primarily a matter of state law. State law authorized the enslaving of people and defined the rights and responsibilities of both the enslaved and the masters. Consequently, state courts, especially in the South, were called upon most often to elaborate and apply the law of slavery.[12]

Despite slavery being a creature of state law, the Supreme Court was regularly called upon to resolve disputes involving slavery, particularly in the years leading up to the Civil War. Of course, the federal courts interpreted and implemented federal statutes as well as the US Constitution, and those sources of law generated some cases that occupied the federal docket. However, federal law was relatively meager in the first decades of the nation's existence and could not compare with the importance and volume of cases generated under state law. The jurisdiction of the federal courts was defined not only by the source of law but also by the parties in the suit. Over the course of the nineteenth century, most of the Court's docket was occupied by so-called diversity cases, in which the parties to the suit were citizens of different states. Because such suits arrived in the federal courts only by virtue of the identity of the litigants, the law to be applied in those cases was borrowed from the states. By virtue of diversity cases, the federal courts heard a substantial number of routine state-law cases, including those involving slavery. Most of those were not about slavery per se, about slavery as a legal institution and practice, but rather were simply cases—from probated wills to disputed contracts—involving a particular form of valuable property, enslaved people. A sizable portion of the cases heard by the Supreme Court that called into question the place of slavery within the law were generated by constitutional provisions and federal statutory provisions. Congress took steps to prohibit American participation in the international slave trade as well to prohibit the importation of enslaved people into the United States. However, Congress also facilitated the recapture of fugitives who had fled across state lines. Meanwhile, state efforts to control the movement of enslaved and formerly enslaved people across state boundaries ran up against federal constitutional constraints.

The federal courts were not simply neutral arbiters when it came to slavery. The Supreme Court in particular was structured to protect slavery. Understanding how requires some appreciation of how the formal design of the Court interacted with established convention. The text of the Constitution specified that there would be a Supreme Court, but the details of its structure were left for Congress to determine by statute. Starting with the Judiciary Act of 1789, the seats on the Supreme Court were attached to judicial circuits. Each circuit consisted of a geographical territory containing a set of lower federal court judges. During the nineteenth century, justices were expected to "ride circuit," regularly travel to sit with the lower federal judges and hear cases at trial and on appeal. Because much of the work of the federal courts involved

local litigants contesting issues of state law, Supreme Court justices were expected to be familiar with the law and social circumstances of the territory
within which they would hear cases. In practice, this meant that each justice
was associated with a distinct circuit. When Congress created a new circuit,
it also created a new seat on the Court. When Congress drew the territorial
boundaries of a judicial circuit, it also determined the pool of lawyers from
which presidents would select Supreme Court nominees.

Drawing the boundaries of judicial circuits was inevitably politicized.[13] The
Judiciary Act of 1789 created six seats on the Supreme Court, connected to the
three circuits that grouped the thirteen original states into northern, central,
and southern regions. The Jeffersonian Judiciary Act of 1802 reorganized the
judicial circuits to create a one-to-one match between the six justices and six
circuits. Three of those circuits were located below the Mason-Dixon Line,
and three were above. The admission of new western states justified the creation of a seventh western circuit (stretching from Ohio to Tennessee) in 1807.
But the rapid western expansion of the early nineteenth century complicated
the organization of the federal judiciary just as it complicated other aspects
of American politics. The newly formed states being carved out of the Louisiana Purchase and the Northwest Territory were producing their own federal
judicial caseload, though at a smaller volume than the more populated and
economically developed states along the eastern seaboard. The creation of new
federal district courts could serve as a stopgap but left the growing new states
disrespected and underserved. There was little political agreement in Congress
on how to redraw circuit boundaries and reorganize the federal court system,
however.

The political success of the Jacksonian Democrats helped break the legislative logjam. After the 1834 elections, Democrats had solid control of both
chambers of Congress and the White House. Seven new states had joined
the Union since the 1807 judiciary bill, and the 25th Congress admitted two
more. With those western states primarily sending Democrats to Congress,
the time was ripe to more fully incorporate them into the structure of the
federal judiciary. The Judiciary Act of 1837 redrew circuit boundaries and reorganized the Court. The size of the Court was increased from seven to nine,
giving the departing Andrew Jackson two seats to fill. The six circuits on the
eastern seaboard were left unchanged, but the western states were reorganized
into three new circuits. Ohio was grouped with other states carved out of the
Northwest Territory to create a single circuit, whereas two other circuits were
composed of western states south of Missouri and Kentucky. The end result
was a nine-justice Supreme Court, with five seats situated in slave states and

four seats in free states. The reorganized Court reflected both partisan and sectional politics. The expanded bench included seven Jacksonians, with three justices from the Deep South and two from border slave states. Although the individual justices changed over succeeding years, the Court itself was not significantly reorganized again until the Republicans dramatically reshaped the federal judiciary in 1863.[14] It is not surprising that Republican editor Horace Greeley would dismiss the Taney Court as "five slaveholders and two or three doughfaces."[15]

## SLAVERY AND THE RULE OF LAW

One of the distinguishing features of judges is their concern for the law. Legal theorist H. L. A. Hart contended that legal systems only function to the extent that those operating inside the system, most notably lawyers and judges, internalize it as a set of normatively obligatory commitments. A well-functioning legal system should be experienced as internally felt duties rather than externally imposed constraints. From the internal point of view, the existence of the legal rule is itself a reason to follow the rule and adopt it as a guide to behavior.[16] Lon Fuller was more particular in emphasizing specific features of the morality of law. To be valid, Fuller insisted, legal rules must be stated at a level of generality that allows them to operate in predictable fashion across a wide range of cases.[17] The rule of law necessitated that parties be able to anticipate, and marshal arguments about, how preexisting rules will be extended to new cases.[18]

Rule-of-law values constitute a distinct normative system. Although broadly consistent with liberalism, the appeal to the rule of law is likely to be more institutionally and professionally specific. A motivating ideology for judges and lawyers, the rule of law might hold less appeal in other communities. Moreover, a commitment to the formal principles of the rule of law might well conflict with the substantive commitments of liberalism. Herbert Wechsler reflected these potential conflicts in his uncertainty about the outcome and reasoning of the Supreme Court in the school desegregation case. Although the expanded rights and equality the justices vindicated in *Brown v. Board of Education* was appealing from the perspective of classical liberal principles as well as of New Deal liberalism, Wechsler worried over whether the result came at the expense of principles of formal neutrality central to the rule of law.[19] Wechsler's specific argument can be and has been criticized, but his general belief that liberal values and rule-of-law values might not always work together is more widely shared.[20]

As a normative system, the rule of law has a variety of elements, but all revolve around a set of central overriding concerns. The rule of law requires that judges adhere to the rules laid down, acting as legal interpreters rather than lawmakers. Doing so necessitates deciding individual disputes in a manner consistent with the existing law. The rules cannot be enforced in an ad hoc fashion or exceptions carved out from general principles. More particularly, the identity of the parties to a case should not affect application of the rules to the legal dispute. Neutral principles should be applied neutrally, without favoritism or bias.

Rule-of-law rhetoric can serve a variety of functions in judicial opinions. It might simply reflect blame avoidance as the judge seeks to displace responsibility for his or her actions to some other authority. In his classic study of how antislavery judges resolved cases involving fugitives, Robert Cover recounts how such judges often showed "a tendency to mechanize the formal requirements" of the law.[21] An emphasis on the judicial obligation to maintain fidelity to the "crystal clear demands" of the law helps deflect attention from those responsible for implementing the law to those responsible for drafting the law, perhaps especially when the demands of the law are not so crystal clear. "The more mechanical the judge's view of the process, the more he externalized responsibility for the result."[22] Of course, the argument from formalism might be genuine. Judicial discretion might be seriously constrained by the language of the law, and judges might well rest on the authority of the lawmaker when seeking to apply the law in cases that come before the bench.

Slavery cases might also have presented tragic choices for judges. Considerations of liberal ideology, or as Cover would have it, considerations of morality and natural law, might point toward using the instruments of the law to assist enslaved people and subvert the slavery system. By contrast, judicial commitments to rule-of-law values might point toward sustaining slavery against the interests of enslaved people when judges operate within a system of positive law that embraces slavery.

My focus here is not on the kind of cases that concerned Cover and provoked ostentatious claims that the law had tied the hands of the judges and prevented them from doing what they otherwise thought would be right in the case before them. Rather, my focus is on the far more routine cases in which faithfully identifying and applying rules in the context of slavery just as the judges would do in any other context was offered as the overriding value at stake in a case. The justices often declined to depart from their normal role as neutral arbiters of the law or to introduce inconsistencies or anomalies into the otherwise seamless web of the law. Successfully integrating cases involving slavery into the larger system of law was itself a normative good. Slavery cases were to be routinized rather than treated as outliers.

Chief Justice John Marshall's opinion in *Mima Queen and Child v. Hepburn* provides an example.[23] A suit for freedom was filed in the District of Columbia, but the trial court held in favor of the slave owner. The case turned on the legal status of the plaintiff's ancestor, now deceased. The plaintiff attempted to marshal testimony from a number of witnesses regarding the ancestor, Mary Queen, but much of it suffered from being hearsay. Many of the witnesses did not have direct knowledge of Mary's situation; they were merely able to report what they had heard from others. For the Supreme Court, the principal question to be decided was whether this testimony fell under the general rule against the introduction of hearsay evidence at trial. A majority of the justices concluded that it did, and they upheld the rulings of the lower court.

The issue for Marshall was whether the Court should carve out an exception to the general hearsay rule in order to tip the scales in favor of enslaved people seeking their manumission.[24] The chief justice was firm in contending that there was no "legal distinction between the assertion of this and any other right" that might justify departing from "general cases in which a right to property may be asserted." Marshall worried that any rule of evidence pronounced in this case would not "be confined to cases of this particular description, but will be extended to others." He wrote, "However the feelings of the individual may be interested on the part of a person claiming freedom," the Court must keep its eye on the broader system of law, where "hearsay evidence is totally inadmissible." The "general rule comprehends the case," and the justices were "not inclined to extend the exceptions further than they have already been carried."[25]

Rule-of-law arguments could also play out in cases involving only the law of slavery. A case involved a suit for freedom by an enslaved woman named Matilda and her children three decades after she had been brought to Virginia from Maryland, on the grounds that the Virginia law at the time of her arrival emancipated an enslaved person brought into the state after a year unless the owner took an oath of state citizenship. There was no evidence that Matilda's owner took the oath, but nonetheless Matilda remained in his service until his death. The problem for the Court was in establishing what presumptions should hold in such a situation. Virginia cases suggested that the owner should be presumed to have taken the oath if he remained in the state for a longer period and continued to enslave the person; the fact of "possession" shifted the burden of proof to the enslaved person. Justice William Johnson emphasized the importance of maintaining settled law. Although Matilda's attorneys encouraged the Supreme Court to see some uncertainty in the state of the law in Virginia, Johnson was unpersuaded. The value of settled law, deference to state courts, and consistency across jurisdictions trumped concern with the freedom of individuals. Although the "ignorance, impotence, and continued state of duress" of those in a "state of bondage" might cast doubt on the appropriateness of a presumption that an enslaved person would seek legal help in a timely fashion if unlawfully retained in bondage, the justices would have to assume that such considerations had been "duly considered by the learned judges of Virginia."[26]

## SLAVERY AND UNION

The concept of union is easily assumed in the modern era. We can readily presume the existence of a perpetual Union, of the stability of the American nation-state and its territorial boundaries. Despite recent examples of the dissolution of modern states, the possibility of the disunion of the United States seems like a distant threat. With the stabilization of American borders, the significance of union as a normative ideology has declined, perhaps replaced by patriotism, what George Kateb has called a "tacit ideology" that elevates a passionate attachment to the community above other goods.[27]

For the first century of the nation's existence, union was a central concept in American political thought. It was "a core value," the means "by which Americans sought to express shared ideals and a common identity."[28] A commitment to "sacred union" could both trump other values and facilitate the realization of other political goals, but fidelity to union had to be constantly reaffirmed just as other core values had to be recollected and upheld. Like other essential concepts within American political discourse, the idea of union was hardly fixed. The concept was open to contestation and reinterpretation, but it could help organize political beliefs and direct debate. Union was a "treasure-trove of the values and images by which Americans sought to comprehend their nature and destiny."[29]

Some of the tensions in the ideal of union were illustrated by the competing toasts offered at the famed Jefferson Day dinner on April 13, 1830. Jackson had been elected president less than two years earlier, but his coalition was fractious. Jackson's own nationalist sensibilities clashed with the more doctrinaire states' rights beliefs of many of his Southern allies. Vice President John C. Calhoun was under pressure from firebrands in his home state of South Carolina to press states' rights to the limit. By 1830, the Capitol was aflame with fights over the protectionist tariff, with nationalists supporting the duties and decentralizers opposing them. States' rights politicians hoped to use the traditional celebration of Jefferson as an occasion to bolster support for their cause; Jackson resolved to reproach them. The evening concluded with leading members of the party offering a series of toasts, many of which praised Jefferson's resistance to the abuses of centralized power. The president was among the last to offer a toast, and he rose to say simply, "Our Union: It must be preserved." The attendees heard the toast as a rebuke and heresy. Senator Robert Hayne at least convinced Jackson to amend his written toast for publication the next day to say "federal union," but the change did little to alter the tone of the statement. Calhoun had been positioned to speak immediately after the president, and his prepared toast cut the other way: "The Union: Next to our liberty, the most dear." Secretary of State Martin Van Buren, who had helped orchestrate Jackson's challenge, spoke last: "Mutual forbearance and reciprocal concession: Through their agency the Union was established. The patriotic spirit from which they emanated will forever sustain it."[30] By the next election, Calhoun had left the administration and Jackson's Democratic Party.

The trio of Jefferson Day toasts displays important features of the idea of union in the first decades of the republic. What sacrifices must be made for the sake of union? On this point, Jackson was willing to agree with nationalist Whigs such as Daniel Webster who argued that liberty and union must work hand-in-hand. In response to Hayne on the Senate floor, Webster had declared that he would not "look beyond the Union, to see what might lie hidden in the dark recess behind. I have not coolly weighed the chances of preserving liberty when the bonds that unite us together shall be broken asunder." Webster would not say "Liberty first and Union afterwards"; for him the only choice was "Liberty *and* Union, now and forever, one and inseparable!"[31] It was in response to Webster's much-discussed formulation, rather than Jackson's surprise toast, that Calhoun had written his own. For Southern radicals, union could not be held up as a value that trumped all others.[32] Union was merely a tool for reaching other, more primary goals, and cries of "union" could not justify sacrificing those larger ends. Van Buren's carefully tempered toast both echoed and foreshadowed the efforts of many nationalist-minded politicians to look for a great compromise that would reconcile the interests of North and South under the overarching framework of union. For such nationalists, preserving the Union both required and justified sacrifice.

The theme of sacrificing values for the sake of union was particularly salient in the context of fugitives. The problem of enslaved people escaping to free jurisdictions was a persistent one for their masters, and the fugitive slave clause of the US Constitution was an important component of the effort in Philadelphia to reach an agreement on a new federal arrangement. The bare constitutional text providing that no fugitive shall be freed as a consequence of the escape "but shall be delivered up on claim of the party to whom such service or labor may be due" left myriad political and legal difficulties to be ironed out. The Fugitive Slave Act of 1793 fleshed out the law by allowing a master or slave catcher to seize a fugitive and obtain a warrant from a local judge authorizing the removal of the individual from the state. Subsequent fugitive slave acts further bolstered the national requirements that localities assist the slave catcher in his work, even as states adopted personal liberty laws designed to obstruct them. As antislavery advocates and Northern "Conscience Whigs" objected to these extensions of the slave power into Northern states, nationalists responded that such sacrifices were the price of union.

Talk of compromise and sacrifice is to be expected in the political arena but is perhaps more surprising in the judicial arena. Nonetheless, a similar discourse of trade-offs and the preeminent value of union appeared in judicial opinions, especially in cases involving the fugitive slave clause.[33] Most prominently, the value of union played a feature role in Justice Joseph Story's 1842 opinion in *Prigg v. Pennsylvania*.[34] Edward Prigg was a slave catcher charged with kidnapping in the Pennsylvania state courts under the authority of an 1826 state personal liberty law. Prigg appealed to the higher authority of the US Constitution and the 1793 Fugitive Slave Act. For the US Supreme Court, the questions at issue were whether the federal statute preempted the conflicting state statute (a familiar problem from the interstate commerce context) and what the constitutional provision required.

Justice Story took the lead in explaining the Court's decision to uphold the federal statute and reject the state law. Though a Massachusetts native, where antislavery agitation was strong and growing by the 1840s, Story took his bearings from the same nationalist philosophy that drove Marshall, Webster, and Henry Clay. Story began by denying that any general rule of interpretation would elucidate the relevant constitutional provisions. Both the components of the constitutional text and the history of its adoption demonstrated "that many of its provisions were matters of compromise of opposing interests and opinions."[35] Story's emphasis on the compromised nature of the Constitution does depart significantly from the type of ringing rhetoric the Marshall Court had deployed when issuing nationalist decisions, but it comports with the way in which Northern moderates sought to deal with the slavery provisions of that document. The "safest rule of interpretation, after all, will be found to be to look to the nature and objects of the particular powers, duties and rights, with all the lights and aids of contemporary history; and to give to the words of each just such operation and force, consistent with their legitimate meaning, as may fairly secure and attain the ends proposed."[36]

The fugitive slave clause was to be given "just such operation and force" as had been attained in the national bargain but no more. Story's approach to thinking about this clause was surprisingly historical in its orientation, almost inviting the kind of state compact analysis favored by the strict constructionists, whom Story generally opposed. "Historically," Story observed, "it is well known, that the object of this clause was to secure to the citizens of the slave-holding states the complete right and title of ownership in their slaves, as property, in every state in the Union into which they might escape from the state where they were held in servitude."[37] Why adhere to this historical bargain? Because, as Story argued, the obligations of union demanded it:

The full recognition of this right and title was indispensable to the security of this species of property in all the slave-holding states; and, indeed, was so vital to the preservation of their domestic interests and institutions, that it cannot be doubted, that it constituted a fundamental article, without the adoption of which the Union could not have been formed. Its true design was, to guard against the doctrines and principles prevalent in the non-slave-holding states, by preventing them from intermeddling with, or obstructing, or abolishing the rights of the owners of slaves.[38]

The fugitive slave clause was "of the last importance to the safety and security of the southern states, and could not have been surrendered by them." Some such guarantee was essential to avoid "the most bitter animosities, and . . . perpetual strife between the different states."[39] Its "intrinsic and practical necessity" to the success of the Union was thus obvious. Judges were then obliged to interpret the provision so that it "shall fully and completely effectuate the whole objects of it." Thus, "no court of justice can be authorized so to construe any clause of the constitution as to defeat its obvious ends," and the obvious purpose of the fugitive slave clause was to maintain "a positive, unqualified right on the part of the owner of the slave" wherever the enslaved person might escape within the Union.[40]

Union played a rather different role in other cases. Justice John McLean, later a dissenter in *Dred Scott,* considered the differences between state and federal regulation of slavery in the 1841 case of *Groves v. Slaughter.*[41] The constitution of the state of Mississippi included a ban on bringing slaves into the state for sale. Among the questions in the case was whether such a state ban interfered with the federal power to regulate interstate commerce. The relationship between the state and federal governments given the interstate commerce clause was a contentious one in the antebellum period, and in this case, McLean distinguished between cases of foreign trade in which the "United States are considered as a unit" and interstate trade. When dealing with the states, federal laws must be "equal and general" and "operate alike on all the states." Congress would not be capable of allowing enslaved people to travel into some states and not others, and similarly the states would not be capable of prohibiting the economic goods of other states. Slavery must be exceptional, separate from commercial regulation, in order to make sense of the anomalous but valid power of the states to exclude enslaved people. Mississippi could prohibit the import of people as slave merchandise. Ohio could ban the enterprise of slavery entirely, and could do so "without trenching upon the commercial power of congress." The "power over slavery belongs to the states respectively" and is "local in its character." Thus, "each state has a right to protect itself against the avarice and intrusion of the slave-dealer; to guard its citizens against the inconvenience and dangers of a slave population." Each state's right to regulate slavery, including the interstate "transfer or sale of slaves" is "higher and deeper than the constitution," for it rests on the "law of self-preservation" of the community, of ultimate concern "to a sovereign state."[42] Preventing the interstate reach of slavery within a Union that contained half slave states and half free states meant respecting the decisions of each locality on how to treat slavery, whether those local decisions permitted or prohibited the practice. Preserving a functional Union meant deferring to state laws regarding slavery and restricting federal power over the movement of enslaved people.[43]

## SLAVERY AND LIBERTY

Liberty is, of course, at the heart of liberal ideology. The liberal consensus thesis contended that Lockean ideals of individual freedom were central to American political thought. Hartz thought that the important "storybook truth about American history" is that Americans had "fled from the feudal and clerical oppressions of the Old World."[44] America was conceived as a New World of freedom. Hartz might not have been completely certain as to the substantive content of the "Lockean creed" that commanded American loyalty, but there was little doubt that freedom from restraint was an important part of the mix.

The freedom to own property, however, might have been just as important to the idea of liberty. Richard Hofstadter concluded, "The sanctity of private property, the right of the individual to dispose of and invest it, the value of opportunity, and the natural evolution of self-interest and self-assertion, within broad legal limits, into a beneficent social order have been staple tenets of the central faith in American political ideologies."[45] Hartz's liberal tradition was likewise the consensus of middle-class strivers who sought to make their own way in the world.

Slavery posed curious contradictions within such an ideological scheme. Slavery denied freedom in a particularly stark way. It denied that a particular class of people within the American society was in fact "born free." But the slavery system also rested on a claim of property. Even if white Americans from national independence forward deplored the international slave trade, which had introduced enslaved people into the country, they laid claim to the financial investments already made. Perhaps the start of the slavery regime had been wrong, but by 1776, or 1820, or 1860, legally acquired property rights were in play, and liberal values emphasized that property was to be respected.

The revolutionary spirit favored liberty over slavery. Jefferson confessed that slavery represented "the most unremitting despotism on the one part, and degrading submissions on the other," but given the social and economic conditions in the South he resigned himself to "the workings of an overruling providence" to accomplish emancipation.[46] The iconoclastic Benjamin Rush went further in linking the abolition of slavery with the fate of America. The "plant of liberty," he warned, "cannot thrive long in the neighborhood of slavery."[47] Jefferson sometimes shared that sentiment; the example of slavery cast doubt on the essential popular belief that "these liberties are the gift of God."[48] As time went on, antislavery activists questioned how an institution such as slavery could be tolerated in "this land of liberty." To make "one man . . . a slave of another" could not be reconciled with "the law of nature, which is the law of God," which had motivated American independence and the founding of the republic.[49]

Especially in jurisdictions with little investment in slavery, the spirit of liberty predominated. In England, Lord Mansfield heard a suit for freedom by James Somerset, held in slavery in Virginia and carried to England. When his master sought to return Somerset to the colonies, the courts were asked to intervene on his behalf. Mansfield admitted that a "contract for sale of a slave is good here; the sale is a matter to which the law properly and readily attaches." However, the actual exertion of coercive authority over the physical body of an enslaved person within the jurisdiction of England was another matter altogether. Mansfield contended that the peculiar nature of slavery precluded its extension beyond the boundaries of states that had specifically authorized it. "The state of slavery is of such a nature, that it is incapable of being introduced on any reasons, moral or political; but only positive law, which preserves its force long after the reasons, occasion, and time itself from whence it was created, is erased from memory: it's so odious, that nothing can be suffered to support it, but positive law."[50] The Supreme Court of Massachusetts took a similar view of slavery after the revolution and the adoption of the state constitution of 1780. Quock Walker claimed to have been emancipated, but Nathaniel Jennison assaulted him as part of an effort to return him to servitude. A jury convicted Jennison of the assault after Chief Justice Cushing instructed them that slavery was not "expressly enacted or established" in the state but existed only by "usage." A "different idea . . . more favorable to the natural rights of mankind, and to that natural, innate desire of Liberty" had gained ground in the United States. The Massachusetts Constitution declared that "all men are born free and equal—and that every subject is entitled to liberty, and to have it guarded by the laws, as well as life and property—and in short is totally repugnant to the idea of being born slaves." Liberty could only be "forfeited by some criminal conduct or given up by personal consent or contract."[51] In other Northern states, legislatures adopted various plans for emancipation, and even some Southern states loosened the rules regarding voluntary manumission.

The federal courts did not follow the path of the King's Bench or the Massachusetts Supreme Court. In both England and Massachusetts, the legality of slavery was put in doubt by the absence of positive law on the subject, allowing judges to create a presumption of liberty in those jurisdictions. The federal courts faced a different legal environment. Local law favored slavery in some of the jurisdictions within which federal judges operated and applied the law. Moreover, both Congress and the US Constitution offered some protection for slavery in federal law and federal territory. Nonetheless, liberal principles would suggest that courts should regard such statutory requirements as exceptions to the general legal rule, exceptions that perhaps should be strictly construed so as to favor liberty to the extent possible. As Lord Mansfield suggested, the law of slavery might be understood against a background of a law of liberty, to be confined only to those narrow circumstances in which it had been authorized.[52]

The justices did sometimes lean in favor of liberty. The case of *Mima Queen and Child* again provides an example. Associate Justice Gabriel Duvall of Maryland wrote a lone dissent to Chief Justice Marshall's ruling in the case. Duvall had only recently joined the bench, having been appointed by President James Madison, after a lengthy stint as comptroller of the US Treasury. *Queen and*

*Child* was his only written dissent.[53] Duvall would not have integrated eviden-
tiary rules for a case of freedom into the general law of hearsay. Whereas Marshall emphasized that the legal rules must be the same whether in the case of
slavery or another case involving property, Duvall emphasized that slavery was
different and that the law should take note of that difference. He drew upon
the experience of his own state. Despite the persistence of slavery in Maryland,
"the law has been for many years settled that on a petition for freedom where
the petitioner claims from an ancestor who has been dead for a great length
of time, the issue may be proved by hearsay evidence." The Maryland decision
turned partly on the similarity between land claims and suits for freedom;
in both cases, the "antiquity of the transactions" might put them outside the
memory of living witnesses, but legitimate claims of legal right still necessitated a just judicial remedy. However, in other ways, the context of slavery was
unique and demanded special consideration by the courts. Duvall wrote:

It appears to me that the reason for admitting hearsay evidence upon a question of
freedom is much stronger than in cases of pedigree or in controversies relative to the
boundaries of land. It will be universally admitted that the right to freedom is more
important than the right of property.

And people of color from their helpless condition under the uncontrolled authority
of a master, are entitled to all reasonable protection.

The ability to vindicate "a natural inherent right" should not turn on "the neglect or
omission of the ancestor" to adequately lay claim to the right.

A similar effort to take into account claims of right and justice made some
appearance in the Court's cases interpreting and applying the congressional
prohibition on American participation in the international slave trade. In one
such case, an American ship with an American crew sailed from Baltimore to
Cuba outfitted for the slave trade and then sailed to Africa. When it was inter-
cepted, the Americans involved claimed that the ship had been sold midpas-
sage to a Spaniard, "who was authorized, by the laws of his country, to carry
on the slave trade." Although the accused argued that the Court should decide
the case "upon principles of law, and not merely upon principles of justice or
morality," Justice Story emphasized that this was no "ordinary trade" but one
"odious in our country" and put "a permanent stain upon the reputation of
all who are concerned in it." The moral stain associated with the slave trade
required particular vigilance to distance the country from it, encouraging the
justices to scrutinize carefully and with skepticism those who might try to
escape detection "under the disguise of foreign flags."[54] Marshall's opinion in
the case of the *Antelope* similarly admitted the moral concerns associated with

the slave trade. Even those whose feelings had been "blunted by familiarity with the practice" could still recognize that the "unnatural traffic" was "abhorrent." Nonetheless, Marshall insisted that a "jurist" could not think merely as a "moralist," and must seek a "legal solution" rooted in the law of nations and not merely in the "law of nature," which endorsed the "natural right to the fruits of his own labour."[55] The Court might not have been willing to denounce the choice of other countries to continue to engage in the slave trade, but neither would it stretch to respect the potential human property found on such ships.

## SLAVERY AND RACE

Race, or more accurately racism, has not usually been regarded as an alternative ideological system within American political thought. Instead, it was traditionally characterized as a matter of political interest or deviant prejudice that did not otherwise inform what we took to be central to the nation's ideals and core values. Merle Curti's pioneering work was representative in understanding its subject matter as a "history of knowledge, of speculation and ideas, and of values."[56] Views about race might fall within the realm of an intellectual history of sociological knowledge and speculation but had little place within the nation's discourse of values. According to this view, the persistence of racial inequalities reflected a failure of liberal ideology to fully control social and political practice to be sure but did not itself demonstrate the presence of an alternative scheme of values or introduce doubts about the basic American commitment to liberalism. Liberalism represented the aspiration, the promise, of American politics, even if there were sometimes gaps between the ideal and the reality.

Recent historical work on conceptions of race within American history has begun to alter that view. Few works are as influential in resituating racism within the American political tradition as Rogers Smith's project on the multiple traditions in American political thought. Cast as a direct response to the Hartzian narrative of a liberal consensus, Smith's project posits instead that American political history has not been dominated by a single system of values but has instead been characterized by multiple traditions. Liberalism has sat beside and competed with republican and inegalitarian value systems for the hearts and minds of Americans. Smith emphasizes that the American civic identity was complex, valuing rights (liberalism) and democracy (republicanism) but also social and political hierarchies in various, often unstable, combinations.[57]

The third category in Smith's multiple traditions is not one of race per se. Rather, it incorporates a variety of distinct ideas about civic identity that are broadly ascriptive and inegalitarian in their perspective. In contrast to basic liberal commitments, which emphasize equality, individualism, and (particularly in the context of immigration and citizenship, of immediate concern to Smith) voluntarism, ascriptive inegalitarian ideas have emphasized the ways in which the American political community is traditional, closed, and hierarchical.[58] Race is among the salient features of a political identity primarily conceptualized as white, Anglo-Saxon, patriarchal, and Protestant and at times has been the most salient feature of the ideal of America. The liberal values that held sway among white men did not necessarily hold sway when the political gaze turned beyond that particular subgroup of the community.

The multiple traditions perspective suggests that racism has itself been a normative value within American political discourse. Its proponents would expect to see a persistent doctrinal commitment in American law and politics to the supremacy of the white race and would expect to see those features of law valorized rather than regretted. White supremacy would be a foundation stone, a starting point for political argument, rather than something to be worked around or shunted aside. The defense of slavery should be prime territory for the elaboration of racism as an American value. As courts struggled to account for slavery within American law, a natural argumentative strategy would have been to appeal to white supremacy—if white supremacy were a normative value from which legal and political arguments could be constructed. Jacksonian America was, according to Smith, the "high noon of the white republic" explicitly defended "in terms of racial superiority rather than strained doctrines of consent," even as the liberal tradition nurtured a growing counternarrative of freedom for all.[59]

The *Dred Scott* case is the overwhelming example of the Court advancing white supremacy as a normative value and legal rationale when resolving a case involving slavery. It is nonetheless a bit striking that *Dred Scott* seems to be an outlier, even for the Jacksonian era.[60] Even as racist rhetoric was becoming increasingly prominent in the political arena, perhaps culminating in the Confederate vice president's address declaring that the new government's "corner-stone rests, upon the great truth that the negro is not equal to the white man," the justices on the US Supreme Court did not generally turn to such arguments.[61] The Court was asked to resolve an increasing number of slavery cases in the 1840s and 1850s as political and legal conflicts between antislavery and proslavery forces became more intense. With *Dred Scott,* the justices hoped to put a final nail in the coffin of the antislavery insurgency. Perhaps the appeal to race was seen as the hammer necessary to end the debate in the late antebellum era, doing the work that arguments such as Story's appeal to the value of union apparently could not.

Chief Justice Roger Taney did not mince words in his majority opinion in *Dred Scott.*[62] The chief justice set out to deny both that Congress could prohibit slavery in the federal territories and that formerly enslaved people could claim diversity-of-citizenship jurisdiction in the federal courts. Taney thought race was most relevant in establishing the latter claim. "The question is simply this: Can a negro, whose ancestors were imported into this country, and sold as slaves, become a member of the political community formed and brought into existence by the Constitution of the United States, and as such become entitled to all the rights, and privileges, and immunities, guaranteed by that instrument to the citizen?" Taney thought the answer to that question depended on who made up the sovereign people that constituted the government and authorized the federal courts to act. Unsurprisingly, Taney emphasized that the Court could not remake the law or "decide upon the justice or injustice, the policy or impolicy" of the constitutional rule; the justices could only "administer it as we find it." But Taney thought the answer was clear:

The question before us is, whether the class of persons described in the plea in abatement compose a portion of this people, and are constituent members of this sovereignty? We think they are not, and that they are not included, and were not intended to be included, under the word "citizens" in the Constitution, and can therefore claim none of the rights and privileges which that instrument provides for and secures to citizens of the United States. On the contrary, they were at that time considered as a subordinate and inferior class of beings, who had been subjugated by the dominant race, and, whether emancipated or not, yet remained subject to their authority, and had no rights or privileges but such as those who held the power and the Government might choose to grant them.[63]

Could formerly enslaved people be among the "constituent members of this sovereignty" and thus federal citizens in the relevant, constitutional sense? Taney denied that they could be, for they were not part of the "dominant race." They were, for all practical purposes, part of an "inferior class of beings" who could not aspire to be part of the body politic. No individual state was authorized to bring them into the larger "political family." Members of this "unfortunate race" could never be "a part of the people," regardless of their legal status as enslaved or free.[64] Taney's infamous opinion in *Dred Scott* provides evidence that liberalism was not the only available political tradition and system of values from which the justices could draw in constructing their appeals.

## CONCLUSION

Judicial discourse about slavery was characterized by multiple traditions, with the justices appealing to liberal ideals to justify their decisions but also to a commitment to union, to the importance of the rule of law, and to the political inferiority of blacks. It goes without saying that the justices generally spoke through the basic grammar of legal argumentation and analysis in the slavery cases, as they did in resolving other legal disputes.[65] However, in attempting to resolve such fundamental and politically salient legal disputes, the justices frequently drew on a larger political discourse that could help explain and justify their actions and the actions of other government officials. The ideas to which they appealed give us insight into the values taken to be commonly held and persuasive within the mainstream legal and political community. The justices rarely cast aside liberal ideals as irrelevant to the law of slavery, but liberal values jostled with other values, sometimes congruent and sometimes incongruous with liberal commitments. The arguments of the justices did not generally suggest that they were embarked on a project of working the law pure so as to best approximate liberal aspirations. Liberal aspirations were always tempered not only by the unfortunate facts on the ground but also by the presence of other ambitions that pulled in different directions.

The Civil War rearranged and remade the materials of American political thought. If, as Hartz suggested, slavery represented a feudal remnant trapped within a young liberal nation, the Civil War could be seen as a purge. If the Hartzian story about the antebellum era was too simplistic, then that suggests that the postbellum era is unlikely to conform to his vision of an untroubled liberal consensus as well. The slavery cases exposed a variety of normative traditions to which the justices could appeal in resolving disputes and clarifying the fundamental requirements of the American political order. Although slavery itself was removed from the constitutional system in the aftermath of the Civil War, the various strands of American political thought were not thereby reconciled and made one. The tensions between liberal ideals and the requirements of the rule of law, the compromises of the Union and the inherited political order, and the scar of race all remained and continued to make themselves felt in the writings of lawyers, judges, and statesmen.

Few legal and political issues have tested American ideals as severely as slavery has. The effort to reconcile the institution of slavery with the commitments of the law and American political ideals broke apart political parties, social movements, and even the nation itself. If the debate over slavery was, in many ways, sui generis within the American political tradition, it nonetheless reveals features of American political thought that are more commonplace. As Smith ably showed, the law and politics of immigration and naturalization can illuminate fundamental features of American political thought. Likewise, the law of slavery can be a window to look onto the wider landscape of American political discourse. The political and ideological resources available to antebellum judges remain vibrant today. Judges still must struggle with the felt injustices of an inherited political order and the temptations of allowing the particular to overwhelm the general. Fortunately, we no longer need to account for slavery within the American constitutional system, but that does not mean that we do not grapple with inequities of our own and temper the aspirations of liberalism with a devotion to other principled commitments.

## NOTES

1. Henry Hart, "The Time Chart of the Justices," *Harvard Law Review* 73 (1959): 99.

2. See Paul Finkelman, *An Imperfect Union* (Chapel Hill: University of North Carolina Press, 1981); Earl M. Maltz, "Slavery, Federalism, and the Structure of the Constitution," *American Journal of Legal History* 36 (1992): 466.

3. Louis Hartz, *The Liberal Tradition in America* (New York: Harcourt, Brace, and World, 1955), 3.

4. For an overview of the status of the Hartzian thesis, see Philip Abbott, "Still Louis Hartz after All These Years: A Defense of the Liberal Society Thesis," and the rejoinders in *Perspectives on Politics* 3 (2005): 93.

5. See, for example, David F. Ericson, *The Shaping of American Liberalism* (Chicago: University of Chicago Press, 1993); Edmund S. Morgan, *American Slavery, American Freedom* (New York: Norton, 1975).

6. John Locke himself doubted that slavery could be reconciled with liberal principles. Locke, *Second Treatise of Government*, in *Two Treatises of Government*, ed. Peter Laslett (New York: Cambridge University Press, 1960), sec. 22–24.

7. For accounts of alternative traditions in the United States, see Rogers M. Smith, *Civic Ideals* (New Haven, CT: Yale University Press, 1997), and the chapters in this volume by James Read, Alan Levine, James Stoner, Jr., and Johnathan O'Neill.

8. Samuel P. Huntington, *American Politics* (Cambridge, MA: Harvard University Press, 1981), 4.

9. Hartz, *Liberal Tradition in America*, 147, 148.

10. I limit myself here to opinions produced by the justices sitting on the US Supreme Court. Many other judges within the federal and state judicial systems were forced to grapple with legal issues posed by the presence of slavery within the United States, and undoubtedly some of those judges could be expected to approach the problem somewhat differently than the justices did.

11. Hartz, *Liberal Tradition in America*, 20.

12. For an excellent overview, see Thomas D. Moore, *Southern Slavery and the Law, 1619–1860* (Chapel Hill: University of North Carolina Press, 1999).

13. On the organization of the federal judiciary in the first part of the nineteenth century, see Russell R. Wheeler and Cynthia Harrison, *Creating the Federal Judicial System* (Washington, DC: Federal Judicial Center, 1989); Justin Crowe, *Building the Judiciary* (Princeton, NJ: Princeton University Press, 2012).

14. In 1842 and 1855, Congress shifted the circuits slightly but did so in a way that did not affect the balance on the Supreme Court. The 1863 statute expanded and restructured the Court to create a seven-to-three Northern majority, and an 1866 statute reorganized the circuits again to create nine seats on the Court, with only one coming from the former Confederacy. See also Howard Gillman, Mark A. Graber, and Keith E. Whittington, *American Constitutionalism*, vol. 1 (New York: Oxford University Press, 2013), 194–196, 254–256.

15. Quoted in Charles Warren, *The Supreme Court in United States History*, vol. 3 (Boston: Little, Brown, 1922), 21.

16. H. L. A. Hart, *The Concept of Law*, 2nd ed. (New York: Oxford University Press, 1994).

17. Lon L. Fuller, *The Morality of Law*, rev. ed. (New Haven, CT: Yale University Press, 1969).

18. Lon L. Fuller, "Adjudication and the Rule of Law," *Proceedings of the American Society of International Law* 54 (1960): 1.

19. Herbert Wechsler, "Toward Neutral Principles of Constitutional Law," *Harvard Law Review* 73 (1959): 1.

20. For one effort to reconcile liberalism with the rule of law, see Judith N. Shklar, *Legalism* (Cambridge, MA: Harvard University Press, 1964).

21. Robert Cover, *Justice Accused* (New Haven, CT: Yale University Press, 1975), 232.

22. Ibid., 233, 234. Cover labels this rhetorical move a "retreat to formalism" and sees it in part as a psychological mechanism. I have elsewhere discussed the strategic utility of such rhetoric in a political context. See Keith E. Whittington, *Political Foundations of Judicial Supremacy* (Princeton, NJ: Princeton University Press, 2007), 134–152.

23. Mima Queen and Child v. Hepburn, 11 U.S. 290 (1813). Robert Cover collects a large number of cases, many in the state courts, that evince this tension between the formal requirements of the law and the call of conscience over slavery. Cover, *Justice Accused*, 201–256. Mark V. Tushnet has explored one notorious North Carolina case; see Tushnet, *Slave Law in the American South* (Lawrence: University Press of Kansas, 2003).

24. Chief Justice John Marshall took a somewhat different approach when considering how general rules of liability for lost or damaged cargo on carrier ships applied to slaves. The "volition" and "feelings" of slaves meant that they could not be treated like other forms of cargo and thus could not be protected against loss in the same way. As a consequence, English rules of strict liability should be modified. Boyce v. Anderson, 27 U.S. 150 (1829). This modification of inherited doctrine reflected the same kinds of legal calculations judges made in other contexts, however, and did not invoke any particular concern with liberal principles of freedom. The dual nature of a slave as both person and property did generate a variety of legal puzzles for judges to attempt to resolve.

25. A secondary issue raised by the case was whether a broadly antislavery juror should be allowed to serve in such a suit for freedom. The Court upheld the ruling of

the trial judge that such a juror was biased and could not serve, despite the difficulties of locating unprejudiced jurors on matters of private right that intersected with "general and public questions." Such concerns foreshadowed current issues with "death-qualified" juries in capital cases.

26. Mason v. Matilda, 25 U.S. 590, 593 (1827). Similarly, Chief Justice Roger Taney emphasized that "a bequest of freedom to the slave stands upon the same principles with a bequest over to a third person." In this case, the application of consistent legal rules benefitted the slave suing for freedom, for the Court was unwilling to regard a conditional bequest of the possession of a slave as "inconsistent with the right of property." The property interest in a slave, as with other property, could be held subject only to the conditions upon which it was acquired. Williams v. Ash, 42 U.S. 1, 14 (1843).

27. George Kateb, "On Patriotism," *Cato Unbound* (March 10, 2008), www.cato-unbound.org/2008/03/10/george-kateb/patriotism.

28. Rogan Kersh, *Dreams of a More Perfect Union* (Ithaca, NY: Cornell University Press, 2001), 2.

29. Paul C. Nagel, *One Nation Indivisible* (New York: Oxford University Press, 1964), 3.

30. Robert V. Remini, *Andrew Jackson and the Course of American Freedom, 1822–1832* (New York: Harper and Row, 1981), 233–237.

31. *The Works of Daniel Webster*, 5th ed., vol. 3, ed. Edward Everett (Boston: Little, Brown 1853), 342.

32. The antislavery cause had its own radicals willing to sacrifice union for other priorities. See Joel Olson, "The Freshness of Fanaticism: The Abolitionist Defense of Zealotry," *Perspectives on Politics* 5 (2007): 685; James B. Stewart, "The Aims and Impacts of Garrisonian Abolitionism, 1840–1860," *Civil War History* 15 (1969): 197.

33. See, for example, In re Martin, 16 F. Cas. 881 (S.D. N.Y., 1800) ("a subject that created great difficulty in the formation of the constitution, and that . . . resulted in a compromise not entirely satisfactory. . . . But whatever our private opinions on the subject of slavery may be, we are bound in good faith to carry into execution the constitutional provisions in relation to it"); Vaughan v. Williams, 28 F. Cas. 1115 (C.C.D. Ind., 1845) ("Whatever opinion may now be entertained . . . they were settled only by a spirit of compromise and of mutual concession. . . . We are not the less bound by its provisions"); Jones v. Van Zandt, 46 U.S. 215 (1847) ("one of its sacred compromises, and which we possess no authority as a judicial body to modify or override").

34. Prigg v. Pennsylvania, 41 U.S. 539 (1842).

35. *Id.*, at 610.

36. *Id.*

37. *Id.*, at 611.

38. *Id.*

39. *Id.*, at 612.

40. *Id.*

41. Groves v. Slaughter, 40 U.S. 449, 507–508 (1841).

42. Justice John McLean's effort to separate the regulation of slavery from the regulation of interstate commerce gained support from his contention that slaves were understood to be, under the federal constitution, people, not property. It was this suggestion

that provoked further argument from other justices, including Justice Henry Baldwin.

43. Justice Baldwin took a different tack. He thought slaves were clearly articles of commerce, and the denial of the privilege of bringing slaves into a territory for sale was a violation of the federal rights of the slave owner. States could, through their police power, prohibit property in slaves entirely, but if they recognized property in slaves, they could not distinguish the slaves of their own residents from the slaves of the residents of other states. Union meant recognizing the equal rights of all citizens and accepting the free flow of interstate trade, including the exchange across state lines of otherwise lawful property.

44. Hartz, *Liberal Tradition in America*, 3.

45. Richard Hofstadter, *The American Political Tradition and the Men Who Made It* (New York: Knopf, 1948), xxxvii.

46. Thomas Jefferson, *Notes on the State of Virginia* (London: John Stockdale, 1787), 270; *The Writings of Thomas Jefferson*, vol. 9, ed. H. A. Washington (New York: Berby and Jackson, 1859), 279.

47. Benjamin Rush, *An Address to the Inhabitants of the British Settlements in America* (Boston: John Boyles, 1773), 28.

48. Jefferson, *Notes on the State of Virginia*, 272.

49. John Kenrick and Rufus King, quoted in David Bryon Davis, *The Problem of Slavery in the Age of Revolution, 1770–1823* (Ithaca, NY: Cornell University Press, 1975), 332. Jefferson, however, tended to move in the opposite direction. See, for example, Thomas W. Merrill's chapter in this volume.

50. Somerset v. Stewart, 12 Geo. 3, 19 (1772).

51. Commonwealth v. Jennison, *Proceedings of the Massachusetts Historical Society* (1873), 294.

52. Unsurprisingly, the Court was not sympathetic to a request that the justices "disregard . . . the constitution and the act of Congress in respect to this subject, on account of the supposed inexpediency and invalidity of all laws recognizing slavery or any right of property in man." A judicial body was unlikely to embrace liberal principles and invocations of the higher law to such a degree that clear provisions of the Constitution itself were to be ignored. *Jones v. Van Zandt*, 231.

53. *Mima Queen and Child*, 298.

54. In re *The Plattsburgh*, 23 U.S. 133, 142 (1825).

55. In re *The Antelope*, 23 U.S. 66, 119–120 (1825).

56. Merle Curti, *The Growth of American Thought* (New York: Harper and Row, 1943), x.

57. Rogers M. Smith, "Beyond Tocqueville, Myrdal, and Hartz: The Multiple Traditions in America," *American Political Science Review* 87 (1993): 549.

58. Rogers M. Smith, *Civic Ideals* (New Haven, CT: Yale University Press, 1997).

59. Ibid., 198.

60. On *Dred Scott*, see Don E. Fehrenbacher, *The Dred Scott Case* (New York: Oxford University Press, 2001); Mark A. Graber, Dred Scott *and the Problem of Constitutional Evil* (New York: Cambridge University Press, 2006).

61. Henry Cleveland, *Alexander Stephens, in Public and Private, with Letters and Speeches* (Philadelphia: National, 1866), 721.

62. Dred Scott v. Sandford, 60 U.S. 393 (1857).

63. *Id.*, at 404–405.

64. *Id.*, at 417, 407, 410.

65. For one account of the grammar of legitimate legal argumentation, see Philip Bobbitt, *Constitutional Fate* (New York: Oxford University Press, 1984).

# CHAPTER 3

# Antebellum Natural Rights Liberalism

DANIEL S. MALACHUK

Like their revolutionary forebears, antebellum American liberals believed in the metaphysical existence of natural rights, and they differed among themselves only on the question of whether to secure those rights for all persons gradually or immediately. In the three decades before the Civil War, that tactical but nonetheless signal difference was most dramatically illustrated in the quarrels between liberals regarding the pace for emancipating enslaved persons: self-identified "abolitionists" urged immediate emancipation, whereas moderate "antislavery" advocates counseled more gradual approaches.

However, modern scholars have misinterpreted this tactical debate as indicative of a deeper, philosophical one to the point of likening immediatist abolitionists such as William Lloyd Garrison to today's "perfectionist" liberals and gradualist antislavery advocates such as Abraham Lincoln to "political" ones. Although this distinction between perfectionist and political liberalism is certainly important today, to trace it so far back in time is to drive an anachronistic wedge right through the middle of antebellum natural rights liberalism.

This is not to say there were no differences among antebellum liberals beyond the tactical; although antebellum liberals were *philosophically* one regarding the metaphysical priority of natural rights, they differed about how to secure those rights—and not just *tactically* about the pace of this work but *politically* about the best regime for this work. The wide political array of natural rights liberals that resulted—including anarchists, cosmopolitans, revolutionary nationalists, and constitutional nationalists—helps to answer the question of whether the Civil War was a revolution or a return: basically, it depends on who you ask. More important than this political question though is the philosophical one raised by this deep consensus about natural rights among antebellum liberals: If liberals then required metaphysical natural rights to end slavery, can political liberals now do the same—when globally there are more enslaved persons than ever before—without natural rights?

## ANTEBELLUM NATURAL RIGHTS LIBERALISM

After much scholarly debate over the past fifty years, that natural rights liberalism began with John Locke's *Two Treatises of Government* (1689) is a settled matter, as is the fact that, although this theory jostled for supremacy in England for a century afterward, Louis Hartz's old claim that American thought "begins [and] stays with Locke, by virtue of an absolute and irrational attachment" is only somewhat exaggerated, at least in the Northern context.[1] When in 1776 Thomas Paine warned in Lockean terms that the persecutory British were "declaring War against the natural rights of all Mankind," his book spoke "common sense" to enough Americans to make it the world's first best-seller.[2] And, as Carl Becker long ago observed, because Thomas Jefferson and his colleagues also believed Locke's natural rights philosophy "self-evident," they paraphrased it so closely in the Declaration of Independence (1776): "that all men are created equal, that they are endowed by their Creator with certain unalienable Rights, that among these are Life, Liberty and the pursuit of Happiness," "that to secure these rights, Governments are instituted among Men, deriving their just powers from the consent of the governed," and "that whenever any Form of Government becomes destructive of these ends, it is the Right of the People to alter or to abolish it, and to institute new Government."[3] As Jefferson would later explain, in crafting the Declaration, he and his colleagues sought "not to find out new principles . . . but to place before mankind the common sense of the subject."[4]

Two generations later, the existence of natural rights remained common sense for the antebellum liberals. Prior to the Civil War, for those liberals seeking to universalize natural rights, the simplest and surest way remained to allude to the Declaration. At Seneca Falls, New York, in 1848, to prove that women have natural rights too, Elizabeth Cady Stanton simply adjusted the Declaration to assert "that all men and women are created equal; that they are endowed by their Creator with certain inalienable rights," and so on.[5] Similarly, in his January 1, 1831, "Inaugural Editorial" to the *Liberator,* Garrison explained that, in "assenting to the 'self-evident truth' maintained in the American Declaration of Independence, 'that all men are created equal, and endowed by their Creator with certain inalienable rights—among which are life, liberty and the pursuit of happiness,' I shall strenuously contend for the immediate enfranchisement of our slave population."[6] This reliance upon the Declaration's natural rights was no passing whim for Garrison; thirty-four years later he brought the *Liberator* to a close with the contention that "no journal . . . has

vindicated . . . the Declaration of Independence, with its self-evident truths—
the rights of human nature, without distinction of race, complexion or sex—
more earnestly or more uncompromisingly."[7]

A few more antebellum liberals help to illustrate just how widespread these
convictions about the Declaration's natural rights were. Consider another
immediatist abolitionist like Garrison, one committed to even more aggressive tactics. In his May 1858 Provisional Constitution and Ordinances for the
People of the United States, John Brown declared (in Lockean terms) that the
current American state was illegitimate because it remained in a state of war
with enslaved persons. As Brown put it in the preamble:

Whereas slavery, throughout its entire existence in the United States, is none other
than a most barbarous, unprovoked, and unjustifiable war of one portion of its citizens
upon another portion . . . in utter disregard and violation of those eternal and self-
evident truths set forth in our Declaration of Independence, we, citizens of the United
States, and the oppressed people who, by a recent decision of the Supreme Court [i.e.,
*Dred Scott v. Sandford*], are declared to have no rights which the white man is bound
to respect, . . . do, for the time being, ordain and establish for ourselves the following
Provisional Constitution and Ordinances, the better to protect our persons, property,
lives, and liberties, and to govern our actions.[8]

As his biographer David S. Reynolds explains, Brown intended the provisional constitution to found a new American state that would—this time—
hold true to its founding principles, an independent mountain society in the
Alleghenies where Brown and those liberated from slavery might live for years
like the Jamaican maroon communities.[9]

Another American abolitionist, the nation's greatest, Frederick Douglass,
shifted tactically from immediatism to gradualism over the course of the 1850s,
but whatever his tactics he always held exactly the same Lockean convictions
as did Jefferson, Stanton, Garrison, and Brown. Douglass was particularly emphatic about the metaphysical status of those natural rights too. "I have always
felt," he wrote in his 1881 *Life and Times*, "that I had on my side all the invisible
forces of the moral government of the universe. Happily for me I have had the
wit to distinguish between what is merely artificial and transient and what is
fundamental and permanent; and resting on the latter, I could cheerfully encounter the former."[10] For Douglass, the "fundamental and permanent" were
natural rights, as several scholars have recently argued. "In the basis as well
as the substance of his moral principle," Peter C. Myers has written, Douglass "followed the Declaration of Independence, which pointedly located the
primary political truths not in positive revelation but instead in 'the Laws of

*Nature* and of *Nature's* God.'" Natural rights were "the substance of Douglass's rational faith."[11] Nicholas Buccola similarly traces Douglass's "natural rights philosophy" to Douglass's belief (in Douglass's own words) in the "civic catechism of the Declaration of Independence."[12]

Douglass's emphasis upon the metaphysical status of natural rights echoed Locke's own. Because all men are "the Workmanship of one Omnipotent, and infinitely wise Maker," Locke famously argued, they are God's "property," and no other's, and thus are "made to last during his [God's], not one another[']s Pleasure."[13] Douglass agreed, insisting that the enslaved person was "a moral and intellectual being" wrongly held by another person instead of by God, for each person bears "the image of God . . . and possess[es] a soul, eternal and indestructible." For Douglass, slavery—in Justin B. Dyer's words—was simply "a violation of the natural moral order" and thus "constituted a peculiar 'crime against God and man.' Douglass's argument," Dyer continues, "presupposed a connection between the moral order and divine providence."[14]

As noted, Douglass retained his rational faith in natural rights even as he shifted tactically from immediatism (like Garrison and Brown) to gradualism; but other consistently moderate antislavery thinkers also shared this faith, which Lincoln (to take the most prominent example) called in fact his "ancient faith." This has been understood by scholars for some time: whether one turns to Becker's 1922 *The Declaration of Independence* or Harry V. Jaffa's 1959 *Crisis of the House Divided,* scholars have long recognized that Lincoln, in Jaffa's words, "believed slavery to be against natural right."[15] Although these and other scholars since have still found many reasons to disagree with each other—for example, about whether Lincoln was racist, whether Lincoln's "ancient faith" drew on the Christian Bible as well as the Declaration, or whether (regardless of Lincoln's belief) natural rights are true or false—there is nonetheless broad consensus that Lincoln himself truly believed in natural rights.[16] What matters is that for Lincoln these rights were indeed *natural,* "grounded," as Dyer explains, "in truth that transcended a particular time and place and found an enduring basis in human nature. Nature, for Lincoln, . . . did not merely denote what is but also supplied norms of what ought to be, and reason, rather than passion, provided the means by which men apprehended those practical axioms. As such the particular . . . norms of a particular polity could be measured against transcendent, rational standards."[17]

Further, as was the case for Garrison, Brown, and Douglass, for Lincoln the Declaration was the central document for American natural rights liberalism. Although he did not begin his career with a singular dedication to the text, when Lincoln returned to politics in the 1850s, the Declaration—partly because of attacks on it by John Calhoun and others—became his touchstone.[18] Indeed, so fervent grew his dedication to the founding document that in an 1861 speech at Philadelphia, Lincoln confessed he "never had a feeling politically that did not spring from the sentiments embodied in the Declaration of Independence"[19] (*Collected Works*, hereafter cited parenthetically as *CW*, with page numbers). What those sentiments amounted to, for Lincoln, was the universality of natural rights. In October 1858, in the seventh and final debate with Stephen Douglas, Lincoln described the meaning of the Declaration this way:

> I think the authors of that notable instrument intended to include all men, but they did not mean to declare all men equal in all respects. They did not mean to say all men were equal in color, size, intellect, moral development or social capacity. They defined with tolerable distinctness in what they did consider all men created equal—equal in certain inalienable rights, among which are life, liberty and the pursuit of happiness. This they said, and this they meant. (*CW* 3:301)

Unlike Brown, though, Lincoln firmly believed that these inalienable rights could be secured only gradually, not with a new nation in the mountains but with the power of the existing Union. In an 1857 speech at Springfield, he explained that the authors of the Declaration, in announcing the inalienable rights, "meant simply to declare [them] so that the enforcement of [these rights] might follow as fast as circumstances should permit": "They meant to set up a standard maxim for free society, which should be familiar to all, and revered by all; constantly looked to, constantly labored for, and even though never perfectly attained, constantly approximated, and thereby constantly spreading and deepening its influence, and augmenting the happiness and value of life to all people of all colors everywhere" (*CW* 2:406). Lincoln was in this way a "gradualist."

So, although antislavery Lincoln agreed with abolitionist Brown about the metaphysical existence of natural rights, he disagreed about the pace at which those rights should be realized universally. *Philosophically*, that is, Lincoln agreed with the abolitionists that the Declaration's natural rights served as "a standard maxim for free society" and thus even as "a spiritual regulator" (as Staughton Lynd once put it) akin "to that of the Biblical injunction 'Be ye perfect.'"[20] *Tactically*, though, Lincoln and the abolitionists differed tremendously. Consider Garrison. Although since even before the founding opponents of slavery had been advocating for the gradual emancipation of enslaved people, in the 1830s Garrison was among the most prominent of a new breed of activists who promoted what came to called "immediatism." Inspired not only by the Declaration's natural rights but also the Second Great Awakening's revivalism, Garrison believed "moral suasion" would spark a kind of conversion experience among white Americans about the righteousness of "the immediate enfranchisement of our slave population," as Garrison called for in 1831. Meeting in New York City in December 1833 to establish the American Anti-Slavery Society (AAS), Garrison demanded immediate emancipation:

More than fifty-seven years have elapsed, since a band of patriots convened in this place, to devise measures for the deliverance of this country from a foreign yoke. The corner-stone upon which they founded the Temple of Freedom was broadly this—"that all men are created equal; that they are endowed by their Creator with certain inalienable rights; that among these are life, LIBERTY, and the pursuit of happiness." At the sound of their trumpet-call, three millions of people rose up as from the sleep of death, and rushed to the strife of blood; deeming it more glorious to die instantly as freemen, than desirable to live one hour as slaves.[21]

Thus far, all of these sentences might have been spoken by Lincoln. However, then Garrison explained to his fellow AAS members, "We have met together for the achievement of an enterprise, without which that of our [founding] fathers is incomplete." And with this statement, Garrison made his turn toward immediate civil disobedience, arguing first "that all those laws which are now in force, admitting the rights of slavery, are therefore, before God, utterly null and void," then second that some of those laws are to be found in the Constitution itself (he mentioned the articles about suppressing insurrections and the three-fifths clause among others), and then third that because these laws perpetuate among even Northerners a "relation to slavery [that] is criminal," that relationship "MUST BE BROKEN UP." Committed like Lincoln to natural rights, Garrison advocated tactics that were the very opposite of Lincoln's: disunion instead of union.[22]

Philosophically one but tactically divided, Lincoln's gradualism and Garrison's immediatism would constitute the great drama of American liberalism until the Civil War rendered the question moot: At what pace should natural rights be universally secured? Unfortunately, however, that disagreement about tactics has so preoccupied—and even misled—modern scholars that we have lost sight of the much more important consensus about natural rights.

## AN ANACHRONISTIC WEDGE

There have always been two major critiques of abolitionism. The first critique, initiated by antebellum proslavery Southerners such as George Fitzhugh, rejected abolition's natural rights as violating the neofeudal ideal it shared with reactionary Europeans such as Joseph de Maistre and Thomas Carlyle.[23] Over the course of the twentieth century, however, explicit theories of hierarchical societies sputtered into "neo-Confederate" sentiments rather than a significant theoretical legacy.

The second critique of abolitionism, though, was made by liberals and included no objection to its natural rights basis. When, for example, the very first immediatist, David Walker, declared in his 1829 appeal that all black persons "must and shall be free"—for could not American whites "see your Declaration [and] understand your own language?"—liberal critics of immediatism did not object to Walker's philosophy; on the contrary, they shared it.[24]

What liberal critics of abolitionism objected to were Walker's immediatist tactics, and in so doing, they initiated an essentially psychological critique of these tactics. Take, for example, the liberal critique of abolitionism developed by Massachusetts senator Daniel Webster. Like the abolitionists, Webster was fundamentally committed to natural rights; we can trace that commitment throughout his entire life. For example, in a November 1799 article, a teenaged Webster, disturbed by Napoleon's recent coup d'état and forsaking of French revolutionary principles, assured his audience that Napoleon's antics would do nothing to challenge Webster's own convictions about natural rights. For when men—unlike Napoleon—justly "take arms to burst those chains that have bound them in slavery, to assert and maintain those privileges which they justly claim as natural rights, their object is noble, and we wish them success."[25] A half-century later, in a February 1850 letter, Webster reiterated these same convictions to the abolitionist Unitarian minister William Furness when he explained that his crafting of the 1850 Compromise—which sought to balance California's entry into the Union as a free state with a law strengthening the Constitution's provision for the return of fugitive slaves (Article 4, Section 2, paragraph 3)—did not at all violate his fundamental belief that (and these are Webster's words) "slavery is a continued and permanent violation of human rights." However, he prudently reasoned, only the "mild influences of Christianity" would ever truly bring slavery to an end; his role as a statesman was to preserve the Union so that it would one day be able to protect the rights of the emancipated. That is why, Webster told Furness, he could in no way countenance the radical tactics of those "breaking up social and political systems, on the warmth, rather than the strength, of a hope that, in such convulsions, the cause of emancipation may be promoted."[26]

Webster alludes here to immediatists such as Garrison, whose extreme tactics—including his 1833 demand that all systems supporting slavery "MUST BE

BROKEN UP"—made them, in Webster's eyes, not fellow natural rights liberals but radicals of a specific and dangerous temperament. Webster diagnosed that temperament a month later in a major March 7, 1850, congressional speech in which he explicitly contrasted his prudent support of the compromise bill with the rabid opposition of the abolitionists. The abolitionists' real problem, Webster explained, was their temperamental inability to compromise. "There will sometimes be found men," Webster observed, "with whom every thing is absolute; absolutely wrong, or absolutely right." Even worse, he added, "they are apt . . . to think that nothing is good but what is perfect, and that there are no compromises or modifications to be made in consideration of difference of opinion or in deference to other men's judgment." Indeed, if they cannot get their way, these fanatics will happily destroy the world. "If their perspicacious vision enables them to detect a spot on the face of the sun, they think that a good reason why the sun should be struck down from heaven. They prefer the chance of running into utter darkness to living in heavenly light, if that heavenly light be not absolutely without any imperfection."[27]

Webster was one of the many antebellum liberals who developed this psychological profile of abolitionists, a profile we have subsequently come to call "perfectionist."[28] The readiness of moderate American thinkers to pathologize abolitionists did not at all slacken with the end of the Civil War or even the start of the civil rights movement; on the contrary, even some of the most astute American scholars continued to rely upon this diagnosis. In his 1964 "The Paranoid Style in American Politics," for example, Richard Hofstadter lumped abolitionists with all of those for whom social conflict is not "something to be mediated or compromised."[29] What is at stake for these "paranoids," Hofstadter explained, "is always a conflict between absolute good and absolute evil, what is necessary is not compromise but the will to fight things out to a finish." Much as Webster in 1850 accused abolitionists of readiness to strike down the sun, Hofstadter in 1964 judged them genocidal because in their view "the enemy is thought of as being totally evil and totally unappeasable, [and therefore] he must be totally eliminated." Indeed, he continued, abolitionism is best understood as a psychological condition, not a political movement, given that the paranoid abolitionist's "enemy is on many counts a projection of the self."[30]

The civil rights movement inspired a generous reconsideration of abolitionism, but the psychoanalytical habit has still been hard for liberal critics of abolitionism to break. In an important 2012 book, *The Abolitionist Imagination*, Andrew M. Delbanco, although admiring the renaissance in abolitionist historiography, nevertheless still contends that the abolitionists exemplified a "persistent impulse in American life."[31] "The sacred rage of abolitionism"—as

Delbanco labels "its moral urgency and uncompromising fervor, its vision of the world purified and perfected"—"has been at work in many holy wars since the war against slavery. One thinks," Delbanco continues, "not only of the war against drink, or of Reagan's Star Wars, but of the war against the gold standard . . . , the 'war to end all wars,' the wars on poverty, on cancer, on drugs, the ongoing war on terror, and, whether we like it or not, the war against abortion."[32] These "parallels should remind us," Delbanco concludes, "that all holy wars . . . from left or from right, bespeak a zeal for combating sin, not tomorrow, not in due time, not, in Lincoln's phrase, by putting it [slavery] 'in the course of ultimate extinction,' but *now*."[33]

Together, then, the critiques of Webster in 1850, Hofstadter in 1964, and Delbanco in 2012 reveal a continuity of focus on abolitionism's *psychological* perfectionism. However, Delbanco's analysis also hints at a new innovation in the liberal critique of abolitionism, entailing two striking claims. The first is that abolitionism was also afflicted by a different kind of perfectionism, a *philosophical* perfectionism, to be defined momentarily. The second is that, in resisting abolitionism's immediatism, antislavery gradualists cultivated an alternative philosophical foundation known as value pluralism, which anticipates the worldview we now associate with political liberalism. So compelling has this innovative interpretation of abolitionist-as-perfectionist-liberal and antislavery-advocate-as-political-liberal become today that it has found expression not only in the work of abolitionism's deftest critics, such as Delbanco, but also in the work of abolitionism's most nuanced champions, such as Eric Foner. However, before turning to this evidence, it will help to first recall the modern liberal critique of philosophical perfectionism upon which these scholars draw.

In his 1971 *A Theory of Justice,* John Rawls codified a new philosophical use of the term "perfectionism" to describe "a teleological theory directing society to arrange institutions and to define the duties and obligations of individuals so as to maximize the achievement of human excellence in art, science, and culture."[34] What advocates of "political liberalism," as Rawls came to call his rival theory, should most object to about perfectionism is not its psychological authoritarianism but its deeper philosophical assumption: its epistemic confidence that a timeless "excellence" not only can be enforced but can even be discovered in the first place. For Rawls, "the fact of reasonable pluralism" means the best we can ever hope to build is an "overlapping consensus" about not a single value or set of values but a range of rival values, held loosely, always in conflict.[35]

Although his is currently the most famous articulation, Rawls himself traced his value pluralism further back into the twentieth century.[36] In a footnote in *Political Liberalism,* Rawls nods to Isaiah Berlin's account of value pluralism as capturing the tragic quality of political life, which is that "the full range of values is too extensive to fit into any one social world." An oppressive regime is oppressive precisely because it refuses to fit that range of values into its social world, of course, but even the well-meaning liberal society, which "may have far more space than other social worlds," "can [still] never be without loss. The basic error," Rawls continues, "is to think that because values are objective . . . they must be compatible. . . . Not all truths can fit into one social world."[37]

For Berlin, one is a value pluralist because there are just too many objective values in the world for any to be held as supreme in a liberal society. In another footnote, in his *Collected Papers,* however, Rawls offers an even more tragic reason to be a value pluralist, one offered by Max Weber. Rawls explains that, whereas Berlin believes political tragedy stems from the fact that there are simply too many objective values to fit harmoniously into any given society, Weber believes "political tragedy arises from the conflict of subjective commitments and resolute wills."[38]

This is arguably the ethos in which abolitionism is being assessed today. Vigorous proponents of metaphysical claims—like the abolitionists for natural rights—are (it is argued) in dangerous denial not only of the wide range of rival values but also of the subjective character of all of those values. Delbanco calls this state of denial "the abolitionist imagination," and against it he champions those nineteenth-century Americans who urged instead an "articulate ambivalence," particularly the antebellum era's two greatest novelists. Look at Herman Melville's devastating portrait of Captain Ahab in *Moby-Dick* (1851), Delbanco writes, for a character who is clearly a sendup of fanatical zealots such as Garrison.[39] In addition, Nathaniel Hawthorne too was keenly attuned (as Henry James observed of his predecessor) to "the high brutality of good intentions" such as those held by the crusading abolitionists.[40] Rather than proselytize for a single set of metaphysical truths like the abolitionists did, this argument goes, Hawthorne and Melville used their fiction to illuminate the politically tragic reality of value pluralism. According to this worldview, no set of values like natural rights stands as a "higher law," as some abolitionists labeled their cause; rather, we must modestly acknowledge the variety of human experiences and surrender to the only order we can ever have in common, the law we write for ourselves. In the same 2012 volume, Wilfred M. McClay comes to Delbanco's aid with this argument, urging that we admire not perfectionist immediatists such as Garrison but political gradualists such as Lincoln, who had a "reverence for the laws" (Lincoln's theme in his 1838 Lyceum Address) and whose "moral heroism resided in his willingness to wait on the very same history that the abolitionist tried to hasten."[41] Perhaps even more admirable, McClay continues, is the literature of this period—again, referring to Melville and Hawthorne, who used it "to stand in the middle, between the ethic of ultimate ends and the ethic of responsibility, fully conscious of both but fully committed to neither."[42]

In situating the novelists between the abolitionists (and their ethic of ultimate ends) and Lincoln (and his ethic of responsibility), McClay alludes here to Weber's description, in "Politics as a Vocation" (1918), of "two fundamentally differing and irreconcilably opposed maxims": the ethic of ultimate aims, in which "the Christian does rightly and leaves the results with the Lord," and the ethic of responsibility, in which "one has to give an account of the foreseeable results of one's action."[43] For Weber, the proponent of ultimate aims "cannot stand up under the ethical irrationality of the world"; he is in this way "a political infant."[44] Abolitionism, McClay points out, had the "accents of Max Weber's ethic of ultimate ends: 'Let justice be done, though the heavens fall!'"; in contrast, there is the other ethic, "the mediating prudential wisdom and statesmanship of an Abraham Lincoln."[45]

In using Weber to map the politics of antislavery advocacy in the antebellum North, McClay reiterates here an argument made earlier in *The Abolitionist Imagination* by Delbanco, who in turn traces it back to the great historian of this period, Foner. According to (what Delbanco calls) "the Foner synthesis," Lincoln took responsibility for the state, whereas the abolitionists took responsibility for its ultimate aims.[46] And, in *The Fiery Trial: Abraham Lincoln and American Slavery* (2010), Foner does indeed invoke Weber's essay to help him explicate the work of both sides. Paying tribute to Lincoln as the great ethicist of responsibility, Foner argues that the abolitionists also deserve our respect for imagining—and compelling Lincoln to imagine too—the ultimate aim, ending slavery. Foner underscores that, in an essay otherwise emphatic about the instrumentalism of most political action, "Weber concluded by noting the symbiotic relationship between political action and moral agitation. 'What is possible,' he wrote, 'would not have been achieved, if, in this world, people had not repeatedly reached for the impossible.'" The abolitionists were important, Foner concludes, "because their agitation helped to establish the context within which politicians like Lincoln operated":

On issue after issue in the 1850's and during the Civil War—the necessity of northern political unity to halt the expansion of slavery; opposition to compromise on this question during the secession crisis; emancipation in the District of Columbia; general emancipation under the Constitution's war power; the arming of black soldiers; amending the Constitution to abolish slavery; extending the right to vote to at least some blacks—Lincoln came to occupy positions first staked out by abolitionists and Radical Republicans.[47]

Delbanco might prefer Lincoln's responsibility ethic, whereas Foner might prefer the abolitionists' ultimate-ends ethic, but remarkably, both of these scholars seem to agree we can best describe antebellum liberalism as divided between these ethics: the perfectionists pursued ultimate aims; the politicos eschewed such metaphysics and exercised power responsibly.

However, this interpretive paradigm drives an anachronistic wedge right through the middle of antebellum natural rights liberalism: between the gradualist liberals such as Webster and Lincoln, on the one hand, and the immediatist abolitionists, on the other. It reassigns the former to the political liberal camp, pledged only to the ethic of responsibility, and the latter to the perfectionist camp, pledged only to the ethic of ultimate aims. As shown in the first section of the chapter, though, these politicians and activists were divided only by their tactics, not by their philosophical presuppositions. All antebellum liberals— from Walker to Webster, from Brown to Lincoln—presupposed that human individuals are endowed by their creator with natural rights.

This point can be made one final time by recalling the famous exchange of Michael J. Sandel and Rawls about the nature of Lincoln's liberalism, for Sandel was effectively objecting to Rawls's attempt to drive an anachronistic wedge into the period and claim Lincoln as a political liberal. Sandel actually began the exchange in 1994, when he contended that in the 1858 Lincoln-Douglas debates a political liberal would have had to side with the arguments of Douglas, not Lincoln. Sandel explained that, whereas Lincoln insisted metaphysically that the Declaration proclaimed all men created equal, Douglas countered politically that the signers of that document did not mean black men. Sandel added that other key resources within the political culture—the Constitution itself, the 1857 *Dred Scott* decision—also supported slavery and even a racial hierarchy (in the case of *Dred*) in various ways. So, Sandel concluded, "to the extent that [Rawls's] political liberalism refuses to invoke perfectionist moral ideals and relies instead on notions of citizenship implicit in the political culture, [Rawls] would have had a hard time explaining in 1858 why Lincoln was right and Douglas was wrong."[48] This is because Lincoln, unlike Douglas, rejected the proslavery political culture of the time and instead introduced an ultimate aim—natural rights—into the debate. To do this is—for thinkers like Rawls, at least—to violate the political liberal's ethic of responsibility.

In response to Sandel, Rawls reasoned that political liberals would in fact side with Lincoln, for they would contend that ending slavery is reasonable. This is because ending slavery, Rawls wrote, "is a clear case of securing the constitutional essential of the equal basic liberties," whereas Douglas's alternative—deferring to popular sovereignty regardless of the position taken on slavery—is not.[49] Recently, John Burt has considered Rawls's defense in more detail and reached a similar conclusion. Against Sandel's portrait of an amoral political liberalism, Burt argues that political liberalism—Rawls's as much as Lincoln's—"is an expression of the conviction that citizens have a crucial moral investment in each other's ethical freedom." Burt offers in support of this claim Rawls's response to Sandel's charges: that is, participants in the original position (alluding to Rawls's famous thought-experiment in A *Theory of Justice*) would never risk allowing slavery.[50]

However, as antebellum liberals recognized, slavery *was* indeed risked by the founders in their "original position" as upheld by the Constitution. Therefore, the only way to challenge a constitutional republic allowing race-based slavery would be to reach outside of that Constitution to some extraconstitutional resource, such as natural rights. And this is precisely what the antebellum liberals—from Walker through Lincoln—did.

Where the antebellum liberals differed from each other was about the kind of political contraptions that might best realize those natural rights. If the current political contraption is actually betraying its philosophical foundation, then perhaps we must "bend" that contraption—as Douglass said of the Constitution, to make sure it is antislavery—or even break it, as John Quincy Adams contemplated as early as 1820 and Brown proposed in 1858. It is to these and other political differences among the antebellum natural rights liberals that this chapter now turns.

## THE POLITICS OF NATURAL RIGHTS LIBERALISM

For decades, we have rightly understood the main political drama of the antebellum years as a struggle between liberals and violent radicals, but we have mistaken the players. The great *philosophical* debate in antebellum America was indeed between liberals and radicals, but the liberals were—across the board—against slavery because of their faith in the natural rights enshrined in the Declaration of Independence. The radicals, on the other hand, were not to be found among the abolitionists but among those proslavery zealots who aggressively rejected the American liberal tradition of natural rights and instead sought—effectively as revolutionaries—to transform the United States into a neofeudal slave empire. Condensing the most recent work of historians, John Stauffer (in his contribution to Delbanco's *The Abolitionist Imagination*) has nicely summarized the key points of this account. Prior to the 1830s, natural rights liberals sought mostly by legal means to bring an end to slavery, which they did throughout the North; slavery's defenders in the South were effectively gradualists themselves in seeking to delay this reckoning only for their region. However, sometime in the 1830s, Southern neofeudalists began to defend slavery as a positive good, not just for the South and Southern west but (disregarding the line drawn in the Missouri Compromise) the Northern west, the North itself (as the *Dred* decision suggested), and even the Caribbean, Mexico, and other parts of South America. Over the next thirty years, in response to this vision of a hemispheric slave empire, more and more white liberals reached the conclusions first grasped by black liberals such as Walker: the abolition of slavery (not its containment in the Old South) was the only way to stop the neofeudal radicals. When Lincoln finally recognized this too, he authored the grandest abolitionist statement of all, the 1863 Emancipation Proclamation.[51] Over the course of these three decades, the natural rights basis of antebellum liberalism came into sharp focus.

Unfortunately, as modern scholars have grown philosophically disenchanted with natural rights, they have backdated their own disenchantment into the antebellum years. This is to some degree understandable. That great fin de siècle intellectual shift—what Weber called "secularization"—has convinced many academics ever since that any appeal to natural rights is too metaphysical, too religious even, to take seriously.[52] So it makes some sense that such scholars have wished to find secularist precursors before the Civil War.

However, this is indeed wishful thinking. Antebellum liberals—dedicated to natural rights, and seeking (with admittedly different tactics) to realize them universally for all persons—were metaphysical, not political, liberals. Given this yawning philosophical canyon between yesteryear's natural rights liberalism and today's political liberalism, what if anything do liberals of the "ancient faith" have to offer political theorists today?

The value of that ancient faith itself will be taken up in the conclusion, but here it should be noted that the great philosophical consensus about natural rights enabled a remarkable range of thinking about the political means—especially the role of the nation-state—for realizing those rights. Four categories are discernable, and this stands in some contrast to modern liberalism. After all, as Peter Singer observed in 2002, nationalism tends to be a given for modern liberals. Pointing specifically to Rawls's *A Theory of Justice*, Singer states, "In setting up his original choice, . . . Rawls simply assumes that the people making the choice all belong to the same society and are choosing principles to achieve justice within their society." That justice might be a global concern is—in the preeminent text of modern liberal theory—"a question [that] *never even arises.*"[53] Many political liberals, including Rawls, have since sought to rectify this oversight, of course, but Singer's general point—that "we have lived with the idea of sovereign states for so long that they have come to be part of the background not only of diplomacy and public policy but also of ethics"—remains germane.[54]

Antebellum liberals, in contrast, had not lived so long with the idea of sovereign states. Moreover, because they believed natural rights to be, well, natural and thus entirely independent of whatever artificial states humans construct, antebellum liberals tended as theorists to be much more open to alternative frameworks for securing the natural rights of all persons. For example, some antebellum liberals even reached the conclusion that any state was inimical to the universal exercise of natural rights. In a set of letters published as a book in 1850, abolitionist Henry C. Wright reasoned that any government was an obstacle to the realization of natural rights because (alluding to the Declaration) "the history of all attempts of man to rule over man . . . demonstrates that an assumption of such power is opposed to nature and to nature's God."[55] Instead, Wright urged that each of us simply "respect the persons and rights of others as thou wouldst have thine respected" by "see[ing] and worship[ing] the Divine in the human" and thus "maintain love and communion with God, by loving and communing with men."[56] In this way "the existence and government of our Creator never did, and never can, conflict with the doctrine of man's absolute inviolability."[57] Anarchists, then, were one of the four categories of antebellum natural rights liberals.

Although agreeing that natural rights means the absolute inviolability of each person, many more antebellum liberals concluded that the nation-state was nonetheless necessary to secure this inviolability. They did not assume the existence of the nation-state, as Rawls does. Rather, they were keenly aware of the nation-state's artificiality and pushed to reengineer the nation-state so as to better secure the natural rights of all persons. These antebellum liberals might be called revolutionary nationalists. For example, increasingly disenchanted with the nation's entrenched commitment to slavery, John Quincy Adams contemplated in 1820 that the United States might require rebuilding. "Slavery is the great and foul stain upon the North American Union," Adams wrote, and for its "total abolition" "a dissolution, at least temporary, of the Union, as now constituted, would be certainly necessary." However, he continued hopefully,

"the Union might then be reorganized on the fundamental principle of emancipation."[58] That Brown similarly hoped the United States might be rebuilt on
the natural rights philosophy of the Declaration is evident not least in his calling his own constitution "provisional."[59] These writers might both be called
revolutionary nationalists.

Unlike the anarchists and the revolutionary nationalists among the antebellum liberals, the third camp is somewhat harder to define. Like the revolutionary nationalists, they understood nation-states to be valuable instruments
for beginning to secure natural rights; however, they ultimately believed these
instruments too provincial to finish the job. As Lynd illustrated, many abolitionists (like many natural rights thinkers from the Enlightenment forward)
thus concluded that the ultimate political organization would have to be global
and that nation-states were merely stepping stones to that end. "Seeking to be
faithful to the principles of the American Revolution," Lynd notes, "abolitionists were driven outside the framework of national allegiance and began to
understand themselves as citizens of the world."[60] Some of the strongest statements about the naturalness of rights and the artificiality of the nation-state
come from this group of theorists. For example, in his 1842 *Duty of the Free
States,* William E. Channing emphasized that, whenever the nation-state unjustly uses law to abridge the natural rights of individuals, we must patiently
recall that "man is not the mere creature of the State. Man is older than nations, and he is to survive nations," implying a supranational future.[61] The
ultimately global aims of Garrison are much clearer simply in his choice of
motto for the *Liberator,* which ran at the top of every issue, "Our Country is
the World—Our Countrymen are all Mankind." As Caleb W. McDaniel has
recently observed, Garrison and his followers "believed both that democracy,
like an ocean, should be ever-restless, and that crossing the ocean was good
for democracy. They were wary," he continues, "about the dangers of too much
national pride in a democracy like theirs, a concern that was both reinforced
by their transatlantic experiences and echoed by transatlantic writers" such as
Giuseppe Mazzini and John Stuart Mill.[62]

Still, although convinced that natural rights had preceded and would
survive nation-states, what positive alternatives to the nation-state did these
theorists actually offer? There is more research to be done here, but a recurring idea is that nation-states might serve as stepping-stones toward a more
global framework, a "nationalist cosmopolitics" also being actively explored
at that time by European liberals.[63] Consider just a couple of examples from
American natural rights liberals following the Civil War. In his 1881 *The Scholar
in a Republic,* Wendell Phillips argued, "The [founding] fathers touched their

highest level when, with stout-hearted and serene faith, they trusted God that it was safe to leave men with all the rights he gave them." Phillips pled for the postwar United States to serve as "the sheet-anchor of the race" of humanity, modeling for the world "gently binding men into commonwealths in order that they may at least melt into brothers."[64] Similarly, in 1871, responding directly to Carlyle's 1867 neofeudalist essay "Shooting Niagara; and After?," poet Walt Whitman's *Democratic Vistas* not only identified "the Secession-Slave-Power" as the preeminent threat to "the People" but went on to imagine new configurations of those people—beyond the national—where natural rights were not only secured but enjoyed to their utmost.[65] In one paragraph's remarkably (for this visionary poet) straightforward argument, Whitman contends that although historically "the First stage" (accomplished with the Revolutionary and Civil Wars) "was the planning and putting on record the political foundation rights of immense masses of people—indeed all people—in the organization of republican National, State, and municipal governments," and "the Second stage relates to material prosperity" (which the industrializing world seemed to promise), "the Third stage," "a sublime and serious Religious Democracy" will come next. In this stage, "everything that has been written, sung, or stated, of old, with reference to humanity under the feudal and oriental institutes, religions, and for other lands, needs to be re-written, re-sung, re-stated, in terms consistent with the institution of these States" so that the United States proves, as the book concludes, to be the "divine Mother not only of material but spiritual worlds," centered upon "the average, the bodily, the concrete, the democratic, the popular, on which all the superstructures of the future are to permanently rest."[66]

A fourth and final category of antebellum natural rights liberalism is the constitutional nationalists. Whereas revolutionary nationalists such as John Quincy Adams and Brown were prepared to break the old and build a new United States to universalize natural rights, others hoped that the existing Constitution, for all its flaws, might better enable this work. Under the sway of Garrison, Douglass began his abolitionist career convinced that the Constitution was a proslavery document and thus to be "broken" (to recall once more Garrison's 1833 language). As recounted by Myers, Douglass retained this position into the 1840s, only beginning to shift around 1847 when he began to publish the *North Star.* The dawning "conviction that the Constitution was an antislavery document," Myers writes of Douglass, "yielded an abolitionism that was restorationist rather than revolutionary."[67] This seems to have happened over the course of the 1850s. Whereas in his 1850 Lecture on Slavery, No. 1, he proclaims slavery to have "become interwoven with all American institutions, and has anchored itself in the very oil of the American Constitution," by 1856 he declared that "all human enactments designed to sustain [slavery are] of no binding authority, and utterly contrary to the Constitution of the United States."[68] In September 1859, despite Brown's beseeching him for two days in a secret Pennsylvania quarry to join the Harpers Ferry Raid, Douglass steadfastly refused to support this revolutionary effort.[69] And, in 1860, Douglass made his most explicit defense of the antislavery Constitution as something we ought to "bend to the cause of freedom and justice."[70]

The exemplary constitutional nationalist, of course, was Lincoln. When his zealous faith in the universality of natural rights is borne in mind, Lincoln's infamous foot-dragging on the question of emancipation becomes proof of his commitment to retain the Constitution as the best framework for securing those natural rights. His reverence for the Constitution, of course, can be traced all the way back to his 1838 Lyceum Address. And, although through the 1850s the Declaration came to be the sacred text of his ancient faith, Lincoln remained committed to the Constitution. In his 1857 reaction to the *Dred Scott* ruling, for example, Lincoln explained that although he considered the decision "erroneous," he nonetheless believed the Supreme Court's "decisions on Constitutional questions, when fully settled, should control, not only the particular cases decided, but the general policy of the country, subject to be disturbed *only* by amendments of the Constitution as provided in that instrument itself. More than this," he added, "would be revolution" (*CW* 2:401, emphasis added), clearly differentiating himself from the revolutionary nationalists. In his First Inaugural Address, in 1861, faced with the secession of multiple states, Lincoln declared that "in view of the Constitution and the laws, the Union is unbroken" and that "as the Constitution itself expressly enjoins upon me" he "shall take care . . . that the laws of the Union be faithfully executed in all the States" (*CW* 4:265). In contrast, "the central idea of secession, is the essence of anarchy" (*CW* 4:268). Issuing the Emancipation Proclamation in 1863 and helping the House to pass the Thirteenth Amendment, abolishing slavery in 1865, Lincoln until the end of his life relied upon constitutional powers to more universally realize "the proposition that all men are created equal" (*CW* 7:23).

## TWO CONCLUSIONS

To come to one of this book's central questions, whether the Civil War was a revolution or a return, the answer would depend on which antebellum natural rights liberal you asked. For constitutional nationalists such as Douglass and

Lincoln, the war enabled a return to the principles set forth in the Declaration. In contrast, had they lived to see it, Brown and John Quincy Adams, the revolutionary nationalists, might have seen in the Civil War and Reconstruction amendments the military and legalistic revolution necessary to build a new republic of natural rights. As suggested above, Phillips would likely find this question of return or revolution moot because nations in his view were merely stepping-stones to a more global securing of natural rights. In helping to found the radical Universal Peace Union in 1866, dedicated to the eradication of war worldwide, the former anarchist Wright would likely have agreed with Phillips.

More philosophically, is the question of natural rights itself moot? In contending that "the Civil War [not only] swept away the slave civilization of the South [but also] almost the whole intellectual culture of the North along with it," Louis Menand nicely articulates a common scholarly assumption.[71] That old intellectual culture—including the metaphysical fiction of natural rights— embarrassed postbellum American intellectuals such as William James; a more thorough rebuking of that old culture came at the hands of European intellectuals such as Charles Darwin, Friedrich Nietzsche, Sigmund Freud, and Weber. And, thus, over time, even liberalism—once the preeminent political theory of natural rights—itself finally shuffled off its metaphysics to become strictly political, still championing human rights but without really believing in them.

Is this enough, though? As long as we continue to read the antebellum period through the lens of Weber, we will feel like we have no choice. But what if we tried on a different lens, perhaps (to offer a final provocation) one forged not by Weber but by a very different champion of the Weimar Republic, Thomas Mann. Following the catastrophe of the Great War, Mann, like Weber, urged liberals to step forward but not merely in defense of an "ethic of responsibility." Instead, in a 1922 lecture titled On the German Republic, Mann sought "to win [his young student auditors] over to the side of the republic, of what is termed democracy, and what I term humanity" by returning, in effect, to natural rights liberalism.[72] This is most evident in Mann's startling turn in this lecture to, of all people, Whitman, "who once said," Mann reports (of *Democratic Vistas*), "that at the core of democracy, finally, there resides a religious element."[73] Yes, perhaps we should hear in such strange old texts as *Democratic Vistas* and On the German Republic only the swan song of natural rights liberalism as performed by two thinkers who lived through the first modern wars but for whatever quirky reasons resisted the lesson of "disenchantment" learned so well by their peers. However, before we bid natural rights liberalism adieu, we must still acknowledge that it liberated four million persons from slavery.

Today, there are about thirty-six million enslaved persons in the world.[74] Are we so sure we can do without Lincoln's ancient faith?

## NOTES

1. Louis Hartz, *The Liberal Tradition in America: An Interpretation of American Political Thought since the Revolution* (New York: Harcourt, 1991), 6. Hartz's claims about Locke's exclusive influence were too extreme, as proven not only by the 1960–1970s "republican synthesis" scholars but also by those who restored liberalism to a new synthesis in the 1980–1990s. For the former, see Bernard Bailyn, *The Ideological Origins of the American Revolution* (Cambridge, MA: Harvard University Press, 1967); Gordon Wood, *The Creation of the American Republic* (Chapel Hill: University of North Carolina Press, 1969); and J. G. A. Pocock, *The Machiavellian Moment* (Princeton, NJ: Princeton University Press, 1975). For the latter, see Isaac Kramnick, *Republicanism and Bourgeois Radicalism: Political Ideology in Late Eighteenth-Century England and America* (Ithaca, NY: Cornell University Press, 1990); Michael P. Zuckert, *Natural Rights and the New Republicanism* (Princeton, NJ: Princeton University Press, 1994) and *The Natural Rights Republic: Studies in the Foundation of the American Political Tradition* (Notre Dame, IN: University of Notre Dame Press, 1996); and James T. Kloppenberg, *The Virtues of Liberalism* (New York: Oxford University Press, 1998). An important challenge to even the moderated claims of the new synthesis is found in Rogers M. Smith, "Beyond Tocqueville, Myrdal, and Hartz: The Multiple Traditions in America," *American Political Science Review* 87, no. 3 (September 1993): 549–566 and *Civic Ideals: Conflicting Visions of Citizenship in U.S. History* (New Haven, CT: Yale University Press, 1997).

2. Thomas Paine, *Common Sense*, ed. Isaac Kramnick (New York: Penguin, 1986), 63.

3. Carl Becker, *The Declaration of Independence: A Study in the History of Political Ideas* (New York: Harcourt, Brace, 1922), 72. Reviewing the Declaration's extensive historiography, Michael Zuckert has more recently confirmed this classic conclusion about Locke's dominance: "We appear then to be left with the old view as the most plausible view, that Locke inspired the Declaration and that it has a basically Lockean meaning." Zuckert, *Natural Rights Republic*, 40

4. Quoted in Zuckert, *Natural Rights Republic*, 1.

5. Cited in Sue Davis, *The Political Thought of Elizabeth Cady Stanton: Women's Rights and the American Political Tradition* (New York: New York University Press, 2008), 50.

6. William Lloyd Garrison, "Inaugural Editorial," *Liberator*, January 1, 1831, in *Against Slavery: An Abolitionist Reader*, ed. Lowance Mason (New York: Penguin, 2000), 104.

7. William Lloyd Garrison, "Valedictory," in *Documents of Upheaval: Selections from William Lloyd Garrison's the Liberator, 1831–1865*, ed. Truman Nelson (New York: Hill and Wang, 1966), 278.

8. John Brown, Provisional Constitution and Ordinances for the People of the

United States, in *The Public Life of Capt. John Brown with an Autobiography of His Childhood and Youth,* by James Redpath (Boston: Thayer and Eldridge, 1860), 234.

9. David S. Reynolds, *John Brown, Abolitionist: The Man Who Killed Slavery, Sparked the Civil War, and Seeded Civil Rights* (New York: Vintage, 2005), 249–254. Brown's idea was not entirely outlandish; on other successful maroon societies within the United States, see Steve Hahn, *The Political Worlds of Slavery and Freedom* (Cambridge, MA: Harvard University Press, 2009), 1–53.

10. Frederick Douglass, *Autobiographies* (New York: Library of America, 1994), 896.

11. Peter C. Myers, *Frederick Douglass: Race and the Rebirth of American Liberalism* (Lawrence: University Press of Kansas, 2008), 49.

12. Nicholas Buccola, *The Political Thought of Frederick Douglass* (New York: New York University Press, 2012), 2, 1.

13. John Locke, *Two Treatises of Government,* ed. Peter Laslett (Cambridge, UK: Cambridge University Press, 1988), 271.

14. Justin B. Dyer, *Natural Law and the Antislavery Constitutional Tradition* (Cambridge, UK: Cambridge University Press, 2012), 182.

15. Becker, *Declaration of Independence;* Harry Jaffa, *Crisis of the House Divided: An Interpretation of the Issues in the Lincoln-Douglas Debates* (Chicago: University of Chicago Press, 2009), 110.

16. For a summary of the debate about Lincoln's racism, see James N. Leiker, "The Difficulties of Understanding Abe: Lincoln's Reconciliation of Racial Inequality and Natural Rights," in *Lincoln Emancipated: The President and the Politics of Race,* ed. B. R. Dirck (DeKalb: Northern Illinois University Press, 2007), 73–98. Lincoln's reliance upon the Bible is considered in Joseph Fornieri, *Abraham Lincoln's Political Faith* (DeKalb: Northern Illinois University Press, 2003). Jaffa expounds upon his disagreement with Becker's assertion that "whether the natural rights philosophy of the Declaration of Independence is true or false is essentially a meaningless question" in introducing the 2009 edition of Jaffa, *Crisis of the House Divided,* v.

17. Dyer, *Natural Law,* 23.

18. Pauline Maier, *American Scripture: Making the Declaration of Independence* (New York: Vintage, 1998), 202.

19. Abraham Lincoln, Speech in Independence Hall, Philadelphia, Pennsylvania, in *The Collected Works of Abraham Lincoln,* vol. 4, ed. Roy P. Basler (New Brunswick: Rutgers University Press, 1953–1955), 240, http://quod.lib.umich.edu/1 /lincoln/.

20. Staughton Lynd, *Intellectual Origins of American Radicalism* (Cambridge, MA: Harvard University Press, 1982), 5.

21. William Lloyd Garrison, "Declaration of Sentiments of the American Anti-Slavery Society," in *Antislavery Political Writings, 1833–1860: A Reader,* ed. C. B. Thompson (Armonk, NY: M.E. Sharpe, 2004), 42.

22. Quotes from ibid., 42, 43, and 44–45.

23. "Society," George Fitzhugh wrote of the American South in 1854, "is in a natural, healthy and contented state. Such was very much the condition of society in middle and southern Europe two centuries ago, before feudalism disappeared and liberty and equality were established." Europe, he argued "must go back to domestic slavery."

Fitzhugh, *Sociology for the South, or the Failure of Free Society* (Richmond, VA: A. Morris, 1854), 306. See also Smith, *Civic Ideals,* 204–205.

24. David Walker, "Appeal to the Colored Citizens of the World," in *Pamphlets of Protest: An Anthology of Early African-American Protest Literature, 1790–1860,* ed. Richard Newman, Patrick Rael, and Philip Lapsansky (New York: Routledge, 2001), 105, 109.

25. Cited by Edwin D. Sanborn, *A Eulogy on Daniel Webster* (Hanover, NH: Dartmouth University Press, 1853), 23.

26. *The Writings and Speeches of Daniel Webster,* vol. 2, ed. F. Webster (Boston: Little, Brown, 1903), 354.

27. Daniel Webster, Speech in the Senate on Compromise Resolutions, in *American Speeches: Political Oratory from the Revolution to the Civil War,* ed. T. Widmer (New York: Library of America, 2006), 490.

28. For example, Sigmund Freud identified the condition in his 1920 "Beyond the Pleasure Principle" as a "driving force that prevents the individual from resting content with any situation he ever contrives, and instead [citing Goethe's *Faust*] 'press[ing] ever onward unbridled, untamed.'" See *Beyond the Pleasure Principle and Other Writings,* trans. J. Reddick (New York: Penguin, 2003), 82.

29. Richard Hofstadter, "The Paranoid Style in American Politics," *Harper's Magazine* (November 1964): 77–86, 82.

30. Ibid., 85.

31. Andrew M. Delbanco, *The Abolitionist Imagination* (Cambridge, MA: Harvard University Press, 2012), 3.

32. Ibid., 47–48.

33. Ibid., 47–48, 48–49.

34. John Rawls, *A Theory of Justice* (Cambridge, MA: Belknap Press of Harvard University Press, 1971), 325.

35. John Rawls, *Political Liberalism,* expanded ed. (New York: Columbia University Press, 2005), xix.

36. For a more complete account of Rawls's reliance upon earlier philosophies of value pluralism, see Peter Lassman, *Pluralism* (Malden, MA: Polity, 2011).

37. Rawls, *Political Liberalism,* 197n.

38. John Rawls, *Collected Papers,* ed. Samuel Freeman (Cambridge, MA: Harvard University Press, 1999), 463n.

39. Delbanco, *Abolitionist Imagination,* 36, 34.

40. Delbanco contends that this reading of American literature has gone out of fashion (ibid., 172n) but a recent, compelling reading of Nathaniel Hawthorne's moderation along these lines is Larry J. Reynolds, *Devils and Rebels: The Making of Hawthorne's Damned Politics* (Ann Arbor: University of Michigan Press, 2008).

41. Wilfred McClay, "Abolition as Master Concept," in Andrew M. Delbanco, *The Abolitionist Imagination* (Cambridge, MA: Harvard University Press, 2012), 135–152, 144. McClay notes that, in contrast to Ahab, Melville offered an admirably Lincolnesque captain in Captain Vere, who in *Billy Budd, Sailor* dispassionately upholds the law as it is written.

42. Ibid., 145.

43. Max Weber, "Politics as a Vocation," in *From Max Weber: Essays in Sociology*, ed. H. H. Gerth and C. W. Mills (New York: Routledge, 1991), 77–128, 120.

44. Ibid., 122.

45. McClay, "Abolition as Master Concept," 142, 143.

46. Delbanco, *Abolitionist Imagination*, 21.

47. Eric Foner, *The Fiery Trial: Abraham Lincoln and American Slavery* (New York: Norton, 2010), xix.

48. Michael J. Sandel, "A Response to Rawls' Political Liberalism," *Liberalism and the Limits of Justice*, 2nd ed. (Cambridge, UK: Cambridge University Press, 1998), 184–218, 202, emphasis added.

49. Rawls, *Political Liberalism*, 484.

50. John Burt, *Lincoln's Tragic Pragmatism: Lincoln, Douglas, and Moral Conflict* (Cambridge, MA: Harvard University Press, 2013), 15, 16–17.

51. John Stauffer, "Fighting the Devil with His Own Fire," in Andrew M. Delbanco, *The Abolitionist Imagination* (Cambridge, MA: Harvard University Press, 2012), 69–78. Of Lincoln's recognition of the radical nature of proslavery advocates, Frederick Douglass observed in his *Life and Times* that the president was ultimately like John Brown in coming to see that the aggressive neofeudalists were implacable foes of natural rights and that "no solid and lasting peace could come short of [their] absolute submission." Douglass, *Autobiographies*, 796.

52. Max Weber, "The Protestant Sects and the Spirit of Capitalism," in *From Max Weber: Essays in Sociology*, ed. H. H. Gerth and C. W. Mills (New York: Routledge, 1991), 302–322, 307.

53. Peter Singer, *One World: The Ethics of Globalization* (New Haven, CT: Yale University Press, 2002), 9. Observing that modern liberals treat the state "as if it were a natural feature of the world that individuals can do no other than accept as they find it," Carole Pateman made this point earlier and more pointedly. See Pateman, *The Problem of Political Obligation: A Critique of Liberal Theory* (Berkeley: University of California Press, 1985), 6.

54. Singer, *One World*, 8.

55. Henry C. Wright, *Anthropology, or, the Science of Man; in Its Bearing on War and Slavery* (Boston: E. Shepard, 1850), 70.

56. Ibid., 62.

57. Ibid., quotes from 62 and 11.

58. Quoted in Dyer, *Natural Law*, 98.

59. See also the parallels drawn between Brown's deeds and Machiavelli's and Rousseau's theories of the founder in Scott John Hammond, "John Brown as Founder: America's Violent Confrontation with Its First Principles" in *Terrible Swift Sword: The Legacy of John Brown*, ed. P. A. Russo and P. Finkelman (Athens: Ohio University Press, 2005), 61–76.

60. Lynd, *Intellectual Origins of American Radicalism*, 132.

61. William E. Channing, *Duty of the Free States, or, Remarks Suggested by the Case of the Creole* (London: John Green, 1842), 11.

62. Caleb W. McDaniel, *The Problem of Democracy in the Age of Slavery: Garrisonian*

*Abolitionists and Transatlantic Reform* (Baton Rouge: Louisiana State University Press, 2013), 14.

63. See Daniel S. Malachuk, "National Cosmopolitics in the Nineteenth Century," in *Cosmopolitics and the Emergence of a Future*, ed. D. Morgan and G. Banham (New York: Palgrave Macmillan, 2007), 139–162.

64. Wendell Phillips, *The Scholar in a Republic* (Boston: Lee and Shepard, 1881), 21.

65. Walt Whitman, *Democratic Vistas*, in *The Collected Writings of Walt Whitman*, vol. 3: *Prose Works, 1892*, ed. F. Stovall (New York: New York University Press, 1964), 361–425, 377.

66. Ibid., quotes from 409–410 and 426.

67. Myers, *Frederick Douglass*, 89.

68. Douglass, Lecture on Slavery, No. 1; Frederick Douglass, "What Is My Duty as an Anti-Slavery Voter?" in *Antislavery Political Writings, 1833–1860: A Reader*, ed. C. B. Thompson (Armonk, NY: M. E. Sharpe, 2004), 206.

69. See the account in John Stauffer, *Giants: The Parallel Lives of Frederick Douglass and Abraham Lincoln* (New York: Hachette, 2008), 159.

70. Frederick Douglass, "The Constitution of the U.S.: Is It Proslavery or Anti-Slavery?" in *Antislavery Political Writings, 1833–1860: A Reader*, ed. C. B. Thompson (Armonk, NY: M. E. Sharpe, 2004), 156.

71. Louis Menand, *The Metaphysical Club: A Story of Ideas in America* (New York: Farrar, Straus, and Giroux, 2002), x.

72. Thomas Mann, On the German Republic, trans. L. S. Rainey, *Modernism/Modernity* 14, no. 1 (January 2007): 109–132, 113–114.

73. Ibid., 124.

74. Including labor, sex, and child slavery, experts estimate there are around 35.8 million enslaved people today. See, for example, Kevin Bales, *Blood and Earth: Modern Slavery, Ecocide, and the Secret to Saving the World* (New York: Random House, 2016).

CHAPTER 4

# Scientific Racism in Antebellum America

ALAN LEVINE

This chapter is a study of one peculiar theory supporting antebellum America's "peculiar institution": scientific racism.[1] It claimed to prove scientifically that the different races of the world were different species deserving different moral and political treatment, and it was thus used to justify slavery. This theory did not cause slavery or the widespread social and political racism in antebellum America. Rather, the science was tainted by the racism prevalent at the time. This sad episode reveals the dangers, temptations, and limits of science. Science must be supplemented by critically reflective moral and political thinking, by the scientists themselves, and by prudent and vigilant citizens and statesmen. When such monitoring goes astray, so too may science.

The scientific racism that flourished in antebellum America included some of the nation's most respected scientists. They formed a school of thought taken seriously in Europe and known there as the "American School" of ethnography. It lasted from the 1830s to the Civil War, and most of its members were, ironically, Northerners. The most important of its thinkers was Samuel George Morton, who was cautious in drawing explicitly political conclusions. He does not seem to have conducted his studies simply to defend slavery in the United States, but his studies do justify it. Morton's arguments were amplified and spread by other scholars, such as George R. Gliddon and Jean Louis Rodolphe Agassiz, and by enthusiastic researchers, such as Josiah Nott. They more clearly emphasized their work's racist implications, and Nott and Gliddon used it explicitly to justify the enslavement of blacks. The actual political influence of this racist science is unclear, but it was known and sought out by some of the most powerful and influential Southern leaders, such as John C. Calhoun, who served as a senator, secretary of war, secretary of state, and vice president of the United States, and James Henry Hammond, governor of and senator from South Carolina, both among the South's leading defenders of slavery as a "positive good."

To understand this particular abuse of science, we have to examine the particular times and contexts in which it developed, and it is that story this chapter aims to tell. These scientists allowed their science to be contaminated by the racial prejudice common in their epoch, which they uncritically internalized and perpetuated. Theirs is the disturbing tale of seemingly well-meaning men who attempted to wrestle with deep and legitimate questions according to some of the best scientific procedures and lights of the day. Still, this led to gross scientific errors. They also fell victim to the all-too-human desires to influence authority and please power, and we see them eager to assist and oblige Southern leaders. One clear lesson is thus the need for science to be truly and only objective and for scientists, citizens, and statesmen to make sure unscientific assumptions are questioned and exposed.

However, although historical understanding helps explain this particular perversion of science, preventing the abuse of science is more complicated than simply insisting that science adhere to its own strict standards. Science alone is insufficient to justify morality or egalitarian politics. Because of its nature and limits, science is perennially vulnerable to abuse, even today.

## THE LIMITS OF SCIENTIFIC RACISM

In studying the American School's justification of slavery, this chapter is neither a comprehensive examination of justifications of slavery nor a comprehensive account of theories of race in antebellum America. Slavery and racial prejudice existed in America long before the scientific movement under review here, and scientific racism was thus neither necessary nor sufficient for these to exist or be justified. Slavery itself is as old as recorded history. The word *slave* derives from "slav," referring to the Eastern European peoples, the population of choice in Europe for enslavement during ancient and medieval times. Race-based slavery—and theories of racial inequality to justify it—came much later and developed in peculiarly American ways largely to meet Southern needs.[2] Far from creating slavery and racism, the ideas of the American School were influenced by their preexistence.

Antebellum America spawned a spectrum of justifications for slavery, worth briefly recounting here to highlight alternatives to the American School's scientific justification. As some people always have, some Southerners enjoyed being masters, being able to impose their will with legal impunity on a group of powerless human beings. The literature on slavery in the South is replete with sadistic masters and overseers, including Frederick Douglass's cruel "slave breaker," Mr. Covey, and Harriet Beecher Stowe's character Simon Legree in

*Uncle Tom's Cabin* (1852), who need no highfalutin justification for their cruel actions.[3] Systematic chronicles of slavery, such as Angelina Grimké and Theodore Weld's *American Slavery as It Is: Testimony of a Thousand Witnesses* (1839), compiled by fierce abolitionists and influential on the abolitionist movement, sicken the reader with their first-person testimonies, including by abusers, of repeated whippings, floggings, rapes, and the infinite other cruelties that made up daily life in the Southern slavery system. Even if the compilers' abolitionist zeal exaggerated some details, the overarching picture of brutality toward enslaved people is one of sadistic cruelty without any apparent moral worry.[4]

Other Southerners justified slavery as useful or necessary. Clearheadedly and hard-heartedly, they justified it as the foundation for their refined life or as necessary to civilization's progress. These people might have flattered themselves as illusion free, as doing what anyone with power would do. A literary example of this is St. Clair in *Uncle Tom's Cabin*, who knows slavery is wrong but confesses that he holds slaves "because my brother Quashy is ignorant and weak, and I am intelligent and strong—because I know how and *can* do it. . . . Because I don't like work, Quashy shall work. Because the sun burns me, Quashy shall stay in the sun. Quashy shall earn the money, and I will spend it. Quashy shall lie down in every puddle, that I may walk over dry-shod."[5] An explicit real-world justification is made by Hammond, who unapologetically averred in his infamous Mud-Sill Speech of 1858:

In all social systems there must be a class to do the menial duties, to perform the drudgery of life. . . . Such a class you must have, or you would not have that other class which leads progress, civilization, and refinement. It constitutes the very mud-sill of society and of political government; and you might as well attempt to build a house in the air, as to build either the one or the other, except on this mud-sill. Fortunately for the South, she found a race adapted to that purpose to her hand. A race inferior to her own, but eminently qualified in temper, in vigor, in docility, in capacity to stand the climate, to answer all her purposes. We use them for our purpose, and call them slaves.[6]

Moral callousness is hard to humanely justify on utilitarian grounds alone, however, and even Hammond here further justifies slavery as rule over an inferior people suited to the role.

The overwhelming majority of Southerners, however, largely hid slavery's horrors from others as well as from themselves. They distanced themselves from slavery's dirtiest requirements, telling themselves sanitized stories or imagining themselves as paternalistic and gentle masters of childlike people who otherwise could not look after themselves. These self-deceptions and the slave owners' "desperate need to deceive themselves" have been carefully documented in a series of books by Eugene Genovese and Elizabeth Fox-Genovese, including *Fatal Self-Deception: Slaveholding Paternalism in the Old South* and *The Mind of the Master Class.*[7] Self-deception included the paternalistic stories Southerners told themselves about their good and happy slaves. Southerners often claimed blacks were unable to take care of themselves and concluded that slavery was actually good for them, uplifting their souls and spurring their progress. Hammond and Calhoun, for example, both claimed slavery was a "positive good" not only for white citizens but for blacks too. Calhoun argued that blacks in Africa had never lived so well or developed their capacities as well as the enslaved people in America's South:

I appeal to facts. Never before has the black race of Central Africa, from the dawn of history to the present day, attained a condition so civilized and so improved, not only physically, but morally and intellectually. It came among us in a low, degraded, and savage condition, and in the course of a few generations it has grown up under the fostering care of our institutions, reviled as they have been, to its present comparatively civilized condition.[8]

Calhoun's argument might have applied to free blacks who had freely chosen to improve themselves based on what American civilization had to offer, but even if exposure to "civilization" improved the condition of enslaved people—and we should be loath to grant this considering their brutalization and the laws forbidding them to learn how to read or write—who would choose chattel slavery for oneself and one's posterity to achieve such goods? Calhoun and Hammond also argued that Africans enslaved in the South were better treated and better cared for than those Hammond called the "white slaves," that is, the white working class in the North, hired not for a lifetime of security and care, as they claimed the enslaved received, but for a fixed term at subsistence wages, and then cast aside.[9]

The alleged paternalistic kindness and dutifulness of Southern whites to civilize and Christianize the people they enslaved was captured in the Southern ideology of "our family, white and black," in which blacks were deemed part of the family, although admittedly a part needing more discipline. The increased intimacies with enslaved people who worked in the house, as opposed to field, might have helped white Southerners varnish reality for themselves. Although much of this paternalistic talk was undoubtedly rhetorical, "useful as a means of mollifying critics of the institution's harshness,"[10] scholars have unearthed evidence from private letters that suggest that some Southerners genuinely believed these sentiments[11]—unless perhaps they were trying to convince other slaveholders as a means also to convince themselves. However this might have been, there was a whole literature in the South, the so-called anti-Tom literature, richly describing what its authors saw as the organic goodness of slavery for everyone in the system, including especially those enslaved.[12] Of course, slave owners' behaviors, such as selling the enslaved people (selling family members?), contradicted their proclaimed self-understanding. And although being unaware of contradictions between one's principles and actions is the most ordinary thing in the world, the gap is not usually so glaringly extreme as in the Southern slavery system. They denied the truth, and probably had to deny it to themselves, because how could they themselves be perpetrators of evil?

These Southern justifications of slavery predate scientific racism, showing that scientific racism caused neither slavery nor the widespread racial prejudice in antebellum America. Of the many justifications for slavery, however, the scientific one is perhaps the most troubling. It is unique precisely because of its propagators: scientists who did not have "dirty hands," that is, any obvious financial self-interest in defending slavery, and who claimed to be pursuing only empirically verifiable truth. Their professional status and methods lent their views undeserved credibility.

## CONTEXTS OF SCIENTIFIC RACISM

The American School's scientific racism emerged to prominence when it did because it spoke to white Americans', Northerners', and Southerners' questions about race and interpreted racial differences in ways relevant to many different interests and agendas. Obviously, their ideas appealed to slave owners who wanted to justify their slavery and feel good about themselves, but, as we saw in the previous section, many justifications of slavery existed. So to truly understand the connection between members of the American School and their followers, we must see how their racist science appealed to their contemporaries in more specific contexts, at least seven of which exist: four political, one scientific, and two religious. These contexts blended to shape what the American School was offering. The four political contexts created the desire in antebellum America for the kind of racist theory they offered. The scientific and religious contexts helped shape their theory's contours. In sharing and propagating so many of their contemporaries' interests and concerns, they incorporated many unscientific threads into their theorizing.

The American School's first political context concerned the experience of ordinary white Americans. Based on their personal experiences with the degraded condition of enslaved Africans and of "wild Indians," many white Americans, Northerners and Southerners alike, wondered whether the Africans and Native Americans were capable of achieving what Caucasians had. It was a widespread question at the time,[13] and a question that frequently arises when peoples with fundamentally different ways of life encounter each other.

A second political context for the American School's racist science was unique to America's great political experiment based on the assertion in the Declaration of Independence that all men are created equal. Given the national creed, the question of the abilities of different races had profound political and philosophical implications for the citizens of the new nation beyond a mere curiosity prompted by their experiences. Many white Americans believed—and hoped—the creed would be proven true, even as their own experiences with Africans and Native Americans raised doubts in their minds. For example, Jefferson famously asserted that all men are created equal and recognized blacks and whites as part of a single human species, even while speculating in his *Notes on the State of Virginia* that the races might have fundamentally different abilities and characteristics.[14] Many Northern antebellum figures, such as Ralph Waldo Emerson, held the same ambiguous attitude. Emerson recognized the fundamental equality of blacks as a matter of moral principle and also expressed reservations about what he saw about their abilities in practice.[15] Throughout the antebellum period, both Americans committed to the Declaration's universal moral equality and Southerners opining inequality craved evidence for their disparate views.

A third political context was the increasingly polarized national discussion of slavery in the 1830s. The national conversation about race broke down after Nat Turner's rebellion (1831). Although this was not the first slave revolt, it aroused in Southerners a fear for their lives and inflamed passions on both sides of the debate. About this time, partly influenced by this event, the political conversation devolved into increasingly shrill mutual recriminations between the abolitionist and the "positive good" camps. One wonders whether the rise of scientific racism that began in the 1830s was propelled by, and a displacement of, the lack of meaningful dialogue in the political sphere. Science, framed as apolitical and as based only on facts, might have risen to prominence amid this breakdown as a way of filling the gap created by the absence of honest conversation.[16]

A fourth political context of the American School's thought is the way both sides of antebellum America's political-philosophical debates on human equality appealed to both science and God. For example, arguing in what is believed to be his last letter against the "chains under which monkish ignorance and superstition" had kept humanity, Jefferson asserted that equality was supported by both science and God. Jefferson averred, "The general spread of the light of science has already laid open to every view the palpable truth, that the mass of mankind has not been born with saddles on their backs, nor a favored few booted and spurred, ready to ride them legitimately, by the grace of God."[17] Thus, although perhaps he speaks as much his hope as fact, for Jefferson science supports human equality, and God does not sanctify inequality, despite what the monks think. The inegalitarian argument culminated in Alexander Stephens's famous Corner-Stone Speech, in which he alleged that science and God taught exactly the opposite of what Jefferson claimed. According to Stephens, "Our new government [the Confederacy] is founded on exactly the opposite idea [of America]; its foundations are laid, its corner-stone rests upon the great truth, that the negro is not equal to the white man; that slavery—subordination to the superior race—is his natural and normal condition." This alleged truth of inequality, Stephens claimed, is supported by science and God. He called inequality a "great physical, philosophical, and moral truth . . . like all other truths in the various departments of science." As a parallel to the experiences of Galileo, Adam Smith, and William Harvey, Stephens claimed inequality was a scientific truth that would ultimately prevail, and he looked "with confidence to the ultimate universal acknowledgment of the truths upon which our system rests." According to his view, the Confederacy thus "is the first government ever instituted upon the principles in strict conformity to nature, and the ordination of Providence."[18] Could science in fact resolve the political problem of human equality? Antebellum Americans wanted to know.

A fifth context had to do with the accepted state of science at the time the American School wrote. In antebellum America, there was no scientific consensus on the question of human equality, let alone human origins, and this scientific indeterminacy is the fifth context in which the American School must be understood. Then-dominant scientific opinion upheld the "unity" hypothesis, in which all human beings are part of a single human species, but the scientists understood that this view had not been scientifically demonstrated. The discipline of science was thus open for the American School to make its own way. In asking whether humanity had one or more origins, its members thus raised legitimate scientific questions with no necessary commitment to racial hierarchy. They aimed to solve a problem well known to many astute but unscientific observers: the question of the "many versus the one," of accounting on the one hand for the similarities of all human beings while on the other hand recognizing their diversity. This is not an easy problem with an obvious answer. Insofar as every human individual is different from every other, some philosophers have argued that all classifications are nonsense, that only individual, particular beings exist.[19] Most observers, however, have found general patterns of differences to be significant. Humans deriving from Africa, Europe, and China are of different skin colors, hair types, religions, mores, cultures, and laws. Although some of these differences, for example, laws and manners, exist only by human convention and human creation, others such as skin color and hair type seem natural. The question was: Are differences in ability and attainment cultural or biological?

Four main scientifico-philosophical answers could be posited to the problem of the many and the one, and all were argued in antebellum America. Two argued that these differences have been there since the beginning of time, and two argued that they came later. If differences existed from the beginning, they existed either from eternity (the ancient view) or because they were created by God. In both of these explanations, the differences were described as permanent and immutable. If the differences came later, they could have been created by God (the third possibility) or originated in reaction to different environments and circumstances (the fourth possibility). It is worth remembering that the contours of our current scientific views on this question developed between Carl Linnaeus's groundbreaking classification in his *Systema Naturae* of 1735 and Charles Darwin's *On the Origin of Species* in 1859. Both Linnaeus and Darwin argued that all human beings are of a single species, but whereas Linnaeus argued that species were fixed by God and unchanging, Darwin argued that species were always changing based on a process of natural selection. The period between Linnaeus and the eventual acceptance of Darwin is exactly when the American School thrived, so the question was not settled in its time. This unsettled scientific consensus is the fifth context in which the American School must be understood.

Unlike both Linnaeus and Darwin, the American school scientists argued that the different races of humans were fundamentally different, immutable (or almost immutable) species. (Their views were thus much closer to Stephens's Confederate beliefs than Jefferson's Declaration.) Like Linnaeus and unlike Darwin, they argued that natural differences came from God, although they differed among themselves on whether the different species were created by God at the beginning of time or later.

In making their arguments, members of the American School explicitly rejected two main contrary theories: the theory of evolution and the traditional teaching of revealed biblical Christianity. Like everyone else at the time, they were trying to articulate their thoughts in the context of an indeterminate science (the fifth context) and all-too-authoritative religious views (the sixth context). Although we today largely accept Darwin's theory of evolution as explaining human (indeed, all living) diversity, Darwin had not yet published his evidence during the heyday of the American School, and in its absence they argued that the idea of the evolution of, or changes within, humanity was unsupported by the known data.[20] As we shall see, in making this argument they sometimes uncritically allowed a then-standard interpretation of the Bible to supply "facts," especially the assumption of the approximately four-thousand-year age of the earth based on biblical chronology, to color their science, with devastating results. Today this assumption seems unscientific and naïvely pious and quaint. However, the American School thinkers accepted it even though they were otherwise at pains to distance themselves from Christianity as traditionally understood. They explicitly discussed and were acutely aware of Galileo's experiences with the Roman Catholic Church and, living in a Christian-majority America, some were at times clearly reluctant to cross the accepted authority of Christianity. They were fully aware that by arguing that there are different species or kinds of humans, they were contradicting the dominant institutionalized interpretations of the Bible, in which all of humanity descended from Adam and later from Noah and were thus of a single species. Yet, after repeated cautious and cautionary statements trying to mollify Christian authorities, they argued that "scientific truth" must take precedence over the Bible. They tried to mitigate the contradiction between their science and received religion by arguing both that the Bible cannot be interpreted literally and by trying to reinterpret the Bible to be consistent with their view of different species of humanity. In short, as was common at the time, they situated their thought in a dialogue between science and Christianity.

Based on their science and their reinterpreted Christianity, they developed a view of biblical polygenesis, of multiple human creations consistent with the Bible, which is their seventh context. Polygenism dates back to ancient times, when thinkers argued that the different peoples of the world had existed in their differences from eternity. After biblical revelation claimed a single human creation, this view became hard to maintain. During the Christian epoch, polygenism was most powerfully argued by Isaac La Peyrère. La Peyrère was a sixteenth-century Jewish convert to Christianity who articulated a theory of biblical polygenism in order to save the Bible from three different kinds of "facts" that seemed to him to contradict it. First, the newly discovered people in the Americas seemed to disprove the Bible's account of the flood and story that all the people of the world were descended from Noah. La Peyrère could imagine how Noah's descendants crossed Eurasia and Africa, but how could they have gotten all the way to the Americas? For asking this exact question and concluding that they could not, Giordano Bruno was burnt at the stake in Rome in 1600. Second, based on the then most authoritatively accepted account of biblical chronology, the world was deemed only about four thousand years old, but early modern Europe encountered ancient civilizations, such as Egypt and China, that according to their own historical records and stories claimed to be older than that and hence older than the world itself. If these civilizations' histories were correct, La Peyrère concluded, the Bible as typically interpreted was not. Third, La Peyrère was aware that the Bible as typically interpreted had internal inconsistencies. For example, if Adam and Eve were the first humans and had only male children, from where did their wives come?[21]

La Peyrère's polygenism aimed to rescue the Bible from these three different kinds of difficulties. He read the Bible as offering two different accounts of human creations. The first human creation was of those he called "gentiles" and is found in Genesis 1. Genesis 1 says that all the people and animals and plants of the earth were created in one day, and La Peyrère argues that they were placed over the entire earth on that day because any earth without animals and humans to enjoy it would be wasted, and God would not do that.[22] According to La Peyrère, a second creation story explains the history of the "chosen" people and is found in Genesis 2. Genesis 2 begins with Adam and Eve, and according to La Peyrère it is the creation story of only the specially chosen people descending from them through Abraham to Jews and Christians.[23] By seeing Genesis 1 as the separate creation of the gentile peoples, La Peyrère explains who Cain and Abel married, how people got to the Americas before the mighty sailors of early modern Europe, and how and why old civilizations could exist, as the flood, he avers, was localized to the Jewish people. La Peyrère used this polygenetic argument to insist that all the people of the world were God's children, part of God's plan, and all equally deserving of respect.[24] Voltaire later offered a nonbiblical view of this polygenetic argument to criticize Europeans' sense of exceptionalism based on Christian pride, which he thought fueled the unjust imperialism of his epoch, and to insist on the equal dignity and rights of all the different peoples on earth.[25] Lord Kames did something similar.[26] In short, polygenism has been a long-existing, if today little-known, thread of Western thought, and it was used in early modern Europe to establish, paradoxically, the fundamental moral unity of humanity.

The American School of scientists in antebellum America, however, used polygenism not to uphold the equal dignity of the different races or species of human beings but to insist on the superiority of the Caucasian and the inferiority of the African, Native American—and, indeed, all other—races. Responding to Americans' burning moral and political questions about the equality of the races and trying to answer the questions scientifically in a Christian age without scientific consensus, their polygenism did not augur universal human equality but instead a justification for racial segregation and the existing slavery of the South. If widely accepted, the polygenism of the American School might have undermined the American experiment in political equality.

## MORTON AND THE AMERICAN ORIGINS OF POLYGENISM

Morton is credited as the American pioneer of the scientific idea that human beings comprise different species. He was not the first to argue this position in America,[27] but Morton offered scientific credibility to the earlier views based on his extensive studies of skulls and other ethnological data and reports. He embraced the idea of different, fixed human species and argued that each was created at its beginning with distinct, immutable characteristics. Comparative skull analysis informed his conclusion that these physical and intellectual characteristics make the other races scientifically inferior to the white race, with the black race being the most inferior. His science was influenced by unscientific prejudice and fatally flawed.

Morton was highly regarded as the founder of the new American School of ethnography and a celebrated scientist in the antebellum period. According to his obituary in the *New York Tribune,* he was "one of the brightest ornaments of our age and country," and "probably no scientific man in America enjoyed a higher reputation among scholars throughout the world, than Dr. Morton."[28] He was a practicing physician and researcher in Philadelphia with two medical degrees, one from the University of Pennsylvania and one from the University of Edinburgh. He was a lecturer at the Pennsylvania Medical College and for more than twenty-five years a member of the Academy of Natural Sciences in Philadelphia, one of the leading American scientific institutions of the day. He was elected its corresponding secretary in 1831 and through that position dealt with leading scientists around the globe on a regular basis. He first established his scientific reputation with a study of the fossils brought back by Lewis and Clark. He published in top journals, but his book publications—*Crania Americana: A Comparative View of the Skulls of Various Aboriginal Nations of North and South America—to Which Is Prefixed an Essay on the Varieties of Human Species* (1839) and *Crania Aegyptiaca, or Observations on Egyptian Ethnography Derived from Anatomy, History, and Monuments* (1844)—introduced the findings for which he is infamous.[29] On the basis of his collection of skulls, the world's largest, he "won his reputation as the great data-gatherer and objectivist of American science, the man who would raise an immature enterprise from the mires of fanciful speculation."[30] Oliver Wendell Holmes praised him for "the severe and cautious character" of his studies, which "from their very nature are permanent data for all future students of ethnology."[31]

Morton's studies focused on the then esteemed scientific method of quantitatively measuring skull sizes, shapes, and the various angles of their parts.[32] Such measurements are standard scientific procedure in determining, for example, whether one population of duck is a different species from another. Morton poured white pepper seed or lead shot into skulls and then measured the content to determine their brain size.[33] Based on his studies, he determined that there were five kinds of humans divided into twenty-two subgroups based on racial mixing. (Morton and his followers did not accept Buffon's definition of a species as based on the possibility of procreation, discussed below.) His measurements show that the Caucasian race has the largest crania and thus the largest brain of any race, whereas the Negro race has the smallest crania and is thus physically and intellectually inferior. Indeed, based on size and angles, Morton concludes that if the skulls of the Negroes were just a few degrees different, "we have an orang outang, or a monkey."[34]

Morton's obnoxious conclusion was based on various assumptions and procedures. Modern scientists debate the validity of Morton's actual physical measurements, and there is evidence of selection bias in his data. Also, his argument is based on the faulty assumption that greater physical brain size translates simply into greater intelligence or aptitude, and this is not correct. The modern scientific consensus is that his conclusions are "false and racist."[35]

Morton did not, however, rely on quantitative measurements alone but rather supplemented his physical science with supposedly empirical ethnographic observations or reports thereof, so his work combined the modern fields of anatomy and anthropology. From anthropological studies he recognized that there can be a diverse range of behaviors within each species of human. For example, he noted, "The moral and intellectual character of the Africans is widely different in different nations."[36] However, rather than infer the importance of politics or culture in creating these different behaviors, he generalized about African behavior and character as such, describing it as "fiery and revengeful," "docile," "remarkably stupid and slothful," and as marked by "indolence, deception and falsehood."[37] In addition to being contradictory— fiery and docile?—these caricatures were supplied by others' interactions with enslaved and formerly enslaved blacks in America and by white, would-be masters in Africa. Morton thus relied on obviously biased ethnological reports.

Morton rejected the idea of social or cultural factors determining racial behavior and argued for multiple creations of humans by noting that the Caucasians and Negroes have been separate races since the oldest reliable records, those of ancient Egypt. He accepted the then prevalent belief based on a reading of the Bible that the entire world was only about four thousand years old. So if the pyramids and other findings in Egypt date back three thousand years and depict races as they exist today, then they have been immutable for at least three thousand of humanity's four thousand years. Arguing against the idea that human development has been affected by climate, an idea he continually attacked throughout both of his main books, he asked why one would believe that the species changed so fundamentally in the first thousand years, but then changed scarcely at all in the next three thousand? He argued as follows:

The recent discoveries in Egypt give additional force to the preceding statement [concerning the origin of species] inasmuch as they show beyond all question, that the Caucasian and the Negro races were as perfectly distinct, in that country upwards of three thousand years ago as they are now: whence it is evident that if the Caucasian was derived from the Negro, or the Negro from the Caucasian, by the action of external causes, the change must have been effected in at most a thousand years; a theory which the subsequent evidence of thirty centuries proves to be a physical impossibility; and we have already ventured to insist that such a commutation could be effected by nothing short of a miracle.[38]

If race had been constant during human history, there was no reason to suppose that social or cultural factors affected it.

In addition to arguing for the fixedness of race since ancient Egypt, Morton further claimed that the characteristics exhibited by the races of his time were identical to the characteristics exhibited by them back then. Morton admired the culture of the ancient Egyptians and could not accept that they were any race but white: none other than the Caucasians, "nor any race of the Negroes, produced the celebrated people who gave birth to the civilization of ancient Egypt, and of whom we may say that the whole world has inherited the principles of its laws, sciences and, perhaps also religion." So, he asserted, just as in the antebellum era, the white race three thousand years ago was the dominant one. Similarly, Morton wove in the idea that the Negro race's historically consistent place was at the bottom. Members of the Negro race in antiquity were treated the same as they were in Morton's day, as servants: "The Negro population of Egypt [were] traffickers, servants and slaves [and] were a very numerous body."[39]

Morton combined his quantitative measurements of skulls with ethnography in order to infer causality: the social position of the Negroes had not changed in three thousand years *because of* their physical and intellectual inferiority to those of the Caucasian race. Negros were well suited to be slaves *because of* their specific characteristics resulting from their smaller brain size. Whereas any other race would resist or collapse under the burden of slavery, Morton alleged that the Negroes thrived in captivity: "The more pliant Negro, yielding to his fate, and accommodating himself to his condition, bore his heavy burden with comparative ease."[40] *Crania Aegyptiaca* acknowledged that many races have been enslaved: "We have unequivocal evidence, historical and monumental, that slavery was among the earliest institutions in Egypt, and that it was imposed on all conquered nations, white as well as black."[41] This supposition might have suggested to Morton that slavery was merely a social, not a racial, institution, but Morton concluded otherwise. He estimated the Negro population to be in the tens of thousands in ancient Egypt, yet observing only a few Negro skulls in the catacombs, he concluded that most could not elevate their social positions sufficiently to have merited an honorable burial. He concluded that the ancient Africans, like the ones of his time, lacked the ability to rise when in competition with other races: "Negroes were numerous in Egypt, but their social position in ancient times was the same that it is now, that of servants and slaves."[42] Together the anatomical and ethnographical evidence thus explained to Morton the Africans' consistently low status.

In his books *Crania Americana* and *Crania Aegyptiaca*, Morton did not dare challenge biblical revelation to suggest that there were different human creations from the beginning.[43] Rather, not wanting to totally reject the dominant biblical account and finding what he deemed compellingly consistent empirical evidence for the fixedness of different racial types, Morton argued that these differences were created by God when He decided to distribute Noah's descendants across the earth. Rather than simply place the same human type into radically different climatic conditions, God at that time generously chose to adapt each kind to its new environment. Morton speculates, "The same Omnipotence that created man, would adapt him at once to the physical, as well as the moral circumstances in which he was to dwell upon the earth."[44] Humans are thus racially fixed with immutable characteristics that do not change based on their environment, but according to Morton the "diversities of organization" of the different racial groups "were coeval with the dispersion of the species."[45] Morton thought this halfway point between the unity and diversity of the species based on an unrecorded and previously unknown intervention by

God was the most "reasonable conclusion" to explain human diversity.[46] Morton thus allowed that the theory of racial species for which he claimed to have provided scientific proof had divine basis; moreover, the political liabilities that corresponded with speciation also had a divine basis.

In sum, despite his international reputation for innovative research based on hard empirical data, Morton's efforts at empirical science were undermined by his reliance on racially prejudiced ethnography, faulty biblical chronology, and selection bias.

## *SPREADING MORTON'S POLYGENETIC IDEAS*

*Crania Americana* became well known in the scientific communities in America and Europe and inspired a number of other respected authors, scholars, and naturalists to take up Morton's argument.[47] The most renowned and influential of these were George R. Gliddon, Louis Agassiz, and Josiah Nott, all of whose science fared little better than Morton's.

An author, scholar, and lecturer, Gliddon was recognized as the leading American Egyptologist. English-born, he grew up in Egypt from an early age because his father was the US consul to Egypt in Alexandria. He lectured on ancient Egypt throughout America to "a great number of literary and scientific societies" and "was met with great success."[48] He became interested in Morton's work, and they struck up a correspondence and intellectual friendship. When Gliddon returned to Egypt as US vice consul, he used his position to provide Morton hundreds of skulls and other materials he requested from Egypt that formed the basis of Morton's *Crania Aegyptiaca*. According to his obituary, "Mr. Gliddon's Egyptian studies naturally led him into the cognate researches, and he became deeply interested in those anthropological subjects which have of late secured so large a degree of attention amongst students, especially as connected with the question of human origins and the diversity and permanence of race."[49] Gliddon did more than simply carry Morton's torch. He amplified and embellished Morton's main racial and polygenetic ideas.

Agassiz is recognized as one of the premiere American scientists of the nineteenth century. Born in Switzerland and a disciple of the great French naturalist and zoologist George Cuvier, Agassiz was the first major European scientist to come to America and stay. He left the University of Neuchâtel, was given a professorship at Harvard, and became the founder and director of its Museum of Contemporary Zoology. (A hall at Harvard still bears his name.) According to Stephen Jay Gould, "No man did more to establish and enhance the prestige of American biology during the nineteenth century."[50] Not a poly-genist in Europe, Agassiz became one in America after his experiences with African Americans and his exposure to Morton's work. He specialized in flora and fauna, arguing that all species were created for their unique environments. His work supported Morton's basic arguments about polygenism and the in-feriority of blacks.

Nott was a renowned physician, scientist, and "fervent southern polemi-cist who defended white supremacy with all the zeal of a South Carolina slave owner while urging the freedom of scientific inquiry from religious ortho-doxy."[51] Born in South Carolina, he received his medical degree from the Uni-versity of Pennsylvania and studied medicine in Paris before settling in Mobile, Alabama, to practice medicine and live the life of a "gentleman." He did groundbreaking research to demonstrate the role of the mosquito in spread-ing malaria and is credited as the first to identify the role of the mosquito in spreading yellow fever.[52] He founded the Medical College of Alabama. Nott was also a fanatical racist all his life. He owned slaves, paid for the first Ameri-can translation of Arthur Gobineau's *Essai sur l'inégalité des races humaines,*[53] and wrote a series of essays and books arguing the natural and irremediable inferiority of blacks and thus their need for and benefits from enslavement. Unlike other white supremacist advocates at the time, Nott argued on the basis of polygenism, which is how he connected with Morton and became one of the main propagators of his thought.

Nott's first publication was on a topic on which all the scientists of the American School agreed—that species were not defined by their ability to pro-create—but it was based on assertion, not science. Nott claimed that the mulat-toes in the American South were less intelligent than their white counterparts but more intelligent than the inferior fully Negro race.[54] His publications on this topic gave Nott an international reputation because he claimed both that the races were different species and that they could produce offspring, whereas Buffon had speculated that interspecies intercourse would not result in off-spring at all. Indeed, reproductive possibility was Buffon's defining criterion of a species, and Nott fundamentally challenged this dominant scientific view. Nott pointed to the many hybrids that had offspring (horses and donkeys, cows and bison) and argued both that Buffon was wrong in his definition of a species and (in a semi-nod to Buffon) that the hybrid offspring of the black and white species would eventually cease to exist as a result of increasing infertility. This is clear from the title of Nott's first essay on race: "The Mulatto a Hybrid: Prob-able Extermination of the Two Races If the Whites and Blacks Are Allowed to Intermarry."[55] In this essay, Nott averred that an island with a hundred males of the white species and a hundred females of the black species would in time be depopulated. This was the fate of humanity, he opined, if interspecies procreation continued. He admitted that statistical evidence for his claim did not exist, that his claim was based only on his observations in Mobile, and that the truth of them depended "upon my veracity alone."[56] However, because his arguments spoke directly to the most heated issues of the day, they attracted great attention, and Nott soon found himself an international sensation.

Like Nott, Morton and Agassiz also challenged Buffon's definition of a species, but with attempted scientific rigor. The polygenists had to challenge this definition because everyone could see that individuals of different races could procreate, yet Morton also accepted travelers' reports that intercourse between Caucasians and aboriginals in Australia rarely resulted in offspring. He attributed this to "a disparity in primordial organization." Morton argued that cross-species sex frequently led to hybridization and thus that *species* must be redefined as "a primordial organic form." Agassiz, in a letter to Morton, applauded this definition: "You have at last furnished science with a true philosophical definition of species." However, what forms were "primordial"? How could they be defined? Morton hypothesized that sex between more distant species was less likely to be fertile, whereas sex between more closely related species was likely to be more fertile.[57]

After Morton's death in 1851, Gliddon and Nott collaborated to spread Morton's message. The result of their collaboration was the seven-hundred-page tome *Types of Mankind; or, Ethnological Researches, Based upon the Ancient Monuments, Paintings, Sculptures, and Crania of Races, and upon Their Natural, Geographical, Philological, and Biblical History*, which served as an extension and popularization of Morton's work.[58] It included essays by them, previously unpublished works by Morton, expositions of Morton's work, and contributions by several leading polygenist scientists in Morton's orbit, including Agassiz. As is frequently the case in such edited volumes, the essays are not entirely consistent on every point, but they make clear, overlapping arguments about crania sizes, racial superiority, and polygenism. *Types of Mankind* also contains several very long essays on biblical interpretation, trying to teach the reader how to read the Bible properly and how to reconcile polygenism with the Bible. The book was both popular and influential. It received five hundred advance subscriptions and eventually sold more than ten thousand copies. Gliddon's obituary says that *Types of Mankind* "has been widely read and produced a profound impression on the educated mind of the country."[59] It represents the culminating breadth of arguments of the American School.[60]

Agassiz's contribution, "Of the Natural Provinces of the Animal World and Their Relation to the Different Types of Man," used biological studies to reinforce the polygenetic argument. It documented the many ecosystems around the world, arguing that the flora and fauna of each ecosystem were designed to thrive in their particular place and not in others. Astonished by the intricacy of this delicate balance, Agassiz believed that the only explanation had to be that they had been created that way from the beginning by God. God thus created not only different species of human beings to thrive in the different environments of the world but created all the different species of animals and plants in the same way. The Bible tells the story only of the creation of the Caucasian race, but, in fact, each race as well as every other living species had its own creation in its own locale, he proposed.

*Types of Mankind* as a whole reinforced the idea that blacks were physically and intellectually inferior to members of the Caucasian race: "Groups of mankind, as we have abundantly seen, differ in their cranial development; and their instincts drive them into lines diverging from each other—giving to each one its typical or national character."[61] "The Negro and other unintellectual types have been shown, in another chapter, to possess heads much smaller, by actual measurements in cubic inches, than the white races."[62] Nott cited Agassiz citing Morton's work to compare the brain of the Negro to that of an "orang-outan" and discussed at length the differing characteristics of the white and black races.[63] "I have looked in vain, during twenty years, for a solitary exception to these characteristic deficiencies among the Negro race"; he concluded that they were incapable of advanced culture.[64]

Unlike many American School publications, *Types of Mankind* systematically argued the consistency of polygenism with scripture through what its authors deemed the proper interpretation of the Bible. Indeed, all of Part 2 (106 pages) of this three-part book is dedicated to interpreting Genesis properly. Much of Part 3 is on "The Art of Writing," in which the authors explain how ancient writers wrote in order to support their interpretation of Genesis in Part 2. In aligning their theory with their interpretation of the Bible, they aimed to accomplish three things: scrupulous accuracy, protection from religious critiques, and making their theory more appealing to the white American public, especially in the South. They cautioned against a too literal interpretation of the Bible: "There is nothing in the language of the Bible which illustrates more strongly the danger of a too rigid enforcement of literal construction than the very loose manner in which *universal terms* are employed. . . . Neither the writers of the Old or New Testament knew anything of the geography of earth much beyond the limits of the Roman empire, nor had they any idea of the spheroidal shape of the globe."[65] So against the idea that all human beings are descended from Adam and Eve, they systematically argued that only the white race is discussed in the first three chapters of Genesis.[66] Because other races exist, "we would be led to infer that our species had its origin not in one, but in many creations."[67] According to them, races started at different points and only over time converged and "amalgamated" to give rise to new races.[68] Despite racial mixing, fundamental racial characteristics are long-standing: "We examine the venerable monuments of Egypt, and we see the Caucasian and the Negro depicted side by side, master and slave, twenty-two centuries before Christ."[69] At the end of a chapter titled "Biblical Ethnology," the authors acknowledged that their views had been "challenged" by traditional Bible scholars, but they decided the reader was "best qualified to decide," and they left it at that. In their worldview, the choice was between a theory of evolution for which there was no evidence; a literal reading of the Bible that could not explain the world's diversity; and polygenism, which best fit the available data.

## POLYGENISM AND POLITICS

The political upshot of the polygenetic argument and scientific understanding of racial characteristics in *Types of Mankind* was an argument for perpetual white dominance and black inferiority. Its authors claimed to find that only the Caucasian race is capable of running a civilization: "Lofty civilization, in all cases has been achieved solely by the 'Caucasian' group."[70] Therefore, if the white race stopped running America, the "whole fabric would doubtless soon fall to ruins."[71] They argued that civilizations in Europe were struggling because they had free blacks in their population.[72] America was doing "better" than Europe, they claimed, because it better understood the correct position of the Negro in society. The Negro could only be in charge of a successful society if "a Negro's head may be changed in form, and enlarged in size."[73] Because that was not happening, black-led societies were incapable of accomplishing anything great.[74] Moreover, they argued that blacks were better off, even improved, by playing a servile role in society: "Negro races, when *domesticated,* are susceptible of a *limited* degree of improvement; but when released from restraint, as in Hayti, they sooner or later relapse into barbarism."[75] Blacks and whites needed to be socially stratified (even when they are free), because blacks' intellectual growth stops before adulthood.[76] Antebellum America's widespread belief in the racial inferiority of blacks now had an underpinning in science.

Although all the American School thinkers accepted the inferiority of blacks as scientifically proven and irremediable, they did not advocate identical political positions. Nott repeatedly and loudly argued that slavery was civilization's only solution for the problem of the inferior black species. Morton did not particularly comment on the political situation. Agassiz strongly opposed slavery, but because he accepted blacks' inferiority as a scientific fact, he urged that the races be kept separate. He lived through the Civil War and welcomed the end of slavery and establishment of equality before the law, but he rejected social equality as disadvantageous to both whites and blacks. According to him, because the races had a "primitive difference," "social equality I deem at all times impracticable. It is a natural impossibility flowing from the very character of the negro race."[77] Agassiz thought that to give blacks total equality in all areas would overburden them and be but "mock-philanthropy": "It seems to us to be mock-philanthropy and mock-philosophy to assume that all races have the same abilities, enjoy the same powers, and show the same natural dispositions, and that in consequence of this equality they are entitled to the same position in human society. History speaks here for itself."[78] Equality would be unnatural and unhelpful to the Negro: "No man has a right to what he is unfit to use. . . . Let us beware of granting too much to the negro race in the beginning, lest it become necessary to recall violently some of the privileges which they may use to our detriment and their own injury."[79] The moderate position was thus separate but equal.

With the advocacy of Gliddon, Nott, and Agassiz (among others), the American School's racist and polygenetic ideas became increasingly popular in the scientific community and in society at large, and their ideas rose to the attention of some of the South's leading political figures, such as Calhoun and Hammond. Although it is testimony to the reach of the American School that the leaders at the top of the Southern cause sought information about and from the American School, there is no evidence that American School science itself was ever used by them or decisively shaped their opinions in any way.

Hammond and Nott were childhood friends and stayed in contact with each other their entire lives. Nott thus presumably gave Hammond all he wanted on the subject—but this turned out not to be much. In 1845 Nott sent him a series of letters on his newfound scientific polygenism, and one of Hammond's other friends gave and discussed with him Morton's *Crania Aegyptiaca* in the same year,[80] but there is no evidence that Hammond requested more information, ever used or repeated their arguments in his public words, or mentioned polygenism to anyone else in his private writings.

In a relationship trumpeted in the "Introduction" of *Types of Mankind* and verified by existing letters, it is clear that Calhoun and the American School thinkers had some contact—but, in truth, the contact and its impact were limited. Calhoun initiated the contact in 1844, seeking a meeting with Gliddon for information regarding his scientific view of the Negro.[81] The immediate context was then secretary of state Calhoun's correspondence with British foreign minister Richard Pakenham over the possible annexation of Texas as a slave state. In Gliddon's words, "Mr. Calhoun declared that he could not foresee what course the negotiation [with England over the annexation of Texas] might take, but wished to be forearmed [with arguments] for any emergency."[82] "He [Calhoun] was convinced that the true difficulties of the subject could not be fully comprehended without first considering the radical differences of humanity's races, which he intended to discuss should he be driven to necessity." To be armed to argue the "radical differences of humanity's races," Calhoun asked Gliddon for "the best sources of information in this country."[83] In a letter dated May 9, 1844, Gliddon introduced Calhoun to Morton: "Sir, in compliance with the wish you expressed, last Monday evening to be placed in possession of the latest ethnographical facts, I now have the gratification of introducing my distinguished friend, Sam[uel] Geo[rge] Morton Esq.[,] M.D."[84] Gliddon explained that Morton was the best source of information on the subject and that he himself was "but a pupil" of Morton's work.[85] Enclosed with Gliddon's May 9 letter to Calhoun was an additional letter from Morton. This letter stated, "Sir, Having been informed by my friend Mr. [George R.] Gliddon of the interest you take in certain Ethnographic questions, I beg your acceptance of a memoir in which, among other subjects, I have briefly inquired into the social position of the Negro race in the earliest periods of authentic history."[86] Morton soon after sent Calhoun copies of *Crania Americana* and *Crania Aegyptiaca,* along with other "minor works."[87] About a week later (May 17, 1844), Gliddon also sent a follow-up letter to Calhoun, with which he enclosed several pamphlets of his own and asserted the main politically relevant point of Morton's research: "Dr. Morton's researches prove, that Negro-Races have ever been *servants* and *slaves,* always distinct from, and subject to, the *Caucasian,* in the remotest of times."[88] Gliddon acknowledged the theory's apparent break with scripture but assured Calhoun that "we have misunderstood the meaning of the *original* Genesis of Moses." He offered Calhoun the services of several likeminded scholars "whenever *you* desire the solution of any *ethnographical* problem, in respect to *African*-subjects. . . . The resources of these gentlemen, when viewed collectively, exceed all others in the world, in a new branch of Science of which Dr. *Morton* is the mastermind. In short, we have any amount of *facts* at our disposal to support and confirm all those doctrines, that, for so long and bright a period, have marked the illustrious career of *John C. Calhoun*."[89]

Despite their eagerness to help, there is no evidence that Calhoun ever again requested their services or used their ideas or that their ideas changed his thinking in any way.[90] To the best of my knowledge, he never mentioned scientific polygenism in any publication or speech or in his private letters. At their initial meeting, Calhoun did discuss with Gliddon a letter he was working on to the US ambassador to France, one Wm. R. King, that was afterward widely published and pilloried by the British press because Calhoun had "intruded Ethnology into diplomatic correspondence."[91] The American School thinkers seemed to take a kind of victory in the mere fact that Calhoun used ethnology. But there is nothing—zero—in the letter related to any of the American School's distinctive ideas. As he had for years previously, Calhoun described the Negro as naturally inferior, but he did not base this on American School science and never described blacks as a different species or from a different human creation. He did decry emancipation as a "mockery" of philanthropy and as a "stale and unfounded plea of philanthropy," as the American School thinkers rejected "the immense evils of false philanthropy," but it is not clear whether Calhoun got this phrase from them, they from him, or if it was in common usage.[92] In any case, this language is not about their science. Calhoun's omission of their ideas in his arguments is especially striking because in this very letter and on several other occasions, Calhoun used other kinds of dubious science and other dubious studies to support his racist position.[93]

Nonetheless, Calhoun maintained a polite but distant contact with American School thinkers. Calhoun traded a handful of letters with them over the subsequent few years, but these letters give no evidence that Calhoun himself sought further instruction from them.[94] He also met with them in Mobile during his two-day stop there November 4–6, 1845, during his retirement tour from government,[95] and it is instructive what Calhoun told them in person about his not using their ideas. He told them, in their words, of "the inconveniences which true ethnological science might have created in philanthropical diplomacy, had it been frankly introduced."[96] Calhoun must have liked that they supported his view of blacks generally, but perhaps he found their views too heretical, and/or perhaps the antibiblical nature of their polygenism was just too high a price to pay for their science, and Calhoun was unwilling to risk alienating his Southern Christian base. However this might have been, he never used their science.

*THE END OF SCIENTIFIC RACISM?*

Polygenetic arguments largely disappeared after the Civil War for two reasons.[97] First, with the defeat of the South and the end of slavery, there no longer was a political need for such an argument to support slavery. Thus, with respect to this particular mode of thought, the Civil War proved a decisive end. Second, Darwin's arguments about the evolution and mutability of species (1859, 1871) provided a new beginning for post–Civil War American science. Evolution became accepted as a clearly superior account of the diversity of human beings within a rubric of fundamental unity. Even the dogmatic Nott recognized Darwin's superiority to his own life's work and had the intellectual credibility to abandon polygenism when confronted with Darwin's theories and evidence. Agassiz, however, never accepted Darwin. After the Civil War he became even more famous as the last great American scientist holding on to creationism, even if he moderated his polygenism to emphasize it for the other animals and not human beings.[98]

The triumph of "good" science in the form of Darwin did not, however, end science's entanglement with racism. Darwin, Darwinists, and social Darwinists were deeply entangled in racist thought. Indeed, the original title of Darwin's work, edited in modern editions presumably to avoid tainting the great theorist of evolution, is *On the Origin of the Species by Means of Natural Selection, or the Preservation of the Favoured Races in the Struggle for Life* (1859). And the role of race is integral to Darwin's thought. One of the three stated goals of his other major work, *The Descent of Man* (1871), is to determine "the value of the differences between the so-called races of man."[99] Darwin vociferously hated slavery,[100] but he concluded that the Caucasian is the most evolved race and the blacks the least. Indeed, he saw but a small gap "between the Negro or Australian and the gorilla."[101] Does this sound familiar?[102] Unlike the members of the American School, Darwin did not think racial groups have immutable characteristics, but this does not mean he thought they would evolve equally. He predicted that all extant races will eventually go extinct, but he averred that the blacks will be the first to go and that the next stage of evolution will come out of the whites.[103] To some Darwinists, the "savages" of Africa represented the "missing link" between lower animals and civilized human beings.[104]

In the decades immediately after the Civil War, Herbert Spencer's so-called social Darwinism of "survival of the fittest" was invoked to justify the extreme inequalities of the day and as a call for governments to consciously promote the fittest individuals and weed out the mentally and physically weak. According to him, "under the natural order of things society is constantly excreting its unhealthy, imbecile, slow, vacillating, faithless members." And, he averred, this is how it should be; he favored the conscious application of a "purifying process" so that "vitiation of the race through the multiplication of its inferior samples is prevented." Otherwise, humanity would be "pressed against the inexorable necessities of its new position" and be "moulded into harmony with them [its weak], and ha[ve] to bear the resulting unhappiness as best it can."[105] Insofar as these ideas were standard fare in American schools after the Civil War, they helped undercut and end Reconstruction's educational efforts to alleviate the condition of the recently freed, downtrodden, formerly enslaved people. Like Calhoun and the American School thinkers, social Darwinists deemed efforts spent on those unworthy of them misguided charity based on "false humanity."[106]

The racism of Darwin's evolution theory was used to promote racism and eugenics in the twentieth century. The move from Darwin's theory of evolution to eugenics was but a small step and happened shortly after Darwin wrote. Indeed, combining Darwin's theory of evolution with Gregor Mendel's gene theory, Darwin's own cousin by marriage, Francis Galton, coined the phrase "eugenics," his call for conscious societal intervention to pass along superior genes so that the species could best evolve. Galton notes, "The influence of man upon the nature of his own race has already been very large, but it has not been intelligently directed, and has in many instances done great harm."[107] The aim of eugenics is to make sure evolution is "intelligently directed." Galton believed there were "differences in intellectual power between men of different races," and he distinguished between "high races," such as his English one, and "low races," such as "the coarse and lazy negro."[108] Galton argued that "the most merciful form of what I have ventured to call 'eugenics' would consist in watching for the indications of superior strains or races, and in so favoring them that their progeny shall outnumber and gradually replace that of the old one."[109] Less merciful forms would involve more active intervention to promote the superior and hinder the inferior.

The racism that existed in Galton's conception of eugenics continued as eugenics blossomed in America during the Progressive era. Every industrialized country developed eugenics movements, but before World War II eugenics thrived most in the United States. Eugenics was championed within the Progressive movement because Progressives shared the same logic of using direct, intelligent government policy to address society's ills.[110] Progressives abhorred the inequalities created during what they deemed the unfettered laissez-faire capitalism of the robber baron era, were frustrated by the many boom-and-bust cycles of the economy, and wanted to cure social ills such as crime, housing shortages, low wages, and problems with immigrants. To achieve their goals, Progressives favored policies of intelligent government intervention, exactly what the eugenics movement wanted with respect to the transmission of genes. They became natural allies as eugenicists claimed that they were able to get at the root cause—bad genes—of many social problems. One of the Progressives' policies was the anti-immigration Johnson Act (1924), which aimed to keep out immigrants of inferior stock. Another policy deemed efficient, rational, and humane was the sterilization of the weak so their offspring could no longer burden them or society. Margaret Sanger, the great proponent of birth control, for example, also campaigned for sterilization to prevent undesirable children from being born. In her work she approvingly cites both Spencer and Charles Davenport, the dean of American eugenics.[111] Like them, she warned about the need to protect the population from the unfit: "the feeble-minded," "the moron," "the mental defective," and "imbecility."[112] "Eugenics," she writes, "seems to me to be valuable in its critical and diagnostic aspects, in emphasizing the danger of irresponsible and uncontrolled fertility of the 'unfit' and the feeble-minded establishing a progressive unbalance in human society and lowering the birth-rate among the 'fit.'"[113] In this spirit, eugenics programs during the Progressive era were instituted in thirty states and resulted in the forced sterilization of at least sixty thousand, and perhaps as many as one hundred thousand, people.[114] The US Supreme Court upheld these sterilizations in the infamous case of *Buck v. Bell*, in which, writing for the 8–1 decision of the Court, Justice Oliver Wendell Holmes wrote, "It is better for the world, if instead of waiting to execute degenerate offspring for crime, or to let them starve for their imbecility, society can prevent those who are manifestly unfit from continuing their kind."[115] Sanger, like most of her American contemporaries, did not explicitly call for eugenics based on race, but it is perhaps notable that in her chapter "The Fertility of the Feeble-Minded," the only example she gives is of a family in "a thickly populated Negro district."[116] In reality, the "undesirable" in America often translated to poor and black, and the sterilization campaigns disproportionately affected these groups.[117]

The Nazis' mass murder of millions of innocents along racial lines drew on and was the culmination of a hundred years of Darwinist and eugenic thought.[118] Many of the leaders of America's eugenics movement also worked with their counterparts in Germany, and some hailed Germany's eugenics experiments under Hitler.[119] Nazism was driven by an absurd, fanatical, and pathological racism, but insofar as it was based on survival of the fittest and government action to achieve a eugenical end, the prevailing science in Germany did not hinder but rather supported the basic structure of Hitler's worldview.[120]

## CONCLUSION

Although it is easy to condemn the American School's scientific racism, science's entanglement with racism has not disappeared—nor is it likely to. The most disturbing part of the American School episode, and the sad entanglement of science in racism more generally, is the stark way in which it raises fundamental issues both about the nature of science itself and about its relation to politics. According to its own modern self-understanding, science is value free. It claims to create knowledge and understanding that in themselves are value neutral and that can be employed for good or evil. Science has no scientific basis for preferring one to the other or even recognizing that there is a moral difference between them. Because science itself is value neutral, it will be deployed according to the moral and political views of its day.

Science's own insistence on its value neutrality and its inability to supply moral guidance both exacerbates the moral problem and heightens the need for overseeing it. Science today might be able to refute theories affirmatively asserting racial inequality, such as those advanced by Morton and Nott. However, it does so at the price of being unable to affirmatively undergird liberal, egalitarian views. Science's current teachings on evolution and on a universe that is merely matter and motion undercut the grounds of anyone having natural rights. Everyone might be equally in the same moral situation according to science, but according to science it is also a situation in which everyone is equally devoid of moral or political natural rights. If that is the case, then science (including social science) alone cannot have a moral preference, let alone be a moral imperative, for choosing liberal egalitarianism over hierarchical racism or the cruelty of a Hitler or Stalin. Indeed, just as the American School science was used to justify slavery and Darwinism was used to justify eugenics and Nazism in the past, so science and scientists can be used by any calamitous political movement.

For all the benefits it has brought—and they are many—science, despite its rationality, cannot solve moral and political dilemmas or be counted on as a reliable support to moderate politics. Science alone cannot justify morality. On the one hand, this is obvious to all self-knowing scientists, and the point might thus seem trivial. On the other hand, it is troubling if the only universally recognized authority of our age leaves citizens and polities without guidance. If science cannot supply the first principles for solving moral and political problems, to what should citizens appeal in making their moral and political judgments? The difficulty in answering this question is partly because of science's radical division of the world into a sphere of so-called facts and a sphere of so-called values. Insofar as scientists must see natural rights merely as values, science cannot support them. Moreover, the reduction of natural rights to mere values is corrosive of the moral foundations of the American regime.

Today, and at least since Friedrich Nietzsche and Michel Foucault, there is a fashionable critique of science in which its distinction between facts and values has been challenged as simplistic and untenable. These critics argue that science can never achieve the value-neutral purity it requires. However, rather than uphold natural rights as possibly true, this critique deems not only science but all thought, including all philosophical and moral claims, to be mere perspective entangled in the values of its author. Insofar as this critique calls into question the idea of truth itself, it undermines moral claims even further because it rejects any basis for any objective claim, moral or otherwise. Science's claims and the radical polemics against those claims have thus inevitably taken us to an intellectual situation in which it is difficult to uphold traditional American principles at all other than as mere values.

Just as the politicians of the antebellum period seem to have been sufficiently skeptical of the American School, we too would do well to be eternally vigilant about science's supposedly neutral claims. We would do equally well to be vigilant in monitoring the radical claims that a priori dismiss every basis for objective truth, including science. With all that can go wrong, scientists, ordinary citizens, and statesmen have a never-ending need for prudence, critical self-understanding, and moderation. Neither science nor its critics can be counted on to moderate politics. Rather, thoughtful citizens must be moderate and circumspect in their deployment of science. In this at least, the politicians of antebellum America who ignored the American School were right.

## NOTES

1. I would like to thank the following people for their comments on earlier drafts of this chapter: Wamaid Levine-Borges, Philip Lyons, Daniel Malachuk, Thomas Merrill, Marianne Noble, Johnathan O'Neill, James Read, James Stoner, Jr., and Matthew Wright. I dedicate this chapter to my daughter, Aimée Brown-Borges. May it help create a better world for you to live in.

2. The best critical accounts of justifications of slavery include David Brion Davis, *Inhuman Bondage: The Rise and Fall of Slavery in the New World* (New York: Oxford University Press, 2006) and Winthrop Jordan, *White over Black: American Attitudes toward the Negro, 1550–1812* (Chapel Hill: University of North Carolina Press, 1968).

3. *Narrative of the Life of Frederick Douglass,* chap. 10, recounts the year Douglass spent with this pious Christian, who made "his reputation as a 'nigger-breaker'" (chap. 9). Describing the harsh work conditions and repeated beatings, Douglass writes, "A

few months of this discipline tamed me. Mr. Covey succeeded in breaking me. I was broken in body, soul, and spirit. My natural elasticity was crushed, my intellect languished, the disposition to read departed, the cheerful spark that lingered about my eyes died; the dark night of slavery closed in upon me; and behold a man transformed into a brute!" Douglass, *Narrative of the Life of Frederick Douglass* (New York: Dover, 1995), 38; orig. pub 1845. In Harriet Beecher Stowe, *Uncle Tom's Cabin* (Boston: J. P. Jewett, 1852), the character Legree is complex but sadistic.

4. There are many documentations of the horrific cruelty of life under slavery. Angelina Grimké and Theodore D. Weld, *American Slavery as It Is: Testimony of a Thousand Witnesses* (New York: American Anti-Slavery Society, 1839) is notable for its influence on the abolitionist movement. This book has the benefit of accounts told not only by witnesses but by participants, black and white, of whippings, beatings, shackles, and near starvation. It includes overseers discussing the pros and cons of treating enslaved people well versus working them to death (typically decided in favor of the latter).

Such cruelty is not, of course, unique to the American South. History is full of tyrants, large and small. Christopher Browning found that among ordinary police officers, not card-carrying Nazis, sent to brutally and systematically murder Jewish civilians, about one-third sadistically enjoyed and embellished their unlimited power, even though none had sought it out. In short, some people like possessing unlimited power. Browning, *Ordinary Men: Reserve Police Battalion 101 and the Final Solution in Poland* (New York: HarperCollins, 1992).

5. Stowe, *Uncle Tom's Cabin,* chap. 19.

6. James Henry Hammond, Mud-Sill Speech, http://www.pbs.org/wgbh/aia/part4/4h3439t.html.

7. Eugene Genovese and Elizabeth Fox-Genovese, *Fatal Self-Deception: Slaveholding Paternalism in the Old South* (Cambridge, UK: Cambridge University Press, 2011), 5; Genovese and Fox-Genovese, *The Mind of the Master Class: History and Faith in the Southern Slaveholders' Worldview* (Cambridge, UK: Cambridge University Press, 2005); *Slavery in White and Black: Class and Race in the Southern Slaveholders' New World Order* (Cambridge, UK: Cambridge University Press, 2008). See also Eugene Genovese, *Roll, Jordan, Roll: The World of the Slaves* (New York: Vintage, 1976); David Brion Davis, *Inhuman Bondage,* esp. chaps. 3, 9, and 10; Lacy K. Ford, *Deliver Us from Evil: The Slavery Question in the Old South* (New York: Oxford University Press, 2011).

8. John Calhoun argued, "Let me not be understood as admitting, even by implication, that the existing relations between the two races in the slaveholding States is an evil: Far otherwise; I hold it to be a good, as it has thus far proved itself to be, to both, and will continue to prove so if not disturbed by the fell spirit of abolition. I appeal to facts. Never before has the black race of Central Africa, from the dawn of history to the present day, attained a condition so civilized and so improved, not only physically, but morally and intellectually. It came among us in a low, degraded, and savage condition, and in the course of a few generations it has grown up under the fostering care of our institutions, reviled as they have been, to its present comparatively civilized condition. This, with the rapid increase of numbers, is conclusive proof of the general happiness of the race, in spite of all the exaggerated tales to the contrary." Calhoun, Speech on the Reception of the Abolition Petitions, Delivered in the Senate, February 6, 1837, in

*Speeches of John C. Calhoun, Delivered in the House of Representatives and in the Senate of the United States,* ed. Richard Crallé (New York: D. Appleton, 1853), 625–633.

9. In a similar vein, see also George Fitzhugh, *Cannibals All!—or Slaves without Masters* (Richmond, VA: A. Morris, 1857).

10. Ford, *Deliver Us from Evil,* 8.

11. This is the main argument of Genovese and Fox-Genovese, *Fatal Self-Deception.* See, for example, 14, 25, 26.

12. The so-called anti-Tom literature gets its name from the authors' intention of refuting the harsh account of slavery depicted in Stowe, *Uncle Tom's Cabin.* See Thomas F. Gossett, Uncle Tom's Cabin *and American Culture.* For representative excerpts of this literature, see http://utc.iath.virginia.edu/proslav/antitoms.html.

13. George M. Fredrickson, *The Black Image in the White Mind: The Debate on Afro-American Character and Destiny, 1817–1914* (Chicago: University of Chicago Press, 2000), includes a comprehensive view of racial attitudes in antebellum times.

14. See Thomas Jefferson, *Notes on the State of Virginia,* in *Life and Selected Writings,* ed. Adrienne Koch and William Peden (New York: Modern Library, 1944), Queries 14 and 18.

15. See Alan Levine and Daniel Malachuk, eds., *A Political Companion to Ralph Waldo Emerson* (Lexington: University Press of Kentucky, 2011) and Fredrickson, *The Black Image in the White Mind.*

16. If so, a lesson of this episode might be the importance of keeping alive real and reflective conversation in public arenas.

17. Thomas Jefferson to Roger Weightman, June 24, 1826, in *Thomas Jefferson: Writings,* ed. Merrill D. Peterson (New York: Library of America, 1984), 1516–1517. The date is ten days before Jefferson died.

18. Alexander Stephens, Corner-Stone Speech, in *Alexander H. Stephens, in Public and Private: With Letters and Speeches, before, during, and since the War,* ed. Henry Cleveland (Philadelphia: National, 1866), 721–722.

19. Consider, for example, nominalists such as William of Ockham and idealists such as Immanuel Kant and G. W. F. Hegel. Ockham holds that only individual beings, and not types, exist. Kant and Hegel argue that universals do not exist in themselves but are constituents of pure reason.

20. It should be noted that Charles Lyell's *Principles of Geology,* greatly influential on the young Charles Darwin, was published in 1830–1833, so there was some but not definitive evidence for evolution available to the American School. For example, Lyell argued that the earth was much older than four thousand years.

21. Isaac La Peyrère, *Pre-Adamitae* (1655), translated into English as two separate works: *A Theological Systeme upon the Presupposition That Men Were before Adam* (London, 1655), hereafter cited as *Men before Adam;* and *Men before Adam, or, a Discourse upon the Twelfth, Thirteenth, and Fourteenth Chapters of the Epistle of Paul to the Romans* (London, 1656), hereafter cited as *Discourse.* The account in this paragraph is summarized by La Peyrère, *Discourse,* Book 1, chap. 8, 22; and *Discourse,* Book 1, chap. 26, 60–61. He concludes that his view makes the Bible "clearer" and more consistent and that with his interpretation "it is wonderfully reconciled" with empirical history. All in all, "by this position, Faith and right Reason are reconciled" (Book 1, chap. 8, 22).

22. La Peyrère, *Men before Adam,* Book 3, chap. 1, 129–134.

23. Ibid., Book 3, chap: 2, 135–140.

24. Ibid., Book 5, chap. 9, 346–351.

25. For example, Voltaire, *Essai sur les Moeurs,* chaps. 11 and 17, attacks the Bible's claim of a single human creation and Europe's consequent pride for considering itself the inheritor of the sole true religion, which justifies its global imperialism.

26. Henry Home, Lord Kames, *Sketches of the History of Man* (1774), http://www.oll .libertyfund.org/titles/kames-sketches-of-the-history-of-man-3-vols.

27. The first publication to argue for polygenism in America was Charles Caldwell, *Thoughts on the Original Unity of the Human Race* (New York: E. Bliss, 1830).

28. Cited in William Stanton, *The Leopard's Spots: Scientific Attitudes toward Race in America, 1815–1859* (Chicago: University of Chicago Press, 1960), 144.

29. Samuel George Morton, *Crania Americana: A Comparative View of the Skulls of Various Aboriginal Nations of North and South America—to Which Is Prefixed an Essay on the Varieties of Human Species* (Philadelphia: J. Dobson, 1839); *Crania Aegyptiaca, or Observations on Egyptian Ethnography Derived from Anatomy, History, and Monuments* (Philadelphia: John Penington, 1844). Morton published his final measurements in 1849; see Stanton, *Leopard's Spots,* 15–17.

30. Stephen Jay Gould, *The Mismeasure of Man* (New York: Norton, 1996), 83.

31. Cited in Stanton, *Leopard's Spots,* 96.

32. These are depicted in a diagram in Morton, *Crania Americana,* 252.

33. Ibid., 252.

34. Ibid., 251.

35. Gould, *Mismeasure of Man,* argues with Morton's calculations based on retabulations of his raw data, concluding: "In short, and to put it bluntly, Morton's summaries are a patchwork of fudging and finagling in the clear interest of controlling a priori convictions. Yet—and this is the most intriguing aspect of the case I find no evidence of conscious fraud; indeed, had Morton been a conscious fudger, he would not have published his data so openly" (86). In light of Gould's critique, a team from the University of Pennsylvania (that today owns and houses Morton's collection of skulls) reanalyzed everything. Its findings are as follows: "In the 2000s, a team of Penn anthropologists, including Penn Museum's Janet Monge, set out to re-measure the Morton Collection and reassess Gould's conclusions. After analyzing a sample of the skulls, they determined that Morton's measurements themselves were correct, even though his conclusions were false and racist" (sign at University of Pennsylvania Museum of Archaeology and Anthropology, August 17, 2016). See also Nicholas Wade, "Scientists Measure the Accuracy of a Racism Claim," *New York Times,* June 14, 2011, D4. However, even if Morton's specific physical measurements were correct, Gould reports several other errors, such as selectively including and omitting skulls in various subcategories, over- and underrepresentation of male (which tend to be larger) and female (which tend to be smaller) skulls, respectively, in different racial groups, and not measuring relative to stature. Larger bodies require larger brains with no implication for intelligence, just as an elephant is not more intelligent than a human because of its larger brain size. Morton's samples of Native Americans, for example, include many small-statured Peruvians, whereas he omitted small-statured, white "Hindoos." Gould also

speculates on other "plausible scenarios" he claims might have further distorted Morton's results (97). Although these latter are mere speculation, Gould's overall analysis based on Morton's own records is convincing.

36. Morton, *Crania Americana,* 87.

37. Ibid.

38. Ibid., 88.

39. Quotes from ibid., 31.

40. Ibid., 75.

41. Morton, *Crania Aegyptiaca,* 59.

42. Ibid., 66.

43. For a suggestive account of the religious-based attacks on Morton's polygenism, see Gould, *Mismeasure of Man,* 101–104.

44. Morton, *Crania Americana,* 2–3.

45. Morton, *Brief Remarks on the Diversities of the Human Species, and on Some Kindred Subjects* (Philadelphia: Merrihew and Thompson, 1842), 8, cited in Stanton, *Leopard's Spots,* 42.

46. Morton, *Crania Americana,* 3.

47. Morton's influence on his followers is acknowledged and direct. The introduction to *Types of Mankind* avers that Morton is the "founder of that school of Ethnography of whose views this book may be regarded as an authentic exponent." George R. Gliddon and Josiah Clark Nott, *Types of Mankind, or, Ethnological Researches, Based upon the Ancient Monuments, Paintings, Sculptures, and Crania of Races, and upon Their Natural, Geographical, Philological, and Biblical History* (Philadelphia: Lippincott, Gramoo, 1855), xviii.

48. *New York Herald,* Gliddon obituary, November 20, 1857.

49. Ibid.

50. Gould, *Mismeasure of Man,* 75.

51. Reginald Horsman, *Josiah Nott of Mobile: Southerner, Physician, and Racial Theorist* (Baton Rouge: Louisiana State University Press, 1987), 81.

52. See, for example, Josiah Clark Nott, "Yellow Fever Contrasted with Bilious Fever—Reasons for Believing It Is a Disease sui generis—Its Mode of Propagation—Remote Cause—Probable Insect or Animalcular Origin, &c.," *New Orleans Medical and Surgical Journal* 4 (1848): 563–601; Nott, "Sketch of the Epidemic of Yellow Fever of 1847, in Mobile," *Charleston Medical Journal and Review* 1 (1848): 1–21.

53. Count A. de Gobineau, *The Moral and Intellectual Diversity of Races, to Which is added an Appendix Containing a Summary of the Latest Scientific Facts Bearing upon the Question of the Unity or Plurality of Species,* trans. H. Hotz (Philadelphia, 1856); the appendix by Nott claimed to set Gobineau right on the question of polygenism. For a discussion of this publication, see Horsman, *Josiah Nott of Mobile,* 204–210.

54. Stanton, *Leopard's Spots,* 66.

55. Josiah Clark Nott, "The Mulatto a Hybrid: Probable Extermination of the Two Races If the Whites and Blacks Are Allowed to Intermarry," *American Journal of the Medical Sciences* 6 (1843).

56. Horsman, *Josiah Nott of Mobile,* 87.

57. Gould, *Mismeasure of Man,* 84–85; Stanton, *Leopard's Spots,* 141.

58. Gliddon and Nott, *Types of Mankind*. The origins of this book are explained on ix–x.

59. Ibid., x; *New York Herald*, Gliddon obituary.

60. The individuals involved in *Types of Mankind* had later publications, but this book represents a fusion and movement unlike any later works.

61. Gliddon and Nott, *Types of Mankind*, 461.

62. Ibid., 403.

63. Ibid., 415–417.

64. Ibid., 456.

65. Ibid., 557.

66. Note the contrast with La Peyrère, who included the creation of all human beings in Genesis I–II.

67. Quoted from Morton's edited manuscript in Gliddon and Nott, *Types of Mankind*, 305.

68. Ibid. For a discussion of "amalgamation" in antebellum America, see Diana Schaub's chapter in this volume.

69. Gliddon and Nott, *Types of Mankind*, 306–307.

70. Ibid., 461.

71. Ibid., 404.

72. Ibid., 405.

73. Ibid., 404.

74. Ibid., 462.

75. Ibid., 461, emphasis added.

76. Ibid., 415 (essay by Agassiz).

77. Gould, *Mismeasure of Man*, 79, 80.

78. Ibid., 79.

79. Ibid., 80.

80. Nott wrote Hammond letters on his new racial views on July 10, July 25, August 12, and September 4, 1845, and another on June 3, 1850. The friend who sent Hammond some of Nott's writings was William Brown Hodgson. Hammond replies to Nott encouragingly on August 3, 1845, and as far as I can tell this single letter is the extent of Hammond's words on any subject specifically related to the American School's views. On these exchanges, see Horsman, *Josiah Nott of Mobile*, 92–93, 100–101, 119–120; Stanton, *Leopard's Spots*, 52–53, esp. 77–78.

81. Gliddon and Nott, *Types of Mankind*, 50.

82. Ibid., 51.

83. Ibid., 50, 51.

84. *The Papers of John C. Calhoun*, vol. 18: *1844*, ed. Clyde N. Wilson (Columbia: University of South Carolina Press, 1988), 462.

85. Ibid.

86. Ibid., 463.

87. Gliddon and Nott, *Types of Mankind*, 50.

88. *Papers of John C. Calhoun*, vol. 18, 532, italics in original.

89. Ibid., 532–533, italics in original.

90. In his otherwise excellent and judicious book *Leopard's Spots*, Stanton seems to

overestimate the effect on Calhoun of this exchange with the American School, writing that Calhoun proceeded with his letter in part because he was "secure in his knowledge acquired from Gliddon and Morton" (62). Calhoun proceeded with his letter, but he did not use any of the American School's evidence or arguments. For a more balanced accounting of the American School's possible influence on Calhoun, see James H. Read, *Majority Rule versus Consensus: The Political Thought of John C. Calhoun* (Lawrence: University Press of Kansas, 2009), 133–134.

91. Gliddon and Nott, *Types of Mankind*, 51.

92. *Papers of John C. Calhoun*, vol. 19: *1844*, 568–578; Gliddon and Nott, *Types of Mankind*, 52.

93. Calhoun repeatedly used data from the 1840 census that he knew, or had every reason to know, were false. The 1840 census was the first to account for the nation's mentally ill. A Dr. Edward Jarvis of Massachusetts studied the census data and found that the number of insane free Negroes in the North greatly outnumbered the number of insane enslaved Negroes in the South. The data indicated a direct continuum: the farther north, the greater the proportion of insane blacks. This led him to surmise, much to the excitement of the South, that slavery was good for the intelligence and morality of blacks. Stanton, *Leopard's Spots,* 58–61. Jarvis later recanted his report after he discovered that Northern towns were lying about the number of insane Negroes they had reported. Why they did this is unclear. Knowing of Jarvis's recantation and the falseness of the original data did not, however, stop Calhoun from using them in his letters to Pakenham and King. Calhoun wrote, "The Census and other authentic documents show that, in all instances in which the States have changed the former relation between the two races, the condition of the African instead of being improved, has become worse. They have invariably sunk into vice and pauperism, accompanied by the bodily and mental inflictions incident thereto—deafness, blindness, insanity, and idiocy, to a degree without example, while in all other States which have retained the ancient relation between them, they have greatly improved in every respect—in number, comfort, intelligence, and morals." *Papers of John C. Calhoun*, vol. 18, 276. Calhoun knowingly used this incorrect social science, but he nowhere used the arguments or data of the American School.

94. According to *Papers of John C. Calhoun,* the sum of their letters, or letters that mention them in any pertinent way, are as follows. Gliddon thanks Calhoun for a confidential favor and offers his latest views on Africans (August 2, 1844 [vol. 19, 503]). Calhoun thanks Morton for his works but says he has not had a chance yet to read them (September 1844 [vol. 19, 689]). Nott sends Calhoun data suggesting that blacks live longer under slavery in Charleston than in freedom in Philadelphia, but this has nothing to do with the distinctively American School argument (October 29, 1844 [vol. 20, 158–160]). Gliddon sends Calhoun his latest antibiblical thoughts (December 26, 1844 [vol. 20, 630–631]). Two people also write Calhoun a total of three letters to tell him of work by American School thinkers. A certain Frederick Hollick, who had met Calhoun once the previous year, writes Calhoun of the importance of Gliddon's work (February 20, 1847 [vol. 24, 181]), and James de Bow twice sends him copies of publications by Nott (November 17, 1847 [vol. 24, 661] and December 26, 1847 [vol. 25, 42]).

Calhoun also had other exchanges with Gliddon and Nott totally unrelated to their science. Gliddon sends two letters asking Calhoun for assistance in keeping the consulship to Egypt in his family after his father dies (July 22, 1844 [vol. 19, 415–418] and August 20, 1844 [vol. 19, 615–616]). Nott writes Calhoun telling him that his son William has fallen ill in Mobile (May 21, 1847 [vol. 24, 373–374]) and that he is doing better (May 28, 1847 [vol. 24, 384–385]). Three letters from Calhoun to his son Andrew mention Nott, hoping that he can help cure his grandson, little Andrew (November 25, 1848 [vol. 26, 141], December 15, 1848 [vol. 26, 173], and May 19, 1849 [vol. 26, 399]). In sum, there is no evidence of a vital intellectual impact by the American School on Calhoun.

95. See *Papers of John C. Calhoun*, vol. 22: *1845–1846*, 251–254. Nott was a part of Mobile's official welcoming delegation.

96. Gliddon and Nott, *Types of Mankind*, 52.

97. Polygenetic arguments live on today among racist, extremely fringe, white-power movements, with their bizarre theories of inferior "mud people" deserving to be slaves.

98. Stanton, *Leopard's Spots*, 189–191.

99. Charles Darwin, *The Descent of Man* (Princeton, NJ: Princeton University Press, 1981 [a photoreproduction of the original 1871 edition published by J. Murray, London]), 3. In this book Darwin discusses skull size and shape in his evaluation of the races (216) and cites the American School thinkers several times: Morton once, Nott and Gliddon five times, and Agassiz nine times.

100. See Gould, *Mismeasure of Man*, 422–423.

101. Darwin, *Descent of Man*, 201. Darwin also writes, "At some future period, not very distant as measured by centuries, the civilised races of man will almost certainly exterminate and replace throughout the world the savage races" (201). Although Darwin writes this matter-of-factly, neither advocating nor lamenting it, the social Darwinists and the eugenicists among his followers actively sought to bring it about.

102. Like the American School thinkers, Darwin also cites skull size and shape in his evaluation of the races (e.g., *Descent of Man*, 216).

103. William H. Jeynes, "Race, Racism, and Darwinism," *Education and Urban Society* 43, no. 5 (2011): 536.

104. Ibid., 537.

105. Herbert Spencer, *Social Statics* (London: Chapman, 1851), in section "Poor Laws," 322, 323, 324. Although Spencer's initial writings predate Darwin, they became popular in Darwin's wake.

106. Jeynes, "Race, Racism, and Darwinism," 542, 547. For a discussion of the consequences of social Darwinism on schools in America during Reconstruction, see 548–550.

107. Francis Galton, *Inquiries into Human Faculty and Its Development* (London: Macmillan, 1883), 308.

108. Ibid., 82–83, 317.

109. Ibid., 307.

110. Thomas C. Leonard, *Illiberal Reformers: Race, Eugenics, and American Economics in the Progressive Era* (Princeton, NJ: Princeton University Press, 2016); Garland E. Allen, "Eugenics and American Social History, 1880–1950" *Genome* 31, no. 2 (1989): 885–889; Donald K. Pickens, *Eugenics and the Progressives* (Nashville, TN: Vanderbilt

University Press, 1968); Mark H. Haller, *Eugenics: Hereditarian Attitudes in American Thought* (New Brunswick, NJ: Rutgers University Press, 1984).

111. For example, in Margaret Sanger, *The Pivot of Civilization* (New York: Brentano's, 1922), a quote from Spencer is the epigram of her chapter "The Cruelty of Charity": "Fostering the good-for-nothing at the expense of the good is an extreme cruelty. It is a deliberate storing up of miseries for future generations. There is no greater curse to posterity than that of bequeathing them an increasing population of imbeciles." She approvingly cites Charles Davenport, the leading American eugenicist, 81.

112. Ibid., 80, 81.

113. Ibid., 104.

114. Elizabeth A. Noren, "Nothing Natural: Social Darwinism, Scientific Racism, and Eugenics in America," *Social Sciences Directory* 2, no. 1 (January 2003): 27.

115. Buck v. Bell, 274 U.S. 200 (1927), cited in Randall Hansen and Desmond King, *Sterilized by the State: Eugenics, Race, and the Population Scare in Twentieth-Century North America* (Cambridge, UK: Cambridge University Press, 2013), 106.

116. Sanger, *Pivot of Civilization*, 84.

117. Hansen and King, *Sterilized by the State*, 237–258; Paul Lombardo, ed., *A Century of Eugenics in America: From the Indiana Experiment to the Human Genome Era* (Bloomington: Indiana University Press, 2011), includes a fascinating essay by Gregory Michael Dorr and Angela Logan that reverses the usual perspective: "'Quality, Not Mere Quantity, Counts': Black Eugenics and the NAACP Baby Contests," 68–92.

118. André Pichot, *The Pure Society: From Darwin to Hitler,* trans. David French (London: Verso, 2009); Richard Weikart, *From Darwin to Hitler: Evolutionary Ethics, Eugenics, and Racism in Germany* (New York: Palgrave Macmillan, 2004).

119. Edwin Black, *War against the Weak: Eugenics and America's Campaign to Create a Master Race* (New York: Four Walls Eight Windows, 2003).

120. Richard Weikart, "The Role of Darwinism in Nazi Racial Thought," *Germanic Studies Review* 36, no. 3 (October 2013): 537–556. See 538 for a powerful and convincing case of six fundamental ways in which Nazi science drew on Darwin.

# CHAPTER 5

# From Calhoun to Secession

JAMES H. READ

Abraham Lincoln, in his July 4, 1861, Message to Congress in Special Session, observed that Southerners possessed "as much pride in and reverence for the history and government of their common country as any other civilized and patriotic people." For that reason, Lincoln argued, secessionist leaders had to argue (deceptively, in his view) that withdrawing a state from the Union involved no violation of law but instead was fully consistent with the common Constitution, to which Americans North and South continued to pay respect,[1]

Secessionist leaders obviously did not share Lincoln's view of the constitutionality of secession, much less his view of slavery. However, in another sense their actions and words confirmed Lincoln's point. Most secessionists did not see themselves as breaking with the US Constitution but as saving it: in exiting the Union they believed they carried the old Constitution in their travelling bags. "We have changed the constituent parts, but not the system of our Government. The Constitution formed by our fathers is that of these Confederate States," Jefferson Davis announced in his February 18, 1861, Inaugural Address as Provisional President of the Confederate States of America.[2] The Confederacy's vice president, Alexander H. Stephens, likewise assured Southerners, "All the essentials of the old constitution, which have endeared it to the hearts of the American people, have been preserved and perpetuated."[3]

For many Southerners, the ties to what Lincoln called the "common country" remained deep and persistent. It is true that the most enthusiastic secessionists—"Fire-Eaters" such as Robert Barnwell Rhett of South Carolina—felt little attachment to the Union and celebrated its dissolution as a "glorious dawn."[4] But more typical was Davis's anguished Farewell Address to the US Senate (January 21, 1861) upon receiving notice that his home state of Mississippi had seceded from the Union. Davis nostalgically recalled "the kind associations which once existed" between Massachusetts and Mississippi and characterized secession as a painful last resort to which his state had been forced by what he viewed as unconstitutional attacks on slavery.[5] Stephens had been friends with Lincoln when they served together in Congress, exchanged letters with him during the secession crisis, and regarded secession as an overreaction to Lincoln's election.[6] Yet Stephens made clear that if Georgia voted to secede, he considered himself constitutionally obligated to follow; he too would advocate secession if Lincoln, after taking office, began implementing territorial restrictions on slavery.[7]

In this chapter, I examine the political and constitutional reasoning of those Southern leaders who claimed to love and revere what Lincoln called the "common country" and its shared Constitution—yet who argued that this shared Constitution obliged them to secede rather than be governed by a president committed to restricting the territorial expansion of slavery. The chapter features Davis of Mississippi (1808–1889), an anguished secessionist, and Stephens of Georgia (1812–1883), a critic of secession who subsequently fully committed to the Confederate cause. For purposes of contrast I discuss Robert Barnwell Rhett of South Carolina (1800–1876), even though he had zero attachment to the Union and minimal commitment to the Constitution, because he learned he had to clothe his secessionism in constitutional dress to be effective. John C. Calhoun of South Carolina (1782–1850) is central to the inquiry, even though he died a decade before secession, because he set the channels within which nearly every Southern leader argued and acted during the secession crisis.

The specific question I address here is: Why did leaders of the Deep South states decide to secede in response to a procedurally fair election and before Lincoln had even taken office? In one sense the answer is clear: to protect and perpetuate the institution of slavery. The secession declarations of South Carolina, Mississippi, Florida, Alabama, Georgia, Louisiana, and Texas abundantly demonstrate this. But the *immediate* threat to slavery before Lincoln took office was not great enough to explain fully why secession commenced when it did. Moreover, secession carried a nontrivial risk of endangering the very institution—slavery—it was designed to perpetuate.

When Lincoln was elected, slavery was still protected by the Constitution. The two previous presidents, Franklin Pierce (term 1853–1857) and James Buchanan (term 1857–1861), had been unusually receptive to the political demands of slaveholders. Slaveholders' supposed constitutional right to hold slave property in any federal territory had been upheld by the Supreme Court in the *Dred Scott* decision (1857). As a presidential candidate, Lincoln had indeed challenged that decision and promised to contain slavery within its current geographical limits wherever possible. But he had pledged to leave it untouched within those limits. In his First Inaugural Address (March 4, 1861), Lincoln repeated his pledge: "I have no purpose, directly or indirectly, to interfere with the institution of slavery in the States where it exists."[8] In the address,

Lincoln even signaled his willingness to support a constitutional amendment that would have explicitly prevented the federal government from interfering with slavery in the states,[9] and that passed both houses of Congress shortly before his inauguration.[10]

Despite pressure from many in his own party, Lincoln conspicuously refused to retreat from his pledge to restrict slavery in the federal territories.[11] Nor did he retreat from his position that the institution of slavery should ultimately be extinguished on American soil over some long and indefinite time frame. But it was far from clear that as president Lincoln would succeed in enacting the territorial restrictions he sought. If the slave states of the lower South had not seceded, thereby forfeiting their representation in Congress, it would have been difficult, at least in the short term, for Lincoln to secure majority support in both the House and Senate for legislation prohibiting slavery in the territories. If such legislation had passed, it would probably have been declared unconstitutional by the US Supreme Court (still led by Chief Justice Roger Taney) unless in the interim Lincoln had the opportunity to appoint several new justices. In short, there were no rational grounds for slaveholders to fear that Lincoln, as president, would begin attacking slavery in the states;[12] even the territorial restrictions he favored could not have been enacted quickly.

Conversely, secession and the prospect of civil war placed the future of slavery at risk. Southern critics of secession pointed this out during secession debates. Benjamin Perry, a South Carolinian critical of the secessionist enthusiasm sweeping the state, argued that the Union "should be saved as a bulwark against abolition."[13] Stephens likewise considered slavery safe in the Union and endangered by disunion (and the actual outcome of the war certainly lends support to that judgment). Davis recognized that secession could be followed by a civil war that might "bring disaster on every portion of the country,"—which, if it came to pass, would hardly leave the institution of slavery untouched. Yet Davis was nevertheless willing "to proclaim our independence, and take the hazard."[14]

There is no question that slaveholders' highest political priority was to protect slavery. That had been true for decades. But in the immediate aftermath of Lincoln's election, it was by no means clear whether slavery was better protected by seceding from the Union or remaining in it. In this chapter I seek to describe how slaveholders' sense that they had been victims of repeated constitutional outrages tipped the scales in favor of secession. Southerners seceded *not only* to defend slavery but also—they argued—to protect the Constitution, a Constitution under which (as they understood it) every state and every citizen, North as well as South, was morally and constitutionally obligated to do everything possible to protect the institution of slavery and render it more secure. Calhoun is essential to the story because he was the first to lay out this understanding of the Constitution in its full breadth and detail. Davis's understanding of the Constitution was nearly indistinguishable from Calhoun's in this respect.

The Constitution, according to this theory, could be dangerously violated without actually transgressing any of its literal provisions. For the Constitution, in this view, was not merely a written document. The Constitution instead represented a code of conduct—partly written, largely unwritten—regulating states and sections in their interactions with each other. That constitutional code, slaveholders believed, was violated when Northern states permitted abolitionist societies to operate within their boundaries, when Northerners introduced legislation to restrict the territorial expansion of slavery—even if that legislation did not pass, and when an antislavery president was elected on a sectional vote even if that election met all the prescribed forms of the Constitution. My principal aim here is not to evaluate this constitutional theory (which I find problematic for reasons that extend beyond its moral blindness to slavery)[15] but to describe how the sense of constitutional outrage it fed convinced Southern leaders that they were justified, indeed obligated, to secede from the Union when Lincoln was elected.

*CALHOUN'S SOUTHERN LEGACY*

Southern leaders across the political spectrum—Whigs as well as Democrats, committed secessionists as well as critics of secession—looked to Calhoun's legacy for guidance and justification in the decade following Calhoun's death in 1850. "Fire-Eater" Rhett of South Carolina, advocating secession since at least 1844 in opposition to Calhoun's efforts at compromise, suggested that in his dying breath Calhoun had signaled to Rhett that the South must secede.[16] At the other end of the Southern spectrum, Stephens of Georgia, who argued against secession but considered himself obligated by his state's decision, drew extensively from Calhoun's legacy to explain and justify his own course of conduct.[17] Davis, who considered Lincoln's election justifiable cause for secession but viewed it as a tragic loss, was a lifelong admirer and political protégé of Calhoun. Davis accompanied Calhoun's body back to South Carolina in 1850, then returned to the Senate to pick up the sectional struggle where Calhoun's had left off. Though he had been dead for more than ten years, Calhoun's legacy was very much alive in the South in 1860, and it importantly shaped how Southern leaders responded to Lincoln's election.

Calhoun was born in 1782, near the close of the Revolutionary War, and died in 1850, a decade before his state of South Carolina became the first to secede from the Union. He served in the US House during the War of 1812, then as President James Monroe's secretary of war, as vice president under John Quincy Adams and Andrew Jackson, as President John Tyler's secretary of state, and as US senator from South Carolina for nearly two decades. He was an innovative political and constitutional theorist who offered an incisive analysis of how majority rule can evolve into majority tyranny and an intriguing, if problematic, consensus model of government as remedy to the pathologies of majority rule.[18]

Calhoun was also a slaveholder and in 1837 became one of the first prominent Southern leaders to defend slavery as a "positive good," not merely a difficult-to-remove evil.[19] At first Calhoun's unapologetic defense of slavery went too far even for some senators from slave states.[20] But by the 1850s Calhoun's view was orthodoxy in the South.

Calhoun's political and constitutional thought, considered as a whole, cannot be dismissed as a mere rationalization for slavery. Many elements of his theory, including his diagnosis of majority tyranny and his consensus model of government, are logically separable from his defense of slavery. But Calhoun himself argued that slavery provided "the most safe and stable basis for free institutions in the world";[21] it was no accident, in his view, that the classical republics of Greece and Rome were slaveholding societies. In contrast, abolitionism (he argued) exhibited majority tyranny at its worst because it clothed the pursuit of Northern political and economic interests in the garb of a moral crusade.

During the first half of Calhoun's long political career (from 1810 until the mid-1820s) he was distinguished for his nationalism. In the late 1820s, principally in response to the 1828 "Tariff of Abominations" (which he saw as an attempt by Northern manufacturers to fleece Southern planters), but also anticipating threats to slavery, he became a committed advocate of full state sovereignty, state nullification of federal law, and a constitutional right of secession. Yet secession was precisely what he hoped to avoid. He envisioned nullification, whereby a state refuses to permit the implementation of a particular federal law within its own boundaries, as a means by which disaffected states could resist federal policies they regarded as unconstitutional or unjust without being driven to the extreme of secession.[22]

Most important about Calhoun's influence on antebellum Southern leaders was its radically double-edged character. Depending on circumstances, Calhoun's example could function either as glue to hold the Union together or as acid hastening its dissolution. Calhoun himself believed his political and constitutional prescriptions, if followed, would resolve sectional disputes and perpetuate the Union. Though he claimed each state had a constitutional right to secede, he contemplated with dread the actual prospect of disunion. In an 1838 letter he compared secession to a bloody "knife of separation through a body politic . . . which has been so long bound together by so many ties, political, social, and commercial." Yet in the same letter, penned at the height of his campaign to ban antislavery speech from the halls of Congress, Calhoun wrote, "We cannot and ought not to live as we are at present, exposed to the continued attacks and assaults of the other portion of the Union." If abolitionist agitation did not ultimately cease, the South would "stand justified before God and man in taking the final step"—secession. But every other means "of arresting the evil" (abolitionism) must first be exhausted.[23]

Calhoun believed that the key to defeating the abolitionist threat, and thus perpetuating both the Union and slavery, lay in coming to a comprehensive national agreement that all branches of the federal government, as well as every state, North as well as South, had a constitutional obligation to do everything in its power to uphold and strengthen the institution of slavery and to refrain from any action or speech that weakened slavery. On December 27, 1837, Calhoun introduced to the US Senate a series of resolutions concerning slavery and the Union.[24] The catalyst for his resolutions was an antislavery memorial passed by the Vermont legislature and presented to the US Senate by one of Vermont's senators. Calhoun characterized Vermont's action as "a deep and dangerous blow into the vitals of our confederacy" because it violated "the mutual and solemn pledge" each state had made, when it entered the Union, to reciprocally uphold and support the institutions of its fellow states. Vermont had also "grossly insulted" slaveholders and the citizens of slaveholding states. The federal government, Calhoun argued, and every one of the state governments, had "a high and sacred trust" to exercise its powers so as to give "increased stability and security to the domestic institutions of the States that compose the Union."[25] These constitutional obligations were to be enforced, if necessary, by the threat of secession. If his resolutions were rejected, Calhoun warned, "he would consider it as throwing down all constitutional barriers in the way of the abolitionists" and a sign to the South that it could not safely remain in the Union.[26]

Beyond his immediate aim, to prevent the US Senate from receiving any abolitionist petitions, Calhoun's purpose in the resolutions was to address a wide range of recent threats to slavery that slave states could not effectively counter simply by blocking the implementation of federal laws within their own boundaries. South Carolina could nullify the protective tariffs of 1828 and 1832 both in theory and in practice by declaring Charleston an "open port" and refusing to collect import duties. But most threats to slavery could not be blocked in any comparable way. No one in Congress was proposing to abolish slavery within the boundaries of South Carolina or any other slave state. Any such proposal would have clearly violated the antebellum Constitution and if attempted would have meant immediate civil war.

Most immediate threats to slavery, instead, concerned action or policy outside the borders of slave states that could not be "nullified" as the tariff had been. Such threats included abolitionist resolutions introduced to Congress, the wider work of abolitionist societies active in Northern states, and proposals to abolish slavery or the slave trade in the District of Columbia (over which Congress has constitutional jurisdiction) and in federally administered western territories. These antislavery initiatives were diverse in origin and character. But what they all had in common was, first, that none of them violated the letter of the US Constitution (and some, like the right of petition, were explicitly guaranteed); and second, that slave states could do little about them by direct action within the boundaries of their own states or by invoking their reserved powers to run their states their own way. (This is why the often-expressed view that slave states before the Civil War only wanted the federal government to "leave them alone" is so misleading.[27]) These threats-beyond-boundaries could be met only by a much more aggressive response and a new interpretation of the Constitution. That was how Calhoun's legacy became decisive in shaping Southern constitutional thought and political strategy in the final decades before the Civil War.

Thus the wider purpose behind Calhoun's December 27, 1837, slavery resolutions was to articulate a constitutional theory that would (1) make it a clear duty of the federal government positively to support and strengthen the institution of slavery, not merely refrain from interfering with it—yet do so in a way that respected the full sovereignty of states; and (2) make clear to Northern states their duty, as members of the federal partnership, not to engage in or tolerate any action by or within their states that threatened slavery.

From the perspective of these constitutional principles, to attack slavery, as Vermont had done by presenting an antislavery memorial to the Senate, was therefore a violation of the Constitution. Calhoun admitted his claim that Vermont had acted unconstitutionally was based upon "no particular portion of the Constitution." (On the contrary, the First Amendment of the Constitution specifically guarantees citizens the right to "petition the government for redress of grievances.") Instead the constitutional principle Vermont had violated by presenting an antislavery memorial was grounded in the Constitution's "general character and structure," and on what Calhoun called "the higher elements of our system."

The Constitution's "higher elements," likewise, in Calhoun's view, prohibited Congress from restricting slavery or the slave trade in the District of Columbia (even though Article I, Section 8 of the Constitution grants Congress the power "to exercise exclusive Legislation in all Cases whatsoever, over such District") or in the federal territories (even though Article IV, Section 3 grants Congress power to "make all needful Rules and Regulations respecting the Territory or other Property belonging to the United States"). To restrict the spread of slavery to new territories, Calhoun's resolutions held, violated the "equality of rights and advantages" that must exist among members of a federal union. To refuse to the slave states "any advantage which would tend to strengthen, or render them more secure, or increase their limits or population by the annexation of new territories or states . . . would be contrary to that equality of rights and advantages which the Constitution was intended to secure alike to all the members of the Union, and would, in effect, disenfranchise the slaveholding states."[28] Moreover, in Calhoun's view, for Congress to provide antislavery proposals of this kind a public platform—even if they were not enacted into law—violated this fundamental constitutional ethic.

This helps us understand why the election of a president in 1860 who publicly condemned slavery and voiced opposition to its future expansion was seen by many Southern leaders as ample justification for secession even before that president had taken office. In his First Inaugural Address, Lincoln asked, "Is it true, then, that any right, plainly written in the Constitution, has been denied? I think not."[29] But from Calhoun's perspective and that of Southern leaders steeped in his thought, such constitutional literalism was beside the point. For Southerners—following Calhoun—the Constitution represented a code of conduct, largely unwritten, Northern voters had violated by electing Lincoln.

Calhoun's six slavery resolutions of December 1837 played a critical role in shaping Southern constitutional thought and political strategy in the years that followed. Rhett, who at the time represented South Carolina in the US House, helped publicize Calhoun's resolutions—though Rhett already sought to push Southern resistance further than Calhoun was willing to go.[30] In May 1860,

Davis introduced to the US Senate a set of resolutions in a substantial portion of which the text was identical to Calhoun's six resolutions of 1837. Stephens, writing after the Civil War to justify his own course of conduct, quoted at length from Calhoun's 1837 slavery resolutions—though Stephens revealingly omitted the passages in which Calhoun's resolutions described the duty of all states to give "increased security and stability" to the institution of slavery.[31]

In 1849 Calhoun penned his Southern Address, which reiterated the main themes and arguments of his 1837 resolutions, updated to address recent developments, including the status of slavery in the vast territories acquired through the Mexican War. The address warned Southerners of a "whole series of aggression and encroachment on our rights," including Northern states' refusal to return fugitive slaves, the continued "systematic agitation" of the slavery question by Northern abolitionist societies, and recent attempts in Congress "to exclude slavery from all the territories of the United States, acquired, or to be acquired." Like his 1837 resolutions, Calhoun's Southern Address argued that in ratifying the Constitution, Northern states had pledged "their faith, in the most solemn manner, sacredly to observe" the constitutional provisions recognizing and protecting slavery. This faith had been repeatedly violated. Even worse, if Northerners succeeded in excluding slavery from all federal territories—the nursing ground of future states—the North would eventually control "a sufficient number of states to give her three fourths of the whole" and thereby abolish slavery by constitutional amendment, contrary to the "true intent" of the document.[32] Calhoun thus recognized the possibility that slavery could in the long run be abolished through regular constitutional channels. He was willing to resort to arms to prevent this from happening.

His address argued that Southerners should sooner secede from the Union than submit to such "aggression and encroachment." But the address did not call for secession. Its purpose instead was to urge Southern political leaders, whether Democrat or Whig, to set aside their party attachments and "be united among yourselves." "If you become united, and prove yourselves in earnest, the North will be brought to a pause, and to a calculation of consequences; and that may lead to a change of measures, and the adoption of a course of policy that may quietly and peaceably terminate this long conflict between the two sections." A firmly united South, in short, would persuade the North to change its behavior: to faithfully return fugitive slaves, suppress abolitionist societies, and recognize slaveholders' right to hold slave property in any federal territory. But if the North was foolish enough to persist in its current course, then Southerners would have to be ready to "resort to all means necessary" to defend their "rights . . . property, prosperity, equality, liberty, and safety." The address did not precisely spell out the circumstances under which secession would become necessary, observing only that "we think it would not be proper to go at present" beyond the formation of a united political front.[33]

Calhoun's Southern Address was signed by 48 of the 124 members of Congress representing Southern states.[34] Rhett (representing South Carolina in the House) and Davis (senator from Mississippi) were among the signers. A majority of Southern Democrats signed the address; most Southern Whigs did not, including Stephens (House member from Georgia). It was not, however, disagreements with Calhoun over slavery that motivated Stephens's opposition to the Southern Address. As we will see, Stephens was no less committed to slavery than Calhoun and frequently invoked Calhoun's authority on matters of constitutional interpretation. What Stephens and other Southern Whigs opposed was Calhoun's effort to form, in the name of Southern unity, what would in effect be an explicitly Southern political party.[35] This threatened to cripple both the Whigs and the Democrats as national political parties. That might indeed have been part of Calhoun's aim in the Southern Address, because he saw national, patronage-fueled political parties as inherently corrupt and inclined to majority despotism.[36] Stephens, however, feared that the formation of a Southern political party was a step toward secession.[37] Like many others (including Stephen Douglas),[38] Stephens saw national political parties that included both Northern and Southern members as critical ties holding the Union together.[39]

As it turned out, in 1860 the fatal split in the Democratic Party was critical in the series of events culminating in secession. Among those engineering that split was Rhett.

## *ROBERT BARNWELL RHETT: ENTHUSIASTIC SECESSIONIST*

In Lincoln's First Inaugural Address, he directed his appeal to those Americans, North and South, "who really love the Union." He acknowledged, however, that there were some Americans "who seek to destroy the Union at all events, and are glad of any pretext to do it." To these he admitted he had nothing to say.[40]

Rhett, the chief architect of South Carolina's secession, was one of those who sought to "destroy the Union at all events." In 1838, as the Senate was debating Calhoun's six slavery resolutions, Rhett drafted House resolutions of his own calling for dissolution of the Union unless the Constitution was amended to give increased protection to slavery.[41] Rhett had publicly decided for secession as early as 1844, when the House of Representatives repealed the "gag rule" and began allowing slavery to be debated in the chamber. Rhett's central argument for secession was that "a people, owning slaves, are mad, or worse than mad, who do not hold their destinies in their own hands."[42] Rhett displayed none of Calhoun's anguish over the prospect of a severed Union. Instead Rhett predicted a glowing future for a wealthy, powerful, expansionist, slaveholding "glorious Southern Confederacy." Continued union with Northerners filled him with disgust.[43] Rhett, who had succeeded Calhoun in 1850 as US senator from South Carolina, resigned in protest in 1852 over South Carolina's unwillingness to secede immediately from the Union.[44] If Lincoln was correct in claiming that most Southerners still possessed "pride in and reverence for the history and government" of the United States, Rhett and the other Fire-Eaters represent exceptions but crucial exceptions because they drove the politics that produced secession.

Rhett recognized that he was an exception. He knew that he was working to dissolve a Union to which most Southerners were still attached. This is what makes his shifting tactics instructive. From 1844 until the early 1850s, Rhett had urged secession as an act of "revolution" on the model of 1776. To call for "revolution" is to claim a natural (not constitutional) right to act against existing constitution and law. During the political crisis of 1850, Rhett proclaimed, "I am a Traitor . . . a Traitor in the great cause of liberty, fighting against tyranny and oppression."[45]

But Rhett found that his call for revolution was not catching on, even in South Carolina. So he changed his approach. Eric Walther, in his study of the Fire-Eaters, writes that by the end of 1851, "Rhett realized that his clarion call for a southern revolution had cost him more support than it attracted." "With this realization came a determination to stand his message on its head. Henceforth, Rhett would not only deny that the South entertained revolutionary intentions but would accuse the North of overthrowing the Constitution and waging an aggressive, methodical campaign against the conservative and passive South."[46] "I have never been an enemy of the constitutional Union," Rhett assured a gathering of Virginia Democrats in 1859. "I am not now."[47] But in fact, behind the scenes, Rhett was working to cripple the Democratic Party nationally, thereby ensuring Republican victory in the 1860 election, because he predicted—correctly, as it turned out—that this outcome would provide the necessary trigger for secession.[48] The prevalent view among Southern leaders had been that secession, if and when that step was taken, had to be "cooperative," that is, the joint and simultaneous act of a united South. Rhett instead predicted (again correctly) that if a single slave state seceded, it could force the other slave states to follow.[49] To work, Rhett's strategy required a constitutional theory that could justify a state's decision unilaterally to secede in response to the results of a procedurally fair election. Calhoun's constitutional theory and political legacy turned out to be essential for this purpose.

Calhoun and Rhett had enjoyed a long-lasting, though often stormy, political friendship.[50] At several key points over the years they pushed in opposite directions. Shortly after supporting Calhoun's presidential campaign, for example, Rhett broke with Calhoun by founding the openly secessionist Bluffton Movement of 1844, which Calhoun effectively squelched. Yet Calhoun until his death continued to work with Rhett.[51]

The central importance, as well as the ambiguity, of Calhoun's legacy is revealed by the (possibly invented) anecdote Rhett told about the dying Calhoun's final political statement.

After Calhoun collapsed in the lobby of the Senate shortly before his death, Rhett claimed, he extended his hand and said: "Ah! Mr. Rhett, my career is nearly done. The great battle must be fought by you younger men." . . . "Had his mighty spirit devised some way to save the Union, consistent with the liberties of the South? Or did he wish to utter there that word which all his lifetime he could not speak, although wrong and oppression tortured him—that word, which dying despair could alone wring from his aching heart—disunion!!"[52]

Rhett's story of Calhoun's supposed dying words is significant, whether accurate or not, because it shows the degree to which committed secessionists depended on Calhoun's legacy to justify actually taking the final, fateful step. If Calhoun could be presented as ultimately endorsing secession, his authority would carry more weight than that of anyone else.

There is no other evidence that Calhoun actually called for secession at the end of his life, nor that he specifically designated Rhett as his political successor. Nevertheless, it is not implausible to conclude, as did at least one reader of the *Charleston Mercury* in 1858, that Rhett represented "the logical consequence of Mr. Calhoun."[53] For in his final speech in the Senate (March 4, 1850), Calhoun had set forth a number of conditions, the fulfillment of which he regarded as morally and constitutionally obligatory. If those conditions were fulfilled, Calhoun argued, it would not only preserve the Union but also "improve and strengthen the Government" to the advantage of all, North and South. If, however, those conditions were not met, it would show that the North was unwilling "to perform her duties under the Constitution," and it was time for the South to separate—peacefully if possible but by force of arms if necessary.[54]

Those conditions were as follows: (1) The Northern states must concede to the South "an equal right in the acquired territory"—meaning the right of slaveholders to bring and securely hold their slave property in all federally owned territories not yet organized as states; (2) the North must "do her duty by causing the stipulations relative to fugitive slaves to be faithfully fulfilled"; (3) the North must "cease the agitation of the slave question"; and (4) the North must consent to a constitutional amendment that "will restore to the South, in substance, the power she possessed of protecting herself, before the equilibrium between the sections was destroyed by the action of this Government." What Calhoun meant here was a constitutional amendment guaranteeing the South veto rights over national policy, which he believed could be best accomplished by creating a kind of dual presidency, one representing the North and the other the South, each with veto rights over national legislation and over the actions of the other copresident. Calhoun added that if the North remained silent in the face of the South's conditions for remaining in the Union, "you compel us to infer by your acts what you intend."[55]

By 1860 two of Calhoun's conditions had arguably been fulfilled, but in equivocal form; the other two remained clearly unfulfilled. The Compromise of 1850, which passed after Calhoun's death, included a strong fugitive slave clause, one that positively obligated public officials in free states, and even private citizens, to cooperate in capturing fugitive slaves. But the law enraged many in the North and triggered several widely publicized actions of resistance.[56] Calhoun's stated conditions had required not merely the passage of a new fugitive slave law but that the obligation to render fugitive slaves be "faithfully fulfilled" by citizens of the North, and that was not the case. The US Supreme Court in the *Dred Scott* decision (1857) ruled that slaveholders had a right to bring and hold slave property in any federal territory—here endorsing one of Calhoun's key constitutional claims—but this ruling was widely denounced in the North, and many Northern leaders, including Lincoln, aimed to limit the scope of the decision as much as possible and eventually to overturn it.[57] No constitutional amendment was enacted to grant the South formal veto rights over all national policy. The "agitation of the slave question" by Northern abolitionist societies continued and increased over the course of the 1850s. For these reasons Rhett could plausibly portray secessionism as the culmination of Calhoun's work, whether or not Calhoun had blessed this course in his dying breath.

But Rhett had to employ some deception to pull off the secessionist act. In particular he had to pretend to support Democratic victory in the 1860 election when in fact he aimed to cripple the party, ensure Republican victory, and thereby trigger secession. The Democratic Convention convened in Charleston, South Carolina, in April 1860. Rhett realized well in advance that if he could persuade delegates from the Deep South to walk out of the convention, it would be enough to "break down the spoils Democracy and, on the election of a Black Republican, [by which Rhett meant any Republican] to dissolve the Union."[58] The Democratic Party was ripe for division over both platform and presidential nominee. Democratic delegates from the Deep South insisted on platform language and on a presidential nominee affirming that slaveholders had a constitutional right to bring slave property to any federal territory, that neither Congress nor a territorial legislature could deprive them of that right, and that Congress had an obligation to enact slave codes in the territories if the territorial authorities failed to do so. But the leading Democratic presidential nominee, Stephen Douglas, remained committed to his "popular sovereignty" policy (embodied in the 1854 Kansas-Nebraska Act), whereby the territorial inhabitants decided whether slavery would be permitted or prohibited in that territory.

Rhett's strategy for splitting the party was to persuade delegates from Deep South states to withdraw from the convention if the party's presidential nominee did not "clearly endorse the expansion of slavery into the territories."[59] When Douglas and the Northern wing of the party refused to comply with that demand, the delegations from Alabama, Mississippi, Louisiana, South Carolina, Florida, Texas, and Georgia walked out of the convention.[60] Many delegates on both sides of the party division appear to have "clung to an opportunistic notion that later on, some persons unknown, in some fashion unknown, would somehow patch up the split."[61] Davis, for example, supported the walkout strategy in hopes of ultimately securing a Democratic presidential nominee more supportive of slavery than Douglas was.[62] But Rhett "hoped to see the Democratic party destroyed" because this "would ensure a Republican victory and provide southerners with the impetus for secession."[63] The sectional split in the Democratic Party did virtually ensure Republican victory in the 1860 presidential election.

In a certain sense Rhett's party-splitting move followed in Calhoun's footsteps. Calhoun's Southern Address of 1849 (which Rhett signed) likewise demanded that Southerners cast off their loyalties to national political parties and unite in uncompromising defense of slavery. The difference is that Calhoun believed splitting the parties and uniting the South would save the Union by causing Northerners to see the light. Rhett entertained no such hopes. He employed a party-splitting strategy precisely to dissolve the Union.[64]

## JEFFERSON DAVIS: ANGUISHED SECESSIONIST

Davis was no less committed to perpetuating and expanding slavery than Rhett was. Yet in contrast to Rhett, an early and enthusiastic secessionist, Davis was a late and anguished secessionist who apprehended the dangers ahead. In his January 21, 1861, Farewell Address to the US Senate, Davis acknowledged that, in seceding from the Union, his home state of Mississippi "surrenders all the benefits, (and they are known to be many,) deprives herself of the advantages, (they are known to be great,)" and "severs all the ties of affection, (and they are close and enduring,) which have bound her to the Union."[65] Davis hoped the North would let the South go in peace but recognized the possibility of a war that could "bring disaster on every portion of the country." Yet despite his attachment to the Union and his recognizing the possibility of horrific war, "a conviction of pressing necessity" had brought Davis and his state to this decision—"a belief that we are to be deprived in the Union of the rights which our fathers bequeathed to us."[66]

In this speech Davis invoked Calhoun by name, whom he described as "a great man" with a "deep-seated attachment to the Union." Calhoun, Davis reminded the Senate, had been "determined to find some remedy for existing ills short of severance of the ties which bound South Carolina to the other States." Calhoun's Union-preserving efforts had failed, and now it was "necessary and proper" to resort to "a different class of remedies."[67] Thus Davis, like Rhett, invoked the deceased Calhoun's legacy to justify the final step—secession which Calhoun himself had not taken. But unlike Rhett, Davis shared Calhoun's attachment to the Union and his view of secession as a tragic last resort. Davis had served the United States as an officer in the Mexican War, as US senator for more than a decade, and as US secretary of war (1853–1857) only a few years before this anguished speech. When he spoke of the personal and political loss occasioned by secession, Davis was not putting on an act.

Davis had long admired Calhoun, whose career served in many respects as a pattern for his own. According to Davis's biographer William Cooper, "Calhoun had exercised an enormous influence on Jefferson Davis."[68] Calhoun, as secretary of war in 1824, had appointed Davis to the US Military Academy; Davis in turn served as secretary of war three decades later. Both Calhoun and Davis served for many years in the US Senate, where they were allies in urging Southern unity during the sectional crisis of 1849–1850. Davis assumed a central role after Calhoun's death in opposing the Compromise of 1850.[69]

Moreover, Davis closely adhered to Calhoun's view of the Constitution and Union.[70] He shared Calhoun's views on the constitutional status of slavery in the territories and defended slavery with arguments similar to Calhoun's. Like Calhoun, Davis believed that rule by a sectional majority was inherently despotic and specifically rejected the principle that "all men are created equal."[71] Both Calhoun and Davis were willing on occasion to accept territorial compromises on slavery, but only on the condition that those compromises preserved equal power for the South and carried no message that slavery was wrong.[72] Davis, like Calhoun, hoped that strong Southern unity would "produce a reaction in the public feeling of the North" in favor of slaveholders' rights and thereby preserve the Union, but he was prepared to secede if the North did not change its ways.[73]

Like Calhoun, Davis believed that each state was fully sovereign and for that reason followed Calhoun in denying that the United States constituted a "nation."[74] And yet until 1861 Davis was in important respects an American nationalist—indeed a *proslavery nationalist*.[75] He saw no tension between his commitment to slavery and state sovereignty, on one side, and his commitment to an energetic, expansive, militarily powerful United States on the other. Nor did he perceive any contradiction between insisting, on one hand, that the federal government had no constitutional authority whatsoever over slavery, and on the other demanding that the federal government vigorously defend the rights of slaveholders "in vessels or in territories, on the high seas, or on the Pacific slope," indeed "wherever our flag floats."[76]

The constitutional assumption that guided many Republicans before the Civil War was that "freedom was national, slavery local"—that is, federal laws and regulations should assume the universal liberty of all persons except where slavery had been specifically authorized by the laws of a state.[77] Davis, following Calhoun, assumed precisely the opposite. He dismissed as "wholly untrue" the notion that "slavery was established by the laws of the states where it is found, and is purely local in its character." On the contrary, Davis insisted, slaves were "recognized as property by the Constitution of the United States" as well as by "the universal admission of mankind."[78] A Northern state, by right of sovereignty, could enact antislavery regulations within its own boundaries, but its authority to do so did not extend beyond those boundaries. Nor were Northern states absolved of their constitutional obligation to render fugitive slaves. In short, slavery was national—indeed also international and universal; whereas freedom (at least for persons of African descent) was merely local. This helps us understand how Davis could be a genuine American patriot and nationalist who nevertheless considered it necessary for his state to secede rather than be governed by a Republican president. For by condemning slavery and proposing to fence it within the boundaries of existing slave states, Republicans (in Davis's view) had stolen from Southerners the American republic they had loved and served. Secession was the only way of preserving what remained of that republic. "We but tread in the path of our fathers when we proclaim our independence, and take the hazard."[79]

In his proslavery nationalism Davis appears to have been oblivious to the enormous political and moral demands he and the slaveholding South were making upon their Northern compatriots. He saw in Northerners' opposition to the indefinite expansion of slavery only an illegitimate desire for political and economic supremacy, an "aggression upon the people of the South." During debate over the Compromise of 1850 (which he opposed because it admitted California as a free state, among other reasons), Davis argued that Southerners "have never claimed from this Federal Government any peculiar advantages for themselves"; they sought no more or less than to be recognized as "the equals of the North."[80] Yet his actual policy demands—that the federal government must not restrict slavery in any way, including in federally owned territories, but instead legitimize and protect slavery "wherever our flag floats"—could not reasonably have been perceived as neutral in the North. Rhett had concluded by the mid-1840s that Northerners would never fully commit to legitimizing and defending the rights of slaveholders, and thus opted for secession. Davis appears instead to have continued to hope, until the day Lincoln won the 1860 election, that if Southerners remained united and uncompromising in their defense of slavery, Northerners would recognize their error, cease their denunciations of slavery, and come to a mutual understanding with the South.

The full extent of Calhoun's influence on Davis is exemplified by the seven resolutions Davis introduced to the US Senate on May 8, 1860.[81] Davis's 1860 resolutions closely followed the slavery resolutions Calhoun introduced in the Senate on December 27, 1837. (Davis, serving in the US military in 1837, carefully noted Calhoun's resolutions and the ensuing debate at the time.)[82] A side-by-side comparison shows that Davis's 1860 resolutions lifted substantial portions of their text—at least half—from Calhoun's 1837 resolutions. Davis's first resolution, for example, held "that in the adoption of the Federal Constitution, the States adopting the same acted severally as free and independent sovereignties, delegating a portion of their powers to be exercised by the Federal Government for the increased security of each against dangers, *domestic* as well as foreign."[83] Calhoun's first resolution from December 1837 reads "that in the adoption of the Federal Constitution, the States adopting the same acted, severally, as free, independent, and sovereign States; and that each, for itself, by its own voluntary assent, entered the Union with the view to its increased security, against all dangers, *domestic* as well as foreign."[84]

Davis's second resolution says the following about abolitionism: "That all such attacks are in manifest violation of the mutual and solemn pledge to protect and defend each other, given by the States respectively on entering into the constitutional compact which formed the Union, and are a manifest breach of faith, and a violation of the most solemn obligations."[85] Calhoun's fourth resolution of 1837 holds "that all such attacks are in manifest violation of the mutual and solemn pledge to protect and defend each other, given by the States, respectively, on entering into the constitutional compact which formed the Union, and, as such is a manifest breach of faith, and a violation of the most solemn obligations, moral and religious."[86]

Every member of the Senate would have known that Davis had adapted Calhoun's resolutions. Davis was making the point that Calhoun's understanding of the Constitution, slavery, and abolitionism was no less true and relevant in 1860 than it was in 1837. Davis explained that he was introducing these resolutions because "here I ask the Senate to declare great truths to-day, and for all time to come, to bring back the popular judgment to the standard of the Constitution."[87] Clearly, for Davis, it was Calhoun who had clarified once and for all "the standard of the Constitution." Davis maintained in 1860 that only such a constitutional understanding could save the Union; Calhoun had argued the same from 1837 until his death.

Thus both Calhoun and Davis adhered to a constitutional understanding that, in the guise of impartiality and noninterference, was in fact affirmatively proslavery and made enormous demands upon the North. There was, however, a subtle but important difference between Calhoun and Davis. Calhoun had a keener sense than Davis did of the degree of opposition such a stance would encounter in the North. This contrast comes across in the only significant political disagreement between the two during Calhoun's lifetime: Calhoun's opposition to the Mexican War in contrast to Davis's enthusiastic support and personal participation. By 1846 Calhoun had already spent nearly a decade combatting antislavery proposals in Congress; he recognized the strength of the antislavery impulse, however pernicious he considered it. For this reason Calhoun opposed the expansionist aims of those calling for war with Mexico, recognizing from the outset that acquiring vast new territories would heighten the slavery conflict and further endanger the Union.[88]

Davis displayed no such awareness. He assumed as a matter of course that the southwestern territories newly acquired from Mexico would become slave territories and slave states and was confident that Northern Democrats (the party whose expansionism caused the war) would show themselves "the natural allies of the South, and will meet us upon just constitutional ground."[89] Throughout the 1850s he continued to believe—contrary to the evidence—that the Democratic Party, North and South, would remain united in defense of what he considered slaveholders' unquestionable rights in the federal territories. He appears to have regarded President Buchanan—who was unusually supportive of slavery—as "the representative northern Democrat."[90] Both Rhett and Davis demanded an uncompromisingly proslavery stance from the Democratic Party in 1860. Rhett, however, did so deliberately to cripple the party and trigger secession. In contrast Davis appeared genuinely shocked when as a result the party became fatally divided, virtually assuring Republican victory in the election.[91] He felt personally betrayed to discover that not even President Buchanan fully supported the South's constitutional claims.[92] Secession, when it occurred, was in his view entirely the fault of the North for its "wanton aggression" upon Southerners. The latter had responded as honor and duty required and therefore were entirely absolved of responsibility for the breakup of the Union that Davis had served and loved.[93]

## ALEXANDER STEPHENS: CRITIC OF SECESSION

President-elect Lincoln on December 22, 1860, wrote a private letter to Stephens of Georgia, who less than two months later became vice president of the Confederate States of America. Lincoln and Stephens had served together in the House of Representatives in the late 1840s as fellow Whigs and critics of the Mexican War. (Both Calhoun and Lincoln had admired Stephens's speeches against the Polk administration's war policy.)[94] Lincoln's phrase in his First Inaugural Address, "We are not enemies, but friends. We must not be enemies"[95] might have been penned with Stephens in mind. Stephens was the type of Southern leader Lincoln hoped would remain loyal to the Union. Lincoln knew that Stephens had argued against secession before the Georgia legislature the previous month. In his letter Lincoln assured Stephens, "as once a friend, and still, I hope, not an enemy," that he would not "*directly, or indirectly,* interfere" with Southerners' slavery system: "The South would be in no more danger in this respect than it was in the days of Washington." But Lincoln did not retreat from his commitment to restricting the territorial expansion of slavery. "You think slavery is *right* and ought to be extended; while we think it is *wrong* and ought to be restricted. That . . . is the only substantial difference."[96] In late 1860 Lincoln still hoped that a leader such as Stephens, and a state such as Georgia, could be persuaded not to secede despite what Lincoln admitted was a "substantial difference" over the future of slavery.[97]

In his antisecession speech at the Georgia legislature's secession debate of November 12–19, 1860, Stephens had observed, "That this Government of our fathers, with all its defects, comes nearer the objects of all good governments than any other on the face of the earth, is my settled conviction."[98] In contrast to South Carolina, where the secession vote was unanimous, Georgia's ultimate decision for secession was fairly close.[99] In that respect Lincoln's appeal to Southern unionists, though ultimately unsuccessful, did not appear hopeless in the months following his election. There were certainly secessionists who did not understand, or pretended not to understand, that Lincoln was not John Brown. But Stephens accurately understood Lincoln's position on slavery. Though he deeply disagreed with Lincoln, he did not misrepresent or caricature him.

In his December 30, 1860, reply to Lincoln's letter, Stephens assured Lincoln that "personally, I am not your enemy—far from it" despite how "widely we may differ politically." Stephens acknowledged, "We both have an earnest desire to preserve and maintain the Union of the States, if it can be done upon the principles and furtherance of the objects for which it was formed." He claimed that he, and the people of the South, entertained no fears that "a Republican Administration, or at least the one about to be inaugurated, would attempt to interfere *directly* and *immediately* with slavery in the States." Stephens thus showed he understood that, at least for the moment, Lincoln and the Republicans would leave slavery alone where it already existed. Stephens denounced the self-righteous attitude of those in Lincoln's party who "simply, and wantonly" put the South "under the bar of public opinion and national condemnation" but implied that Lincoln's own antislavery statements did not display that insulting tone.[100] Thus Stephens presented himself, and by extension the people of the South, as free of personal enmity toward the people of the North, capable of appreciating their shared love of country, willing to tolerate respectfully voiced differences of opinion, and accurate in his understanding of the president-elect's position on slavery.[101]

Yet despite all this, Stephens made clear that he *would* support secession if Lincoln succeeded in putting his policies into practice. "If the policy of Mr. Lincoln and his Republican associates shall be carried out, or attempted to be carried out, no man in Georgia will be more willing or ready than myself to defend our rights, interest, and honor at every hazard and to the last extremity," he told the Georgia legislature. Lincoln's policy, Stephens noted, was "for

using the power of the General Government against the extension of our institutions." Echoing Calhoun's 1837 resolutions, Stephens argued that to exclude
slavery from federal territories would violate that "perfect equality between all
the States and the citizens of all the States in the Territories, under the Constitution of the United States" and would therefore justify secession. If Lincoln
were to repeal or weaken the fugitive slave laws, Stephens added, this would
also justify secession. But "I do not think his bare election sufficient cause. . . . I
would wait for an act of aggression."[102] Stephens's continued unionism was thus
conditioned upon Lincoln's inability to implement the central elements of the
platform upon which he had been elected.

Stephens considered it essential that Georgia have adequate constitutional
justification for any action it took. "In my judgment, the election of no man,
constitutionally chosen to that high office, is sufficient cause for any State to
separate from the Union. . . . To make a point of resistance to the Government,
to withdraw from it because a man has been constitutionally elected, puts us in
the wrong. . . . The result was different from what we wished; but the election
has been constitutionally held."[103] Stephens here voiced a principle Lincoln later
emphasized in his July 4, 1861, Message to Congress in Special Session: that
free government cannot endure unless those who lose a fair election respect
its results instead of resorting to armed resistance. Furthermore, Stephens argued, Lincoln himself would be "bound by the constitutional checks which are
thrown around him, which at this time render him powerless to do any great
mischief. . . . The House of Representatives is largely in a majority against him.
. . . In the Senate he will also be powerless." Why then "disrupt the ties of the
Union, when his hands are tied"?[104] Stephens here implicitly made the point
that if Georgia intended to keep Lincoln's action within constitutional limits,
Georgia too had to display respect for constitutional forms.

If in the six months between Lincoln's election and the battle at Fort Sumter there existed some window of opportunity for avoiding civil war, Stephens
and Georgia exemplified that window. It is conceivable that Stephens's position
might have prevailed in Georgia,[105] which in turn might have strengthened
unionism in other Southern states. Yet the conditions Stephens placed upon
his continued willingness to oppose secession show how narrow that window
would have been even if his position had prevailed in Georgia and some other
slave states.[106]

Stephens had long made clear that, despite his unionism, he believed just
as strongly in the rightness of slavery as any secessionist did.[107] He remained a
unionist longer than many other Southerners in part because he believed slavery was safe in the Union and fully protected by the Constitution. In July 1860

he had written that he considered "slavery much more secure in the Union than out of it."[108] At the Georgia secession debate he asked, "Have we not at the South, as well as at the North, grown great, prosperous, and happy under its operation?" Secession, on the other hand, was fraught with great dangers: Southerners might "in an evil hour rashly pull down and destroy those institutions, which the patriotic hand of our fathers labored so hard to build up."[109]

After Georgia seceded and Stephens became vice president of the Confederacy, he delivered his notorious Corner-Stone Speech (March 21, 1861), in which he proclaimed, "Our new government is founded upon . . . the great truth that the negro is not equal to the white man; that slavery, subordination to the superior race is his natural and normal condition."[110] In fact, Stephens simply voiced here what nearly every Confederate leader believed. Except for its explicit commitment to racial hierarchy, which he admitted was a major change, the Confederate Constitution as Stephens described it was fundamentally the old US Constitution with a few improvements on points of detail.[111] Thus even in committing himself fully to the secessionist cause, Stephens reinforced Lincoln's observation that most Southerners still possessed "pride in and reverence for the history and government" of the "common country" and its "national Constitution."[112]

But the US Constitution Stephens defended in arguing against Georgia's secession was not the Constitution as Lincoln understood it; it was much closer to Calhoun's Constitution. Stephens, like Calhoun, argued that each state was fully sovereign and as such had a constitutional right to secede from the Union. Stephens promised the Georgia legislature, "Should Georgia determine to go out of the Union . . . though my views might not agree with them . . . I shall bow to the will of the people."[113] After the war Stephens defended this position at length, drawing from a state-compact theory of the Union virtually identical to Calhoun's.[114] Stephens also followed Calhoun in denying that the federal government could ever constitutionally employ force against a state, for any reason—a point he especially emphasized in his December 30, 1860, letter to Lincoln. "The Union was formed by the consent of Independent Sovereign States. . . . Under our system, as I view it, there is no rightful power in the General Government to coerce a state."[115] After the war, in *A Constitutional View of the Late War between the States,* Stephens supported this position by incorporating a forty-five-page extract from Calhoun's February 26, 1833, Senate speech denouncing the force bill (which authorized President Andrew Jackson to enforce federal tariff laws despite South Carolina's ordinance of nullification).[116]

Thus for Stephens, as for most Southern leaders, by 1860 Calhoun stood as the leading authority on the US Constitution, and this significantly shaped the choices Southern leaders made during the secession crisis. Stephens granted Calhoun this stature even though, in contrast to Davis, Stephens had never been a political disciple of Calhoun and in fact had frequently crossed swords with him when they both served in Congress. In 1849 Stephens had strongly opposed Calhoun's call for a Southern political party, which Stephens believed threatened the Union.[117] Stephens supported the Compromise of 1850, in contrast to Davis, who followed in Calhoun's footsteps by opposing it.[118]

It is true that by 1860 Stephens was echoing Calhoun's argument, affirmed in Chief Justice Taney's *Dred Scott* opinion, that slavery could not be constitutionally excluded from any federal territories. But Stephens had not always taken this view. A survey of Stephens's shifting constitutional positions with respect to slavery in the territories shows that his initial view was very different from Calhoun's, but over time he moved increasingly in Calhoun's direction. During the dispute in 1848 over the status of slavery in the territories acquired from Mexico, Stephens argued that because Mexico had abolished slavery in 1829, slavery remained forbidden there unless and until specifically authorized by the action of the US Congress. At that time Stephens "flatly denied Calhoun's position—that slavery, protected by the Constitution, would automatically follow it and the flag into new territories."[119] (As noted above, Davis echoed Calhoun on this point.) In doing so Stephens was not motivated by opposition to slavery. Yet he was willing, at least in 1848, to accept the de facto free territory status of the Mexican Cession in order to take an explosive, potentially Union-threatening question off the table.

But Calhoun's constitutional theory had by the late 1850s become in effect the common political currency of the South, a currency eventually employed even by those like Stephens who once had declined to follow Calhoun's lead.

## SECESSION: CONSTITUTIONAL OR REVOLUTIONARY?

Southerners believed their states had a right to secede. But that by itself explains very little about *why* the slave states seceded or about how they framed the act. Given most Southerners' strong attachment to both Constitution and Union, and the prospect that secession could trigger bloody conflict and risk the future of slavery, Southerners' abstract belief in a right of secession does not explain their decision actually to go forward with it. What I have sought to describe above, drawing from Calhoun's political and constitutional thought, are the specific political conditions and frames of mind that persuaded Southern leaders such as Davis that secession was not merely permissible but necessary—indeed the only principled course of action under the circumstances.

The purpose of secession was to protect and perpetuate the institution of slavery. But because it was not immediately clear whether slavery would be safer within the Union or out of it, a sense of repeated constitutional injury—that Calhoun's legacy continually renewed—played a key role in convincing Southern leaders that Lincoln's election was itself sufficient justification for secession. Slave-state leaders unquestionably had an enormous political and economic interest in slavery. But that does not mean the constitutional arguments they made can be dismissed. For their constitutional commitments actively shaped *how they understood* their interests and the political strategies they adopted to defend those interests. The same applies, of course, to the interests and constitutional views of those who voted for Lincoln. How Americans understood the Constitution during the sectional crisis mattered. They would have acted differently had they understood the Constitution differently.

The legacy of Calhoun was evident not only in the decision to secede but in the legal framing of secession ordinances and in the public justifications advanced for the act. This was clearest in South Carolina, the first state to secede and the one in which we would expect Calhoun's influence to be significant. But Calhoun's constitutional influence is discernable to varying degrees in the other secession declarations and ordinances of the Deep South states that seceded before Lincoln took office (Mississippi, Florida, Georgia, Alabama, Louisiana, and Texas). I will focus here on how South Carolina framed the act of secession.

In principle, secession can be understood either as an extralegal or as a legal act—either as an act permitted by standing law or one whose justification lies somewhere outside existing law. To invoke a natural "right of revolution," as the American colonists did in 1776, is to seek an extralegal justification. The Declaration of Independence does not claim that the British Constitution authorizes the act but instead justifies it on the basis of Britain's alleged repeated violation of the "unalienable rights" belonging to all human beings. Lincoln too admitted in his First Inaugural Address that the American people possessed a *"revolutionary* right to dismember, or overthrow" their government. He also acknowledged that if "a majority should deprive a minority of any clearly written constitutional right, it might, in a moral point of view, justify revolution—certainly would, if such right were a vital one."[120] But Lincoln knew any right-of-revolution justification for secession was weak under the circumstances. Certainly no "long train of abuses" could have been attributed to either Lincoln himself or to the federal government on December 20, 1860, the date of South Carolina's secession from the Union.

Moreover, a right-of-revolution justification was vulnerable because of the high regard for the US Constitution expressed by all sides in the slavery and secession crisis. Lincoln observed in his July 4, 1861, Message to Congress in Special Session that secessionists would have failed if their plan were seen as involving "*violation* of law"; instead they argued that secession could be effected "*consistently* with the national Constitution."[121] There were indeed some secessionists, such as Rhett, who in the early 1850s had proudly characterized Southern secession as "revolution," but the rhetoric of revolution proved counterproductive and—with the help of Calhoun's constitutional theory—secessionists of all stripes learned to frame the act in constitutional language. By 1860 the assumption had become nearly universal in the South that each state was fully sovereign and as such could legally and constitutionally secede from the Union for any reason at all. Meanwhile other states were obligated by the shared Constitution to permit the seceding state to depart in peace.

The US Constitution was conspicuously silent on the question of secession. (So too was the Constitution of the Confederate States of America.) Thus any constitutional argument for or against secession necessarily took an extratextual form. Calhoun grounded a right of secession on what he argued was the inherent logic of the process by which the US Constitution was ratified. Because each state, exercising its sovereignty, ratified the document individually and separately, and because each state could have chosen not to ratify and thus remain outside the Union, it followed necessarily (Calhoun argued) that states retained their sovereignty intact throughout all stages of the process and could constitutionally revoke their act of ratification and exit the Union at any time.[122]

Lincoln characterized such constitutional theory as "an insidious debauching of the public mind."[123] Whether debauched or not, the constitutional argument worked. Thus in 1860–1861 most (though not all) seceding states followed the lead of South Carolina in framing the act as a literal *unsigning* of the Constitution—as the revocation of a specifically dated past act by which that state ratified or otherwise affirmed the US Constitution.[124] South Carolina's December 20, 1860, Ordinance of Secession (a separate, briefer document than the Declaration of Causes of Secession) reads as follows in its entirety: "That the Ordinance adopted by us in Convention, on the twenty-third day of May in the year of our Lord One Thousand Seven hundred and eighty-eight, whereby the Constitution of the United States of America was ratified, and also all Acts and parts of Acts of the General Assembly of this State, ratifying amendment of the said Constitution, are here by repealed; and that the union now subsisting between South Carolina and other States, under the name of 'The United States of America,' is hereby dissolved." To frame secession as a purely constitutional act was essential for enlisting the kind of constitutional reverence Lincoln referred to in his July 4, 1861, Message to Congress in Special Session.

To portray secession as a constitutional act, rather than invoking the *natural* right of revolution, was important for another reason: natural rights claims could likewise be made by slaves or by abolitionists on their behalf. By the logic of natural right, slaves would have as much right to "secede" from slave owners as slave owners had to secede from the Union. If the escalating logic of revolution took that course, secessionists would then have effected precisely the opposite of what they intended, which was to render slavery more secure. If instead secession was viewed as a constitutional right inhering not in individuals but in states as corporate bodies, then slaves obviously could not make comparable claims.

Calhoun himself specifically rejected the philosophy of natural rights—the notion that human beings were by nature free and equal—which the Declaration of Independence had invoked. A number of "great and dangerous errors," Calhoun wrote, originate in "the prevalent opinion that all men are born free and equal;—than which nothing can be more unfounded and false."[125] He made clear that abolitionism was among these "most false and dangerous of political errors" resulting from the mistaken theory that "all men are born free and equal."[126] Thomas Jefferson, Calhoun added, had made a mistake in inserting such dangerous language into the Declaration of Independence. Moreover, it was unnecessary for justifying the colonists' decision to break with Britain. "Breach of our chartered principles, and lawless encroachment on our acknowledged and well established rights by the parent country, were the real causes, and of themselves sufficient, without resorting to any other, to justify the step."[127] Thus the colonies, in Calhoun's view, apparently had a right under the British Constitution to break with the British Empire; natural rights arguments were superfluous and pernicious.

It would logically follow that secession in the American context should likewise refer to constitutional forms and chartered principles and avoid invoking a right of revolution. As it turned out, no seceding state, with the possible exception of Tennessee, principally grounded the act on the natural right of revolution. But the constitutional justification, and the parallels with Calhoun's own constitutional theory, are clearest in South Carolina.

As noted above, South Carolina's secession ordinance, consistent with the notion that a sovereign state can secede for any reason at all, is a straightforward unsigning of the Constitution. But South Carolina published a separate document, Declaration of the Immediate Causes Which Induce and Justify the Secession of South Carolina from the Federal Union.[128] The constitutional case for secession closely followed the criteria Calhoun himself had laid out in his March 4, 1850, Senate speech and used those criteria to argue that secession had been justified since at least 1852. (Rhett chaired the committee that produced this declaration; the principal drafter was Christopher Memminger.) The first grievance the declaration lists as justifying secession is that "fourteen of the States have deliberately refused, for years past, to fulfill their constitutional obligations" to return fugitive slaves. This grievance, it is important to note, was not directed against the federal government (which, the declaration itself reports, had enacted fugitive slave laws) but against the behavior of fellow states and their citizens, which had "enacted laws which either nullify the Acts of Congress or render useless any attempt to execute them." Because of such behavior the constitutional compact "has been deliberately broken" and "the consequence follows that South Carolina is released from her obligation."

The next specific justification for secession likewise concerns the conduct of Northern *states*, not that of the federal government. "Fifteen of the States . . . have assumed the right of deciding upon the propriety of our domestic institutions. . . . They have denounced as sinful the institution of slavery; they have permitted open establishment among them of societies, whose avowed object is to disturb the peace and eloign [carry off] the property of the citizens of other States." Calhoun had made clear in his final Senate speech that Northern states must cease "the agitation of the slave question" if the South were to remain in the Union. That by 1860 the Northern states had not suppressed such societies but instead had continually "permitted" their "open establishment among them" was, according to the declaration, just cause for secession. There were actually two separate injuries alleged here: first, the insult from Northern states when they presumed themselves morally superior and entitled to pass judgment on "the propriety of our domestic institutions"; and second, the danger that abolitionist "books and pictures" would incite slaves to "servile insurrection."[129]

Neither of these two central justifications for secession referred to actions by the federal government; the Declaration of Causes did not allege any "long train of abuses" by the federal government (though it charged Northern states with a pattern of violations). The federal abuses listed as justifying secession were placed instead in a hypothetical future. The election of a president "whose opinions and purposes are hostile to slavery" and whose party "has announced that the South shall be excluded from the common territory" (another of Calhoun's criteria for secession) justified immediate separation from the Union because on March 4, 1861, the federal government "will have become" the open enemy of the slaveholding states, following upon the pattern already set by Northern states for more than a decade.

South Carolina's act of secession thus was not presented as an act of revolution but as a constitutional act, justified by Northerners' violations of that Constitution. But apart from Northern states' unwillingness to comply with fugitive slave laws, the alleged constitutional violations listed in the declaration—such as "denouncing as sinful the institution of slavery"—were violations only in the wider, extratextual, code-of-conduct sense Calhoun had set forth in 1837. In this way and many others, Calhoun's legacy was essential for enabling secessionists, including Fire-Eaters such as Rhett, who had once spoken the language of revolution, to characterize secession as a purely legal and constitutional act and to persuade Southerners that they had been victims of deep and persistent constitutional injuries.

## CONCLUSION

Lincoln was correct in observing that most Southerners remained attached to "the history and government of their common country." This was certainly true for Calhoun, Davis, Stephens, and many other Southern leaders whom this chapter might have portrayed. Rhett, who did not share that attachment, had to operate politically among a Southern majority who did. Some secessions occur among peoples who regard each other as deeply foreign. The Southern state secession of 1860–1861 was not of that kind.

But Lincoln's hope that a shared Constitution and political traditions, enduring "bonds of affection," and "mystic chords of memory"[130] would enable Americans to resolve the secession crisis proved misplaced. In many respects the presence of a shared Constitution heightened the dispute, just as bitter religious wars are sometimes fought among rival devotees of the same sacred text.

The American Civil War has sometimes been portrayed as resulting from a "tragic misunderstanding" between North and South.[131] It is certainly true that both sides underestimated the other side's willingness to fight. It is also the case, as Daniel Crofts points out, that secessionist demagogues persuaded many Southerners, contrary to fact, that Lincoln and the Republicans were "bloodthirsty abolitionists."[132] But whether more accurate judgment in this respect would have radically altered the course of events is an open question. Davis, as noted above, foresaw the possibility of a horribly destructive war, but this did not deter him. Lincoln and Stephens appear to have understood each other with perfect clarity during the secession crisis. Yet Stephens had warned that he would support secession if Lincoln, after taking office, began implementing territorial restrictions on slavery. Lincoln refused to retract that commitment. Between Lincoln and Stephens the real tragedy was that there was no misunderstanding. South Carolina's Declaration of the Causes of Secession accurately noted that Lincoln believed "the public mind must rest in the belief that slavery is in the course of ultimate extinction"[133] but treated this as sufficient justification for secession.

On the other hand, the evidence presented in the chapter does not entirely support the "irrepressible conflict"[134] thesis—or at least the version of the thesis that holds that long, bloody civil war over slavery had been inevitably building for decades.[135] Certainly the room for movement on either side following Lincoln's election to the presidency was extremely narrow; Stephens effectively exhausted that field, at least as far as the lower South was concerned. Lincoln would not back down on his commitment to territorial restrictions, and the slave states would not back down on their opposition to such restrictions.

But Stephens's argument that Lincoln could be prevented from enacting his restrictive agenda if the slave states remained in the Union cannot be easily dismissed, and it opens up a field of political scenarios not limited to civil war. Some of these scenarios are morally disturbing, entailing, for instance, political capitulation on the part of Republican members of Congress or a backlash from Northern voters against the Republican Party in future elections. Stephens himself speculated that if the South refrained from secession, "by 1875 or 1890 Massachusetts" might "vote with South Carolina and Georgia upon all those questions that now distract the country and threaten its peace and existence."[136] That scenarios other than civil war might have been possible does not necessarily mean they were attractive ones.

But it is impossible adequately to evaluate the question of alternatives to civil war if we begin only after Lincoln's election. An unfractured Democratic Party in 1860 might have altered the course of events. The tensions within the party existed in any case, but breaking up the convention and throwing the election to the Republicans was, at least in Rhett's case, a deliberate strategy.

Going back further, presidents and Supreme Court justices somewhat less favorable to the extreme proslavery position during the 1850s might have dampened Southerners' conviction that their demands were constitutionally beyond question as well as their expectation that they could continue to dominate the federal government in the future as they had in the past.

In this respect Davis is especially instructive. For Davis—whose outlook was more typical of the Deep South than Rhett's was—it was not hatred of the Union that motivated secession but a certain view of what the Union ought to be, in his own experience had often been, and could have continued to be had it not been betrayed by the election of an openly antislavery president. In Davis's view (as well as Calhoun's), the United States was a Union in which slavery had been constitutionally blessed from the very beginning, in which a slaveholder was considered as good a man as any other—if not better, in which abolitionism was regarded as unconstitutional as well as unpatriotic, and in which one section of the country did not presume to tell another what to do (except when that section had right on its side, as Southerners believed they did).

To what degree Davis's (and Calhoun's) view of the Constitution accurately reflected what was intended with respect to slavery when the Constitution was framed and ratified is a question that would take us too far afield.[137] What matters here is that over the course of Davis's own political career, the federal government *had* usually operated as the slavery-friendly agency he believed it should be. It was true that slavery had been under attack in 1850, but this was succeeded by the slavery-friendly presidencies of Pierce, for whom Davis served as secretary of war, and Buchanan. Until Lincoln's election, Davis had reasonable grounds for believing that slaveholders would continue to prevail whenever slavery was challenged. Don Fehrenbacher observes, "The policy of the federal government down through the years, despite several conspicuous exceptions, had been predominantly supportive of slavery. . . . That was the impression given by the national capital. That was the image presented in diplomacy to the rest of the world. And that had become the law of the land by edict of the Supreme Court. . . . But with Lincoln's election, all was suddenly changed."[138] The bitterest divorces occur when one learns that one's partner is in truth very different than one has imagined him or her to be. Southern leaders initiated the political divorce of 1860–1861 for similar reasons.

Finally, if we are looking for crucial moments in antebellum history that set the channels tending toward secession and civil war (though perhaps not with iron necessity), we should carefully examine the revolution in Southern constitutional thought inaugurated by Calhoun. It is true that many of the elements in Calhoun's view of slavery and the Constitution were anticipated by others. But he assembled those elements into a comprehensive political and constitutional vision of unrivalled breadth and detail. Calhoun's defense of slavery was made incalculably stronger by the way in which he interwove slavery with everything else in his constitutional fabric.

Slaveholders and slave states would have had a powerful political, economic, and psychological interest in defending the institution of slavery whether Calhoun had come along or not. What Calhoun did was to provide slaveholders a good constitutional conscience that they would otherwise have lacked. To be seen as defending an institution out of simple self-interest—whether it be slavery, monarchy, or anything else—is to play a politically weak hand. A *constitutional* defense was essential if slavery was to endure, one that extended beyond the specific constitutional clauses that protected slavery without naming it. For antislavery leaders had discovered many ways to act against slavery without violating the letter of the Constitution.

Calhoun's constitutional revolution did far more than merely engage slave-holders' self-interest. By presenting itself as the formula for saving a troubled Union, Calhoun's constitutional vision appealed to the shared love of a common country. It connected defense of slavery with all of the other things a constitution is supposed to do, including ensuring equality among citizens and preventing majority tyranny. From Calhoun's sweeping perspective, for Congress to restrict—or even to debate whether to restrict—slavery in federal territories was not just an incursion on property rights. It was at the same time corrupt party politics, a violation of state sovereignty, the tyranny of a sectional majority over a sectional minority, the violation of a solemn obligation binding on all states and their citizens to defend and strengthen the institution of slavery, and the destruction of republican equality—for it meant that one class of citizens (Northerners) had access to federal lands while another (Southerners) was unjustly excluded. (To point out that Southerners themselves would not be excluded from the territories—they just had to show up without slaves—would from Calhoun's perspective simply reinforce the point.) For Northern states to permit abolitionist societies to operate was likewise in Calhoun's view a perversion of constitutional equality because it presumed that one class of citizens, and one group of states, could set themselves up as morally superior to another. (Calhoun did not of course extend this principle of republican equality to persons of African descent.)

By elevating to the level of a constitutional violation every restriction on slavery, actual or proposed, every instance of antislavery speech, and every perceived insult to the South, and then sanctioning those alleged constitutional prohibitions with threats of secession, Calhoun set an example—subsequently followed by other Southern leaders—that radically narrowed the range of what democratic politics would be permitted to address. If there was any chance of resolving the slavery conflict peacefully, it could not have been accomplished in the first few months of 1861. It would have had to be the painstaking political work of decades. Calhoun helped ensure that such a politics was foreclosed before it could commence. Calhoun's denigration of democratic politics—accomplished in the name of purifying and elevating politics—prepared the ground for Southern leaders' judgment after November 1860 that losing a fairly conducted election was adequate justification for secession.

## NOTES

1. Abraham Lincoln, Message to Congress in Special Session, July 4, 1861, in *Abraham Lincoln: Speeches and Writings, 1859–1865,* ed. Don E. Fehrenbacher (New York: Library of America, 1989), 254–255.

2. Jefferson Davis, Inaugural Address as Provisional President of the Confederate States of America, February 18, 1861, in *Jefferson Davis: The Essential Writings,* ed. William J. Cooper, Jr. (New York: Library of America, 2004), 202.

3. Alexander H. Stephens, Corner-Stone Speech, March 21, 1861, http://teaching americanhistory.org/library/document/cornerstone-speech/.

4. Eric H. Walther, *The Fire-Eaters* (Baton Rouge: Louisiana State University Press, 1992), 154.

5. Jefferson Davis, Farewell Address in US Senate, January 21, 1861, in *Jefferson Davis: The Essential Writings,* ed. William J. Cooper, Jr. (New York: Library of America, 2004), 190–194.

6. Thomas E. Schott, *Alexander H. Stephens of Georgia: A Biography* (Baton Rouge: Louisiana State University Press, 1988), 307, 310.

7. See Alexander H. Stephens, Unionist Speech, in *Secession Debated: Georgia's Showdown in 1860,* ed. William W. Freehling and Craig M. Simpson (New York: Oxford University Press, 1992), 51–79.

8. Abraham Lincoln, First Inaugural Address, March 4, 1861, in *Abraham Lincoln: Speeches and Writings, 1859–1865,* ed. Don E. Fehrenbacher (New York: Library of America, 1989), 215.

9. Ibid., 222.

10. For the story of this slavery-protecting amendment (never ratified), including Lincoln's decision to give it his support, see Daniel W. Crofts, *Lincoln and the Politics of Slavery: The Other Thirteenth Amendment and the Struggle to Save the Union* (Chapel Hill: University of North Carolina Press, 2016).

11. See, for example, Abraham Lincoln to Lyman Trumbull, December 10, 1860, in *Abraham Lincoln: Speeches and Writings, 1859–1865,* ed. Don E. Fehrenbacher (New York: Library of America, 1989), 190; Abraham Lincoln to William Kellogg, December 11, 1860, in ibid., 191; Abraham Lincoln to John A. Gilmer, December 15, 1860, in ibid., 192. See also Crofts, *Lincoln and the Politics of Slavery,* 109–111, 132. Lincoln refused to support the proposed Crittenden Compromise, which would have permitted the spread of slavery to the territories. Crofts, *Lincoln and the Politics of Slavery,* 116.

12. Crofts, in *Lincoln and the Politics of Slavery,* points out that despite Lincoln's assurances to the contrary, many citizens of slave states apparently believed Lincoln would aggressively attack slavery in the states after he took office: "Hyperbolic white Southerners decided that all Republicans were bloodthirsty abolitionists" (12). Though I acknowledge that many Southerners held inaccurate views of Lincoln's intentions, I am more struck by the degree to which secessionist leaders *accurately* understood Lincoln's views and yet were willing to secede and risk civil war. The South Carolina Declaration of the Causes of Secession does not misrepresent Lincoln's position on slavery.

13. Quoted in David M. Potter, *The Impending Crisis: 1848–1861* (New York: Harper and Row, 1976), 475.

14. Davis, Farewell Address in US Senate, 194.

15. John C. Calhoun's own version of proslavery constitutional theory is critically examined in James H. Read, *Majority Rule versus Consensus: The Political Thought of John C. Calhoun* (Lawrence: University Press of Kansas, 2009), 85–117.

16. Walther, *Fire-Eaters,* 141–142.

17. Alexander H. Stephens, *A Constitutional View of the Late War between the States,* 2 vols. (Philadelphia: National, 1867). See esp. vol. 1, 343–406 for Stephens's commentary on John C. Calhoun.

18. John C. Calhoun's analysis of majority tyranny and his proposed remedy, which he called the concurrent majority, are set forth in *A Disquisition on Government,* in *The Papers of John C. Calhoun,* vol. 28: *1849–1850,* ed. Clyde N. Wilson and Shirley B. Cook (Columbia: University of South Carolina Press, 1959–2003), 3–67. For critical examination of Calhoun's consensus model of government, see Read, *Majority Rule versus Consensus,* 160–195.

19. John C. Calhoun, Remarks on Receiving Abolition Petitions, February 6, 1837, in *The Papers of John C. Calhoun,* vol. 13: *1835–1837,* ed. Clyde N. Wilson (Columbia: University of South Carolina Press, 1959–2003), 395.

20. See, for instance, John C. Calhoun's exchange with Senator William Cabell Rives of Virginia. Rives's remarks are omitted from *The Papers of John C. Calhoun* but included in *Union and Liberty: The Political Philosophy of John C. Calhoun,* ed. Ross M. Lence (Indianapolis: Liberty Fund, 1992), 466–469. For an extended discussion of Calhoun's defense of slavery, see Read, *Majority Rule versus Consensus,* 118–159.

21. John C. Calhoun, Further Remarks in Debate on His Fifth Resolution, January 10, 1838, in *The Papers of John C. Calhoun,* vol. 14: *1837–1839,* ed. Clyde N. Wilson (Columbia: University of South Carolina Press, 1959–2003), 84.

22. John C. Calhoun's clearest exposition of nullification theory comes in his Fort Hill Address, of 1831, in *The Papers of John C. Calhoun,* vol. 11: *1829–1832,* ed. Clyde N. Wilson (Columbia: University of South Carolina Press, 1959–2003), 413–439.

23. John C. Calhoun to Anna Maria Calhoun Clemson, January 25, 1838, in *The Papers of John C. Calhoun,* vol. 14: *1837–1839,* ed. Clyde N. Wilson (Columbia: University of South Carolina Press, 1959–2003), 107. For Calhoun's efforts to ban abolitionist speech both in and outside the halls of Congress, see Read, *Majority Rule versus Consensus,* 98–106.

24. John C. Calhoun, Resolutions on Abolition and the Union, December 27, 1837,

in *The Papers of John C. Calhoun,* vol. 14: *1837–1839,* ed. Clyde N. Wilson (Columbia: University of South Carolina Press, 1959–2003), 31–32.

25. John C. Calhoun, Remarks on the Vermont Abolition Memorial, December 19, 1837, in *The Papers of John C. Calhoun,* vol. 14: *1837–1839,* ed. Clyde N. Wilson (Columbia: University of South Carolina Press, 1959–2003), 13–14; Calhoun, Remarks on Amending His Third Resolution, January 4, 1838, in *The Papers of John C. Calhoun,* vol. 14: *1837–1839,* ed. Clyde N. Wilson (Columbia: University of South Carolina Press, 1959–2003), 54. For discussion of this episode, see Read, *Majority Rule versus Consensus,* 98–106; and Sotirios A. Barber, *The Fallacies of States' Rights* (Cambridge, MA: Harvard University Press, 2013), 128–130.

26. *Papers of John C. Calhoun,* vol. 14, 37.

27. For a critique of the traditional view that slave states merely demanded that the federal government leave them alone and remain neutral on slavery, see Read, *Majority Rule versus Consensus,* 87–89.

28. Calhoun, Resolutions on Abolition and the Union, 32.

29. *Abraham Lincoln,* 219.

30. William C. Davis, *Rhett: The Turbulent Life and Times of a Fire-Eater* (Columbia: University of South Carolina Press, 2001), 111–112.

31. Stephens, *Constitutional View,* vol. 1, 398–401.

32. John C. Calhoun, Southern Address, in *The Works of John C. Calhoun,* vol. 6, ed. Richard K. Crallé (Columbia, SC: A. S. Johnston, 1851), 290–313, http://eweb.furman .edu/~benson/docs/calhoun.htm.

33. Ibid.

34. Michael F. Holt, *The Rise and Fall of the American Whig Party: Jacksonian Politics and the Onset of the Civil War* (New York: Oxford University Press, 2003), 387.

35. Schott, *Alexander H. Stephens,* 96–101; Holt, *Rise and Fall,* 385–390.

36. For Calhoun's critique of political parties, see Read, *Majority Rule versus Consensus,* 13–14, 49–51, 193–194; John G. Grove, *John C. Calhoun's Theory of Republicanism* (Lawrence: University Press of Kansas, 2016), 79–91.

37. Schott, *Alexander H. Stephens,* 100.

38. Stephen Douglas's opening observation in his first 1858 debate with Abraham Lincoln was that both the Democrats and the Whigs (before the latter's demise) had been truly national parties that could proclaim their principles "in Louisiana and Massachusetts alike," unlike the Republican Party, which Douglas criticized as sectional. First Joint Debate, Ottawa, August 21, 1858, in *The Lincoln-Douglas Debates,* ed. Robert W. Johannsen (New York: Oxford University Press, 1965), 37.

39. On the continued resilience of national political parties in the late 1840s despite both parties' internal disagreements over slavery, see Joel H. Silbey, *Party over Section: The Rough and Ready Presidential Election of 1848* (Lawrence: University Press of Kansas, 2009). But by the early 1850s issues such as banks, tariffs, and internal improvements that had structured national party competition between Democrats and Whigs had become increasingly irrelevant; see Michael F. Holt, *The Political Crisis of the 1850s* (New York: Norton, 1983). For the fruitless attempt of the Constitutional Union Party in 1860 to defuse the slavery crisis by reviving these old issues, see Holt, *The Election of*

*1860: "A Campaign Fraught with Consequences"* (Lawrence: University Press of Kansas, 2017), 76–77.

40. *Abraham Lincoln*, 219.

41. Davis, *Rhett*, 112.

42. Walther, *Fire-Eaters*, 126, 132.

43. Ibid., 145–150.

44. Ibid., 145.

45. Ibid., 143.

46. Ibid. See also Davis, *Rhett*, 148–151, for the tepid Southern response during the mid-1850s to Rhett's repeated calls for secession.

47. Walther, *Fire-Eaters*, 152.

48. Ibid., 151–154. See also Davis, *Rhett*, 387–389.

49. Walther, *Fire-Eaters*, 134, 139–141.

50. Ibid., 121–142.

51. Ibid., 123–124, 130–135, 141–142, 145–146.

52. Ibid., 141. Walther implies that Robert Barnwell Rhett might well have invented this scene to claim for himself the role of Calhoun's handpicked successor.

53. Ibid., 149.

54. John C. Calhoun, Speech on the Admission of California and the General State of the Union, March 4, 1850, in *Union and Liberty: The Political Philosophy of John C. Calhoun*, ed. Ross M. Lence (Indianapolis, IN: Liberty Fund, 1992), 600–601.

55. John C. Calhoun's dual executive proposal is described in detail in his *Discourse on the Constitution, in Union and Liberty: The Political Philosophy of John C. Calhoun*, ed. Ross M. Lence (Indianapolis, IN: Liberty Fund, 1992), 274–277.

56. Potter, *Impending Crisis*, 121–144. See also Albert J. Von Frank, *The Trials of Anthony Burns: Freedom and Slavery in Emerson's Boston* (Cambridge, MA: Harvard University Press, 1998).

57. See Mark A. Graber, *Dred Scott and the Problem of Constitutional Evil* (New York: Cambridge University Press, 2006).

58. Robert Barnwell Rhett to William Porcher Miles, January 29, 1860, quoted in Walther, *Fire-Eaters*, 151.

59. Ibid.

60. Potter, *Impending Crisis*, 407–425.

61. Ibid., 414.

62. William J. Cooper, Jr., *Jefferson Davis: American* (New York: Knopf, 2000), 311–314. Davis hoped to secure the Democratic presidential nomination for Caleb Cushing of Massachusetts, who was strongly proslavery.

63. Walther, *Fire-Eaters*, 151.

64. My narrative here of the Democrats' split focuses on Robert Barnwell Rhett and his deliberate party-dividing tactics. For a broader narrative that includes actors who drove the party division without necessarily aiming to destroy the party, see Holt, *Election of 1860*, 50–66, 115–133; and Potter, *Impending Crisis*, 407–425.

65. Cooper, *Jefferson Davis: American*, 192.

66. Ibid., 193.

67. Ibid., 191.

68. Ibid., 196.

69. Ibid., 28, 179–183.

70. "Davis was convinced that Calhoun had enunciated the correct interpretation of both the constitutional and political Union." Ibid., 196.

71. For views of the Constitution, Union, majority tyranny, and slavery that parallel John C. Calhoun's, see, for example, Jefferson Davis to Malcolm D. Haynes, August 18, 1849, in *Jefferson Davis: The Essential Writings*, ed. William J. Cooper, Jr. (New York: Library of America, 2004), 64–71; Davis, Speech in the US Senate, August 13, 1850, in ibid., 81–87.

72. For example, Jefferson Davis suggested in 1850 that the dangerous sectional conflict "might be adjusted, without compromise of principle, by a division of the territory between the two sections of the Union," but such a compromise would have to permit slavery to expand southward "toward the equator," and it could not express any negative judgment on the institution of slavery itself. Davis, Speech in the US Senate, March 8, 1850, in *Jefferson Davis: The Essential Writings*, ed. William J. Cooper, Jr. (New York: Library of America, 2004), 78–79. See also Cooper, *Jefferson Davis: American*, 172–173.

73. Jefferson Davis to Lowndes County Citizens, November 22, 1850, in *Jefferson Davis: The Essential Writings*, ed. William J. Cooper, Jr. (New York: Library of America, 2004), 90.

74. Davis to Haynes, August 18, 1849, 65. For John C. Calhoun's initial embrace and subsequent denial of American nationhood, see Read, *Majority Rule versus Consensus*, 53–84.

75. For the argument that John C. Calhoun too was in certain respects a proslavery nationalist because for him protecting slavery took precedence over states' rights, see Barber, *Fallacies of States' Rights*, 128–130. See also Read, *Majority Rule versus Consensus*, 87–89, 99–106.

76. Davis to Haynes, August 18, 1849, 71.

77. James Oakes, *Freedom National: The Destruction of Slavery in the United States, 1861–1865* (New York: Norton, 2013). For a contrasting narrative, see Crofts, *Lincoln and the Politics of Slavery*, who argues that Oakes exaggerates the extent to which most Republicans were committed to the "freedom national" principle before the war (276–278).

78. Davis to Haynes, August 18, 1849, 69. For a description of proslavery constitutional theory, see Don E. Fehrenbacher, *The Slaveholding Republic: An Account of the United States Government's Relations to Slavery* (New York: Oxford University Press, 2002).

79. *Jefferson Davis: The Essential Writings*, 194.

80. Davis, Speech in the US Senate, August 13, 1850, 83.

81. Davis, Speech in the US Senate, May 8, 1860, 172.

82. Jefferson Davis to Joseph Emory Davis, January 2, 1838, in *Jefferson Davis: The Essential Writings*, ed. William J. Cooper, Jr. (New York: Library of America, 2004), 15.

83. *Jefferson Davis: The Essential Writings*, 172.

84. Calhoun, Resolutions on Abolition and the Union, 31.

85. *Jefferson Davis: The Essential Writings*, 173.

86. Calhoun, Resolutions on Abolition and the Union, 32.

87. *Jefferson Davis: The Essential Writings*, 174.

88. John Niven, *John C. Calhoun and the Price of Union* (Baton Rouge: Louisiana State University Press, 1989), 301–305. Jefferson Davis, as a member of the US House at the time, voted for war and then left his congressional seat to command a Mississippi regiment in the war. Cooper, *Jefferson Davis: American*, 123–157.

89. Jefferson Davis to Charles J. Searles, September 19, 1847, in *Jefferson Davis: The Essential Writings*, ed. William J. Cooper, Jr. (New York: Library of America, 2004), 53.

90. Cooper, *Jefferson Davis: American*, 287.

91. Ibid., 311–315.

92. Jefferson Davis to J. J. Pettus, January 4, 1861, in *Jefferson Davis: The Essential Writings*, ed. William J. Cooper, Jr. (New York: Library of America, 2004), 185–186.

93. Davis, Inaugural Address as Provisional President, 199–200.

94. Schott, *Alexander H. Stephens*, 73, 81.

95. Lincoln, First Inaugural Address, 224.

96. Abraham Lincoln to Alexander H. Stephens, December 22, 1860, in *Abraham Lincoln: Speeches and Writings, 1859–1865*, ed. Don E. Fehrenbacher (New York: Library of America, 1989), 194.

97. Crofts, *Lincoln and the Politics of Slavery*, 131–132, discusses Lincoln's exchange of letters with Alexander Stephens as well as Lincoln's correspondence around the same time with John A. Gilmer, a North Carolina unionist Lincoln considered appointing to a cabinet post.

98. Alexander H. Stephens, Unionist Speech, November 14, 1860, in *Secession Debated: Georgia's Showdown in 1860*, ed. William W. Freehling and Craig M. Simpson (New York: Oxford University Press, 1992), 59.

99. On January 2, 1861, Georgia held an election to select delegates to a special convention to consider the question of secession. Nearly 80 percent of Georgia's eligible voters turned out, and those who participated appear to have been nearly evenly divided on the question. On January 19, 1861, the delegates selected in that election voted 166–130 in favor of secession. William W. Freehling and Craig M. Simpson, "Introduction," in *Secession Debated: Georgia's Showdown in 1860*, ed. Freehling and Simpson (New York: Oxford University Press, 1992), xx–xi. In contrast, South Carolina's convention had voted unanimously in favor of secession on December 20, 1860.

100. Indeed, Abraham Lincoln consistently strove to distance himself from the self-righteous tone characteristic of many other antislavery leaders. For example, Lincoln remarked in his October 16, 1854, speech against the Kansas-Nebraska Act that the Southern people "are just what we would be in their situation. If slavery did not now exist among them, they would not introduce it. If it did now exist among us, we should not instantly give it up." *Abraham Lincoln: Speeches and Writings, 1832–1858*, ed. Don E. Fehrenbacher (New York: Library of America, 1989), 315.

101. Alexander H. Stephens to Abraham Lincoln, December 30, 1860, in Stephens, *Constitutional View*, vol. 2, 267–270.

102. Stephens, Unionist Speech, 69–70.

103. Ibid., 55–56.

104. Ibid., 56–58.

105. An important historical and biographical puzzle is why Alexander Stephens, after having spoken effectively against secession before the Georgia legislature in November 1860, was largely inactive during the campaign leading up to the January 2, 1861, popular vote to select convention delegates. The popular vote was nearly evenly divided between supporters and opponents of secession, and thus Stephens's active participation might have tipped the balance. Schott, *Alexander H. Stephens,* 311–322.

106. Here my reading of the available possibilities for compromise in late 1860 and early 1861 is more restricted than Crofts's view, who in *Lincoln and the Politics of Slavery* suggests there might have been wider room for compromise if rank-and-file Southerners had been disabused of the Fire-Eaters' misrepresentation of Abraham Lincoln and the Republicans as abolitionists in disguise. In my view a compromise preventing civil war would have been extremely difficult (though not altogether impossible) even assuming that Southerners had a fully accurate understanding of Lincoln's views—as Stephens himself clearly did.

107. Schott, *Alexander H. Stephens,* 62, 146.

108. Alexander H. Stephens to J. Henly Smith, July 10, 1860, quoted in Potter, *Impending Crisis,* 475.

109. Stephens, Unionist Speech, 63, 66.

110. Stephens, Corner-Stone Speech.

111. Ibid.

112. Lincoln, Message to Congress in Special Session, July 4, 1861, 255.

113. Stephens, Unionist Speech, 75.

114. Stephens, *Constitutional View,* vol. 1, 18–22.

115. Ibid., vol. 2, 270.

116. Ibid., vol. 1, 343–388.

117. Schott, *Alexander H. Stephens,* 97–101.

118. Ibid., 122–135.

119. Ibid., 89.

120. Lincoln, First Inaugural Address, 219, 222.

121. Lincoln, Message to Congress in Special Session, 254–255.

122. John C. Calhoun sets out this argument most comprehensively in *A Discourse on the Constitution and Government of the United States,* in *Union and Liberty: The Political Philosophy of John C. Calhoun,* ed. Ross M. Lence (Indianapolis, IN: Liberty Fund, 1992), esp. 81–101, 212–213.

123. Lincoln, Message to Congress in Special Session, 255.

124. http://www.teachingushistory.org/lessons/ordinance.htm. Georgia, Virginia, and North Carolina—which, like South Carolina, were among the original states ratifying the Constitution—also framed the secession ordinance as a revocation of that specifically dated act. The secession ordinances of Louisiana, Texas, and Arkansas, not among the original states ratifying the Constitution, used a similar format but substituted the dated act by which their territorial legislature resolved to accept the authority of the US Constitution. The secession ordinances of Florida, Alabama, Tennessee, and Mississippi did not take the form of revoking any specific past act of ratification.

125. Calhoun, *Disquisition on Government,* 34, 36.

126. John C. Calhoun, Speech on the Oregon Bill, June 27, 1848, in *The Papers of John C. Calhoun,* vol. 25: *1847–1848,* ed. Clyde N. Wilson and Shirley B. Cook (Columbia: University of South Carolina Press, 1959–2003), 534–536.

127. Ibid.

128. South Carolina, Declaration of the Immediate Causes Which Induce and Justify the Secession of South Carolina from the Federal Union, http://avalon.law.yale.edu/19th_century/csa_scarsec.asp.

129. Ibid.

130. Lincoln, First Inaugural Address, 224.

131. The reader can verify this with an Internet search of the terms *American Civil War* and *tragic misunderstanding.* Authors who employ the phrase include Bruce Catton in *The Civil War* (Boston: Houghton Mifflin, 1960), 23.

132. Crofts, *Lincoln and the Politics of Slavery,* 12. Some secessionists did portray Abraham Lincoln as nearly indistinguishable from John Brown, whether tactically or out of conviction. See William A. Link, *The Roots of Secession: Slavery and Politics in Antebellum Virginia* (Chapel Hill: University of North Carolina Press, 2003), 217–218.

133. South Carolina, Declaration of the Immediate Causes. The document quotes accurately from Lincoln's House Divided Speech, June 16, 1858, in *Abraham Lincoln: Speeches and Writings, 1832–1858,* ed. Don E. Fehrenbacher (New York: Library of America, 1989), 426.

134. The phrase "irrepressible conflict" was employed before the Civil War, especially by antislavery writers, though it was not then intended to project a horrific civil war. See, for example, New York senator William Henry Seward, On the Irrepressible Conflict, October 25, 1858, http://www.nyhistory.com/central/conflct.htm. Seward later became Abraham Lincoln's secretary of state and assisted in drafting his First Inaugural Address.

135. For a recent survey of historical literature on this question, see Frank Towers, "Another Look at Inevitability: The Upper South and the Limits of Compromise in the Secession Crisis," *Tennessee Historical Quarterly* 70, no. 2 (Summer 2011): 108–125. Towers himself argues that secession and civil war were "nearly inevitable." "Was the Civil War Inevitable?" is a common essay question in college and high school courses in the United States, which the reader can confirm with an Internet search.

136. Stephens, Unionist Speech, 62.

137. The recorded debates of the Constitutional Convention of 1787 do not support John C. Calhoun's claim that Northern states understood themselves as making a solemn moral and constitutional obligation to protect and defend slavery against threats and restrictions of every kind when they agreed to the three-fifths and fugitive slave clauses. See Read, *Majority Rule versus Consensus,* 115–116. For comparison of the historical Constitution with the proslavery interpretation of it, see Fehrenbacher, *Slaveholding Republic,* 15–47.

138. Fehrenbacher, *Slaveholding Republic,* 296.

# Part Two

## *Hard Choices*

# CHAPTER 6

# Lincoln and "The Public Estimate of the Negro"

## From Anti-Amalgamation to Antislavery

DIANA J. SCHAUB

In his postwar assessment of Abraham Lincoln, Frederick Douglass made the case that Lincoln's statesmanship during the war hinged on his symbiotic relationship with Northern public opinion.[1] The "primary and essential condition" for Lincoln's twin accomplishments of union and abolition was "the earnest sympathy and the powerful cooperation of his loyal fellow-countrymen." Douglass was all too aware of the deficiencies of that public opinion, especially as "viewed from the genuine abolition ground." To the extent that Lincoln accommodated himself to "the prejudices common to his countrymen towards the colored race," he appeared to Douglass and his friends as "tardy, cold, dull, and indifferent." However, Douglass also indicated that democratic statesmen ought to be evaluated by a quite different standard: "Measuring him by the sentiment of his country, a sentiment he was bound as a statesman to consult, he was swift, zealous, radical, and determined." On Douglass's mature understanding, Lincoln's relationship to public opinion was equal parts accommodation and transformation, with a judicious accommodation to white prejudice actually serving as the indispensable pathway to society-wide transformation.

Lincoln's own understanding of the state of white opinion regarding blacks—and the severe constraints it placed on political maneuver—is displayed in his speeches throughout the 1850s.[2] Noting the rhetorical bind in which Lincoln found himself, particularly in notoriously antiblack Illinois, many scholars would echo Lewis E. Lehrman's conclusion that "Lincoln probably took as advanced an anti-slavery position as any Illinois politician could sustain and hope to be elected to statewide office."[3] Without dissenting at all from that eminently reasonable judgment, my aim is to look more closely at the structure of Lincoln's speeches (first the Peoria Address,[4] but more especially the *Dred Scott* Speech) to see how he navigated those treacherous waters.

Attention to these texts (in juxtaposition to the texts of Lincoln's opponents) reveals that Lincoln not only succeeds in finding the precise positioning that avoids political suicide; he does much more. He is a practitioner of rhetoric, in the classical sense, as the art of soul leading. He conforms as far as he must to public opinion but with a view to informing and reforming that opinion. In this chapter, I am not trying to ascertain the nature of Lincoln's own full position on the question of race (or to gauge the distance between his expressed position and his full position), but I do hope to demonstrate that the amelioration of racial prejudice is one of his objects. Of course, it would tell us something about Lincoln's own soul to know where he is leading the souls of others.

## PREJUDICE AND INJUSTICE

Lincoln's first acknowledgment of white prejudice occurs in the Peoria Address, delivered in October 1854 and, like so many of Lincoln's speeches, crafted in explicit reply to a speech by the other Douglas, Stephen A., the author of the repeal of the Missouri Compromise, against which Lincoln inveighs. The passage appears as a digression from his main line of argument. After giving a history of the nation's "policy of prohibiting slavery in new territory" and stating his thesis that the repeal of the Missouri Compromise is wrong in both "direct effect" and "prospective principle," Lincoln pauses: "Before proceeding, let me say that I think I have no prejudice against the Southern people. They are just what we would be in their situation."[5] Recognizing their "wolf by the ear" dilemma, he sympathizes with conscience-stricken Southerners.[6] His sympathy leads him to conduct an interesting thought experiment: what would happen "if all earthly power were given to me."[7] He runs through the options: (1) "Free all the slaves, and send them to Liberia." His verdict on this solution of immediate emancipation followed by immediate expatriation is that it would be disastrous for the freedpeople themselves ("Landed there in a day, they would all perish in the next ten days") as well as being materially impossible to execute ("There are not surplus shipping and surplus money enough . . . to carry them there in many times ten days"). Note that Lincoln evaluates the plan first from the black perspective, then the white.[8]

(2) "Free them all, and keep them among us as underlings." His verdict on this solution is again given first from the black perspective. Lincoln says he is not sure "that this betters their condition." In his own survey of the available options, Douglass amply confirmed Lincoln's fears about this particular course. Making the freedpeople "a degraded caste" would, according to Douglass, "be to lacerate and depress the spirit of the Negro, and make him a scourge

and a curse to the country." "Do anything else with us," Douglass pleaded, "but plunge us not into this hopeless pit."[9] Regardless of whether freedom without equality is better or worse than slavery from the black perspective, Lincoln reiterates his conviction that he "would not hold one in slavery, at any rate."[10]

(3) "Free them, and make them politically and socially, our equals." His verdict on this solution, toward which the ordering of the presentation seems to be driving, is considered exclusively from the white perspective. Lincoln's silence about the black response to this option suggests that it—and it alone—would meet with black approval. Resistance to it arises entirely from the "feelings" of whites, including Lincoln's own. (Douglass was apparently not wrong to speak of Lincoln's "unfriendly feeling."[11]) Lincoln's analysis, however, is highly nuanced, for although stating that "my own feelings will not admit of" the fullest equality, he also considers a hypothetical "if mine would." Apparently, Lincoln's feelings are not so fixed that he cannot imagine them being different. Yet, it turns out that Lincoln's feelings scarcely matter because all concerned "well know" that the feelings "of the great mass of white people" will not tolerate full equality. When Lincoln wonders "whether this feeling accords with justice and sound judgment," he pretty frankly implies that it does not. It is an invidious prejudice. However, again, that scarcely matters because "a universal feeling, whether well or ill founded, can not be safely disregarded."[12] His conclusion is that immediate equality is impossible.

Unlike the controversy over the extension of slavery, in which the proper course to be pursued was crystal clear to Lincoln, the problem of the existing institution was unsolvable even for a tyrant possessed of "all earthly power" because earthly power, unlike divine power, cannot contravene the laws of physics or correct the vagaries of the human heart. Yet, Lincoln does not abandon his quest. His final suggestion is a modest, nontyrannical one: "It does seem to me that systems of gradual emancipation might be adopted."[13] Gradualism addresses the wrong of slavery while introducing some separation between the issue of slavery and the more problematic issue of race relations. It was, after all, the entanglement of slavery and race (or, more precisely, the undecided question of the status of blacks postslavery) that increasingly stymied antislavery action.[14] It might not be so bad to delay the day of racial reckoning.[15]

Remarkably, in the course of two paragraphs, Lincoln transforms his initial expression of sympathy for white Southerners into an endorsement of gradual emancipation for black slaves (although he still refrains from blaming "our brethren of the south"[16]). Lincoln is a practitioner of rhetorical jujitsu. What he does in small compass in these two paragraphs with respect to slavery in the states, he does over the course of the entire Peoria Address with respect to slavery in the territories. The most dramatic instance is his treatment of the claim that "equal justice to the South" (i.e., respect for "property" rights) demands opening the territories to slavery. Lincoln translates this claim into the most brutal language: "That is to say, inasmuch as you do not object to my taking my hog to Nebraska, therefore I must not object to you taking your slave. Now, I admit this is perfectly logical, if there is no difference between hogs and negroes."[17] Here Lincoln does confront the entanglement of slavery and race (although without reference to postslavery race relations), in the most direct way. At issue is "the humanity of the negro."[18] He then instances the Southerners' own behavior—they outlawed the African slave trade, they shun social intercourse with slave dealers, they sometimes free enslaved people—to prove that they too recognize the fact of shared humanity: "In all these cases it is your sense of justice, and human sympathy, continually telling you, that the poor negro has some natural right to himself—that those who deny it, and make mere merchandise of him, deserve kickings, contempt and death."[19]

This moment is the fulcrum of the speech. Having summoned up these human sympathies and not incidentally having introduced the notion of natural right, Lincoln continues for the rest of the speech to recur to them periodically, interweaving these more heartfelt general appeals with more specific historical and constitutional arguments. Thus, a few pages later, he refers to "the abundance of man's heart"—out of which the condemnation of slavery emerges and will do so eternally because "you still can not repeal human nature."[20]

Near the end of the speech, Lincoln brings this theme of public sentiment to its denouement, so to speak. He arrays the "great mistake" of Douglas, who has "no very vivid impression that the negro is a human" against "the totally different view" held by "the great mass of mankind": "They consider slavery a great moral wrong; and their feeling against it, is not evanescent, but eternal. It lies at the very foundation of their sense of justice; and it cannot be trifled with.—It is a great and durable element of popular action, and I think, no statesman can safely disregard it."[21]

This passage cries out to be paired with the passage near the beginning of the Peoria Address that also spoke of a "feeling" that "can not be safely disregarded."[22] The echoes in language are striking, although the content of the two feelings could not be more opposed. The first feeling, common to "the great mass of white people," was dead set against political equality for blacks. Lincoln had more than hinted that this feeling was "ill-founded." He had also, just barely, floated the possibility that this prejudice might be subject to change, at least in his own case, and thereby he demonstrated that it was not "eternal," although neither could it be said to be "evanescent." Contrasting at every point, the second feeling belongs not to "the great mass of white people" but to "the great mass of mankind" (white people included). This feeling against slavery is not only just but foundational to the sense of justice. Whereas white prejudice interferes with wise action (as when it vetoes schemes of gradual emancipation), antislavery sentiment can inspire action even after a long period of moral inanition—perhaps especially when a "statesman" revives and directs it. This "statesman" is a new element not present in the first passage.

The stunning matchup between these two passages suggests that even in a speech such as the Peoria Address—massively long, with many joints and moving parts—there is a dominant purpose, with a structured rhetoric designed to achieve it. The purpose is to shift the audience away from its anti-black sentiment by eliciting its antislavery sentiment. A listener to Lincoln's three-hour oration might not be conscious of the parallelism of these two passages, while nonetheless being moved (by the intervening arguments) in the direction Lincoln intends. A reader, by contrast, has the immense advantage of being able to discover the pairing and study the precision of Lincoln's formulations, which, in combination, reveal his deep grasp of the statesman's relation to public sentiment in both its self-interested and justice-loving dimensions, neither of which can be "safely disregarded."[23]

## "OUR FATHERS DID NOT REGARD THE NEGRO RACE AS ANY KIN TO THEM"

Between the Kansas-Nebraska Act of 1854 and the *Dred Scott* decision of 1857, the difficulty of making the move Lincoln wanted his audiences to make increased significantly. Chief Justice Roger Taney, whether in ignorance or malfeasance, had made a mockery of his own professed commitment to originalism by claiming that at the time of the nation's founding (and throughout the century previous), the "unhappy black race . . . were never thought of or spoken of except as property."[24] In his smack-down dissent, Justice Curtis exposed Taney's egregious errors of fact, meticulously citing chapter and verse from the state constitutions to prove that "at the time of the ratification of the Articles of Confederation, all free native-born inhabitants of the States of New Hampshire, Massachusetts, New York, New Jersey, and North Carolina, though descended from African slaves, were not only citizens of those States, but such of them as had the other necessary qualifications possessed the franchise of electors, on equal terms with other citizens."[25]

Free black men took part in the adoption of the nation's fundamental charters. How did Taney manage retroactively to strip these voters of their participation in "We the People"? Although he mentions "the legislation and histories of the time," in fact, Taney relies on something much more nebulous: "the state of public opinion," which he characterizes, or mischaracterizes, as uniformly hostile to blacks. With a pretense of superior compassion, Taney writes, "It is difficult at this day to realize the state of public opinion in relation to that unfortunate race, which prevailed in the civilized and enlightened portions of the world at the time of the Declaration of Independence, and when the Constitution of the United States was framed and adopted."[26]

Interestingly, the only legislative evidence Taney gives of the "prevailing opinion" that blacks were "regarded as beings of an inferior order . . . and so far inferior that they had no rights which the white man was bound to respect"[27] are two laws from the early 1700s relating to intermarriage between Negroes, mulattoes, and whites. It seems a decidedly strange choice inasmuch as the existence of laws punishing those who entered into such marital unions (or laws banning the unions outright) seems to indicate that the line separating the races was not as bright as Taney claims. There were whites who did not find all members of the African race "altogether unfit to associate with," perhaps even some who were willing to risk the sentence of seven years' servitude. Although Taney claims these laws made "no distinction" between "the free negro or mulatto and the slave," that claim is at odds with the passage he cites in which "mulattoes born of white women" were not sentenced to slavery if they intermarried with whites but were instead punished as the whites themselves were, becoming "servants during the term of seven years."[28]

Taney is not wrong that there were persistent legislative attempts to affix "this stigma, of the deepest degradation . . . upon the whole race" and to erect "a perpetual and impassable barrier" between the races.[29] However, his purpose in citing these, and only these, particular laws relating to sexual contact seems less a matter of historical accuracy than an underhanded way of triggering the contemporary fear of what was called *amalgamation*.[30] A dispassionate survey of the status of blacks under colonial law would have recognized jarring contradictions and ambivalences in their position—classed as property but also possessed of personality. So, for instance, an early Maryland law sought to encourage the importation of slaves by making clear that conversion to Christianity did not work their freedom. Thus, masters should not neglect Christian instruction; any such neglect would be to "the great displeasure of Almighty God and the prejudice of the Soules of those poor people."[31] Personhood can be seen in the long-standing respect accorded the right of an enslaved person to petition a court for freedom (a right protected by statute in South Carolina and Georgia). As often as not, blacks could actually meet with a fair hearing. An interesting 1974 study by Ross M. Kimmel, focused on Maryland, captures some of these complexities:

While statutory law helps us somewhat to understand the legal status of blacks in colonial Maryland, it is really only a point of departure. Case law, on the other hand, provides a closer look at the legal dynamics of race relations. The numerous surviving freedom petitions filed by blacks and mulattoes, for example, show that, despite a clearly stated statutory presumption that blackness meant slavery, there evolved in Maryland a common law presumption that exceptions could be made. The Provincial Court, the county courts, and the other special courts which heard slave freedom suits showed a consistent tendency to judge each case on its individual merits and to grant petitioners their freedom when the evidence warranted it.[32]

There was also respect for the right to a jury trial in criminal cases—and, perverse as it might seem, to be accused of a crime is an acknowledgment of one's standing as a morally accountable being.

On June 12, 1857, just a few weeks after the revised full text of Taney's opinion was released to the public,[33] Douglas delivered his Remarks on Kansas, Utah, and the *Dred Scott* Decision.[34] He was delighted to follow Taney's lead. Indeed, he made the focus on "amalgamation" more explicit and more virulently racist. He abandoned the references to "that unfortunate race" and the formulations Taney employed to suggest impartial reportage, as in, for instance, "They had for more than a century before *been regarded as* beings of an inferior order."[35] Douglas frankly affirms what he too takes to be the verdict of the founding era that "the African race" ranks among the world's "inferior races." Further, he endorses "the truth of the proposition that amalgamation is degrading, demoralizing, disease and death." He argues that the aim of "our revolutionary fathers" was "to preserve the purity of the white race" and to "prevent any species of amalgamation, political, social or domestic."[36]

Tellingly, it is the "domestic" possibility—the ultimate consequence of realized equality—that most alarms him: "Our fathers did not regard the negro race as any kin to them, and determined so to lay the foundations of society and government that they should never be of any kin to their posterity."[37] The conclusion of Douglas's discussion of the *Dred Scott* case implies that the reason for the decision was to prevent this outcome. By denying all possibility of black citizenship, the Court saves white men—who are, after all, men of principle—from ever having to "authorize negroes to marry white women on an equality with white men."[38]

But when you confer upon the African race the privileges of citizenship, and put them upon an equality with white men at the polls, in the jury box, on the bench, in the executive chair, and in the councils of the nation, upon what principle will you deny their equality at the festive board and in the domestic circle[?]

The Supreme Court of the United States has decided that, under the constitution, a negro is not and cannot be a citizen.[39]

## VINDICATING THE FOUNDERS

In drafting his response, Lincoln was well aware of what he was contending with. "Amalgamation" had been either the central topic or the pervasive subtext in the remarks of both Taney and Douglas. Although Taney's antiblack animus was not put in the rabble-rousing form the popular politician favored, it was just as strongly expressed. Indeed, Taney's survey of public opinion concluded by suggesting that intermarriage was equivalent to "unnatural" bestiality because members of the African race were "looked upon as so far below [the white race] in the scale of created beings."[40]

Not surprisingly then, Lincoln's *Dred Scott* Speech, delivered June 26, 1857, is the one in which he most directly addresses "the public estimate of the negro" both in the founding era and his own.[41] The speech contains two distinct discussions of "amalgamation" (§25 and §§35–42), discussions that create a frame for his most extensive explication of the meaning of the Declaration of Independence (§§26–34)—an explication rivaled only by the more concise and poetic treatment in the Gettysburg Address. Yet another significant feature of Lincoln's *Dred Scott* Speech is that, because of its focus on what Douglas euphemistically called "the domestic circle," women are featured throughout. It is a daring speech, with talk of polygamy, concubinage, and rape. Interestingly though, it almost entirely avoids mention of "white women" or "black men." Lincoln's rhetorical jujitsu involves a unique focus on black women and black girls (about which more later).

Senator Douglas had given his speech at the invitation of an Illinois grand jury. Its members had specified the subject matter, naming three controversial areas of public policy. As an answer to Douglas's command performance, Lincoln's speech touches on the same three issues. Lincoln, however, entertains them in a different order and weights them quite differently. Lincoln acknowledges the shift by first specifying the sequence in which Douglas addressed "the several subjects of Kansas, the *Dred Scott* decision, and Utah" (§1) and then highlighting his reconfiguration by saying "I begin with Utah" (§2). Schematically, their respective orderings and proportions look like this:

| Douglas Speech | | Lincoln Speech | |
| --- | --- | --- | --- |
| Topic | # of paragraphs | Topic | # of paragraphs |
| Kansas | 3 | Utah | 2 |
| *Dred Scott* | 22 | Kansas | 5 |
| Utah | 13 | *Dred Scott* | 39 |

No wonder Douglas's speech is known as Remarks on Kansas, Utah, and the *Dred Scott* Decision, whereas Lincoln's is known as the *Dred Scott* Speech. Lincoln not only dispatches the other two topics quickly but also subtly links and subordinates each of them to his treatment of the *Dred Scott* decision, creating thereby a more cohesive argument despite a superficial impression of discrete parts.[42]

Lincoln's main purpose in this speech is to correct a dangerous misreading of the Declaration put forth by his Democratic political opponents. Lincoln's generation, no less than our own, struggled to make sense of the stark contrast between the Declaration's ringing endorsement of mankind's natural equality and the ongoing existence of chattel slavery. No one—at least in that era—wanted to denounce the founders as hypocrites. (Today, of course, there is not so much compunction on this score.) One way to rescue the founders from the charge that they said one thing and did the opposite is simply to read blacks out of the Declaration. That is what both Taney and Douglas do. It is immensely convenient that their vindication of the founders also vindicates the status quo of the 1850s. Here is Douglas:

Can any sane man believe that the signers of the Declaration of Independence . . . intended *to place* the negro race on an equal footing with the white race? If such had been their purpose would they not have abolished slavery and converted every negro into a citizen on the day on which they put forth the Declaration of Independence? . . .

No one can vindicate the character, motives, and conduct of the signers, . . . except upon the hypothesis that they referred to the white race alone, and not to the African, when they declared all men to have been created equal.[43]

Taney reasons similarly, declaring the framers "great men" and as such "incapable of asserting principles inconsistent with those on which they were acting."[44]

Lincoln is perhaps no less interested in vindicating the founders, but he does not take the easy, self-congratulatory route.[45] Lincoln rejects the white supremacist interpretation of the Declaration as nonsensical—he says it does "obvious violence to the plain, unmistakable language of the Declaration," the language of inclusion, not exclusion.[46] At the same time, he honestly acknowledges the distance between the founders' theoretical principles and their political practice. He does not think that the gap between words and deeds made them hypocrites, however. Lincoln reminds his audience that democratic statesmen—constrained as they always are by tradition and public opinion—are not free to "place" folks, whether black or white, instantly on a footing of full equality. That limitation does not mean that the words of the Declaration are empty platitudes. Properly understood, they vitalize and guide political life.

Here is the justly famous, central passage from Lincoln's speech:

I think the authors of that notable instrument intended to include *all* men, but they did not intend to declare all men equal *in all respects.* They did not mean to say all were equal in color, size, intellect, moral developments, or social capacity. They defined with tolerable distinctness, in what respects they did consider all men created equal—equal in "certain inalienable rights, among which are life, liberty, and the pursuit of happiness." This they said, and this meant. They did not mean to assert the obvious untruth, that all were then actually enjoying that equality, nor yet, that they were about to confer it immediately upon them. In fact they had no power to confer such a boon. They meant simply to declare the *right,* so that the *enforcement* of it might follow as fast as circumstances should permit. They meant to set up a standard maxim for free society, which could be familiar to all, and revered by all; constantly looked to, constantly labored for, and even though never perfectly attained, constantly approximated, and thereby constantly spreading and deepening its influence, and augmenting the happiness and value of life to all people of all colors everywhere.

According to Lincoln, human beings are equal, but they are not equal every which way.[47] They are equal only in a highly specific way. Before specifying that way, however, Lincoln first details some of the manifold ways in which humans are unlike one another: he says they are not the same in "color, size, intellect, moral developments, or social capacity." That is an intriguing list. A little reflection shows how carefully constructed it is—ascending from simpler, physical differences to more complex, multidimensional differences—and how it aims to be comprehensive, capturing the tremendous variety of humanity: in appearance, in faculties, and in character.[48] The list also hints at a difficult question: What account, if any, must be taken of these inequalities in a just political system? For present purposes, we can concentrate on the first category: color.

Given that Lincoln's dispute with Taney and Douglas concerned the founders' view of black people, it is not surprising that Lincoln begins by acknowledging a difference that presents itself to all eyes. Human beings do not look the same; they come in different colors. In the speech Douglas had given, he spoke repeatedly of the "African race" and "other inferior races"; he also spoke of the "superior" "white race."[49] Taney had done the same, referring to "negroes of the African race" and "the enslaved African race," always in juxtaposition to "the dominant race," that is, "the white race."[50] Lincoln, by contrast, rarely utters the term "race."[51] Instead of dividing human beings into fixed categories, Lincoln presents the difference between blacks and whites as a purely superficial difference of skin tone. (Frederick Douglass, too, understood race as a mere matter of complexion.) Moreover, in other writings, Lincoln points out that skin tone is not actually binary (black and white) but a matter of degree (lighter and darker). Thus, he warns slaveholders that if they regard whiteness as a title to mastery, they cannot escape the logical conclusion that they themselves should be enslaved to the first person who comes along with paler skin than their own.[52] By speaking of color rather than race, Lincoln suggests the existence of a spectrum of infinite gradations. Although he highlights the visible differences of color within what he calls "the whole human family," he hints at the individual rather than class character of those differences. He bridges the racial divide with a rainbow, such that by the end of this passage he is able to envision "all people of all colors everywhere" enjoying the benefits of "free society."

Having acknowledged the scope of differences among men, Lincoln returns to the matter of our essential similarity. What is the precise respect in which human beings are alike? Lincoln quotes directly from the Declaration: we possess "inalienable rights," which is to say, rights that belong to us by virtue of the kind of creature we are. According to Lincoln, there should be no confusion about the meaning of equality. Equality is not some vague generality. Quite the contrary—the Declaration offers a definition of its central concept. Equality means equality with respect to natural rights. None of the significant differences among human beings—which might loom larger than they ought in the minds of the audience—invalidates the equal entitlement to "life, liberty, and the pursuit of happiness." Rights are not contingent on anything but membership in what Lincoln calls the "human family." This phrase is a direct riposte to Stephen Douglas, who had insisted that "our fathers did not regard the negro race as any kin to them."[53]

Lincoln's next step in his analysis of the Declaration is crucial to his moral vindication of the revolutionary generation. He considers again what the authors did not intend to say. Although they were deadly serious about the truth of human equality, they knew full well that not all were, as Lincoln puts it, "actually enjoying that equality." Indeed, by their assessment, they themselves were not enjoying equal rights; that, after all, is why they wrote the Declaration: to present to the world the evidence of their oppression as justification for their independence from Great Britain.

By focusing on what the founders did not mean to say, Lincoln reminds his audience of how insecure rights are and how often they are violated. Most people in most times and most places have not enjoyed the equality to which they are entitled. What did the authors of the Declaration propose to do about this nearly universal disrespect for the natural rights of man? According to Lincoln, "they had no power" to set the world "immediately" to rights. Indeed, it was pretty unclear whether the colonists would have sufficient power to reclaim their own usurped rights, much less anyone else's.

Having dashed any utopian hopes about perfect equality, Lincoln concludes with two ringing sentences stating what the founders did mean. They declared "the *right*," and by doing so generated the expectation that "the *enforcement*" would follow as soon as possible, which is to say, as speedily as prudence permits. Whereas the declaration of right is universal and absolute, the enforcement of right is dependent upon circumstances. To take the case of black slavery: by the premises of the Declaration, it is undeniable that black persons possess a natural right to liberty wrongfully denied by the laws and practices of the colonists. The rectification of that injustice was neither quick nor easy. As it turned out, it required a Civil War, followed by the Thirteenth, Fourteenth, and Fifteenth Amendments to the Constitution and a long, torturous process of societal reconstruction stretching over the next century and into our own.

However, what must be emphasized is Lincoln's conviction that the declaration of right in 1776 was itself epoch-making. It established a lodestar—or what Lincoln calls a "standard maxim"—guiding incremental improvement or at least shining the torch of reason on oppression. Without that clearly articulated standard, there would be no inherent pressure for reform. This is a truly new thing: a government that has within itself a principle of self-correction. Fidelity to the origins—indeed, fidelity to the point of reverence—becomes the engine of perpetual progress.[54] According to Lincoln, the spread of equal liberty is not limited to the United States. The Declaration of Independence is global in its reach not because the United States will impose regime change by force but because awareness of the foundations of free society moves people longingly toward it. Knowledge of the truth ("familiar to all") produces attachment to the truth ("revered by all"), which in turn produces action on behalf of the truth ("constantly labored for").

## THE DAUGHTERS OF DRED SCOTT

For good reason, this "standard maxim" passage is often quoted by admirers of Lincoln.[55] However, to grasp how Lincoln readies his contemporary audience to receive this interpretation of the Declaration's equality principle, it is necessary to pay attention to what might be called the ground-clearing passages. Most of those are directed against Douglas, but there is one section devoted to refuting Taney (§§19–23).[56] Having asserted that Taney's decision was "based on assumed historical facts which were not really true," Lincoln relies on Curtis's dissent to prove that blacks *could* be citizens because, contra Taney, some blacks *were* enfranchised citizens at the time of the founding. Sticking to the legal specifics, Curtis had declined to take up the question of the state of public opinion regarding blacks; his refusal to do so was itself a criticism of Taney's soft, unjudicial methodology. Lincoln, however—out of his awareness that "in this and like communities, public sentiment is everything"[57]—did not want to leave unchallenged Taney's misrepresentation of that public sentiment. According to Lincoln, the chief justice had assumed "that the public estimate of the black man is more favorable *now* than it was in the days of the Revolution." To prove that assumption "mistaken" and "grossly incorrect," Lincoln details concrete changes that collectively illustrate a hardening of opinion toward blacks, such as the disfranchisement of free blacks, the introduction of legal impediments to voluntary manumission, the introduction into state constitutions of restraints on the legislative power to emancipate slaves, the spread of slavery to new territories (via the Kansas-Nebraska Act), and the restraints on congressional power over slavery in the territories (via the *Dred Scott* decision)—all culminating in bold attacks on the Declaration's equality principle.

Thus, Lincoln's defense of the revolutionary generation becomes a biting criticism of his contemporary generation. The section concludes with a metaphorical description of the situation of "the black man":

Mammon is after him; ambition follows, and philosophy follows, and the Theology of the day is fast joining the cry. They have him in his prison house; they have searched his person, and left no prying instrument with him. One after another they have closed the heavy iron doors upon him, and now they have him, as it were, bolted in with a lock of a hundred keys, which can never be unlocked without the concurrence of every key; the keys in the hands of a hundred different men, and they scattered to a hundred different and distant places; and they stand musing as to what invention, in all the dominions of mind and matter, can be produced to make the impossibility of his escape more complete than it is.

Through this prison house image, Lincoln once again (as in the Peoria Address) requires whites to view the world—the world of white power—from the black perspective. It is an image that taxes the white imagination. Think of the alternative. Lincoln could have said something like: "Taney is wrong. It wasn't the founding era but our own that regards blacks as nothing but property." In the Peoria Address, however, Lincoln had indicated that he did not believe it was actually possible to regard a human being as merely property. One cannot, consistently, live a lie. That was why so much of Southern life and practice could be called upon to testify against the "peculiar institution." This image of the prison house (unlike a lament about commodification) insists on the humanity, the personhood, of the incarcerated. Ominously, the passage as a whole confirms what Lincoln had averred privately in a letter to George Robertson on August 15, 1855: "There is no peaceful extinction of slavery in prospect for us."[58]

Toward Taney, Lincoln is blunt but respectful, speaking impersonally of his mistaken assumptions and errors of fact. The polemic against Douglas is different, full of satiric sallies, relentlessly skewering Douglas's character along with his policy positions. Lincoln begins with the situation in the Utah Territory, where the Mormons were taking up arms against the US government, although he does not spend much time on the practical question of what to do about the Mormon Rebellion.[59] Instead, he deftly shifts the discussion to the underlying moral question of polygamy.[60] The Republican Platform of 1856 had linked polygamy and slavery, denouncing them as "twin relics of barbarism" and calling upon Congress to prohibit both practices in the territories.[61] It is worth noting that the main reason polygamy was considered barbarous was because it involved the subordination of women to the patriarchal authority of men. Furthermore, because family structure and political structure are linked, sexual despotism in the household was regarded as the handmaiden of despotic theocratic rule.[62]

What Lincoln tries to do is force his political opponent, Stephen Douglas, to take a position on the morality or immorality of polygamy—something Douglas had absolutely refused to do on the subject of slavery; he professed not to care whether voters in the territories embraced or rejected slavery. According to Douglas's doctrine of popular sovereignty, residents of the territories had a sacred right to decide all matters for themselves on the basis of local majority rule. Lincoln is testing the limits of Douglas's view that majorities—majorities composed of white males—can do whatever they like (whether it be to keep a stable of black men as slave labor or a stable of white women as sex slaves). He is trying to puncture Douglas's stance of nonjudgmentalism, or moral neutrality. Although Douglas can perhaps get away with saying he does not care one way or the other about slavery because the nation is about evenly split on that issue, he cannot adopt that strategy with respect to Mormon polygamy because it triggers vehement public outrage. (Remember, the reason the Mormons were all the way out in the Utah desert was because they had been chased out of every other place they had tried to settle.)

After pressuring Douglas on the polygamy issue (and then making a few barbed remarks about the situation in Kansas[63]), Lincoln arrives at his main topic: the *Dred Scott* decision.[64] Quite surprisingly, this discussion turns out to involve yet another controversial form of sexual union. Just about the only thing about which Douglas did express moral disapproval was any kind of intimate mixing between the races. When Republicans insisted that slavery was wrong and that all human beings had a natural right to liberty, Douglas argued that must mean Republicans endorsed full social and political equality for blacks, or, as he summarized it: if the Declaration of Independence applies to the "African race," that would "authorize negroes to marry white women on an equality with white men."[65] Douglas did all he could to stoke white fear— which is to say white male fear—of "amalgamation," the fear that a daughter of theirs would bring home a Negro, the *Guess Who's Coming to Dinner* kind of fear. Female supporters of Douglas even embroidered their dresses with the slogan "White Men or None."[66]

The first element of Lincoln's rejoinder is simply to expose the tactical nature of Douglas's racism. "If he can, by much drumming and repeating, fasten the odium of that idea [amalgamation] upon his adversaries," then Douglas might be able to salvage his political career (which, Lincoln argues, was increasingly imperiled by the fallout from the Nebraska bill).[67] In order to call out Douglas on this tactic, Lincoln must make explicit the underlying public sentiment that supports it: "There is a natural disgust in the minds of nearly all white people, to the idea of an indiscriminate amalgamation of the white and black races." Statements of this type provoke disgust in modern readers and lead to doubts about Lincoln's own views.[68]

Before joining in the denunciation, we should note a few curious features of Lincoln's formulation. Although he calls the disgust "natural," he also indicates that not all whites share this animus; thus, it is possible that Lincoln counts himself among the nondisgusted minority. He also says the objection is to "indiscriminate" amalgamation. One might wonder about the meaning of that qualifier. Setting aside race for the moment, does anyone recommend or practice "indiscriminate" mixing in their associations with others? Individuals choose their friends and partners deliberately. Would a more discriminating amalgamation (for instance, political but not social) be acceptable to more whites? By war's end, Lincoln would announce himself in favor of qualified suffrage for blacks as a first step toward political equality. We should also remember that black thinkers, at least through W. E. B. DuBois, granted that whites had a legitimate interest in protecting themselves against "indiscriminate" amalgamation. Here is DuBois, writing in 1899:

That the Negro race has an appalling work of social reform before it need hardly be said. Simply because the ancestors of the present white inhabitants of America went out of their way barbarously to mistreat and enslave the ancestors of the present black inhabitants, gives those blacks no right to ask that the civilization and morality of the land be seriously menaced for their benefit. Men have a right to demand that the members of a civilized community be civilized; that the fabric of human culture, so laboriously woven, be not wantonly or ignorantly destroyed.[69]

Such concerns were part of what led Booker T. Washington to believe that the remediation of educational and economic disparities was the pathway to bettered race relations—in other words, that much of the race problem was actually a class problem. Lincoln's word "indiscriminate," which can certainly sustain such a reading, should perhaps mitigate our contemporary outrage. There is a further oddity in Lincoln's formulation: he attributes this "natural disgust" to "minds" in reaction to an "idea." This was not how the "scientific" advance guard of the anti-amalgamation movement conceived the matter. Leading ethnologists such as Josiah Clark Nott and Samuel George Morton were arguing that white repugnance to mixing with blacks was "instinctual," thus confirming their new doctrine of polygenesis (the view that the races were different species, of separate creation, despite the fact of interfertility).[70] Lincoln's formulation—which preserves the possibility of dialogue and critique—gives no credence to such pernicious speculations.

Finally, and most importantly, we should never forget that the reason Lincoln mentions white resistance at all is because he is attempting to neutralize its interference with the antislavery cause. This paragraph starts with the reference to the "natural disgust" of whites but ends with a declaration of the "natural right" of blacks. It is yet another exhibition of Lincoln's ability to move from accommodating white prejudice to transforming and transcending it.

How does he accomplish the move in this instance? In light of the inflamed state of public opinion, he must find a way to challenge his opponent's equation of abolition with amalgamation. Here is what he says:

Now I protest against that counterfeit logic which concludes that, because I do not want a black woman for a *slave* I must necessarily want her for a *wife.* I need not have her for either, I can just leave her alone. In some respects she certainly is not my equal; but in her natural right to eat the bread she earns with her own hands without asking leave of any one else, she is my equal, and the equal of all others.[71]

Note that Lincoln avoids any mention of the black man/white woman pairing, the surefire trigger for white anxiety. Instead he speaks of a black woman and then shows the illogic of Douglas's claim by making himself the illustrative example. Lincoln hates slavery and yet does not seek a black wife. By personalizing the issue, Lincoln manages to deny that he is any kind of advocate for intermarriage, but he does so without giving any credence to the overheated fears of the white racial imagination. His example skirts all those nasty stereotypes about predatory black men. Instead, in a deft rhetorical move, he turns his disavowal of race mixing into an endorsement of the essential equality and independence of women.

Speaking of this hypothetical black woman, Lincoln says he need not "have her" as either a slave or a wife. He can just let her be, allow her to go about her business as a self-determining agent. Lincoln's stance is not unlike that set forth by Frederick Douglass, in his 1865 speech "What the Black Man Wants":

What I ask for the Negro is not benevolence, not pity, not sympathy, but simply *justice*. The American people have always been anxious to know what they shall do with us. . . . I have had but one answer from the beginning. Do nothing with us! Your doing with us has already played the mischief with us. Do nothing with us! . . . All I ask is, give [the Negro] a chance to stand on his own legs! Let him alone! If you see him on his way to school, let him alone, don't disturb him! If you see him going to the dinner-table at a hotel, let him go! If you see him going to the ballot-box, let him alone, don't disturb him! If you see him going into a work-shop, just let him alone, your interference is doing him a positive injury.[72]

Lincoln's statement embodies this same liberal attitude—liberal in the authentic sense of leaving individuals free to exercise their talents and pursue their interests.[73]

Having accorded this black woman equal respect, Lincoln moves immediately to his consideration of the meaning of the Declaration's equality clause—the passage I have already discussed at some length. Nothing could be clearer than that, for Lincoln, "all men" includes not only black men, but all women as well, since his leading example of a person entitled to natural rights is a black woman.

Directly after finishing his long commentary on the individual rights doctrine of the Declaration, Lincoln returns once more to this matter of race mixing (§§35–42). Because Douglas is frightening whites in the free states away from their belief in individual rights by hinting that black freedom would endanger the purity of white womanhood, Lincoln must tack back to address these concerns. This is an admission of sorts that his earlier disavowal, being limited to a description of his own desires and behavior, did not fully meet the case. The issue is not whether Lincoln must himself engage in the ultimate social mixing, but whether someone with his views must allow others to do so. His initial response (§35) is to say: "Agreed for once—a thousand times agreed. There are white men enough to marry all the white women, and black men enough to marry all the black women; and so let them be married." Lincoln cheerfully, even humorously, acknowledges that folks tend to stick to "their own" when it comes to marriage; his ready agreement has the effect of defusing Douglas's attempt to stir up racial chauvinism. I quote from DuBois again, who uses a similar delaying tactic to stave off such fears:

There is a tendency on the part of many white people to approach the Negro question from the side which just now is of least pressing importance, namely, that of the social intermingling of races. The old query: Would you want your sister to marry a Nigger? still stands as a grim sentinel to stop much rational discussion. . . . The whole discussion is little less than foolish; perhaps a century from to-day we may find ourselves seriously discussing such questions of social policy, but it is certain that just as long as one group deems it a serious *mésalliance* to marry with another just so long few marriages will take place, and it will need neither law nor argument to guide human choice in such a matter.[74]

And then, Lincoln's argument takes a bold turn. Citing the available census statistics on the number and residence of mixed-race individuals, Lincoln proves that the real cause of amalgamation—this thing that so horrifies Douglas—is slavery. The problem is not marriage between whites and free black people. The problem is rape of black women by white masters. Lincoln is well aware that slavery violates not only the right to the fruits of one's labor but the right to the integrity of one's body. He points out that where freedom exists, and especially where civic equality exists, mixed-race unions are rare. New Hampshire, "the State," he says, "which goes the farthest toward equality between the races," has the fewest mulattoes. This is a classic instance of Lincoln's brilliant redirection. He has taken the white fear of race mixing and shown how it ought to lead those who have that fear to endorse not only black freedom but civic equality (or at least a greater degree of civic equality).

Today, interracial marriage is no longer controversial. That welcome change can make it difficult for us to appreciate the strategy behind Lincoln's language. We expect all good people to be ostentatiously antiracist. While the case can be made that Lincoln himself is free of racial prejudice, he certainly does not make a big show of being morally outraged by racist views.[75] He knows that attacking the core beliefs of one's audience does not generally win you any friends or any votes. Instead, through his cool, numerical analysis, Lincoln tries to persuade even racial bigots that they ought to rethink their policy preferences. He is willing to exploit white chauvinism in order to further the antislavery cause—and in such a way that chauvinism itself, instead of being reified, is (to borrow a phrase) put in the course of ultimate extinction.[76]

The final step in his argument (§§37–38) involves a shift in tone. It is as if he has now prepared his audience to hear a higher type of appeal. Lincoln reminds us that the *Dred Scott* case, in which the slave Dred Scott was suing for his freedom, involved not just a black man but "his wife and two daughters." With respect to this black family, Lincoln says, "We desired the court to have held that they were citizens so far at least as to entitle them to a hearing as to whether they were free or not; and then, also, that they were in fact and in law really free." Why did Lincoln care about Dred Scott, his wife, and two daughters? What was at stake? Here is what Lincoln says: "Could we have had our way, the chances of these black girls ever mixing their blood with that of white people, would have been diminished at least to the extent that it could not have been without their consent." Lincoln enshrines the notion of consent not only in the public, political realm but in the private, sexual realm. Lincoln is not outraged by race mixing but by the violent and nonconsensual aspect of such mixing as occurs, inevitably, under slavery.[77]

Lincoln contrasts his policy favoring black freedom with the effects of Douglas's endorsement of the *Dred Scott* decision. "But Judge Douglas," he says, "is delighted to have them decided to be slaves, and not human enough to have a hearing . . . and thus left subject to the forced concubinage of their masters, and liable to become the mothers of mulattoes in spite of themselves." I find this to be a profoundly empathetic statement. Lincoln has managed to move his listeners from Douglas's horror at the thought of "the mixing of blood by the white and black races" to sympathy for the daughters of Dred Scott now sent back to the real horrors of slavery. In place of those bigoted caricatures of black men, he encourages his male listeners to put themselves in the shoes of Dred Scott, the father of vulnerable daughters—daughters he will be powerless to protect from the depredations of the slave system.

The argument has come full circle. Lincoln knows his audience is repelled by polygamy. He has now shown that American slavery, at least for women, is often a form of polygamy, the worst kind of polygamy, "forced concubinage." Although not making any specific accusation against Dred Scott's master,

Lincoln nonetheless indicates that "a percentage of masters . . . are inclined to exercise this particular power which they hold over their female slaves."

At the close of his speech, Lincoln sums up the three planks of the Republican position: "that the negro is a man, that his bondage is cruelly wrong, and that the field of his oppression ought not to be enlarged." All three derive from his understanding of the Declaration. Throughout the decade of the 1850s, Lincoln uses his oratorical powers to revive Americans' faith in human equality. Uniquely in the *Dred Scott* Speech, he seeks to strengthen the antislavery sentiments of his audience—sentiments Lincoln believes lie at the very foundation of our sense of justice—by his subtle focus on the fate of women. Lincoln manages to expand our human sympathies without sacrificing analytic rigor and without descending into either overt emotionalism or demagogic appeals to anger, as so many of the abolitionist orators do.

In the concluding section of the *Dred Scott* Speech, through an analysis of colonization, Lincoln offers a final reflection on "public sentiment."[78] In the Peoria Address, he had indicated that while colonization could not be accomplished quickly, it might be doable "in the long run."[79] Here he indicates that the project needs "a hearty will." Significantly, he defines "will" as compounded "from the two elements of moral sense and self-interest." The two must operate in tandem for what is will-worthy to be effectually brought to pass. "Will" is something that requires "forming"—and when formed, it is synonymous with "public sentiment." Lincoln's reference to "the children of Israel," who "went out of Egyptian bondage in a body," makes the case for the God-stamped morality of colonization; if the listener remembers the fate of the Egyptian oppressors, it makes the self-interest case in the strongest possible terms as well. However, as Lincoln knows, the American/Egyptian self-interest in black/Israelite liberty is being obscured. The last paragraph brings into focus the degenerative effect of Douglas's 1854 Kansas-Nebraska Act, which severed any connection between moral sense and self-interest: "It will be ever hard to find many men who will send a slave to Liberia, and pay his passage, while they can send him to a new country, Kansas, for instance, and sell him for fifteen hundred dollars, and the rise." These last words of the *Dred Scott* Speech are a trenchant illustration of Lincoln's thesis in the Peoria Address. In that speech Lincoln said that he hated Douglas's repeal of the Missouri Compromise because it corrupted Americans into "criticizing the Declaration of Independence, and insisting that there is no right principle of action but *self-interest.*"[80] Lincoln's aim in all of these speeches is to reattach self-interest to moral sense. Closing the yawning gap between them requires Lincoln to build word bridges, sometimes temporary ones, made occasionally from materials that modern readers find dubious or distasteful but that are marvels of construction.

## NOTES

1. Frederick Douglass, Oration in Memory of Abraham Lincoln, Delivered at the Unveiling of the Freedmen's Monument in Memory of Abraham Lincoln, in Lincoln Park, Washington, DC, April 14, 1876, in *The Life and Writings of Frederick Douglass*, vol. 4, ed. Philip S. Foner (New York: International, 1975), 309–319.

2. Abraham Lincoln's early Temperance Address should also be consulted for its treatment of the general topic of reform and rhetoric. Lincoln, Address Delivered before the Springfield Washington Temperance Society, February 22, 1842, in *Abraham Lincoln: His Speeches and Writings*, ed. Roy P. Basler (New York: Da Capo, 2001), 131–141.

3. Lewis E. Lehrman, *Lincoln at Peoria: The Turning Point* (Mechanicsburg, PA: Stackpole, 2008), 141–142.

4. Abraham Lincoln, The Repeal of the Missouri Compromise and the Propriety of Its Restoration: Speech at Peoria, Illinois, in Reply to Senator Douglas, October 16, 1854, in *Abraham Lincoln: His Speeches and Writings*, ed. Roy P. Basler (New York: Da Capo, 2001), 283–323.

5. Ibid., 285, 291.

6. Two years earlier, in his eulogy on Henry Clay, Abraham Lincoln had quoted the passage containing Thomas Jefferson's grim metaphor for the conflict between justice and self-preservation; see Lincoln, Eulogy on Henry Clay Delivered in the State House at Springfield, Illinois, July 6, 1852, in *Abraham Lincoln: His Speeches and Writings*, ed. Roy P. Basler (New York: Da Capo, 2001), 273.

7. Abraham Lincoln, 291. Here Lincoln imagines himself as Aristotle's *pambasileus*, the one person with "authority over all matters" (*Politics*, Book 3, chap. 14, 1285b-33).

8. Abraham Lincoln, 292. Lincoln is generally known as an advocate of colonization, so it is interesting that he here presents it in a form (that of instantaneous accomplishment) that leads him to reject it. At the same time, he does indicate that colonization, as a long-term undertaking, might be feasible or at least that "high hope" could attach to its feasibility (a somewhat more qualified endorsement). See the conclusion of Lincoln, Eulogy on Henry Clay, for a more extended explanation of what hope he saw in colonization.

Not surprisingly, the meaning of Lincoln's advocacy of colonization is contested. At one extreme is Lerone Bennett, Jr., *Forced into Glory: Abraham Lincoln's White Dream* (Chicago: Johnson, 1999), who describes Lincoln as relentlessly pursuing ethnic cleansing through plans to deport all blacks. John Burt, in his careful review of the issue, reaches a different scholarly conclusion:

Where Lincoln had enthusiasm for colonization, he had enthusiasm for it as an anti-slavery strategy, and as a means of "restoring a captive people to their long-lost father-land." Where (as is more typical) he embraced colonization grudgingly, he embraced it either as a concession to the persistence of white racism, and black resentment of it, since those things would make a common political culture hard to maintain, or he embraced it strategically, simply as a way to have a ready answer to the politically devastating question of what his plans were for the former slaves; but Lincoln never embraced colonization in order to eliminate black economic competition with the labor of whites, or . . . as a means of purifying the United States to lily-whiteness.

In sum, for Lincoln, colonization "usually served a rhetorical rather than a policy purpose." Burt, *Lincoln's Tragic Pragmatism: Lincoln, Douglas, and Moral Conflict* (Cambridge, MA: Harvard University Press, 2013), 359, 361–362.

9. Frederick Douglass, The Present and Future of the Colored Race in America, a Speech Delivered in the Church of the Puritans, New York, in May 1863, in *The Life and Writings of Frederick Douglass,* vol. 3, ed. Philip S. Foner (New York: International, 1975), 351. As a result of disfranchisement, sharecropping, segregation, discrimination, and lynching, this is what happened post-Reconstruction.

10. *Abraham Lincoln,* 292.

11. Douglass, Oration in Memory of Abraham Lincoln, 315.

12. *Abraham Lincoln,* 292.

13. Ibid., 292.

14. Alexis de Tocqueville, in his famous chapter "On the Three Races That Inhabit the United States," shows how the very ease of ridding the Northern states of slavery made it harder for the Southern states to follow suit. De Tocqueville, *Democracy in America,* trans. Harvey C. Mansfield and Delba Winthrop (Chicago: University of Chicago Press, 2000), 339–341.

15. In Abraham Lincoln's Annual Message to Congress in December 1862, as the Emancipation Proclamation was about to take effect, he sketched an alternative: a comprehensive plan for gradual emancipation. The first thing he said in its defense was, "*The time* spares both races from the evils of sudden derangement." *Abraham Lincoln,* 681 (emphasis added).

16. Ibid., 292.

17. Ibid., 301.

18. Ibid.

19. Ibid., 302.

20. Ibid., 309. John Channing Briggs has a wonderfully rich examination of the biblical and Shakespearean allusions in this portion of the speech, which he describes as a "calculated outburst." Briggs, *Lincoln's Speeches Reconsidered* (Baltimore, MD: Johns Hopkins University Press, 2005), 154–159.

21. *Abraham Lincoln,* 322.

22. The parallel passages are found in ibid., 292 and 322.

23. Harry V. Jaffa notes the parallelism of the two passages in Jaffa, *Crisis of the House Divided: An Interpretation of the Issues in the Lincoln-Douglas Debates* (Chicago: University of Chicago Press, 1959), 376–377 and Jaffa, *A New Birth of Freedom: Abraham Lincoln and the Coming of the Civil War* (Lanham, MD: Rowman and Littlefield, 2000), 337–338. He explains the pairing in terms of the Declaration's twin principles

of consent and equality. In obedience to this dual imperative, Lincoln's statesmanship sought "the highest degree of equality for which general consent could be obtained" (377). I wring a slight change on Jaffa's invaluable insights by attaching significance to the movement (or ascent) in the Peoria Address from the "consent" passage to the "equality" passage.

24. Dred Scott v. Sandford, 60 U.S. 393 (1857), Chief Justice Roger Taney writing for the Court.

25. *Id.*, at 573.

26. *Id.*, at 407.

27. *Id.*

28. *Id.*, at 409, 408.

29. *Id.*, at 409.

30. The term *amalgamation*, borrowed from metallurgy, had been used to describe race mixing since the 1820s. It was especially pressed into service in the North to resist the abolitionists, who were routinely called "amalgamationists." Later, in 1864, in response to the Emancipation Proclamation, a new term would be coined: *miscegenation*. Like amalgamation, miscegenation had a pseudoscientific ring to it. For its devisers— who had combined *miscere*, "to mix," with *genus*, or "race"— it offered the advantage of meaning one thing, and one thing only. See Elise Lemire, *"Miscegenation": Making Race in America* (Philadelphia: University of Pennsylvania Press, 2002), who finds there were three periods of amalgamation hysteria between 1776 and 1865.

31. For the text of this 1671 law, see Archives of Maryland, vol. 2, 272: http://msa.maryland.gov/megafile/msa/speccol/sc2900/sc2908/000001/000002/html/am2--272.html.

32. Ross M. Kimmel, "Blacks before the Law in Colonial Maryland," Archives of Maryland, http://msa.maryland.gov/msa/speccol/sc5300/sc5348/html/title.html.

33. Although the decision was announced on March 6, 1857, Chief Justice Roger Taney undertook revisions in response to Justice Curtis's dissent. Thus, Curtis's tour de force held the field for weeks before the final text of the majority opinion was entered into the record toward the end of May. See Don E. Fehrenbacher, *The Dred Scott Case: Its Significance in American Law and Politics* (New York: Oxford University Press, 1978), 314–321.

34. Stephen Douglas, Remarks on Kansas, Utah, and the *Dred Scott* Decision. I cite a facsimile of the speech printed in a pamphlet by the Chicago Daily Times Book and Job Office, https://archive.org/stream/remarksofhonstep5702doug#page/no/mode/2up.

35. Dred Scott, 60 U.S. 407 (emphasis added).

36. Douglas, Remarks, 11.

37. Ibid.

38. Ibid., 8.

39. Ibid., 11.

40. Dred Scott, 60 U.S. 409.

41. Abraham Lincoln, The *Dred Scott* Decision: Speech at Springfield, Illinois, June 26, 1857, in *Abraham Lincoln: His Speeches and Writings*, ed. Roy P. Basler (New York: Da Capo, 2001), 352–365. The speech has forty-two paragraphs; in-text references are by paragraph number. John Burt notes, "The central theme of Lincoln's attack on the

*Dred Scott* decision was his attack upon its racism, not upon its immediate political aims, because it was the racism of the decision that most corroded the habits of thought that democracies cannot survive losing." Burt, *Lincoln's Tragic Pragmatism,* 553.

42. In fairness to Stephen Douglas, it should be noted that he does attempt to justify his stance on all three issues under the rubric of "the rights of self-government"—although in the case of Utah, he argues that the right ought to be revoked, "blotting the territorial government out of existence" because the Mormons had become "alien enemies and outlaws." Douglas, Remarks, 13.

43. Ibid., 9 (emphasis added).

44. Dred Scott, 60 U.S. 410.

45. In his dissent, Justice Curtis had stated, "This is not the place to vindicate their memory." Nonetheless, he said enough to establish that his view coincided with that of Lincoln:

> I shall not enter into an examination of the existing opinions of that period respecting the African race, nor into any discussion concerning the meaning of those who asserted, in the Declaration of Independence, that all men are created equal; that they are endowed by their Creator with certain inalienable rights; that among these are life, liberty, and the pursuit of happiness. My own opinion is, that a calm comparison of these assertions of universal abstract truths, and of their own individual opinions and acts, would not leave these men under any reproach of inconsistency; that the great truths they asserted on that solemn occasion, they were ready and anxious to make effectual, wherever a necessary regard to circumstances, which no statesman can disregard without producing more evil than good, would allow; and that it would not be just to them, nor true in itself, to allege that they intended to say that the Creator of all men had endowed the white race, exclusively, with the great natural rights which the Declaration of Independence asserts. But this is not the place to vindicate their memory. As I conceive, we should deal here, not with such disputes, if there can be a dispute concerning this subject, but with those substantial facts evinced by the written Constitutions of States, and by the notorious practice under them. And they show, in a manner which no argument can obscure, that in some of the original thirteen States, free colored persons, before and at the time of the formation of the Constitution, were citizens of those States. Dred Scott, 60 U.S. 574–575.

46. *Abraham Lincoln,* 360–361. All in-text Lincoln quotes for the remainder of this section are from §26. Chief Justice Roger Taney, by the way, had admitted that the terms of the Declaration "would seem to embrace the whole human family, and if they were used in a similar instrument at this day would be so understood." Dred Scott, 60 U.S. 410.

47. Kurt Vonnegut, Jr., provides a dystopic vision of a United States in which "nobody was smarter than anybody else. Nobody was better looking than anybody else. Nobody was stronger or quicker than anybody else." Vonnegut, "Harrison Bergeron," in *Welcome to the Monkey House* (New York: Dial, 1968), 7–14.

48. For a full treatment of the elements in the list, see Diana J. Schaub, "Abraham

Lincoln's Commentary on the 'Plain Unmistakable Language' of the Declaration of Independence," in *Liberal Moments: Reading Liberal Texts,* ed. Ewa Atanassow and Alan S. Kahan (London: Bloomsbury, 2017). This section of the chapter contains material drawn from that article.

49. Douglas, Remarks, 8, 9, 10, 11.

50. Dred Scott, 60 U.S. 403, 405, 406, 407, 408.

51. When Abraham Lincoln did so, it was usually to summarize the position of his opponents, as when he said that "Judge Douglas is especially horrified at the thought of the mixing of blood by the white and black races" or when he noted, with satirical import, that "the French, Germans and other white people of the world are all gone to pot along with the Judge's inferior races." When speaking in his own voice, he tended to use the phrases "white and black people," "free colored persons," and even "free Americans of African descent." Justice Curtis, also, avoided the term "race," instead speaking of "colored persons" or "persons of color descended from Africans held in slavery." Dred Scott, 60 U.S. 574.

52. Abraham Lincoln, Fragment on Slavery, in *Abraham Lincoln: His Speeches and Writings,* ed. Roy P. Basler (New York: Da Capo, 2001), 58.

53. Douglas, Remarks, 11.

54. Abraham Lincoln attached great significance to "reverence," beginning with his Lyceum Address in 1838—the first of his many reflections on what it means to conserve a revolutionary founding. Lincoln, The Perpetuation of Our Political Institutions: Address before the Young Men's Lyceum of Springfield, Illinois, January 27, 1838, in *Abraham Lincoln: His Speeches and Writings,* ed. Roy P. Basler (New York: Da Capo, 2001), 76–85.

55. The material in this section is an expanded version of what appears in Diana J. Schaub, "Abraham Lincoln and the Daughters of *Dred Scott:* A Reflection on the Declaration of Independence," in *When in the Course of Human Events: 1776 at Home, Abroad, and in American Memory,* ed. Will R. Jordan (Macon, GA: Mercer University Press, 2018), 194–214.

56. The attacks on Stephen Douglas come in five waves: on Utah (§§2–3); on Kansas (§§4–8); on the character of judicial precedent (§§9–18); on the meaning of the Declaration (§§24–34); and on "the mixing of blood" (§§35–42).

57. Abraham Lincoln, First Debate, at Ottawa, Illinois, August 21, 1858, in *Abraham Lincoln: His Speeches and Writings,* ed. Roy P. Basler (New York: Da Capo, 2001), 458.

58. Ibid., 331.

59. Stephen Douglas, in his speech, had come out in favor of extremely strong measures revoking Utah's territorial status, thus in effect denying the residents of Utah "popular sovereignty," the centerpiece of Douglas's policy for the territories. Lincoln hammered Douglas for his hypocrisy, claiming that his readiness to abandon popular sovereignty for Utah proved that the doctrine was "a mere deceitful pretense for the benefit of slavery." *Abraham Lincoln: His Speeches and Writings,* ed. Roy P. Basler (New York: Da Capo, 2001), 353.

60. Plural marriage was then part of the religious doctrine of the Church of Jesus Christ of Latter-Day Saints. One-third of Mormon women were estimated to be in polygamous marriages.

61. This plank was the third of nine resolutions. See http://www.presidency.ucsb .edu/ws/?pid=29619.

62. See the reasoning in Reynolds v. United States, 98 U.S. 145 (1878):

Marriage, while from its very nature a sacred obligation, is nevertheless, in most civilized nations, a civil contract, and usually regulated by law. Upon it society may be said to be built, and out of its fruits spring social relations and social obligations and duties, with which government is necessarily required to deal. In fact, according as monogamous or polygamous marriages are allowed, do we find the principles on which the government of the people, to a greater or less extent, rests. Professor Lieber says, polygamy leads to the patriarchal principle, and which, when applied to large communities, fetters the people in stationary despotism, while that principle cannot long exist in connection with monogamy. (166)

63. These remarks also highlight Douglas's dishonesty.

64. There is another intervening attack on Douglas. In the course of explaining his view of the proper weight that attaches to judicial precedent, Lincoln convicts Douglas (who accused Lincoln of seditious disrespect for the Court) of hypocrisy by reminding the audience of Douglas's criticisms of the Court at the time of the bank decision: "It would be interesting for him to look over his recent speech, and see how exactly his fierce philippics against us for resisting Supreme Court decisions, fall upon his own head." *Abraham Lincoln: His Speeches and Writings,* ed. Roy P. Basler (New York: Da Capo, 2001), 357.

65. Douglas, Remarks, 8. As Eric Foner points out, "'Social equality' was more a term of abuse than a legal or analytical category." It did not mean natural rights, civil rights, or political rights. It was code for "interracial sexual relations and marriage." Foner, *The Fiery Trial: Abraham Lincoln and American Slavery* (New York: Norton, 2010), 118.

66. Allen C. Guelzo, *Lincoln and Douglas: The Debates That Defined America* (New York: Simon and Schuster, 2008), 186, 219.

67. *Abraham Lincoln,* 359–360. This first discussion of "amalgamation" is in §25.

68. George M. Fredrickson traces the emergence in the past forty years of scholars "fixated on what they take to be Lincoln's dyed-in-the-wool racism," regarding him "as just another American white supremacist"; on the other side of this "historiographic polarization" are scholars who "view Lincoln as a consistent and effective opponent of slavery and a sincere, if sometimes politically covert, champion of racial equality." Fredrickson, *Big Enough to Be Inconsistent: Abraham Lincoln Confronts Slavery and Race* (Cambridge, MA: Harvard University Press, 2008), x. Fredrickson attempts to delineate a nuanced and politically contextualized middle ground between the hagiographers and the debunkers. Similarly thoughtful and fair-minded is Henry Louis Gates, Jr., in the substantial essay that opens his edited anthology of all of Lincoln's comments on the topics of race and slavery. Gates, *Lincoln on Race and Slavery* (Princeton, NJ: Princeton University Press, 2009). Although the collection is a valuable sourcebook, it is always important to resituate these excerpts in the longer pieces to which they belong before hazarding any interpretation of their meaning.

Gates, who admits he is not a Lincoln scholar, has made important discoveries through his fresh engagement with the material: "One of the most striking conclusions that a close reading of Lincoln's speeches and writings yielded to me was that 'slavery,' 'race,' and 'colonization' were quite often three separate issues for him"—a compartmentalization that "far too many scholars" fail to see, and, as a result, they "blur distinctions that were important to him and to his contemporaries" (xx–xxi).

69. W. E. B. DuBois, *The Philadelphia Negro*, in *African-American Social and Political Thought: 1850–1920*, ed. Howard Brotz (New Brunswick, NJ: Transaction, 1992), 503.

70. Lemire, *"Miscegenation,"* 111–114. For a full treatment of "scientific" racism, see the chapter by Alan Levine in this volume.

71. *Abraham Lincoln*, 360.

72. Frederick Douglass, What the Black Man Wants: Speech at the Annual Meeting of the Massachusetts Anti-Slavery Society at Boston, April 1865, in *The Life and Writings of Frederick Douglass*, vol. 4, ed. Philip S. Foner (New York: International, 1975), 164.

73. Lemire reads this passage differently: "There is nothing attractive, he implies, about a black woman when he repeatedly insists that he 'can just let her alone.' . . . He bases his insistence of non-interest on a belief in black physical inferiority" (138) Although such a belief was prevalent at the time, I see no textual reason to ascribe it to Lincoln. Doing so fails to recognize the purpose of this passage. I suspect as well that contemporary listeners are put off by Lincoln saying that this woman is in some respects not his equal. I must say I am not at all bothered by that because I do not regard myself (or indeed anyone I have ever met) as Lincoln's equal, except, of course, in the respect he mentions: that of having an equal natural right to enjoy the fruits of one's own labor.

74. DuBois, *Philadelphia Negro*, 506.

75. Despite his attribution to Abraham Lincoln of "unfriendly feelings" toward blacks, Frederick Douglass concluded his oration by hailing Lincoln as "our friend and liberator" (319), Douglass credited Lincoln not only with the Emancipation Proclamation but with "measures approved and vigorously pressed by him" that began to dismantle "prejudice and proscription" (314).

76. Harry Jaffa says of this passage, "In slyly pointing out that where there was the greatest equality there was the least miscegenation, [Lincoln] drew from the premises of racial bigotry a forceful argument for racial equality. Here is a profound intimation of how little Lincoln actually shared the general opinions on race that dominated the political discourse of his time." Jaffa, *New Birth of Freedom*, 330–331. Speaking more generally, John Burt also notes the forward thrust of Lincoln's formulations: "Despite repeated denials that he favored racial equality, Lincoln consistently chose the arguments that would lay the groundwork for racial equality later, and rejected arguments that would have supported preventing the spread of slavery into the territories but that would have ruled racial equality out." Burt, *Lincoln's Tragic Pragmatism*, 335.

77. It is true that Lincoln swore to stand by the laws banning mixed-race marriages in the Charleston debate. Once again, though, he played that endorsement for a joke, vowing to uphold the statutes for the sake of "Judge Douglas and his friends," who "seem to be in great apprehension that they might [marry Negroes], if there were no

law to keep them from it," suggesting further that Douglas be kept in the Illinois State Legislature (and out of the US Senate) so that he could fight any attempt to repeal the restraining order against his runaway desires. Quoted in *The Lincoln-Douglas Debates of 1858,* ed. Robert W. Johannsen (New York: Oxford University Press, 1965), 163.

78. Lincoln's advocacy of colonization is often troubling to contemporary readers. As an anonymous reviewer queried, "If he believed in equality, why would he even consider colonization?" It is certainly true that if someone today were to float the idea of the voluntary departure of blacks en masse from the United States, it would rightly be regarded as obnoxious and at odds with the notion of equal citizenship. However, the question as applied to antebellum America is anachronistic. In fact, many of those who supported colonization in that time (from white leaders such as Henry Clay to black leaders such as Martin Delany and Henry Highland Garnett) did so because they believed in black equality and wanted to improve the chances of its realization. Referring to the passage about colonization in Lincoln's Eulogy on Henry Clay, George Fredrickson says: "Although Lincoln was advocating a separation of the races, he did so in this instance without suggesting that the races were inherently unequal in capacities. Blacks, he implied, have capabilities, perhaps as great as those of whites, but they could realize them only in Africa or at least outside the United States" because of the obstacle of white prejudice. Fredrickson, *Big Enough to Be Inconsistent,* 58. According to Henry Louis Gates, Jr., Lincoln "continued to contemplate colonization for much of his term as president because of an equally genuine concern that the huge number of slaves who would ultimately be freed by the Thirteenth Amendment would never be accepted by the former Confederates and white people in the North. . . . It was certainly not unreasonable for Lincoln, and anyone else who took a moment to think about it, [to realize] that it would be extraordinarily difficult to assimilate this mass of former slaves into an integrated American society without extended social, political, and economic conflict." Gates, *Lincoln on Race and Slavery,* xxvi.

79. *Abraham Lincoln,* 292.

80. Ibid., 291.

# CHAPTER 7

# Why Did Lincoln Go to War?

STEVEN B. SMITH

Dictatorship is like the act of self-defense. . . . The argument has been repeated ever since—first and foremost by Abraham Lincoln: when the body of the constitution is under threat, it must be safeguarded through a temporary suspension of the constitution.—Carl Schmitt

A decent society will not go to war except for a just cause. But what it will do during a war will depend to a certain extent on what the enemy—possibly an absolutely unscrupulous and savage enemy—forces it to do. There are no limits which can be assigned in advance.—Leo Strauss

When and under what conditions will democracies fight to protect themselves from internal disunity? This question was raised by German émigré and political scientist Karl Loewenstein in his definitive article "Militant Democracy and Fundamental Rights."[1] Writing in the wake of the Nazi seizure of power, Loewenstein was concerned with the inability or unwillingness of democracies to protect themselves from the rise of extremist parties. This was a problem not unique to but exacerbated in Weimar Germany, where elements of both the left and the right contested the government's legitimacy. When is it acceptable to use force against those who contest the very premises of democratic self-government? "Government," Loewenstein wrote, "is intended for governing."[2] When the organs of government are under attack, governments are empowered to use whatever powers are at their disposal to reaffirm their authority. Loewenstein's theory of militant democracy is also at the core of Abraham Lincoln's response to the crisis of secessionism in 1860. However, how far is it possible for a constitutional government to go? Can a constitutional government use force—even suspend constitutional liberties and rule of law—in order to prevent its dismemberment? Can it go to war to do so? These were the questions with which Lincoln had to contend as he took the oath of office as president of the United States.

*THE ELECTION OF 1860 AND THE THREAT OF DISUNION*

Virtually no sooner had Lincoln been elected as the sixteenth president than the state of South Carolina passed by a unanimous vote its Ordinance of Secession, declaring that the union of South Carolina with all the other states, both North and South, was henceforth dissolved. This act met with delirious enthusiasm and was soon followed by the states of Mississippi, Florida, Alabama, Georgia, Louisiana, and Texas. A convention with delegates from seven Southern states met in Montgomery, Alabama, to draft a new constitution for themselves and begin proceedings of secession. A former Mississippi senator, Jefferson Davis, was nominated as the president of the new provisional Confederate government a month before Lincoln even arrived in the nation's capital.[3]

What was it—every student of the period is inclined to ask—that made the election of Lincoln so unacceptable as to require the dissolution of the Union? He had repeatedly said that he had no intention to interfere with slavery where it existed but only to restrict its spread to places where it did not yet exist. In the months prior to Lincoln's inauguration, several makeshift proposals were suggested for heading off the secession crisis. One of them, the Crittenden Compromise—so named after Senator John Crittenden from Kentucky—would have extended the old Missouri Compromise line all the way to the Pacific with the understanding that slavery would be perpetually accepted south of the line and prohibited north of it. This proposal was supported by the Washington Peace Conference, convened in February 1861, which included representatives from twenty-one states, including former president John Tyler.[4] This conference proved as unacceptable to Lincoln, whose policy was to oppose all further extension of slavery, as it was to the secessionists, who believed it was their lawful right to extend slavery. Did this mean that the Republican Committee of Thirteen, which voted against the Crittenden Compromise, killed any chance for peace? "Probably not," James McPherson concludes. "Neither Crittenden's nor any other compromise could have stopped secession in the lower South. No compromise could undo the event that triggered disunion: Lincoln's election by a solid North."[5]

It is often argued, with some justice, that Lincoln seriously underestimated the secession crisis.[6] He viewed the threat of secession largely as a bluff to extract further concessions along the lines of the Crittenden Compromise. Lincoln expressed his faith in the loyalty of the majority of the Southern population in a passage written for delivery in a speech given by Lyman Trumbull just over two weeks after his election:

Disunionists *per se* are now in hot haste to get out of the Union, precisely because they perceived they cannot, much longer, maintain apprehension among the Southern people that their homes, and firesides, and lives, are to be endangered by the action of the Federal Government. With such *"Now or never"* is the maxim. I am rather glad of this military preparation in the South. It will enable the people the more easily to suppress any uprisings there, which their misrepresentations of purposes may have encouraged.[7]

As this passage makes clear, Lincoln tended to see the talk of secession as the work of a small group of Southern firebrands—the "Now or never" lobby— who had managed to exert undue influence over the majority of the Southern population. When push came to shove, he believed that the mass of Southerners would remain loyal to the Union. He was wrong. "Lincoln's obtuseness to the secession threat was probably the greatest political misjudgment of his life," Allen Guelzo has written.[8] The doctrine of state sovereignty had been drummed into Southern opinion as completely as the doctrine of unionism held sway in the North. Furthermore, the belief in state sovereignty proved inseparable from slavery. It might be asked—as I think Lincoln believed—what interest the vast majority of Southerners who were not slave owners could possibly have in sustaining an institution in which they had no share. Why would a small subsistence-level farmer fight to preserve slavery for the wealthy planter oligarchy? This is a question that has bedeviled all students of the Civil War and American history. The sad but inevitable conclusion is that the appeal of racial domination—what George Fredrickson called *Herrenvolk* democracy—proved more attractive than the appeal of the Union. In America race has always trumped class. This appeal to race and racial hierarchy was—and remains—the tragedy of American politics.[9]

However, if Lincoln might have underestimated secession fervor, it might equally be argued that the South seriously overplayed its hand. None believed that the North would go to war to preserve the Union, and it was further believed that if the North attempted a naval blockade of Southern ports, then the European powers, especially England and France, would intervene on behalf of the South. To be sure, secession was not universally popular in the South and was manipulated by extremist minorities in the states of the Deep South who rammed their agenda through the various state conventions before there was even an adequate chance to deliberate on the matter. Nevertheless, it might still be asked: What was the immediate danger? Lincoln did not come into office with an overwhelming mandate. He would have—and could have—done no more than prevent the spread of slavery to any newly acquired territory. He had repeatedly pledged to support the fugitive slave laws then on the books, accepted the constitutionality of the *Dred Scott* decision, and denied any attempt to abolish slavery in the District of Columbia or the slave trade among the slave states. Why did the Southern rejectionists not simply decide to bide their time and hope for an outcome more to their liking in the next election? This question is frequently asked with a sense of exasperation by those who regard politics as an endless back and forth of the political pendulum as public opinion shifts first one way, then another. What is certainly true is that by choosing to secede, Southerners brought a quicker and certainly more violent end to slavery than had they stayed in the Union. Had the South not seceded— who knows?—Lincoln might have been just another in a list of uninspired one-term presidents, and slavery could have lasted well into the twentieth century.[10]

The answer is that in politics—as in love and war—people are inclined to forget where their best interests lie and let their passions carry them away. Despite the objection that Lincoln represented no material threat to their interests, those in the South regarded the election of Lincoln not just as another swing of the pendulum but as a decisive statement—at least by a sizable portion of Northern opinion—that slavery was no longer merely something about which Americans could continue to agree to disagree. The election of Lincoln had declared that to a large body of the population, slavery was a moral wrong that, even if it could not be eliminated, could no longer be granted equal moral status. And this to the South was deemed intolerable. It was an assault not so much on their interests but on their identity, their entire way of life, inseparable from slavery. When it comes to matters of moral identity, what we demand is recognition, at the very least toleration, but the idea that some regard our moral identity as somehow tainted or unclean is no longer tolerable. This is what the election of 1860 said to the South, that its very identity could no longer be seen as morally equal to that of the North. What the South rejected in Lincoln had little to do with his policy but everything to do with what he and his political party represented. "If one issue sent the slave states fleeing from the Union," James Oakes has written, "this was it: the Republican Party had elected a president who did not believe there was a constitutional right of property in slaves."[11]

The right of secession, it was argued, had deep roots in the American political tradition going back to the founding of the nation. The American Revolution began with an act of secession from the British Empire. The Declaration of Independence included the right of rebellion as one of the chief rights to be exercised whenever government becomes oppressive and intolerable. The

Constitution itself was ratified not by some national plebiscite but by the individual states, at which time each could vote on whether to accept or reject the new arrangements. Was not the right of withdrawal—the right of peaceful exit—crucial to our understanding of free government? This doctrine of the inherent sovereignty of each individual state was given expression in John C. Calhoun's nullification thesis and held as virtual dogma throughout the South. The Union appeared to those in the South as a treaty of alliance, from which exit might be painful but that still gave each state ultimate authority to decide whether to remain or withdraw its allegiance. The question is whether this reading of the Constitution holds water, whether any Constitution can allow for its own dissolution.[12]

To be sure, the Constitution is silent on this matter. There is nothing in the text that either affirms or denies a state's right to secede. Lincoln would argue—as we will see—that to admit the right of secession is a virtual nonsequitur. Lincoln in fact never admitted a right to secession. There is no such thing as a state that allows for its own dissolution. The seceding states he always said were in a state of rebellion and had therefore put themselves outside the Constitution. Lord Charnwood, by no means sympathetic to the right of secession, provides a characteristically beautiful expression of the painful moral dilemma faced by those of the North and the South with all the elements of a Greek tragedy:

In no other contest of history are those elements of human affairs on which tragic dramatists are prone to dwell so clearly marked as in the American Civil War. No unsophisticated person now, except in ignorance of the cause of the war, can hesitate as to which side enlists his sympathy, or can regard the victory of the North otherwise than as the costly and imperfect triumph of the right. But the wrong side—emphatically wrong—is not lacking in dignity or human worth; the long-drawn agony of the struggle is not purely horrible to contemplate; there is nothing that in this case makes us reluctant to acknowledge the merits of the men who took arms in the evil cause.[13]

When Lincoln arrived in Washington under cloak of darkness because of rumors of planned assassination, the representatives of seven Southern states had already drawn up a new constitution and inaugurated their own provisional president. Lincoln's First Inaugural Address was delivered on March 4, 1861, on the steps of the still-unfinished capitol building. The oath of office was administered by Chief Justice Roger Taney, who had signed the *Dred Scott* decision into law just three years before. Never before in history had so much hung in the balance.

## "*THE UNION OF THESE STATES IS PERPETUAL*"

Of all the presidential inaugurals ever spoken, Lincoln's first is the one most clearly devoted to the theme of constitutional government. It is less a speech than a lecture on the meaning and scope of political authority. According to Lincoln's law partner and first biographer, William Herndon, Lincoln began working on the speech in late January. Among the works he chose to consult in writing the speech were Henry Clay's speech on the Compromise of 1850, Andrew Jackson's proclamation against nullification, a copy of the US Constitution, and Daniel Webster's 1830 speech against Robert Hayne, which, according to Herndon, Lincoln regarded as "the grandest specimen of American oratory."[14] The First Inaugural Address, along with his Message to Congress in Special Session of July 4, 1861, constitute the essence of Lincoln's political philosophy. It behooves us to read both of them carefully.

At the core of Lincoln's inaugural speech is a debate over the foundation and limits of free government, or "self-government," as Lincoln called it. Is the government the result of a compact between the states in which each of the parties to the compact retains its sovereign rights as it had before, or is the government a union in which not the states but the people as a whole are sovereign? Is the Union one and indivisible, as the Whig tradition of Webster and Clay maintained, or a confederation of discrete entities, as John Taylor of Caroline and Calhoun believed? The debate goes back to the very name of our government: the United States. Is the emphasis to be put on the first word or the second, on the Union or the states? Do we call the war the Civil War, as favored in the North, or the War between the States, as favored in the South? These questions provide the crucial background of Lincoln's address.[15]

"In compliance with a custom as old as the government itself, I appear before you," are Lincoln's first words, the reference to custom and age clearly intended to mollify the doubts of his critics (324).[16] The speech, as Harry Jaffa has noted, had to be "firm but not belligerent," trying to find a basis for consensus among friend and foe alike.[17] Accordingly, Lincoln continues with a series of specific pledges he hopes will assuage his critics that he bears them no hostile intentions, that he will willingly, even "cheerfully," maintain the territorial integrity and "domestic institutions" of each state, including the enforcement of existing slavery legislation. On this basis, he then claims to take the oath of office with "no mental reservations" and with "no purpose to construe the Constitution or laws by any hypercritical rules," this last phrase suggesting that he would not bring his own private conscience or other external standard to bear on constitutional matters. Lincoln even goes as far as to quote the entire fugitive slave clause from the Constitution and points out that he has sworn to uphold this law "as much as any other" (326). To be sure, he goes on to acknowledge a difference of opinion over how that act is to be enforced, whether it is the duty of the national government to return fugitives or the responsibility of slaveholders, who would be obliged to press their case in state courts. "But surely that difference is not a very material one," Lincoln adds, stating that "it can be of little consequence . . . by which authority it is done" (326).[18]

After engaging in these preliminaries, Lincoln turns to the real subject of the address: "It is seventy-two years since the first inauguration of a President under our national Constitution" (326). Recognizing the difficulty of the task before him, he notes that of his fifteen predecessors, many had to navigate specific perils, but for the first time a disruption of the federal Union is now not merely threatened but "formidably attempted." On what basis, then, is this proposed secession to be resisted? Here Lincoln's tone shifts. He employs a number of arguments—philosophical, historical, and legal—to support his case that the Union is permanent and more than simply the sum of its parts. He then goes on to state the nub of his thesis as follows:

I hold that in contemplation of universal law, and of the Constitution, the Union of these States is perpetual. Perpetuity is implied, if not expressed, in the fundamental law of all national governments. It is safe to assert that no government proper, ever had a provision in its organic law for its own termination. Continue to execute all the express provisions of our national Constitution, and the Union will endure forever—it being impossible to destroy it, except by some action not provided for in the instrument itself. (326–327)

This is a crucial passage. It is often argued that Lincoln entertained a "mystical" idea of the Union that had no foundation in history or law.[19] Yet here we see that Lincoln's fundamental concern has nothing mystical about it at all. His concern is with the elementary conditions of self-government. The right of self-preservation is not only something that pertains to individuals but to forms of government. A government unable to sustain itself through free and fair elections can no longer claim to be a government. His reference here to what he calls the "fundamental law" or "organic law" of all constitutions entails the argument for the perpetuity of such a government. There is simply no such thing as a Constitution that allows for its own dissolution. The most fundamental right entailed by the Constitution is the right to self-preservation. Lincoln claims to find evidence for this right in the presidential oath of office to "preserve, protect, and defend" the Constitution from dismemberment or attack.

Lincoln next attempts to sustain his philosophical account of the "organic law" of all constitutions with a historical argument about the US Constitution. His claim, simply put, is that the states of the Union only have their existence through the Constitution, not the Constitution through the states:

Descending from these general principles, we find the proposition that, in legal contemplation, the Union is perpetual, confirmed by the history of the Union itself. The Union is much older than the Constitution. It was formed in fact, by the Articles of Association in 1774. It was matured and continued by the Declaration of Independence in 1776. It was further matured and the faith of all the then thirteen states expressly plighted and engaged that it should be perpetual by the Articles of Confederation in 1778. And finally, in 1787, one of the declared objects for ordaining and establishing the Constitution, was "*to form a more perfect union.*" (327)

Lincoln here articulates the national theory of the Constitution. On this view, the Union was brought into being not by the independent states but by a collective act of the people as a whole. "We, the people," not "we the representatives of the states" are the opening words of the preamble of the Constitution. But Lincoln added his own historical reconstruction of how this Union came about. The Union, he tells his audience, was born in 1774 with the Articles of Association, matured two years later with the Declaration of Independence, and further consolidated under the Articles of Confederation. Finally, the Constitution, with the claim to create a "more perfect union," conferred a national identity on what was still a less-than-perfect form of association. Lincoln draws from this the inevitable conclusion: no state has the right to constitutionally withdraw from the Union, secession is an act of rebellion, and the constitutional power to suppress rebellion is therefore unquestionable. QED.

Lincoln next turns from high constitutional theorizing to a series of practical questions he had addressed many times in his debates with Stephen A. Douglas and in the Cooper Union Speech. There are many issues, he contends, to which the Constitution simply provides no answer. If the majority could simply deprive the minority of its rights, this might be enough to justify revolution. Think, he asks. Has this ever been the case? There are many cases in which the Constitution is silent, and people will have to agree to disagree:

But no organic law can ever be framed with a provision specifically applicable to every question which may occur in practical administration. No foresight can anticipate, nor any document of reasonable length contain express provisions for all possible questions. Shall fugitives from labor be surrendered by national or by State authority? The Constitution does not expressly say. *May* Congress prohibit slavery in the territories?

The Constitution does not expressly say. *Must* Congress protect slavery in the territories? The Constitution does not expressly say. (328–329)

The point at issue between Lincoln and his secessionist critics is the oldest one in political theory: Who governs? For the states of the South, the law of the land had been decided by the Taney Court's *Dred Scott* ruling. In their view, the states of the North appeared to be in violation of the Constitution with the election of Lincoln and his stated desire to put slavery on the path of "ultimate extinction." Lincoln argued, by contrast, that not the Court but the people are sovereign in a free state. To argue that matters are to be "irrevocably fixed" by the decision of the Court is to argue that the people have ceased to be their own rulers and have resigned their government to that "eminent tribunal." The primary remedy for real or alleged usurpations by governments is through changing the officers of those governments by free elections and not by seeking redress in the courts.

As the president-elect, Lincoln hopes to exercise caution, fully recognizing that this reticence could be mistaken for inaction. He will fulfill his constitutional duties to the best of his abilities unless the American people, his "rightful master," withhold the means. These duties include the occupation and possession of government properties, the collection of taxes and imposts, and the delivery of the mail in all parts of the Union. All of this can be done, Lincoln enjoins, without invasion and with "no using of force against or among the people anywhere." He goes as far as to concede that if local hostility should prevent federal officials from carrying out their duties, he will not attempt to replace them with "obnoxious strangers" to secure those ends, even though it would be his right to do so. "There was a strong note of contingency in the line of action announced in the inaugural," David Potter writes.[20] His frequent use of the passive voice is an indication of the degree to which he believes affairs are out of his own hands. "The course here indicated will be followed," Lincoln announced, "unless current events and experience, shall show a modification, or change, to be proper" (328).

Lincoln then goes on to parse the logic of secession. In a free government, there is no alternative but to accept the judgment of the majority, constrained by constitutional guarantees for the rights of minorities. If the minority refuses to be governed by the majority, there is no other foundation for self-government. If a minority will secede rather than acquiesce, Lincoln warns of the danger of an infinite regress. It will only be a matter of time until some minority of the minority demands another secession and so on, ad infinitum. The result will be a cycle of ungovernability:

Plainly, the central idea of secession, is the essence of anarchy. A majority, held in restraint by constitutional checks, and limitations, and always changing easily, with deliberate changes of popular opinions and sentiments, is the only true sovereign of a free people. Whoever rejects it, does of necessity, fly to anarchy or despotism. Unanimity is impossible; the rule of a minority, as a permanent arrangement, is wholly inadmissible; so that, rejecting the majority principle, anarchy or despotism in some form, is all that is left. (329)

The core issue separating the two sides can be stated simply: "One section of the country believes slavery is *right,* and ought to be extended, while the other believes it is *wrong* and ought not be extended" (330). Will the call for separation resolve or exacerbate this problem? Lincoln affirms the latter. The great body of the people both North and South, he attests, continues to abide by "the dry legal obligation" of the law. This would almost certainly cease after separation. The restrictions on the slave trade—outlawed since 1808—would be lifted in the South, whereas the obligation to return fugitives would be ignored in the North. Lincoln then goes on to argue for the impossibility of separation. "Physically speaking," he says, "we cannot separate. We cannot remove our respective section from each other, nor build an impassable wall between them" (330). He compares disunion to a divorce, but one in which the couple must continue to live together in the same house. Unlike actual husbands and wives who can simply go their own separate ways, North and South would continue to coexist side by side in continual contact. "Is it possible," he asks rhetorically, "then to make that intercourse more advantageous or more satisfactory, *after* separation than *before?*" (330).

The theme of the final paragraphs of the speech is firm but conciliatory. "This life-long pattern of yielding and resisting, of deferring to other views yet refusing to abandon principle is at work throughout the speech" and nowhere more memorably than in the peroration, John Channing Briggs writes.[21] "Why should there not be a patient confidence in the ultimate justice of the people?" Lincoln asks (331). He urges the citizens to "think calmly and *well,*" adding that nothing can be lost by "taking time." He calls upon "intelligence, patriotism, Christianity, and a firm reliance" upon God, "who has never forsaken this favored land," as the best means of resolving the dispute. After having initially sought to assuage his audience about his pacific intentions, Lincoln now begins to unsheathe the sword. The choice between war and peace rests entirely in the hands of his "dissatisfied fellow countrymen," he warns. "You can have no conflict without yourselves being the aggressors." Lincoln will not begin a conflict, but he also cautions that he will not shrink from one. "*You* have no oath registered in Heaven to destroy the government, while *I* shall have the most solemn one to 'preserve, protect, and defend' it" (331–332). Lincoln's reference to his oath of office suggests that he would not stand idly by and watch the Union be dismembered but would be prepared to act to preserve it. The question is, Just what was Lincoln entitled to do?

The most memorable part of the First Inaugural Address is its closing lines appealing to "the better angels of our nature." What does he mean by this poetic interjection in what is otherwise a lecture on constitutional law? First, it should be noted these words were not originally a part of Lincoln's draft of the speech. When Lincoln arrived in Washington on February 23, he was still at work on the speech and gave the draft to Seward, by then Lincoln's designated secretary of state, to read it and make some suggestions. Seward responded with a seven-page letter suggesting some forty-nine changes, the most important being the final paragraph. Originally, the speech had ended with the paragraph beginning "In your hands, my dissatisfied countrymen and not mine, is the momentous issue of civil war." However, this paragraph had originally ended with a reference to Matthew 10:34, in which Jesus speaks of bringing judgment to earth. "With you and not with me is the solemn question, 'Will it be peace or a sword?'"

Seward thought this far too militant and suggested more conciliatory language. What he proposed was the following:

I close. We are not, we must not be aliens or enemies, but fellow countrymen and brethren. Although passion has strained our bonds of affection too hardly they must not, I am sure they will not be broken. The mystic chords which proceeding from so many battlefields and so many patriot graves pass through all the hearts and all the hearths in this broad continent of ours will yet again harmonize in their ancient music when breathed upon by the guardian angel of the nation.

Lincoln then made his own changes to Seward's text:

I am loath to close. We are not enemies but friends. We must not be enemies. Though passion may have strained, it must not break our bonds of affection. The mystic chords of memory, stretching from every battlefield and patriot grave to every living heart and hearthstone all over this broad land, will yet swell the chorus of the Union when again touched, as surely they will be, by the better angels of our nature. (332)

Lincoln's changes are deeply revealing. Seward's "I close" directly signals the end of the speech. Lincoln's "I am loath to close" suggests not only reluctance but fear of what will happen when he does. Seward's "mystic chords" become Lincoln's "mystic chords of memory." The theme of memory and forgetfulness is something that goes back as far as Lincoln's Lyceum Address. In that speech he addressed the fading of historical memory. What invading armies had been unable to accomplish, "the silent artillery of time" might lead us to forget—our past (13–14). His point is that only a collective memory linking the battlefield to the hearthstone can make a people what they are. People are what they are through the memories they share with others. This, of course, is the original meaning of patriotism. Erase memory, and you erase peoplehood. And what Seward called "the guardian angel of the nation" became for Lincoln "the better angels of our nature." "Lincoln's tenor voice offered a peroration, or conclusion, of memorable words on the meaning of America that reach across time," Ronald C. White has written. "Each element in his conclusion spoke across the growing divide to mutual feelings of union."[22]

## "THIS IS ESSENTIALLY A PEOPLE'S CONTEST"

On March 5, 1861, the day after his inauguration, Lincoln received a letter from Major Robert Anderson stating that he could no longer hold the military garrison at Fort Sumter without reinforcements. This represented the first crisis of the new administration. The new president consulted with his cabinet on how to respond. General Winfield Scott claimed that the fort could not be held with less than twenty-five thousand troops, which would take weeks to train and transport. Others favored abandoning the fort as a lost cause and retreating to Fort Pickens, a more defensible outpost. Seward began working informally with a Southern delegation that would allow for the peaceful surrender of the fort. Several weeks passed, with no decision in sight, until Lincoln dispatched a letter informing the governor of South Carolina of his intention to send provisions only for the relief of the troops being starved into submission. His purpose was to avoid provocation but to assert his right to control and support federal properties. This act was deemed unacceptable to the South, and on April 12, the first shots were fired. The bombardment of Fort Sumter lasted for two days, culminating in Anderson's surrender and evacuation of the fort. It was the first time in American history that the flag had been fired upon by its own citizens.

If Lincoln's first actions as commander in chief were tentative and obscure, he makes clear his justification for declaring war in his July 4, 1861, Message to Congress in Special Session. In this message, more than in the First Inaugural Address, Lincoln sets out his reasons for engagement, giving the war not just a military but a philosophical rationale. Here he reprises the events leading up to the outbreak of war, showing how the Southern states took certain "illegal actions" and were hoping to enlist the aid and recognition of "Foreign Powers" to accomplish their plans. Only after outlining the background conditions leading up to war does Lincoln set these events in the context of world history. "This issue," he opines, "embraces more than the fate of these United States. It presents to the whole family of man, the question, whether a constitutional republic, or a democracy—a government of the people, by the same people—can, or cannot, maintain its territorial integrity, against its own domestic foes" (337–338). Lincoln states the question as follows: "Is there, in all republics, this inherent and fatal weakness? Must a government, of necessity, be too *strong* for the liberties of its own people, or too *weak* to maintain its own existence?" (338). At fate, then, is nothing less than the future of self-government.

Lincoln admits the extraordinary measures his government had taken to respond to the crisis. A call was sent out for raising a militia of seventy-five thousand troops and a proclamation issued for closing the ports of areas then in rebellion. "So far," Lincoln conjectures, "all was believed to be strictly legal" (339). Subsequent calls were made for volunteers to serve for three years as well as for additional provisions for the army and navy. These measures, "whether strictly legal or not," were required by "public necessity" and required only congressional ratification (339). Lincoln then ventured into more debatable territory. In certain cases, the rights of habeas corpus had been suspended, and people had been detained without recourse to trial or due process. Lincoln admits that the legality of these actions has been questioned by the Taney Court but that such measures had been pursued "very sparingly." In any case, the question returns to the right of a government to preserve itself:

The whole of the laws which were required to be faithfully executed, were being resisted, and failing of execution, in nearly one-third of the States. Must they be allowed to finally fail of execution, even had it been perfectly clear, that by the use of the means necessary for their execution, some single law, made in such extreme tenderness of the citizen's liberty, that practically, it relieves more of the guilty, than of the innocent should, to a very limited extent, be violated? To state the question more directly, are all the laws *but one* to go unexecuted, and the government itself go to pieces, lest that one be violated? Even in such a case, would not the official oath be broken, if the government should be overthrown, when it was believed that disregarding the single law, would tend to preserve it? (340)

Did Lincoln use his position as wartime commander in chief to override the Constitution? Had he become a dictator in the Schmittian sense, in which the state of exception had in effect become the norm?[23] This suspicion has dogged his prosecution of the war by legions of writers who have doubted Lincoln's commitment to civil liberties.[24] The debate turns on his suspension of habeas corpus in the case of *Ex Parte Merryman,* alluded to above. John Merryman was a Maryland militia officer at the time the war broke out. Maryland, on the capital's border, was a hotbed of antiunionist sentiment. On May 25, 1861, he was arrested by Union troops for engaging in acts of sabotage and training Confederate troops. On Lincoln's orders, Merryman was detained without trial. No less a personage than Roger Taney himself came to Merryman's defense, demanding that he be produced for a civil trial or released. Lincoln, Taney claimed, had overstepped his presidential bounds because only the Congress, not the president, could suspend habeas corpus.

Lincoln's appeal not only to his oath of office but to the requirements of "public safety" points to a doctrine of *necessity* that he claimed conferred certain exceptional powers in wartime. Necessity is a philosophical concept often put in opposition to choice or will. To appeal to necessity would appear to invoke the language of fatalism or determinism, that is, the belief that whatever happens is bound to happen and cannot be otherwise. It would also seem tantamount to a denial of moral responsibility. We cannot be held responsible for something about which we have no choice. This is clearly *not* what Lincoln meant by the term, although in a famous letter he once said that he did not so much shape events as events shaped him (418). This seeming admission of passivity in the face of larger forces at work suggests some doctrine of historical or even cosmic determinism at work behind our actions. This idea of fate at work has even led one of Lincoln's principal modern biographers to claim that this belief accounted for the essential "passivity" of Lincoln's character and his failure to take bold action.[25]

Lincoln's bold and swift action to curtail internal dissidents is hardly evidence of passivity or inaction. Rather, his conception of necessity in wartime is something closer to what I would call *constitutional necessity,* that is, actions that must be taken in order to preserve not only the Constitution but constitutional government. This is not the same as the moral promise implied in the oath of office but is closer to doing what you believe a situation requires. Actions can be judged constitutional only if they are undertaken to preserve the Constitution. The limits of these actions cannot be specified in advance simply because it is not possible to anticipate all situations. There might be extraordinary moments in which extraordinary measures are required. No constitution can specify beforehand what kinds of measures might be necessary to preserve it. Therefore, actions undertaken to preserve the Constitution and its way of life are deemed constitutional. At various times, Lincoln called on this doctrine of necessity to justify such extreme measures as the suspension of habeas corpus, the arrest of political dissenters, the closing of opposition newspapers, and the substitution of civil trials with military tribunals, just as he would later call on "military necessity" as one of the reasons for issuing the Emancipation Proclamation.[26]

Lincoln's defense of these extraordinary actions—actions that have led to the popular view that he had assumed dictatorial powers—is based on the priority of the Constitution. He cites Article I, Section 9: "The privilege of the writ of habeas corpus, shall not be suspended unless when, in cases of rebellion or invasion the public safety may require it" (340). If the Constitution requires the executive to provide for the execution of all the laws, it follows that he or she must also be equipped with the constitutional means to do so. If the current rebellion has led to the suspension of the laws in one-third of the Union, then the suspension of habeas corpus is a necessary means to prevent the rebellion from spreading. Is this not a moment when public safety requires it, he asks rhetorically, to which he answers his own question as follows: "It was decided that we have a case of rebellion and the public safety does require the qualified suspension of the privilege of the writ which was authorized to be made" (340).

At long last, Lincoln lays out his political theory of war. His case turns on what might at first glance appear to be a linguistic point of little importance, but Lincoln is finely attuned to the importance of language, and herein lies the rub. "It might seem at first thought to be of little difference whether the present movement at the South be called 'secession' or 'rebellion,'" he writes (341). No one of the framers ever believed, he argues, that secession was a right of the states (more of this in a moment) so that what we are witnessing is rebellion, not secession. Knowing that the people of the South, "just like any civilized and patriotic people," would resist a call to rebellion, he embarks on a new strategy:

Accordingly, they commenced an insidious debauching of the public mind. They invented an ingenious sophism, which, if conceded, was followed by perfectly logical steps, through all the incidents to the complete destruction of the Union. The sophism itself is that any state of the Union may, *consistently* with the national Constitution, and therefore *lawfully* and *peacefully* withdraw from the Union without the consent of the Union or of any other state. . . . With rebellion thus sugar-coated, they have been drugging the public mind of their section for more than thirty years; and, until at length, they have brought many good men to a willingness to take up arms against the government the day *after* some assemblage of men have enacted the farcical pretense of taking their State out of the Union who could have been brought to no such thing the day *before*. (342)

Lincoln's reference to an "ingenious sophism"—and presumably the sophist behind it—is an unmistakable reference to Calhoun. His claim that Calhoun had been "drugging" the mind of the South for a period of more than thirty years takes this back to the Nullification Crisis of the 1830s. It was the nullificationist thesis that any state has the right to nullify or invalidate a piece of national legislation it deems unconstitutional. Nullification was not a call to secession, but it paved the way to it. It was the logical conclusion of the compact theory of the Union, which regarded the Union as an agreement between the individual, sovereign states. The idea of the sovereign rights of the individual states is behind the rage for secession or, as Lincoln insists upon calling it, "rebellion." He refers to the "so-called seceded States," suggesting that he will not even use the term without qualification. Even the terms "drugging" and "debauching" suggest that secession is the result of a conspiracy to corrupt an entire section in order to make rebellion seem defensible. Acts of violence against the federal authority, Lincoln had warned in his First Inaugural Address, were not acts of war—protected by the laws of war—but "insurrectionary or revolutionary" crimes. "The secessionists were not enemies in war," John Witt has written; "they were criminals subject to punishment for treason."[27]

There is simply no such thing as a right of secession, Lincoln insists. "This sophism," he continues, "derives much—perhaps the whole—of its currency, from the assumption, that there is some omnipotent, and sacred supremacy pertaining to a *State*" (342). And yet—he repeats but also develops an argument he outlined in his First Inaugural Address—the states have never existed outside of the Union. "The new ones," he remarks, "took the designation of States on coming into the Union" (342). Still others, such as those purchased as part of the Louisiana Territory, have actually been bought and paid for out of federal monies. "By conquest, or purchase, the Union gave each of them, whatever of independence, and liberty, it has. The Union is older than any of the States and, in fact, it created them as States" (343). Many of these states, Lincoln suggests, have contracted debts to the federal government, and secession is simply a mask for avoiding their obligations.

Most revealingly, Lincoln writes, the seceding states have adopted constitutions that parody the very national Constitution they have rejected. Do these constitutions admit a right of secession? If not, they stand condemned of repudiating the very right they claim for themselves. If so, it will only be a matter of time until a minority of a minority claims this right for itself in order to avoid its obligations to the rest and casts doubt on whether these new state constitutions were passed by a majority. Lincoln spends considerable time on the case of Virginia, which has allowed a "giant insurrection" to take place within its borders, as well as the loyalty of those unionists who would later break off to form West Virginia (338–339). "There is much reason to believe," he notes, "that the Union men are the majority in many, if not in every one, of the so-called seceded States" (344). Many of these states have written new Declarations of Independence, but, "unlike the good old one, penned by Jefferson," they have avoided the words "all men are created equal." In the provisional Confederate Constitution, Lincoln wonders, why have they dropped the familiar "We, the people" in the preamble and replaced it with the tortuous circumlocution, "We, the deputies of the sovereign and independent States"? What do they have to hide? "Why this deliberate pressing out of view, the rights of men, and the authority of the people?" Lincoln asks rhetorically (345).

Lincoln attempts to answer these questions at the very end of the Message to Congress in Special Session. He notes that the aim of the Constitution is to provide a republican form of government to each one of its members. To preserve constitutional government for all, extraordinary measures are now being undertaken. These measures, such as the "qualified suspension" of habeas corpus, deemed unconstitutional by Taney and others, are means to the essential end of preserving the form of government established by the founders. Lincoln finally turns to the ultimate issue at stake:

This is essentially a People's contest. On the side of the Union, it is a struggle for maintaining in the world that form, and substance of government whose leading object is, to elevate the condition of men—to lift artificial weights from all shoulders—to clear the paths of laudable pursuit for all—to afford all, an unfettered start, and a fair chance, in the race of life. Yielding to partial, and temporary departures, from necessity, this is the leading object of the government for whose existence we contend. (345)

In declaring the war a "People's contest," Lincoln means it will be decided not by the states or the Court but the people, or at least their armies, in the field of battle.

Lincoln wraps up his message, as he would the Gettysburg Address, by noting the unfinished business at hand. "Our popular government has often been called an experiment," he writes. "Two points in it, our people have already settled—the successful *establishing* and the successful *administering* of it. One still remains—its successful *maintenance* against a formidable internal attempt to overthrow it" (346). In describing this form of government as an "experiment," Lincoln alludes to its provisional nature. As with any experiment, we cannot know in advance what the result will be. What will guarantee its survival? It will depend above all on the degree of belief or popular commitment to it. Among other things, it is a test to see whether a free people—a sovereign people, not an aggregate of states—can preserve itself from dismemberment. Can such a government long endure? "It is now for them to demonstrate to the world, that those who can fairly carry an election, can also suppress a rebellion—that ballots are the rightful, and peaceful successor, of bullets" (346). Lincoln's use of the phrase "to demonstrate to the world" is clearly a reminder of the Declaration's "let Facts be submitted to a candid world." Lincoln wants it never to be forgotten that what is at stake in the war is more than a sectional or regional conflict but nothing less than the future of self-government.

At the conclusion of his message, Lincoln turns from the active to the passive voice. It is with the "deepest regret," he notes, that the executive finds the war power "forced upon him." He has no choice but to perform his duty or let the Union perish. It is for the "people themselves," not their elected officials, to decide this fate. Lincoln then distinguishes between himself as a "private citizen" and his role as chief executive. As a citizen, he could not have consented to let the Union perish, whereas it is to him as the president others have entrusted this task. "In full view of his great responsibility," he writes, "he has, so far, done what he deemed his duty" (347). However, as executive, Lincoln cannot perform this task alone. "You will now," he enjoins Congress, "according to your own judgment, perform yours." He can only hope that the will of Congress will accord with the will of the executive and that all who have been disturbed will have a "speedy restoration" of their rights. It is worth recalling the final words of his message: "And having thus chosen our course, without guile, and with pure purpose; let us renew our trust in God, and go forward without fear, and with manly hearts" (347).

### LINCOLN'S "WEIMAR" MOMENT

The First Inaugural Address and the July 4 Message to Congress in Special Session were Lincoln's fullest accounts of his reasons for going to war. The arguments over states' rights, the extent of federal authority, and executive power remain even today the chief locus of American politics. These matters are by no means settled by the Constitution but are the subject of ongoing political discussion, debate, and realignment. The crisis of 1860 did nothing more than put these issues into their boldest relief. How we view these issues shapes the way we think of Lincoln, or maybe the way we think of Lincoln determines the way we think of these issues. Lincoln in 1860 was the savior of the Union at the moment of its supreme crisis, a worthy companion to Winston Churchill eighty years later in 1940. The comparisons are worth considering. The days and weeks following Lincoln's election, the hesitancies, the uncertainties, but in the final instance his decision to respond to the Southern aggression at Fort Sumter was a unifying decision, bringing together not only Republicans but former rivals such as Douglas and James Buchanan, almost as much as Churchill brought together a unified front in the face of an arguably much greater menace.[28]

The comparison of Lincoln in 1860 and Churchill in 1940 is tempting but misleading. As severe as was the crisis confronting Lincoln, the Confederacy was not Nazi Germany, and Calhoun was not Goebbels.[29] What Lincoln faced was not an all-out attack on civilization but an attack on the future of democratic self-government, a very different thing. The antebellum South was a civilization; Nazi Germany was an anticivilization, the only regime that knew no other principle than murderous hatred of the Jews. Precisely this distinction allowed Churchill to claim that the American Civil War was the last war fought by gentlemen. This statement alone is sufficient to distinguish the two cases.

If a comparison to Germany is to be made, I would call it —even at the risk of anachronism—Lincoln's "Weimar moment." The problem with the Weimar Republic was that it was weak. Its single moment of greatness, Leo Strauss remarked, was its response to the murder of Walter Rathenau, the Jewish minister of foreign affairs. Otherwise, "it presented the sorry spectacle of justice without a sword or of justice unable to use the sword."[30] The issue facing Lincoln was whether a democracy would fight to preserve itself from dismemberment. Like the leaders of Weimar, Lincoln confronted the choice of whether the United States would become what Loewenstein subsequently called a "militant democracy." For Loewenstein, this term meant something like the suspension of constitutional law and the assumption of emergency powers to save democracy from itself. "If democracy believes in the superiority of its fundamental values," he wrote in response to the Nazi seizure of power, "it must live up to the demands of the hour, and every possible effort must be made to rescue it, even at the risk and cost of violating fundamental principles."[31]

The question is whether Lincoln's decision to go to war required him to adopt the kind of extraconstitutional measures Loewenstein assumed are required. Did the president's suspension of habeas corpus and other extraordinary acts overstep the boundaries of a constitutional executive and resort to dictatorial power? Did he believe that the protection of the Constitution requires a suspension of the Constitution, as Carl Schmitt argued, or that there are no assignable limits to what a government might do in its self-defense, as Leo Strauss suggested? Lincoln answered both of these questions with a decisive "No." He exercised his wartime powers as commander in chief with prudence and judgment. Lincoln kept his head while others around him were losing theirs. His own secretary of state, William Seward, seriously suggested instigating a war against France or Spain as a way of rallying national unity![32] Lincoln always maintained—as in the arrest of antiwar agitator Clement Vallandigham—that his departures from the Constitution were themselves authorized by the Constitution (403–404, 408–411).[33]

Constitutional powers must be prepared to deal with bad times as well as good without giving way to government by fiat. As Nomi Lazar has aptly put it, "Emergency powers are justified—when they are justified—because they embody principles that already function under normal circumstances."[34] In other words, states of emergency do not automatically require a suspension of democratic norms and procedures but should be regarded as continuous with them. "Order is a value also, and it animates the day-to-day life of the state alongside liberal values," Lazar notes. "Rights are derogated for the sake of order every day."[35]

Lincoln showed how it was possible even in an extreme situation to operate within the broad limits of the Constitution and the rule of law. He claimed more than once that his wartime powers were only temporary and would cease with the end of hostilities (404). He resisted the temptation to extend the Emancipation Proclamation to the border states on the grounds that he would find himself outside the rule of law and in "the boundless field of absolutism" (416). He refused to assume dictatorial powers when others around him were urging him to do so. "I have heard in such a way as to believe it of your recently saying that both the Army and the Government needed a Dictator," he wrote to General Joseph Hooker on the occasion of appointing him to the head of the Army of the Potomac. "Of course it was not *for* this, but in spite of it, that I have given you the command" (398).

Most importantly, Lincoln refused to suspend elections even during a time of civil war. In a text titled simply Memorandum of Probable Failure of Re-Election dated August 23, 1864, Lincoln mused on the real possibility that he would be a one-term president whose efforts would go for naught. "This morning, as for some days past," Lincoln mused, "it seems exceedingly probable that this Administration will not be re-elected. Then it will be my duty to so co-operate with the President elect, as to save the Union between the election and the inauguration; as he will have secured his election on such ground that he cannot possibly save it afterwards" (424). A victory gained at the expense of nullifying free elections would not be a victory worth having.

Lincoln's decision to go ahead with the election of 1864 has been called "the greatest glory" of his presidency.[36] This might be a slight—but only a slight—exaggeration. I would call the Emancipation Proclamation Lincoln's finest hour. However, fortunately, his gloomy predictions did not come to pass. Shortly after he wrote this note, General William Tecumseh Sherman's armies subdued Atlanta, Flag Officer David Farragut's navy bottled up the Confederate harbor at Mobile Bay, and Lincoln won reelection in a landslide. And yet Lincoln knew a war that would end up destroying constitutional procedures would not be a war worth winning. "Must a government, of necessity, be too *strong* for the liberties of its own people, or too *weak* to maintain its own existence?" he had asked in his Fourth of July Message to Congress in Special Session (338).

To his infinite credit, Lincoln realized that free elections should not be sacrificed even in a moment of crisis because the cost would be the end of constitutional government itself. For constitutional leadership, the ends do *not* justify the means. Constitutional leadership is necessarily limited or bounded leadership. It is in this possibility of a leader operating within the limits of constitutional restraint that the hope of our republic rests. Lincoln entertained an unsentimental trust in the judgment of the American people, whom in his First Inaugural Address he had called his "rightful master," a subtle dig at the masters who held sway in the South. "Seldom in history," Ralph Waldo Emerson wrote in a letter shortly after the election, "was so much staked upon a popular vote. I suppose never in history."[37]

## NOTES

Epigraphs: Carl Schmitt, *Dictatorship. From the Origin of the Modern Concept of Sovereignty to Proletarian Class Struggle*, trans. Michael Hoelzl and Graham Wood (Cambridge, UK: Polity, 2014), 118; Leo Strauss, *Natural Right and History* (Chicago: University of Chicago Press, 1953), 160.

1. Karl Loewenstein, "Militant Democracy and Fundamental Rights," *American Political Science Review* 31 (1937): 417–432; see also Alexander S. Kirshner, *A Theory of Militant Democracy: The Ethics of Combatting Political Extremism* (New Haven, CT: Yale University Press, 2014).

2. Loewenstein, "Militant Democracy and Fundamental Rights," 432.

3. For useful discussions of the secession conference, see William J. Cooper, *We Have the War upon Us: The Onset of the Civil War, November 1860–April 1861* (New York: Knopf, 2012), 181–193; James McPherson, *Battle Cry of Freedom: The Civil War Era* (New York: Oxford University Press, 1988), 257–259.

4. For the background, see Russell McClintock, *Lincoln and the Decision for War: The Northern Response to Secession* (Chapel Hill: University of North Carolina Press, 2008), 176–180, 183–185; see also Cooper, *We Have the War upon Us*, 173–184, 199–201.

5. McPherson, *Battle Cry of Freedom*, 254; see also David M. Potter, *The Impending*

*Crisis, 1848–1861* (New York: Harper and Row, 1976), 530–532; Cooper, *We Have the War upon Us,* 3–8, 102–112, 180–181.

6. See Potter, *Impending Crisis,* 432–433; McPherson, *Battle Cry of Freedom,* 230–231; for a recent attempt to exonerate Lincoln's role during the secession winter, see Harold Holzer, *Lincoln President Elect: Abraham Lincoln and the Great Secession Winter, 1860–1861* (New York: Simon and Schuster, 2008). See also William H. Freehling, *The Road to Disunion:* vol. 2: *Secessionists Triumphant, 1854–1861* (New York: Oxford University Press, 2007).

7. Cited in John Burt, *Lincoln's Tragic Pragmatism: Lincoln, Douglas, and Moral Conflict* (Cambridge, MA: Harvard University Press, 2013), 625; see also McClintock, *Lincoln and the Decision for War,* 51–53.

8. Allen C. Guelzo, *Abraham Lincoln: Redeemer President* (Grand Rapids, MI: Eerdmans, 1999), 254; see also David Potter, *Lincoln and His Party in the Secession Crisis* (New Haven, CT: Yale University Press, 1942), 19: "Throughout the crisis leading to military conflict, this Republican failure to comprehend the reality of secession remained a basic factor."

9. See the canonical study by George Fredrickson, *The Black Image in the White Mind: The Debate on Afro-American Character and Destiny, 1817–1914* (New York: Harper and Row, 1971).

10. For the best study of Abraham Lincoln's changing views on slavery, from colonization to compensated emancipation to full emancipation, see Eric Foner, *The Fiery Trial: Abraham Lincoln and American Slavery* (New York: Norton, 2010).

11. James Oakes, *Freedom National: The Destruction of Slavery in the United States, 1861–1865* (New York: Norton, 2013), 56–57.

12. For the debate over the right of secession, see Allen Buchanan, *Secession: The Morality of Political Divorce from Fort Sumter to Lithuania and Quebec* (Boulder, CO: Westview, 1991); Sanford Levinson, ed., *Nullification and Secession in Modern Constitutional Thought* (Lawrence: University Press of Kansas, 2016).

13. Lord Charnwood, *Abraham Lincoln* (Lanham, MD: Madison, 1996), 132, 134–135.

14. William Herndon, *Life of Lincoln* (New York: Da Capo, 1983), 386.

15. For the role of this debate, especially in the early republic, see Rogan Kersh, *Dreams of a More Perfect Union* (Ithaca, NY: Cornell University Press, 2001); see also Samuel Beer, *To Make a Nation: The Rediscovery of Federalism* (Cambridge, MA: Harvard University Press, 1993).

16. All page references in the text are to Steven B. Smith, ed., *The Writings of Abraham Lincoln* (New Haven, CT: Yale University Press, 2012).

17. Harry V. Jaffa, *A New Birth of Freedom: Abraham Lincoln and the Coming of the Civil War* (Lanham, MD: Rowman and Littlefield, 2000), 259.

18. See Oakes, *Freedom National,* 75–78.

19. See Edmund Wilson, *Patriotic Gore: Studies in the Literature of the American Civil War* (New York: Norton, 1994), 99, 106.

20. Potter, *Impending Crisis,* 570; see also McPherson, *Battle Cry of Freedom,* 230–231.

21. John Channing Briggs, *Lincoln's Speeches Reconsidered* (Baltimore, MD: Johns Hopkins University Press, 2005), 299.

22. Ronald C. White, *The Eloquent President: A Portrait of Lincoln through His Words* (New York: Random House, 2005), 91; see also Burt, *Lincoln's Tragic Pragmatism,* 644–646.

23. For the state of exception, see Carl Schmitt, *Political Theology,* trans. George Schwab (Cambridge: Massachusetts Institute of Technology Press, 1988), 5–13.

24. See Mark E. Neely, Jr., *The Fate of Liberty: Abraham Lincoln and Civil Liberties* (New York: Oxford University Press, 1991), 133–150; George Kateb, *Lincoln's Political Thought* (Cambridge, MA: Harvard University Press, 2015), 146–152.

25. David Herbert Donald, *Lincoln* (New York: Simon and Schuster, 1995).

26. For Abraham Lincoln's doctrine of necessity, see David Bromwich, "Lincoln's Constitutional Necessity," in Bromwich, *Moral Imagination: Essays* (Princeton, NJ: Princeton University Press, 2014), 118–159; see also Oakes, *Freedom National,* 34 42.

27. John Fabian Witt, *Lincoln's Code: The Laws of War in American History* (New York: Free Press, 2012), 142.

28. See John Lucas, *Five Days in London, May 1940* (New Haven, CT: Yale University Press, 1999).

29. The continual comparison of Abraham Lincoln and Winston Churchill helps to disfigure Jaffa's otherwise admirable *New Birth of Freedom,* 49, 100, 124 126, 259–260; the comparison of John C. Calhoun with Joseph Goebbels has come up with the recent debate about renaming Yale's Calhoun College; see "What's in a Name?" *Yale Alumni Magazine* (May–June 2016).

30. Leo Strauss, "Preface to 'Spinoza's Critique of Religion,'" in Strauss, *Liberalism Ancient and Modern* (New York: Basic Books, 1968), 224.

31. Loewenstein, "Militant Democracy and Fundamental Rights," 432.

32. See McPherson, *Battle Cry of Freedom,* 270–271; McClintock, *Lincoln and the Decision for War,* 236–237.

33. For the constitutionality of the Vallandigham case, see Daniel Farber, *Lincoln's Constitution* (Chicago: University of Chicago Press, 2003), 170–175; see also Witt, *Lincoln's Code,* 271–273.

34. Nomi Claire Lazar, *States of Emergency in Liberal Democracies* (Cambridge, UK: Cambridge University Press, 2009), 5.

35. Ibid.

36. Bromwich, "Lincoln's Constitutional Necessity," 157.

37. Cited in Charnwood, *Abraham Lincoln,* 305.

# CHAPTER 8

# The Lincolnian Constitution

CALEB VERBOIS

Despite the legion of books and articles written about Abraham Lincoln, it seems there is always more ground to cover in the actions of one of America's most significant statesmen. Lincoln's commitment to constitutionalism is worth special emphasis. At first glance, this might seem strange, especially given various critiques of Lincoln both during the Civil War and from modern historians, that he did not give careful enough consideration to constitutional forms. As Arthur Schlesinger, Jr., famously said, Lincoln marked "the beginning of a fateful evolution" toward an out-of-control presidency.[1] However, Lincoln himself argued against this thesis. He did not see his actions as making a permanent change because he thought they were *only* justified by the extraordinary circumstances of the Civil War; he took great care to justify even his most extreme acts as constitutional. The half-century after Lincoln's presidency suggests he was right because in the general absence of any major crises, presidents in the second half of the nineteenth century were some of the weakest in American history. Thus, despite the difficulties in governing the country during the Civil War, Lincoln's commitment to constitutionalism was unwavering, as this chapter will show through a careful examination of three of Lincoln's most controversial actions: his unilateral action to call up the militia in 1861, his suspension of habeas corpus, and the Emancipation Proclamation. Each of these actions was extraordinary and, some have argued, unconstitutional, but in each case, Lincoln made a clear argument for the lawfulness of his actions. In doing so he upheld his long-standing support for the Constitution and avoided becoming the dangerous demagogue he warned about in his Lyceum Address.[2]

## LINCOLN'S CONSTITUTION

When Lincoln stepped into the White House, he became the leader of a deeply divided nation. Seven states had already seceded. He immediately began to take a number of controversial actions to protect Washington, DC, and preserve the Union. In his July 4, 1861, Message to Congress in Special Session, in which he justified those actions, he asked, "Is there in all republics this inherent and fatal weakness? Must a government of necessity be too *strong* for the liberties of its people, or too *weak* to maintain its own existence?"[3] Lincoln concluded that the answer was "No." His argument rested on a specific understanding of the way the Constitution was intended to work:

The whole of the laws which were required to be faithfully executed were being resisted, and failing of execution in nearly one third of the States. Must they be allowed to finally fail of execution, even had it been perfectly clear that by the use of the means necessary to their execution some single law . . . should to a very limited extent be violated? To state the question more directly: are all the laws *but one* to go unexecuted, and the government itself go to pieces, lest that one be violated? Even in such a case, would not the official oath be broken if the government should be overthrown, when it was believed that disregarding the single law would tend to preserve it? But it was not believed that this question was presented. *It was not believed that any law was violated.* The provision of the Constitution that "the privilege of the writ of *habeas corpus* shall not be suspended unless when, in cases of rebellion or invasion, the public safety may require it," is equivalent to a provision—is a provision—that such privilege may be suspended when, in case of rebellion or invasion, the public safety *does* require it.[4]

Lincoln made two very different arguments. First, he suggested that it would be better for one law to be violated than for the whole country to collapse. This does not sound like an argument designed to uphold the Constitution at all costs but rather an argument to violate the Constitution to uphold the Union. If, as I have already suggested, Lincoln really did want to uphold the Constitution at all costs, the obvious question is, Why did he make such an argument? I think there are three reasons.

First, Lincoln brought up this possibility because he was well aware that the argument for violating the Constitution had been made before his presidency. Lincoln might or might not have read Locke's argument for prerogative, but he was certainly familiar with Thomas Jefferson's case for extraconstitutional prerogative power.[5] Jefferson, in keeping with Locke, had argued for the legitimacy of prerogative power, which is simply the power of the executive to act without the sanction of, or indeed, in direct violation of, the law and the Constitution. This appealed to Jefferson because it was convenient, at least when he was president, and because it allowed the president to act as he considered necessary without establishing that power as precedent.[6] Prerogative holds out the promise of allowing maximum presidential flexibility within the confines of a narrow interpretation of the Constitution. As we shall see, Lincoln offered a distinct alternative to prerogative theory. He rejected the idea that he could violate the Constitution as needed and instead offered an alternative, constitutionalized justification for extraordinary uses of presidential power. Second, Lincoln made this argument because he was a good lawyer. He recognized that some members of Congress might not agree with his reading of the Constitution and hoped they might instead accept this one. Finally, Lincoln made the argument for prerogative explicit in order to show that he did not rely on it.

Lincoln asked, "Are all the laws but one to go unexecuted . . . lest that one be violated?" He answered his own question—in the negative—"But it was not believed that this question was presented. *It was not believed that any law was violated.*"[7] This was his primary claim: not that his actions were legitimate because they were necessary violations of his constitutional role but that they were legitimate because they were a necessary use of his extraordinary—but constitutional—powers as president. Lincoln echoed Alexander Hamilton's argument from the controversy surrounding George Washington's 1793 Neutrality Proclamation: "The Constitution itself is silent as to which or who is to exercise the power; and as the provision was plainly made for a dangerous emergency, it cannot be believed the Framers of the instrument intended that in every case the danger should run its course until Congress could be called together."[8] Lincoln refused to simply assert that he could act illegally or unconstitutionally if he deemed it necessary. He knew there were boundaries to his power; he could not simply free all slaves, for example, but the war allowed him to fully exercise all of the powers of the presidency in a way he did not think would be legitimate outside of the context of war. And as is clearly demonstrated by Lincoln's speech, the separation of powers is not destroyed by such executive action, because the president frequently has to defend his actions later in order to receive congressional approval for further measures. Together, Lincoln's calling out of the militia, his partial suspension of the writ of habeas corpus, and the Emancipation Proclamation show a president struggling to hold the country together *while* maintaining the integrity of the Constitution rather than *ignoring* the Constitution to hold it together.[9]

Importantly, Lincoln does not argue that the constitutional framers anticipated all future contingencies, such as a need for extraordinary executive power in a civil war. Rather, he argues that they anticipated a general need. To put it another way, if one is creating a constitution to bind democratic officials within a particular range of powers, one must provide for a real dilemma: How to provide future political actors sufficient power to deal with emergencies?

It is not sufficient to allow for an amendment process because that would, by definition, be too unwieldy and slow in a real emergency. There are only three possible solutions to this problem. The first is to conclude that future political actors in your system might simply lack the sufficient power to act in an emergency, with the corresponding consequence that your regime might fail. The second is to conclude, with Locke and Jefferson, that an element of your political system, such as the executive, may violate the constitution in an emergency in order to preserve the regime. The third is to create a constitutional regime that itself recognizes the difference between ordinary time and extraordinary time and grants an executive correspondingly more power in extraordinary times.

The first of these three solutions should be considered a failure for the obvious reason that no constitution can anticipate all future necessities and would thus doom the regime to eventual and inevitable failure. The second and third share an obvious danger. They both can encourage presidential overreach. However, the US Constitution has its own structural restraints on such overreaching, such as the power of the purse and the Damoclean sword of impeachment. However, the second solution, Lockean prerogative, denies these constitutional restraints because the only recourse against prerogative is an "*appeal to Heaven*,"[10] Locke's way of referring to an armed revolution.[11] Arguably, Lockean prerogative can even override congressional power of the purse.[12] In a real sense, this disconnects the Lockean executive from any meaningful democratic check. In contrast, though Lincoln's actions strained the bounds of his constitutional office, he was always restricted by a need to appeal to Congress for funds and legislation. A Lockean executive in similar circumstances would not be restrained.

The genius of the Constitution, which Lincoln fully appreciated, is that it is flexible enough to allow the executive to act in emergencies without undermining the legitimacy of the Constitution itself. That is why, far from demonstrating Lincoln's antipathy toward the Constitution and laws, his actions in calling out the militia, suspending the writ of habeas corpus, and signing the Emancipation Proclamation demonstrate his belief that the Constitution contains within itself the ability to react and stretch to a great crisis—in fact, that the Constitution operates differently in extraordinary times than in ordinary times. Therefore, he did not need to appeal to prerogative power to violate the Constitution because that would both violate his oath and eviscerate the Constitution. Rather, he needed to understand the Constitution properly and justify his actions to a watching world.

## THE MILITIA

The Constitution clearly grants Congress, not the president, the power to call up the militia; thus Lincoln's calling up the militia without congressional approval has been seen as a violation of his constitutional authority: "Of all his exercises of executive power, Lincoln's military actions in April and May 1861—calling up the militia, increasing the size of the army and the navy, blockading and seizing the vessels in particular ports—most closely approached extralegal Lockean prerogative."[13] However, long before the Civil War, Congress had delegated to the president the authority to call up the militia in emergencies. The Militia Act of 1792, used by Washington to put down the Whiskey Rebellion in 1794, gave the president the authority to use the state militias to respond to an invasion by a foreign nation or Native American nation, or "whenever the laws of the United States shall be opposed or the execution thereof obstructed, in any state, by combinations too powerful to be suppressed by the ordinary course of judicial proceedings."[14] Importantly, the decision on when this might be necessary was put solely in the hands of the president.[15] The law was expanded twice more to cover any instances of insurrection and to allow the president to call the militia to arms for six months at his discretion.[16] Thus, well before Lincoln became president, more than sufficient legal authority had been established for the president to call up the militia.[17] As Richard Brookhiser notes, Lincoln "echo(ed) Washington's language in his own call for militia."[18] Both Washington and Lincoln consciously lifted phrases directly from the 1792 Militia Act.[19]

Given this precedent, Lincoln's calling up the militia is not an example of a president acting on prerogative grounds. Instead, it is an illustration of how Lincoln thought the Constitution and laws were supposed to work in extraordinary times. Lincoln explained his view in detail in a letter to Erastus Corning, a Democratic congressman from New York who had written to Lincoln criticizing his conduct of the war. In his answer, Lincoln defended his actions and his understanding of the Constitution:

If I be wrong on this question of constitutional power, my error lies in believing that certain proceedings are constitutional when, in cases of rebellion or Invasion, the public Safety requires them, which would not be constitutional when, in absence of rebellion or invasion, the public Safety does not require them: in other words, that the Constitution is not in its application in all respects the same in cases of Rebellion or invasion, involving the public safety, as it is in times of profound peace and public security. The Constitution itself makes the distinction; and I can no more be persuaded that the government can constitutionally take no strong measure in time of rebellion, because it can be shown that the same could not be lawfully taken in time of peace, than I can be persuaded that a particular drug is not good medicine for a sick man, because it can be shown to not be good food for a well one. Nor am I able to appreciate the danger apprehended by the meeting, [the May 16, 1863, meeting in Albany, which Corning chaired, the resolutions of which he sent to Lincoln] that the American people will, by means of military arrests during the rebellion, lose the right of public discussion, the liberty of speech and the press, the law of evidence, trial by jury, and Habeas corpus, throughout the indefinite peaceful future which I trust lies before them, any more than I am able to believe that a man could contract so strong an appetite for emetics during temporary illness, as to persist in feeding upon them through the remainder of his healthful life.[20]

In this paragraph Lincoln laid out two important points. First, in times of great danger, some governmental actions that would normally be prohibited become legal. The Constitution and congressional law make a distinction between normal and extraordinary times, such as a war with a foreign power or an internal rebellion.[21] The state militias are not needed by the federal government in normal times. However, in extraordinary times, if the militias are needed and Congress is not in session, the president might have to act quickly. Thus, Lincoln's decision to call up the militia should not be interpreted as an example of prerogative power. Instead, it is a constitutionally and legislatively approved action because of the emergency at the time—not an extraconstitutional action necessary to resolve the emergency. This subtle distinction is important. For Locke, Jefferson, or any other prerogative theorist, any action that would not normally be permitted during routine times *must* be an example of prerogative power. However, this is not how the Constitution was designed. According to Lincoln, the Constitution itself is flexible enough to allow political actors to deal with emergencies without going outside of constitutional law.

Second, as Lincoln's argument about the sick man shows, extraordinary but constitutional acts in emergencies do not permanently change the meaning of the Constitution in normal times. Lincoln argued directly against the ratchet effect—the idea that after one president asserts a power, all future presidents may continue to use it. Lincoln's example shows that civil liberties such as the writ of habeas corpus could be curtailed during the Civil War without being permanently reduced after the war. Presidents can take strong, necessary, and constitutional actions during a war without starting an epidemic of future presidents acting in the same way during peacetime. Because the Constitution still applies during a crisis, Lincoln could maintain a distinction between ordinary and extraordinary times without appealing to prerogative.[22]

## THE SUSPENSION OF HABEAS CORPUS

Lincoln had a more difficult time arguing that he had the constitutional power to suspend habeas corpus. Congress, after all, had legislatively recognized the distinction between ordinary and extraordinary times when it came to calling up the militia. It had not made such a distinction over habeas corpus. The only substantial federal law on habeas corpus was the 1789 Judicial Act, which established in federal courts a right to habeas corpus.[23] In fact, there was very little debate over habeas corpus after the Constitution was signed. Two points are worth mentioning. First, the Constitution does not give an affirmative power to suspend the writ. Instead, it negatively says the writ may only be suspended in cases of rebellion or invasion.[24] Second, nothing in the Constitution explicitly says where the power to suspend the writ lies.

Lincoln's critics argued, not without reason, that because the power to suspend habeas corpus is mentioned in Article I of the Constitution, which deals with Congress, only Congress may suspend habeas corpus. Lincoln gave a two-part answer. First, he suggested that the suspension of the writ was an example of the distinction between ordinary and extraordinary times, which the Constitution justifies, as he mentioned in the letter to Corning quoted earlier. Lincoln argued: "The provision of the Constitution that 'the privilege of the writ of *habeas corpus* shall not be suspended unless when, in cases of rebellion or invasion, the public safety may require it,' is equivalent to a provision—is a provision—that such privilege may be suspended when, in case of rebellion or invasion, the public safety *does* require it."[25] Second, Lincoln suggested that because the suspension of the writ was mentioned in Section 9 of Article I, which contains limitations on Congress rather than powers, "The Constitution itself is silent as to which or who is to exercise the power; and as the provision was plainly made for a dangerous emergency, it cannot be believed the Framers of the instrument intended that in every case the danger should run its course until Congress could be called together."[26] Or, as Herbert Storing puts it, "The Constitution must be read—was meant to be read—in light of necessity. . . . The Constitution is meant to be commodious and elastic enough to meet the demands of necessity and yet retain its character as law."[27] However, as Lincoln's own speech to Congress demonstrated, the separation of powers was not harmed by his actions as president because he had to defend his emergency actions in order to receive congressional approval for further measures. Importantly, Lincoln's argument assumed that Congress would question the president's actions, not simply rubber stamp everything he did.

Lincoln's suspension of the writ is a prime example of a president acting during an emergency in an area where the Constitution is vague and Congress could not be called to act. After all, the reason Lincoln needed to suspend habeas corpus on his own was that there was so much civil unrest in Baltimore that neither Union troops nor members of Congress could get safely from the North to Washington, DC. Lincoln himself had to sneak through the city in disguise. Baltimore, as the largest city in a border state where slavery was legal, was not at all sure it wanted to side with the Union. In fact, Baltimore was in such an uproar that in mid-April five hundred Pennsylvania troops were attacked with bricks. Baltimore's mayor told Lincoln that other Union troops would have to "fight their way at every step" to pass through Baltimore and that "the responsibility for the bloodshed will not rest upon me."[28] The bloody scene was repeated the next day when a group of volunteers detrained in Baltimore to walk two miles to their next train, and a mob attacked them. The troops fired in defense, and the "riot left four soldiers and twelve civilians dead."[29] Governor Hicks of Maryland and Mayor George William Brown of Baltimore tried to convince Lincoln to stop sending troops through Baltimore, and a few days later a Baltimore committee asked that no Union troops move through the state at all, but the president was adamant that the troops were working for the benefit of the country.[30]

Lincoln argued that his decision to suspend habeas corpus in response to the Baltimore unrest was necessary because of the danger to the Union as a whole, and the capital in particular, and justified by his understanding that the Constitution had to be read in light of necessity. However, he also argued that it was justified by precedent.[31] Lincoln appealed to General Andrew Jackson's suspension of the writ during the War of 1812 and the subsequent congressional approval of Jackson:

After the Battle of New Orleans and while the fact that the treaty of peace had been concluded was well known in the city, but before official knowledge of it had arrived, General Jackson still maintained martial or military law. . . . It may be remarked—first, that we had the same Constitution then as now; secondly, that we then had a case of invasion, and now have a case of rebellion; and, thirdly, that the permanent right of the people to public discussion, the liberty of speech and of the press, the trial by jury, the law of evidence, and the *habeas corpus* suffered no detriment whatever by the conduct of General Jackson, or its *subsequent approval by the American Congress.*[32]

In appealing to Jackson's precedent, Lincoln again rejected the ratchet argument, asserting that the writ of habeas corpus was not permanently harmed by its temporary suspension by Jackson. However, Lincoln's adversaries both in Congress and on the Supreme Court pushed back, questioning the legality and constitutionality of his actions. Democrats in Congress were particularly outraged. However, they had a difficult time arguing against Lincoln given that just twenty years earlier, they had supported Jackson's imposition of martial law in the refund debate.[33] In the 1840s, Jackson, retired from the presidency by then, asked Congress to retroactively support his implementation of martial law as commanding general in New Orleans in 1812 by refunding the fine imposed by a Louisiana judge at the time, both to solidify his legacy and to establish the precedent that the executive could establish martial law in times of great need. The Democratic Congress obliged Jackson, though with some opposition. This became an important precedent for Lincoln.[34]

When Lincoln asked Congress to pass a law confirming his suspension of habeas corpus in September 1862, Congress was at first divided over the question of whether Congress alone possessed the right of suspension. Democrats in Congress studiously avoided mentioning the Jacksonian precedent and initially opposed the bill. However, their opposition was short-lived.[35] The problem was political. In addition to the inconvenient fact that most Democrats in Congress supported martial law in Jackson's refund debate, the Democratic presidential hopeful in 1864 was General George B. McClellan. McClellan had been involved in the military arrests of Maryland legislators in 1861 and therefore could not oppose Lincoln on martial law or the suspension of the writ without appearing hypocritical. This led the Democrats to quietly drop the issue.[36]

Thus, despite some initial objections, Congress eventually determined that it could retroactively ratify Lincoln's decisions. Senator Justin Morrill of Vermont concluded, "So long as Lincoln acted within the constitutional scope of the government, Congress could ratify acts he performed in absence of its prior consent."[37] In fact, in Morrill's mind, congressional ratification was really superfluous because Lincoln's actions were "necessarily and logically deducible from the powers conferred upon [him] in the U.S. Constitution."[38] Daniel Farber similarly notes, "If prior congressional authorization was needed, it probably did exist. . . . This source of authority was the militia act." Farber notes that in *Ex Parte Field* the federal circuit court concluded, "The statutes empowering

Lincoln to call out the militia also implicitly authorized him to declare martial law, and hence to suspend habeas."[39]

The more sustained disagreement came from the Supreme Court. In *Ex Parte Merryman*, Chief Justice Roger Taney wrote, "I can only say that if the authority which the constitution has confided to the judiciary department and judicial officers, may thus, upon any pretext or under any circumstances, be usurped by the military power, at its discretion, the people of the United States are no longer living under a government of laws."[40] However, although Taney's decision has typically been viewed as a strong defense of civil liberties,[41] it was a radical departure from his earlier position on the subject. Taney, appointed to the Supreme Court by Jackson, had strongly supported the former president in the refund debate despite the fact that Jackson had acted only on his authority as a military general without civilian support, precisely what Taney rejected in *Merryman*. Taney argued that any opposition to Jackson's action must be partisan in nature: "Future ages will be amazed that such conduct as that of Judge Hall could find defenders or apologists in this count[r]y, and how there could be any difficulty in stigmatizing the disgraceful proceeding in the manner it deserves. . . . Unfortunately the bitter feelings engendered by party conflicts too often render men blind to the principles of justice."[42] Nonetheless, Taney argued that under Lincoln, the military was usurping the Constitution "upon any pretext," but in fact, the situation was rather more serious. As mentioned above, in the Pratt Street Riot, in Baltimore, four soldiers had been killed and thirty-six wounded, along with twelve dead civilians, when they attempted to change trains. After this Governor Hicks actually had some railroad tracks destroyed in an attempt to prevent Lincoln from sending any more troops through Baltimore.[43] In short, in Baltimore there were active riots and rebellions against the federal government, and Taney rejected Lincoln's justification for suspending the writ, whereas in New Orleans, there were rumors of British spies and sympathizers but no actual rebellion or destruction, and Taney supported Jackson's decision to suspend the writ on his authority as a general.

There are only three possible reasons Taney would support Jackson, and not Lincoln, in suspending the writ, and none are satisfactory. First, Taney might have supported Jackson because he was a military officer "on the ground" and needed to act quickly. However, in *Merryman*, Taney actually objected to *military officers* usurping constitutional protections at the slightest provocation despite the fact that they were acting on Lincoln's orders. Second, Jackson was fined by a state judge, and that might have offended Taney because, as Chief Justice John Marshall had noted in *Bollman*, only federal courts had authority over habeas corpus petitions. However, in Taney's letter to Jackson, he mentioned traitors in New Orleans, the nefarious influence of the National Bank and paper money in attacking Jackson's motives, and what he saw as Judge Hall's obvious disgraceful actions, but he made no mention of the problem of a state judge fining a federal official.

The third reason Taney might have supported Jackson and not Lincoln is, of course, partisanship: "Taney was either disingenuous when writing Jackson, when there was really nothing to be gained by such an act, or *Ex Parte Merryman* reflected his own partisan motivations, the very motivation that he had accused Whigs of in the 1840s."[44] As James Simon notes, "Taney systematically reduced the president's constitutional powers to Lilliputian proportions. Here Taney displayed the artistry of a partisan trial lawyer rather than the detachment of a judge."[45] Simon goes on to note that Taney's understanding of presidential power here was "starkly at odds with Taney's own reading of presidential power when he had been President Jackson's Attorney General."[46] Moreover, when the governor of Rhode Island wanted to use martial law to put down an armed insurrection, Taney as chief justice supported him, writing that the power "is essential to the existence of every government, essential to the preservation of order and free institutions, and is necessary to the State of this Union as to any other government."[47] As a result, partly because of Taney's inconsistency and hypocrisy, partly because Lincoln ignored Taney, and partly because Congress supported the president against Taney, the *Merryman* decision had little practical effect.

According to Lincoln, the president must act within the bounds of the Constitution, regardless of the circumstances. He can argue for a broad reading of the Constitution but not that he should be allowed to go outside of it. Because of this, the strength of a presidential claim to authority is linked to the strength of the constitutional argument. If the constitutional rationale is weak, so is the claim to authority. In contrast, if a president makes a claim of authority based on extraconstitutional prerogative power, he only needs to claim necessity. It is inherently difficult to argue about what qualifies as "necessity." Although legal and constitutional arguments can be complicated, they are much more concrete than claims about necessity. Moreover, as Justice David Davis's decision in *Ex Parte Milligan,* the post–Civil War case that dealt with the constitutionality of Lincoln's suspension of habeas corpus, demonstrates, any constitutional presidential use of power is subject to judicial review, whereas prerogative actions by definition cannot be checked by another body. Lincoln's presidency shows that a president can act decisively under a broad reading of constitutional power yet still be limited by the Constitution. However, it is important to recognize that much of that limitation is political in nature—Congress has to be willing to act against the president. At least in Lincoln's mind, Congress can legitimately disagree. There is no room for Congress to disagree with prerogative.

In Lincoln's thinking, that is the real danger of prerogative—it is not limited by the Constitution. As Lincoln famously noted in his Lyceum Address, the Constitution has to be preserved and upheld in order for the public to remain attached to it.[48] The basic criticism of Lincoln is that he violated the Constitution and the law. However, prerogative power does not solve that problem. After all, that is what prerogative is—a violation of the Constitution—the very thing Lincoln sought to avoid above all else. As Justice Davis noted in *Milligan*:

> No doctrine, involving more pernicious consequences, was ever invented by the wit of man than that any of its provisions can be suspended during any of the great exigencies of government. Such a doctrine leads directly to anarchy or despotism, but the theory of necessity on which it is based is false; *for the government, within the Constitution, has all the powers granted to it, which are necessary to preserve its existence.*[49]

Although both Justice Davis's decision in *Milligan* and Taney's decision in *Merryman* took issue with Lincoln's suspension of habeas corpus, they did so for very different reasons.[50] Taney, in *Merryman*, as already noted, asserted that the president had no authority to suspend the writ at all, and furthermore, that suspension was unnecessary because the civilian courts were open. Lincoln argued that the whole state of Maryland, and especially Baltimore, was virtually in a state of revolt, if not rebellion, and that the governor and secessionists were actively impeding the movement of Union troops. In contrast, in *Milligan*, though Davis sharply criticized the government, he did not object to Lincoln's suspension of habeas corpus on principle but rather objected to the specifics of application of martial law in Indiana. Because Indiana was not in active rebellion, and its civilian courts were open, there was no justification to deny Milligan the writ and a jury trial. The Court concluded that the federal government could institute martial law in some circumstances but only when there was actually a war or an ongoing rebellion, and it could only delay trial for a citizen during a crisis, not change the means of that trial.[51]

In short, Davis very clearly rejected the doctrine of extraconstitutional prerogative power, and he argued that Lincoln had crossed the line in bringing civilians to trial in military court while civilian courts were operating. However, though the Court ruled against Lincoln posthumously in *Milligan*, it had no difficulty concluding that the Constitution allowed for the suspension of habeas corpus during a crisis.[52] Taney objected to the very idea of the executive suspending the writ. Davis objected to the suspension of the writ, the establishment of martial law, and the military trial of civilians in an area not in rebellion. The two cases are substantially different. Moreover, Davis emphatically rejected the notion of extraconstitutional prerogative power, the idea that the executive can violate the Constitution in an emergency, because prerogative leads to "pernicious consequences" and is based on a *false* "theory of necessity" because the US Constitution readily gives all necessary powers to the government.

## THE EMANCIPATION PROCLAMATION

In the previous two examples, Lincoln's critics thought he had gone too far, but Lincoln argued that his actions fit with the proper understanding of the Constitution. In the case of the Emancipation Proclamation, Lincoln's allies worried he had not gone far enough. As Mark Neely notes, "One cannot be certain without public opinion polls, but it seems likely that the most unpopular measure taken by President Lincoln in the first year of the war was his revocation of Frémont's emancipation proclamation for Missouri."[53] Lincoln argued that Frémont's proclamation was "*purely political* and not within the range of *military* law, or necessity."[54] Lincoln went on to explain that a general could of course seize private property for military necessity on a temporary basis, but he could not for all time declare that the property no longer belonged to the original owner. To do otherwise was simply "dictatorship." He concluded, "I do not say Congress might not with propriety pass a law (for emancipation). . . . What I object to, is, that I as President, shall expressly or impliedly seize and exercise the permanent legislative functions of the government."[55] Lincoln's initial objection to emancipation was not that slavery was right but that emancipation could not be justified constitutionally as a purely political action. As he said during his First Inaugural Address, "I have no purpose . . . to interfere with the institution of slavery. . . . I believe I have no lawful right to do so."[56] For Lincoln, "the law had to be settled by lawmakers, in Congress, in the states, and by himself as president."[57]

However, as Lincoln understood, the Constitution operates differently in times of war and rebellion than it does in times of peace. Lincoln made this clear when he declared that his Emancipation Proclamation in 1863 was justified "by virtue of the power in me vested as Commander-in-Chief, of the Army and Navy of the United States in time of actual armed rebellion against authority and government of the United States, and as a fit and necessary war measure for suppressing said rebellion."[58]

Lincoln's critics have long insisted that the Emancipation Proclamation was hypocritical because it carefully listed each state, indeed, each county still under Southern military control and only freed slaves in those areas.[59] In other words, they charge that Lincoln's proclamation was ineffectual and only designed to gain the support of European allies such as Britain and France without actually freeing any slaves. However, this charge misses the reason Lincoln carefully listed areas under Southern control. Lincoln specifically declined to free slaves in the Union because he did not believe he had the constitutional authority to do so. Those areas were not in active rebellion, so the president could not free slaves there any more than he could have freed slaves in the South in the absence of the Civil War. As Lucas Morel notes, when Lincoln's treasury secretary asked him to apply the Emancipation Proclamation to Union-controlled territory in Virginia and Louisiana, Lincoln refused because it was not militarily necessary. He said, "Would I not give up all footing upon the constitution or law? Would I not thus be in the boundless field of absolutism?"[60] Lincoln refused to violate the Constitution through prerogative power. However, as a president acting against a rebellion, he could use his expanded powers to emancipate slaves—with the goal of weakening the South militarily.[61] Thus, executive emancipation was justified as a wartime measure, when it could never be justified during peace.[62] However, as Lincoln recognized, for emancipation to last after the war, it had to be supported by a permanent constitutional amendment.[63] This is why the Emancipation Proclamation is a prime example of how Lincoln understood the limits of his constitutional power and how they could be expanded, temporarily, in a time of rebellion.

## CONSTITUTIONALISM AND LINCOLN'S REJECTION OF PREROGATIVE

The critical point to note about each of these three cases—calling up the militia, suspending habeas corpus, and the Emancipation Proclamation—is that Lincoln could have chosen another path. He could have claimed that as president he had Lockean prerogative power to violate the law and the Constitution for the common good. Indeed, some of his strongest allies urged him to do so. However, despite the most vociferous claims of his opponents, who often accused him of violating the Constitution, Lincoln repeatedly refused to do so.

Instead, Lincoln made serious, compelling arguments for the constitutionality of his actions. His militia decision was the easiest case because Congress itself had foreseen the need for the president to act unilaterally and provided for it through legislation. His suspension of the writ of habeas corpus stood, at first because he ignored Taney and then later because Congress supported him legislatively. His use of military arrests and tribunals stood until after the war, and even then, the Court in *Milligan* only suggested that it was inappropriate to use military tribunals in territories not actively revolting or in a state of war, not that the use of military law or tribunals was itself unconstitutional. And the Emancipation Proclamation was accepted as a legitimate wartime act and made permanent by the passage of the Thirteenth Amendment. The end result was that Congress and the Court agreed with Lincoln's argument that, as Justice Robert Jackson would later quip, the Constitution is not "a suicide pact,"[64] and that the explicit and implicit powers of the president are sufficient for any necessary action to protect the republic.

Lincoln pushed his office to the limits of his power, but he stayed within those limits because he valued fidelity to the Constitution. Unlike Jefferson, who specifically avoided making his constitutional qualms about the Louisiana Purchase public and asked his allies in Congress to pass controversial legislation "sub-silentio,"[65] Lincoln defended his actions directly to Congress and asked for the support of that body. Lincoln argued that it was his duty to ensure that the laws were executed and maintained that his extraordinary actions were taken only to ensure that he fulfilled his constitutional oath.

The problem with the use of prerogative in the American constitutional system is that it assumes there are serious flaws in the Constitution: it is not sufficient for all emergencies, and it can be violated whenever the president makes an argument that it is necessary to contravene it or simply acts in secret. And that is the seductive danger of prerogative—it enables the president to act on his own, outside the bounds of the Constitution, in secret. However, for Lincoln as well as for James Madison and Hamilton, every violation of the Constitution, whether in public or in secret, damages the underlying belief in the document and weakens the public's support for the country.[66]

In his dissent in *Korematsu v. United States,* Justice Jackson argued for a bend-but-not-break approach to the knotty issue of the constitutionality of the mass internment of Japanese Americans in World War II:

If we cannot confine military expedients by the Constitution, neither would I distort the Constitution to approve all that the military may deem expedient.... Once a judicial opinion rationalizes such an order to show that it conforms to the Constitution, or rather rationalizes the Constitution to show that the Constitution sanctions such an order, the Court for all times has validated the principle of racial discrimination in criminal procedure and of transplanting American citizens. The principle then lies about like a loaded weapon ready for the hand of any authority that can bring forward a plausible claim of urgent need.[67]

Jackson's argument is a powerful one, and it has often been used against any claim of inherent presidential power. Jackson argued that the forced imprisonment of the Japanese could not be justified by constitutional principle. It could only be justified by expediency. It was illegal but necessary. But as Storing notes, "The difficulty is that prerogative—even Arthur Schlesinger's 'emergency prerogative'—is a loaded pistol too; and, all things considered, a more dangerous one. Do we want to save our Constitution by admitting that we must at times resort to nonconstitutional, plebiscitary dictatorship? The question would then be, shall we abide by the Constitution or not?"[68] Note that although Justice Jackson dissented from the Court's approval of President Franklin D. Roosevelt's internment policy, he made an argument for prerogative power. In arguing that a judicial order in favor of internment lies about like a loaded gun ready to be used in less exigent circumstances, he was arguing that the Court was wrong to justify internment as constitutional. However, that did not mean for Jackson that the internment policy was unjustified. It was simply unconstitutional: "It would be impracticable and dangerous idealism to expect or insist that each specific military command in an area of probable operations will conform to conventional tests of constitutionality. When an area is so beset that it must be put under military control at all, the paramount consideration is that its measures be successful, rather than legal. The armed services must protect a society, not merely its Constitution."[69] However, as Storing notes, this is at least as dangerous a conclusion. Under Jackson's reading, there is no reason for the military and the president to feel the need to justify their actions as constitutional as long as they can claim they are necessary. And, as Jackson helpfully notes, the Court has no capacity to judge necessity: "In the very nature of things, military decisions are not susceptible of intelligent judicial appraisal."[70] So Jackson's support of prerogative actually removes any judicial check from actions of "military necessity."

Rather than being a safer way to control the executive, prerogative actually makes the presidency more dangerous. Allowing the president to take any action he deems necessary as long as he justifies it as such is far too great an authority. Instead of limiting presidential actions to those that are absolutely necessary, Lockean prerogative actually makes it more likely presidents will take actions beyond their authority. If presidents can avoid "parchment barriers" by simply claiming necessity, what is there to stop them from claiming necessity at every turn? If the president can use Lockean prerogative to violate the Constitution, how can he be held accountable, and by whom? The public only has the option to speak through elections once every four years. And Locke's conclusion that the only recourse from unjust prerogative is "an appeal to heaven" is not a sufficient answer for a representative democracy.

Lincoln showed us a very different and much preferable answer to the need for emergency action in a constitutional republic. He agreed with Madison that "it is in vain to oppose constitutional barriers to the impulse of self-preservation. *It is worse than in vain; because it plants in the Constitution itself necessary usurpations of power, every precedent of which is a germ of unnecessary and multiplied repetitions.*"[71] This was part of Madison's argument that the Constitution needed to be expansive enough to allow for acts necessary for its preservation. Without that, the government would eventually usurp its constitutional power in order to protect the country, and every time it did so would set a dangerous precedent—that the Constitution provided an insufficient government and that the public could only be protected by its violation. Indeed, this was one of the primary reasons Madison and Hamilton both initially opposed the Bill of Rights: "Repeated violations of these parchment barriers [state bills of rights] have been committed by overbearing majorities in every State."[72] Madison noted particularly that in a rebellion or insurrection the "suspension of the Habeas Corpus" would be dictated, and "no written provisions on earth would prevent the measure. . . . The best security against the evils is to remove the pretext for them."[73] For both Madison and Hamilton, the solution was to ensure, in Hamilton's words, that "a power equal to every possible contingency must exist somewhere in government."[74] Hamilton's claim cuts directly against the logic of extraconstitutional prerogative. For Hamilton, because it is impossible to foresee all emergencies, government should be given a large enough grant of power to deal with any circumstance.[75]

Lincoln built on this understanding of the Constitution—that it needed to be read broadly in necessity but that it must be followed at all costs. As he noted, "If the laws be continually despised and disregarded, if their rights to be secure in their persons and property, are held by no better tenure than the caprice of a mob, the alienation of their affections from the Government is the natural consequence; and to that, sooner or later, it must come."[76] An executive wielding the prerogative power to violate the law at his discretion alone is little different than a mob. Both are capricious actors, justifying their decisions with fear, and both are free of any control or limitation. They are antithetical to constitutional government.

In the final analysis, prerogative is not a reasonable alternative to a strong, constitutional presidency. It is not supported by the constitutional or historical record, and in attempting to solve one problem it creates a far more dangerous crisis. After all, is it really advisable to embrace a theory that suggests we must violate the Constitution in order to save it? Perhaps it would be wiser to take a second look at Lincoln's example and regain "a reverence for the constitution."[77] Lincoln's commitment to constitutionalism during the greatest crisis in American history is perhaps his most enduring contribution to the American republic—not least because that is what made emancipation effective and irreversible. It should not be forgotten.

This commitment to constitutionalism shows the importance of Lincoln for our modern era. Lincoln is one of the principal historical examples of an American political figure taking the Constitution seriously and attempting to justify his preferred policies under the Constitution rather than simply altering or ignoring the Constitution when convenient. This is also why Lincoln's actions during the Civil War should be seen as a *renewal* of America's constitutional commitments, not a refounding. Throughout his career, Lincoln consistently referred back to the Declaration of Independence, the Constitution, and the intent of the founders. His first major public statement on government and law, the Lyceum Address, was a treatise on the importance of upholding the Constitution and the law. Throughout his campaigns for the Senate in 1858 and the presidency in 1860, and consistently during his administration, he insisted on the need to uphold the Constitution and, in so doing, carved a path between those willing to abandon the Constitution or the Union. During the Civil War, he was determined to preserve the Union *by* constitutional means and to give a public justification for the constitutionality of his actions. That, I submit, is at the heart of why Lincoln should still be regarded as one of the greatest American presidents—he not only held the nation together during great peril and set in motion the emancipation of all slaves but he did so within the constraints of the Constitution. In doing so, he left a clear example by which to measure future executives.

## NOTES

1. Arthur M. Schlesinger, Jr., *The Imperial Presidency* (Boston: Houghton Mifflin, 2004), 61, orig. pub. 1973, cited in Herbert J. Storing, *Toward a More Perfect Union: Writings of Herbert J. Storing*, ed. Joseph M. Bessette (Washington, DC: American Enterprise Institute Press, 1995), 382, 379.

2. Abraham Lincoln, The Perpetuation of Our Political Institutions: Address to the Young Men's Lyceum of Springfield, Illinois, January 27, 1838, in *Abraham Lincoln: His Speeches and Writings,* ed. Roy P. Basler (New York: Da Capo, 2001), 76–84; hereafter cited as Lyceum Address.

3. Abraham Lincoln, Message to Congress in Special Session, July 4, 1861, in *Abraham Lincoln: His Speeches and Writings,* ed. Roy P. Basler (New York: Da Capo, 2001), 598; see also 601.

4. Ibid., 600–601 (emphasis added on "It was not believed that any law was violated").

5. "What Abraham Lincoln Read: An Evaluative and Annotated List," *Journal of the Abraham Lincoln Association* 28, no. 2 (2007): 62.

6. Thomas Jefferson to John B. Colvin, September 20, 1810, in *The Works of Thomas Jefferson,* ed. Paul Leicester Ford (New York: G. P. Putnam's Sons, 1904–1905). See also Benjamin Wittes, *Law and the Long War* (New York: Penguin, 2008); Benjamin Kleinerman, *The Discretionary President* (Lawrence: University Press of Kansas, 2009); Daniel P. Franklin, *Extraordinary Measures: The Exercise of Prerogative Powers in the United States* (Pittsburgh, PA: University of Pittsburgh Press, 1991); Jeremy Bailey, *Thomas Jefferson and Executive Power* (Cambridge, UK: Cambridge University Press, 2007); John Locke, *Second Treatise on Civil Government,* in Locke, *Two Treatises of Government,* ed. Peter Laslett (Cambridge, UK: Cambridge University Press, 1988), chap. 14; Daniel Farber, *Lincoln's Constitution* (Chicago: University of Chicago Press, 2003), esp. 121–132.

7. Lincoln, Message to Congress in Special Session, 601 (emphasis added).

8. Ibid. Notably, Lincoln made this claim despite the fact that the suspension of the writ of habeas corpus is mentioned in Article I, Section 9, not Article II. See Farber, *Lincoln's Constitution,* 136–143, for a slightly different take. Farber suggests that Lincoln's calling up the militia was legitimate, but the request for additional volunteers and especially his "transfer of federal funds are probably best regarded as unconstitutional." Farber suggests Lincoln did not even try to defend them. This is a substantial critique, because clearly Congress has authority over the purse. Yet even Farber notes that Congress subsequently endorsed Lincoln's actions. Moreover, as his speech on July 1, 1861, before Congress could meet, demonstrates, it seems that Lincoln did defend his actions, all of them, as legitimate not because he could violate the Constitution through prerogative power but because he was tasked with preserving the Constitution until Congress could meet. Farber himself notes that "the constitutional verdict on Lincoln's bold initial response to secession is almost entirely favorable" (143).

9. Note that there is a substantial record of disagreement here. See James G. Randall, *Constitutional Problems under Lincoln* (Urbana: University of Illinois Press, 1951), 118–139, as an example. Even he, however, admits that the Constitution is largely silent on the question of whether the executive or Congress may suspend habeas corpus and that "the essential question is not who suspends, but whether the emergency actually calls for summary arrest."

10. Locke, *Second Treatise,* chap. 14, sec. 168.

11. Russ J. Corbett, *The Lockean Commonwealth* (Albany: State University of New York Press, 2009), 93.

12. Ibid., 90. Importantly, although Lincoln's calling up the militia might have incurred some initial costs before Congress met, his authorizing of the militia was specifically supported by statute, and President George Washington had already used the same statute to authorize the militia. Moreover, when Lincoln addressed Congress on July 4, 1861, in addition to justifying the actions he had taken before Congress met, he

also requested funds for dealing with the rebellion. Congress responded enthusiastically, authorizing 25 percent more than Lincoln requested.

13. Sean Mattie, "Prerogative and the Rule of Law in John Locke and the Lincoln Presidency," *Review of Politics* 67, no. 1 (Winter 2005): 92; US Const., art. 1, sec. 8.

14. Militia Act of 1792, sec. 2, http://www.constitution.org/mil/mil_act_1792.htm. In total, there are five versions of the statute: Calling Forth Act of 1792, 1 Stat. 264 (repealed 1795), chap. 28; Militia Act of 1795, 1 Stat. 424 (repealed in part 1861 and current version at 10 U.S.C. §§ 331–335 [2000]), chap. 36; Insurrection Act of 1807, 2 Stat. 443 (current version at 10 U.S.C. §§ 331–335 [2000]), chap. 39; and Suppression of the Rebellion Act of 1861, 12 Stat. 281 (current version at 10 U.S.C. §§ 331–335 [2000]) chap. 25.

15. The legislation specifically said "that whenever it may be necessary, in the judgment of the President, to use the military force." Militia Act of 1795, 2 Stat., chap. 36, sec. 3.

16. Ibid., sec. 1, 2. See Carol M. Highsmith and Ted Landphair, *The Library of Congress, American Memory: A Century of Lawmaking for a New Nation* (Golden, CO: Fulcrum, 1994).

17. Moreover, the Militia Act was expanded again in 1861 when Congress assembled in July, after which it remained virtually unchanged until the year 2000. The 1861 Act expanded the president's power to use the militia to "execute the laws" to allow him to call up the militia (and the federal armed forces) until sixty days after the beginning of the next legislative session, unless Congress were to intervene with a veto-proof resolution, whenever, in his judgment, it became "impracticable . . . to enforce . . . the laws of the United States within any State or Territory." Stephen I. Vladeck, "Emergency Powers and the Militia Acts," *Yale Law Journal* 114, no. 1 (October 2004): 166.

18. Richard Brookhiser, *Founder's Son* (New York: Basic Books, 2014), 202.

19. Ibid,

20. Abraham Lincoln to Erastus Corning and Others, June 12, 1863, in *Abraham Lincoln: His Speeches and Writings*, ed. Roy P. Basler (New York: Da Capo, 2001), 705. See also Stephen Engle's very good work, *Gathering to Save a Nation. Lincoln and the Union's War Governors* (Chapel Hill: University of North Carolina Press, 2016), 299–305.

21. As Lincoln mentioned, he was referring, of course, to the recognition in the Constitution that the writ of habeas corpus cannot be suspended except in cases of rebellion or invasion, a clear acknowledgment that normal rules can be altered in an emergency. Also, as already noted, congressional laws authorizing the president to call up the militia in an emergency also recognize this contingency.

22. It is also important to note that Lincoln's letter to Corning was a private explanation of his understanding of how the Constitution works differently in a crisis than during ordinary times. Lincoln was well aware of the long-standing history of presidential letters becoming public documents. This letter was turned into a pamphlet that sold a half million copies (see Brookhiser, *Founder's Son,* 208). However, the original focus of the letter was not on the militia; instead, it was about the much more difficult problem of military tribunals and the suspension of habeas corpus.

23. Justice Marshall noted in Ex Parte Bollman, 8 U.S. 75 (1807), that the Judicial Act gave federal courts exclusive habeas corpus authority over federal prisoners.

24. US Const., art. 1, sec. 9, cl. 2.

25. Lincoln, Message to Congress in Special Session, July 4, 1861, 600–601 (emphasis original).

26. Ibid., 601.

27. Storing, *Toward a More Perfect Union*, 382.

28. Engle, *Gathering to Save a Nation*, 45; see also 45–47, 57–60.

29. Ibid., 46. See also James F. Simon, *Lincoln and Chief Justice Taney: Slavery, Secession, and the President's War Powers* (New York: Simon and Schuster, 2006), 183–187.

30. Simon, *Lincoln and Chief Justice Taney*, 185.

31. I focus on Andrew Jackson's precedent, but Daniel Farber notes other examples as well, such as in 1777 when the Continental Congress "recommended that disloyal persons in Delaware and Pennsylvania be taken into custody." Farber, *Lincoln's Constitution*, 159. Notably, one might distinguish these cases because it was the Continental Congress acting. However, in 1777 there was no executive, and Congress was actually enforcing the suspension of the writ as an executive.

32. Lincoln to Corning and Others, June 12, 1863, 699–708 (emphasis added).

33. Matthew Warshauer, *Andrew Jackson and the Politics of Martial Law* (Knoxville: University of Tennessee Press, 2006), 226.

34. Note as well that the final outcome of the removal debate provides a sharp counterpoint to James Randall's argument against Lincoln on habeas corpus. Randall incorrectly argues that Andrew Jackson's contempt fine from Judge D. A. Hall was a vindication of civil authority, but in reality, Jackson won the long game. See Randall, *Constitutional Problems under Lincoln*, 145.

35. Mark Neely, *The Fate of Liberty: Abraham Lincoln and Civil Liberties* (New York: Oxford University Press, 1991), 203, 207.

36. "It seems that little changed since politicians debated martial law in the 1840s. . . . More often than not, partisanship outweighed ideology." Warshauer, *Andrew Jackson*, 232, 235.

37. Henry Archibald Cox, *War, Foreign Affairs, and Constitutional Power: 1829–1901* (Pensacola, FL: Ballinger, 1984), 219.

38. Senator Justin Morrill, *Congressional Globe* 31: 392. Cox notes, "If the authority for these executive actions was implied from expressly granted power, then Morrill's perception of the power Lincoln relied upon was akin to the implied powers of Congress granted in the 'sweeping' clause of the Constitution" (see US Const., art. 1, cl. 18). Cox, *War, Foreign Affairs, and Constitutional Power*, 219.

39. Farber, *Lincoln's Constitution*, 162. Farber goes on to note that although the Court never directly addressed habeas corpus, its opinion in *Moyer v. Peabody*, 212 U.S. 78 (1909), written by Oliver Wendell Holmes, came to the obvious conclusion that if the government has the power to use deadly force against people, it has the power to detain them. See also Randall, *Constitutional Problems under Lincoln*, 128–129.

40. Ex Parte Merryman, 17 F. Cas. 144 (1861). See also Simon, *Lincoln and Chief Justice Taney*, 190–199.

41. Carl B. Swisher, *History of the Supreme Court of the United States: The Taney Period, 1836–1864* (New York: Macmillan, 1974), 852. Similarly, Goldsmith declared, "Taney courageously wrote a decision for the circuit court . . . charging Lincoln with

violating the Constitution." *The Growth of Presidential Power: A Documented History*, vol. 2, ed. William M. Goldsmith (New York: Chelsea House, 1974), 960–961.

42. Roger Taney to Andrew Jackson, April 28, 1843, in *Jackson Correspondence*, vol. 6, ed. John Bassett (Washington DC: Carnegie Institute of Washington, 1926–1935), 217.

43. Simon, *Lincoln and Chief Justice Taney*, 185.

44. Warshauer, *Andrew Jackson*, 211.

45. Simon, *Lincoln and Chief Justice Taney*, 192–193.

46. Ibid., 193.

47. Ibid. See also Farber, *Lincoln's Constitution*, 148–149.

48. Lincoln, Lyceum Address, 76–84.

49. Ex Parte Milligan, 71 U.S. 2, 121 (1866) (emphasis added).

50. For more detail on the limited use of the *Ex Parte Milligan* decision see Neely, *Fate of Liberty*, esp. chap. 8, "The Irrelevance of the *Milligan* Decision."

51. Ex Parte Milligan, 71 U.S. 2, 125–127 (1866).

52. Justice Davis concluded, "Unquestionably, there is then an exigency which demands that the government, if it should see fit in the exercise of a proper discretion to make arrests, should not be required to produce the persons arrested in answer to a writ of habeas corpus. The Constitution goes no further. It does not say after a writ of habeas corpus is denied a citizen, that he shall be tried otherwise than by the course of the common law; if it had intended this result, it was easy by the use of direct words to have accomplished it." Ibid., 125–126.

53. Neely, *Fate of Liberty*, 49. See also Engle, *Gathering to Save a Nation*, 118.

54. Abraham Lincoln to O. H. Browning, September 22, 1861, in *Abraham Lincoln: His Speeches and Writings*, ed. Roy P. Basler (New York: Da Capo, 2001), 613–615.

55. Ibid.

56. Abraham Lincoln, First Inaugural Address, March 4, 1861, in *Abraham Lincoln: His Speeches and Writings*, ed. Roy P. Basler (New York: Da Capo, 2001), 579–590.

57. Brookhiser, *Founder's Son*, 223.

58. Abraham Lincoln, Emancipation Proclamation, January 1, 1863, in *Abraham Lincoln: His Speeches and Writings*, ed. Roy P. Basler (New York: Da Capo), 689–692; Abraham Lincoln to James Conkling, August 26, 1863, in ibid., 720. See also Brookhiser, *Founder's Son*, 226–227.

59. See, for example, Lerone Bennett, Jr., *Forced into Glory: Abraham Lincoln's White Dream* (Chicago: Johnson, 2001).

60. Abraham Lincoln to Salmon Chase, September 2, 1863, in *Collected Works of Abraham Lincoln*, vol. 6, ed. Roy P. Basler (New Brunswick, NJ: Rutgers University Press, 1953), 429. See also Lucas Morel, "Forced into Gory Lincoln Revisionism," in *Lincoln's American Dream*, ed. Kenneth L. Deutsch and Joseph R. Fornieri (Washington, DC: Potomac, 2005), 205–206.

61. Mark Landy and Sidney Milkis, *The American Presidency*, 5th ed. (Washington, DC: Congressional Quarterly Press, 2008), 163. James Randall similarly notes that Lincoln used extreme caution regarding emancipation to "place the whole policy frankly on the basis of the war power." Randall, *Constitutional Problems under Lincoln*, 45.

62. See also Farber, *Lincoln's Constitution*, 154–157: "Lincoln was correct about the law of war. . . . The lawfulness of seizing enemy property is confirmed by the U.S.

Constitution, which empowers Congress to 'make Rules concerning Captures on Land and Water.'"

63. Neely, *Fate of Liberty*, 221.

64. Terminiello v. Chicago, 337 U.S. 136 (1949). This does not imply that Lincoln set a *new* precedent for Justice Jackson but rather that both recognize the same basic truth about our founding document.

65. See Thomas Jefferson to James Madison, August 18, 1803, in *The Works of Thomas Jefferson*, vol. 8, ed. Paul Leicester Ford (New York: G. P. Putnam's Sons, 1904–1905), 245; Thomas Jefferson to John Breckinridge, August 18, 1803, in ibid., 245; Thomas Jefferson to Thomas Paine, August 18, 1803, in ibid., 245. Jefferson writes to Paine that it is "prudent to say nothing on that subject, but to do sub-silentio what shall be found necessary." See also Thomas Jefferson to Wilson Cary Nicholas, September 7, 1803, in ibid., 247.

66. James Madison, "*Federalist* No. 41," in *The Federalist Papers*, ed. George W. Carey and James McClellan (Indianapolis, IN: Liberty Fund, 2011), 208; Lincoln, Lyceum Address, 76–84.

67. Korematsu v. United States, 323 U.S. 214, 247 (1944).

68. Storing, *Toward a More Perfect Union*, 380.

69. Korematsu, at 244.

70. *Id.*, at 245.

71. Madison, "*Federalist* No. 41," 225 (emphasis added).

72. James Madison to Thomas Jefferson, October 17, 1788, in *The Papers of James Madison*, vol. 11, ed. William T. Hutchinson and William M. E. Rachal (Charlottesville: University Press of Virginia, 1977), 297–300.

73. Ibid.

74. Alexander Hamilton, "*Federalist* No. 26," in *The Federalist Papers*, ed. Clinton Rossiter (New York: Penguin, 2003), 138.

75. Alexander Hamilton, "*Federalist* No. 23," in *The Federalist Papers*, ed. Clinton Rossiter (New York: Penguin, 2003).

76. Lincoln, Lyceum Address, 76–84.

77. Ibid.

# CHAPTER 9

# To Preserve, Protect, and Defend

## The Emancipation Proclamation

W. B. ALLEN

In the war for the American Union, the Confederate States of America refused to pay the price of victory—slavery—and therefore paid the price of defeat, slavery. This conundrum best explains not only the reason for the war but the course of the war. Moreover, the conundrum had slowly arisen and become manifest since the American Revolution. The reality of slavery is that it is the viper at the breast—the enemy within—in every society at war throughout history.[1] The decision by the Confederacy to go to war and to oppose the strength of its erstwhile Northern counterpart, while retaining slavery, was therefore suicidal. For its only chance to win lay in simultaneously gaining an accession of strength and eliminating its chief vulnerability through wholesale manumission.

By contrast, the Union required *only* to persist in maintaining a pristine freedom from slavery in order to prevail in the war. The observation that the Union enjoyed purity on the question of slavery is not to be taken hyperbolically. For it is patent that the Constitution effected tacit recognition of slavery and that the Fugitive Slave Acts of 1793 and 1850 both entwined federal laws and regulations with slavery. Yet it remained true at least until the hour of the *Dred Scott* decision that never in the history of the Constitution in America had any person legally acknowledged to be free ever been reduced to slavery. In consequence, there neither was nor needed to be a federal slave code (*this despite the legal existence of slavery in the federal city*). The Union's antebellum pristine freedom from slavery[2] became the animating subject of the debate over the Kansas-Nebraska Act and the *Dred Scott* decision in which Abraham Lincoln made a "Caesar's wife" platform on the question of slavery the animating question of American politics. Lincoln embraced that position as a legal obligation deriving from his oath to "preserve, protect, and defend" the Union under the Constitution.

Now, the federal government had never positively endorsed slavery on its own terms, as opposed to accepting the unavoidability of an evil where it presumably could not be changed. In the view of Justice Joseph Story in *Prigg v. Pennsylvania* (later held by the Republican Party), freedom for all persons is the national assumption, whereas slavery only existed by virtue of state or local law. To be sure, the continuing reality of slavery, accepted but not endorsed by the constitutional order, presented an enduring dilemma for the Union. That dilemma was well illustrated during the war in the problem Lincoln and other Union leaders faced of the "contraband," slaves who had escaped thanks to the war. On the one hand, the Union could surely use those persons to aid in the war effort in a variety of ways. On the other hand, the easiest legal solution to the problem, treating the slaves as contraband similar to the homes and possessions of rebelling Southerners, paradoxically ceded the main point in contention between the North and the South, whether human beings could be property at all. From a narrow legal point of view, the Union could make use of the "contraband" against the slaveholders only by becoming a slave master in its own name.

This dilemma, and the deeper dilemma of preserving the purity of the Union in the face of the reality of slavery, sheds light on one of the great controversies about Lincoln's handling of the war, the timing and meaning of the Emancipation Proclamation. Many committed antislavery advocates then, and many scholars today, fault Lincoln for moving too slowly on emancipation. In their view, he was dragged unwillingly to the just deed, thus confirming their view that Lincoln was above all a man of political expediency, not a man of principle. Yet this view overlooks the true dimensions of the problem facing Lincoln. For Lincoln cared not just about emancipating the slaves but also about preserving the Constitution, and with it the possibility of democratic self-governance. If Lincoln had acted arbitrarily to emancipate the slaves, he would have undermined the constitutional basis of his own authority, lost the support of the public, and made it much more likely that the border states would secede. That price was too high, and not simply because of the short-term political considerations of keeping the border states in the fold. Nonetheless, Lincoln realized that the commitment to preserving the Union's purity on the slavery question—never willingly endorsing or extending the institution—would sooner or later require emancipation, especially as the war produced more and more escaped slaves, whose legal status would have to be decided one way or the other. Contra the still widespread view that Lincoln was compelled by circumstances out of his control to emancipate the slaves, this chapter shows that Lincoln's awareness of the requirement to preserve and protect the Union's purity led him to emancipation in the time and the fashion that he accomplished it.

Just as the Confederacy could not prevail in the war without ending slavery, the Union could not prevail without ending slavery. That truth has animated the historical narratives that portray Lincoln as being dragged toward an emancipation policy despite his disinclination to any initiative beyond protecting the Union's purity.[3] The narrative proposed here places the subject in a different perspective, however, revealing that in the end it was precisely the requirement to preserve and protect the Union's purity that required Lincoln to embrace emancipation independently of lobbying for and against that position.

## REVISING THE NARRATIVE

A revised narrative begins with the Revolutionary War and evolves through the major political events touching slavery in the antebellum era. Additionally, it reveals that Lincoln was wrong in citing a conspiracy among Stephen Douglas, Franklin Pierce, Roger Taney, and James Buchanan as endangering the Union's purity.[4] For the reality was that Chief Justice Taney had already signaled the eventual outcome of the *Dred Scott* case as early as 1842, when he wrote an energetic dissent in the case of *Prigg v. Pennsylvania* (the outcome of which Taney approved). However, to demonstrate the relevance of prior historical moments, it will be most helpful first to recapture the context in which the decision for emancipation arose during the war.

Moreover, to set the stage for that context, it is helpful to recall the conundrum the seceding states faced in light of the express position articulated by Lincoln and the Republican Party Platform. Inasmuch as Lincoln and the platform insisted that there was no intent to affect the constitutional status of slavery in the slaveholding states, it followed that the only threat to slavery was the threat to limit its expansion into new territories. Because secession practically accomplished that very result, it would appear to have played into Republican hands. That is too simple a reading, however. For Lincoln believed that slavery bottled up in the existing slaveholding states was slavery doomed to be what Alexander Stephens called "evanescent" in the Corner-Stone Speech on March 21, 1861.[5] Secessionists, however, failed to entertain the danger in the prospect of a regionalized slavery with an imminently minority master class and no fugitive return cooperation. Unionists at the same time failed to reckon on the doom of slavery from secession itself. Both failures underscored the greater meaning of the war for the Union as a war for freedom broadly.

In other words, Lincoln's "hands-off" policy was in fact a strategy to destroy slavery. Given that strategic reality, however, one might plausibly inquire whether the act of secession itself did not give Lincoln and the Republicans what they wanted—namely, slavery bottled up in the South (albeit a South no longer part of the Union). Not only did the Southern leaders fail to perceive that implication of secession, but the Northern leaders failed to regard it as the accomplishment of their prime objective. This, in turn, forces us to see that there was a goal beyond that of the gradual extinction of slavery that necessitated the defense of the Union per se. That goal tacitly made emancipation the end because the Union could remain preeminent on no other foundation.[6]

## LINCOLN AND THE CONTRABAND

A famous painting by Jean Leon Gerome Ferris, *Lincoln and the Contraband,* celebrates an emancipating Lincoln while unwittingly revealing what made emancipation necessary. The contraband policy, by which slaves escaped to find freedom in Union Army encampments, was anything but an emancipation policy. For it received and regulated the slaves as the "property" of the enemy combatants. In doing so the contraband policy made increasingly urgent the necessity for general law and policy governing the "personal property" of the rebels as the war unfolded. Other forms of property could readily be confiscated, detailed records kept, and return or compensation as appropriate anticipated upon the end of hostilities. To treat people who had been slaves similarly, however, would entail the necessity of the equivalent of a "federal slave code," which would preserve the status of these persons as property. When viewed in the context of the manifest military advantage in receiving and even recruiting slaves to Union forces (both to weaken the adversary and to strengthen Union forces through intelligence and manpower), it becomes equally manifest that a decision had to be taken concerning how to treat them (i.e., whether they were ever to be subject to being returned to their owners or emancipated once and for all upon being received in Union lines). The initial ad hoc decision to label them "contraband" created a tacit response to that question that ran counter to Union purity on the question of slavery.

Less than a month after hostilities opened at Fort Sumter on April 12, 1861, questions about what to do with the slaves had already emerged. Thomas Gantt, a Missouri unionist, inquired of Brigadier General William Harney, commander in the Department of the West, whether "the United States Government" intended to "interfere with the institution of negro slavery in Missouri or any slave State, or to impair the security of that description of property."[7] Harney,

Jean Leon Gerome Ferris, *Lincoln and the Contraband*

in reply, observed that "already since the commencement of these unhappy disturbances, slaves have escaped from their owners, and have sought refuge in the camps of United States troops. . . . They were carefully sent back to their owners."[8] This inquiry and reply structured what became the most paradoxical development of the war, namely, the attempt to enforce for persons in rebellion against the Constitution a constitutional right to the return of fugitive slaves. Nor was it long before the paradox was revealed in its fullest measure.

By May 27, 1861, General Benjamin Butler was reporting that the question had become "very serious," having already previously initiated and reported the contraband policy. "Squads" of fugitives were entering the Department of Virginia camp, bringing women and children with them. Moreover, several of these escapees had been put to work by the Confederates constructing batteries, from which Butler had received fire. Butler thought, "As a military question it would seem to be a measure of necessity to deprive their masters of their services."[9] Butler received the slaves as "contraband" and referred to his superiors for a ruling as to what was appropriate. He queried, "Shall they [the Confederates] be allowed the use of *this property* against the United States, and we not be allowed its use in aid of the United States?" To be sure, Butler made clear that he was alive to the "question of humanity" as well as to the "political question" involved in this judgment, over and above the military question. Nevertheless, there was scarce time for a full-scale deliberation because decisions were required in the field at once.

What in rapid succession followed Butler's initial attempt to solve the problem were an altogether inadequate First Confiscation Act by Congress on August 6, 1861;[10] General John Frémont's general emancipation under martial law in Missouri on August 30, 1861, and Lincoln's September 11 revocation of that order; an emancipation proposal by Secretary of War Simon Cameron (soon replaced by Edwin Stanton) on December 1, 1861; the introduction of a new, Lincoln-approved Code of War on April 24, 1862, justifying emancipation as an act of military necessity;[11] and a general emancipation decree by General David Hunter in the South Carolina, Georgia, and Florida Departments, revoked by Lincoln on May 19, 1862.[12] Along the way to Lincoln's firm insistence that he, and he alone, could make the decision on emancipation,[13] Congress had proceeded to forbid the return of fugitive slaves on March 13, 1862,[14] to end slavery in the District of Columbia (April 16, 1862),[15] and to prohibit it in the territories (June 19, 1862) while being very near to completing the Second Confiscation Act (finally approved July 17, 1862), which would come very close to demanding in so many words a proclamation of emancipation from the president.[16] Thus, in little more than a year and independently of all the lobbying that had transpired, events had moved the country ineluctably toward emancipation, leaving in balance only the question of how the president would manage the question while still managing the strategy of the war (tied strongly to an effort to retain slaveholding border states in the Union).

Although I think the lobbying has often been overstated in terms of its influence, it does no harm to observe certain symbolic attempts to influence the president. One of the earliest arrived from the pen of John Jay, grandson of the abolitionist architect of the Jay Treaty, on June 29, 1861 (prior to Congress assembling to respond to the war, which had already begun). Jay called for enactment of a general confiscation of "the lands and personal property of all citizens [or] persons who shall be found levying war against the United States," to be forfeit during their natural lives. He explained himself: "If the act is made to include all property real or *personal* to which the offender is entitled under or by virtue of the laws of the state where the same is situated, it would necessarily include *Slaves* & would perhaps go far towards relieving the Government of some of the nice and difficult questions that are likely to arise in reference to that class of persons."[17]

The issue would become fully as delicate as Jay foresaw, whether in the form of General William Tecumseh Sherman's early resolves about handling the "contraband" problem by returning the slaves to their masters as expeditiously as possible[18] or in that of the steely message from Governor Andrew of Massachusetts that his state "does not send her citizens forth to become the hunters of men or to engage in the seizure and return to captivity of persons claimed to be fugitive slaves, without any recognition of even the forms of law."[19]

In January 1862, B. H. Wright sent Lincoln a full-blown plan of emancipation, notable for its sensitivity to the constitutional niceties (no attainders beyond the life of the person adjudged and no general power of manumission in the federal government). He urged, accordingly, strategic adherence to the Constitution, seeking indirect pathways to a "way . . . provided by the present war for the extinction of Slavery. . . . It is one of the designs of Providence working through events."[20] At the same time the administration received representations from unionist slaveholders in Maryland who protested that they were forcibly resisted by Union troops when they attempted to retrieve fugitives known to be in the army encampment.[21]

Then in June 1862, Lincoln heard from pacifist cum-warrior Elihu Burritt encouraging him to read the fullest emancipation significance into the pending Second Confiscation Act and to recoil from it as a hot ember tossed among dried timbers. Burritt read the measure as an unconstitutional bill of attainder that would require the federal government to process confiscated property, including slave property, in such a manner as to convey it securely to new owners after the punished rebels had been replaced. In effect, Burritt argued, that kind of confiscation would necessitate a federal slave code.[22]

Finally, Benjamin Bannan wrote to Lincoln on July 24, 1862, soliciting "a decree of general emancipation, which would be hailed as the greatest stroke of policy that any government ever practiced, not only by the people of this Nation, but throughout the whole Christian world, and would immortalize the man who dared do it—he would stand second to no man who ever lived. It would give a death-blow to the Rebellion—save at least one hundred thousand lives, and not less than Five hundred millions of treasure—With such a result before you, how can you hesitate any longer[?]"[23]

As we shall observe, Lincoln had presented to his cabinet as near to a general emancipation as he thought he had constitutional power to effectuate two days before the newspaper editor's letter to him was written. And he had naturally made the decision long before that. We may place Bannan's letter, therefore, in company with the other, more famous newspaper editor's letter that elicited from Lincoln one of the finest examples of his prudent statesmanship. That other letter came from Horace Greeley, published August 19, 1862,[24] and drew from Lincoln the famous reply:

As to the policy I "seem to be pursuing," as you say, I have not meant to leave any one in doubt.

I would save the Union. I would save it the shortest way under the Constitution. The sooner the national authority can be restored the nearer the Union will be "the Union as it was." If there be those who would not save the Union unless they could at the same time save slavery, I do not agree with them. If there be those who would not save the Union unless they could at the same time destroy slavery, I do not agree with them. My paramount object in this struggle is to save the Union, and is not either to save or to destroy slavery. If I could save the Union without freeing any slave I would do it, and if I could save it by freeing all the slaves I would do it; and if I could save it by freeing some and leaving others alone, I would also do that. What I do about slavery and the colored race, I do because I believe it helps to save the Union; and what I forbear, I forbear because I do not believe it would help to save the Union. I shall do less whenever I shall believe what I am doing hurts the cause, and I shall do more whenever I shall believe doing more will help the cause. I shall try to correct errors when shown to be errors; and I shall adopt new views so fast as they shall appear to be true views.

I have here stated my purpose according to my view of official duty; and I intend no modification of my oft-expressed personal wish that all men every where could be free.[25]

Lincoln conveyed by this evasion both his readiness to declare practically general emancipation and, at the same time, his readiness to accept the defected states back into the fold. It must be understood, however, that Lincoln himself had a firm understanding of which of those prospects was the more likely. The fact that he had already committed to emancipation reveals his judgment of the likely outcome. Lincoln arrived at that result by meticulously weighing not merely the politics but the substance of the matter.

## RULE OF LAW

The antecedent conditions of the Emancipation Proclamation illustrate with singular clarity the nonprocedural, nonlegalistic significance of the rule of law.[26] In July 1862 Congress enacted the Second Confiscation Act, a measure designed in the middle of the war for the Union to provide legal stability to the growing phenomenon of slaves both escaping from masters and fleeing behind Union lines or being taken by Union forces.

President Lincoln generally approved of the purposes of the Second Confiscation Act, for he had been much vexed by irregular practices dealing with the question of slavery and its impact during the war. Most notably, General Frémont's proclamation of emancipation Lincoln had had to overturn, for it was an improper assumption of authority that operated to undermine strategic objectives in the conduct of the war. From the beginning, the president had been careful to persuade border states to remain loyal by reassuring them that nothing would be done to interfere with their peculiar domestic institution (while encouraging abolition with compensation).

Additionally, the issues of employing not merely slaves but also black citizens in the armed forces of the United States had been a sensitive and controversial matter. Yet, the flood of fugitives behind Union lines necessitated the development of practices to employ them in the service at least of strengthening logistical support for Union forces. Many generals, therefore, had been forced to question exactly how to understand the legal status of these items of property, chattel, which had fallen into their "possession" as a consequence of the war.

At the same time, the supreme commander of Union forces, General George McClellan, was determined to ensure that the war would be conducted with an explicit guarantee not to interfere with the institution of slavery—that is, to preserve the "property" interest of the slaveholders. He was at best negligent in complying with the instructions of the commander in chief for the conduct of the war, in large part because of his concern to preserve slavery intact. It was no accident, therefore, that in 1864, after he had been removed from command, he became the nominee of the political party that opposed Lincoln's reelection, running on a platform of "peace with slavery."

In the midst of debates occasioned by these multiple concerns, therefore, Congress determined to clarify matters once and for all. By then it had been accepted to enlist black soldiers, in all-black units commanded by white officers initially. However, it remained unclear just how far the Union could go toward receiving and even targeting slave property as a legitimate military initiative. The purpose of the Second Confiscation Act was to establish that slave property could be commandeered or otherwise made use of on exactly the same terms as any other "property" belonging to enemy combatants, especially in the cases where such "property" supported the ability to carry on the rebellion. More than two hundred thousand black citizens and ex-slaves ultimately served in the Union Army—a nonnegligible accession of strength.


## SLAVERY AND THE LAWS OF WAR

However, here a complication intervened. We understand that complication best by placing it in a context of historical developments that enables us to understand why the procedures for dealing with slave property are not as clear-cut as those dealing with other "property." Five facts and events are pertinent in this respect.

First, never in the history of America had any person legally acknowledged to be free ever been reduced to slavery. That is to say, the legal rule had consistently been that free persons may not be reduced to slavery (de facto abuses notwithstanding). In this, America followed the rule descending from *Somerset against Stewart,* a British ruling that only positive law could establish slavery. The common law recognized only freedom, and that 1772 reading pertained to the prerevolutionary American colonies equally with the soil of Great Britain.[27]

Second, this legal and moral fact took on special significance in the 1795–1796 handling of and debate about the Jay Treaty, which finally regularized American-British relations in terms of the Treaty of Paris, which concluded the Revolutionary War in 1783. The heart of the debate reveals how extensively George Washington responded to moral imperatives above legal niceties. The Jay Treaty aimed to settle outstanding claims, to get Britain finally to evacuate the western territories of the United States, to establish reasonable terms of commercial exchange, and to effectuate appropriate compensation for damaged or appropriated properties. Within this last area a sensitive issue arose, triggering immense opposition to the treaty. One extant claim for compensation was for runaway or "carried away" slaves. John Jay, an early abolitionist, simply did not honor this expectation and returned a treaty silent on the question. Washington's decision to ratify the treaty was effectively a decision to dismiss the justice of the claims for compensation or repatriation of the slaves.

The basis for this decision is laid out in compelling clarity by Alexander Hamilton, who at Washington's direction produced a series of thirty-eight "Defence" essays (under the pseudonym "Camillus") devoted to the Jay Treaty[28] and several other essays under the names of "Horatius" and "Philo Camillus."[29] Hamilton saw the problem of slavery as a moral problem, in which the request for repatriation of slaves (the original request by the Confederation Congress in the Treaty of Paris [1783]) was "odious" to the law of nations and natural right. The slaves, whether captured or defecting, received their liberty from the British, and the demand for their return amounted to a demand to reduce free persons to slavery. Insofar as they were in fact free persons, not "property," the demand for compensation was inconsistent with legal as well as moral norms (especially the recently decided *Somerset* case in Britain).[30] More importantly still, if they were taken as "property," then the laws of war could have treated them as booty and therefore also potentially not subject to reclaim.

Washington directed Hamilton to defend the Jay Treaty with a long list of considerations to which Washington sought a response. By such directions Washington revealed his intentions. Thus, Washington decided to ratify and defend the Jay Treaty without the slavery provision on the grounds announced by Hamilton that "Reason, Religion, Philosophy, Policy" guided the decision.[31]

Third, the prohibition of the foreign slave trade clarified the slavery option by the manner in which the international slave trade ended, when the constitutional limitation expired. President Thomas Jefferson and Secretary of State James Madison initiated the process in 1807 with apparent pleasure. They encountered a difficulty, however, that no one had anticipated.

It centered on the question of what to do with any contraband (that is, ships and slave cargo) that might be apprehended. Jefferson's original proposal envisioned a traditional disposal (sale) of contraband in the interest of the government. However, other parties, especially Quakers, pointed to the grand paradox that would involve the United States selling Africans as a means of denying that privilege to American citizens in the name of the rights of humanity.[32] Madison's speech of 1789—we treat persons as property in law to be able to prevent their being treated as property in practice—resonated loudly.

The first major debate over constitutional interpretation within the Congress took place in the House of Representatives on May 13, 1789. The subject was slavery, and it carried with it all of the ambiguous assumptions that freighted the several compromise provisions on the subject in the Constitution. It is to be remembered that the slave trade clause (Article I, Section 9), by which slavery could not be prohibited by Congress until the year 1808 but by which Congress could impose an import tax on slaves, produced contrary interpretations even at the time, ranging from the more familiar Southern claims that "we got all that we could" on behalf of slavery, to the less well-known but extraordinary claim by James Wilson that "I consider this as laying the foundation for banishing slavery out of this country."[33]

The House debate shows how far the hopeful interpretation prevailed over the shameful interpretation. On the surface it seems that the shameful interpretation prevailed, for the House voted by a large majority not to impose the constitutionally permitted impost on slaves. Further investigation reveals, however, that the vote was carried primarily by the Northern and eastern antislavery votes, cast by those who acted in this case on the principle enunciated by men such as Fisher Ames and Roger Sherman that "no one appeared to be prepared for the discussion."

Madison, however, was prepared to discuss the matter and most reluctant to yield to counsels of caution on a matter that others feared could abort the Union:

I cannot concur with gentlemen who think the present an improper time or place to enter into a discussion of the proposed motion. . . . There may be some inconsistency in combining the ideas which gentlemen have expressed, that is, considering the human race as a species of property; but the evil does not arise from adopting the clause now proposed; it is from the importation to which it relates.

Our object in enumerating persons on paper with merchandise, is to prevent the practice of treating them as such. . . .

The dictates of humanity, the principles of the people, the national safety and happiness, and prudent policy, require it of us. . . . I conceive the Constitution, in this particular, was formed in order that the Government, whilst it was restrained from laying a total prohibition, might be able to give some testimony of the sense of America with respect to the African trade. . . .

It is to be hoped, that by expressing a national disapprobation of this trade, we may destroy it, and save ourselves from reproaches, and our posterity the imbecility ever attendant on a country filled with slaves. . . . If there is any one point in which it is clearly the policy of this nation, so far as we constitutionally can, to vary the practice obtaining under some of the state governments, it is this.

To Madison, it appears, the slavery option was such that it could, and should, be subjected to calculated disincentives.[34]

It quickly became clear that Jefferson's 1807 proposal involved a mere oversight. Yet, it was immensely difficult to discern what else might be done. The counterproposal, that the Africans be freed rather than sold, was the immediate cause, which touched off a heated debate that produced the first compromise on slavery admitting the existence of irreconcilable differences between North and South. Here, for the first time, was an explicit threat of civil war over the institution of slavery, and an accommodation that recognized that "easterners" must not be asked to turn their backs on the founding and principles of humanity, whereas "Southerners" must not be asked to participate in a condemnation of their own way of life.[35] Therefore, the Northern proposal, effectively to free the "cargo" within the United States and even within the slave states, was amended, first, to freeing them only in the North (i.e., indenturing them for a term of years at a stipulated wage), and, ultimately, remanding them to such provisions as might be made in the states where they happened to be found, with the tacit understanding that they were not to be dealt with as property.

Fourth, the War of 1812 recreated and intensified the Treaty of Paris dilemma from the Revolutionary War.[36] Indeed, the problem was far worse because the British far more systematically cultivated slave defections during the

War of 1812.[37] Alarms spread throughout the slaveholding South not only about runaways but also about slave rebellions fomented by the prospect of liberation. Runaways were quickly spirited away by British warships to territories in the Caribbean and elsewhere. Moreover, it took little more than gaining a toehold behind British lines in Florida or onboard British vessels for slaves to be recognized as free. As a war tactic, it made great sense for the British to maraud through the Chesapeake area and the Gulf Coast seeking to undermine American strength by instigating instability in slaveholding regions. A large slave population presents a natural war-fighting target.

As the War of 1812 closed, the United States and Britain settled terms in the 1815 Treaty of Ghent, in which President Madison and Secretary of State James Monroe carefully inserted (through the aegis of their minister to the United Kingdom, John Quincy Adams) very specific language regarding the return of or compensation for slave property lost during the war. Article V of the 1818 convention to implement that treaty reads in part:

Whereas it was agreed by the first Article of the Treaty of Ghent, that "All Territory, Places, and Possessions whatsoever taken by either Party from the other during the War, or which may be taken after the signing of this Treaty, excepting only the Islands hereinafter mentioned, shall be restored without delay"; . . . and whereas under the aforesaid Article, *the United States claim for their Citizens, and as their private Property, the Restitution of, or full Compensation for all Slaves who, at the date of the Exchange of the Ratifications of the said Treaty,* were in any Territory, Places, or Possessions whatsoever directed by the said Treaty to be restored to the United States, but then still occupied by the British Forces, whether such Slaves were, at the date aforesaid, on Shore, or on board any British Vessel lying in Waters within the Territory or Jurisdiction of the United States; and whereas differences have arisen, whether, by the true intent and meaning of the aforesaid Article of the Treaty of Ghent the United States are entitled to the Restitution of, or full Compensation for all or any Slaves as above described, the High Contracting Parties hereby agree to refer the said differences to some Friendly Sovereign or State to be named for that purpose; and The High Contracting Parties further engage to consider the decision of such Friendly Sovereign or State, to be final and conclusive on all the Matters referred.[38]

In this article the contracting parties are careful to confine the US claim to "property" to those not already removed beyond US jurisdiction. Whether Adams did this knowingly, we do not know.[39] We do know that he spent the next ten years defending a broader interpretation of the passage than the language suggests (though the language necessarily suggests the prospect of reducing to slavery in the United States persons legally judged free). Perhaps he was seeking to establish bona fides with his Southern constituency, as Witt suspects. Or, perhaps, he knew what he was doing originally and did what he did subsequently to conceal the *scienter* element of his negotiations.[40] Even then there is controversy concerning actual liability, which eventually was resolved only by reference to the tsar of Russia as arbitrator, who in 1822, when Monroe was president and John Quincy Adams was secretary of state, finally assigned limited compensatory payment to the United States (subsequently used partially to settle slaveholder claims) but returned not a single person to slavery.

The Treaty of Ghent experience was the closest the United States as an entity ever came to establishing property in slaves, in doing which it would have incurred moreover the obligation to develop a slave code, however limited. The eventual resolution through cash payments rather than the actual return of persons averted that necessity. However, the experience underscores just how important it eventually became for the slaveholding states to win federal acknowledgment of a constitutional foundation for slavery. The fact that the Ghent arbitration occurred within the same time frame and context as the Missouri Compromise, which enshrined the "freedom national, slavery sectional" rationale, serves only to underscore just how tentative were the early decisions about the legal status of slavery. It might be fairly said that Madison, Monroe, and Adams (three successive presidents) very nearly repudiated the Washington/Hamilton line of interpretation during and after the War of 1812, averting that consequence largely as a result of British intransigence (despite Britain's not yet having abolished slavery, which arrived only in 1832) and an arbitration decision that "split the baby."

Fifth, as Jefferson had foreseen, however, the Missouri Compromise would not permanently settle the question domestically. And nothing so thoroughly conveys the lingering instability of the slavery question than the decision in *Prigg v. Pennsylvania* in 1842. In that Supreme Court decision, Justice Story wrote for a majority that overturned a Pennsylvania statute that interfered with efforts to obtain the return of a runaway slave. Story, who remains the finest legal analyst of the Constitution to have served on the Supreme Court, wrote an opinion notable both for clarifying the constitutional status of slavery and for the declaration that Congress had evacuated the field of legislation regarding the status of slavery in the nation at large. No state, whether free or slave, had any right to intrude upon the federal constitutional regime in relation to slavery.[41] As soon as the Compromise of 1850, this decision would imperil the "personal liberty" laws in Northern states, an apparent victory for the slaveholding states. Nevertheless, in 1842, Chief Justice Taney found it necessary not merely to concur in the majority ruling in *Prigg* but also to dissent from the deciding opinion's subordination of state lawmaking power to congressional direction.

The Court . . . decides that the power to provide a remedy for this right is vested exclusively in Congress; and that all laws upon the subject passed by a state, since the adoption of the Constitution of the United States, are null and void; even although they were intended, in good faith, to protect the owner in the exercise of his rights of property, and do not conflict in any degree with the act of Congress.

. . . the law of Pennsylvania, under which the plaintiff in error was prosecuted, is clearly in conflict with the Constitution of the United States, as well as with the law of 1793. But as the question is discussed in the opinion of the Court, and as I do not assent either to the doctrine or the reasoning by which it is maintained, I proceed to state very briefly my objections.

The opinion of the Court maintains that . . . the state authorities are prohibited from interfering for the purpose of protecting the right of the master and aiding him in the recovery of his property. I think the states are not prohibited, and that, on the contrary, it is enjoined upon them as a duty to protect and support the owner where he is endeavoring to obtain possession of his property found within their respective territories.

The language used in the Constitution . . . contains no words prohibiting the several states from passing laws to enforce this right. They are in express terms forbidden to make any regulation that shall impair it. But there the prohibition stops. And according to the settled rules of construction for all written instruments, the prohibition being confined to laws injurious to the right, the power to pass laws to support and enforce it, is necessarily implied. *And the words of the article which direct that the fugitive "shall be delivered up," seem evidently designed to impose it as a duty upon the people of the several states to pass laws to carry into execution, in good faith, the compact into which they thus solemnly entered with each other. The Constitution of the United States, and every article and clause in it, is a part of the law of every state in the Union; and is the paramount law.* The right of the master, therefore, to seize his fugitive slave, is the law of each state; and no state has the power to abrogate or alter it. And why may not a state protect a right of property, acknowledged by its own paramount law? Besides, the laws of the different states, in all other cases, constantly protect the citizens of other states in their rights of property, when it is found within their respective territories; and no one doubts their power to do so. . . . *I perceive no reason for establishing, by implication, a different rule in this instance; where, by the national compact, this right of property is recognised as an existing right in every state of the Union. . . .*

I cannot understand the rule of construction by which a positive and express stipulation for the security of certain individual rights of property in the several states, is held to imply a prohibition to the states to pass any laws to guard and protect them. . . .

It has not heretofore been supposed necessary, in order to justify these laws, to refer them to such questionable powers [as] internal and local police. They were believed to stand upon surer and firmer grounds. They were passed, not with reference merely to the safety and protection of the state itself; but in order to secure the delivery of the fugitive slave to his lawful owner. They were passed by the state in the performance of a duty believed to be enjoined upon it by the Constitution of the United States.[42]

The chief justice, in short, maintains that the right of property in slaves is national as early as 1842, which, by implication, undermines the Missouri Compromise and prepares for it to be deliberately jettisoned in 1854 in the Kansas-Nebraska Act (if that had not already been accomplished in 1850). Although so-called free states might yet elect not to maintain slavery on the strength of their internal police power, they could not constitutionally avoid recognizing slavery as legitimate usage under the Constitution.

## DERIVING LAW FROM NECESSITY

In these five events, therefore, we see a mosaic that captures the dimensions of the role of slavery and race in American politics. That role must be considered against the backdrop of the principles of the regime because actions touching upon slavery and race bear heavy implications for those principles, and vice versa. This does not result from any cultural or traditional pattern so much as from the conscious choices with which Americans wrestled at every turn in the nation's history, up to and including the decisions of the present generation.

It was especially obvious in the 1807 struggle to end the slave trade: from the moment slavery was in any degree limited, the question of race arose. The free states did not desire the imposed presence of black immigration, whereas the slave states did not desire to multiply the numbers of free blacks in their communities. The answer to that question rests, in turn, not only on the fact that the consciously chosen principles of the regime entail equality and liberty for all humans but, far more importantly, that they require an open, heterogeneous society. The decisions made on this question in the aftermath of the war for American Union, in the form of the postwar amendments and civil rights legislation, indicate a positive if grudging response to the latter.

Although it would be inaccurate to assert that no one prior to the last half of the nineteenth century imagined an interracial society founded on the principles of the Declaration of Independence, that question is of minimal concern here. First, it is of minimal concern because subordinate to the question of whether the Declaration was understood to include all human beings, it was without regard to the practical implications of that principle. Second, it is of minimal concern because the status of slavery and race under the Constitution—and how to legislate in regard to it—has never been a single question. Madison's concern to avoid the "imbecility" of a country filled with slaves does not *require* the corollary of turning slaves into free citizens in the republic. The 1807 slave trade debate reveals, however, that such a question arises the moment the freedom of the African is conceded. Nothing so perfectly illustrates this relationship as the Reconstruction amendments, added to the Constitution in the immediate aftermath of the war.

## EMANCIPATION AT LAST

These reflections return us to the dilemmas Lincoln faced in the midst of the war, especially the Second Confiscation Act. Lincoln had intended to veto the act because of a particular concern he had about the operation of the attainder, but by implication also the status of the "contraband." In the end, he did sign the act after a joint resolution in Congress addressing his general concern. However, he took the rather extraordinary step, after signing the act, of enclosing the *draft* of the veto message that he had intended to send, to entrench the legal principle that concerned him. Moreover, he then prepared a proclamation to announce the act, to which he added an unanticipated, previously unannounced commitment to issue an "emancipation proclamation." Lincoln's reasons for taking these two steps illustrate the nature of the rule of law.

After enumerating his agreement with provisions of the act, Lincoln then proceeded to specify the problem attracting a proposed veto:

That to which I chiefly object, pervades most parts of the Act, but more distinctly appears in the first, second, seventh and eighth sections. It is the sum of those provisions which results in the divesting of title forever. For the causes of treason, and the ingredients of treason, not amounting to the full crime, it declares forfeiture, extending beyond the lives of the guilty parties; whereas the Constitution of the United States declares that "no attainder of treason shall work corruption of blood, or forfeiture, except during the life of the person attainted." True, there is to be no formal attainder in this case; still I think the greater punishment can not be constitutionally inflicted, in a different form, for the same offence—With great respect, I am constrained to say I think this feature of the act is unconstitutional—It would not be difficult to modify it—I may remark that *this provision of the Constitution, put in language borrowed from Great Britain, applies only in this country as I understand, to real, or landed estate.*

Again, this act, by proceedings *in rem* forfeits property, for the ingredients of treason, without a conviction of the supposed criminal, or a personal hearing given him in any proceeding—That we may not touch property lying within our reach, because we can not give personal notice to an owner who is absent endeavoring to destroy the government is certainly not very satisfactory; still the owner may not be thus engaged, and I think a reasonable time should be provided for such parties to appear and have a personal hearing. Similar provisions are not uncommon in connection with proceedings *in rem*.[43]

We observe Lincoln's scrupulousness in dealing with the property of rebellious subjects according to the rule of law. For no property were such procedures more necessary than for personal property, as opposed to property in rem. This is especially pertinent because Lincoln applies the rule to *all* property, recognizing that the law facilitates seizures that would transfer that property to the United States. As he undertook to convey this message on July 17, 1862, although signing the Second Confiscation Act, he had already prepared the proclamation to announce the act, which would follow in just five days:

In pursuance of the sixth section of the act of Congress entitled "An act to suppress insurrection and to punish treason and rebellion, to seize and collect property of rebels, and for other purposes," approved July 17, 1862, and which act, and the Joint Resolution explanatory thereof, are herewith published, I, Abraham Lincoln, President of the United States, do hereby proclaim to and warn all persons within the contemplation of said sixth section to cease participating in, aiding, countenancing, or abetting the existing rebellion . . . on pain of the forfeitures and seizures, as within and by said sixth section provided. . . . As a fit and necessary military measure for effecting this object, I, as a Commander-In-Chief of the Army and Navy of the United States, do order and declare that on the first day of January in the year of our Lord one thousand, eight hundred and sixty-three, all persons held as slaves within any state or states wherein the constitutional authority of the United States shall not then be practically recognized, submitted to, and maintained, shall then, thenceforward, and forever, be free.[44]

This proclamation of emancipation—and it is not a mere draft, inasmuch as Lincoln delayed issuing it upon persuasion to await a military victory (such as Antietam in September 1862)—surprised virtually all participants in the discussions of 1862. It follows a most emphatic letter from General McClellan of July 7, 1862, that declared: "A declaration of radical views, especially upon slavery, will rapidly disintegrate our present armies."[45] Lincoln, however, had larger issues to deal with, urgent since the opening of the war and especially the First Confiscation Act of 1861, which conferred "contraband" status on slaves used by Confederates to further the war effort.[46] In short, the Union had fallen into the trap it fell into in 1795–1796, 1807, and 1815, inadvertently coming into the ownership of slaves. The very term "contraband" applies legally to property. Lincoln was at pains both to ensure the rule of law as to property and to avoid subjecting human beings to that rule. Thus, he prepared to approve the Second Confiscation Act (which made slaves Union property) at the same time he prepared to declare the "contraband" free persons, so as to avoid subjecting them to continuing status as chattels and also to avoid placing the Union in the uncomfortable relation of having to deal with them as "property."

Lincoln's perspective involved the rule of law at a higher level than mere lawmaking. He proposed to keep the nation true to itself, and to its moral heritage, while guiding it through the emergency in such a manner as neither to constrain nor to yield to contingencies that would compromise that moral heritage. To that extent his decisions reflect the different relation in which he stood to the law than every other officer—legislative, judicial or otherwise. That difference was first manifested in Lincoln's Message to Congress in Special Session on July 4, 1861, to respond to the outbreak of hostilities. Among the many factors Lincoln reviewed with Congress, most taking on a constitutional cast, one above all signalized the view Lincoln took regarding his obligations to the Constitution. That one was the suspension of the writ of habeas corpus; Lincoln maintained that his oath required him to preserve "the whole of the laws" to the extent possible, even if at the expense of "some single law."

He posed to Congress the famous query: "To state the question more directly, are all the laws, *but one*, to go unexecuted and the government itself go to pieces, lest that one be violated?"[47] As the balance of Lincoln's defense of having suspended the writ of habeas corpus demonstrated, he derived a *legal* responsibility to act on behalf of the Constitution from his constitutionally prescribed oath, which gave him moral obligations and hence a different status than that of the other officers of government. Lincoln dealt with emancipation on the same foundation, whereupon even the argument of "military necessity" depends. The difference in status is reflected in the difference in oaths sworn by the president and every other officer of the government. Lesser officers swear:

I, (name), do solemnly swear (or affirm) that I will support and defend the Constitution of the United States against all enemies, foreign and domestic; that I will bear true faith and allegiance to the same; that I take this obligation freely, without any mental reservation or purpose of evasion; and that I will well and faithfully discharge the duties of the office on which I am about to enter. [So help me God.][48]

By contrast, the president swears, "I do solemnly swear (or affirm) that I will faithfully execute the Office of the President of the United States, and will to the best of my Ability, preserve, protect and defend the Constitution of the United States."[49] Lincoln did not believe he was required to await a judicially settled interpretation of that legal obligation to act on the basis of it. And it is fair to insist that, in his view, nothing preserves and protects the Constitution as visibly as the continuing influence of liberty and the rule of law. Because this is a constitutional and not merely a statutory requirement, the president claimed authority to act within the law directly from his oath.[50] Lincoln did so throughout his tenure and, as the president, was the only constitutional officer so empowered.

## NOTES

1. See Toni Ahrens, "Emancipation," in *Encyclopedia of African American History,* vol. 1: *From the Colonial Period to the Age of Frederick Douglass,* ed. Paul Finkelman (New York: Oxford University Press, 2006), 463: "During the Revolution, the British promised freedom to any slaves who would bear arms against the rebels. Thousands of slaves elected to take this option; others fled their homes not to join the British but to resettle with their families in nonslave states."

2. A status formalized in the Missouri Compromise, which yielded the slogan "Freedom national; slavery local." See James Oakes, *Freedom National: The Destruction of Slavery in the United States, 1861–1865* (New York: Norton, 2013).

3. See the exchange between James McPherson and Ira Berlin in Michael Vorenberg, *The Emancipation Proclamation: A Brief History with Documents* (Boston: Bedford/St. Martin's, 2010), 128–151.

4. The conspiracy charge was given its strongest appearance of credibility by James Buchanan's anticipation of the *Dred Scott* decision in his Inaugural Address days prior to the ruling issued by the Supreme Court. Lincoln laid out the schema of a conspiracy in his House Divided Speech, June 16, 1858, delivered at the Republican State Convention in Springfield, Illinois. See *The Collected Works of Abraham Lincoln,* vol. 2, ed. Roy P. Basler (New Brunswick, NJ: Rutgers University Press, 1953), 461.

5. An impromptu speech delivered in Savannah, Georgia, by the vice president of the Confederacy, in *America's War: Talking about the Civil War and Emancipation on Their 150th Anniversaries,* ed. Edward L. Ayers (Chicago and Washington, DC: American Library Association and National Endowment for the Humanities, 2012), 51.

6. See ibid., 41–57, for the tacit exchange between Abraham Lincoln's First Inaugural Address of March 4, 1861, and Alexander Stephens's Corner-Stone Speech of March 21, 1861, provided side-by-side.

7. Thomas T. Gantt to Brigadier General W. S. Harney, May 14, 1861, Letters Sent, ser. 5481, Department of the West, US Army Continental Commands, Record Group 393, Pt. 1, National Archives, vol. 2, DMo, 202–204; Brigadier General William S. Harney to Thomas T. Gantt, Esq., May 14, 1861, in ibid. (also available at Freedmen and Southern Society Project, http://www.freedmen.umd.edu/Gantt-Harney.html).

8. Ibid.

9. General Benjamin F. Butler to General-in-Chief Winfield Scott, May 27, 1861, in Box 99, 1861. Letters Received Irregular, Secretary of War, Record Group 107, National Archives (also available at Freedmen and Southern Society Project, http://www.freed men.umd.edu/Butlerhtml).

10. See Allen C. Guelzo's general discussion in Guelzo, *Lincoln's Emancipation Proclamation: The End of Slavery in America* (New York: Simon and Schuster, 2004), 41–46. See also Oakes's discussion of "Trumbull's Amendment" in *Freedom National*, 118–122.

11. See John Fabian Witt, *Lincoln's Code: The Laws of War in American History* (New York: Free Press, 2012). Witt quotes Lincoln's August 26, 1863, letter to James C. Conkling:

> You dislike the emancipation proclamation; and, perhaps, would have it retracted. You say it is unconstitutional—I think differently. I think the constitution invests its commander-in-chief, with the law of war, in time of war. The most that can be said, if so much, is, that slaves are property. Is there—has there ever been—any question that by the law of war, property, both of enemies and friends, may be taken when needed? And is it not needed whenever taking it, helps us, or hurts the enemy? Armies, the world over, destroy enemies' property when they can not use it; and even destroy their own to keep it from the enemy. Civilized belligerents do all in their power to help themselves, or hurt the enemy, except a few things regarded as barbarous or cruel. Among the exceptions are the massacre of vanquished foes, and non-combatants, male and female (138)

12. See "Chronology," in Vorenberg, *Emancipation Proclamation*, 153–157, for a listing of all of these events (except for the Code of War).

13. This position was based on the logic of war and connected to Lincoln's position that the Constitution gave Congress no power over slavery in the states where it existed.

14. Law Enacting an Additional Article of War, U.S. Statutes at Large, Treaties, and Proclamations of the United States of America, vol. 12 (Boston: 1863), 354 (also available at Freedmen and Southern Society Project, http://www.freedmen.umd.edu/art war.htm).

15. In opposition to the April 1, 1862, Resolution by the Washington, DC, City Council, which announced that "a large majority of the people of this community is adverse to the *unqualified* abolition of slavery in this district at the present critical juncture in our national affairs." Freedmen and Southern Society Project, http://www .freedmen.umd.edu/DCCouncil.html.

16. Second Confiscation Act, sec. 6 and 9, replacing the original sec. 9 of House Resolution 471 and calling for "proclamation" of the forfeiture of property, while declaring slaves "captives of war" immediately freed. A bill to suppress insurrection, to punish treason and rebellion, to seize and confiscate the property of rebels, and for

other purposes, *Journal of the Senate* (1862), 815–816 (also available at http://memory
.loc.gov/cgi-bin/query/r?ammem/hlaw:@field%28DOCID+@lit%28sj054163%29
%29).

17. John Jay to Abraham Lincoln, June 29, 1861, in Abraham Lincoln Papers at the
Library of Congress, transcribed and annotated by the Lincoln Studies Center, Knox
College, Galesburg, Illinois.

18. See Brigadier General A. McD. McCook to Brigadier General W. T. Sherman,
November 5, 1861, in Miscellaneous Records, ser. 3534, Department of the Ohio, US
Army Continental Commands, Record Group 393, pt. 1, National Archives, vol. 2, Do,
p. 91; Brigadier General W. T. Sherman to Brigadier General A. McD. McCook, No-
vember 8, 1861, in Letters Sent, ser. 866, Department of the Cumberland, U.S. Army
Continental Commands, Record Group 393, pt. 1, National Archives (also available
at Freedmen and Southern Society Project, http://www.freedmen.umd.edu/McCook
-Sherman.html). On the other hand, see Sherman's letter to the adjutant general of the
US Army, December 15, 1861, in s-1491 1861, Letters Received, ser. 12, Adjutant General's
Office, Record Group 94, National Archives: "It is really a question for the Government
to decide what is to be done with the Contrabands." A day earlier,

> Sherman had informed the adjutant general that the "immense" amount of military
> labor in the Union-occupied Sea Islands was all being "done by volunteer soldiers."
> "The Negro labor expected to be obtained here is so far almost a failure. They are
> disinclined to labor, and will evidently not work to our satisfaction without those
> aids to which they have ever been accustomed, viz. the driver and the lash. A sud-
> den change of condition from servitude to apparent freedom is more than their
> intellects can stand, and this circumstance alone renders it a very serious question
> what is to be done with the negroes who will hereafter be found on conquered soil."

See *The War of the Rebellion: A Compilation of the Official Records of the Union and
Confederate Armies*, ser. 1, vol. 6, ed. Robert N. Scott (Washington, DC: 1880–1901),
203–204.

19. John A. Andrew (governor of Massachusetts) to Simon Cameron (secretary of
war), December 7, 1861, in M-1250 1861, Letters Received, ser. 12, Record Group 94, National Archives (also available at Freedmen and Southern Society Project, http://www
.freedmen.umd.edu/Andrew.html).

20. B. H. Wright to Abraham Lincoln, January 22, 1862, in Abraham Lincoln Papers
at the Library of Congress, transcribed and annotated by the Lincoln Studies Center,
Knox College, Galesburg, Illinois.

21. Jno. H. Bayne et al. to Hon. E. M. Stanton, March 10, 1862, enclosing affidavit of
A. J. Smoot, March 1, 1862, in M-387 1862, Letters Received, Secretary of War, Record
Group 107, National Archives (also available at Freedmen and Southern Society Proj-
ect, "Maryland Legislators to the Secretary of War, Enclosing Affidavit of a Maryland
Slaveholder," http://www.freedmen.umd.edu/Smoot.html).

22. Elihu Burritt to Abraham Lincoln, June 2, 1862, in Abraham Lincoln Papers at
the Library of Congress.

23. Benjamin Bannan to Abraham Lincoln, July 24, 1862, in Abraham Lincoln Papers at the Library of Congress.

24. Horace Greeley, "The Prayer of Twenty Millions," *Tribune*, August 20, 1862.

25. *Collected Works of Abraham Lincoln*, vol. 5, 388–389.

26. This helps to explain the prosaic character of the proclamation. See Harold Holzer, *Emancipating Lincoln: The Proclamation in Text, Context, and Memory* (Cambridge, MA: Harvard University Press, 2012), 85–87.

27. Somerset against Stewart, 12 Geo. 3, King's Bench, May 14, 1772, http://www.commonlii.org/int/cases/EngR/1772/57.pdf.

28. Camillus, "Defence No. III," July 1795, in *Papers of Alexander Hamilton*, vol. 18, ed. Harold C. Syrett (New York: Columbia University Press, 1973), 519.

29. Horatius, "Horatius No. II," in *Papers of Alexander Hamilton*, vol. 19, ed. Harold C. Syrett (New York: Columbia University Press, 1973), 76; Camillus, "Defence No. V," in *Papers of Alexander Hamilton*, vol. 18, ed. Harold C. Syrett (New York: Columbia University Press, 1973), 94, and so forth.

30. Somerset against Stewart, Lofft 1–18; 11 Harg. State Trials 339; 20 Howell's State Trials 1, 79–82; 98 Eng Rep 499–510 (King's Bench, June 22, 1772).

31. See Camillus, "Defence No. III," 519.

32. Madison's speech is found in 9th Congress, May 13, 1789, *Annals of Congress*, Committee of the Whole.

33. Pennsylvania State Ratifying Convention, December 3, 1787.

34. See my discussion of Madison's House speech in W. B. Allen, "A New Birth of Freedom: Fulfillment or Derailment," in *Slavery and Its Consequences: The Constitution, Equality, and Race*, ed. Robert A. Goldwin (Washington, DC, and Lanham, MD: American Enterprise Institute and University Press of America, 1988), 4; Madison's speech, May 13, 1789.

35. In this the Southerners echoed their forebears' reaction to Jefferson's draft language for the Declaration of Independence, which condemned the slave trade.

36. "During the Revolution, the British promised freedom to any slaves who would bear arms against the rebels. Thousands of slaves elected to take this option; others fled their homes not to join the British but to resettle with their families in nonslave states." Ahrens, "Emancipation," 463.

37. Glen Allen Smith, *The Slaves' Gamble: Choosing Sides in the War of 1812* (New York: Palgrave Macmillan, 2013) An illustration of the situation arose when an American privateer captured a British ship with twenty-two former slaves in the crew. "The owners of the American ship asserted that the slaves were property who should be exchanged with the British. Despite the owners' position, the slaves were handed over to British officials—in some cases more than two years later (late June 1816). The debate over property rights, slave restitution, and spoils of war continued to work its way through Congress and diplomatic channels for years to come" (57).

38. http://avalon.law.yale.edu/19th_century/ghent.asp#_blank.

39. See Witt, *Lincoln's Code*, 75.

40. John Quincy Adams did obtain a different article in which he obligated Britain to assist in enforcing the ban on the foreign slave trade and through which he was able to develop capital punishment in the United States for those found guilty of the attempt.

41. Prigg v. Pennsylvania, 41 U.S. 539 (1842), Justice Joseph Story writing for the Court.

42. *Id.*, Chief Justice Taney's dissent (emphasis added).

43. Abraham Lincoln to Congress, July 17, 1862, *Journal of the Senate*, 872.

44. Abraham Lincoln, Preliminary Draft of Emancipation Proclamation, July 22, 1862, in Abraham Lincoln Papers at the Library of Congress.

45. George B. McClellan to Abraham Lincoln, Memo: Thoughts on Political and Military Affairs, July 07, 1862. *Abraham Lincoln Papers at the Library of Congress.*

46. http://www.history.com/topics/emancipation-proclamation#a1.

47. *Collected Works of Abraham Lincoln*, vol. 4, 430.

48. 5 U.S.C. § 3331.

49. US Const., art. II, sec. 1, cl. 8.

50. See Guelzo, *Lincoln's Emancipation Proclamation*, 218–219.

# CHAPTER 10

# The Case of the Confederate Constitution

JAMES R. STONER, JR.

In his magnificent study *The Radicalism of the American Revolution,* historian Gordon Wood makes an argument that exalts the greatness of that revolution but diminishes the honor of those who made it.[1] The world the revolutionary generation found was monarchical, and the world they left behind was democratic, but they only half intended the change of regime. Propelled by an ideology of republicanism, they sought to vindicate the capacity of mankind to govern themselves through wisdom and virtue—through public deliberation and adherence to the rule of law—but in slipping out of the monarchical noose, they unraveled the whole fabric of social deference and interpersonal connection that had formed them into the remarkable men they were. The democratic world that emerged was characterized by individualism, ambition, self-interestedness, restiveness, and a self-assured egalitarianism; good birth, higher education, inherited wealth, and social graces were no longer the marks of virtue and so of likely success and achievement. George Washington and Thomas Jefferson were "out"; Andrew Jackson and Martin Van Buren were "in." This genuine democracy was something radically new, in Wood's telling, but it was not the "new order of the ages" the founders intended. Unlike so many other revolutionaries over time, they were not destroyed by the forces they unleashed, but their hopes faded, and they became strangers in the great republic they launched.

Now, if Wood is right—no student of Alexis de Tocqueville can deny that much of what he says is compelling—then there is a prima facie case to justify, or at least explain, those a generation later who aimed to dissolve the Union and who created the Confederate States of America. Like the American revolutionaries themselves, they claimed to be restoring the ancient constitution of their country, betrayed by those who administered its government. Against partisan and acquisitive democracy, they aimed to vindicate republicanism, the devotion of virtuous people to a higher purpose, public good, and political liberty. As president of the Confederacy, Jefferson Davis said in his First Inaugural Address:

The declared purpose of the compact of the Union from which we have withdrawn was to "establish justice, insure domestic tranquillity, provide for the common defense, promote the general welfare, and secure the blessings of liberty to ourselves and our posterity;" and when, in the judgment of the sovereign States composing this Confederacy, it has been perverted from the purposes for which it was ordained, and ceased to answer the ends for which it was established, a peaceful appeal to the ballot box declared that, so far as they are concerned, the Government created by that compact should cease to exist. In this they merely asserted the right which the Declaration of Independence of July 4, 1776, defined to be "inalienable." Of the time and occasion of its exercise they as sovereigns were the final judges, each for itself. The impartial and enlightened verdict of mankind will vindicate the rectitude of our conduct; and He who knows the hearts of men will judge of the sincerity with which we have labored to preserve the Government of our fathers in its spirit.[2]

As the revolutionary founders' achievement must be judged by the Constitution they wrote in 1787 and ratified in 1788, so an "enlightened and impartial" verdict on secession requires an assessment of the Confederate Constitution. Did that constitution merit its authors' claim to be the true successor of the US Constitution of 1787 and 1788, against that all-too-living document the founders' successors, from John Marshall to Jackson, had twisted into something different from what it was meant to be? The Confederacy began, as Davis made plain, with a constitutional claim—the legitimacy of secession—and they quickly wrote a constitution, actually two constitutions, one provisional and one permanent, in February and March 1861, respectively. I will say a little about secession—though it goes unmentioned in either constitution—but my aim is not to lay out in great detail the case in its favor or the case against.[3] Instead, by looking at the Confederate Constitution(s) in comparison with the Constitution of the United States as it then existed, I want to address the question of whether their claim to conserve the Spirit of 1776, and of 1787, deserves respect.

Even to ask such a question must seem peculiar to the minds of many historians and constitutional progressives.[4] If on the one hand social change is driven by forces that human beings might touch and color but cannot control, and if on the other hand constitutions are living documents that morph alongside social change, then nothing done by the emerging democracy of early America can be condemned as a betrayal of the founders' intentions, and the Confederates can be dismissed—or perhaps, because their actions precipitated so many deaths, condemned—as men who could not adjust to history, who could not face change. However, that way of thinking is not open to those today who profess to be originalists, who look to the original founders for authority and wisdom even still, despite the apparent failure of their handiwork in 1861. On the contrary, facing the constitutional thought of the Confederates is imperative if we are to have a full understanding of the original constitutionalism of the founding. It is, after all, the implicit and sometimes explicit charge of the living constitutionalists that recourse to the original Constitution invokes an instrument designed by a slaveholding elite to impose their purposes, now widely recognized to be nefarious. Moreover, the interpretation of the Thirteenth, Fourteenth, and Fifteenth Amendments—whether they complete the founders' Constitution or radically revise it—takes on new light when these amendments are compared with the changes in the Constitution of 1787–1788 made for the Southern states by the Confederate Constitution. Again, a liberal historian can bury the past for practical purposes even as he or she exhumes it for intellectual ones. A constitutional conservative, by contrast, has to come to present terms with the Constitution's preservation, or purported preservation, of the past.

## THE PATH TO THE CONFEDERATE CONSTITUTION

Secession was the most extreme of three approaches developed by the Democratic and before that the Jeffersonian Republican Party to address the question of what should be done about unconstitutional federal laws. The Federalist solution was simple and to us more familiar: what today we call judicial review, the authority of the judiciary to declare statutes they find to contradict the Constitution null and void. This solution, however, had two problems. First, not all offending statutes might give rise to legal cases in which their constitutionality might be tested, or tested in a timely way; this remains an issue in the twenty-first century, despite twentieth-century innovations such as declaratory judgments and modern doctrines of standing. Second, if sovereignty is in the people, in whose name the Constitution was established, rather than the judges, hardly the only officials required to take an oath to uphold it, what could be done if the people were convinced the courts were wrong in their interpretation of the Constitution, upholding offensive legislation or striking down laws essential to the ends of government? To neither difficulty did the process of amendment seem adequate; it was one thing to make the Constitution difficult to innovate upon but quite another to make it difficult to preserve.

Although the Jeffersonians did not in general reject judicial review, their view of the Constitution as a compact among the states gave them additional recourse in the face of unconstitutional federal legislation. In his Virginia Resolutions in 1798, James Madison had used the term "interposition" to assert a state's response in such circumstances, by which he meant at least the ability of a state to communicate with sister states directly, not through Congress, to determine what concerted action might be appropriate; Thomas Jefferson's Kentucky Resolutions the same year had raised the possibility of nullification, that is, of a state's declaring a federal law null and void within its jurisdiction.[5] In the 1798 crisis, although no further states accepted the invitations of Virginia and Kentucky to make official protest, the offending statutes, the Alien and Sedition Acts, expired of their own accord in 1801, and the chief protestors found themselves in possession of the federal executive authority as a result of the ordinary constitutional process of election. Nullification returned three decades later when the state of South Carolina, under the leadership of John C. Calhoun, purported to nullify a federal tariff act, only to be met with a congressional force bill, passed with the blessing of President Jackson—though a crisis was averted by the passage of a compromise tariff act grudgingly accepted by the South Carolinians.[6]

Secession would take matters a step further than nullification, not merely suppressing a particular exercise of federal authority but severing the bond of union, but it likewise supposed the sovereignty of the states and nature of the Constitution as a compact. In the law of nations, after all, states were not ordinarily obliged by a treaty their partners had violated, so if the Constitution were a treaty, unconstitutional action by a majority of its members would effectively dissolve it or at any rate justify those states claiming the violation dissolved their relation to the others. Like nullification, the theory of secession was not dreamed up first in South Carolina; it had been proposed by the states of New England at the Hartford Convention in the winter of 1814–1815, though an end to the war whose prosecution they thought unconstitutional averted a crisis in that instance too.[7] In 1860, there was no fortuitous avoidance of the issue: the states of the Deep South saw the election of a Republican president without a single electoral vote from the slave states and of Republican majorities in both houses of Congress as the entrenchment of abolitionism in the federal government, and they anticipated disregard of the Fugitive Slave Acts, the abolition of slavery in Washington, DC, and its prohibition in the territories, the latter in defiance of the 1857 Supreme Court decision in *Dred Scott v. Sandford,* which the Republicans for their part saw as deeply mistaken and unworthy of respect as binding precedent. Before Lincoln took the oath of office and sought in his First Inaugural Address to reassure the slave states of his commitment not to interfere with slavery where it was established in the states, seven states had purported to secede from the Union, forming their own confederacy, writing a constitution, and inaugurating a president of their own.[8]

Secession proceeded state by state, apparently a risky strategy in that South Carolina in 1832 had found itself alone in nullifying the tariff, and Virginia and Kentucky found their 1798 resolutions rejected by the other legislatures to which they were sent. The formal practice developed in South Carolina in December 1860 was for the state legislature to call back into session the convention that had ratified the Constitution in 1788, prompting the election of delegates, and then in convention to proceed with rescission of the earlier ratification, enactment of an ordinance of secession, and issuance of a call for the formation of a new confederacy. Details varied state by state, with referenda conducted in states such as Texas and Virginia, but all with remarkable speed and concert. In addition to South Carolina, the states of Mississippi, Georgia, Alabama, Florida, and Louisiana had declared their secession by late January and sent delegates to a congress in Montgomery, Alabama, in early February, with Texas (where secession was delayed by the opposition of Governor Sam Houston) joining the others later that month. Like the Articles Congress in the 1780s, each state voted as a delegation in the Montgomery Congress, adopting a provisional constitution that kept that congress in power for a year, electing a president by congressional vote, and getting to work immediately on drafting a permanent constitution. Meanwhile, the senators and representatives of the seceding states had withdrawn from Washington, where the US Congress was in session over the winter months, sometimes giving farewell speeches to the bodies from which they resigned.[9]

It is notable that even the provisional Confederate Constitution was patterned on the Constitution of the United States rather than on the Articles of Confederation, and this despite the fact that the initial Confederate Congress gave each state a single vote and allowed it to choose the size of its delegation, as under the Articles. The permanent Confederate Constitution made its Congress bicameral and adopted proportional representation in the House and two senators per state in the Senate, exactly as under the United States. Despite its name, the Confederacy was not an attempt to repeal the US Constitution and restore the Articles; instead, its claim was to be the true successor to that Constitution, which its member states emphatically considered to have been theirs too, at least until it was perverted. Our question here is what evidence appears in their document to support or undercut that claim.

## TWO CONSTITUTIONS

Let us compare, then, the US and the Confederate Constitutions[10] on six dimensions in which they differ: state sovereignty, the powers of the central government, legislative-executive process, judicial process, slavery, and citizenship. To anticipate, on the first four matters, the Confederates innovated a little, but in the spirit of perfecting rather than reorienting the Constitution. On the question of slavery, however, the change was explicit and emphatic, whereas the question of citizenship was resolved ambivalently except insofar as it was expected that blacks would never have a share.

First, though the Confederacy was formed after the assertion of state sovereignty in the ordinances of secession, the changes in the document were subtler than one might expect. To be sure, the preamble was reworded to remove language—"more perfect Union," "common defense," "general welfare"—alleged by the early nationalists to support their interpretation of the Constitution, thereby to reinforce the secessionists' claims. Echoing the Articles of Confederation, the states were explicitly called "sovereign" and "independent," and instead of a "more perfect Union" they claimed to be forming merely a "permanent federal government." Beyond that, however, indication of enhanced sovereignty in the states or provision for greater state independence is difficult to find. There are a few small things. It would be possible for a state legislature to impeach a federal official whose jurisdiction is entirely within a single state (Article I, Section 2). States that shared a river could make compacts to improve its navigation between themselves without congressional monitoring (Article I, Section 10). Admission of new states would be by a two-thirds vote, not a simple majority (Article IV, Section 3), and ratification would be by five rather than nine (Article VII). Amendments could be proposed only by a convention, not by Congress, though ratification was either by state legislatures or state conventions just as in the United States—and ought to have been a little easier because two-thirds rather than three-quarters of the states were needed for an amendment to go into effect (Article V). The Confederate Constitution included all the twelve amendments added to the US Constitution, not as addenda but inserted into the text as appropriate; where the Tenth Amendment appears (Article VI, Section 6), the powers not delegated were reserved to "the States, respectively, or to the people thereof," the last word having been added apparently to make clear that the people were constituted state by state, not in the nation as a whole. Although, as we will see, the powers of the federal government were altered, the clause restricting the reach of those powers remained the "truism" Marshall said it was; not even the qualifier "expressly," omitted in the Tenth Amendment in comparison with the provision in the articles it echoed, made a return.[11] Again, the Confederates would no doubt claim that this was what one could have expected: their secession was proof of their opinion that the *text* of the Constitution preserved state sovereignty, the threat having come from those who misread it. The guaranty clause and the supremacy clause remained in Articles IV and VI, respectively, virtually unchanged.

Second, the powers of the central government, expressed in Article I, Section 8, were almost identical in the two documents, the changes generally being declaratory of the Jeffersonian or Democratic interpretation of clauses borrowed from the old Constitution, not introductory of something entirely new. Taxation was limited in its purpose to the raising of revenue, presumably to rule out regulation by high taxes; the controversial reference to "the general welfare" was removed from the clause as well, limiting the purpose of government spending to "provid[ing] for the common defense and carry[ing] on the Government" (Article I, Section 8, Subsection 1). Bounties, duties, and taxes could not "be laid to promote or foster any branch of industry," whether by encouragement or discouragement, echoing the long-standing Southern complaint against the tariff, not to mention the opposition to Alexander Hamilton's *Report on Manufactures*. The power to regulate commerce was repeated exactly, but appended to it was the Jeffersonian-Jacksonian insistence that "neither this, nor any other clause contained in the Constitution, shall ever be construed to delegate the power to Congress to appropriate money for any internal improvement intended to facilitate commerce," though an exception was made for maintaining lighthouses, improving harbors, and dredging rivers, provided these activities were funded by navigation duties (Article I, Section 8, Clause 3). A later clause permitted the power to tax exports, strictly prohibited in the US Constitution, if two-thirds of Congress agreed (Article I, Section 9, Clause 6). The Post Office—source of much controversy during the age of abolitionist mailings and of course of much patronage, not to mention the one federal institution in the South Lincoln pledged to keep open in his First Inaugural Address the same month—was allowed to be reestablished, but it was given only two years to operate with tax monies, after which it was required to be self-supporting (which, in fact, in the ensuing years it became; Article I, Section 8, Clause 7). All the powers concerning the military were identical to those in the US Constitution except, as throughout the document, every reference to the "United States" was changed to the "Confederate States"

(Article I, Section 8, Clauses 10–16)—a choice of no small importance because the Confederacy was in the event destined to institute conscription even before the United States did.[12]

Third, leaving aside for a moment the provisions concerning slavery, the most innovative aspect of the Confederate Constitution was its treatment of legislative-executive relations. Here the drafters rather imitated the founders than copied their text: as in 1787, the current political science of constitutional design focused on the separation of powers and took Montesquieu's analysis of the English Constitution as authoritative, so the Confederates looked to the England of their day with its development of ministerial government anchored in Parliament for new ideas. They retained the presidency and even the corrected Electoral College system, inserting the Twelfth Amendment into their Article II. Their Congress—after the first year of the unicameral provisional government—had a House and a Senate elected mostly on the American design. However, several innovations were introduced into the legislative process apparently to strengthen legislative-executive cooperation on the new British model. First, the principal officers of the government were allowed to speak on the floor of either House of Congress, or rather, Congress was allowed to invite them to speak. Alexander Stephens, vice president of the Confederacy and active in its Constitution's design, admits he would have

preferred that this principle should have gone further, and required the President to select his constitutional advisers from the Senate and House of Representatives. That would have conformed entirely to the practice in the British Parliament, which, in my judgment, is one of the wisest provisions in the British constitution. It is the only feature that saves that government. It is that which gives it stability in its facility to change its administration. Ours, as it is, is a great approximation to the right principle.[13]

In the provisional government, where Congress was a single house and the states voted as units, ministers had constitutional permission to speak on the floor, and apparently some did. In the permanent Constitution, that permission was dependent on Congress, although apparently it never was granted. Still, the model of the executive as initiator of legislation and the legislature as the sounding board was written into the new appropriations process, where not only were the ends of appropriations limited, as discussed above, but the traditional role of Congress in appropriations was replaced by a privilege given to the president and chief officers: bills appropriating funds that *they* recommended could pass with a simple majority, whereas congressionally initiated bills required a two-thirds vote to pass (Article I, Section 9, Clause 9).

Appropriation bills were commanded to be precise and specific, and extra compensation for any contractor or agent after the fact was prohibited (Article I, Section 9, Clause 10). Moreover, the president was given the power to veto single lines in an appropriation bill while signing the rest, and although there was the familiar provision for a two-thirds override, this enhanced veto power not only bespoke fiscal restraint but increased presidential power: no longer could Congress force the executive's hand by presenting an entire bill to "take or leave" (Article I, Section 7, Clause 2). The line-item veto was the one unambiguous contribution of the Confederate Constitution to the American constitutional tradition because it was later adopted by a number of the states, North and South, and even attempted at the federal level in the late twentieth century. Similarly required, and similarly adopted by some states, was the Confederate Constitution's insistence that all legislation have a single purpose (Article I, Section 9, Clause 20). The restrictions on the appropriations and legislative processes probably represented in part an aspiration toward frugal government, but they also represented a rejection of politics as usual, the competition of parties and factions, the practices of logrolling and deal making, and the messiness of democratic assemblies.[14]

A similar disdain for ordinary party politics probably lay behind the other major innovation on this score, the single presidential term of six years. This was an issue—or two issues, term length and eligibility for reelection—extensively debated at the Philadelphia Convention, with votes going back and forth over the course of the summer. Stephens makes the case for a longer term, which he calls "a decidedly conservative change": "It will remove from the incumbent all temptation to use his office or exert the powers confided to him for any objects of personal ambition. The only incentive to that higher ambition which should move and actuate one holding such high trust in his hands, will be the good of the people, the advancement, prosperity, happiness, safety, honor, and true glory of the confederacy."

This is the ideology of republicanism that historian Wood attributes to the founders, now adopted to change their handiwork. The enemy is party competition, which frequent elections promote, and perhaps none so much as the election and reelection of the president, which had quickly become the focus and occasion for party formation in the young United States, whether it was intended or foreseen by the founders. Of course, the Confederacy did not last long enough for Davis to complete the six-year term to which he was elected in the fall of 1861 (without competition) and into which he was inaugurated in February 1862, after a year as congressionally elected president of the provisional government. Nevertheless, it is a fact that regular political parties did not emerge during the life of the Confederacy despite continued fierce party competition in the Union during the same period.

Perhaps it was their confidence in overcoming party rancor that made the Confederates nonchalant when it came to courts, our fourth point of comparison. The judiciary article of the US Constitution was for the most part repeated word for word, with a few interesting omissions: the phrase "law and equity" was left out of the case or controversy clause, and federal diversity jurisdiction—the jurisdiction of federal courts to entertain suits between citizens of different states for no reason beyond their different citizenship—was abolished. Doing so would not only have reduced the caseload of the federal courts, leaving most suits in the hands of state judges, but also would have reduced the opportunities for federal judges to interfere in the interpretation of state law, something Justice Joseph Story had developed into a system of what came to be called "federal common law." The Eleventh Amendment, effectively declaring state sovereign immunity in rebuttal of *Chisholm v. Georgia,* was incorporated into Article III. The provisional Constitution had appointed a district judge for each state, all of whom were to sit together as a Supreme Court. The permanent Constitution instead copied the US federal model, though as a matter of practice in the three remaining years after the Constitution's coming into effect, the Confederate Supreme Court was never organized and never sat.[15]

Thus far, in discussing the form of sovereignty, the powers of Congress, the redesign of legislative-executive relations, and the judiciary, the Confederate Constitution appeared mostly traditional even when it did not simply repeat the founders' text: declaring in writing certain interpretations controversial in the early republic, choosing a few innovations that approximated the latest political science from Britain, and reverting to a proposal at the Philadelphia Convention that might easily claim the endorsement of Washington, whom, after all, the Confederates put on their seal.

However, in their treatment of slavery, innovation was decisive, at least in the sense of declaring in writing in a constitutional text practices the founders had hidden. The word "slave" first appeared in the three-fifths clause, adopted from the US Constitution and governing the apportionment of representatives, replacing the reference to "other persons." This new attitude toward slavery became apparent in the prohibitions on Congress in Article I, Section 9, where the US Constitution's expired provision permitting the importation of slaves until 1808 was replaced with a constitutional prohibition on the international slave trade; no longer was this referred to by the circumlocution of 1787 but explicitly as "the importation of negroes of the African race"; the exception was that slaves could be imported from the United States, although the

Confederate Congress was allowed the power to suppress that too, should it choose to do so. The big addition was a permanent guarantee of slavery, in so many words, inserted into an existing clause: "No bill of attainder, ex post facto law, or law denying or impairing the right of property in negro slaves shall be passed" by the Confederate Congress. The fugitive slave clause remained, of course, now explicitly referring to persons who escaped slavery rather than to persons "held to service or labour in one state, under the laws thereof." Explicit provision was made to protect the right of transit of slaveholders moving through other states in addition to their home state. The issue in *Dred Scott,* whether slavery could be prohibited in the territories, was now settled in the new text: the power of Congress to acquire and govern new territories was explicitly given —this had been disputed from the time of the Louisiana Purchase through the decision in *Dred Scott*—but this concession to the national sentiment was immediately qualified by reiteration of protection for slavery: "In all such territory the institution of negro slavery, as it now exists in the Confederate States, shall be recognized and protected by Congress and by the Territorial government; and the inhabitants of the several Confederate States and Territories shall have the right to take to such Territory any slaves lawfully held by them in any of the States or Territories of the Confederate States" (Article IV, Section 3, Clause 3).

Although concern over transit acknowledges the possibility that some states might in the future abolish slavery, the clauses prohibiting the Confederate Congress from interfering with slavery and requiring recognition of slavery in the territories were clearly meant to entrench slavery under the auspices of the Confederacy itself. The requirement of a two-thirds vote in both houses to admit a state likewise ensured that the politics of the Missouri Compromise, balancing slavery and freedom, would not reappear.

Stephens's notorious Corner-Stone Speech, from which I have been quoting, was given later in the month the Confederate Constitution was adopted, and although it began by expounding and exalting that Constitution, which he had played a part in forming, he saved his most extravagant praise for the slavery provisions just recounted. Of the new government, he said: "Its foundations are laid, its corner-stone rests, upon the great truth that the negro is not equal to the white man; that slavery, subordination to the superior race, is his natural and normal condition. This, our new government, is the first, in the history of the world, based upon this great physical, philosophical, and moral truth."[16]

The mention not only of slavery—an institution alluded to in the US Constitution, but a word never mentioned there—but of *Negro* slavery, makes explicit in the constitutional document the racial basis of the practice, known to all of course but now boldly proclaimed, as Stephens suggested, as a constitutional principle. Whatever the postwar reinterpretation of the Confederacy and its purpose, even by Stephens himself in his monumental tome, *A Constitutional View of the Late War between the States,* as a dispute over states' rights, the Confederate Constitution quite consciously departed from the Constitution of the United States to make race-based slavery no longer an evil to be regretted, minimized, and hidden but a "positive good" to be proclaimed.[17]

Finally, what was the meaning of the Confederate Constitution for citizenship? Remember that this Constitution was written before the Fourteenth Amendment defined US citizenship. The Constitution of 1787 had given Congress the power to establish "an uniform rule of naturalization," but the states were left to determine the qualifications of voters even in federal elections, the rule being that those enfranchised to vote for the more popular house in the state assembly were enfranchised to vote for members of the federal House of Representatives, originally the only officers elected by the people in every state (the state legislatures deciding, in different ways, who could vote for presidential electors and the Senate being elected by the legislatures themselves). The Supreme Court in the *Dred Scott* case had distinguished citizenship of the United States from state citizenship and had determined that people of African descent, even if free, could not be citizens of the United States. Although the Lincoln administration was to ignore this doctrine and issue passports to free African Americans, the Confederacy decided to specify citizenship in its written Constitution, explicitly making only "citizens of the Confederate States" and "no person of foreign birth" eligible to vote if they also satisfied the state rule. The "uniform rule" clause became a "uniform law" clause, but the power remained in Congress to define citizenship; despite the "corner-stone," there was no clause that explicitly restricted citizenship to whites. The president was to be "a natural born citizen of the Confederate States, or a citizen thereof at the time of the adoption of this Constitution, or a citizen thereof born in the United States prior to the 20th of December, 1860"—the last clause presumably to allow Virginians and the like, not yet part of the Confederacy when the Constitution was adopted, to be eligible after their state joined the others, the date of the South Carolina secession ordinance apparently being recognized as the birthdate of the new nation.

Was this to be a Southern nation? Perhaps in the aspiration to republican devotion to the common good there was a rhetoric of nationhood; clearly in the insistence upon "negro slavery" there was a definition of the outsider and a confident purpose to dominate, sometimes seen as the hallmarks of classical republicanism by its critics. If the subsequent sense of Southern nationalism was forged on the battlefields of the war, there nevertheless must have been a common will of sorts that led people into the forge, something more akin to a way of life thought threatened, not just a vague sense of home, for the Southern homeland was not attacked until much later in the fighting. There is in the preamble to the Confederate Constitution, as there was in the provisional Constitution but not in the US Constitution, invocation of "the favor and guidance of Almighty God," presuming perhaps a shared faith and perceived higher purpose, but the prohibition on religious tests for office was untouched, as was the First Amendment, which appears word for word in Article I, Section 9, Clause 12.[18] The Confederate citizens had been "naturally born" citizens of the United States, and if their Constitution threw a switch that sent them down a different track, that Constitution itself seems to have been made for Americans and seems to have been content to take them as they were. It goes without saying that there was nothing about civic education in this Constitution's text, any more than there had been in the US Constitution.

## CONCLUSION

Were secession and the Confederacy, then, a good-faith attempt to recover the republicanism of the original Constitution against a majoritarian democracy that had transformed it into something never intended by the founders? There is some evidence for that, in the aspiration for a republican government that transcended the bitterness of partisan division, apparent in the longer nonrenewable presidential term, in the tightening of executive control of the budgetary process, and in the explicit emphasis on citizenship in the clauses on voting and officeholding. At the same time, there was no effort to roll back universal male suffrage for the white population, with the states, most of them staunchly democratic, left in control of the franchise.[19] The imitation of British cabinet government was not a glance back to the founding but in some respects an anticipation of the future; Woodrow Wilson's endorsement of "congressional government" after the Civil War further marks him as a son of the Confederacy, not simply a Progressive, or illustrates the way in which the Confederates themselves thought theirs was the path of progress. Still, however much American practice in the founding era left in place the inequality of the races, the principle of equal natural rights articulated by Virginians such as Jefferson and Madison and put in practice by Washington in his last will and testament were repudiated in the Confederate Constitution, explicitly in its text and in

Stephens's defense of its new cornerstone. Washington's image might have been placed on its seal, but it is hard to imagine the author of the Farewell Address countenancing disunion or the testator who manumitted the blacks enslaved on his estate accepting the perpetuation of an institution he came to despise.[20]

Did the Confederate Constitution contribute to the political development of American constitutionalism, or was it simply a dead end? To argue the first, one might suggest that the reintegration of the Southern states into the Union after the war was probably facilitated by the fact that the states had continued to operate under a constitution whose basic processes of government were very similar to the one they left and to which they later returned. No doubt this complicated Reconstruction; the "indestructibility" of the states of the Confederacy was not just a legal fiction of the US Supreme Court but an empirical fact, so the Union did not find the political landscape as clear for rebuilding after the war as the physical landscape of those areas swept by Union troops. The Union's success in a way proved that its Constitution was not a mere compact, but in a sense the Confederates proved the same by adopting a strong central government employing a similar constitutional framework, strong at least in its war power, which at the time was what mattered most. Of course, as Publius had recognized at the outset, dividing America into separate confederacies would make each of those more uniform—more a nation, perhaps—and thus probably made the Civil War bloodier, for the spirit of compromise was abandoned when there was resort to force and was less needed among those partial confederacies whose interests and sentiments were substantially the same. Ironically, although the Confederacy was built by asserting the right of secession, its Constitution and its experience rather helped build a "solid South" than an anarchy of Southern states.

That points, I think, to several other consequences of Confederate constitutionalism that outlasted the short tenure of the document. The Confederacy had no developed, competitive political parties, and for almost a century after Reconstruction, the South, too, had minimal partisan competition.[21] Similarly, of course, the racial hierarchy explicitly tied to slavery in the document long outlasted the end of slavery, or at least, after the experiment of Reconstruction, it was restored. The military institutions of the South, left in place by the Confederate Constitution with only a change at the top of the hierarchy of command, likewise persisted, and by the twentieth century Southern troops were reintegrated into federal forces, so to speak, fighting under the Stars and Stripes. And then, of course, there are the devices first developed by the Confederate Constitution and later adopted by many of the states, the line-item veto, the single-issue requirement, and even at the federal level the eventual establishment of an independent postal service, though one that has yet at this writing to pay its own way.

The Confederate Constitution broke with common law by renouncing diversity jurisdiction and by explicitly endorsing slavery, and doing so on the basis of race; its neglect of the judicial power and denial of rights to a whole race, while asserting formal protection of legislatively established rights of masters, no doubt colored subsequent Southern history, with its peculiar combination of legal formalism and extralegal violence. By contrast, the end of slavery in the US Constitution ushered in a new era of civil rights, or at least of federal guarantees of civil rights, and the federal judiciary soon ensured that this included a whole array of common-law privileges and immunities, even if not always implemented under the clause including those words and even though blocked in their practical enforcement on behalf of the freedpeople in the states of the failed Confederacy. The Confederate Constitution in the end indicates a road not taken by American constitutional republicanism; its explicit references to slavery and to race highlight in retrospect the original US Constitution's avoidance of both in its language, and also indicate by contrast the way the Union changed the Constitution after the Civil War. However, given the continuity of the states and of the constitutional tradition, perhaps it ought to be conceded that the Confederate Constitution opened vistas—some of them sinister—that sometimes helped and sometimes tempted those on the restored Union road.

## NOTES

1. Gordon Wood, *The Radicalism of the American Revolution* (New York: Knopf, 1991).

2. Jefferson Davis, Inaugural Address, February 18, 1861, in *Messages and Papers of the Confederacy*, vol. 1, ed. James D. Richardson (Nashville, TN: United States Publishing, 1906), 32–33 (also available at http://avalon.law.yale.edu/19th_century/csa_csainau.asp).

3. See Chapters 5 and 7 of the present volume.

4. See Marshall L. DeRosa, *Confederate Constitution of 1861: An Inquiry into American Constitutionalism* (Columbia: University of Missouri Press, 1991); he makes the case that the Confederates sought to restore the republicanism of the antifederalists.

5. See Gordon Wood, *Empire of Liberty: A History of the Early Republic, 1789–1815* (New York: Oxford University Press, 2009), 269–271. The resolutions can be found on Yale's Avalon website: Kentucky at http://avalon.law.yale.edu/18th_century/kenres.asp and Virginia at http://avalon.law.yale.edu/18th_century/virres.asp.

6. See Daniel Walker Howe, *What Hath God Wrought: The Transformation of America, 1815–1848* (New York: Oxford University Press, 2007), 395–410.

7. Ibid., 68–69.

8. James M. McPherson, *Battle Cry of Freedom: The Civil War Era* (New York: Oxford University Press, 1988), chaps. 7–8; see this also for the events described in the following paragraph.

9. A detailed account of the proceedings and the process of drafting the two constitutions can be found in Charles Robert Lee, Jr., *The Confederate Constitutions* (Chapel Hill: University of North Carolina Press, 1963).

10. I rely on the versions in Richardson, *Messages and Papers of the Confederacy*, vol. 1, 3–14, 37–54. Numbers in the text refer to the permanent Constitution. Both documents are available at Yale's Avalon site: provisional, http://avalon.law.yale.edu/19th _century/csa_csapro.asp, and permanent, http://avalon.law.yale.edu/19th_century/csa _csa.asp.

11. See Articles of Confederation, art. 2.

12. See Timothy S. Huebner, *Liberty and Union: The Civil War Era and American Constitutionalism* (Lawrence: University Press of Kansas, 2016), 257–260. It might also be noted that the habeas corpus clause appears in Article I, Section 9, exactly as it is written in the US Constitution, but its use during the war was quite different: Jefferson Davis goes to Congress to request suspension, gets it once, only to see it expire and to meet stiff opposition when he seeks its renewal; in fact, some state judges used habeas corpus to provide relief from conscription later in the war. See ibid., 270–275.

13. Alexander H. Stephens, Corner-Stone Speech, March 21, 1861, in *The Civil War: The First Year Told by Those Who Lived It,* ed. Aaron Sheehan-Dean, Stephen W. Sears, and Brooks D. Simpson (New York: Library of America, 2011), 224–225 (also available at http://teachingamericanhistory.org/library/document/cornerstone-speech/). Another contemporaneous account of the Confederate Constitution, also by a delegate to the Congress that wrote it, is Robert H. Smith, *An Address to the Citizens of Alabama on the Constitution and Laws of the Confederate States of America, March 30, 1861* (Mobile, AL: Mobile Daily Register, 1861).

14. This aspiration figures prominently in the analysis of George C. Rable, *The Confederate Republic: A Revolution against Politics* (Chapel Hill: University of North Carolina Press, 1994). See also Huebner, *Liberty and Union,* 251, which also includes a helpful discussion of the failure of Confederate financial policy, which their institutional innovations in no way helped prevent.

15. DeRosa argues that the Confederates, having seen the nationalist tendencies of the Supreme Court under John Marshall, deliberately left the judicial power principally in the hands of the states. DeRosa, *Confederate Constitution of 1861,* chap. 6.

16. Stephens, Corner-Stone Speech, 226. See also Smith, *Address to the Citizens of Alabama,* 16–19, who concludes that from Africans captured into slavery "have sprung about four millions of improved, civilized, hardy and happy laborers."

17. See Alexander H. Stephens, *A Constitutional View of the Late War between the States* (Philadelphia: National, 1868), 10, where the cause of the war is said to have been not slavery (which just happened to be the "question" of the moment) but "a conflict in principle [that] arose from different and opposing ideas as to the nature of what is known as the General Government. The contest was between those who held it to

be strictly Federal in its character, and those who maintained that it was thoroughly National."

18. Famously, Judah Benjamin, the first Jewish member of an American cabinet, served in several prominent roles in Jefferson Davis's government.

19. However, see Rable, *Confederate Republic,* 49, who notes that counting enslaved people for the purpose of apportionment in states such as South Carolina effectively gave the few large slaveholders in the low country "rotten boroughs" and diminished the vote of the poorer, upcountry whites.

20. See Jeffrey Morrison, "Prologue: A Second American Revolution? George Washington and the Origins of the Civil War," in *Constitutionalism in the Approach and Aftermath of the Civil War,* ed. Paul D. Moreno and Johnathan O'Neill (New York: Fordham University Press, 2013), 6–26.

21. Rable concludes with a similar point. *Confederate Republic,* 302.

# Part Three

*Pyrrhic Victories?*

# CHAPTER 11

# Completing the Constitution

## The Reconstruction Amendments

MICHAEL ZUCKERT

The Civil War and its aftermath, Reconstruction, were responsible for many changes in American life, none of more lasting significance than the three amendments added to the Constitution between 1865 and 1870. These three were the most far-reaching amendments to the Constitution to that date and arguably remain so today. The amendments in succession abolished slavery in all of the United States, established the basic civil rights of the new freedmen (and of all persons in the United States), and established a right against discrimination on the basis of race in the right to vote. In a formula a bit too simple but not entirely misleading, one can say that the amendments dealt in turn with natural rights (Thirteenth), with civil rights (Fourteenth), and with political rights (Fifteenth).

Although an order appears in the sequence of the amendments, it is clear this order was not premeditated. When Congress debated and passed the Thirteenth Amendment in 1865, no one saw it as the first installment in a series of new amendments. One common way to understand the trio of amendments is to see each as going further than the preceding one, with the Republican sponsors of the amendments coming to recognize more was needed than was yet accomplished to provide adequately for the new freedmen. However, that is not the only way to understand the sequence of amendments, for some see the Thirteenth as the most far-reaching and the others as merely clarifying implications of the Thirteenth or making explicit the status of the legislation that could constitutionally occur under the Thirteenth Amendment.

The ambiguity regarding the relation of the amendments to each other parallels a disagreement that existed among the drafters of the amendments, among Supreme Court justices attempting to interpret the amendments, and among scholars attempting to understand the language and history of the amendments. Two polar positions dominate the scholarly discussions and reflect disagreements among the drafters and the justices: some see the amendments as working a constitutional transformation, a revolution, if you will. The scholars at this pole tend to emphasize the primacy of the Thirteenth Amendment over the other two.[1] At the other pole are those who see in the majority of the political leaders and the people of the 1860s a distaste for radical action and an attachment to the Constitution as it was, with some changes for the sake of doing away with slavery and providing protection for the freedmen without going as far as a constitutional revolution.[2] These scholars tend to emphasize the Fourteenth Amendment and see it as going beyond its predecessor. However, they do not see any of the amendments as working a fundamental change in the constitutional system. In particular, they do not see the amendments as overturning the federalism of the original Constitution, whereby the central government possesses only certain delegated powers, and the states remain the bodies that do most of the governing and retain jurisdiction over the basic rights of person and property. At the extreme, these scholars say the Constitution was changed "only a little."[3]

The debate over the general character of the change in the Constitution wrought by the Reconstruction amendments smolders on because there is real evidence to which each side can appeal. That fact derives from two aspects of the surge of legislation producing the amendments. On the one hand, there were different factions within the Republican Party pressing for different kinds of constitutional outcomes. We can almost identify the so-called radicals with the constitutional revolution position and the so-called moderate Republicans with the "changed only a little" position. One can, therefore, find advocates for both positions in the historical record. On the other hand, as with all political action, we must not identify the advocacy positions of any of the partisans with the outcome, for the outcome might represent some third position, perhaps a middle ground between the two poles, or, if one can conceive the polar positions as actually existing on a continuum of less to more radical, the outcome will be that point along the continuum at which a majority (in the case of amending the Constitution, a two-thirds majority) can be found. Where that point is will depend, of course, on the distribution of devotees along the various positions on the continuum. Thus, for example, if the radical constitutional revolutionaries possessed the needed two-thirds majority, they could produce an outcome to their liking. However, if they did not, the outcome would have to have shifted toward the more moderate one to that point at which the needed majority could be formed.[4] Much good work on the amendments has been done by scholars who trace the interactions of the radical and moderate wings of the Republican Party. Most of the work of that kind begins from the observation that the radicals did not command the two-thirds majority needed to produce the constitutional revolution some of them sought.

In this chapter, I will argue that neither of the usual interpretations offered by scholars actually captures the character of what the Reconstruction amendments were intended to accomplish. The change effected by these amendments was not a constitutional revolution or the Constitution changed "only a little." Instead of either of these outcomes, I shall argue, these amendments aimed at "completing the Constitution."

This idea can best be understood if we revert for a moment to the original Constitution as seen by its chief drafter, James Madison. Perhaps surprisingly, Madison, the reputed "father of the Constitution," was on the whole displeased with the final product that emerged from the Constitutional Convention. It is well known that he was distressed by the so-called great compromise, whereby the large states achieved their goal of population-based representation in one branch of the legislature and the small states achieved their goal of equal representation for each state in the other branch. However, that was not the main source of his disappointment. More important was the failure of the convention to adopt two institutions he thought necessary to the future health of the American republic.

The first institution had to do with federalism. Before the convention began, Madison had given much thought to the operation of federal systems. He concluded that they had nearly irresistible tendencies to centrifugal motion in which the member states failed to stay "in their proper orbits" around the federal authorities by failing to honor their obligations to those authorities or to each other. They encroached on the powers of the central authorities or of the other member states, or they failed to fulfill their obligations to the federation, by, for example, not paying their financial assessments. The result was friction within the federation, "imbecility" of the federal government, and eventually the collapse of the system. He saw the weak Articles of Confederation as merely a replay of the standard course of federal failures.

Because the centrifugal forces are so strong, Madison concluded that the remedy must be equally strong: he wished to arm Congress with a power to "negative," that is, to veto, all laws passed by states contrary to the Constitution. This is a power that in modified form exists in the Supreme Court now, but for a variety of reasons Madison did not consider the Court as valid or effective with that power as Congress could be.

Even more radically, Madison famously concluded that the relatively small republic states were far more likely to commit injustice in legislation than the federal government was because of the greater likelihood of majority factions carrying the day in the states. This aspect of Madison's thinking is well known through his widely read *Federalist Paper* 10. Less well known is the institution he wanted to place in the Constitution to respond to the problem of injustice in state legislation. Parallel to the negative power for the sake of keeping the federal system in order, he sought a more far-reaching congressional power to negative "all laws whatsoever" passed by the states, with that power to be used to promote justice, stability, and wisdom in the state laws.[5] In this case, Congress would not be limited to enforcing the constitutional text but would be free to apply its best judgment about wisdom, justice, and stability. The more limited form of the negative would function to keep the states in their proper constitutional "orbits"; that is, it would deal with interstate and state-federal relations. The more expansive version of the negative would operate to secure desired qualities of law within the states. It was a very radical idea for the time it was proposed.

Scholars who take note of these two institutions for which Madison advocated at the Constitutional Convention often take them as evidence that he was a strong nationalist in 1787. This is a large mistake and leads to many misunderstandings of Madison and of the Constitution he sought. His aim is better conceived as "corrective federalism." That is to say, he sought a system in which most basic governing would remain in the states, but the federal government would possess these strong powers to correct the states when, in the judgment of Congress, they went astray in one or another of the various ways I have mentioned. The Constitution he sought would not have worked a constitutional revolution over the Constitution adopted, for the basic distribution of power within the federal system would have been unaffected, and the basic power of the states to govern themselves and to deal with most aspects of the rights of persons and property would have remained unimpaired. However, it would not have been only a small change over the Constitution accepted, for Congress would have had these strong powers to intervene and correct state actions it disapproved. Congress would not, however, have had the power to exercise positive legislative power in the areas in which it would have had these corrective powers. That would be the important difference between Madison's favored Constitution and a truly national one of the sort affirmed by the partisans of the constitutional revolution theory of the Reconstruction amendments.

Lacking the two institutions of corrective federalism, the Constitution was importantly incomplete in Madison's eyes, and he was quite pessimistic about its future in 1787. The Constitution lasted somewhat better than he thought it would, but the Civil War was after all a great constitutional failure in which the system suffered from the flaws Madison pointed out and eventually came apart along the fault lines he identified. For what is secession but the most centrifugal of events? If Congress had had the power to negative all state laws, could South Carolina or the other Southern states have passed secession ordinances? If Congress had had the power to negative all state laws, could the states have engaged in the practices that so roused sectional antipathies and eventually led to war? Had Madison's preferred constitution been adopted, could it be said that slavery in the states was completely beyond the power of Congress?

This is not the place to engage in speculations about alternative American histories. My point in bringing up Madison's idea of corrective federalism and his analysis of the Constitution as incomplete is for the sake of suggesting that these ideas provide a better way to conceive of the Reconstruction amendments: the amendments attempt to complete the Constitution by instituting a system of corrective federalism, neither the centralizing revolution of some nor the minimal constitutional change of others. This is not to say that the framers of the post–Civil War amendments were patterning their actions after Madison's proposals—they seem to have been ignorant of those proposals. It is not even to say that they had a clear blueprint for corrective federalism in mind when they began their work with the Thirteenth Amendment, but that they came to a similar (but very differently implemented) idea through their realization of the weaknesses of the original Constitution— the weaknesses Madison had identified—and through their continuing commitment to a genuinely federal system, just as Madison was from the start and always committed to a federal system. Put otherwise, their commitment to federalism prevented them from going where the constitutional revolutionists claim they went, but their commitment to justice and rights in the states prevented them from accepting only minimal changes in the Constitution. Without realizing it, they went a long way toward "completing the Constitution" as Madison thought it should be.

## THE THIRTEENTH AMENDMENT

The story of the Thirteenth Amendment does not begin in 1864, when it was first proposed in Congress; in one sense it goes back to 1619, when the first enslaved Africans arrived in America, but for our purposes let us begin in 1863 with President Abraham Lincoln's Emancipation Proclamation. It might have seemed that with the Emancipation Proclamation, an amendment prohibiting slavery would not be necessary. Indeed, Lincoln's proclamation declared the slaves to which it applied "henceforward to be free," which the preliminary proclamation clarified to mean "forever free."[6] The president himself favored an amendment, however, because he recognized two important limitations of his proclamation. First, it was issued under his authority as commander in chief as a war measure. It would deprive the Confederacy of one of its major resources during the war, the slave labor that allowed the South to mobilize a much larger proportion of its white population for military service than it could without that labor. The proclamation also provided for taking the formerly enslaved people into the Union Army, adding substantially to Union military capability. However, Lincoln was uncertain that the courts—the arbiters of the Constitution—would recognize the postwar validity of his act of emancipation. He had a reasonable fear that a policy enacted under war powers would not legally outlast the war on which it was premised. The war powers origin of Lincoln's emancipation limited what he had accomplished in yet another way: he could emancipate slaves only in those parts of the United States at that time in rebellion. That meant Lincoln could not as a war measure end the practice of slavery in the loyal border states or in those parts of the Confederacy under Union control on the date of emancipation. Although he accepted the possibly limited legal force of the proclamation after the war ended, he nonetheless believed that it had tremendous moral force that would powerfully work toward complete and undeniably legal emancipation. The proclamation provided for the service of formerly enslaved men in the army, an opportunity many took. All told, nearly two hundred thousand black soldiers fought in the Union Army, providing nearly 10 percent of the army. Lincoln and many others believed that if these men fought and in large numbers died for the Union, the nation had a moral obligation to permanently end their enslavement. Many who favored the Thirteenth Amendment saw themselves as living up to that moral obligation.

Some thought the amendment unnecessary, or, paradoxically to our ears, unconstitutional. Many of the abolitionists had developed a constitutional theory to the effect that Congress always had possessed constitutional authority to abolish slavery in the states. This was an extremely controversial and distinctly minority view, however. Advocates of this view looked to various parts of the Constitution for the authority to abolish slavery. Some, for example, looked to Article IV, Section 4 of the Constitution, which provided, "The United States shall guarantee to every state in this Union a republican form of government." Constitutional abolitionists argued this provision implied that Congress had the power to guarantee, that is, provide, republican government, which, they argued, was incompatible with slavery, for slavery is a denial of the political equality characteristic of republicanism. Senator Charles

Sumner thought the Thirteenth Amendment unnecessary and in one sense undesirable, for it seemed to deny the constitutional theory that Congress already possessed power to undo slavery and merely needed to exercise its power.[7] Alternatively, Sumner and other constitutional abolitionists appealed to the due process clause of the Fifth Amendment, which provided, "No person should be deprived of life, liberty, or property without due process of law." In a very unorthodox reading of this clause because it was directly contrary to a well-known Supreme Court ruling, Sumner and others held that this clause forbade slavery in the states and empowered Congress to uproot slavery where it existed.[8] However, very few in Congress took this view of the Constitution seriously.[9]

A constitutional argument with much more traction in the debate was the claim that such an amendment would be unconstitutional. Congress discussed the Thirteenth Amendment intensively on two different occasions, once in the 38th Congress, when the amendment itself was up for consideration, and again in the 39th Congress, when the civil rights bill was debated. The two discussions were quite different in character, and therefore ought to be considered separately.[10]

To the modern eye, the debates on the Thirteenth Amendment in the 38th Congress have a distinctly odd look, for the central issue that preoccupied members of Congress was, in effect, whether the proposed amendment to the Constitution was itself constitutional.[11] Opponents set the terms of the debate by charging that the proposal deviated from the fundamental principles of the Constitution and thus could not (or at least morally and politically should not) be adopted. Proponents responded that the amendment was indeed congruent with or even in some sense demanded by the principles of the Constitution. In other words, the debate posed the question of whether the amendment was fundamentally consistent with and therefore completed the Constitution, as proponents claimed, or rather overturned the Constitution, as opponents claimed.

Garrett Davis, Democratic senator from Kentucky, considered it "irrefragably true, that the power of amending the Constitution does not authorize the abolition of slavery." Indeed, he denied that "the power of amending the Constitution is illimitable."[12] Joseph Edgerton, Democratic representative from Indiana, drew the conclusion from Davis's premise: "So long as the Federal Union exists there is not and should not be any political power short of the free consent of each slaveholding State that can rightfully abolish slavery in the United States."[13]

These Democrats could not deny entirely the existence of the amending power, but they believed that a sound interpretation of the document as a whole implicitly limited the amending power. These opponents of the amendment generally agreed that the line distinguishing valid from invalid exercise of the amending power was crossed when, as here, there was an effort to reach the internal structuring of the member states. Fernando Wood of New York said it very clearly: "There was an implied and solemn understanding [at the time of the adoption of the Constitution] that the local and domestic institutions of the States should not be attempted to be interfered with in any manner so as to be drawn within the sphere of Federal authority." Without that understanding, Wood asked, "Does anyone suppose . . . that the Constitution would have been ratified by any of the States?"[14] Representative Edgerton made the same point: "The assertion of power or right in a majority of the States, either through legislation of the Federal Government or through amendments of the Constitution, to interfere with or control the domestic institutions of a State, such, for example, as slavery, essentially repudiates the principle upon which the union was formed, namely the political equality of the States."[15] This amendment, said Representative Samuel Cox of Ohio, would "change the . . . form and structure of our federative system in its most essential feature."[16]

That "most essential feature," Cox explained a week later, is "the principle of self-government over state affairs." The Union, properly understood, extends only to "three classes of functions": relations to foreign states, relations between the states, and "certain powers which . . . to be useful and effective must be general and uniform in their operation throughout the country."[17] The proposed amendment then "breaks down . . . the distinction between the spheres of the States and national governments,"[18] a distinction implicit in the entire fabric of the Constitution and explicitly affirmed in the Ninth and Tenth Amendments. As Wood put it, "These articles are the general rules for the construction and interpretation of the entire instrument. Powers already granted may be modified, enlarged, or taken away by an amendment, but those which are retained by the people, or reserved to them, or to the states, cannot be delegated to the United States, except by the unanimous consent of all the States."[19] Their point was not, as Alan Grimes would have it, to affirm that "slavery was such an essential part of our constitutional system that to allow Congress to abolish it would be tantamount to an unconstitutional change in the form of government."[20] Rather, as Senator Davis said: "Property is a matter of State or domestic institution. The General Government does not legitimately, and was never intended to have, any jurisdiction or authority over the subject of property. . . . That is a great and fundamental feature of our Federal and State systems of government."[21]

By crossing this line, the opponents believed, the Republican majority was introducing "a revolutionary change in the Government." If this amendment could be passed, then, claimed Edgerton of Indiana, other amendments "might, with equal propriety, be aimed at any other local law or institution of a state." Amendments might, for example, abolish freedom of religion or regulate marriages. In a word, "the principle of the proposed amendment is the principle of consolidation. . . . It is absurd to call a Federal Union wherein such a principle of consolidation has been introduced into its fundamental laws a union of free and equal States."[22] "Where will it end, when once begun?" asked Cox of Ohio. "Should we amend the Constitution so as to change the relation of parent and child, guardian and ward, husband and wife, the laws of inheritance, the laws of legitimacy?"[23] Senator Davis of Kentucky captured the Democratic concern perfectly when he insisted, "The power of amendment as now proposed to be exercised," not so much the amendment itself, "imparts a power that would revolutionize the whole Government, and that would invest the amending power with a faculty of destroying and revolutionizing the whole Government."[24]

Whereas the opponents of the amendment saw it as working a constitutional revolution merely by its attempt to regulate the internal matters of the member states, the proponents rejected the constitutional revolution label and instead saw the amendment as a fulfillment or completion of the original Constitution. The amendment's proponents largely accepted the constitutional principle regarding the use of the amending power as explained by Thomas Davis of New York during the House debate:

When it appears to the people that there exists in the land an institution inconsistent with that Constitution, inconsistent with the principles of our government, we . . . propose to them, in accordance with that Constitution, to determine . . . whether or not they will amend it, and thereby remove the evil, there is nothing despotic, nothing wrong . . . in that we propose nothing which is not constitutional, nothing which is not just.[25]

Very early in the Senate debate, Republican Henry Wilson attempted to explain the inconsistency the amendment attempted to remove:

Cannot we hear amid the wild rushing roar of this war storm the voice of Him who rides upon the winds and rules the tempest saying unto us, "You cannot have peace until you secure liberty to all who are subject to your laws?" Sir, this declaration must be heeded. It has been whispered into the ears of this nation since first we pronounced life, liberty, and the pursuit of happiness to be the inalienable rights of all men.

On the basis of that pronouncement, Americans established "our free Government," with which slavery is "incompatible."[26] A familiar theme in Republican political thought was the primacy of the principles of the Declaration of Independence within the American political order—a theme given its consummate expression by Lincoln, but one widely shared inside and outside of Congress.[27] Surely the most eloquent statement of the point in these debates was by Sumner, who believed, "It is only necessary to carry the Republic back to its baptismal vows, and the declared sentiments of its origins. There is the Declaration of Independence: let its solemn promises be redeemed. There is the Constitution: let it speak, according to the promises of the Declaration."[28] Not internal self-governance or states' rights, but "the promises of the Declaration" are the ground of the American constitutional order, according to the drafters of the amendment.

The supporters went further in their efforts to prove the amendment's legitimacy. Slavery, they said, was not only "incompatible with our free Government," in that it directly countered "the great objects for which the Constitution was established" but also "it has confronted the Constitution itself, and prevented the enforcement of its most vital provisions."[29] Senator Wilson had in mind the violation not only of the spirit of the Constitution that slavery itself constituted but also the direct violation of the Constitution's letter to which slavery led.

Wilson and the other Republicans were especially concerned about the privileges and immunities clause of Article IV, Section 2. William Kelley, Republican representative from Pennsylvania, asked one of his Democratic colleagues, "Does he not know that for more than thirty years those dear friends of his, for whose institutions he and his party plead so fervently, have, not withstanding [sic] this right so specifically guaranteed, denied not only the right of asylum, but the right of transit through their States to us, who doubted the wisdom or divinity of chattel slavery?"[30] Southern states not only violated the privileges and immunities of citizens of Northern states but also turned against their own citizens. Said John A. Kasson, Republican of Iowa:

You cannot go into a State of the North in which you do not find refugees from Southern States who have been driven from the States in the South where they had a right to live as citizens, because of the tyranny which this institution exercised over public feeling and public opinion, and even over the laws of those States. . . . Who does not know that we have abundant proof that numbers of men in the State of Texas, Germans who had settled there, quiet and peaceable men, have been foully murdered in cold blood because they were known to be anti-slavery in sentiment?[31]

Among the privileges and immunities secured by the Constitution were not only the rights to asylum and transit but also those rights identified in the Bill of Rights. According to Senator Wilson, these rights "belong to every American citizen . . . wherever he may be within the jurisdiction of the United States." However, he asked, "how have these rights essential to liberty been respected in those sections of the Union where slavery held the reins of local authority and directed the thoughts, prejudices, and passions of the people?"[32] According to Wilson, all the rights identified in the First Amendment had been dishonored in the slave states. "The Constitution may declare the right, but slavery ever will, as it ever has, trample upon the Constitution and prevent the enjoyment of the right."

The cause of this dismal record of disrespect for the Constitution was the institution of slavery. "What then shall we do?" asked Wilson. "Abolish slavery. How? By amending our national Constitution. Why? Because slavery is incompatible with free government." The amendment was necessary, said Representative Kasson, "to carry into effect one clause of the Constitution [Article IV, Section 2], which has been disobeyed in nearly every slave State of the Union for some twenty or twenty-five, or thirty years past."[33] The abolition of slavery, then, was compatible with the Constitution because it would remove the chief spur to persistent violation of the Constitution. The amendment would allow other important provisions of the Constitution to come into their own. In this sense, the abolition of slavery represented an enforcement or completion of the original Constitution.

## THE THIRTEENTH AMENDMENT: A DEFECTIVE COMPLETION

The supporters and opponents of the Thirteenth Amendment took on the question of whether it completed or revolutionized the Constitution. As is the case with all genuine constitutional disputes, there was something serious to be said on both sides, but those who argued for the amendment had the stronger case. The original Constitution did not simply embody state autonomy respecting all matters of internal governance and ordering. One need think only of Article I, Section 10, which set limits on the powers of the states, for example, to make ex post facto laws or to impair the obligations of contract. These express limits were in fact transformed and truncated versions of Madison's proposed universal negative, which would have had a much larger and less-defined scope.

From Madison's perspective, the aspiration to "complete the Constitution" was clearly legitimate. Indeed, there was a remarkable parallel between

Madison's perception of what the system required and what the amendment's framers attempted to supply. Madison saw his universal negative as serving two purposes: making rights secure in the states and guarding against encroachments by states on each other and on the federal government. The Thirteenth Amendment was intended to improve the security of rights within the states by directly forbidding the most blatant violation of rights by the states and by removing the goad that prompted them to intrude on the rights of citizens of other states, on the prerogatives of other states, and on the powers of the federal government.

Yet the amendment differed greatly from Madison's proposal. Madison attempted to institute a political process that would operate to review every action by the states; the amendment proceeded instead more according to the model adopted in the original Constitution as a substitute for Madison's process—an explicit constitutional limitation to be enforced by the courts and, at least in this case, by Congress as well. The Constitution as adopted, and as amended, is much more legalistic than Madison thought desirable.

Yet, the amendment goes beyond Madison's negative power in two respects. Congressional power under the amendment is not necessarily limited only to a negative, or disallowing, power. And in committing the entire nation against slavery, the amendment has a clearer substantive commitment than did Madison's procedural solution. Indeed, it remains a case for great speculation as to how the negative power would have been used regarding slavery if adopted, and it is an intriguing question as to what Madison himself anticipated on this score.

Although the amendment parallels in several ways Madison's favored device, it must be judged inadequate as a completion of the Constitution. Immediate subsequent history—two further amendments adopted hardly before the ink was dry on the certificates of ratification for the Thirteenth—shows that clearly enough. The chief failing of the amendment lay in the lack of proper thought given to the meaning and implications of the commitment to emancipation.

There were two key questions that few members of the 38th Congress recognized. The first question concerned the issue: What, if any, positive rights or claims follow from the abolition of slavery? The framers of the amendment tended to take for granted a narrower view of the implications of emancipation, but without evidence of having thought very much about the question. Do, as many modern scholars claim, certain empowerments, for example, a right to vote, or certain immunities, for example, freedom from discrimination and other forms of unequal treatment, follow from the abolition of slavery?

The historical situation suggests the general understanding at the time was that the prohibition of slavery was compatible with both denial of some or even many rights and the imposition of unequal laws on the African Americans, for this was the prevailing legal arrangement in many of the Northern states.[34]

Because the United States constitutes a federal system, a second question arose. In a unitary system, it would be enough to settle what positive rights flowed from emancipation, but in the dual constitutional system of the United States, the further question existed of which government had the power and responsibility to provide for those rights. The framers of the amendment hardly considered this second question because they hardly confronted the first. Expecting all good things to flow nearly spontaneously from abolition, they could avoid the hard choices about American federalism the second question posed. For if emancipation had positive implications, then it might not be possible to leave responsibility for securing such rights where it had been—with the states. And if that responsibility were transferred to the federal government, that would indeed make for the constitutional revolution of which some speak. However, the amendment's drafters had not seen this far ahead and certainly in 1864–1865 never made any such commitments.

## THE THIRTEENTH AMENDMENT AND THE CIVIL RIGHTS BILL

Events soon led Congress to take up the two questions it had mostly ignored when originally debating the Thirteenth Amendment. In the wake of emancipation, the Southern states began passing the laws that became known as the Black Codes. The Republicans saw these as a Southern effort to snatch slavery from the jaws of freedom, to evade the Thirteenth Amendment, and to undo the results of the war. Republican activist and former Civil War general Carl Schurz, on a fact-finding mission to the South, found that the Black Codes reflected the widespread view that "the negro exists for the special object of raising cotton, rice, and sugar *for the Whites,* and that it is illegitimate for him to indulge, like other people, in the pursuit of his own happiness in his own way." As Schurz quoted an officer of the Freedman's Bureau, "The whites deem the blacks their property by natural right, and however much they may admit that the relations of masters and slaves have been destroyed . . . they still have an ingrained feeling that blacks at large belong to the whites at large. . . . An ingrained feeling like this is apt to bring forth that sort of class legislation which produces laws to govern one class with no other view than to benefit another."[35]

The Black Codes were "class legislation" that denied many of the rights and liberties usually taken for granted as part of free status. Especially onerous provisions were set forth, applying to blacks only. For example, in one Louisiana town, blacks were forbidden to own or rent property. Blacks were also forbidden to reside there unless they were "in the regular service of some white person or former owner."[36] Severe limits were put on the rights of blacks to engage in commerce, to receive an education, to appeal to the courts for protection, and to testify in court.

Republican outrage led to efforts to undo the Black Codes. Early in 1866, a proposal for a new amendment was discussed in Congress, and a civil rights bill was introduced at nearly the same time. The Civil Rights Act of 1866 prohibited the restrictive codes being adopted in the South and set penalties for all persons "acting under color of law" who attempted to enforce their provisions. Section 1 of the bill defined citizens in much the same terms as the Fourteenth Amendment later did, and then went on to provide:

Such citizens, of every race and color, without regard to any previous condition of slavery . . . shall have the same right, in every State and Territory in the United States, to make and enforce contracts, to sue, be parties, and give evidence, to inherit, purchase, lease, sell, hold, and convey real and personal property, and to full and equal benefit of all laws and proceedings for the security of person and property, as is enjoyed by white citizens.

It was defended as an exercise of Congress's powers under Section 2 of the Thirteenth Amendment. The main argument in favor of the bill held that to be free meant to possess the sort of rights mentioned in the bill and to have them protected by law. Thus, if one's right to make contracts is not recognized and enforced, one is not treated as a free person, with the free will to incur legal rights and responsibilities via agreements with other free wills. In this manner the bill responded to the first question posed by the amendment procuring emancipation—not being enslaved means being recognized by law as free, capable of doing all the kinds of things listed in the bill.

This answer was not by any means uncontroversial. Although there was a certain theoretical force to the argument raised on behalf of the bill, there was a good deal of history and experience that spoke otherwise. As President Andrew Johnson said in his veto message of the bill: "A perfect equality of the white and colored races is attempted to be fixed by Federal law in every state of the union over the vast field of state jurisdiction covered by these enumerated rights. In no one of these can any State ever exercise any power of discrimination between the different races. In the exercise of State policy over matters exclusively affecting the people of each State it has frequently been thought expedient to discriminate between the two races."[37] And indeed it had been, for in many of the Northern states where slavery was forbidden, it was not understood that the free status thus secured, established, or implied all the rights enumerated in the bill. So, for example, Ohio, a state carved out of the old Northwest Territory, required free blacks "to post a five-hundred dollar bond before they could enter the state."[38] In other words, the practice in the United States implicitly recognized a status between slavery and full freedom and equality wherein the enumerated rights were not legally recognized for all. Likewise, the spare language of the Thirteenth Amendment had been taken from the Northwest Ordinance of 1787, and in the many years since 1787 it had not been generally understood to bestow or legally require the rights listed in the act.

Johnson also noted the possible implications for federalism of the civil rights bill. "Hitherto every subject embraced in the enumeration of rights contained in this bill has been considered as exclusively belonging to the states."[39] Johnson did not deny that there were some constitutional limitations on the states in their custody of these matters, but he wondered if the rationale for the bill did not imply that Congress would have power to replace all state legislation if it so wished. He protested on behalf of traditional federalism. Did the country, without being aware of it, cancel altogether the traditional federal distribution of powers between state and nation when it adopted the Thirteenth Amendment to end slavery?

One man who had his doubts was John Bingham, moderate Republican representative from Ohio. Bingham was a particularly important doubter, for he became the chief drafter of the Fourteenth Amendment. Bingham and many other moderates accepted the goal of the civil rights bill—to protect the listed rights against hostile state legislation—but they doubted that the Thirteenth Amendment could properly be read to provide a constitutional basis for the legislation. Bingham and others thus pushed for a new amendment to put congressional power to pass the civil rights bill beyond doubt and at the same time to do two other important things. First, the new amendment would of itself provide the protections sought in the civil rights bill by directly forbidding the state violations the bill prohibited. Second, and more subtly, the new amendment would undergird the bill with a more confined and precise constitutional theory than the one used by some to defend it under the Thirteenth Amendment. The new amendment would in effect resolve the ambiguities and uncertainties of interpretation of the Thirteenth Amendment.

## THE FOURTEENTH AMENDMENT

At least part of the purpose, then, of the Fourteenth Amendment was to provide an assured constitutional foundation for the Civil Rights Act of 1866.
Some of the later Supreme Court justices as well as some of the scholars of the
"changed only a little" persuasion go as far as to consider the meaning of the
amendment to be just the same as and no more than that of the bill. That is
doubtful for a number of reasons, one of which is that the draft of the amendment was introduced in Congress before the civil rights bill. Moreover, the language of the two pieces of legislation is altogether different. The civil rights bill
contains a discrete and specific list of rights protected. The amendment speaks
in grand and far more general terms of privileges and immunities of citizens
of the United States, of due process and the equal protection of the law, which
the states are forbidden to deny to any persons. That chronology and more
general language speak against the simple identification of the civil rights bill
and the amendment, but that language poses its own problems, for these terms
seem of indefinite meaning and scope, opening the way for those who take
the Reconstruction amendments to have produced a constitutional revolution.

Yet, broad and perhaps vague as the language of the amendment is, it is
language with precedent in the unamended Constitution, as in the privileges
and immunities clause in Article IV, Section 2, and the due process clause of
the Fifth Amendment. These terms were not devoid of meaning. Perhaps most
significant, judging from the statements of Bingham, these terms were chosen
with great deliberateness and were meant to have a clear meaning. Bingham
and others made statements during the debates on the amendment that jibe
with the idea that the intent was to "complete the Constitution," neither to
simply reaffirm it nor to revolutionize it. Bingham said at one point, "I am perfectly confidant [*sic*]" that the provisions of the proposed Fourteenth Amendment "would have been [in the original Constitution] but for the fact that
[their] insertion . . . would have been utterly incompatible with the existence
of slavery in any state."[40] Like Madison, the drafters of the Fourteenth Amendment concluded that the Constitution was incomplete not only because it had
allowed slavery but also because it had failed to sufficiently provide for the
general security of rights. The Thirteenth Amendment undid the cause of the
incompleteness, but the Fourteenth was to do the completing.

Taking a cue from Bingham's efforts to use precise language in his final draft
of the amendment, let us take our bearings from that language in attempting to
discern just how the amendment was to "complete the Constitution." Structur-
ally, the amendment operates in terms of five pairs of concepts, each of which

elucidates the others and each member of which delimits and defines the other. These structural pairs provide the key to the amendment's meaning.

The first sentence defines two forms of citizenship—citizens of the United States and citizens of the states.[41] The text then contrasts "citizens of the United States" and "persons." Associated with citizens are "privilege and immunities"; associated with persons are certain other matters, the most easily identified the famous triad of rights, "life, liberty, and property." A fourth pair of terms relates to the two clauses that deal with persons: states are prohibited from depriving persons of the above rights without due process of law, and states are forbidden to deny persons equal protection of the laws. Finally, a fifth pair contrasts the prohibition of the states from doing certain things with the empowerment (in Section 5) of the Congress to "enforce" the amendment.

To summarize the five pairs:

- citizens of the United States—citizens of states
- citizens—persons
- privileges and immunities—rights
- due process of law—protection of the laws
- prohibition against state action—congressional powers

The amendment opens by setting up two kinds of citizenship. Given that it goes on to speak of privileges and immunities of US citizens but not those of state citizens, we are justified in drawing two conclusions. First, there is a difference between the privileges and immunities inherent in each kind of citizenship; otherwise, the amendment could have proceeded without any need to distinguish which sort of citizenship and which sorts of privileges and immunities were of concern. Second, the amendment limits itself to the privileges and immunities of US citizens; other than defining who state citizens are and distinguishing the two kinds of citizens from each other, the amendment has no further concern to secure the privileges and immunities of state citizens. The Fourteenth Amendment thus contemplates the continued existence of a dual, or federal, system. As part of the Constitution for the general government, the amendment sensibly limits itself to the privileges and immunities inhering in citizenship in the government of which it is the constitutive document.

The next two pairs are intimately connected; citizens of the United States have privileges and immunities, and persons have rights.[42] This too makes sense. Privileges and immunities are special, not possessed by everyone as a matter of right. A privilege is something over and above the basic; immunity is freedom from some burden. In contrast, the Declaration of Independence says rights belong to "all men," or in more general language, to all persons. These natural or universal rights are not "privileges" or "immunities"; they are not special to some, not exceptions in any way. The rights of persons—life, liberty, and property—are natural rights because all human beings possess them independently of any human law. Natural rights predate government, which came into existence solely to protect those rights.[43]

The rights identified in the amendment are the familiar natural rights, but what are the "privileges and immunities of citizens of the United States"? Because privileges and immunities belong to citizens of the United States, and because the fundamental document governing the United States is the Constitution, it would seem reasonable to conclude that the privileges and immunities are special rights enjoyed by the citizens of the United States by virtue of the Constitution. As opposed to natural rights, privileges and immunities are conventional, or constitutional, rights.

Where does the Constitution establish the constitutional rights of US citizens? It does so in several places, though most clearly in the Bill of Rights. The Bill of Rights lists some of the rights possessed by citizens of the United States; for example, freedom of speech, the right to a jury trial, and the right to be free from the threat of cruel and unusual punishment (i.e., an immunity). However, the rights identified in the Bill of Rights are not the only privileges and immunities of citizens of the United States. In the notorious *Dred Scott v. Sandford* case, for example, Chief Justice Roger Taney identified the right to sue in federal court as a privilege of US citizenship. The right to participate in the government of the United States, as regulated by law, is another privilege of US citizenship. Article I, Sections 9 and 10 of the Constitution list a series of prohibitions against the Congress and the states respectively, that would also qualify, it seems, as privileges or immunities of US citizens.

Privileges and immunities are over and above natural rights. The former are not natural and universal because they are incidents of citizenship; that is, they depend for their existence on the prior existence of government, which is itself an artificial thing. Thus, Justice Bushrod Washington, in the most extended early judicial explication of privileges and immunities, emphasized their connection to government: privileges and immunities are matters that "belong of right to the citizens of all free governments; and which have at all times been enjoyed by the citizens of the several states which compose this union." Privileges and immunities depend on the variable character of government. They have at least an element of the purely conventional, for they are defined in the laws, customs, and constitutions of specific states and nations.

Some privileges and immunities have the character of specifications of rights. For example, persons have a natural right to property. After government comes into existence, persons may be deprived of their property only under certain conditions and if done with due process of law. For example, a person accused of violating a law must be able to know the charges and to present evidence before an impartial judge. In the Anglo-American legal system, certain conventions have evolved as to which qualify as proper procedures, many of which are spelled out in the Bill of Rights. Although these procedures protect natural rights, they do not have the same status as natural rights themselves. Moreover, it would be difficult to say that they are uniquely required in order to secure rights. They are the specific, but conventional, procedures that have arisen within a polity, but some other procedures could do as well or nearly so, or even better. They are thus the privileges and immunities possessed by citizens of this polity. Other privileges and immunities center on sharing in the governance of "free societies." These cannot be natural, strictly speaking, for government is not natural. These must be over and above the natural rights because there can be no natural right to govern an entity that does not exist in nature.

The original Constitution vested or recognized certain special rights in citizens of the United States and set out a legal requirement that the government of the United States must respect these rights. For the most part, however, the original Constitution did not say that the states must respect these special rights. In the famous case of *Barron v. Baltimore*, the Supreme Court had confirmed that point—the Bill of Rights did not hold against the states. That was part of the incompleteness of the Constitution.

The privileges and immunities clause of the Fourteenth Amendment was meant to remedy this situation. The special rights of US citizens were now to be protected against adverse actions by the states. The Fourteenth Amendment's privileges and immunities clause was intended, in other words, to incorporate the Bill of Rights and to secure other privileges and immunities against usurpation by the states.

Whereas citizens of the United States possess special privileges and immunities, all "persons" are to be given certain protection in their universal, or natural, rights. Of course, all persons "possessed" these rights prior to the Fourteenth Amendment, but they did not possess them as constitutional rights. To take the most blatant example: enslaved people had a natural right to life and liberty, but the Constitution did not secure them that right. It did not directly deny them the right, but it did not prevent the states from denying them that right. The Fourteenth Amendment was meant to correct that, and this was probably its most important intended achievement. The amendment was to provide a new constitutional right (a civil right) to people's natural rights.

The provision of constitutional rights is a somewhat complex matter in itself and is extraordinarily complex in a federal system. That double complexity is what underlies the next two pairs of concepts in the amendment. Let us first think of the problem as it would appear in a unitary system of government. Government exists, says the Declaration of Independence, in order to secure the inalienable rights of human beings. Government's relation to these rights, however, is twofold. The primary task of "securing rights" is to *supply* protection to the rights. This means that government must do something positive and active—make laws that secure rights, define the terms of the rights, and provide police, courts, and the like. To do this properly, governments cannot act according to mere whim, however. They must announce in advance what the rules are, how things are to be done, and what behavior by persons will call down the force of the community upon them. That is, governments must operate according to what John Locke called "known and settled standing law." The law exists for the sake of securing rights; it does so by providing protection to persons. Thus, the positive task of government in securing rights can be stated in terms of the duty of governments to supply "protection of the laws." This is what the Fourteenth Amendment means in its equal protection clause. States have a duty to supply equal protection of the laws, that is, as much protection in rights to all classes as to the most favored class in the protection of its rights.

Government's relation to securing rights can be complex. Government can fail in two ways—in not supplying protection (e.g., standing by while thugs shoot innocent people) or in itself being a threat to rights. Governments have duties not only of a positive sort (to supply protection of the laws) but of a negative sort as well: not to oppress, or to act against citizens only with due process of law. Government can deprive citizens of natural rights—for example, to life, liberty, and property—only if the person has violated a law and the government has properly established that fact—before an independent judge, in a setting where the accused person has a right to challenge the government's claim, and so on. The due process clause of the Fourteenth Amendment secures to all persons a constitutional right to this sort of "negative" protection of their natural rights against the states.

Hence, the due process and the equal protection clauses perfectly complement each other: each provides a constitutional right to one aspect of the security of natural rights, the negative and positive aspects, respectively.

Now we can add in the last dimension of complexity, the one that results from the federal system, which relates to the fifth pair of concepts. The Fourteenth Amendment established a constitutional right to citizens' natural rights, but it did so in the form of prohibitions against actions by the states. This signals a very important intention in the amendment—not to overturn but only to correct the traditional federal system. In the traditional federal system, the states did the bulk of governing. The government of the United States had relatively few (though very important) tasks assigned to it. The Fourteenth Amendment did not mean to change this. The great bulk of rights protecting was to continue to occur in the states. They were to do this, however, in accordance with the limits imposed on them by the amendment.

In the first instance, those limits—the privileges and immunities clause, the due process clause, and the equal protection clause—impose a moral and quasilegal duty on all officers of the state to follow the dictates of the amendment. However, the amendment does not leave matters there. Enforcement measures are inherent. The first line of enforcement is the court system. Just as the courts have the power to enforce limitations against the states in the original Constitution, so courts have this power under the Fourteenth Amendment. Article I, Section 10, for example, says that no state shall pass any "law impairing the Obligation of Contracts." Under this clause, the Supreme Court had, prior to the Civil War, held quite a few state laws unconstitutional. Under the Fourteenth Amendment, the courts would now do the same with state actions that violated the amendment.

Section 5 of the Fourteenth Amendment empowers Congress as another agency for enforcing the prohibitions against the states. It can, for example, pass laws punishing state officers who deprive persons of life, liberty, or property without due process of law. The amendment gives Congress power to supervise the states in their exercise of their primary powers. However, there is another and potentially further-reaching enforcement power under the Fourteenth Amendment. If a state fails to protect natural rights, then Congress may enforce the constitutional right to protection of the laws by supplying that protection itself. An example occurred shortly after ratification of the Fourteenth Amendment. The Ku Klux Klan arose in many Southern states and committed acts of violence and intimidation against blacks. These acts were committed often in collusion with state officials; the states would not or could not curb the Klan. Thus, Congress, when convinced the states had failed to provide protection of the laws, intervened to provide protection against the Klan. As long as Congress waited to see that there was a real failure by the states to do their duty, this was perfectly constitutional under the meaning and intent of the Fourteenth Amendment.

One can summarize the achievement of the Fourteenth Amendment in three shorthand doctrines: (1) incorporation of the Bill of Rights through the privileges and immunities clause; (2) establishment of new constitutional rights to one's natural rights through the due process and equal protection clauses and, thereby, a constitutional duty in the states to secure the preexisting natural rights of persons within their jurisdictions; and (3) the "state-failure doctrine" of congressional power to enforce rights.

Although the Fourteenth Amendment employs a very different device than Madison's universal negative, the Fourteenth Amendment's connection to his perception of the direction in which the Constitution needed to be supplemented is fairly clear. The amendment establishes the principle that the federal government possesses a general supervisory power over the states with respect to the most important matters. It leaves no room for the idea that the states are sovereign or autonomous. It establishes the two orders of government as *one system* in which the states are not superior to the federal government, although the federal government is not simply and totally superior to the states either. If the states perform properly, there is little or no actual transference of governing activity from the states to the federal government, but there is a clear establishment of constitutional devices for keeping the states in orbit.

Likewise, the Fourteenth Amendment directly establishes the protection for rights in the states that Madison sought in 1787. Instead of the political device of a congressional veto, we have a legalistic device, but nonetheless a device intended to achieve something similar to Madison's veto. It is another form of corrective federalism.

The Fourteenth Amendment thus represents the dominant understanding of the new constitutional order held by its drafters: the core of the American political order is the commitment to the principles of the Declaration of Independence (i.e., that government exists to protect natural rights). Such a commitment was present in the original Constitution and is reaffirmed in the Fourteenth Amendment. At the same time, the American republic is a federal republic, a system of divided authorities in which the states conduct the greatest amount of governing, including rights protection. Most of the Republicans, contrary to President Johnson's fears, valued this federal system as much as they sought to put rights protection on a more secure footing. In 1871, when Congress considered a bill to extend the powers of the general government further into the states than they had ever gone before, Bingham said: "Do gentlemen say that by so legislating we would strike down the rights of the states? God forbid. I believe our dual system of government essential to our national existence. . . . The nation cannot be without the state governments to localize and enforce the rights of the people under the Constitution. . . . No right reserved by the Constitution to the states should be impaired."

Bingham's conception of the relation between the rights of persons, the states, and the general government was thus complex. The principles of right, both natural and legal, in this regime are national, and the federal government must be armed with power to make those principles effective. This did not mean, however, that the national power must supplant the states in their ordinary custody of these national principles. He did not believe it would be good for the states to cease making and enforcing the laws that secure and regulate the privileges and immunities of citizens and the life, liberty, and property of persons. Even so, the claims of the states to these areas of legislation are not absolute. When the system faces an unavoidable choice between rights protection and federalism, the Fourteenth Amendment mandates the primacy of rights.

## THE FIFTEENTH AMENDMENT

Suffrage for the freedmen was a question that kept recurring from the first moments of Reconstruction until the passage of the Fifteenth Amendment in 1870. Not to follow the subject all the way back to the beginning, we can look first at Section 2 of the Fourteenth Amendment for some of the prehistory of the Fifteenth Amendment. (So far, we have discussed only Sections 1 and 5 of the Fourteenth.) Section 2 was necessary in the first place as a response to the end of slavery, for the original Constitution had established a formula for state representation in the lower house of Congress that an enslaved person should count as three-fifths of a free person. Section 2 of the Fourteenth Amendment affirmed what was implied by the abolition of slavery—that a formerly enslaved person should be considered in the population count for representation just as all free persons always had—as a full person.

Beyond that, Section 2 provides that if the states deny any of their male citizens who have reached the age of twenty-one years the right to vote in federal elections, the population base on which its representation is calculated is to be reduced "in the proportion which the number of such male citizens shall bear to the whole number of male citizens, twenty-one years of age in such state." Section 2 thus leaves the setting of voting qualifications with the states and in particular does not prohibit the states from denying the freedmen the vote. It merely provides an incentive for the states to grant them the vote. Another implication of this provision in Section 2 is that the various classes of rights covered in Section 1 of the amendment does not include the right to vote, for if it did, the states would outright be prohibited from denying to any person the right to vote.

The Fifteenth Amendment does not go as far as to remove from the states all control over suffrage qualifications. Unlike the other two Reconstruction amendments, it speaks explicitly in the language of race, for it forbids the states (and the United States as well) from denying or abridging "the right of citizens . . . to vote . . . on account of race, color, or previous condition of servitude." This language, it should be noted, allows states to deny the vote on other bases, such as education level, literacy, sex, age, and whatever other criteria the states might choose to impose. For much of its history the amendment proved less than effective at procuring the vote for the freedmen and their descendants, for it allowed the states to use other criteria that proved largely to be proxies for race, such as literacy tests administered in a racially biased way. The drafters of the amendment were aware of this possibility, which is one reason an alternative version of the amendment, establishing universal male suffrage, was seriously considered at the time. Congress settled on the form the amendment took for a combination of two reasons: first, the prevalence of the view that some qualifications for the vote were legitimately imposed, or at least that the states should be free to impose such; second, the same respect for maintaining much of the traditional federal system as we saw at work in the drafting of the Fourteenth Amendment.

The Fifteenth Amendment clearly takes a somewhat different approach to completing the Constitution than that taken in the Fourteenth. The corrective federal mechanism of Madison's negative power and of the Fourteenth Amendment are not as evident here. The aim here is more to affect the political process that produces policy rather than to police or correct the policy outcomes. However, the Fifteenth does share something very important with the corrective federalism devices. It indicates a desire to see that governance in the American constitutional Union remain largely a state affair, with the Constitution and instruments of Union governance setting certain parameters or possessing certain corrective powers but not supplanting the states in their sphere of authority.


## CONCLUSION

The three Reconstruction amendments, especially the Fourteenth, have proven the most dynamic parts of the Constitution in the 150 years since their adoption. Even to begin to retrace their role in American life in that century and a half would require much space, but suffice it to say, there is hardly an issue with a constitutional dimension that does not involve and turn on the amendments.

So, for example, the protection of economic liberty in the late nineteenth and early twentieth centuries, the movement to apply the Bill of Rights to the states, the civil rights revolution, the women's rights movement, the affirmation of an abortion right, and now of rights of same-sex marriage—all these and more trace to the Reconstruction amendments. What we think of as the modern Constitution would be unthinkable without the Reconstruction amendments and the major changes they effected in the federal system, in the relations between citizens and their own states and in the kinds of protections for the rights of persons the amendments supply.

The constitutional revolution and the "changed only a little" interpretations have analogues in the larger and later debates over the meaning of the Fourteenth Amendment, with some, such as Justice William Brennan, taking a position rather like the constitutional revolution interpretation, arguing that questions of justice, morality, and natural law are now proper objects of the judiciary's consideration, and others, such as Robert Bork, taking a position rather like the "changed only a little" interpretation, arguing that the Court's job is only to police the constitutional structure of government. Understanding the spirit of the Reconstruction amendments as "corrective federalism" would provide us a better guide through these constitutional thickets than either of these problematic extremes.

## NOTES

1. Jacobus ten Broek, *Equal under the Law* (New York: Collier, 1965); Alexander Tsesis, *The Thirteenth Amendment and American Freedom* (New York: New York University Press, 2004).

2. Raoul Berger, *Government by Judiciary: The Transformation of the Fourteenth Amendment* (Cambridge, MA: Harvard University Press, 1977); Berger, *The Fourteenth Amendment and the Bill of Rights* (Norman: University of Oklahoma Press, 1989).

3. M. E. Bradford, "Changed Only a Little: The Reconstruction Amendments and the Nomocratic Constitution of 1787," *Wake Forest Law Review* 24 (October 1989): 573–598.

4. There is a group of scholars who write as though the radicals controlled legislative outcomes in 1865–1866. Not only Jacobus ten Broek but other scholars such as Sidney Buchanan, Alexander Tsesis, Robert Kaczorowski, and William B. Glidden assume that the radicals were able to set the terms and meanings for the new amendments. Consider the chapters by Tsesis and Kaczorowski in *The Promises of Liberty: The History and Contemporary Relevance of the Thirteenth Amendment*, ed. Alexander Tsesis (New York: Columbia University Press, 2010), 1–23, 304–315. See also William B. Glidden, *Congress and the Fourteenth Amendment* (Lanham, MD: Lexington, 2013), 13–28. On the actual strength of the radicals in Congress, see, for example, A. J. Langguth,

*After Lincoln: How the North Won the Civil War and Lost the Peace* (New York: Simon and Schuster, 2014), 120. More sober are scholars who recognize the limits of the ability of the radicals to control outcomes in the 39th Congress. See Earl M. Maltz, *Civil Rights, the Constitution, and Congress, 1863–1869* (Lawrence: University Press of Kansas, 1990).

5. Max Farrand, *Records of the Federal Convention of 1787,* vol. 1 (New Haven, CT: Yale University Press, 1966), 164–173 (June 8, 1787).

6. *Abraham Lincoln: Speeches and Writings,* vol. 2, ed. Don E. Fehrenbacher (New York: Library of America, 1989), 424–425.

7. Charles Sumner, Speech in the Senate, April 8, 1864, *Congressional Globe,* 32nd Cong., 1st sess. (1864): 1474–1482; Langguth, *After Lincoln,* 23–24.

8. Barron v. Baltimore, 7 Pet. 243 (1833).

9. ten Broek, *Equal under the Law,* 170–171n.22; see also G. Sidney Buchanan, "The Quest for Freedom: A Legal History of the Thirteenth Amendment," *Houston Law Review* 12, no. 1 (1975): 321, 357, 590.

10. Many treatments of the Thirteenth Amendment collapse the two discussions, much to the detriment of understanding both. See, for example, Michael Curtis, *No State Shall Abridge* (Durham, NC: Duke University Press, 1986), 48–49; Harold Hyman and William Wiecek, *Equal Justice under Law* (New York: HarperCollins, 1982), 386–404.

11. Herman Belz, *A New Birth of Freedom: The Republican Party and Freedman's Rights, 1861–1866* (Westport, CT: Greenwood, 1976), 122.

12. *Congressional Globe,* 38th Cong., 1st sess. (1864): 1489.

13. Ibid., 2985.

14. Ibid., 2941.

15. Ibid, 2985.

16. *Congressional Globe,* 38th Cong., 2nd sess. (1865), 125.

17. Ibid., 242.

18. Ibid.

19. *Congressional Globe,* 38th Cong., 1st sess. (1864): 2941.

20. Alan Grimes, *Democracy and the Amendments to the Constitution* (Lanham, MD: Lexington, 1978), 37.

21. *Congressional Globe,* 38th Cong., 1st sess. (1864): 1489.

22. Ibid., 2986.

23. *Congressional Globe,* 38th Cong., 2nd sess. (1865): 242.

24. *Congressional Globe,* 38th Cong., 1st sess. (1864): 1498.

25. *Congressional Globe,* 38th Cong., 2nd sess. (1865): 155.

26. *Congressional Globe,* 38th Cong., 1st sess. (1864): 1202.

27. For a beautiful account of Lincoln and the relation between the Declaration of Independence and the Constitution, see Harry V. Jaffa, *Crisis of the House Divided: An Interpretation of the Issues in the Lincoln-Douglas Debates* (Chicago: University of Chicago Press, 1959). See also Alexander Tsesis, "The Thirteenth Amendment's Revolutionary Aims," in *Promises of Liberty: The History and Contemporary Relevance of the Thirteenth Amendment,* ed. Alexander Tsesis (New York: Columbia University Press, 2010), 2–7; Glidden, *Congress and the Fourteenth Amendment,* 15–18.

28. *Congressional Globe,* 38th Cong., 1st sess. (1864): 1482.

29. Ibid., 1202.

30. Ibid., 2984.

31. *Congressional Globe,* 38th Cong., 2nd sess. (1865): 193.

32. *Congressional Globe,* 38th Cong. 1st sess. (1864): 1202.

33. *Congressional Globe,* 38th Cong., 2nd sess. (1865): 193.

34. For a somewhat extreme statement, see Chief Justice Roger Taney's summary of the legal status of free blacks in the North in his infamous opinion in *Dred Scott v. Sandford,* 60 U.S. 393 (1857).

35. Carl Schurz, "Report on the States of South Carolina, Georgia, Alabama, Mississippi, and Louisiana," *Senate Executive Documents for the First Session of the Thirty-Ninth Congress of the United States of America,* vol. 1 (Washington, DC: Government Printing Office, 1866), 21.

36. Ibid., 23.

37. Andrew Johnson, Veto Message on the Civil Rights Act of 1866, March 27, 1866, in *A Compilation of the Messages and Papers of the President,* vol. 8, ed. James V. Richardson (Washington, DC: Government Printing Office, 1893), 3605.

38. Langguth, *After Lincoln,* 195.

39. Johnson, Veto Message, 3605.

40. *Congressional Globe,* 39th Cong., 1st sess. (1866): 1090.

41. I realize it is a widely accepted view that the distinction between the two citizenships (or the privileges and immunities thereof) is an invention of the Supreme Court in the *Slaughterhouse Cases.* Although much of what the Court said in the *Slaughterhouse Cases* was erroneous, this distinction is warranted both by the text and by the history of the amendment. On the latter, consider Bingham's theory of privileges and immunities, as presented in the debate on the admission of Oregon to statehood, February 11, 1859. *Congressional Globe,* 35th Cong., 2nd sess. (1859): 982–985. The distinction goes back even further. It figures importantly in Chief Justice Roger Taney's opinion in *Dred Scott v. Sandford,* 60 U.S. 393 (1857).

42. Some scholars have denied the significance of the distinction between "citizen" and "person." Apart from the argument presented here, the historical record makes clear that the distinction was intentional. See, for example, *Congressional Globe,* 35th Cong., 2nd sess. (1859): 983.

43. For an explication of nature and natural rights, see Michael P. Zuckert, "Thomas Jefferson on Nature and Natural Rights," in *The Framers and Fundamental Rights,* ed. Robert Licht (Washington, DC: American Enterprise Institute Press, 1991). For testimony as to the widespread acceptance of the natural rights philosophy by the framers of the amendment, consult the index entries for "natural rights" and "Declaration of Independence" in Alfred Avins, *The Reconstruction Amendments' Debates: The Legislative History and Contemporary Debates in Congress on the 13th, 14th, and 15th Amendments* (Richmond, VA: Commission on Constitutional Government, 1967). My reading of the congressional debates suggests that Avins's index, itself substantial, much understates the evidence on the presence of the natural rights philosophy.

CHAPTER 12

# The Politics of Reconstruction and the Problem of Self-Government

PHILIP B. LYONS

As I would not be a *slave*, so I would not be a *master*. This expresses my idea of democracy. Whatever differs from this, to the extent of the difference, is no democracy.
—Abraham Lincoln

Although many historians consider Reconstruction a failure,[1] few if any have tried to draw political lessons for the practice of self-government from that tragic outcome.[2] Leaders at the time were adrift on uncharted waters. Never before had the US government faced the need to reconcile eight million mostly prejudiced whites accustomed to domination to treating blacks as equals and fellow citizens. Neither the Declaration of Independence nor the US Constitution provided guidance as to how Reconstruction should be conducted. The effort was further complicated by the fact that the ruling Republican Party was split between moderates and radicals—between the former's more prudent approach to seeking Southern white consent in establishing relatively just governments and the latter's more idealistic policy of establishing purer just governments but via force and without such consent. After Lincoln was removed from the scene by an assassin's bullet, the course of Reconstruction depended upon the outcome of the struggle between these two wings of the Republican Party. From the characteristics of this struggle and the attempts to transcend it, lessons can be drawn for meeting the challenge of self-government. For without statesmanship, the fate of Reconstruction depended on which side pursued its approach not only with the best arguments but also by other means, fair or foul.

The result of the Republicans' internal factional struggle was a framework for Reconstruction that all but guaranteed failure in the eleven defeated states. The framework adopted encouraged the rise of such extremism in the Southern states that federal military intervention seemed the only recourse for protecting rights. However, the prospect of this alarmed many Republicans over the threat such intervention posed to the vitality of the states and the nation's system of federalism. This gave rise to a third faction of Republicans, the Liberal Republican Party, who victoriously argued that because federal interference would make matters worse, it was better to relegate civil rights enforcement to the very states foremost in violating the rights of blacks. Thus, the cause of civil rights was set back a hundred years, along with the prospect of curbing the spirit of mastery. As the greatest challenge to self-government our country has ever faced, Reconstruction has much to teach us about the capacity of the majority to take the steps necessary to establish equality for all, black as well as white.

This chapter begins by analyzing the different approaches toward Reconstruction advocated at the time. The main views were those of the moderate and radical Republicans, the two wings of the dominant party of the era, and this chapter describes how the strengths and weaknesses of each came to light in their struggles over the Fourteenth Amendment and the Congressional Reconstruction Act (CRA). In particular, the chapter shows how the uncompromising demands of the radical Republicans, coupled with President Ulysses S. Grant's radical Reconstruction proclivities, undermined Reconstruction in many of the defeated states. I argue that Lincoln's thoughts and actions managing Reconstruction in Louisiana during the war illustrate the kind of statesmanship required to transcend the positions of the various factions. I further argue that those few state leaders who followed in Lincoln's footsteps attempted and in one case achieved one of the rare successes of the Reconstruction era. Lincoln's Reconstruction statesmanship thus serves as a benchmark for determining better and worse ways to secure civil rights in situations of horrible prejudice and after the horrors of civil war.

## MODERATE VERSUS RADICAL REPUBLICANS

The moderate and radical Republicans shared the same goal but advocated very different means to attain it. Both shared a common cause—the promotion of just government for all Americans. In the context of Reconstruction and Southern white racism, the great problem was securing rights for the recently freed blacks. Accordingly, both Republican factions voted for the joint resolution that later was ratified as the Thirteenth Amendment, abolishing slavery. Both also decried the ongoing horrors of racial violence in the South. For example, moderate William Fessenden (R-ME) noted in the *Report of the Joint Committee on Reconstruction* that the feeling in many parts of the South toward the freedmen, especially by uneducated and ignorant whites, was one of vindictive and malicious hatred, frequently leading to acts of cruelty, oppression, and murder that the local authorities were at "no pains to prevent or punish."[3] Similarly, from his tour of the South arranged by radical Senator Charles Sumner (R-MA), General Carl Schurz reported that in South Carolina, for example, "a spirit of bitterness and persecution manifests itself towards the negroes. They are shot and abused outside the immediate protection of our forces by men who announce their determination to take the law into their own hands."[4] Both wings of the Republican Party wanted to end this violent lawlessness.

Moderate and radical Republicans differed greatly on the proposed means to achieve this shared end. For the radicals, fighting for immediate and full black rights was an all-encompassing passion. Radical Republican leaders such as Senator Sumner and Congressman Thaddeus Stevens (R-PA) had "a genuine desire to do justice to the Negro."[5] The radicals thought Southerners so disloyal, so hostile to the Negro, and so prejudiced that establishing just governments required the use of force. The moderates thought it essential to seek the consent of white Southerners to establish long-lasting, just governments. Although they recognized that such consent meant, regrettably, moving more slowly, they feared that without it the whole process of Reconstruction would fail.

A leading radical, Congressman Samuel Shellabarger (R-OH), wanted to suspend the rights of US citizenship for former rebels. According to him, the defeated states were not ready for readmission to the Union and would not be unless white citizens were reeducated under the control of a truly loyal authority backed by military force. Other radicals thought sweeping reforms of Southern institutions necessary for eradicating Southern racial prejudice, to force Southern whites to accept blacks as equals. Until that day, just government could not be based on the consent of the white majority but only on the freedmen and those few loyal, trustworthy people who had remained faithful to the Union during the war.

In contrast, moderate Republicans opposed the temporary suspension of white citizens' rights in the South. They felt that a genuine change of heart could not be achieved by coercion; affirmations of loyalty under such circumstances were worthless and would simply mask bitter resentment and the hostility of a populace preparing for the day when the tables would be turned. A major leader of the moderates, Congressman John A. Bingham (R-OH), thought the majority of local whites had to be treated as equals, as fellow citizens, as deserving of a share in political rule provided they accepted responsibility to protect the civil rights of blacks as well as whites. Exceptions would have to be made for those who, by abandoning their office under the United States to join the rebellion, had blatantly shown their contempt for the US Constitution. Nevertheless, moderate Republicans favored the immediate application as far as practical of the principles of equality and consent, of treating Southern whites as still possessed of the right of self-government. They were convinced of the need for white support in the South if the new Republican free-state governments were to survive.

Each Republican faction thought the other's approach inimical to the common cause. Moderates feared that radical Republican policy risked transforming the victors into despots and rendering the vanquished even more fiercely resolved to resist Reconstruction. Radical Republicans believed the moderates underestimated the extent of disloyalty and prejudice in the South; they feared that the moderates would allow disloyal, unreconstructed, would-be masters to rule the Southern states.

Each position contained elements essential for successful Reconstruction. The radicals brought to the table a passionate and unyielding concern for the protection of the rights of blacks and white loyalists who had risked all for the Union cause. Moderates knew that the long-term safety of blacks and white Union loyalists depended ultimately on attracting widespread white Southern support. Any coherent Reconstruction policy had to incorporate elements of each approach. For Reconstruction to succeed, dissent among those Lincoln called "the friends of freedom" had to be overcome and transcended.[6] This is what Lincoln attempted to do in reorganizing Louisiana.

## LINCOLN'S RECONSTRUCTION STATESMANSHIP AND THE TWO REPUBLICAN POSITIONS

President Lincoln concentrated on building a political community enjoying sufficient white support to reduce the need for force but tolerate its use as necessary for rights protection. The key was building such a foundation—something of which neither the moderate nor the radical Republicans spoke—for free-state governments that both attracted white consent (the moderates' goal) and protected black rights (the radicals' aim). Lincoln's solution at the outset was limited black suffrage. His approach addressed both moderate and radical Republican concerns but transcended them by avoiding the weaknesses of each.

Quickly finding Louisiana's radical Republican leader, Thomas J. Durant,

impossible to work with because of his idealistic demand for a total reorienta-
tion of society—ridding it of all its evils, not just slavery—the president worked
through the moderate Republican general, Nathaniel P. Banks, commander of
the Department of the Gulf. The president backed the general's plan to avoid
holding a constitutional convention that would air every issue under the sun
before first electing state officers. For the understanding in holding such an
election was that slavery was already abolished by decree, thus not antagonizing Louisianans' sensibilities by forcing them to vote against an institution they
knew was dead. Such prudence was typical of moderate Republicans.

With the general's backing, a moderate Republican, Michael J. Hahn, was
elected governor on March 4, 1864, and an election of delegates to a state constitutional convention was scheduled for later in the month. Their task was
to build a larger basis of consent to Reconstruction in the state. Therefore,
Lincoln reacted positively to a request from the New Orleans freeborn black
community, containing many well-educated professionals, with a "suggestion"
to Governor Hahn for his private consideration:

Now you are about to have a Convention, which, among other things, will probably
define the elective franchise. I barely suggest for your private consideration whether
some of the colored people be let in—as, for instance, the very intelligent and especially
those who have fought gallantly in our ranks. They would probably help, in some trying
time to come, to keep the jewel of liberty in the family of freedom.[7]

The president saw such meritorious blacks as most likely to be of service to
the free state. That Lincoln suggested including meritorious blacks reflected
his belief that mere accommodation of Southern feelings was not enough and
that a political constituency had to be built to defend "the jewel of liberty," to
fulfill the responsibilities of the government for rights protection. To add these
freeborn blacks to the mix of political elements in Louisiana would advance
the cause of freedom. They would help counterbalance planter influence.

Pursuant to Lincoln's urging, Banks and Hahn ensured that the state Constitutional Convention met the needs of a majority of whites as well as advanced the status of blacks. The objective was shaping a political community
likely to support a new free-state government created by the new state Constitution. Therefore, none of the delegates to the state Constitutional Convention
was of the old slaveholding regime.[8] The majority represented white farmers
who favored the abolition of slavery. "'The emancipation of Africans,' concluded a delegate from Rapides, 'will prove to be . . . the true liberation and
emancipation of the poor white laboring classes of the South.'"[9] The new state

Constitution abolished slavery, repudiated the rebel debt, and reduced the political power of the wealthy white planters in the new state legislature.[10] Blacks and whites were declared equal before the law.[11]

Lincoln understood that prudence dictated limits on how far equal rights could be pressed *at that time*. To lay the groundwork for further advance in the future was sufficient. Although the delegates favored emancipation, they did not accept blacks as their equals. Banks and Hahn successfully pressed them to authorize the legislature with power in the future to "pass laws extending the suffrage to such other persons, citizens of the United States, as by military service, by taxation to support the government, or by intellectual fitness, may be entitled thereto."[12] The concession accommodated the interests of the local white moderates by postponing the extension of the franchise and, when it was granted, limiting it by criteria most likely to prove acceptable to whites. To have asked for more risked uniting Louisiana's white moderates with its white conservatives against the new state Constitution. The president was pleased. He proudly described the new charter as an excellent new constitution—"better for the poor black man than we have in Illinois."[13]

How much Lincoln's approach was different from that of the radical Republicans in Congress was evident from their reaction to the new free-state Constitution. It did not please them. They declared that General Banks was the real founder of the new government, which only 10 percent, not a majority, of white Louisianans had participated in establishing. In effect, they wanted to overcome white prejudice against blacks by a fait accompli. Therefore, they came up with a plan of their own.

Passed July 4, 1864, the Wade-Davis bill provided that as soon as a majority of the white males swore allegiance to the Constitution of the United States, procedures would be set in motion for the adoption of a new state constitution that proscribed all ex-Confederate officials and soldiers from voting and holding public office, abolished slavery, and repudiated Confederate debt. Only those who could swear the ironclad oath—those who had not aided the rebellion in any way, shape, or form—would be eligible to vote for delegates to the Constitutional Convention and later vote to ratify the charter after it was drafted. Because it short-circuited the political work needed to expand white support for a free-state government that provided for the eventual acceptance of enfranchisement, at least of qualified blacks, the Wade-Davis bill reflected the radical Republican disregard for consent. It failed to address the problem that had troubled Lincoln from the beginning—how to win over a majority to support a loyal government.[14] The Wade-Davis bill practically guaranteed that no government that enjoyed the consent of the governed would be formed by these procedures. A Wade-Davis government would be an outcast in a hostile political environment.

Lincoln pocket vetoed the Wade-Davis bill and proclaimed his own Reconstruction policy on July 8, 1864. He would not abandon the approach he had used in Louisiana. He would not neglect the element of white consent. Declaring that he was "unprepared, by a formal approval of this Bill, to be inflexibly committed to any single plan of restoration,"[15] he would not abandon constructive efforts to build a political force that would reconcile ex-rebels to rejoining the Union on the North's terms. The bill did not provide any incentive for the majority of white Southerners to do so. The radical Republicans had proposed a measure that precluded working with the majority of local whites but instead antagonized them.

Realizing that Lincoln was in a stronger position after winning reelection November 8, 1864, radical Republicans offered a compromise bill on December 15, 1864, that included the recognition of Louisiana, the procedures of Wade-Davis, and a solution to the problem of Wade-Davis—getting Reconstruction started—by enrolling "all male citizens" as voters.[16] However, because this allowed universal black male enfranchisement, the bill provided nothing to weaken prevailing white prejudice against blacks voting.

Though pleased with the measure, Lincoln told General Banks and Postmaster Blair that he liked it "with the exception of one or two things which he thought might conceal a feature which might be objectionable to some"—that all black men without qualification were to be made jurors and voters under the temporary governments.[17] Lincoln thought that mandating universal male suffrage at the outset would inflame the race issue. It would risk losing the support he wanted for the new government from Louisiana whites. Lincoln believed the surest practical means to achieve universal male suffrage that included black men was, paradoxically, to start only with the best qualified.[18] The new state government would then have to work to build support for extending the franchise.

Nor would that task be an easy one. White prejudice at the time was so extensive and so virulent that to attempt to oppose it by extending the franchise to all men immediately would create terrible backlash. Three factors made racial hatred so intense then in comparison to racism today: the more widespread publicly accepted conviction that blacks were inferior, anger that 180,000 blacks had fought for the South's defeat, and contempt toward them for having submitted to slavery. Yet there was a critical weakness of the moderate Republican position; they might not be able to convince local whites to accept the bargain offered—to wield political power in exchange for protecting the rights of the qualified. It was this weakness Lincoln addressed in his last public address, after radical Republicans filibustered the bill granting recognition to Louisiana so that it never came up for a vote in late February 1865.

On April 11, 1865, the president called for congressional recognition of Louisiana. His argument not only included radical and moderate Republican objectives but also transcended the views of each with an elaboration of how decent free-state government would have to work to achieve a successful Reconstruction. With congressional recognition, he declared, "We encourage the hearts, and nerve the arms of the 12,000 [Louisiana voters swearing allegiance to the Union] to adhere to their work, and argue for it, and proselyte for it, and fight for it, and feed it, and grow it, and ripen it to a complete success. The colored man too, in seeing all united for him, is inspired with vigilance, and energy, and daring, to the same end."[19] Here in compact form is much of Lincoln's thought about how a "tangible nucleus" of activists could act to make the new government a success. They would argue for it, proselytize for it, and fight for it, and by so doing they would gain more converts. The measures taken would be crucial for winning over new supporters. If the measures were good, they would feed the government and cause it to grow in public acceptance, the equivalent of being ripened to a complete success. Its actions and its laws would create a political dynamic that attracted adherents and reduced opposition. A Southern state government that could help resolve issues that affected the citizens generally, such as the federal cotton tax, tariffs on imported goods, greater economic diversification, internal improvements, economic growth, and financial and currency stability would attract votes.[20] It would pit whites' prejudices against their interests. Lincoln calculated that such a government would be least likely to come under siege by white opposition.

Lincoln's idea that progress on issues of common interest had the potential to secure adherents to the government was confirmed as described below by the case of Florida under Governor Ossian Bingley Hart,[21] the most successful Reconstruction governor of all. As Lincoln understood and Hart demonstrated, political dynamism fueled by the contagious enthusiasm that comes from passing good laws would attract support. But would twelve thousand white Louisianans unite for the black people? Yes, they would support those who could contribute to the success of the new government. Also, by conditioning black suffrage on merit, Lincoln reduced the prospect of black political domination. Blacks too would see this new regime as their best hope for advancement, see that their interests and rights depended upon its acceptance, and consequently be energized to seek a fuller franchise in the future.

Lincoln's approach thus incorporated both moderate and radical views. He understood that the radical Republican fixation on disloyalty and the use of force could not be the governing principle for a successful Republican Reconstruction policy. He understood that a free-state government that commanded the popular support of the people and had the political strength to enforce rights protection against bigoted whites was necessary for success. Lincoln also understood that moderate Republicanism would fail if it did not provide effective law enforcement. Accordingly, Lincoln did not want to leave the embryonic free-state governments in isolation. He understood that additional security, judicial and military, needed to remain close at hand. The president thus wanted all the major departments of the federal government to reestablish themselves within the Southern states, especially the War Department and the Office of the Attorney General. Federal forces had to make sure that everything "like domestic violence or insurrection should be suppressed; but that public authorities and private citizens should remain unmolested if not found in actual hostility to the Government of the Union."[22] In contrast to the moderate Republicans, Lincoln was prepared to use force if the effort to cultivate a loyal state government was in danger of being overwhelmed by hostile whites.[23]

Although Lincoln's Reconstruction work resolved the conflict between the moderate and radical Republicans by addressing the concerns of both, President Andrew Johnson's pro-South bias and racial prejudice inflamed the conflict between the two groups of Republicans. His poor leadership and poor ideas meant that Congress, by default, would have to take on the unenviable task of reintroducing American founding ideals to the people of the South. This responsibility brought on further conflict between the moderate and radical factions.

## DRAFTING THE FOURTEENTH AMENDMENT

After Johnson became president, the centerpiece of moderate Republican policy was the joint resolution drafted in the spring of 1866, which two years later was ratified as the Fourteenth Amendment. Though prudent in advocating a policy that sought the consent of Southern whites in exchange for protection of the rights of all, the moderate Republicans did not have much leverage to ensure that Southern whites kept their side of the bargain. Nor did they have much notion of how to build a constituency that would support a moderate Republican regime, so they left a good deal of leeway for leaders in the defeated states to devise moderate regimes on their own. However, without the progressive government Lincoln envisaged, these governments did not have popular support for the use of force against offending whites. These strengths and weaknesses of the moderate approach are apparent in an analysis of the arguments moderate Republicans made when drafting the key sections of the amendment. Though justly famous as a bulwark of rights protection for future generations, it was weak as a Reconstruction measure, considering the widespread hostility of Southern whites to Reconstruction. That the framers of the amendment were aware of how the victory on the battlefield was at risk of being lost is evident from the findings in the report of the Joint Committee on Reconstruction. Elections in the South for state officers and members of Congress "had resulted, almost everywhere in the defeat of candidates who had been true to the Union." Instead, "notorious and unpardoned rebels" had been elected—"men who could not take the prescribed oath of office, and who made no secret of their hostility to the government and the people of the United States."[24]

Despite their awareness of conditions in the South, the moderate Republicans insisted on treating all but a few of the rebels as equals. A guiding rule for them was captured by the immensely influential Swiss diplomat Emer de Vattel's admonition, "If the conquered country is really to be subject to the conqueror as its lawful sovereign, he must rule it according to the ends for which civil government has been established."[25] They vested Southern whites in the defeated states with the initial responsibility for protecting the privileges and immunities of citizens of the United States and providing all persons within their jurisdiction due process and equal protection of the law. Radical Republicans did not disagree that the states should be held responsible for rights protection and providing due process and equal protection. However, they did not believe the states would do so without sweeping economic, political, and social reforms, during which time the US Constitution and its Bill of Rights, they argued, would need to be suspended in those states.

The weakness of the moderates' policy is reflected in the legislative history, in the drafting of the provisions of the amendment dealing with the political consequences for representation in the US House of Representatives (Section 2), in punishment (Section 3), and in securing the privileges and immunities of citizens of the United States (Sections 1 and 5).

The most urgent issue before Congress was the unintended effect of the Thirteenth Amendment, rewarding Southern states with increased representation in the US House of Representatives because each black was now counted as a whole person rather than three-fifths of a person. This would have given the former Confederate states thirteen representatives in addition to the nineteen they already had for their black residents. If nothing were done, the leader of the radical Republicans in the House, Congressman Stevens (R-PA), said, the South's new total, counting the fifty-one for their white residents, would be eighty-three Democrats, which, when combined with Democratic representatives elected in the North would give them a majority in Congress and in the Electoral College. "They will then at the very first election," he predicted, "take possession of the White House and Halls of Congress."[26] Stevens proposed a harsh all-or-nothing measure that would cut off any additional representation a state could receive as long as it denied the franchise to anyone on the basis of race or color. If a state did so, all persons of such race or color were to be excluded from the basis of representation.[27] He did not believe the South would voluntarily enfranchise blacks. It had to be forced to do so by redistributing property to the freedmen. When blacks became economically independent, they could force whites to treat them as equals. For Stevens the terms of the Declaration of Independence would not be honored unless a reign of force prepared the way.

Senator George H. Williams (R-OR) offered a moderate Republican alternative, close to that of the final version, reducing representation of a state only in the proportion the number of those denied the vote bore to the total number of male voters. The Joint Committee agreed to this on April 25, 1866.[28] With this language, the initiative rested entirely with the Southern states to extend blacks the franchise. This was consistent with the overall moderate Republican approach of presenting the South a bargain: the defeated states could gain greater representation in the US House of Representatives in proportion as they enfranchised freedmen.

However, the undesirable effect of this provision came under attack from another leading moderate, a great admirer of Lincoln, Senator William Stewart (R-NV). His moderate colleagues had gone too far in conciliating Southern whites. He wanted them to take a stronger stand, to avoid solidifying the control of whites over blacks. Moderates had to move in the direction Lincoln had taken—building a constituency that would prevent racists from entrenching themselves in power. Far from addressing the problem of race, he thought the moderate Williams's version would exacerbate racial discrimination. Racial prejudice was so virulent in the South that native whites would never take advantage of such a slight incentive as Williams proposed. Rather, the measure would strengthen rebel elements. With the ballot firmly under their control, they would have every reason to consolidate control of their state governments.[29] Stewart's remedy was to expand the franchise for all men by imposing impartial standards applicable to all, such as education, property, and moral character.

The second issue of punishment for ex-rebels, who some thought should be proscribed from exercising political power, raised the greatest controversy. The alternatives were disfranchisement, a bar on holding public office, or shunting off punishment into a separate piece of legislation. Although the moderate Republicans made a strong argument against the radical Republican position on disfranchisement, their own language, which became that of the final version—a bar on officeholding—assumed a receptivity in the South not yet cultivated and was not present under the Johnson state governments in 1866. The moderates might have had more success if they had taken the third alternative of shunting off punishment into separate legislation.

Radical Republicans favored excluding for five years all persons who voluntarily aided the late insurrection from the right to vote for representatives in Congress, and for elections for president and vice president of the United States.[30] If the Senate struck this language, Congressman Stevens warned, the House would "be filled with yelling secessionists and hissing copperheads." "Give us the third section," he cried, "or give us nothing." To the members who complained that the provision was too punitive, he demanded, "Too strong for what? Too strong for their stomachs, but not for the people. It is too lenient for my hard heart. Not only to 1870 but to 18070, every rebel who shed the blood of loyal men should be prevented from exercising any power in this Government."[31] Stung by Stevens's criticism that he wanted too quickly to readmit those who had so recently borne arms against the Union, Congressman Martin Thayer (R PA) asked the leader whether he could build "a penitentiary big enough to hold eight million [Southern white] people?" "Yes, sir," Stevens replied, "a penitentiary which is built at the point of the bayonet down below, and if they undertake to come here we will shoot them. That is the way to take care of these people."[32]

Moderate Republicans feared that disfranchisement would make Southern whites less inclined to cooperate in Reconstruction. They wanted the language dropped. They wanted all white men to vote in forming the new state governments. Because the formerly rebellious states were still ruled by Johnson appointees, it seemed premature to expect good results from all white men voting. Senator Stewart's main concern was that the people in the Southern states be left as free as possible to establish governments of their own choosing. According to him, there were only two choices for dealing with the dangers that threatened the peace and prosperity of the country—disfranchisement of the rebels by military power or amnesty and suffrage for the rebels. Only the latter was consistent with the grand principles upon which the United States was founded. The senator warned that the radicals' punitive provision would foster minority governments that could only be sustained by the bayonet.

Considering the failure in framing the provision on representation to enfranchise blacks and now the proposed disfranchisement of so many whites, he said, "instead of liberating four million blacks, it will enslave eight million whites."[33] Rule by a minority of loyal whites could only survive with military backing.[34] No good would follow from Stevens's punitive measure. "We do not wish to punish the South," for it has "already been sufficiently scourged and annihilated." Either we give rebels the ballot "or they must be driven out of the country, for if we retain them here as disfranchised enemies, the extraordinary powers necessarily devolved upon the few whom you trust with political rights must make them tyrants." No matter how loyal that minority government ruling over a disfranchised majority, anarchy and discord would be the inevitable result.[35]

As an alternative to disfranchisement, moderate Republicans preferred a bar on officeholding. As the amendment read, only a limited number of rebels were barred from holding office—those public officials, state or federal, civil or military, who had sworn an oath to uphold the Constitution of the United States—and then engaged in rebellion. Consistent with the moderate Republican intention that Southern whites be encouraged to participate in the work of Reconstruction, this was the extent to which the core—the leadership of the South during the war—was to be proscribed from political power. The much greater number who had fought for or aided the rebellion was not affected. Because they were allowed to vote, the provision went part of the way toward meeting Senator Stewart's bold proposal for general amnesty, although the test oath would still bar them from federal office.[36] Thus the punishment section of the joint resolution (Section 3) was not primarily a security measure for black and white loyalists in the South. It was a measure of individual justice, to punish not all those who had fought against the Union but only those who, in fighting against the Union, violated their oaths as federal or state officeholders to support the Constitution. It was an attempt to narrow the punishment for rebellion to an identifiable class of leaders, and even this punishment could be lifted for individuals by a two-thirds vote in Congress.[37] Because Congress avoided blanket punishment of the South, the punitive provision was a victory of sorts for the moderate Republicans. Far from being a poison pill, the provision was more of an olive branch extended to Southern whites.

Here the commitment of the moderates to the ideals of the Declaration of Independence appeared most divorced from reality. Though their emphasis on consent was wise because Reconstruction could not succeed without it, to insist on it at that time was premature. It had to be cultivated. Moderate Republicans' fear of the radical Republican alternative of disfranchisement and despotic rule in the South drew them to the opposite extreme, to embrace practically full enfranchisement for Southern whites with the few exceptions noted. Because even this provision antagonized the South, the moderates might have been better advised to heed Bingham's ideas of leaving out a punishment section of the amendment and instead proposing it as an act of ordinary legislation. The most important priority was to get the South to commit to rights protection as provided in Sections 1 and 5 and then count on the real work of Reconstruction—building the political foundation for rights protection to begin.

Unlike Lincoln, the moderates had not thought about an intermediate stage between vesting the Southern states with the initial responsibility for protecting rights and the stark alternative, if they did not, of congressional enforcement. That intermediate stage would have been the work of statesmen, building free-state governments that would actually protect the rights of blacks and white Union loyalists. This gap in moderate Republican thinking is all the more surprising because of their awareness of the extent of disloyalty in the South. Bingham, for example, pointed to a "conspiracy extending through every State late in insurrection . . . among those returning rebels . . . to take possession of the legislative power of this country, and accomplish by corrupt legislation what they failed to accomplish by arms."[38]

As the father of both Sections 1 and 5, for securing rights protection, Bingham incidentally made a strong case for the amendment enabling the Constitution to be implemented as originally intended.[39] The conditions the South had to meet—protecting the rights of its citizens—were spelled out in Section 1 of the joint resolution, and the consequences for violating these conditions were specified in Section 5. There was little disagreement between the moderate and radical Republicans over the language of these two sections. They were the primary safeguards for blacks and white Union loyalists. Moderate Republican Bingham's language let Southern whites wield only so much political power as was considered safe. At the heart of these two sections is a bargain that the states would continue to bear primary responsibility for rights protection. Only if they denied or abridged the rights of citizens or due process and equal protection for all persons within their jurisdiction would Congress, per Section 5, enforce these protections with "appropriate legislation." Direct federal enforcement without allowing the states to act as first responders was not consistent with moderate Republican policy. It would reduce the states to a condition of dependency.

Because ex-rebels dominated many of President Johnson's state governments, it came as no surprise that ten of the former rebel states over the fall and winter of 1866–1867 refused to ratify the Fourteenth Amendment.[40] Southern leaders were particularly incensed over the punitive Section 3 barring some of their favorites from public office. For example, a former Whig turned Democrat, Governor Jonathan Worth of North Carolina, found the proscriptive section of the amendment intolerable: "No Southern State, where the people are free to vote, will adopt it. If we are to be degraded we will retain some self-esteem by not making it self-abasement."[41] Congress now had to devise a new framework dealing directly with the political forces in the defeated states.

## THE CONGRESSIONAL RECONSTRUCTION ACT (CRA)

Because ten of the Southern states had rejected the Fourteenth Amendment by early 1867, Congress had to make a new start on Reconstruction that would have some chance of overcoming Southern resistance.[42] New constitutional conventions had to meet, and new governments had to be established. The moderates now had to contend with newly energized radicals in drafting legislation for dealing with the South. Because the radical Republicans were determined that the Southern aristocracy had to be removed from political power and have its economic power destroyed, and that blacks and their white allies gain the upper hand politically, they scorned the halfway measures advanced by the moderates. Although the latter saw disaster in the radical Republican plans, they in their weakness failed to rally the votes necessary to secure a Reconstruction act that would have provided a better chance for the survival of the new governments. The result was the Congressional Reconstruction Act (CRA), which compounded the weaknesses of both moderate and radical Republicans, a recipe for factionalism in the Southern states and subsequent hundred years of failure.

The radicals proposed a substitute for the Fourteenth Amendment that would provide the security required. Legal governments could be formed only after all disloyal citizens had been purged from political power. Such persons would be allowed neither to vote nor hold office until five years after they had filed their intention to be restored to citizenship and swear allegiance to the United States.[43] Even more radical, Congressman Shellabarger (R-OH) believed the disloyal deserved a real "stamp of detestation," to be permanently disabled from either voting or holding political office. Traitors included those who had engaged in guerrilla warfare and those who wrote in support of the rebellion.

All should forfeit their citizenship.[44] All should be thrust from the protection of the Constitution. Stevens readily accepted Shellabarger's amendment.

Moderates feared that despotism would result from the radicals' policy. They were quick to denounce treating Southerners as conquered subjects. Their emphasis was on the rights of citizens, not on how to establish a political foundation for governments that would protect those rights. Bingham said that the radicals' position offended Americans' deepest beliefs and would introduce greater lawlessness into the lives of Southern people. The radicals would remove the protections provided by the Fourteenth Amendment. They would withhold the administration of justice and effective enforcement of the law by suspending any obligation of the federal government to the citizens of the defeated states. The people in the South remained US citizens, subject to the direct authority of the central government and enjoying complete protection of their rights without respect to race, color, or previous condition of servitude in such tribunals as Congress saw fit to establish or by recognizing the tribunals already established.[45] If Shellabarger's measure became law, Congressman William E. Dodge (R-NY) claimed, nearly the entire white population of the South would be degraded and the blacks elevated above them, to the injury of both races.[46]

The burden was on the moderate Republicans to advance an alternative to Stevens's proposal. They proposed a military bill that later became the CRA. It declared the Johnson state governments merely pretended governments under the control of unrepentant leaders of the rebellion who could "afford no adequate protection for life or property but countenance and encourage lawlessness and crime." To restore peace and good order until loyal republican governments could be established, the ten Southern states were to be divided into five military districts. Each was to be placed under a military commander whose duty it was to provide protection to all peaceable and law-abiding persons, to suppress violence, and to have offenders tried in civil courts or in military tribunals, as he so chose.[47] The weakness of the bill lay in handing the initiative to the radical Republicans.

The radicals liked the bill. They saw it as possibly inaugurating open-ended military occupation for long enough that truly radical economic, political, and social reforms could be effected. When presented the radical Republican handiwork of the House, a pure open-ended military bill with no escape, the moderate Republican Senate leader, John Sherman (R-OH), erupted: "I will not," he declared, "supersede one form of oligarchy in which the blacks were slaves by another in which the whites are disfranchised outcasts. Let us introduce no such horrid deformity into the American Union." We "want neither black nor white oligarchies."[48] Then the moderates gave up their strongest safeguard against such "horrid deformity."

Determined that the radical Republicans not turn the military bill into a means of tyrannizing the South, the moderate Republicans felt they had to amend the bill to give the people in the Southern states an "escape road," a choice for coming out from under military control by establishing governments that conformed to the Fourteenth Amendment. To prevent the radical Republicans from closing off such an escape, they gave up their strongest card for attracting Southern white consent. They abandoned limited suffrage for black men in favor of universal male suffrage.

Now the radical Republicans had the advantage of insisting on this as a condition for "escape." Though moderate Senator Sherman (R-OH) tried to hold the line at limited suffrage for blacks, the radical Republicans forced him in caucus to accept universal male suffrage. Now the bill provided for that, with exceptions for those who had participated in the rebellion to be determined by the states.[49]

Even with this concession, most radicals refused to support legislation with an "escape road" because they feared that the governments coming out from under military rule would still be dominated by the disloyal. They imposed additional conditions on the establishment of free-state governments by settling on a strategy for preventing the rise of moderate republicanism in the South.[50] They recruited Democrats in the House more than willing to defeat the moderate version of the military bill, for the more radical the measure, the more likely the Republicans would fail to enact any law and leave the responsibility of Reconstruction to the South.[51] With the aid of Democratic votes, the radicals imposed conditions for the formation of these governments that made it less likely these states would be ruled by the disloyal. They mandated disfranchisement and authorized additional restrictions to be imposed at the discretion of the state governments.[52] In recruiting the Democrats to help defeat the moderate Republican version of the military bill, the radicals would not accept free-state governments based on the consent of the governed, both black and white. The moderates were defeated by a group of Republicans who did not believe in any role for a significant number of whites in the states affected. Consequently, the chances for the exercise of Reconstruction statesmanship were slim.

The issue now was whether those favored by the conditions set in these congressional acts—blacks and white loyalists—would find it possible to establish state governments that had a chance of surviving. The prospects were not good. Even if they were to accept the provisions of the proposed constitutional amendment, Southern whites had little hope of being able to share in the control of their own governments or to work constructively with the new rulers. The electorates in most of the Southern states would turn out to be majority black.[53] Because of the proscriptions on Southern whites qualified to handle political responsibilities, the CRA cleared the way for carpetbaggers to gain election to public offices in the South. It opened up the prospect of bitter factional struggles between the moderate Republicans in the states attempting to find a middle ground with local whites and the radical Republicans intent on ruling independently of local majority white consent. Southern Democrats were not encouraged to compromise when such divisions between Republicans afforded opportunities for getting rid of Republican governments altogether.

## RECONSTRUCTION IN THE DEFEATED STATES

The effect of the CRA was to weaken the moderates and strengthen the radicals in the affected states. Reconstruction in all eleven defeated states was adversely affected with one exception, Florida. The harm inflicted by the CRA took three different forms: (1) mistaken confidence that a Republican state government could survive without significant white support (Georgia, Mississippi, North Carolina); (2) weakened bargaining power of moderate Republican governors trying to gain the cooperation of moderate Democrats (Alabama, South Carolina, Tennessee); and (3) the imprudent interventions by President Grant on behalf of radicals in lieu of moderate Republican governors where the latter had a greater chance of surviving (Louisiana, Texas).[54]

Mississippi's failed Reconstruction typified the first category, the mistaken confidence of the radical Republican governor. Governor Adelbert Ames thought his administration could survive, especially after Grant's two-to-one victory in 1872, without addressing the legitimate concerns of Mississippi's white taxpayers. Ames's single-minded mission in life was to relieve the hardships of blacks.[55] To help alleviate the plight of formerly enslaved people, Ames increased property taxes so much that "many planters and farmers saw their land fall to the sheriff's hammer."[56] The critical issue was whether moderate Democrats would prevail over racist thugs ("White Liners") in getting rid of Republican rule. In defiance of the white taxpayers in Warren County, Ames ordered their black tax collector, forced out of office for failing to give a new bond after his old securities proved worthless, to round up a posse to take back his office. The result was a race riot in which three hundred blacks and two whites were killed. Because no one was ever held accountable for the slaughter, the White Liners felt vindicated. They concluded that if the level of violence was kept below the level of an armed insurrection that would trigger a real show of federal force, the state government could be overthrown. Thus, Ames's determination to promote black interests and his indifference to the legitimate concerns of whites brought on blacks' worst nightmare—a state under the control of the White Liners.[57]

Alabama's failed Reconstruction typified the second category of problems, weakened leverage of moderate Republicans attempting to balance radical demands and at the same time attract moderate Democratic support. There the adverse impact of the CRA was evident in the lack of bargaining power two moderate Republican governors had in attempting to achieve political balance and preventing the state from being "redeemed" by the Democrats. Governor William H. Smith (1868–1870) knew that the Republican Party could not survive if its primary constituency was only blacks and carpetbaggers. To gain more white support, Governor Smith failed to take effective measures to protect blacks from Klan attacks. To defeat the influence of the carpetbaggers, he sought votes of white farmers who had no use for the Negro. By catering to the prejudices of the white majority and simultaneously trying to appease the radicals by allowing repeat voting to swell the Republican vote, the governor energized the extremes in both parties. He unintentionally paved the way for the destruction of the Republican Party in the state. Republicans had chosen appeasement of the prejudiced rather than a vigorous stand against the violence of the Klan. Their candidate in a subsequent election, David P. Lewis, ran on a platform that sloughed off responsibility for enforcing civil rights to the federal government, which handed the hard-liners a strategy for victory. If the Republicans were so fearful of antagonizing prejudiced Alabamans that they abandoned the black vote, then the Democrats could win by making race the issue in the 1874 campaign, which they did and won.

Particularly unfortunate were the cases of failed Reconstruction in the third category, where strong moderate leaders overcame the radical Republican influence of the CRA and might have established successful Republican governments. An adviser to Congress during the drafting of the CRA, President Grant adhered for the most part to radical Republican policy and opposed good moderate leaders. He interfered to engineer the downfall of such leaders, for example, in Louisiana.[58] Committed to Reconstruction, Louisiana's two extraordinary Republican leaders were undermined by President Grant. Governor Henry C. Warmoth, the most skilled politician in the state, and the statesmanlike African American leader Pinckney Benton Stewart Pinchback worked so well together that they were the greatest hope for Republican government in Louisiana. Pinchback advised Warmoth on how to preserve their alliance. In an attempt to balance the interests of white as well as black Louisianans, Governor Warmoth had not aggressively advanced the cause of blacks. Yet, because Pinchback believed Warmoth could keep the Republican Party in power, the governor retained the support of the most powerful black leader in the state.

Because of his decision to veto a strong public accommodations bill and other failures to advance the cause of Negroes in the state, Warmoth incurred attack from the federal employees in the New Orleans Customs House, the self-declared champions of black people, who, with few exceptions, were radical Republicans.[59] Because they had Grant's ear, they convinced him that Warmoth had to go. At the insistence of the customs house radicals, the administration managed to steal the 1872 gubernatorial election for customs house radical William Pitt Kellogg. He survived the hatred of local whites and stayed in office only because of federal bayonets. So enraged was Warmoth with Grant's intervention that he left the Republican Party for the Liberal Republican Party. His departure destroyed Louisiana's best chance for successful Reconstruction. Even Grant recognized his error. Come the 1876 election, he simply acquiesced to the prospect that a Democrat would win and thought that best for the state.[60]

The only success of Reconstruction was in Florida, where a shrewd statesman overcame the bias of the CRA to accomplish more in his short fifteen months in office than Lincoln did in Louisiana. When the radical Republicans seized control of the state Constitutional Convention in 1868, other Republicans took alarm and sent a private train to pick up moderate Republican leader Hart in Jacksonville for help in writing a moderate alternative charter.[61] He secured the military's recommendation to Congress to adopt his charter instead of the radical Republican one.

Hart succeeded because he put together the coalition for which Lincoln strove. He met the fear of white Floridians of blacks dominating the state government with a deft compromise in drafting the moderate state Constitution—reenfranchisement of whites in exchange for enfranchisement of blacks. However, to allay white fears of a Negro-dominated legislature, Hart's Constitution capped legislative apportionment for the most populous districts at four representatives.[62] The extensive appointment power vested in the governor also operated as a discretionary check on Negro officeholding.[63] The Hart Constitution reduced the ability of radical Republicans to operate outside the system and had the advantage of forcing ambitious blacks to become skillful players within the system. To deny radicals power as a bloc guaranteed a bi-racial framework within which moderate blacks could wield political power without being viewed as threatening Negro domination. The compromise did not eliminate black influence but did check radical influence. It set the stage for blacks willing to work within the framework of the state Republican Party to exercise much greater influence than they could have hoped for shouting radical demands from the sidelines. Their fears assuaged by the Hart Constitution's checks on black power, whites also supported this arrangement. Florida's black citizens were happy with Hart's Lincolnesque arrangement, and their hopes proved justified. After four years of factional warfare, which did nothing for blacks and prevented the state from being placed on a firm financial foundation, blacks were ready to act on their own judgment of what was in their interest and that of the state. They were the decisive voice in securing Hart's nomination and election as governor of Florida in 1872.

After taking office, Hart secured a strong civil rights measure with the help of Senate Democrats who had been wartime loyalists. In Hamiltonian fashion, he placed the state's credit on a sound basis with the issuance of thirty-year bonds. By facing down violent Klan opposition, the governor earned the respect of Florida's black citizens and succeeded in altering public opinion in the state, attracting support not only from Republicans dismayed by the spectacle of factional warfare but also from many Democrats who came around to support Hart and his successful administration. Had the CRA been constructed along the lines of Hart's Constitution, there might have been other successful Reconstruction efforts in the Southern states.

## *A COMPARISON OF THE THREE APPROACHES TO RECONSTRUCTION*

It remains to compare the three approaches on their ability to meet the challenge of shaping majorities to embrace rights protection. Measured against such a standard, the radical Republicans came up short. They were the ones most deeply attached to the interests and rights of Negroes, but they lacked the prudence to advance those interests and rights effectively; in fact, just the opposite. Their influence at both the federal and state levels split the party and polarized the extremes between their own faction and that of the hard-line Democrats. Their rigidity and unbounded suspicion of Southern whites undermined moderates of both parties and unintentionally paved the way for extremists to prevail. Their very idealism led to measures that defeated the objective of Reconstruction—mitigating the spirit of mastery in the South.

The moderate Republicans demonstrated greater political judgment in taking a more comprehensive view of the whole: that Southern white support was critical if blacks were to benefit and Reconstruction succeed. Yet with their concession on universal male suffrage to provide an escape from open-ended military occupation, the moderate Republicans weakened the leverage their counterparts in the states had for dealing with the fears of local whites. Furthermore, moderate Republican ambivalence about white supremacy and belief that whites should be in charge and avoid political domination by Negroes, especially in majority-minority states, undercut their bargaining power with moderate Democrats. After having yielded on the issue of qualified suffrage, some moderate Republicans' white supremacism made it more difficult for them to drive a hard bargain for rights protection. There was a fine line between, on the one hand, assuaging fears of local whites with measures that kept whites in control yet genuinely designed to foster the interests and rights of blacks and, on the other hand, determination to keep blacks in a subordinate position. In the best case, in Florida, whites were clearly in charge under the leadership of a benevolent moderate Republican governor who accumulated sufficient political power to ensure that blacks rose within the system.

In comparison with both moderate and radical Republicans, Lincoln knew from his devotion to the principles of the Declaration of Independence and his political experience that these great tenets could not be secured without the consent of the governed, which meant, practically, that black rights could not be secured fully all at once, as the radicals wanted. Like the moderates, he understood that white consent was essential to establishing republican government. He showed how the political forces in a state had to be managed to place racial prejudice—the spirit of mastery—in the course of ultimate extinction. He provided an example in the free-state government of Louisiana of how to construct a regime that addressed the demands of both radical and moderate Republicans, a dynamic government capable of enjoying sufficient white support to tolerate the coercive measures necessary to protect black rights. By identifying their interests with such a government, the freedmen would have had the best practical chance of advancement. By succeeding in improving conditions in lands devastated by the war, this new government would pit the interest of local whites against their prejudice, the best means of placing racial discrimination on the defensive. Conceivably, racial prejudice was too strong for even Lincoln's approach to have worked, but at least he provided a model by means of which practical self-government could overcome a huge barrier to equality for all.

## CONCLUSION

The failure of Reconstruction led to the abandonment of establishing free-state governments providing rights protection. Indeed, the failure of Reconstruction gave rise to the argument that the *federal* government had no business even trying to protect the rights of citizens in the Southern states, even forcing state governments to do so. A group calling itself the Liberal Republican Party argued that the attempt by the federal government to enforce civil rights, for example, by the Ku Klux Klan Act of 1871, threatened the vitality of the states. A former moderate, Senator Lyman Trumbull (R-IL), argued that acting on the authority of the Fourteenth Amendment to protect black rights in the South would annihilate the states.[64] Another former moderate, Senator Schurz (R-MO), proposed benign neglect of black rights as a public health measure, for "the rights and liberties of the whole American people [were] of still higher importance than the interests of those in the South whose dangers and sufferings appeal so strongly to our sympathy."[65] And the standard-bearer of the liberal Republican Party, Horace Greeley, called upon Americans to "clasp hands across the bloody chasm" and put the war and Reconstruction and, by implication, the civil rights of blacks behind them. Although the legal promise of equality from the founding era was formally fulfilled by the Reconstruction amendments, the reality of enforcing them, which required public support, would take a century to catch up.

For example, the language of the Fifteenth Amendment, ratified in February 1870, accommodated the intense opposition to black suffrage at the time. Although the radical Republicans had hoped to capitalize on their success of imposing universal male suffrage on the defeated South in the CRA three years before, they did not succeed in imposing it nationwide. The disastrous state elections of 1867, in which key Republican governors in the North went down to defeat over the issue of Negro suffrage, counseled prudence. Republicans in Congress turned to the moderates for the proposed amendment, embracing impartial, not universal, suffrage. Though the text extended the franchise to black men in the North and secured the vote of Negroes in the South, it prohibited denial of the vote based only on race, color, or previous condition of servitude. It did not bar denial of the vote based on sex, education, or property.

The failures in self-government to institutionalize full black equality during the Reconstruction era reveal the outcome of the Civil War neither as a radical break from nor the complete fulfillment of the principles of 1776. Although the Reconstruction amendments were continuous with the principles of 1776, and the abolition of slavery was a huge improvement in racial equality, the political follow-through was lacking. Therefore, Reconstruction only formally, and not in actual practice, embodied the principles of 1776.

Only when public opinion shifted after World War II did a new civil rights era begin. However, despite tremendous advances in civil rights enforcement, a conflict that bore distinct similarities to that between radical and moderate Republicans of Reconstruction reappeared. For example, one of the most remarkable achievements of the twentieth century, the Civil Rights Act of 1964, guaranteeing equality of opportunity without regard to race, color, religion, sex, or national origin, passed only because of assurances that it prohibited racial balancing and quotas. However, a year later, President Lyndon B. Johnson declared that such equal opportunity was not fair, that we had to move beyond it to equality of result.[66] The federal government then pursued equal results via quotas in many areas of education, employment, and business. Such unresolved conflicts seem to require something beyond the ordinary capabilities of a democratic people. The major ones require statesmanship that rises above the opposing sides of the conflict; in this case, the desire of the radicals to invoke the power of the state to achieve equality of result and that of the moderates insisting on equality of opportunity to preserve individual responsibility. As of yet, no such statesman has come forth to tap the better angels of our nature, to address the concerns of these present-day radicals and moderates with a dynamic initiative that energizes blacks and whites to join in common cause for the good of the country.

## NOTES

Epigraph: *The Collected Works of Abraham Lincoln,* vol. 2, ed. Roy P. Basler (New Brunswick, NJ: Rutgers University Press, 1953), 532.

1. Michael Les Benedict, *A Compromise of Principle: Congressional Republicans and Reconstruction, 1863–1869* (New York: Norton, 1974), 243; Les Benedict, *Preserving the Constitution: Essays on Politics and the Constitution in the Reconstruction Era* (New York: Fordham University Press, 2006), 107; William R. Brock, *An American Crisis: Congress and Reconstruction, 1865–1867* (New York: Harper and Row, 1963), 203, 206; Douglas R. Egerton, *The Wars of Reconstruction: The Brief Violent History of America's Most Progressive Era* (New York: Bloomberg, 2014), 346–347; Eric Foner, *Reconstruction: America's Unfinished Revolution, 1863–1867* (New York: Harper and Row, 1988),

160–161, 443; William Gillette, *Retreat from Reconstruction, 1869–1879* (Baton Rouge: Louisiana State University Press, 1979), 184; Larry G. Kincaid, "The Legislative Origins of the Military Reconstruction Act" (PhD diss., Johns Hopkins University, 1968), 271; Michael Perman, *Reunion without Compromise: The South and Reconstruction, 1865–1868* (Cambridge, UK: Cambridge University Press, 1973), 11–12, 347; Brooks D. Simpson, *The Reconstruction Presidents,* 2nd ed. (Lawrence: University Press of Kansas, 2009), 162.

2. Most historians take the side of the Radical Republicans and a few that of the moderates; only one, to my knowledge, LaWanda Cox, sees the necessity of a Reconstruction statesman relying on both force and consent.

3. US House, *Report of the Joint Committee on Reconstruction,* House Report 30, 39th Cong., 1st sess. (1866), xvii.

4. US Senate, 39th Cong., 1st sess., *Senate Executive Document No. 2 (December 9, 1865) on Report of Maj. General Carl Schurz Conditions of the South (States of South Carolina, Georgia, Alabama, Mississippi, and Louisiana), transmitted by President Andrew Johnson,* 18.

5. Kenneth M. Stampp, *The Era of Reconstruction, 1865–1877* (New York: Knopf, 1965), 103.

6. Abraham Lincoln, Last Public Address, April 11, 1865, in *The Collected Works of Abraham Lincoln,* vol. 8, ed. Roy P. Basler (New Brunswick, NJ: Rutgers University Press, 1953), 401.

7. *Collected Works of Abraham Lincoln,* vol. 7, 243.

8. Roger W. Shugg, *Origins of the Class Struggle in Louisiana: A Social History of White Farmers and Laborers during Slavery and After, 1840–1875* (Baton Rouge: Louisiana State University Press, 1968), 203.

9. Ibid., 205.

10. Constitution of Louisiana—1864, in *Federal and State Constitutions,* vol. 3, ed. Francis N. Thorpe (Washington, DC: US Government Printing Office, 1909), 1429, 1444, 1430, respectively.

11. Ibid., 1442.

12. Ibid., 1433.

13. Abraham Lincoln to General Stephen A. Hurlbut, November 14, 1864, in *The Collected Works of Abraham Lincoln,* vol. 8, ed. Roy P. Basler (New Brunswick, NJ: Rutgers University Press, 1953), 107. The Illinois Constitution, to which Lincoln referred, did not give the state legislature authority to extend the suffrage to blacks, prohibited free blacks from settling in the state, and forbade slave owners from bringing enslaved people into the state to set them free. Constitution of Illinois—1848, in *Federal and State Constitutions,* vol. 2, ed. Francis N. Thorpe (Washington, DC: US Government Printing Office, 1909), 1002, 1009.

14. "The question at once is presented in whom [in a reorganized government] this [ruling] power is vested: and the practical matter for decision is how to keep the rebellious population from overwhelming and outvoting the loyal minority." Abraham Lincoln, quoted in *Lincoln and the Civil War in the Diaries and Letters of John Hay,* ed. Tyler Dennett (New York: Dodd, Mead, 1939), 113.

15. Abraham Lincoln, Proclamation Concerning Reconstruction, July 8, 1864, in

*The Collected Works of Abraham Lincoln,* vol. 7, ed. Roy P. Basler (New Brunswick, NJ: Rutgers University Press, 1953), 433.

16. House Resolution 602, 38th Cong., 2nd sess. (December 15, 1864), sec. 7, 8, and 10.

17. Dennett, *Lincoln and the Civil War,* 244–245.

18. Lincoln was ahead of his time in advocating qualified suffrage for blacks. For example, the wording and voting on the Fifteenth Amendment, ratified in 1870, "indicated . . . that property qualifications and literacy tests would not be outlawed." William Gillette, *The Right to Vote: Politics and the Passage of the Fifteenth Amendment* (Baltimore: Johns Hopkins University Press, 1969), 170.

19. *Collected Works of Abraham Lincoln,* vol. 8, 404.

20. The Republicans in Congress had enacted a 2.5 percent tax per pound on cotton, which hurt both the freedmen and former masters. Roger Phillip Leemhuis, "James L. Orr: The Civil War and Reconstruction Years" (PhD diss., University of Wisconsin, 1970), 177. Orr was governor of South Carolina, 1865–1868.

21. See infra, 339–340; Philip B. Lyons, *Statesmanship and Reconstruction: Moderate versus Radical Republicans on Restoring the Union after the Civil War* (Lanham, MD: Lexington, 2014), 271–275.

22. *Albany Evening Journal,* January 15, 1875.

23. Radical Republican George S. Boutwell (R MA) declared Lincoln prepared to use force if a state government fell into the wrong hands. US House, 39th Cong., 1st sess., *Congressional Globe* (February 13, 1867): 1208R. (An "L," "M," or "R" indicates the left hand, middle, or right-hand column on the page, respectively.) According to the president's interpretation of the Republican guaranty clause of the US Constitution, the federal government could always come to the aid of the loyal elements in the states if in danger of being overwhelmed by hostile forces. Foner, *Reconstruction,* 192.

24. US House, *Report of the Joint Committee on Reconstruction,* x.

25. Emer de Vattel, *The Law of Nations,* vol. 3 (Philadelphia: Johnson, 1863), chap. 13, sec. 201, 389.

26. US House, 39th Cong., 1st sess., *Congressional Globe* (December 18, 1865): 74L.

27. US House, 39th Cong., 1st sess., *Congressional Globe* (January 22, 1866): 351M.

28. The Williams version eventually became the final Section 2 of the Fourteenth Amendment. Senator Henderson (R-MO) said Williams's language "encourages to give the ballot, because it gives power in the same proportion as the ballot is given." US House, 39th Cong., 1st sess., *Congressional Globe* (June 8, 1866): 3033M. The Joint Committee report spoke of the provision "being in its nature gentle and persuasive" for extending the ballot (xiii).

29. US House, 39th Cong., 1st sess., *Congressional Globe* (May 9, 1866): 2503M.

30. Benjamin B. Kendrick, "The Journal of the Joint Committee of Fifteen on Reconstruction: 39th Congress, 1865–1867" (PhD diss., Columbia University, 1914), 104–105.

31. US House, 39th Cong., 1st sess., *Congressional Globe* (May 10, 1866): 2544M.

32. Ibid.

33. US House, 39th Cong., 1st sess., *Congressional Globe* (May 24, 1866): 2803M.

34. Ibid., 2800L.

35. Ibid., 2800R.

36. The test oath was the ironclad oath.

37. Radical Republicans resisted lifting the ironclad oath for those whose disabilities had been removed per Section 3 of the proposed Fourteenth Amendment. Finally, two years later, on July 11, 1868, Congress voted to substitute a simple loyalty oath in lieu of the ironclad test oath for such beneficiaries of congressional action. Harold M. Hyman, *Era of the Oath: Northern Loyalty Tests during the Civil War and Reconstruction* (Philadelphia: University of Pennsylvania Press, 1964), 132, 135.

38. US House, 39th Cong., 1st sess., *Congressional Globe* (February 28, 1866): 1092L–M.

39. John Bingham persuasively argued that from the beginning, the protection of rights was a responsibility of governments throughout the land. Federal and state officials had always been bound by the Constitution's supremacy clause (art. VI, cl. 2). Only because the executive and judicial officials of the slave states utterly disregarded their sworn oaths was this commitment to rights protection rendered ineffective. US House, 35th Congress, 2nd sess., *Congressional Globe* (February 11, 1859): 984L.

40. The amendment was sent to the states for ratification shortly after final passage by Congress, June 13, 1866, and was ratified July 9, 1868.

41. *The Correspondence of Jonathan Worth,* vol. 2, ed. J. G. De Roulhac Hamilton (Raleigh, NC: Edwards and Broughton, 1909), 666.

42. In the 39th Congress, 2nd session, which convened December 3, 1866, the legislators took up the legislation that was to become the Congressional Reconstruction Act (CRA). The CRA was actually four pieces of legislation; the major one passed March 2, 1867, and supplements thereto passed March 23, 1867; July 9, 1867; and March 11, 1868.

43. US House, 39th Cong., 2nd sess., *Congressional Globe* (January 3, 1867): 250M–R.

44. US House, 39th Cong., 2nd sess., *Congressional Globe* (January 24, 1867): 721R.

45. US House, 39th Cong., 2nd sess., *Congressional Globe* (January 28, 1867): 817M.

46. US House, 39th Cong., 2nd sess., *Congressional Globe* (January 1, 1867): 628R, 629M.

47. US House, 39th Cong., 2nd sess., *Congressional Globe* (February 6, 1867): 1037L.

48. US House, 39th Cong., 2nd sess., *Congressional Globe* (February 19, 1867) 1564L, 1563R. Although Senator John Sherman's statement might sound antiblack to the modern ear, his emphasis is on oligarchies of any sort, especially of white over black or black over white. Either would be "horrid deformities" of the Union.

49. Senator John Sherman was vindicated three years later when the Republicans adopted impartial suffrage for the text of the proposed Fifteenth Amendment.

50. Well aware of third-party movements in the Southern states to attract moderates and bury Radical Republicanism, Congressman Thaddeus Stevens (R-PA) and other Radical Republicans were determined to keep the South so well suppressed that such movements could never get under way. Thomas B. Alexander, *Thomas R. Nelson of East Tennessee* (Nashville: East Tennessee Historical Commission, 1956), 169.

51. From the Democrats' point of view, if the issue of ratification of the Fourteenth Amendment remained deadlocked, "the Republicans might either have to surrender entirely or else take such drastic measures—disfranchisement and Negro suffrage—as to drive a large contingent of moderate Republicans into the Democrat party and bring the Democrats great numbers of moderate votes." Benedict, *Compromise of Principle,*

462. Senator William Stewart said that the Democrats voted with the Radical Republicans to make the military bill a "bad bill." US House, 39th Cong., 2nd sess., *Congressional Globe* (February 15, 1867): 1366M.

52. See Congressional Reconstruction Act (CRA), 14 U.S. Stat. 429, sec. 5; First Supplementary Reconstruction Act, 5 U.S. Stat. 2, sec. 1; and still further restrictions per the Second Supplementary Reconstruction Act, 15 U.S. Stat. 14, sec. 5.

53. With a racial breakdown of the new electorates created by the acts, C. Vann Woodward shows just how harsh the impact on the South was: "The number of whites disfranchised is unknown and unknowable, but it is evident from a comparison of population and registration figures that the number was rather large in some states. While only two states had a colored majority of population, five states were given a colored majority of registered voters. . . . The two states with a preponderance of Negroes in population, South Carolina and Mississippi, had overwhelming majorities of colored voters." Woodward, *The Burden of Southern History*, rev. ed. (Baton Rouge: Louisiana State University Press, 1968), 98–99.

54. Radical Republican intransigence defeated an early effort in Virginia in 1866 to unite the radical and moderate wings of the party. Although President Ulysses Grant finally made the right decision whom to back as governor of Arkansas, it was too late. He had been outwitted by the Democrats and was helpless to undo an election that brought a Republican leaning Democrat into office. The president had stolen an election in Louisiana and could not afford the public outcry over stealing another one.

55. Upon assuming command in Mississippi, Governor Adelbert Ames "admitted to himself that he had found his mission in life." Blanche Ames Ames, *Adelbert Ames, 1835–1933* (New York: Argosy-Antiquarian, 1964), 240. (Blanche Ames Ames was a daughter of the governor.)

56. William C. Harris, *The Day of the Carpetbagger: Republican Reconstruction in Mississippi* (Baton Rouge: Louisiana State University Press, 1979), 334.

57. With the Democrats in control of the legislature, after the election of November 2, 1875, Governor Adelbert Ames resigned March 28, 1876, rather than stand trial on trumped-up impeachment charges.

58. Similar interference occurred in Texas, where the president backed the weaker, Radical Republican candidate.

59. "By the standards of the reconstruction states, the federal establishment in Louisiana was a colossus." Ted Tunnell, *Crucible of Reconstruction: War, Radicalism, and Race in Louisiana, 1862–1877* (Baton Rouge: Louisiana State University Press, 1984), 149.

60. Allan Nevins, *Hamilton Fish: The Inner History of the Grant Administration* (New York: Dodd, Mead, 1936), 854.

61. Canter Brown, Jr., *Ossian Bingley Hart: Florida's Loyalist Reconstruction Governor* (Baton Rouge: Louisiana State University Press, 1997), 209.

62. Constitution of Florida—1868, art. XVII, sec. 28, in *Federal and State Constitutions*, vol. 2, ed. Francis N. Thorpe (Washington, DC: US Government Printing Office, 1909), 729.

63. Constitution of Florida—1868, art. VI, sec. 19, in ibid., 712. The governor had the power of appointing all members of the state judiciary, the state supreme court, and the

circuit and county courts with the advice and consent of the state senate. Ibid., art. VII, secs. 3, 7, 9, 712, 713. For justices of the peace he enjoyed the sole power of appointment. Ibid., art. VII, sec. 15, 714.

64. US House, 41st Cong., 1st sess., *Congressional Globe* (April 11, 1871): 577L.

65. US House, 41st Cong., 1st sess., *Congressional Globe* (April 14, 1871): 687M.

66. "You do not take a person who, for years, has been hobbled by chains and liberate him, bring him up to the starting line of a race and then say, 'You are free to compete with all the others,' and still justly believe that you have been completely fair." Lyndon B. Johnson, To Fulfill These Rights: Commencement Address at Howard University, June 4, 1965, in *Public Papers of the President: Lyndon B. Johnson, 1965,* vol. 2 (Washington, DC: US Government Printing Office, 1966), 636.

# CHAPTER 13

# "A School for the Moral Education of the Nation"

## Frederick Douglass on the Meaning of the Civil War

PETER C. MYERS

"Republics have proverbially short memories." So observed Frederick Douglass on the day Abraham Lincoln died, prefacing his hope that thenceforward it would be different—that the long anguish of war, brought to its piercing culmination by the great president's murder, would set America on a course of redemption from which it would not again stray.[1]

In his concern about republics' forgetfulness, Douglass was in venerable company. In the near aftermath of the country's first war, Thomas Jefferson confessed his own fear: "From the conclusion of this war we shall be going downhill. . . . [The people] will be forgotten . . . and their rights disregarded. They will forget themselves, but in the sole faculty of making money, and will never think of uniting to effect a due respect for their rights."[2] When, nearing his death in 1826, Jefferson issued his valedictory concerning the Declaration of Independence ("May it be to the world . . . the signal of arousing men to burst [their] chains"),[3] he was offering as much a prayer as a prediction. In another letter, written only a year earlier, the elder statesman sounded undertones of wistfulness and foreboding as he recalled how the Declaration expressed "the harmonizing sentiments of the day"—quietly suggesting that the great revolutionary charter's power to harmonize might have belonged to a *bygone* day and that his fellow citizens were lapsing from their revolutionary faith, just as he had long before expected.[4] What worried the elder Jefferson also worried a young Lincoln, who, glimpsing the approaching crisis in the perpetuation of America's political institutions, remarked in 1838, "I do not mean to say, that the scenes of the revolution *are now* or *ever will* be entirely forgotten; but that like every thing else, they must fade upon the memory of the world, and grow more and more dim with the lapse of time. . . . Passion has helped us; but can do so no more. It will in [the] future be our enemy."[5]

The forgetfulness these great men feared above all signified a fading not of glorious battle scenes but of revolutionary ideas. They regarded the conflict that issued in the Civil War as a contest, at the deepest level, not of bullets or even of material interests but instead of moral and political principles. It was a contest between mutually antagonistic *first* principles, and its primary protagonists were not soldiers or generals or even the political decision makers as such but instead the opposing pedagogues—the ablest, most influential shapers and articulators of public sentiment. "In this and like communities," Lincoln observed, "public sentiment is everything. . . . He who moulds public sentiment goes deeper than he who enacts statutes or pronounces decisions."[6] On one side of the conflict stood John C. Calhoun and his acolytes—Calhoun standing out among the slaveholding South's eminent purveyors of what Lincoln called the "ingenious sophism" of constitutional secession and the still deeper sophisms in support of slavery.[7] On the other side stood the party of Lincoln, defending the Declaration's principles as the "sheet anchor of American republicanism," the "apple of gold" that the Constitution (the "picture of silver" in his biblical metaphor) was framed to preserve and adorn.[8]

Lincoln is justly revered as the greatest defender of the founders' principles, but in his title to greatness in this effort, he does not stand alone. Preparing and succeeding his heroic stand against the abandonment of those principles were others, most notably the radical abolitionists, comparably heroic and (for better and for worse) singularly zealous in their commitment to the antislavery cause. Foremost among those, maintaining his station long after Lincoln's death and long too after other radical abolitionists had left the field, was Douglass, the man Lincoln himself reportedly judged perhaps the most meritorious in the nation.[9]

Douglass fully shared Lincoln's dedication to the founding principles. "No people," he stated on July 4, 1862, "ever entered upon the pathway of nations, with higher and grander ideas of justice, liberty and humanity than ourselves."[10] He also shared Lincoln's assessment of the war as fundamentally a conflict over first principles. Two months after the shooting began, he told a Rochester audience that the conflict "sweeps the whole horizon of human rights, powers, duties and responsibilities. The grand primal principles which form the basis of human society, are here."[11] Years after the clashing of armies had ceased, on Decoration Day (later Memorial Day), 1878, he reiterated with emphasis: "The sectional character of the war was merely accidental. . . . It was a war of ideas, a battle of principles and ideas . . . a war between the old and new, slavery and freedom, barbarism and civilization; between a government based upon the broadest and grandest declaration of human rights the world ever heard or read, and another pretended government, based upon an open, bold, and shocking denial of all rights, except the right of the strongest."[12]

Shortly after Lincoln issued the Emancipation Proclamation, Douglass commented, "The war now on our hands is sometimes described as a school for the moral education of the nation. I like the designation. It certainly is a school, and a very severe and costly one."[13] As severe and costly as the war was, however, Douglass was acutely aware that its events—the heroic actions, the outrages, the grievous losses, the strategies and tactics well and ill conceived— would not suffice in themselves to teach the proper moral lessons. A school needs a schoolmaster, and great as Lincoln's contribution was in that capacity, a successor was needed. In the speeches and writings of Frederick Douglass, we find the most sustained and comprehensive effort in the era to instruct Americans in the sources and enduring significance of their great national conflagration.

## THE FUNDAMENTAL CAUSE

In his Second Inaugural Address, the speech Douglass admired as "a sacred effort," Lincoln explained, "All knew that this interest"—the "peculiar and powerful" interest in slaves —"was, somehow, the cause of the war."[14] One might expect such knowledge, in at least one respect, to be especially clear and compelling for those who had personally experienced subjection to slavery. So it was for Douglass, in more palpable and in more refined senses. In his analysis as in Lincoln's, slavery was both the final cause and the efficient cause of the war.

For Douglass in contrast to Lincoln, however, to claim that slavery was the rebellion's final cause entailed first and foremost an immediate public commitment by the Union or loyalist forces to abolition as their indispensable, nonnegotiable objective. From beginning to end he insisted, "No war but an Abolition war; no peace but an Abolition peace."[15] His zealous impatience on this crucial point reflected, at bottom, his understanding of what slavery essentially *was*. Against the mendacious evasions and euphemisms of slaveholders and their apologists, Douglass contended that slavery was no benign, paternal, tutelary, or civilizing power; radically to the contrary, the South's "peculiar institution" signified the purest form of despotism. Slavery stood for "the complete destruction of all that dignifies and ennobles human character." It signified the utter negation of law and right in human relations. In the Lockean language Douglass regularly employed, slavery licensed the exercise of "absolute and arbitrary power"; it was a state of war between enslaver and enslaved, with slaveholders waging "a direct war upon human nature."[16]

Douglass's Lockean understanding of slavery as an ongoing state of war implied that the conflict between slavery and freedom or free institutions in America was indeed "irrepressible," as Senator William Seward (later Lincoln's secretary of state) declared in a famous 1858 speech.[17] Taking this position, Douglass stood as a mirror opposite of Calhoun. Whereas Calhoun had contended, "Abolition and the Union cannot co-exist,"[18] Douglass maintained that slavery and a Union dedicated to freedom cannot coexist. Douglass's conception of slavery as a state of war implied still more: the conflict was not only irrepressible, it was *ongoing* and had been so for a very long time. For Douglass, the true war at the core of the irrepressible conflict had commenced at least two centuries before the firing upon Fort Sumter and had been prosecuted all the while in an utterly one-sided fashion, awaiting the mass of nonslaveholding Americans to recognize and join it. The history of the nineteenth century through the 1850s was a history, on the one hand, of steady, arrogant encroachment by proslavery forces and, on the other, of timorous evasion and appeasement by the broad, nonslaveholding majority.[19]

For abolitionists, then, the notion of an irrepressible, inevitable conflict in no way counseled an attitude of patience. Contrary to Lincoln's retrospective at his Second Inaugural Address, the war against slavery would not simply "come" via seemingly impersonal agency; war against slaves (and to a lesser degree, their advocates) was already under way, and the question was how to redirect it to the slaveholders. From the 1830s through the 1850s, radical abolitionists labored as gadflies to awaken the nation, or at least its nonslaveholding majority, to the moral gravity of its abandonment of its revolutionary heritage and, therewith, of the first principles of just, republican government. As we will see, the effort to move the nation to cease its evasions and so to rise against the evil of slavery and slavery's spirit was an effort that engaged Douglass at every stage of his long career.

## THE OPENING OF THE NORTHERN MIND

The problem was not simply that Americans had relinquished their devotion to rights. White Americans North and South, Douglass conceded, were certainly lovers of rights in their way. Their respective understandings of rights differed radically, of course, but the common problem was that for the most part, their concern for rights was narrowly selfish; they clamored for their *own* rights even as they ignored or denied the rights of others.[20] For slavery's adversaries, then, one possible approach was to try to persuade others out of their selfishness and into a respect and concern for the rights of all. The attempt to persuade by means of pure moralizing—by a combination of shaming invective and appeals to moral sympathy for those enslaved—came with greatest energy from Douglass's early abolitionist mentor William Lloyd Garrison and his followers, who meant by those means to persuade slaveholders and nonslaveholders alike.

Long a believer in the saving power of moral truth, Douglass found the Garrisonians' purified reliance on "the foolishness of preaching" initially appealing;[21] slavery's characteristic seclusion and suppression of opposition indicated to him that it could not survive in a regime of genuine free speech. As late as 1863 he declared, "Had the right of free discussion been preserved during the last thirty years . . . we should now have no Slavery to breed rebellion."[22] Well before that, however, he recognized the futility of that approach. "Slaveholders are in earnest," he observed in 1857, "and mean to cling to their slaves as long as they can, and to the bitter end."[23] However great the power of speech, it could not by itself overcome slaveholders' will and power to deny it a proper hearing. Douglass came to the conclusion that abolition could be effected only by the application of coercive pressure in one form or another. He aligned himself with the political faction of radical abolitionists, preferring that the requisite pressure come via the agencies of constitutional government, themselves under the pressure of nonslaveholding voting majorities.[24] To awaken the latter to the moral crisis that confronted them, however, Douglass had to begin with an appeal grounded in the primacy of interest.

In part via the fecklessness of Garrisonian moral suasion, by the 1850s experience had taught Douglass a lesson he might have encountered in the work of John Locke. Even where "manifest Acts of Tyranny" are present, Locke wrote, it is impossible for a "few oppressed men to *disturb the Government,* where the Body of the People do not think themselves concerned." He added, however, that where such "illegal Acts have extended to the Majority of the people; or . . . seem to threaten all . . . how they will be hindered from resisting . . . I cannot tell."[25] Even as slavery's hold on the nation's governing institutions seemed more secure with each passing year, even as its depredations in fact and in law seemed ever more extensive, Douglass grew more optimistic in his expectation of slavery's impending demise. In response to the Court's "devilish decision" in *Dred Scott v. Sandford* (1857), he yet insisted, "My hopes were never brighter than now." Actions such as that ruling, meant to stifle abolitionist agitation, would actually serve to broaden and amplify it. "The wisdom of the crafty has been confounded," Douglass argued; "the finger of the Almighty may be seen bringing good out of evil." The hinge of this argument was his expectation of the ruling's effect on Northern, nonslaveholding whites. It had been the "moral blindness of the American people [to] persuade themselves that they are safe, though the rights of others may be struck down." Step by step, they were coming to see that by a series of governmental actions in the 1850s, including *Dred Scott*, "the white man's liberty has been marked out for the same grave with the black man's. The ballot box is desecrated, God's law set at nought [*sic*], armed legislators stalk the halls of Congress, freedom of speech is beaten down in the Senate. The rivers and highways are infested by border ruffians, and white men are made to feel the iron heel of slavery." By its own arrogance or in reaction to abolitionist goading, Douglass reasoned, the slave power had set itself on a course of self-destructive overreaching. As the long-standing "black reasons" for abolition were augmented by such increasingly importunate "white" reasons—or in Locke's words, as slavery's "illegal Acts" extended to the majority—the status of slavery in the American republic, momentary appearances to the contrary notwithstanding, grew ever more insecure.[26]

In a retrospective view of events leading to the war, Douglass thought that attacks by proslavery Southerners on Northern whites' rights and interests indeed proved decisive: "Nothing on the part of the South in the dark and terrible days of slavery did half so much to arouse the hatred of the North against the infernal institution . . . as their absolute denial of the freedom of speech in their midst upon everything touching that question."[27] However that might be, with the attack on Fort Sumter and the administration's response, proslavery forces produced their culminating act of overreach. "The slaveholders themselves have saved our cause from ruin!" Douglass declared, and the response to that attack effected a radical change in his judgment of his Northern compatriots. "The Government is aroused, the dead North is alive, and its divided people united," he enthused. "Never was a change so sudden, so universal, and so portentous." He greeted the outbreak of the Civil War—the loyalist nation's determination finally to make war against those who had long warred upon its principles—with unrestrained joy: "For this consummation we have watched and wished with fear and trembling. God be praised! that it has come at last."[28]

## ABOLITION WAR

Discovering his despair over Northerners' moral and political will to have been overwrought, Douglass was convinced that the Civil War signified—could only be intelligible, let alone worth fighting, *if* it signified—the "consumma-tion" of his and fellow abolitionists' long struggle, the end of slavery. Not only, however, did he see the end from the beginning, Douglass insisted on the end *at* the beginning. His insistence on the public, explicit prosecution of an aboli-tion war from the outset set him at odds, for a time, with Lincoln, who doubted that Northern public opinion had changed so quickly and radically as Doug-lass seemed to think and who also judged that a policy that alienated loyalist slaveholding states such as Kentucky would be fatal to the Union cause. Eager to see the war's public justification placed on clearer, higher moral ground, Douglass spent roughly a year and a half, from early 1861 to late 1862, harshly denouncing Lincoln and his administration for what he viewed as incoherence and imbecility in waging a war to restore the Union without eradicating the evil that had fractured it.[29] Even as Douglass was excoriating the president for continuing the calamitous course charted by his predecessor, however, Lincoln was preparing the action that would prompt a radical change in Douglass's opinion.

When Lincoln issued his preliminary Emancipation Proclamation in Sep-tember 1862, Douglass began to see that Lincoln was quite far from the "excel-lent slave-hound" that he had castigated in reaction to Lincoln's First Inaugural Address, that his disagreement with the president on the war's objective was in fact much narrower than he had supposed.[30] He greeted even this preliminary proclamation with profound exultation—"Oh! long enslaved millions . . . the hour of your deliverance draws nigh!"[31]—and anxiously awaited the deliver-ance of the final proclamation in January. He described the reaction at the Boston gathering he had attended, when the momentous news finally came over the wires late that New Year's Day: "I never saw joy before." A month later he told a Cooper Institute audience that Lincoln's action was "the greatest event of our nation's history."[32]

Douglass's joy upon receiving the word, at long last, of a concrete, official emancipation order did not preclude critical analysis. Sharing none of Lin-coln's constitutional scruples about federally mandated abolition, he criticized the proclamation's carefully circumscribed policy: "To me it seems a blunder that Slavery was not declared abolished everywhere in the Republic."[33] The president's preoccupation with constitutional propriety led him, needlessly in Douglass's judgment, to diminish the proclamation's moral clarity and luster. In his final autobiography, *Life and Times of Frederick Douglass,* he extended that criticism, recalling radical abolitionists' objections that the proclamation "was a measure apparently inspired by the low motive of military necessity, and . . . would become inoperative and useless when military necessity should cease." Viewed from that radical perspective, it appeared "extremely defective." Yet that perspective, he was quick to add, focused on particular, near-term shortcomings rather than the larger, longer significance of Lincoln's action. "For my own part," Douglass explained in *Life and Times*, "I took the proclamation ... for a little more than it purported; and saw on its spirit, a life and power far beyond its letter."[34]

Self-serving as it might be, that recollection was accurate. In his February 1863 speech at the Cooper Institute, Douglass declared that however momentarily limited Lincoln's proclamation was, "I hail it as the doom of slavery in all the States. ... It is a mighty event for the bondman, but it is a still mightier event for the nation at large, and mighty as it is for both ... it is still mightier when viewed in its relation to the cause of truth and justice throughout the world. ... Henceforth [January 1, 1863] shall take rank with the Fourth of July. Henceforth it becomes the date of a new and glorious era in the history of American liberty."[35]

The proclamation's grand significance, Douglass believed, was to herald the destruction of slavery in the modern world's preeminent republic; it was to herald the new birth of freedom and the new life for republican government to which Lincoln would rededicate the nation later that same year at Gettysburg. Yet, a most troubling question remained. If emancipation were, by Lincoln's momentous act, established as the meaning of the war, one was yet compelled to ask: What is the meaning of emancipation?

## A NEW BIRTH OF FREEDOM

In Douglass's interpretation the liberationist significance of the Civil War was complex and far reaching. In its primary, most immediately pressing significance, however, the question attending emancipation concerned the particular fate of the freedpeople, and at the heart of that question, in turn, appeared the long bedeviling question of race—of black-white race relations. "The Negro"—not simply slavery in itself—"is the test of American civilization," Douglass declared in 1859, as intersectional tensions neared the breaking point. He added in 1863, in the midst of the full-blown war, "The relation subsisting between the white and colored people of this country, is of all other questions, the great, paramount, imperative, and all commanding question for this age and the nation to solve."[36]

The implication was that emancipation could not be properly comprehended by the abolition of chattel slavery alone. "Slavery has been fruitful in giving itself names," Douglass noted as he admonished the American Anti-Slavery Society in 1865 that its work was not completed, "and it will call itself by yet another name; and you and I and all of us had better wait and see what new form this old monster will assume, in what new skin this old snake will come forth."[37] There was no tenable middle ground between chattel slavery and full freedom. Emancipation in its full and proper meaning entailed abolition of slavery formal and informal, in law and in spirit alike. In an early 1864 address, The Mission of the War, Douglass included the following principles in the platform upon which he urged "every loyal man" to stand: "That we regard the whole colored population of the country ... as our countrymen ... entitled to all the rights, protection, and opportunities for achieving distinction enjoyed by any other class of our countrymen," and therefore that "we shall favor ... invest[ing] the black man everywhere with the right to vote and be voted for, and remov[ing] all discriminations against his rights on account of his color."[38] Thus demanding that the freedmen and all black men be accorded respect and protection in the full array of rights essential to citizenship, Douglass held the right of suffrage to be paramount. "Slavery is not abolished until the black man has the ballot." Absent that, the freedpeople, so called, would simply become slaves to society at large rather than to individual slaveholders.[39]

For Douglass, however, equality in civil and political rights was not the full meaning of victory in an emancipationist war. Full and proper equality and final victory in that war could not be achieved by changes in laws alone. What he wrote in an antisegregation editorial before the war remained his conviction after it: "The unnatural, unreasoning and malignant prejudice" against blacks "is the secret of most of our social troubles. . This prejudice it is which we are to meet, encounter, and subdue, before any essential change for the better can take place in our condition."[40] The spirit of slavery endures, he reiterated in 1892, in "the prejudice, hate and contempt in which we are still held by the people, who for more than two hundred years doomed us to this cruel and degrading condition."[41] Full and proper emancipation entailed effectual, not merely formal, emancipation, and securing effectual emancipation entailed the eradication of the enduring, nationwide sentiment of racial prejudice. Full and proper emancipation, in other words, entailed the achievement both of civil and political equality and of the still more controversial dimension of equality, then known as "social equality."

The concept of social equality, or social rights, was ambiguous. So far as it signified a "right to enter into social relations with anybody" irrespective of the other's choosing, or a right to be regarded as in all respects the social equal of another, Douglass insisted that it rested "upon an entirely different basis" than civil equality and made no part of black Americans' legitimate demands.[42] So far as it signified access on equal terms to public accommodations, however, or nonsegregated public schools, or the right to purchase a home in a neighborhood of one's choosing, or the right to form mutually agreeable personal associations—that last right reaching the heart of the matter, as it portended racial amalgamation—Douglass held such equality to be squarely within the realm of legitimate civil equality. "I would not be understood as advocating intermarriage between the two races," he explained, but his nonadvocacy in no way signified opposition: "I would not be understood as deprecating it." He simply regarded it, as with social equality in general, as a private matter, "a matter between individuals," to which opposition was baseless and ephemeral.[43] He confidently expected that over time marriages across color lines would become common and unremarkable: "My strongest conviction as to the future of the negro . . . is . . . that he will be absorbed, assimilated, and will only appear finally . . . in the features of a blended race." The "tendency of the age," he observed, "is unification, not isolation." He held assimilation to be "our true policy and our national destiny" for reasons grounded not only in history but also, more deeply, in nature: "Races and varieties of the human family appear and disappear, but humanity remains and will remain forever."[44]

This approving prediction of racial amalgamation is indicative of the revolutionary change Douglass envisioned, for which he contended as the true meaning and legacy of the Civil War. "The arduous task of the future," he argued in late 1862, was "to make the Southern people see and appreciate Republican Government"—an effort in reeducation aiming at "nothing less than a radical revolution in all the modes of thought which have flourished under the blighting slave system."[45] The political and cultural revolution he had in mind was more than regional in scope. A true abolition war, he maintained in The Mission of the War, would entail a "grand moral revolution in the mind and heart of the *nation*."[46] In a companion speech delivered the previous month, he elaborated in the spirit of the apostle Paul. "What business, then, have we to fight for the old Union? . . . We are fighting for something incomparably better than the old Union. We are fighting for unity; unity of idea, unity of sentiment, unity of object, unity of institutions, in which there shall be no North, no South, no East, no West, no black, no white, but a solidarity of the nation, making every slave free, and every free man a voter."[47] Upon the ratification of the Fifteenth Amendment, which seemed to guarantee the crucial right of suffrage to the freedmen, Douglass could scarcely contain his enthusiasm: "At last, at last, the black man has a future. . . . We have ourselves, we have a country, and we have a future in common with other men. . . . *Never was revolution more complete.*"[48]


## A GRAND POLITICS OF INTEGRATION

In form though certainly not in substance, Douglass was a zealous American apostle of what Friedrich Nietzsche called "grand politics."[49] "Something of a hero worshiper by nature," as he confessed, he harbored a lifelong fascination with greatness in its various dimensions.[50] As the crisis of his time moved him to reflect upon great principles and causes, so it drew his thoughts to human greatness—to the greatness of heroic individuals as well as of nations and peoples. Great crises provided opportunities for greatness, both for individuals and collectives, and the Civil War was a preeminent case in point. A prominent part of Douglass's endeavor to moralize the nation's memory of the Civil War was his effort to inspire veneration for its greatest heroes, foremost among whom, in his ranking, stood Lincoln and John Brown, the statesman and the holy warrior of the antislavery cause. In this context one must note also Douglass's effort to cultivate his own heroic image in his autobiographies, as he acknowledged near the close of the 1881 edition of *Life and Times*.[51] He believed, however, that "only a great people can produce and support great men."[52] His veneration of individual greatness, worthy in itself, was also instrumental to his larger enterprise of propagating among his fellow citizens a deeper appreciation of and devotion to the exemplary greatness of America's national mission—and a concomitant respect for the peculiar greatness of black Americans' contribution to it.

Like Lincoln, Douglass characterized the Civil War in its larger meaning as a Christian allegory of national transgression, suffering, atonement, and redemption.[53] Douglass went beyond Lincoln, however, in his understanding of the particular role of black Americans in that allegory. "It is part of the settled order of Providence that the cross must ever precede the crown," he told a suffragist meeting in 1886, applying to that cause a truth he applied also to the nation at large and, most powerfully of all, to his fellow black Americans. "The colored people," he told a literary society of young black men in 1855, had "a special mission to perform in the United States—a mission which none but themselves could perform."[54] That mission far transcended the liberation and social elevation of their own group. "Let it be remembered," he told an English audience in 1860, "that neither self-culture, nor any other kind of culture, can amount to much in this world, unless joined to some truly unselfish and noble purpose."[55] It was the distinctive, luminous virtue of Brown, as Douglass saw it, to sacrifice his life to liberate others from an oppression from which he personally was exempted by his color. "[Patrick] Henry loved liberty for himself," he remarked in a commemorative address at Harpers Ferry, "but this man loved liberty for all men, and for those most despised and scorned, as well as for those most esteemed and honored."[56] In Douglass's hortative vision of the Civil War's full meaning and legacy, black Americans as a class would play a similar role, displaying similar virtue. Naturally loving liberty for themselves, their labors and example would prepare its extension to untold others. To an audience of Boston abolitionists in 1862, Douglass declared:

My friends, the destiny of the colored American . . . is the destiny of America. . . . The allotments of Providence seem to make the black man of America the open book out of which the American people are to learn lessons of wisdom, power, and goodness—more sublime and glorious than any yet attained by the nations of the old or the new world. Over the bleeding back of the American bondman we shall learn mercy. In the very extreme difference of color and features of the Negro and the Anglo-Saxon, shall be learned the highest ideas of the sacredness of man and the fullness and perfection of human brotherhood.[57]

In its fullest meaning, the Civil War as Douglass interpreted it signified a revolution far more profound and extensive than the original American Revolution. The Union victory signified a victory for a grand, encompassing principle of unity—of human unity in liberty—marking the advent of an era of integration unprecedented in American or world history. The Emancipation Proclamation, Douglass remarked, "contemplates one glorious homogeneous people."[58] Viewing them from one angle, he affirmed the standard Republican position that the Reconstruction amendments signified a continuation of, not a departure from, the prewar Constitution's design, with both informed by the Declaration's fundamental principle of equal natural rights. Shortly after the ratification of those amendments, Douglass chided his "friends" in the Democratic Party that the real author of the Fourteenth Amendment was Thomas Jefferson.[59] In another respect, however, he contended that the postwar amendments effected a radical, profoundly significant alteration of the constitutional design, one pursuant to the proclamation's larger objective of national homogeneity. "The true doctrine," he wrote to Gerrit Smith in objecting to the Supreme Court's *Slaughterhouse Cases* ruling, "is one nation, one country, one citizenship and one law for all the people." At times, apparently for prudential reasons and again in keeping with mainstream Republicans,

Douglass presented suffrage for the freedmen as a means of returning home rule to the ex-rebel states, thus as a measure consistent with the principle of states' rights. His deeper conviction, however, seems to have been that in principle the Union victory "swept away . . . the pretension of sovereignty of the individual states" and likewise "abolished sectionalism," as he contended in an 1889 demand for effectual voting rights.[60] Of Southern fears of constitutional centralization, he was simply dismissive: "I have no fear of centralization while the ballot is in the hands of the American people."[61]

That particular fearlessness points also to the surprising further reach of the proclamation's national homogeneity principle, as Douglass conceived it— beyond federal relations to the design of the general, or national, government itself. The cause of national homogencity was inseparable, in his view, from the perfection of republican government, and the principle of popular representation as secured by universal suffrage was indispensable to both. As the most prominent spokesman of the most oppressed minority group in American society, Douglass was surprisingly fearless of the danger of unchecked majority rule. The crucial proviso, however, was that the vote be secure for all. "We have recently been told," he said to a St. Louis audience in early 1867, "that majorities can be as destructive and more arbitrary than individual despots. . . . If this is the truth, I think that we ought to part with Republican government at once." He readily conceded that "majorities can be despotic and have been arbitrary," but he insisted that such arbitrariness is a danger always and only "to unrepresented classes." The simple remedy, then, was "a consistent republic in which there shall be no unrepresented classes." The consolidation of the nation, along with the securing of the people's liberties, entailed the constitution of majority-rule, republican government. "I am here tonight," Douglass told that same audience, earnestly beneath the partisan jest, "as a democrat, a genuine democrat dyed in the wool . . . to advocate a genuine democratic republic."[62]

Yet the constituting of a purified, democratic republican government required more than universal suffrage. To establish such a government, Douglass argued, we must "free it from everything that looks toward monarchy. . . . Blot out from it everything antagonistic of republicanism declared by the fathers." As he made clear, however, what he judged antagonistic to the fathers' republicanism included features the fathers themselves thought essential to constitutional government. He proceeded to call for the virtual elimination of the independent chief executive, including not only the drastic curtailment of presidential appointment and patronage powers but also the complete abolition of the presidential veto, which he considered "alien to every idea of republican government."[63] Douglass made this speech in the heat of a struggle between President Andrew Johnson and radical Republicans in Congress, angered by Johnson's vetoes of their Reconstruction measures. Yet he expressed similar support for a democratized constitutional scheme and similar hostility to the Constitution's design of checks and balances well before and well after the contention of the Johnson years.[64]

Moreover, Douglass's desires for national, democratic homogeneity extended well beyond the elimination of arbitrary divisions of governmental power at the constitutional level. In his expansive interpretation, the Union victory entailed the abolition of *all* morally arbitrary divisions, at least in their public or societal operations. "I believe in unity of all good causes," he told a suffragist convention in 1868.[65] By the same principle that abolished slavery, discriminations in rights by sex (his disagreements with suffragists over the Fifteenth Amendment notwithstanding) were marked for extinction. So, too, were those grounded in religious creed, along with those grounded in national origin. Particularly revealing are his views on this latter point.

"We have undertaken . . . a new experiment," Douglass told a gathering of Republicans in 1871.[66] When Alexander Hamilton stated, in the initial essay of *The Federalist,* that the American experiment was to determine whether "societies of men are really capable or not, of establishing good government from reflection and choice," he had actually understated the question, as it now appeared in the light of emancipation and the postwar amendments. The question went beyond whether republican government, government by "reflection and choice," is possible for *a* or *any* society of human beings; the new or succeeding question was whether republican government is possible in a universally inclusive society, or whether the universal principles upon which it is properly founded can be honored in a society whose members are bound together by no particularist, subrational, or extrarational ties of blood, common history, or religious creed but only by their common profession of those principles themselves. "With equal suffrage in our hands," Douglass proclaimed, "we are beyond the power of families, nationalities or races. . . . Our national genius welcomes humanity from every quarter." The "great experiment," then, was "to establish the truth, or the falsehood, the possibility or impossibility of all nations, kindreds, tongues, and peoples, living harmoniously, happily, prosperously and successfully under one government, . . . to realize the Christian idea that of one blood God has made all nations to dwell on all the Christian earth."[67]

This great experiment portended both an expansion and a qualification of the homogeneity in which Douglass found the central meaning of emancipation. The "blended," amalgamated nationality he envisioned in a future America was to comprise more than the descendants of the black, white, and red people who inhabited the country in his day; and more important, the blending or amalgamation Douglass had in mind was cultural and moral in character, not merely racial or phenotypic. The scope and complexity of his humanitarian, assimilationist position appeared most clearly in his speech Our Composite Nationality, delivered in late 1869, in which Douglass defended, against nativist objections, the opening of borders and opportunities to Chinese immigrants. He defended that policy on grounds of inevitability and material interest but more strongly on grounds of moral interest and principle. The biblical wisdom applied, he contended, to nations no less than to individuals: "It is not good for man to be alone." A policy of insularity, reflecting a desire for racial, ethnic, national, or cultural purity would effect the degradation, not the preservation or elevation, of any people or nation that attempted it. "All great qualities are never found in any one man or in any one race," Douglass observed, and "all . . . varieties of men are improvable." These facts taken together constitute a strong argument for a welcoming policy, he contended, because contact with various others would serve "to temper, modify, round and complete the whole man and the whole nation." Arguing for a virtually open immigration policy, Douglass did not ignore the practical conditions of assimilation. "We should incorporate [immigrants] into the American body politic," he advised, "as fast as they learn our language and comprehend the duties of citizenship." The larger point, however, is that the national homogeneity he viewed as the core principle and ultimate aspiration of emancipation was at once dynamic and universally inclusive. It was to comprehend an ever-changing mix of peoples and cultures, bound together as Americans by the humanitarian, natural rights principles upon which the country was founded.[68]

As his argument in Our Composite Nationality makes clear, despite his language elsewhere Douglass conceived of this integrationist policy in truth not as an experiment, not as an exercise in rational or scientific discovery, but rather as a moral mission. Patriotism was to be subsumed into humanitarianism, which he embraced as the nation's true, unifying, and justifying civil religion.[69] As he sought to convince his fellow citizens of the wisdom of openness to Chinese and other immigrants, he endeavored once again to instruct them in first principles—the first principles of America as of republican and just government: "Our geographical position . . . our fundamental principles of government, world-embracing in their scope and character, our vast resources . . . and our already existing composite population, all conspire to one grand end, and that is, to make us the [most] perfect national illustration of the unity and dignity of the human family that the world has ever seen."[70] That, for Douglass, was the meaning and mission of America, for whose vindication the Civil War had been waged.

## THE IRREPRESSIBLE CONFLICT CONTINUED

Douglass was unquestionably a man moved, on occasion, to flights of zealous enthusiasm. To this observation, however, we must hasten to add that in his sober, settled understanding, Douglass harbored no illusions that the abolition war's full promise would be realized immediately or inevitably. Of the magnitude and the difficulty of the task that remained in completing the Union victory, he was acutely aware.

The primary task and difficulty lay in eradicating the spirit of slavery and rebellion, still very much alive after the Confederate surrender on the battlefield. Douglass saw the problem clearly long before the war's end, commenting in late 1862, "It would be absurd and ridiculous to expect that the conquered traitors will at once cordially cooperate with the Federal Government. . . . The master will carry into the new relation of liberty much of the insolence, caprice and pretention exercised by him while the admitted lord of the lash."[71] His reflections after the fact confirmed those concerns. He wrote in *Life and Times:*

History does not furnish an example of emancipation under conditions less friendly to the emancipated class, than this American example. . . . Liberty came to the freedmen of the United States, not in mercy but in wrath; not by moral choice but by military necessity; not by the generous action of the people among whom they were to live, and whose goodwill was essential to the success of the measure, but by strangers, foreigners, invaders, trespassers, aliens, and enemies. The very manner of their emancipation invited to the heads of the freedmen the bitterest hostility of race and class. . . . He is a poor student of the human heart who does not see that the old master class would naturally employ every power and means in their reach to make the great measure of emancipation unsuccessful and utterly odious.[72]

The powerful natural difficulty posed by the sentiments of Southern whites was compounded by others no less natural, stemming from the sentiments of their erstwhile compatriots in the North. One of those difficulties was the limited trustworthiness of white Northerners' motivations in the war against slavery. "A man that hates Slavery only for what it does to the white man," Douglass worried, "stands ready to embrace it the moment its injuries are confined to the black man."[73] A further difficulty among Northern whites was simple war weariness, strengthening their desire for reconciliation and dulling their appreciation of the moral stakes of the conflict. Near the end of Reconstruction, Douglass observed, "Men cannot, ought not, and will not quarrel and fight forever . . . [and this is] much more true when men are of the same race. . . . So sure as the stars shine in the heavens . . . so sure will the white people North and South abandon their quarrel and become friends. . . . Now when this mighty quarrel has ceased . . . the question for us is: in what position will this stupendous reconciliation leave the colored people?"[74]

The great danger, as he saw it, was that a Northern population all too eager for reconciliation would join a Southern population humiliated and vengeful in defeat in promulgating a minimalist understanding of the meaning of the Union victory—minimizing together the slavery now prohibited and the liberty now guaranteed. Douglass's efforts to propagate an expansively moralized understanding of the war, far from merely celebratory or triumphalist in nature, were conceived as measures taken in an ongoing war, now against the impulses for amoral reconciliation and the malignant cause they would sustain. He sounded a keynote of those efforts in his speech on Decoration Day 1871, reminding those yet disposed to listen of the danger of republican forgetfulness:

We are sometimes asked in the name of patriotism to forget the merits of this fearful struggle, and to remember with equal admiration those who struck at the nation's life, and those who struck to save it—those who fought for slavery and those who fought for liberty and justice. I am no minister of malice. I would not strike the fallen. . . . But may my right hand forget its cunning, and may my tongue cleave to the roof of my mouth, if I forget the difference between the parties to that terrible, protracted and bloody conflict.[75]

Douglass found himself compelled to issue such reminders repeatedly and with increasing intensity for the rest of his life. In another Decoration Day address in 1878, he commented on the emerging evidence that President Rutherford B. Hayes's "experiment" in conciliating the lately rebellious states by returning self-rule to them was proving a disastrous failure. "No candid man," Douglass observed, "can fail to see that we are still afflicted by the painful sequences both of slavery and of the late rebellion." Amid such circumstances, it was imperative to remind the nation of what, in any event, must never be forgotten: "There was a right side and a wrong side in the late war," and "if the observance of this memorial day has any apology, office, or significance, it is derived from the moral character of the war."[76] His commitment to the ongoing struggle for the war's moral legacy appears also to have been the primary determinant of the controversial position he took in opposing the "Exodus," the large-scale migration of Southern blacks to western states in the late 1870s. Douglass cited a variety of reasons supporting his initial judgment, but his deepest objection appeared in his view of the movement as "a surrender, a premature, disheartening surrender" of what had been won in the Union's—the nation's—victory. The Exodus "leaves the whole question of equal rights on the soil of the South open and still to be settled. . . . If the people of this country cannot be protected in every State of this Union . . . the late rebellion has triumphed."[77]

That sense of struggle for the moral significance of the war, with the fear that the larger war was being lost, intensified throughout the 1880s and 1890s and persisted all the way to Douglass's death in 1895. It animated his response to the Supreme Court's ruling in the *Civil Rights Cases* (1883), a ruling, he declared, that "swept over the land like a cyclone leaving moral desolation in its track." The ruling constituted "one more shocking development of that moral weakness in high places which has attended the conflict between the spirit of liberty and the spirit of slavery." His disappointment focused particularly on the Republican Party, the only major party from which it was possible to hope for a commitment to liberty for all. "We have been . . . wounded in the house of our friends," he lamented, wounded by a Court composed entirely of Republican appointees.[78] In his last great protest speech, delivered in January 1894, he offered this gloomy appraisal: "Principles which we all thought to have been firmly and permanently settled by the late war have been boldly assaulted and overthrown by the defeated party. Rebel rule is now nearly complete in many states, and it is gradually capturing the nation's Congress. The cause lost in the war is the cause regained in peace, and the cause gained in war is the cause lost in peace."[79]

As Douglass's life came to its end, the forces of liberty and civilization had become once again reluctant to recognize or join the struggle, as they had in the antebellum period. Then as in that earlier day, however, although the war had not been won, the cause was not lost, could not be lost more than temporarily. The "irrepressible conflict" was "still in progress."[80] It must ever be in progress, Douglass was convinced, so long as liberty and rights for all were not secured and so long as the human spirit remained alive. "The pit of hell is said to be bottomless," he said the year before he died, and he knew not "how low the moral sentiment of this republic may yet fall." Yet he retained his "hope and trust all will come out right in the end," and it was in that spirit that he concluded, once again calling his fellow citizens to remember—to remember the better angels of their nature, as expressed in the action by which their ancestors had made and declared themselves a people, and a people unlike any other:

Could I be heard by this great nation, I would call to mind the sublime and glorious truths with which, at its birth, it saluted a listening world. Its voice, then, was as the trump of an archangel. . . . It announced the advent of a nation, based upon human brotherhood and the self-evident truths of liberty and equality. Its mission was the redemption of the world from the bondage of ages. Apply these sublime and glorious truths to the situation now before you. . . . Recognize the fact that the rights of the humblest citizens are as worthy of protection as are those of the highest and . . . based upon the eternal principles of truth, justice, and humanity, with no class having cause for complaint or grievance, your Republic will stand and flourish forever.[81]

## CONCLUSION

"To live is to battle," Douglass once remarked, and in the great contest over the nation's character and principles no one battled in a more sustained and instructive manner than did he.[82] The occasion for those words was his eulogy on Garrison, his great comrade in rhetorical arms, and he spoke them in a spirit of zestful admiration and gratitude rather than of resignation. For a man such as Douglass, longing to be a heroic warrior for liberty, it was a profound blessing, or at least a remarkable good fortune, to take part in a momentous battle for the liberation of millions, for the very soul of a great nation, and perhaps for something grander still—for the fate of liberty in the entire modern world. "Generations unborn will envy us the felicity," he remarked, "of having been born at a time when such noble work could be accomplished."[83]

Students of the American founding will note the close resemblance between that expression of gratitude and prominent founders' expressions of gratitude for the opportunity to perform their own, no less momentous, work. "You and I," wrote John Adams in 1776, "have been sent into life at a time when the greatest lawgivers of antiquity would have wished to live. . . . When, before the present epocha, had three millions of people full power and a fair opportunity to form and establish the wisest and happiest government that human wisdom can contrive?"[84] In Douglass's understanding, this circumstantial resemblance reflected a profound continuity: the great work in which he participated and the work of the revolutionary fathers were of a piece, signifying successive moments in a single grand revolution from which would emerge history's first fully free, fully republican, universally inclusive political order. Although prominent founders did harbor the skepticism of their day regarding the possibility of an America fully integrated across lines of race or color, the universal principles they inscribed into the republic's two foundational documents, the Declaration of Independence and the US Constitution, not only comprehended but also lent moral authority and even moral urgency to the broad integrationist vision Douglass and others who labored to complete the founders' work would champion. For Douglass, the Civil War signified both a return and an advance, with the advance contingent upon the return; the founders' core principles were permanently true, sufficient unto themselves, and indispensable to free, just, republican government. As it did for Lincoln at Gettysburg, the Civil War signified for Douglass a rebirth or refounding—not a replacement but rather a rededication to and fulfillment of those original principles.

In its still broader significance, the heart or vital spirit of Douglass's complex understanding of the Civil War consists in a progressive, Jeffersonian, at times even providential hopefulness, tempered by a Thucydidean and Machiavellian realism. As Jefferson had bequeathed to the world his hopeful conviction that "all eyes are opened, or opening, to the rights of man," so Douglass declared a month following the Emancipation Proclamation, "I believe in the millennium—the final perfection of the [human] race."[85] More than twenty years later, commemorating emancipation in Great Britain's colonies and in the United States, he reiterated, "No incidents connected with the progress of modern civilization are more significant of the upward tendency of human nature . . . than those two."[86] And yet the war also could be taken, as Machiavelli would have observed,[87] to illustrate republics' recurrent need to be recalled, dramatically and violently, to the first principles from which they naturally tend to lapse, just as the war and its aftermath could be taken as shattering reminders of the Thucydidean truths of the fragility of civilization and the permanent, irresolvable tension between justice and interest.[88] Douglass soberly acknowledged such truths throughout his long career. We drew attention at the outset to his observation of republics' proverbial forgetfulness. At the start of the war, he reflected further, "The human heart is a seat of constant war."[89] He told a suffragist convention in 1868 that it was not only "habitual" but "eminently natural" for "men and women too to be clamorous for their own rights" while ignoring or denying the rights of others.[90] In a speech a few years before his death he conceded, "The world was never yet without prejudice" of one kind or another.[91]

His occasional expressions of millennialist enthusiasm notwithstanding, Douglass knew the future was uncertain. Animating his seemingly confident predictions regarding the true legacy of the war, the coming triumph of justice, and the eradication of arbitrary power in all its forms in America and the modern world was a substantial measure of moral exhortation, a summoning of moral energies to make it so. To enable our work, he maintained, we need faith.[92] He also recognized, however, that a properly inspirational faith could not be only or mainly a faith in things unseen. The Union victory and emancipation were massive historical and moral facts. They demonstrated, in Douglass's argument, that republican (or human) forgetfulness is not invincible; that moral progress is evident in the nation's history as in the particular histories of its white and black citizens; and that great events, as directed and interpreted by great individuals, can become moving, inspiring forces in the achievement of moral reform. The American Revolution, with its invocation of natural, permanent principles of justice, would light the way for a succeeding generation of reformers in the Civil War era, and the like could be true—could be made true—of the Civil War, lighting the way for future reformers and substantiating the hope for a still grander moral consummation in the years to come.

Finally, as to how the great events of Douglass's day and the arguments whereby he influenced and interpreted them might serve to light a path through the race related controversies of our own time, a few general considerations must suffice. At the level of first principles or ultimate aspirations, Douglass's vision of justice in America appears remarkably similar to the "dream" articulated by Martin Luther King, Jr., in his most famous speech. Eighty years prior to King's speech, Douglass encouraged a convention of black men to work faithfully for a day in which race "will cease to have any civil, political, or moral significance."[93] Justice consists primarily in the securing of natural rights for all, and natural rights are properties of human beings as a universal class, not of any particular racial group. One's color or particular racial or ethnic identity can have no qualifying or disqualifying effect on one's status as a moral being.[94] With respect to the application of these principles, however, Douglass's thinking was often complicated by circumstantial or contextual considerations a fact that underscores the need for caution on our part as we consider how Douglass's thinking might help us work through our own controversies, amid significantly different contextual particulars.

At the center of race-related controversies in the post–civil rights era is the question whether special race classifications are needful or useful for purposes of repairing the injuries or elevating the condition of historically downtrodden groups, with the descendants of African American slaves still accorded paradigmatic status among such groups. On the employment of race classifications even for such purportedly benign or antiracist purposes, Douglass's various statements suggest a principled aversion to such policies, tempered or softened by circumstantial considerations. Commending the principle of race neutrality to an antislavery gathering in 1862, he warned against the dangers of placing his or any other group, based on racial identity, outside the common rules of right and responsibility: "The broadest and bitterest of the black man's misfortunes is the fact that he is everywhere regarded and treated as an exception to the principles and maxims which apply to other men."[95] In a similar spirit decades later, at a time when racial Darwinism had become intellectually fashionable, he decried a tendency "now so generally prevailing" to valorize racial identity. "We hear, since Emancipation," he remarked, "much said by our modern colored leaders in commendation of race pride, race love, race effort, race superiority, race men, and the like." Expecting his admonition to be "more useful than palatable," he contended that such talk signified "a great mistake. . . . In all this talk of race, the motive may be good, but the method is bad. It is an effort to cast out Satan by Beelzebub."[96]

Yet, by his strong condemnation of race pride on general principle, Douglass did not mean that appeals to race solidarity or the formation of race-specific associations could never be approved on grounds of provisional, circumstantial necessity. He defended the organizing of "colored" conventions, for instance, on the ground that "white men are already in convention against us."[97] Moreover, at the level of race-related policy, in the very same speech in which he condemned black leaders' talk of race pride, he endorsed the general idea of race-focused reparative justice. "It is sometimes said that we have done enough for the negro," he remarked, but those who say such things forget that for the "terrible wrongs" at issue, no compensation could suffice:

If the American people could put a school-house in every valley of the south, a church on every hill-top; supply with a teacher and preacher each respectively, and welcome the descendants of the former slaves to all the moral and intellectual benefits of the one and the other, without money and without price, such a sacrifice would not compensate their children for the terrible wrong done to their fathers and mothers by their enslavement and enforced degradation.[98]

Taking the long view, Frederick Douglass regarded the Civil War as a great triumph, one that heralded still greater triumphs, for a grand politics of integration. That was the cause he embraced as his own, laboring to advance it with single mind, whole heart, and energy second to none among his own contemporaries from the beginning to the end of his six-decade career of public activism. To carry forward Douglass's integrationist legacy in our own day would require, first, that one carefully assess the natures and strengths of the main threats to integration, or the main forces of disintegration, presently at work. It would require, more pointedly, a resolute insistence that there can be no genuine integration apart from elevation, comprehending both the material and the moral elevation of those who suffer the effects of historic injustices. For the present-day integrationist working in the spirit of Douglass, the difficult task is to promote, so far as possible, the repairing of damages wrought by those injustices while yet resisting an upsurgent enthusiasm for, and institutionalizing of, a new form of racial identity politics. Stated in the simpler language of Douglass's friend Lincoln, it is to keep or to place the perennially divisive idea of race in the course of its ultimate extinction.

## NOTES

1. Frederick Douglass, Our Martyred President, April 15, 1865, in *The Frederick Douglass Papers,* ser. 1, vol. 4, ed. John W. Blassingame and John R. McKivigan (New Haven, CT: Yale University Press, 1979–1992), 76–77 (hereafter cited as *Douglass Papers*).

2. Thomas Jefferson, *Notes on the State of Virginia*, Query 17, in *The Essential Jefferson,* ed. Jean Yarbrough (Indianapolis, IN: Hackett, 2006), 129 (hereafter cited as *Essential Jefferson*).

3. Thomas Jefferson to Roger Weightman, June 24, 1826, in *Essential Jefferson,* 277.

4. Thomas Jefferson to Henry Lee, May 8, 1825, in *Essential Jefferson*; Jefferson, *Notes on the State of Virginia,* 129, 267.

5. Abraham Lincoln, The Perpetuation of Our Political Institutions, January 27, 1838, in *Abraham Lincoln: His Speeches and Writings,* ed. Roy P. Basler (New York: Da Capo, 2001), 84 (hereafter cited as *Speeches and Writings*).

6. Abraham Lincoln, Debate at Ottawa, Illinois, August 21, 1858, in *Speeches and Writings,* 458.

7. Abraham Lincoln, Message to Congress in Special Session, July 4, 1861, in *Speeches and Writings,* 602–603.

8. Abraham Lincoln, The Repeal of the Missouri Compromise and the Propriety of Its Restoration, October 16, 1854, in *Speeches and Writings*; Lincoln, Fragment: The Constitution and the Union, in ibid., 304, 513. See also Proverbs 25:11.

9. See *In Memoriam: Frederick Douglass,* ed. Helen Pitts Douglass (Freeport, NY: Books for Libraries Press, 1971), 71, orig. pub. 1897.

10. Frederick Douglass, Slavery and the Irrepressible Conflict, August 1, 1860, in *Douglass Papers,* vol. 3, 382; Douglass, The Slaveholders' Rebellion, July 4, 1862, in ibid., 529.

11. Frederick Douglass, The Decision of the Hour, June 16, 1861, in *The Life and Writings of Frederick Douglass,* vol. 3, ed. Philip S. Foner (New York: International, 1950–1975), 118 (hereafter cited as *Life and Writings*); see also *Douglass Papers,* vol. 3, 436.

12. Frederick Douglass, There Was a Right Side in the Late War, May 30, 1878, in *Douglass Papers,* ser. 1, vol. 4, 490.

13. Frederick Douglass, The Proclamation and a Negro Army, February 1863, in *Life and Writings,* vol. 3, 332.

14. Frederick Douglass, *The Life and Times of Frederick Douglass,* in *The Frederick Douglass Papers,* ser. 2, vol. 3, ed. John R. McKivigan (New Haven, CT: Yale University Press, 2013), 287 (hereafter cited as *Life and Times*); Abraham Lincoln, Second Inaugural Address, March 4, 1865, in *Speeches and Writings,* 792.

15. Frederick Douglass, The Mission of the War, February 13, 1864, in *Life and Writings,* vol. 3, 403; see also ibid., 114–115.

16. *Douglass Papers,* ser. 1, vol. 3, 441; ibid., vol. 2, 267; ibid., vol. 3, 127.

17. Douglass, Slavery and the Irrepressible Conflict, 376.

18. John C. Calhoun, Speech on the Reception of Abolition Petitions, in *Union and Liberty: The Political Philosophy of John C. Calhoun,* ed. Ross M. Lence (Indianapolis, IN: Liberty Fund, 1992), 472.

19. See, for example, Douglass, *Life and Writings,* vol. 3, 247–248; ibid., vol. 5, 177–179; *Douglass Papers,* ser. 1, vol. 4, 495.

20. Douglass, *Life and Writings,* vol. 2, 495; *Douglass Papers,* ser. 1, vol. 4, 173.

21. Douglass, *Life and Writings,* vol. 5, 244; *Douglass Papers,* ser. 1, vol. 5, 476–477; see also *Douglass Papers,* ser. 1, vol. 3, 422. On "the foolishness of preaching," see I Corinthians 1:21.

22. Douglass, *Life and Writings,* vol. 3, 328.

23. Frederick Douglass, The *Dred Scott* Decision, May 1857, in *Douglass Papers,* ser. 1, vol. 3, 164.

24. Frederick Douglass, Is It Right and Wise to Kill a Kidnapper?, in *Life and Writings,* vol. 2, 284–289.

25. John Locke, *The Second Treatise of Government,* in Locke, *Two Treatises of Government,* ed. Peter Laslett (Cambridge, UK: Cambridge University Press, 1988), secs. 208–209, 404–405.

26. Douglass, *Dred Scott* Decision, 167, 169, 171–172.

27. Frederick Douglass, "Liberty of Speech South," May 4, 1871, in *Life and Writings,* vol. 4, 245.

28. Frederick Douglass, "The Fall of Sumter," May 1861, in *Life and Writings,* vol. 3, 89–91; Douglass, "Sudden Revolution in Northern Sentiment," May 1861, in *Life and Writings,* vol. 3, 89–91, 92.

29. For Frederick Douglass's criticisms of Abraham Lincoln during this period, see, for example, *Life and Writings,* vol. 3, 159–162, 185–187, 202–208, 250–259.

30. On the fundamental concord between Abraham Lincoln and Frederick Douglass on the war's objective, see James Oakes, *The Radical and the Republican: Frederick Douglass, Abraham Lincoln, and the Triumph of Antislavery Politics* (New York: Norton, 2007); Allen Guelzo, *Lincoln's Emancipation Proclamation: The End of Slavery in America* (New York: Simon and Schuster, 2004), esp. 1–109.

31. Douglass, *Life and Writings,* vol. 3, 273, 277.

32. *Douglass Papers,* vol. 3, 568, 549.

33. Douglass, Proclamation and Negro Army, 333.

34. *Douglass Papers,* ser. 2, vol. 3, 277.

35. Douglass, Proclamation and Negro Army, 321–323.

36. Frederick Douglass, "Our Western Tour," March 25, 1859, in *Life and Writings,*

vol. 5, 422; Douglass, The Present and Future of the Colored Race in America, May 1863, in *Life and Writings*, vol. 3, 347. See also *Life and Writings*, vol. 2, 289.

37. Frederick Douglass, In What New Skin Will the Old Snake Come Forth? May 10, 1865, in *Douglass Papers*, ser. 1, vol. 4, 85.

38. Douglass, *Life and Writings*, vol. 3, 393–394.

39. Ibid., 81, 83; Frederick Douglass, What the Black Man Wants, in *Douglass Papers*, ser. 1, vol. 4, 62.

40. Frederick Douglass, "Shameful Abandonment of Principle," May 30, 1850, in *Life and Writings*, vol. 2, 122; see also Douglass, *Life and Times*, in *Douglass Papers*, ser. 2, vol. 3, 201.

41. Frederick Douglass, "Introduction to the Reason Why the Colored American Is Not in the World's Columbian Exposition," in *Life and Writings*, vol. 4, 471–472.

42. Frederick Douglass, This Decision Has Humbled the Nation, October 22, 1883, in *Douglass Papers*, ser. 1, vol. 5, 122–123; Douglass, New Hampshire for the Republicans, February 26, 1875, in *Douglass Papers*, ser. 1, vol. 4, 405–406.

43. Frederick Douglass, The Future of the Colored Race, May 1866, in *Life and Writings*, vol. 4, 193; Douglass, Decision Has Humbled the Nation, 123.

44. Douglass, Future of the Colored Race, 195–196; Frederick Douglass, "The Future of the Negro," in *Life and Writings*, vol. 4, 412; Frederick Douglass, The United States Cannot Remain Half-Slave and Half-Free, in *Life and Writings*, vol. 4, 370; see also Douglass, *Life and Writings*, vol. 1, 418; Douglass, *Life and Writings*, vol. 3, 264–266, 286; *Douglass Papers*, ser. 1, vol. 4, 205.

45. Frederick Douglass, "The Work of the Future," November 1862, in *Life and Writings*, vol. 3, 292.

46. Douglass, Mission of the War, 390 (emphasis added).

47. Frederick Douglass, Our Work Is Not Done, December 3, 1863, in *Life and Writings*, vol. 3, 386. See also Galatians 3:28.

48. Frederick Douglass, At Last, at Last, the Black Man Has a Future, April 22, 1870, in *Douglass Papers*, ser. 1, vol. 4, 266–267 (emphasis added); see also *Douglass Papers*, ser. 1, vol. 4, 361.

49. Friedrich Nietzsche, Aphorism 208, *Beyond Good and Evil*, in *The Complete Works of Friedrich Nietzsche*, vol. 8, ed. Adrian del Caro (Stanford, CA: Stanford University Press, 2014), 111.

50. Frederick Douglass, *My Bondage and My Freedom*, in *Douglass: Autobiographies* (New York: Library of America, 1994), 362. See also Douglass, *Life and Writings*, vol. 2, 177; *Douglass Papers*, ser. 1, vol. 4, 187, 418; *Douglass Papers*, ser. 1, vol. 5, 548.

51. *Douglass Papers*, ser. 2, vol. 3, 372–373.

52. Frederick Douglass, William the Silent, February 8, 1869, in *Douglass Papers*, ser. 1, vol. 4, 187.

53. Lincoln, Second Inaugural Address, 792–793.

54. Frederick Douglass, Advice to Black Youth, February 1, 1855, in *Douglass Papers*, ser. 1, vol. 3, 3.

55. Frederick Douglass, The Trials and Triumphs of Self-Made Men, January 4, 1860, in *Douglass Papers*, ser. 1, vol. 3, 300.

56. Frederick Douglass, Did John Brown Fail?, May 30, 1881, in *Douglass Papers,* ser. 1, vol. 5, 22. In this speech and, in fact, since Brown's raid, Douglass extolled Brown in the most glowing terms as a hero and martyr, even as the captain of a vanguard strike force in what might be considered, in hindsight, an initial skirmish in the Civil War. Yet at the time of the raid itself, Douglass's opinion was mixed. He had declined Brown's direct invitation to take part in the Harpers Ferry raid because he judged it not only suicidal but also gravely imprudent as a public act; it would signify an attack on the US government and thereby (as with Garrisonian disunionism) stain the abolition movement with anti-Americanism. See Frederick Douglass to the *Rochester (NY) Democrat and American,* October 31, 1859, in *Life and Writings,* vol. 2, 461–462; Douglass, *Life and Times,* in *Douglass Papers,* ser. 2, vol. 3, 236–251.

57. Frederick Douglass, The Future of the Negro People of the Slave States, February 12, 1862, in *Life and Writings,* vol. 3, 225. See also Douglass, *Life and Writings,* vol. 5, 240.

58. Frederick Douglass, "Emancipation Proclaimed," October 1862, in *Life and Writings,* vol. 3, 274.

59. Douglass, At Last, at Last, 271–272.

60. Frederick Douglass to Gerrit Smith, July 3, 1874, in *Life and Writings,* vol. 4, 306; Douglass, One Country, One Law, One Liberty for All Citizens, January 1889, in *Douglass Papers,* ser. 1, vol. 5, 400. On black voting rights as supportive of states' rights, see Douglass, "Reconstruction," December 1866, in *Life and Writings,* vol. 4, 199.

61. Douglass, New Hampshire for the Republicans, 405.

62. Frederick Douglass, Sources of Danger to the Republic, February 7, 1867, in *Douglass Papers,* ser. 1, vol. 4, 158, 164–165.

63. Ibid., 158, 162–168.

64. He endorsed a more radically democratic constitutionalism as early as 1851 and as late as 1883. See Frederick Douglass, "Is Civil Government Right?," in *Life and Writings,* vol. 5, 211–212; Douglass, Decision Has Humbled the Nation, 115.

65. Frederick Douglass, Equal Rights for All, May 14, 1868, in *Douglass Papers,* ser. 1, vol. 4, 176.

66. Frederick Douglass, We Need a True, Strong, and Principled Party, March 29, 1871, in *Douglass Papers,* ser. 1, vol. 4, 282.

67. Douglass, Trials and Triumphs of Self-Made Men, 572; Douglass, We Need a True, Strong, and Principled Party, 283.

68. Frederick Douglass, Our Composite Nationality, December 7, 1869, in *Douglass Papers,* ser. 1, vol. 4, 254–256.

69. See, for example, Douglass, *Life and Writings,* vol. 4, 523; *Douglass Papers,* ser. 1, vol. 4, 241–243, 253; *Douglass Papers,* ser. 1, vol. 5, 572.

70. *Douglass Papers,* ser. 1, vol. 4, 253.

71. Douglass, "Work of the Future," 291–292.

72. *Douglass Papers,* ser. 2, vol. 3, 477.

73. Douglass, Proclamation and Negro Army, 330.

74. Frederick Douglass, Celebrating the Past, Anticipating the Future, April 14, 1875, in *Douglass Papers,* ser. 1, vol. 4, 417.

75. Frederick Douglass, The Unknown Dead, May 30, 1871, in *Douglass Papers,* ser. 1, vol. 4, 290–291.

76. Douglass, There Was a Right Side, 485, 491.

77. Frederick Douglass, The Negro Exodus from the Gulf States, September 12, 1879, in *Life and Writings*, vol. 4, 336. Among Douglass's other objections to the Exodus was a political concern: the migration out of the South, he argued, "takes colored voters from a section of the country where they are sufficiently numerous to elect some of their number to places of honor and profit, and places them in a country where their proportion to other classes will be so small as not to be recognized as a political element" (338–339). A few years later, however, Douglass retracted his opposition to the Exodus, citing a fuller awareness of the difficulties then confronting Southern blacks; see Douglass, Strong to Suffer, and Yet Strong to Strive, April 16, 1886, in *Douglass Papers*, ser. 1, vol. 5, 232–233.

78. Frederick Douglass, The *Civil Rights Cases*, October 88, 1883, in *Douglass Papers*, ser. 1, vol. 5, 112.

79. Frederick Douglass, Why Is the Negro Lynched? January 1894, in *Life and Writings*, vol. 4, 511.

80. Frederick Douglass, The Nation's Problem, April 16, 1889, in *Douglass Papers*, ser. 1, vol. 5, 423.

81. Frederick Douglass, Lessons of the Hour, in *Douglass Papers*, ser. 1, vol. 5, 596, 607.

82. Frederick Douglass, This Is a Sad and Mournful Hour, June 2, 1879, in *Douglass Papers*, ser. 1, vol. 4, 507. On the soul of the nation, see Douglass, *Life and Writings*, vol. 3, 339, 395; Douglass, *Life and Writings*, vol. 4, 225.

83. Frederick Douglass, "The Do-Nothing Policy," September 12, 1856, in *Life and Writings*, vol. 2, 404; Douglass, The Revolution of 1848, in *Life and Writings*, vol. 1, 323. See also *Douglass Papers*, ser. 1, vol. 3, 544.

84. John Adams, *Thoughts on Government*, in *John Adams: Revolutionary Writings*, ed. C. Bradley Thompson (Indianapolis, IN: Liberty Fund, 2000), 293 (also available at http://oll.libertyfund.org/titles/adams-revolutionary-writings)

85. Douglass, Proclamation and Negro Army, 552

86. Frederick Douglass, Great Britain's Example Is High, Noble, and Grand, August 6, 1885, in *Douglass Papers*, ser. 1, vol. 5, 193.

87. Niccolò Machiavelli, *Discourses on Livy*, Book 3, trans. Harvey C. Mansfield and Nathan Tarcov (Chicago: University of Chicago Press, 1996), chap. 1, 209–212.

88. Thucydides, *The Peloponnesian War*, trans. Steven Lattimore (Indianapolis, IN: Hackett, 1998), 37–38, 97–102, 164–172, 295–300.

89. Douglass, Decision of the Hour, 119.

90. Douglass, Equal Rights for All, 173.

91. Frederick Douglass, The Negro Problem, October 21, 1890, in *Douglass Papers*, ser. 1, vol. 5, 456, 455.

92. Frederick Douglass, "Danger to the Abolition Cause," June 1861, in *Life and Writings*, vol. 3, 112.

93. Frederick Douglass, Address to the People of the United States, September 24, 1883, in *Life and Writings*, vol. 4, 380.

94. Frederick Douglass, The Blessings of Liberty and Education, in *Douglass Papers*, ser. 1, vol. 5, 625–626.

95. Douglass, Future of the Negro People of the Slave States, 218; see also *Douglass Papers,* ser. 1, vol. 4, 49.

96. Douglass, Blessings of Liberty and Education, 625; *Douglass Papers,* ser. 1, vol. 5, 411. See also Matthew 12:22–28.

97. Douglass, Address to the People of the United States, 377–378; *Douglass Papers,* ser. 1, vol. 4, 90–91.

98. Douglass, Blessings of Liberty and Education, 624.

# CHAPTER 14

# The South and American Constitutionalism after the Civil War

JOHNATHAN O'NEILL

How should the modern scholar understand the South and American constitutionalism? On the one hand, there are deeply rooted constitutional precedents to support the racist assumptions long characteristic of Southern culture. Indeed, slavery was protected by the original Constitution, and during the antebellum period the South's views on slavery and the nature of the Union were in the mainstream of American political thought. The ensuing period of segregation also was "constitutional" insofar as the practice was widely accepted by the polity at large. On the other hand, if one wants to condemn the South's racist constitutionalism, the relativistic positivism of modern scholarship is not adequate to the task.[1] Social science positivism is committed to being value free and scientific and thus unable scientifically to uphold any moral principle, such as equality, or to decry any moral evil, such as racism. A better approach is to consider the South's attitudes from the perspective of the natural rights principles of the American regime. These are the most appropriate measure of Southern thinkers' postwar relationship to the founding and the Constitution. This chapter applies this standard to Southern thought after the war, showing that its leading exponents rejected or failed adequately to confront the founding proposition that "all men are created equal." When the major constitutional and political changes of the twentieth century more fully realized the Declaration's natural rights principles in the South, it was an undeniably great achievement.

However, despite being tainted by racism, Southern voices raised legitimate concerns in the aftermath of the Civil War. Increasingly lost because of the association with racism were well-founded Southern criticisms of the nation's drift into ever more centralized government, crass consumerism, and leveling egalitarianism.

This chapter both analyzes the failings of Southern constitutionalism after the Civil War and highlights the South's legitimate cultural and political critiques. It shows the often intimate connections between the South's racist views and its otherwise valid critiques and (to the extent possible) tries to disentangle them from each other.

## CONFEDERATE APOLOGISTS FOR THE CIVIL WAR

The first post–Civil War Southern histories of the conflict defended the South's established antebellum views. The most significant of these histories were by Jefferson Davis, president of the Confederacy; Alexander Stephens, its vice president; Albert Taylor Bledsoe, the Confederate undersecretary of war; and Edward Albert Pollard, a Confederate journalist.[2] Each expended considerable energy to defend state sovereignty, the compact theory of the Union, the constitutional legitimacy of secession, and opposition to government centralization in the North. The South, said Stephens, had been fighting for the "Sovereign Right of Local Self-government."[3] Its defeat, said Bledsoe, meant that the basis of the federal government had shifted from "compact to that of conquest." The North's "tendency to consolidation in the central power" had finally won.[4] "Under and in spite of the Constitution," the North had become the majority "faction" of James Madison's *Federalist Paper* 10. For Bledsoe, Northern victory was "the fall of the Republic, and the rise of a despotism."[5] Stephens allowed that there was still time to avert the slide into despotism and imperial rule but insisted that "the great and vital question now is: Shall the Federal Government be arrested in its progress, and be brought back to original principles, or shall it be permitted to go on in its present tendencies and rapid strides, until it reaches complete Consolidation[?]"[6] It is apparent from these early apologias for the South that the result of the war had distanced their authors from the belief in the progress of human liberty that had characterized pre–Civil War "Whiggish" historical writing.[7] How could it be, they lamented, that constitutionally limited government and local self-determination had lost to centralization and imperial control?

This Southern post–Civil War conception of political liberty, though serious and significant, failed to address slavery. Indeed, slavery did not appear in these histories as having any moral aspect. It was merely a factor in the larger sectional cum economic and civilizational conflict these writers agreed was the fundamental cause of the war. Slavery "was not a moral dispute." Analysis of its place in the story should not be obscured "by irrelevant issues and the glamour of ethical illusions."[8] Indeed, said Davis, "slavery" was a misnomer for the "mildest and most humane" form of "servitude" that Africans had experienced in the South, where providence had seen fit to place them so that they might be "Christian[ized]" and "improve[d]."[9] Moreover, slavery was the basis of the leisure that ennobled the culture and refined the manners of Southern civilization.[10] These authors' defense of the South did not attempt to justify slavery, yet denied the moral high ground to the North by observing that it too had profited from it. Ultimately the moral question could not be eluded, and everyone knew the foundational premise of the South's position. As Stephens said in the notorious Corner-Stone Speech on the eve of the war, the Confederacy was built "upon the great truth that the negro is not equal to the white man; that slavery[,] subordination to the superior race[,] is his natural and normal condition." The Constitution of the Union "rested upon the assumption of the equality of races. This was an error."[11] However much at the level of theory the South's later arguments for local self-government, states' rights, or secession might be distinguished from racism and slavery, in practice they were inseparable.

Nevertheless, the South had to contend with the meaning of the brute fact of defeat. Postwar Southern writers immediately set about this task. Probably no one did so with as much insight and prescience as Pollard. In the remarkable conclusion to his *The Lost Cause* (1867), he emphasized what would become the South's main refrains almost down to our times: the wrongness of Reconstruction understood as both an assertion of federal power and an attempt at racial equality, and the crassness of the North's materialistic culture. In sounding the first theme, Pollard asserted the clear limits of what the war had decided: "The doctrine of secession was extinguished" and "the restoration of the Union and the abolition of slavery" were settled, but "only so far as political formulas were necessarily involved in these have they been affected by the conclusion." The Southern people "surrendered in the war what the war has conquered; but they cannot be expected to give up what was not involved in the war, and voluntarily abandon their political schools for the dogma of Consolidation." Moreover, there was much the war had not decided: "The war did not decide negro equality; it did not decide negro suffrage; it did not decide State Rights, although it might have exploded their abuse; it did not decide the orthodoxy of the Democratic party." Pollard insisted that states' rights could endure: "It is for the South to preserve every remnant of her rights, and even, though parting with the doctrine of secession, to beware of the extremity of surrendering State Rights in gross." In making these statements, he accurately forecast how the South would approach the constitutional system until well into the twentieth century.[12]

Pollard's second hope that would define the Southern reaction to the Civil War was that defeat did not condemn the South to the base materialism and petty individualism of the North. His antimodernist, antimaterialist cultural critique is worth quoting at length:

> It is to be feared that in the present condition of the Southern States, losses will be experienced greater than the immediate inflictions of fire and sword. The danger is that they will lose their literature, their former habits of thought, their intellectual self-assertion, while they are too intent upon recovering the mere *material* prosperity, ravaged and impaired by the war. There are certain coarse advisers who tell the Southern people that the great ends of their lives now are to repair their stock of national wealth; to bring in Northern capital and labour; to build mills and factories and hotels and gilded caravansaries; and to make themselves rivals in the clattering and garish enterprise of the North. This advice has its proper place. But there are higher objects than the Yankee *magna bona* of money and display, and loftier aspirations than the civilization of material things. In the life of nations, as in that of the individual, there is something better than pelf, and the coarse prosperity of dollars and cents.[13]

As we shall see below, Pollard's themes—the condemnation of Reconstruction and Northern materialism—trod a path that Southern intellectuals went down repeatedly in their assessments of the meaning of the war for the American polity.

The next section of this chapter analyzes Southern intellectuals' attack on the wrongness of Reconstruction (Pollard's first theme), and the following section explores their indictment of the crass materialism of the North (Pollard's second theme). In making these arguments, Southern intellectuals sometimes proved prescient in foreseeing some of the ills of the rise of big government as well as the development of vulgarity in American culture. However, despite these insights, the tragedy of the South after the Civil War was related to its faults beforehand: it could not shake itself of racism. The South's continuing entanglement with racism tarnished its thinkers' critiques, which otherwise might have helped the reconstructed nation deal with the legitimate concerns Southerners raised.

## THE LIMITS OF RECONSTRUCTION IN PRACTICE AND THOUGHT

Though the South lost on the questions of secession and slavery, the story of Reconstruction (1865–1877) told by modern scholarship is how briefly it lasted and how little change it wrought. In this sense Pollard's hopes were vindicated in practice perhaps more than he expected they would be. To be sure, slavery was abolished by the Thirteenth Amendment, federal citizenship defined and civil rights protected by the Fourteenth, and racial discrimination in voting forbidden by the Fifteenth. Through these amendments the radicals in the Republican Party sought to bring the Constitution and Southern life into accord with the principles of liberty, equality, and consent announced in the Declaration of Independence but left unrealized because of slavery. And for a short time, the federal government enforced the amendments through its military presence in the South and its oversight of the region's elections. Modern scholarship concludes that Reconstruction was short-lived and limited not only because of Southern intransigence and racial violence but also because of the North's waning appetite for the thorough remaking of Southern society required to enforce the constitutional principles of Northern victory.[14]

Secession was delegitimized, but most political actors– Southern and Northern– remained very much committed to a decentralized federal polity. Lasting change would have required a substantial shift in the balance of federalism and a long-term military presence in the South. Scholars have shown there was never nearly enough public support for such a change.[15] The postwar constitutional understanding of federalism was articulated, and much of its shape was forecast, in the important case of *Texas v. White* (1869). To determine whether the state of Texas could recover title to US bonds sold by its Confederate government during the war, the Court had to rule on the question of secession. Chief Justice Salmon Chase wrote that the admission of Texas into the Union "was something more than a compact; it was the incorporation of a new member into the political body. And it was final. The union between Texas and the other States was as complete, as perpetual, and as indissoluble as the union between the original States." The Texas secession ordinance and the acts of its Confederate legislature "were absolutely null. They were utterly without operation in law." However, having thus dispensed with secession according to the quintessentially Lincolnian theory of the Union, Chase underscored the traditional federal polity's respect for the states: "Not only, therefore, can there be no loss of separate and independent autonomy to the States through their union under the Constitution, but it may be not unreasonably said that the preservation of the States, and the maintenance of their governments, are as much within the design and care of the Constitution as the preservation of the Union and the maintenance of the National government. The Constitution, in all its provisions, looks to an indestructible Union composed of indestructible States."[16] Thus was secession cast into the dustbin of history and the balance of federalism recalibrated, yet without creating the modern centralized regulatory state.

Although the Reconstruction amendments wrote freedom into the Constitution and created the legal-constitutional tools to transform the South, they could not create the political will to do so. Likewise, the Supreme Court's interpretive approach to the amendments provided ample room for federal oversight of the South and a thorough vindication of the newly announced rights of African Americans, had the American people insisted that Congress take such action.[17] Absent broad support from the polity, and given its own unwillingness to revolutionize the federal system, the Court managed to secure only some aspects of liberty for the freedpeople. It treated Reconstruction as a political question insusceptible to active judicial intervention, thus accepting the polity's broader commitment to the retention of a decentralized federal system in which African Americans remained subjugated.[18] To the detriment of the freedpeople, its jurisprudence focused on preserving the self-governing prerogatives of the states within the federal system while also maintaining the inherited legal distinctions between civil and political rights and between state and private action. An uncomplicated political lesson from this experience is that the pace of cultural change is significantly slower than a decisive military victory or the capacity to engross words on parchment. Another way of putting it, in the realistic but still melancholy words of historian Michael Les Benedict, is that during Reconstruction "Republicans sought to establish democratic constitutional government but in the process threatened constitutional liberty, as white southerners understood it. . . . To southern Conservatives, the war against those [Republican state] constitutions was a struggle not against liberty and democracy but for them."[19] The Southern conception of liberty and self-government simply could not be so quickly expanded to include formerly enslaved people.

After the war, then, Congress and American public opinion acquiesced as notable Supreme Court opinions upheld the segregation and disfranchisement that Southern states relentlessly imposed on African Americans. The *Slaughterhouse Cases* (1873), while not dealing with race as such, made it clear that the Court did not think the Fourteenth Amendment's protections for the civil rights of formerly enslaved people had effectuated a wholesale revolution in federalism. It held that butchers who protested a locally licensed monopoly over the slaughtering trade did not have a new federal right the Fourteenth Amendment could vindicate. In giving the federal government the power to protect the civil rights of formerly enslaved people from state violation, the amendment had not meant to transfer all responsibility for the protection of all civil rights from the states to the federal government, said the Court. To have done so would have made the Court a "perpetual censor upon all legislation of the States, on the civil rights of their own citizens."[20]

Likewise, the Court insisted that the Fourteenth Amendment authorized federal legislation only against state actions that denied rights but not against such actions by private individuals. It similarly accepted that although the Thirteenth and Fifteenth Amendments could reach the discriminatory actions of private individuals, the government was required to show explicitly that they were motivated by racial hostility rather than ordinary criminal intent. In practice this approach relegated black victims to racially biased state criminal justice systems[21] and permitted racial discrimination in privately owned businesses that served the public, such as inns and theaters.[22] These trends reached a culmination of sorts when the Court retreated from its earlier prohibition on racial classification by endorsing the infamous "separate but equal" rule for public transportation in *Plessy v. Ferguson* (1896).[23] Its principle was rapidly extended to most other public contexts.

With respect to nondiscrimination in voting, under the Fifteenth Amendment, the Court at first narrowly read its enforcement section. It sought to preserve primary local control over the regulation of elections while strictly limiting federal oversight to matters of race.[24] This approach had the perverse effect of encouraging Southern states to create facially neutral devices, such as literacy tests and poll taxes, that disfranchised nearly all African Americans and many poor whites. The Court upheld each of these devices.[25] Along the way, the Senate failed in 1890–1891 to pass a bill sponsored by Henry Cabot Lodge that would have strengthened federal authority to protect the voting rights of African Americans in the South.[26] No such attempt was again made for well over half a century. Additionally, by the very early twentieth century most Southern states had successfully implemented the "white primary," thus ensuring that African Americans were kept out of the political process at this crucial early stage. Both developments ensured that the South was a white-dominated, one-party political system until the late 1960s.[27]

During this long era of second-class citizenship for African Americans, the first wave of professional historical writing on Reconstruction took shape. It clung to the premise of racial inferiority that Pollard's *Lost Cause* had hoped would be undisturbed by the result of the war. The sanction of scholarship was thus given to the North's retreat from Reconstruction and the South's reassertion of white supremacy. For more than half a century the South won the intellectual battle for the meaning of the war despite its surrender at Appomattox. Only after World War II did scholars begin to describe Reconstruction as a tragedy in which the South, with Northern complicity, had successfully evaded the postwar amendments and thus negated America's natural rights principles. This modern view gradually replaced the older interpretation. However, in the early twentieth century nearly all scholars ratified and justified Southern actions. How and why did the nation reach a judgment about the Civil War and Reconstruction that largely endorsed the Southern rejection of natural rights and human equality?

The older literature on Reconstruction, called the "Dunning" school of historiography, is well known to American historians. William A. Dunning and his mentor, John W. Burgess at Columbia University, were its founders. The major theme of this interpretation, as stated by Dunning, was "the struggle through which the southern whites, subjugated by adversaries of their own race, thwarted the scheme which threatened permanent subjection to another race."[28] The premise of this theme was white supremacy and the incapacity of the freedpeople for self-restraint and self-government. Dunning's work was clear enough on this point, expressing the racist assumptions prevalent in his era. He wrote that the

ultimate root of the trouble in the South had been, not the institution of slavery, but the coexistence in one society of two races so distinct in characteristics as to render coalescence impossible; that slavery had been a *modus vivendi* through which social life was possible; and that, after its disappearance, its place must be taken by some set of conditions which, if more humane and beneficent in accidents, must in essence express the same fact of racial inequality.[29]

The assertion of federal authority in the South during Reconstruction was "in support of a social and political system in which all the forces that made for civilization were dominated by a mass of barbarous freedmen."[30] Based on this view, Dunning praised the conciliatory, white supremacist policies of President Andrew Johnson; condemned the Republicans as vindictive radicals bent on humiliating the prostrate South; distorted the record of Republican state governments; and rationalized the violence of the Ku Klux Klan. Sanity was said to have returned with white rule and the conclusion of Reconstruction in 1877.[31]

Dunning's many students propagated this perspective in a series of monographic studies of individual states, making it the orthodoxy of the historical profession until the mid-twentieth century. Its core premise of black incapacity meant that Republican efforts to remake the South based on liberty, equality, and consent had been unjust and impossible. The natural rights principles of the founding were no more applicable to African Americans after the Civil War than they had been before it. The Dunning school was also the basis of the popular understanding of Reconstruction, as illustrated in Claude G. Bowers's best-selling *The Tragic Era* (1929) and Thomas G. Dixon's *The Clansman* (1905), which D. W. Griffith famously filmed as *Birth of a Nation* (1915). The treatment of Reconstruction as a tragic mistake soon righted made it possible to exempt the nation from any sustained concern about justice for the freedpeople and their descendants.

This interpretation also fostered sectional reconciliation and national integration. These were major goals for Burgess, who was not only Dunning's mentor but also a leader in the early attempt to organize American political science into a discipline oriented around G. W. F. Hegel's theory of the state. Scholars have long understood that Burgess was fundamentally a Hegelian,[32] but few have analyzed the connection between this intellectual inheritance and his interpretation of Reconstruction. Doing so shows just how much the pro-Southern view, with its concomitant rejection of natural rights, was propagated by the Hegelian philosophical principles embedded in the professionalization of scholarship in the early twentieth century.[33]

Hegel's influence on Burgess produced a forthright rejection of the American theory of natural rights and social contract as the appropriate measure for the meaning of the Civil War and Reconstruction. Rather, Hegel held that all legitimate authority derived from the "state," understood as the ethic or spirit of the political community, which stood behind and legitimated all law and government. History was the rational and inevitable progress of the state as it realized and effectuated the universal principles of civilization.[34] Applying this view to the Civil War, Burgess was sure that "the spirit of civilization" was at work beyond the conscious intentions of the Republican Party. The war was progressive in a Hegelian sense because "the United States were lagging in the march of modern civilization. Slavery and 'State sovereignty' were the fetters which held them back." Accordingly, the "meaning of secession" in the "plan of universal history" was to bring the end of slavery and state sovereignty, "to provoke the Nation to strike them off at one fell blow, and free itself, and assert its supremacy, forevermore."[35]

Although Burgess's notion of progress thus rejected both slavery and any local resistance to the sovereignty of the national "state," it also contained a rigorous and fully theorized racism.[36] The "Teutonic nations" were the most advanced and were "particularly endowed with the capacity of establishing national states." They were "intrusted, in the general economy of history" to "carry the political civilization of the modern world into those parts of the world inhabited by unpolitical and barbaric races."[37] Colonization was necessary, and likely sometimes force: "The civilized states have a claim upon the uncivilized populations, as well as a duty towards them, and that claim is that they shall become civilized; and if they cannot accomplish their own civilization, then must they submit to the powers that can do it for them."[38]

On this account, progress could have only one leader: the "Teutonic element, when dominant, should never surrender the balance of political power. . . . Under certain circumstances it should not even permit participation of the other elements in political power."[39] Burgess's judgment on Reconstruction was thus perfectly consistent with his general philosophical principles: "It was a great wrong to civilization to put the white race of the South under the domination of the negro race. The claim that there is nothing in the color of the skin from the point of view of political ethics is a great sophism. A black skin means membership in a race of men which has never of itself succeeded in subjecting passion to reason, has never, therefore, created any civilization of any kind." Granting political power to the freedpeople, he concluded, was "to establish barbarism in power over civilization. The supposed disloyalty, or even the actual disloyalty, of the white population will not justify this."[40]

The Dunning-Burgess view of Reconstruction constituted a putatively objective body of scientific knowledge consonant with the racist premises of the older Southern view. Acceptance of it functioned to mark one as a professional scholar. Its substance encouraged the reconciliation of North and South insofar as Northerners too agreed that Reconstruction was a dreadful mistake.[41] However, as Burgess made abundantly clear, the return of sectional comity via scholarly consensus was premised on rejecting the founding American principle of natural human equality, a rejection of which had always grounded the Southern position. The Spanish-American War helpfully clarified this point: "The Republican party, in its work of imposing the sovereignty of the United States upon eight millions of Asiatics, has changed its views in regard to the political relation of races and has at last virtually accepted the ideas of the South upon that subject." Southern whites needed no longer fear that the Republicans "will ever again give themselves over to the vain imagination of the political equality of man. It is this change of mind and heart on the part of the North . . . which has caused the now much-talked-of reconciliation."[42]

Though Burgess's condemnation of Reconstruction was clearly derived from Hegelian state theory, that perspective ultimately was too foreign to the American experience accurately to understand its politics. As one scholar has written, Burgess's Hegelianism "was perpetually frustrated of an object." Americans simply did not think of their national life with "any sense of the purposes of the State." However, it is ironic that as early twentieth-century American political science developed away from the theories of Burgess and his ilk, it remained incapable of reaching a sounder philosophical judgment about why Reconstruction was tragically limited. The new generation of scholars who attacked the formalism and abstraction of German state theory replaced its misconceived ethics with pragmatism and a putatively "scientific" analysis of the social process. This new behavioralism in political science abjured defending at the level of theory but assumed in practice the first principles of the American founding and the constitutional order based on them.[43] Only by proper attention to these things could a truer conclusion about the period be reached.

W. E. B. DuBois did thoroughly attack the pro-Southern Dunning-Burgess view during the era of its dominance, albeit from a basis also distant from America's first principles. He argued that Reconstruction briefly brought substantial benefits to the South, including its first real taste of democratic government, its first free public schools, and a substantial increase in needed social legislation.[44] He also excoriated the racism that pervaded the Dunning-Burgess interpretation in a memorably acerbic postscript to his massive book on the era.[45] DuBois quite properly "assum[ed] the truth" of natural human equality, insisting on the "essential humanity of Negroes, in their ability to be educated, to do the work of the modern world, to take their place as equal citizens with others," though he knew this precept would "seriously curtail" his audience in early twentieth-century America.[46] However, he offhandedly dismissed constitutional principles as an explanation for the coming of the war and the shaping of the Reconstruction settlement. Instead, he regarded the Marxist dogma of class struggle as the best explanation of Reconstruction and of social life more generally. DuBois's brave and influential indictment of the racist scholarly consensus, like that consensus itself, was not grounded in reengagement with America's founding principles.

The Marxist-inflected class analysis of Progressivism, which so influenced DuBois, sat alongside the Dunning-Burgess view of the Civil War and Reconstruction in the early twentieth century. This approach also significantly influenced Southern assessments of how the war affected the region's place in the constitutional order, though in ways much different than that of DuBois. The Progressive interpretation was advanced by Charles A. Beard, who, with his wife, Mary, echoed the postwar Confederate apologists by arguing that the conflict was a "social revolution," a "cataclysm in which the capitalists, laborers, and farmers of the North and West drove from power in the national government the planting aristocracy of the South."[47] After the Northern victory in this "Second American Revolution," Northern industrialists captured the federal government, a development the South had long resisted. Northern dominance meant renewal of the protective tariff, national banking legislation, a method of war financing that bound capitalists to Union victory, federal subsidies for railroads, and newfound encouragement of immigration to staff Northern factories.[48] Beard also was a major source of the "conspiracy theory" of the Fourteenth Amendment, which held that its framers had intended it to protect corporate "persons" from state taxation and regulation as much or more than to protect formerly enslaved people.[49] Though subsequently discounted in favor of the more accurate "Negro freedom" theory first articulated in the *Slaughterhouse Cases,* the conspiracy theory supported the notion that the Supreme Court's pre–New Deal suspicion of economic regulation served the same Northern capitalist interests at the root of the war.[50] Again, like the post-war Confederate apologists, the Beards slighted the issue of slavery and treated emancipation mostly as a question about property relationships: "Whatever may be the ethical view of the transaction," they wrote, freeing enslaved people was "the most stupendous act of sequestration in the history of Anglo-Saxon jurisprudence."[51] This approach disgusted DuBois. Momentarily eliding his own Marxism, he observed that in the Beards' "sweeping mechanistic interpretation" one was left "with a comfortable feeling that nothing right or wrong is involved."[52] Indeed, a subsequent analyst of this scholarship concluded that the Beards' consistent condemnation of the supposed economic results of Union victory supported the old Confederate view.[53] As exemplified by the Beards, the strong element of economic determinism in Progressive scholarship sustained the Southern claim that the war was simply a sectional economic rivalry absent any conflict about the meaning of natural rights.

The Progressive line of analysis remained central to pro-Southern scholarship for much of the rest of the twentieth century. The South had long complained of Northern economic domination before the war.[54] Afterward, as we have seen, both Confederate apologists and Beardian Progressives held that the Civil War's fundamental significance was the victory of Northern industrial capitalism. This framework was forcefully elaborated in C. Vann Woodward's influential neo-Beardian account, *The Origins of the New South, 1877–1913* (1951), which argued that the North had intentionally and successfully made the South into a dependent "colonial economy" after Reconstruction.[55] Ever since, empirical and interpretive disputes about this thesis have been major features of historical writing about the South.[56] Scholars have reached no consensus about just how much of Southern economic underdevelopment can be charged to the legacy of slavery, the destruction of the war, the policies of the federal government and private business that favored Northern industry, the scarcity of capital in the region, the economic choices of Southerners them-selves, or perhaps even a secret Yankee-capitalist plot.[57] To the extent that the colonial thesis alleged a never-proven Northern conspiracy, modern historians increasingly find it unpersuasive.[58] Though there might be some element of truth in the more general thesis, too much emphasis on it avoids confronting the South's relationship to America's founding principles.

A claim allied to the colonial thesis, also prominent among both the Con-federate apologists and Beardians, was that Union victory installed the capital-ist North's modern "Leviathan" state of centralization, bureaucratic rule, and regulatory direction.[59] The contrary, however, is true. As several scholars have noted, after the conflict, the wartime assertion of central state authority was quickly rolled back, as was the size of the army. Regulation of the industrial economy was minimal and confused for decades and did not produce anything like an intrusive modern bureaucracy. Payments to Union veterans and des-titute mothers were more often seen as a lesson in the extravagances of party patronage than as model for the modern welfare state. Tariff, banking, and monetary policies reasserted constitutionally legitimate federal powers under-mined before the war—they were not the extrusions of a revolutionary new statist order. The more constitutionally contestable federal subsidy to private railroads is best understood as the result of a government too weak to take on the task of construction, combined with the reluctance of private capital to do so.[60] As one scholar has concluded, it is "difficult to conjure out of these a 'con-solidating,' or even nascent, spirit of étatisme remotely like that exhibited in most European nations at the time."[61] As Leonard D. White put it in his impor-tant study, "An old timer in Washington looking backward from the vantage point of the late 1890s would have found the government establishment bigger but not much different from its essential nature in 1870." "Volume of activity had increased, but not new functions or activities."[62] In America the shift to-ward the regulatory-administrative state resulted not from the Civil War and Reconstruction but from Progressivism and the New Deal. Still, the view that the result of the war brought what Pollard so feared in *The Lost Cause*—the victory of the Northern capitalist-statist juggernaut—had a long reach. Much of the South accepted it despite the region's often welcoming experience of federal power in the eras of Progressive and New Deal state-building. As with the colonial thesis, blaming the intrusive modern American state on Union victory in the Civil War cast the South as a victim, ignoring the violations of the natural and civil rights of African Americans that historically had charac-terized Southern life absent federal oversight or force of arms.

## THE CULTURAL CRITIQUE: SOUTHERN AGRARIANISM ON
## AMERICAN CONSTITUTIONALISM

Just as Pollard's argument on the limits of Reconstruction developed into a full-blown critique of Northern selfishness and racial naïveté in the Dunning-Burgess and Beardian interpretations of the Civil War and Reconstruction, so too was his argument on the North's cultural degeneration more fully elaborated. It was a major theme in the work of the famous Vanderbilt University Agrarians. Scholars have long understood, as did the original Agrarians, that as a body of thought it was more of a shared cultural and intellectual dispensation than a unified political movement with an agreed agenda.[63] The Agrarians and those they influenced chose differing philosophical and political paths as time passed. Yet their core ideas are readily identifiable. Most fundamentally, Agrarianism was a literary and cultural critique of the modern society created by Northern industrial capitalism. The Agrarians arrayed against it a semiromantic affirmation of the South's traditional, rural communities, calling for their preservation against the consumerist greed and tawdry self-absorption that the scientific and industrial North called "progress." The Agrarians did not think industrialism could be wholly avoided. However, they believed that the necessary condition of the South's endurance as a distinctive culture, and as shelter for human liberty in the dawning age of statist collectivism, was that it remain rooted economically in agriculture and independent property ownership. Moreover, the Agrarians agreed that the economics and culture of industrialism, along with the attendant centralization of power in the federal government, was an invasion from the North—just as in 1861.[64] Thus, the Agrarians' trenchant and often poignant condemnation of modern materialism and individualism was tied to their condemnation of the North and its direction of the constitutional order. The Agrarians severely criticized American constitutional development and occasionally tried to steer the New Deal to the benefit of the South, all while still condoning racism and segregation.

Frank L. Owsley, a noted historian, was the thinker who most directly applied the general Agrarian perspective to constitutional and political issues. In *I'll Take My Stand* (1930), Owsley explicitly praised the Dunning view of Reconstruction, stating that it was a necessary corrective for returning the South to its "true philosophy" as against Northern distortion and self-righteousness.[65] He denied that slavery was an authentic reason for the war, and he was sure that Reconstruction was a disaster. It had empowered "former slaves, some of whom could still remember the taste of human flesh and the bulk of them hardly three generations removed from cannibalism. These half-savage blacks were armed" and lorded it over the white population with the help of vindictive Northern politicians and the Union Army.[66]

Owsley never doubted white supremacy, but he insisted that slavery was only a subcomponent of the larger economic and civilizational struggle between North and South. Combining some of the interpretations of historian Frederick Jackson Turner, and especially Beard, with the basic position of the postwar Confederate apologists, Owsley wrote that the "irrepressible conflict" resulting in the Civil War was between "two divergent economic and social systems, two civilizations, in fact."[67] The "eternal struggle between the agrarian South and the commercial and industrial North" was always "to control the government either in its [the North's or the South's] own interest or, negatively, to prevent the other section from controlling it in its interests."[68] From these opposed socioeconomic bases emerged the opposed political philosophies of the sections: "centralization in the North and state rights in the South."[69] The North's interests required "positive legislation exploitative of the agrarian South," hence the assertion of federal law on behalf of commerce and industry. The South "demanded only to be let alone." Hence "state rights" was a "defense mechanism" that had "no positive program" other than protection of the South's inherited way of life. Along with "literal interpretation of the Constitution," the South appealed to states' rights to stop the encroachment of the North and assure "local self-government."[70] Northern victory meant "intolerance, crusading, standardizing alike in industry and life. The South had to be crushed out [because] it impeded the progress of the machine."[71]

Owsley's sectional, Agrarian loyalties clearly dictated his view of constitutional issues. He even deemphasized states' rights, as we have seen, arguing that before the war it had been more of a tactical defense than a foundational constitutional principle.[72] Accordingly, he could not take seriously Northern critics of Progressive statist regulation who appealed to states' rights or federalism. Tutored by Beard's economic determinist view of the Constitution, he saw in such appeals only Northern self-delusion that obfuscated corporate greed, in the interest of which the North would continue to dominate the South.[73]

Indeed, Owsley was hopeful that the assertion of federal authority under the New Deal could be turned in favor of the Agrarians' yeoman farmer ideal. He made this clear in "The Pillars of Agrarianism" (1935), which undertook the most explicit policy analyses and recommendations of any of the Agrarians' work. His central, Agrarian principle was that land ownership must be made more widespread so that the nation's economy was neither controlled by industrial plutocrats nor permitted to drift into communism or fascism. The federal government should buy land from absentee owners, insurance companies, and banks and distribute eighty-acre plots to landless tenants, along with a simple house, some livestock, and a cash advance. The land could not be mortgaged or sold. Subsistence crops would be encouraged, and the unemployed could be brought from cities to farm.[74]

However, to keep the industrial North from once again dominating the agrarian South would, in Owsley's vision, require fundamental constitutional change. Because the "United States is less a nation than an empire made up of a congeries of regions marked off by geographic, climatic, and racial characteristics," the South would never be treated fairly under the current governing arrangement. What was needed was "a new constitutional deal" that accounted for the conflicting regional interests and mores. Owsley then sketched a "new set-up [for] the federal government," redefining authority into semiautonomous regions with significant control over their own economic policies and with sectional representation on the Supreme Court.[75]

In another essay a year later, Owsley took aim at the Constitution in an even more derisive and Beardian-inflected attack. The Constitution should not be treated with "reverence" or regarded as "sacrosanct." It had "repudiated many of the fundamental principles" of the American Revolution and removed "the Federal government as far as possible from the sound of *vox populi*[, placing] it in the hands of the few men of wealth." The centralizing Hamiltonian Federalists, a political dispensation said to include post–Civil War Republicans and their nefarious Fourteenth Amendment, had made the Supreme Court the tool of the wealthy at the expense of the rest of country, especially the South. Owsley concluded that the constitutional system was irredeemable. "We need a new constitution which will reconstruct the Federal government from center to circumference."[76] Getting rid of both the old Constitution and the hidebound fixation on states' rights was necessary to move toward subnational regional governments that could protect the agrarian South. Building on Owsley's ideas, his Agrarian colleague Donald Davidson was equally sure that regional differences could not be accommodated under the Constitution. Satisfactory change would require a "sweeping revision of the constitutional fabric." To advance the Agrarian program there was no means "left but to operate upon the historic document itself."[77] Davidson even suggested that the new regional governments he advocated might be armed with Calhoun's principle of nullification.[78]

The thinking of Owsley and Davidson shows that the Agrarians who most directly analyzed the constitutional system were prepared fundamentally to revise or abandon it, and rather quickly, in favor of what they regarded as Southern sectional interests. Agrarians agreed that the South had been consistently threatened and subjugated by the constitutional system. From there it was a short step to reject American constitutionalism along with modern industrial society.

## THE SOUTHERN VOICE IN MODERN CONSERVATISM

After World War II, Southern power in Congress diminished, and a new conservative movement formed around William F. Buckley, Jr., and the *National Review*. Agrarian ideas continued to develop in this new context and contributed to postwar traditionalist conservatism. A crucial figure here is Richard M. Weaver. He sought to fashion Agrarianism into a philosophically deeper and more explicitly Christian humanist doctrine. This was a significant achievement, and it derived fundamentally from his quintessentially Agrarian perspective on the results of the Civil War. However, like the postwar Confederate apologists, of whom he was the first modern analyst, he continued to see constitutional protections for the equal rights of African Americans as inseparable from the dehumanizing and authoritarian aspects of modern materialism and statism. To be sure, at midcentury Weaver could appeal to long-standing tradition insofar as segregation was constitutional when measured by the established mores of the South and their ratification in Supreme Court precedents. However, that state of affairs traduced both the principles of the American founding and the purpose of the Reconstruction amendments, and Weaver's theory ultimately could not respond to these crucial facts.

Weaver had studied under the Agrarians at Vanderbilt University and spent most of his career in the English Department at the University of Chicago. His 1948 book, *Ideas Have Consequences*, attempted to generalize the Agrarian disposition in response to Progressive liberalism in both its statist and cultural relativist forms. He traced the root of the modern problem to William of Occam and the birth of nominalism in the fourteenth century. It had successfully displaced the philosophical realism achieved in the medieval synthesis of Greek philosophy and Christianity. Long-term decline had set in, Weaver argued, after humans had become the measure of all things. Like his Agrarian mentors, Weaver poignantly condemned the materialism, selfishness, and leveling egalitarianism left to modern people. His reassertion of the old idea that society must have an ethical basis has remained central to American traditionalist conservatism.[79]

In the culture of the South, Weaver found a humanistic rebuke to the modernity he so despised. He hoped that the basic lineaments of Southern conservatism could help America resist cultural decline. This position was stated most clearly in his posthumously published book on post–Civil War Southern thought, actually his doctoral dissertation and the basis of all his later writing. He found in the thought of the postwar South a "religious agrarian order in struggle against the forces of modernism." In fact, it was the "the last non-materialist civilization in the Western World."[80] By clinging to the old ways after the Civil War, the South had "prepared itself for the longer run" against "a future of nihilism, urged on by the demoniacal force of technology and by our own moral defeatism."[81] In a statement that suggested his view of both the fate of the old South and his fear for the future of Western civilization, Weaver declared, "The most assured way to undermine civilization is to surrender to criteria of uniformity and objectivity." He warned of the dawning age of the monolithic state and its "completely pervasive authority, backed by an oligarchy of scientists—that is the situation into which forces are hurrying us."[82]

One of the South's failings after the war, he wrote, was that it did not "study its position until it arrived at metaphysical foundations." What it needed was "a Burke or a Hegel; it produced lawyers and journalists."[83] In attempting to supply the philosophical foundation the South had lacked, Weaver's mature works argued that civilization emerged from a people's attempt to express its relationship to the absolute and eternal. The resulting culture was rooted in sentiment, myth, and poetry. Moreover, culture was inherently discriminatory and hierarchical—and most importantly, it was exclusive.

Precisely this understanding of culture, although profound and insightful, put Weaver on the side of segregation rather than with the natural rights–inspired claims for legal equality being made by African Americans. As an antimodern protest rooted in white Southern cultural identity, Agrarianism ultimately had no place for African Americans as full members of the political community.[84] Weaver's stance thus revealed how Agrarianism lacked the philosophical resources to accept the justice in the claims of the civil rights movement.[85] For example, in an essay from 1957 on "The South and the American Union," Weaver confidently recapitulated the neo-Confederate, Beardian, Dunningite, and Agrarian views of the meaning of the Civil War and Reconstruction discussed above, emphasizing that, in the wake of *Brown v. Board of Education* (1954), the South was determined "not to be assimilated into the national pattern, but to preserve her character" by resisting "nationalization and centralization of authority."[86] The South "maintained the standards of white civilization" and had no desire to be "turned into something like those 'mixed sections' found in large Northern cities. . . . For such reasons, the

Supreme Court's decretal has to it the look of a second installment of Reconstruction."[87] Of course that was precisely the point when it came to the topic of legal equality, although Weaver meant the reference to Reconstruction as the most profound dismissal. He saw federally mandated desegregation as only "the new forward motion of the centralizing and regimenting impulse" that had for so long subjugated the South and was now threatening all of Western civilization.[88] Constitutionalism, for this philosophically informed Southern critic of modernity, was little more than an appeal to states' rights in defense of segregation.

An even more extreme conflation of constitutionalism with the Southern states' rights defense of segregation was exemplified by Davidson, another original Agrarian. In the 1950s he had a substantial role in "massive resistance" efforts through the Tennessee Federation for Constitutional Government. Both Davidson and Weaver defended segregation as a matter of states' rights in the pages of the *National Review,* a stance the magazine itself endorsed in the 1950s. The notorious "Southern Manifesto" (1956), composed by Southern members of Congress in response to *Brown,* took very much the same stance and was formally titled a "Declaration of Constitutional Principles."[89]

Because the South invoked states' rights most vehemently when its racial order was threatened, as in the New Deal–era antilynching and fair employment struggles,[90] Americans sympathetic to the civil rights movement often concluded that such appeals could be nothing more than a mask for racism and segregation. Although figures such as James J. Kilpatrick and Strom Thurmond were racists,[91] the association of local self-government with racism was a historical contingency rather than a requirement of logic or constitutional principle. Regrettably, the result, lamented by scholars as diverse as Vernon Parrington and Eugene Genovese, has been to prevent any appeal to states' rights from resisting either the corporate exploitation or federal regulation that continually removed ever greater swaths of American life from local control.[92] This poisoning of any appeal to states' rights by its association with racism, slavery, and segregation is one of the signal lessons we glean from an analysis of the South's relationship to the constitutional order after the Civil War.

Prominent Southern voices in American politics haltingly abandoned overt racism during the post-1960s conservative ascendance.[93] The most historically and philosophically informed heir of the Agrarian tradition in this period was M. E. Bradford. A student of Davidson's trained at Vanderbilt University primarily as a scholar of Southern literature, Bradford carried the core themes of Agrarianism into the 1980s and early 1990s. He too decried the tawdry and soul-destroying materialism and banality of modern life, and likewise lamented the centralization of power supposedly wrought by Union victory in the Civil War. Most fundamentally, like the Agrarians, he was a defender of Southern culture. It was "a way of life, and not a goal for life, which requires a deference prior to all analysis."[94] To defend Southern culture, Bradford found it necessary to add something the primarily literary core of Agrarianism had lacked—a sustained inquiry into the principles of the American founding.[95] This effort led him to a forthright rejection of the claim that natural rights were the basis of the American project and to a vehement condemnation of Abraham Lincoln for his dedication to this idea.

Bradford is properly categorized within the traditionalist branch of modern American conservatism, though his orientation emerged more from Southern culture and history than from Edmund Burke or Russell Kirk.[96] Still, like Kirk, he argued that the rebellious American colonists fought to continue their practice of local self-government and to defend their traditional, common-law rights from a distant but meddling empire. The founding of America was thus a conservative act and by no means a revolutionary upheaval. For Bradford the famous second paragraph of the Declaration of Independence was not an announcement of the doctrine of natural rights and social contract but rather a statement about thirteen sets of corporate peoples separating, as such, from the British Empire. According to him,

"We," in that second sentence, signifies the colonials as the citizenry of the distinct colonies, not as individuals, but rather in their corporate capacity. Therefore, the following "all men" [were] created equal in their right to expect from any government to which they might submit freedom from corporate bondage. . . . [They] are persons prudent together, respectful of the law which makes them one, even though forced to stand henceforth apart: equal as one free state is as free as another.[97]

Therefore, Bradford also rejected the claim that natural rights and human equality were the definitive American ends that the Constitution was meant to secure. The Constitution for him was

not an instrumental, substantive document drawn up to foster the favorite capital-letter abstractions of the millenarians. It is more concerned with what government will *not* do for each of us than with the positive description of acceptable conduct, which is left to local and idiosyncratic definition—to society, local customs, and tested ways. Most important, it is not about enforcing the abstract "rights of man" or some theory of perfect justice and aboriginal equality.[98]

In this view, the constitutional order was less modern and more circumspect than what had become of it. Bradford's Constitution was essentially structural and procedural, establishing only the methods by which a religious, republican, and diverse people deliberated and governed itself under God.

To distinguish this view from the mistaken one that elevated the Declaration, Bradford followed George Carey and Willmoore Kendall in adopting Michael Oakeshott's distinction between "nomocratic" and "teleocratic" political orders.[99] A nomocratic order establishes modes for conducting official business in accord with the established customs of society, whereas a teleocratic order seeks the ever-fuller realization of an abstract end or goal. According to Bradford (and Kendall and Carey), the Constitution originally had been nomocratic—encouraging moderation and deliberation about common concerns according to set procedures and limits—but it had become increasingly teleocratic, transformed by the crusade for greater equality and more rights, often in the name of the Declaration of Independence. America had shifted from a nomocratic to a teleocratic regime, and Bradford regarded this change as the source of the nation's constitutional and political ills.

Lincoln was Bradford's primary culprit. In acid and derisive language, Bradford attacked Lincoln for having wed the Union war effort to the teleology of rights and equality. Lincoln had used this approach not only to demonize the South but also to overcome once and for all its properly more limited conception of constitutionalism. Bradford saw Union victory as the true beginning of American decline. Lincoln made the idea of natural rights into a messianic, ideological doctrine of radical individualism and egalitarianism that had all but effaced the true nature of American constitutionalism.[100] He bequeathed to Americans an authoritarian politics that made government sovereign over what was once a Christian humanist, locally based set of regional cultures. In the late twentieth century this corruption of the original Constitution advanced through the federal destruction of states' rights and local self-government, typically effectuated by the Supreme Court.

Bradford hoped that his recovery of the Southern perspective on American constitutionalism would help reverse the decline of the republic. The South could help sustain those who resisted modern liberalism and modern statism. However, his attack on natural rights and Lincoln was a crucial choice. It derived from his failure, and that of the larger Agrarian tradition, to accept that slavery was the foundation of the economic and social system whose culture they so lauded. The tone of the old South was not set, as Bradford and the Agrarians would have it, primarily by middling farmers and "plain folk." Rather, the arbiters of Southern culture were the aristocratic planters whose success in the international capitalist economy depended on slavery.[101] Turning a blind eye to slavery enabled Bradford to minimize freedom and equality as the core principles of the founding, while also exempting modern Southern thought from fully confronting them.[102]

## CONCLUSION

Bradford offered the most theoretically and historically sophisticated pro-Southern rejection of America's natural rights social-contract constitutionalism since the beginning of the twentieth century. We have seen that some such rejection, from the Confederate apologists to Dunning and Burgess, through the Agrarians to Weaver and finally Bradford, typified the Southern perspective on the constitutional order after the Civil War. The Reconstruction amendments did rearticulate America's founding principles, but the North was unwilling to enforce this understanding of liberty, equality, and consent against Southern whites' vigorous opposition. Moreover, loyalty to federalism and local self-government, in both North and South, was a political reality that further prevented Southern race relations from reflecting the founders' principles until well into the twentieth century. A major legacy of this history was the poisoning of appeals to states' rights and local self-government by their association in American politics with slavery, secession, and segregation.

Although there was no longer a coherent and distinctive Southern tradition in American constitutional politics by the close of the twentieth century, let us conclude by briefly considering two current questions derived from the Southern thought examined here. First, in modern America, is it any longer possible to uphold a moderate and constitutional version of equality that limits what can be done in the name of this principle? Second, can localism be preserved without invoking federal authority to limit the reach of the market?

The question of equality was addressed perhaps most philosophically by Bradford, who regarded the political discourse built on it as inherently millennial and utopian.[103] In America, he said, its demands were continually expanding as a result of the civil rights movement and the Warren Court and the associated capacity of modern egalitarians to dismiss as racist anyone who opposed them. Bradford held that the new equality leveled cultural and intellectual distinctions, politicized ever more aspects of life, and required an authoritarian government that endangered liberty. Though modern egalitarianism had deep roots, he hoped that the American tradition, especially its Southern elements, contained the resources to resist. However, he came near to despairing of any success. Despite Bradford and the Southern tradition's mistaken denial of natural human equality, it remains true that America still dearly needs a version of equality that fully protects our constitutional rights without leveling all distinctions or homogenizing all differences.

The question about federal authority and the market was best stated by Eugene Genovese, the great erstwhile Marxist historian of the antebellum South. He always extolled the South's antimaterialism and rich culture of localism, but he also called to account the Agrarians, and Bradford specifically, for failing to confront slavery and racism in their rush to condemn federal authority. In Genovese's words, Southern conservatives were caught in a conundrum:

The logic of their political philosophy and constitutional principles leads to a program to limit government interference in civil society to a bare minimum. The logic of their commitment to the defense of what are now loosely called "traditional values" in a society in which the market dominates not only the economy but the society itself compels them to consider government interference as the only feasible way to sustain a society in which those values can survive.[104]

This problem too remains for Americans who wish both to abide by constitutional limitations and to protect from modern assault the traditions and beliefs of local cultures. The Southern experience in the twentieth century provides no immediately reassuring answers to either of the fundamental questions that emerged from it.

Accordingly, consideration of the Southern perspective on the Constitution after the Civil War brings a sense of both achievement and loss. The nation endured the Civil War and Reconstruction: it did not have to be refounded on different principles in order to defeat slavery and secession. Though the era was a renewal and reassertion of America's founding principles, in the South they were too long delayed and resisted. After the South was more thoroughly reconstructed for a second time in the twentieth century, it was better reconciled to what it had so long opposed. However, lost, or nearly lost, were culturally based resistance to consumerist materialism and uniformity as well as the capacity effectively to defend local tradition and self-government from the modern American state. The Southern perspective can never be shorn of its association with the worst offenses to American principles, but we should not let its tragic connection with slavery and racism efface its salutary insights. At our peril do we ignore either the South's powerful indictment of the baser aspects of modern American life or the questions it raises about the legitimate reach of government and the ever greater demand for equality.

## NOTES

1. Herman Belz, "The South and the American Constitutional Tradition at the Bicentennial," in *An Uncertain Tradition: Constitutionalism and the History of the South,* ed. Kermit L. Hall and James W. Ely, Jr. (Athens: University of Georgia Press, 1989), 17–59.

2. Jefferson Davis, *The Rise and Fall of the Confederate Government,* 2 vols. (New York: Appleton, 1881); Albert Taylor Bledsoe, *Is Davis a Traitor?* (Baltimore, MD: Innes, 1866); Alexander H. Stephens, *A Constitutional View of the Late War between the States,* 2 vols. (Philadelphia: National, 1868–1870); Edward A. Pollard, *The Lost Cause* (New York: E. B. Treat, 1867). The crucial introduction to this literature is Richard M. Weaver, *The Southern Tradition at Bay: A History of Postbellum Thought* (New Rochelle, NY: Arlington House, 1968), 112–138.

3. Stephens, *Constitutional View,* vol. 2, iii.

4. Bledsoe, *Is Davis a Traitor?,* v, 8.

5. Ibid., 250.

6. Stephens, *Constitutional View,* vol. 2, 668.

7. Michael Les Benedict, "A Constitutional Crisis," in *Writing the Civil War: The Quest to Understand,* ed. James M. McPherson and William J. Cooper, Jr. (Columbia: University of South Carolina Press, 1998), 155–156.

8. Pollard, *Lost Cause,* 47; Davis, *Rise and Fall,* vol. 1, 1–14, quote at 14.

9. Davis, *Rise and Fall,* vol. 1, 78, 517–518. See also Pollard, *Lost Cause,* 49.

10. Pollard, *Lost Cause,* 50–51.

11. http://teachingamericanhistory.org/library/document/cornerstone-speech.

12. Pollard, *Lost Cause,* 750, 752.

13. Ibid., 751 (emphasis in original).

14. For a recent overview of the massive literature, see Thomas J. Brown, ed., *Reconstructions: New Perspectives on the Postbellum United States* (New York: Oxford University Press, 2006).

15. The importance of federalism is well expressed in the work of two leading constitutional historians of Reconstruction. See, for example, Herman Belz, "The Constitution and Reconstruction," in *The Facts of Reconstruction: Essays in Honor of John Hope Franklin,* ed. Eric Anderson and Alfred A. Moss, Jr. (Baton Rouge: Louisiana State University Press, 1991), 189–217; Michael Les Benedict, *Preserving the Constitution: Essays on Politics and the Constitution in the Reconstruction Era* (New York: Fordham University Press, 2006).

16. Texas v. White, 74 U.S. 700, 726, 725 (1869).

17. A point recently reiterated by Michael Les Benedict, "At Every Fireside: Constitutional Politics in the Age of Reconstruction," in *Constitutionalism in the Approach and Aftermath of the Civil War,* ed. Paul D. Moreno and Johnathan O'Neill (New York: Fordham University Press, 2013), 158, 160.

18. Alfred H. Kelly, Winfred A. Harbison, and Herman Belz, *The American Constitution: Its Origins and Development,* 7th ed., vol. 1 (New York: Norton, 1991), 352, 361.

19. Michael Les Benedict, "The Problem of Constitutionalism and Constitutional

Liberty in the Reconstruction South," in *An Uncertain Tradition: Constitutionalism and the History of the South,* ed. Kermit L. Hall and James W. Ely, Jr. (Athens: University of Georgia Press, 1989),242.

20. Slaughterhouse Cases, 83 U.S. 36, 78 (1873).

21. United States v. Cruikshank, 92 U.S. 542 (1876).

22. Civil Rights Cases, 109 U.S. 3 (1883).

23. Plessy v. Ferguson, 163 U.S. 537 (1896).

24. United States v. Reese, 92 U.S. 214 (1876).

25. Williams v. Mississippi, 170 U.S. 213 (1898).

26. Michael Perman, *The Southern Political Tradition* (Baton Rouge: Louisiana State University Press, 2012), 42.

27. A process traced in ibid.

28. William Archibald Dunning, *Reconstruction: Political and Economic, 1865–1877* (New York: Harper, 1907), xv.

29. William Archibald Dunning, *Essays on the Civil War and Reconstruction* (New York: Macmillan, 1897), 384. This statement is not offered as Dunning's personal view, though his work as a whole makes it plain that it was.

30. Dunning, *Reconstruction,* 212.

31. For an overview of how Dunning's racist assumptions affected his historical judgment, see Alan D. Harper, "William A. Dunning: The Historian as Nemesis," *Civil War History* 10 (1964): 54–66.

32. Bernard Edward Brown, *American Conservatives: The Political Thought of Francis Lieber and John W. Burgess* (New York: Columbia University Press, 1951).

33. The connection is noted in passing by Hugh Tulloch, *The Debate on the American Civil War Era* (Manchester, UK: Manchester University Press, 1999), 212, and in slightly more detail by Benedict, "Constitutional Crisis," 159.

34. John W. Burgess, *Political Science and Comparative Constitutional Law,* vol. 1 (Boston: Ginn, 1890), 59–67; Brown, *American Conservatives,* 141–145; John W. Burgess, "The American Commonwealth: Changes in Its Relation to the Nation," *Political Science Quarterly* 1 (1886): 9, 17.

35. John W. Burgess, *The Civil War and the Constitution, 1859–1865,* vol. 1 (New York: Scribner's, 1901), 134, 135.

36. Brown, *American Conservatives,* 132–134.

37. Burgess, *Political Science and Comparative Constitutional Law,* vol. 1, 44, 45.

38. Ibid., 46.

39. Ibid., 44–45.

40. John W. Burgess, *Reconstruction and the Constitution, 1866–1876* (New York: Scribner's, 1902), 133–134.

41. Peter Novick, *That Noble Dream: The "Objectivity Question" and the American Historical Profession* (Cambridge, UK: Cambridge University Press, 1988), 74–80.

42. Burgess, *Reconstruction and the Constitution,* 298. Dunning makes a similar point in *Essays on the Civil War,* 384–385.

43. Bernard Crick, *The American Science of Politics: Its Origins and Conditions* (Berkeley: University of California Press, 1959), 30 (quote), 31 (quote), 96–100, 236–237, 245–248.

44. W. E. B DuBois, "Reconstruction and Its Benefits," *American Historical Review* 15 (1910): 781–799.

45. W. E. B. DuBois, *Black Reconstruction in America* (New York: Free Press, 1998), orig. pub. 1935.

46. Ibid., xix, 725. This book also set the agenda for much modern revisionist scholarship on Reconstruction by focusing on the centrality of the experiences of formerly enslaved people.

47. Charles A. Beard and Mary R. Beard, *The Rise of American Civilization,* vol. 2 (New York: Macmillan, 1927), 54.

48. Ibid., 107–111.

49. Ibid., 111–114.

50. Herman Belz, "The Civil War Amendments to the Constitution: The Relevance of Original Intent," *Constitutional Commentary* 5 (1988): 115, 117–122.

51. Beard and Beard, *American Civilization,* vol. 2, 100.

52. DuBois, *Black Reconstruction,* 714–715.

53. Thomas J. Pressly, *Americans Interpret Their Civil War* (Princeton, NJ: Princeton University Press, 1954), 116, 247.

54. Joseph J. Persky, *The Burden of Dependency: Colonial Themes in Southern Economic Thought* (Baltimore, MD: Johns Hopkins University Press, 1992).

55. C. Vann Woodward, *The Origins of the New South, 1877–1913* (Baton Rouge: Louisiana State University Press, 1951).

56. A good overview is John B. Boles and Bethany L. Johnson, eds., *Origins of the New South Fifty Years Later: The Continuing Influence of a Historical Classic* (Baton Rouge: Louisiana State University Press, 2003).

57. See generally Joseph P. Reidy, "Economic Consequences of the Civil War and Reconstruction," in *A Companion to the American South,* ed. John B. Boles (London: Blackwell, 2002), 303–317; Peter A. Coclanis and Scott Marler, "The Economics of Reconstruction," in *A Companion to the Civil War and Reconstruction,* ed. Lacy K. Ford (London: Blackwell, 2005), 342–365.

58. William J. Cooper, Jr., and Thomas E. Terrill, *The American South: A History,* 4th ed., vol. 2 (Lanham, MD: Rowman and Littlefield, 2009), 841; Sheldon Hackney, "'Origins of the New South in Retrospect,' Thirty Years Later" (orig. pub. 1972), in *Origins of the New South Fifty Years Later: The Continuing Influence of a Historical Classic* (Baton Rouge: Louisiana State University Press, 2003), 41–42, 55–56. Reidy well states the scholarly transition away from older, cruder Marxist interpretations by noting, "Woodward's colonial analogy might serve again as a starting point, provided that his emphasis on the structural relationships of political and economic domination gives way to one rooted in the human interactions that alternately advanced, retarded, or simply accommodated to the encounter with metropolitan industrial capitalism." Reidy, "Economic Consequences," 315–316.

59. The most prominent defender of this view has been Richard Bensel, *Yankee Leviathan: The Origins of Central State Authority in America, 1859–1877* (Cambridge, UK: Cambridge University Press, 1990).

60. Paul D. Moreno, "'The Legitimate Object of Government': Constitutional Problems of Civil War–Era Republican Policy," in *Constitutionalism in the Approach and*

*Aftermath of the Civil War,* ed. Paul D. Moreno and Johnathan O'Neill (New York: Fordham University Press, 2013), 179, 175; Moreno, *The American State from the Civil War to the New Deal* (Cambridge, UK: Cambridge University Press, 2013), 7–22. See also Morton Keller, *America's Three Regimes: A New Political History* (New York: Oxford University Press, 2007), 131–134.

61. Rogan Kersh, *Dreams of a More Perfect Union* (Ithaca, NY: Cornell University Press, 2001), 231.

62. Leonard D. White, *The Republican Era, 1869–1901: A Study in Administrative History* (New York: Macmillan, 1958), 2; Paul D. Moreno, "Legitimate Object of Government," in *Constitutionalism in the Approach and Aftermath of the Civil War,* ed. Paul D. Moreno and Johnathan O'Neill (New York: Fordham University Press, 2013), 179.

63. My understanding has been informed by Michael O'Brien, *The Idea of the American South, 1920–1971* (Baltimore, MD: Johns Hopkins University Press, 1979); Paul Conkin, *The Southern Agrarians* (Knoxville: University of Tennessee Press, 1988); Mark G. Malvasi, *The Unregenerate South: The Agrarian Thought of John Crow Ransome, Allen Tate, and Donald Davidson* (Baton Rouge: Louisiana State University Press, 1997); Paul V. Murphy, *The Rebuke of History: The Southern Agrarians and American Conservative Thought* (Chapel Hill: University of North Carolina Press, 2001). Here I draw on my initial treatment of Agrarianism in Johnathan O'Neill, "The First Conservatives: The Constitutional Challenge to Progressivism," July 2011, http://www.heritage.org, 4–6.

64. Twelve Southerners, *I'll Take My Stand: The South and the Agrarian Tradition* (New York: Harper, 1930), x–xi, 15–19, 193–194, 202–206.

65. Ibid., 66, 67 (quote).

66. Ibid., 62. Owsley gave no evidence to substantiate the sensational claim of cannibalism.

67. Ibid., 72.

68. Ibid., 73. Owsley frequently acknowledged the influence of Turner, Beard, and his own teacher William E. Dodd. See Edward S. Shapiro, "Frank L. Owsley and the Defense of Southern Identity," *Tennessee Historical Quarterly* 36 (1977): 75, 78–80, 80n8.

69. Twelve Southerners, *I'll Take My Stand,* 76.

70. Ibid., 85, 87, 88.

71. Ibid., 91.

72. Owsley's first book, *State Rights in the Confederacy* (Chicago: University of Chicago Press, 1925), argued that fixation on states' rights undermined the shared Southern identity and unity necessary for the South to have won the Civil War.

73. Twelve Southerners, *I'll Take My Stand,* 86–87.

74. Frank Owsley, "The Pillars of Agrarianism," in *The South: Old and New Frontiers—Selected Essays of Frank Lawrence Owsley,* ed. Harriet Chappell Owsley (Athens: University Press of Georgia, 1969), 182–184.

75. Ibid., 186–187.

76. Frank Owsley, "The Foundations of Democracy," in *Who Owns America? A New Declaration of Independence,* ed. Herbert Agar and Allen Tate (Boston: Houghton Mifflin, 1936), 55, 53, 58.

77. Donald Davidson, "That This Nation May Endure—the Need for Political

Regionalism," in *Who Owns America? A New Declaration of Independence,* ed. Herbert Agar and Allen Tate (Boston: Houghton Mifflin, 1936), 125, 127.

78. Owsley, "That This Nation May Endure," 132. A good treatment of Davidson's sectionalism as derived from Agrarianism is Malvasi, *Unregenerate South,* 189–200.

79. Richard M. Weaver, *Ideas Have Consequences* (Chicago: University of Chicago Press, 1948).

80. Weaver, *Southern Tradition,* 44, 391, italics omitted.

81. Ibid., 388, 391.

82. Ibid., 37, 393.

83. Ibid., 389. Richard Weaver makes clear his view that Agrarianism must be given a deeper philosophical expression. Weaver, "Agrarianism in Exile," in *The Southern Essays of Richard M. Weaver,* ed. George M. Curtis, III, and James J. Thompson, Jr. (Indianapolis, IN: Liberty Fund, 1987), 29–49. He attempted this perhaps most incisively in Weaver, *Visions of Order: The Cultural Crisis of Our Time* (Baton Rouge: Louisiana State University Press, 1964), chap. 1.

84. Murphy, *Rebuke of History,* 177–178. He does not make the point explicitly in terms of natural rights.

85. Even Richard Weaver's strong endorsement of property as a counter to collectivist statism was not expressed in terms of natural rights. See Robert A. Preston, "The Relation of Intellect and Will in the Thought of Richard Weaver," in *The Dilemmas of American Conservatism,* ed. Kenneth L. Deutsch and Ethan Fishman (Lexington: University Press of Kentucky, 2010), 73–74.

86. *The Southern Essays of Richard M. Weaver,* ed. George M. Curtis, III, and James J. Thompson, Jr. (Indianapolis, IN: Liberty Fund, 1987), 250, 251.

87. Ibid., 253.

88. Ibid., 254.

89. Murphy, *Rebuke of History,* 202–205. Another exemplar is James Jackson Kilpatrick, *The Sovereign States: Notes of a Citizen of Virginia* (Chicago: Regnery, 1957).

90. Ira Katznelson, *Fear Itself: The New Deal and the Origins of Our Time* (New York: Norton, 2013).

91. William P. Hustwit, *James J. Kilpatrick: Salesman for Segregation* (Chapel Hill: University of North Carolina Press, 2013); Joseph Crespino, *Strom Thurmond's America* (New York: Hill and Wang, 2012).

92. Eugene D. Genovese, *The Southern Tradition: The Achievements and Limitations of an American Conservatism* (Cambridge, MA: Harvard University Press, 1994), 28–29, 54.

93. The South's movement from racist segregation to more mainstream conservatism is a story well told in Hustwit, *James J. Kilpatrick,* and Crespino, *Strom Thurmond's America.*

94. M. E. Bradford, "Not in Memoriam, but in Affirmation," in Fifteen Southerners, *Why the South Will Survive* (Athens: University of Georgia Press, 1981), 222.

95. This point is emphasized in James McClellan, "Walking the Levee with Mel Bradford," in *A Defender of Southern Conservatism: M. E. Bradford and His Achievements,* ed. Clyde N. Wilson (Columbia: University of Missouri Press, 1999), 35–57. This

volume is indispensable for understanding Bradford's thought. See also Malvasi, *Unregenerate South*, 232–250; Murphy, *Rebuke of History*, 227–234, 244–245, 251–252.

96. This and the following two paragraphs incorporate material from my treatment of traditionalist conservatism in Johnathan O'Neill, "Constitutional Conservatism and American Conservatism," in *Nomos LVI: American Conservatism*, ed. Sanford V. Levinson, Joel Parker, and Melissa S. Williams (New York: New York University Press, 2016), 305–306.

97. M. E. Bradford, "The Heresy of Equality: Bradford Replies to Jaffa," *Modern Age* 20 (1976): 62, 68 (quote).

98. M. E. Bradford, *Original Intentions: On the Making and Ratification of the United States Constitution* (Athens: University of Georgia Press, 1993), 13 (emphasis added, citation omitted).

99. Willmoore Kendall and George W. Carey, *The Basic Symbols of the American Political Tradition* (Washington, DC: Catholic University Press, 1995, xxii–xxiii, orig. pub. 1970; Bradford, *Original Intentions*, 33, 104–105; Bradford, "Not in Memoriam," 220.

100. Bradford, "Heresy of Equality"; M. E. Bradford, *Remembering Who We Are: Observations of a Southern Conservative* (Athens: University of Georgia Press, 1985), 143–156. See also Kendall and Carey, *Basic Symbols*.

101. Malvasi, *Unregenerate South*, 244–247; Elizabeth Fox Genovese and Eugene D. Genovese, "M. E. Bradford's Historical Vision," in *A Defender of Southern Conservatism: M. E. Bradford and His Achievements*, ed. Clyde N. Wilson (Columbia: University of Missouri Press, 1999), 84–85; Genovese, *Southern Tradition*, 79–80; Murphy, *Rebuke of History*, 261–262.

102. Genovese and Genovese, "M. E. Bradford's Historical Vision," 82–83.

103. See esp. Bradford, *Remembering Who We Are*, 47–54.

104. Genovese, *Southern Tradition*, 74.

# Contributors

William B. Allen is professor emeritus and was dean of the James Madison College at Michigan State University. He is the author of several books on American political thought, including *Rethinking Uncle Tom: The Political Philosophy of Harriet Beecher Stowe* (Lanham, MD: Lexington, 2008). He is editor of *George Washington: A Collection* (Indianapolis, IN: Liberty Fund, 1988).

Alan Levine is associate professor of government and founding director of the Political Theory Institute in the School of Public Affairs at American University in Washington, DC. He is the author of *Sensual Philosophy: Toleration, Skepticism, and Montaigne's Politics of the Self* (Lanham, MD: Lexington, 2001). He is editor of *Early Modern Skepticism and the Origins of Toleration* (Lanham, MD: Lexington, 1999), and (with Daniel S. Malachuk) of *A Political Companion to Ralph Waldo Emerson* (Lexington: University Press of Kentucky, 2011).

Philip B. Lyons is an independent scholar in Washington, DC, retired from the US Equal Employment Opportunity Commission. He is the author of *Statesmanship and Reconstruction: Moderate versus Radical Republicans on Restoring the Union after the Civil War* (Lanham, MD: Lexington, 2014).

Daniel S. Malachuk is professor of English at Western Illinois University. He is the author of *Two Cities: The Political Thought of American Transcendentalism* (Lawrence: University Press of Kansas, 2016) and *Perfection, the State, and Victorian Liberalism* (New York: Palgrave Macmillan, 2005). He is editor (with Alan Levine) of *A Political Companion to Ralph Waldo Emerson* (Lexington: University Press of Kentucky, 2011).

Thomas W. Merrill is associate professor of government and director of special programs of the Political Theory Institute in the School of Public Affairs at American University in Washington, DC. He is the author of *Hume and the Politics of Enlightenment* (Cambridge, UK: Cambridge University Press, 2015). He is editor (with Yuval Levin and Adam Schulman) of *Apples of Gold in Pictures of Silver: Honoring the Work of Leon R. Kass* (Lanham, MD: Lexington,

2010) and (with Edmund Pellegrino and Adam Schulman) of *Human Dignity and Bioethics* (Notre Dame, IN: Notre Dame University Press, 2011).

Peter C. Myers is professor of political science at the University of Wisconsin, Eau Claire. He is the author of *Frederick Douglass: Race and the Rebirth of American Liberalism* (Lawrence: University Press of Kansas, 2008) and *Our Only Star and Compass: Locke and the Struggle for Political Rationality* (Lanham, MD: Rowman and Littlefield, 1999).

Johnathan O'Neill is professor of history at Georgia Southern University. He is the author of *Originalism in American Law and Politics: A Constitutional History* (Baltimore, MD: Johns Hopkins University Press, 2005). He is editor (with Paul Moreno) of *Constitutionalism in the Approach and Aftermath of the Civil War* (New York: Fordham University Press, 2013), (with Joseph Postell) of *Toward an American Conservatism: The Birth of Constitutional Conservatism during the Progressive Era* (New York: Palgrave Macmillan, 2013), and (with Gary McDowell) of *America and Enlightenment Constitutionalism* (New York: Palgrave Macmillan, 2006).

James H. Read is professor of political science at the College of St. Benedict/ St. John's University. He is the author of *Majority Rule versus Consensus: The Political Thought of John C. Calhoun* (Lawrence: University Press of Kansas, 2009), *Doorstep Democracy: Face-to-Face Politics in the Heartland* (Minneapolis: University of Minnesota Press, 2008), and *Power versus Liberty: Madison, Hamilton, Wilson, and Jefferson* (Charlottesville: University of Virginia Press, 2000).

Diana J. Schaub is professor of political science at Loyola University Maryland. She is the author of *Erotic Liberalism: Women and Revolution in Montesquieu's Persian Letters* (Lanham, MD: Rowman and Littlefield, 1995). She is editor (with Amy Kass and Leon Kass) of *What So Proudly We Hail: The American Soul in Story, Speech, and Song* (Wilmington, DE: Intercollegiate Studies Institute Books, 2011).

Steven B. Smith is Alfred Cowles Professor of Government and Philosophy at Yale University. He is the author of *Modernity and Its Discontents* (New Haven, CT: Yale University Press, 2016), *Political Philosophy* (New Haven, CT: Yale University Press, 2012), *Reading Leo Strauss* (Chicago: University of Chicago Press, 2006), *Spinoza's Book of Life: Freedom and Redemption in the Ethics* (New

Haven, CT: Yale University Press, 2003), *Spinoza, Liberalism, and the Question of Jewish Identity* (New Haven, CT: Yale University Press, 1998), and *Hegel's Critique of Liberalism: Rights in Context* (Chicago: University of Chicago Press, 1989). He is editor of *The Writings of Abraham Lincoln* (New Haven, CT: Yale University Press, 2012).

James R. Stoner, Jr., is Hermann Moyse Professor and director of the Eric Vogelin Institute at Louisiana State University. He is the author of *Common-Law Liberty: Rethinking American Constitutionalism* (Lawrence: University Press of Kansas, 2003) and *Common Law and Liberal Theory: Coke, Hobbes, and the Origins of American Constitutionalism* (Lawrence: University Press of Kansas, 1992). He is editor (with Harold James) of *The Thriving Society: On the Social Conditions of Human Flourishing* (Princeton, NJ: Witherspoon Institute, 2015), (with Donna Hughes) of *The Social Costs of Pornography* (Princeton, NJ: Witherspoon Institute, 2010), and (with Samuel Gregg) of *Rethinking Business Management: Examining the Foundations of Business Education* (Princeton, NJ: Witherspoon Institute, 2008).

Caleb Verbois is associate professor of political science at Grove City College and an affiliated scholar at the John Jay Institute. A University of Virginia PhD, he teaches American politics and political theory and focuses on American constitutional thought and political development.

Keith E. Whittington is William Nelson Cromwell Professor of Politics at Princeton University. He is the author of *Political Foundations of Judicial Supremacy: The Presidency, the Supreme Court, and Constitutional Leadership in U.S. History* (Princeton, NJ: Princeton University Press, 2009), *Constitutional Construction: Divided Powers and Constitutional Meaning* (Cambridge, MA: Harvard University Press, 2001), and *Constitutional Interpretation: Textual Meaning, Original Intent, and Judicial Review* (Lawrence: University Press of Kansas, 1999). He is editor (with Howard Gillman and Mark Graber) of *American Constitutionalism*, 2nd ed. (Oxford, UK: Oxford University Press, 2016), among others.

Michael Zuckert is Nancy Reeves Dreux Professor of Political Science at the University of Notre Dame. He is the author (with Catherine H. Zuckert) of *Leo Strauss and the Problem of Political Philosophy* (Chicago: University of Chicago Press, 2014) and *The Truth about Leo Strauss: Political Philosophy and American Democracy* (Chicago: University of Chicago Press, 2008). He is also the author of *Launching Liberalism: On Lockean Political Philosophy* (Lawrence: University Press of Kansas, 2002), *Natural Rights and the New Republicanism* (Princeton, NJ: Princeton University Press, 1994), and *The Natural Rights Republic: Studies in the Foundation of the American Political Tradition* (Notre Dame, IN: Notre Dame University Press, 1996). He is editor of *The Spirit of Religion and the Spirit of Liberty: The Tocqueville Thesis Revisited* (Chicago: University of Chicago Press, 2017).

# Index